The Cambridge Handbook of Task-Based Language Teaching

Task-based language teaching (TBLT) is an innovative approach to language teaching which emphasises the importance of engaging learners' natural abilities for acquiring language incidentally. The speed with which the field is expanding makes it difficult to keep up with recent developments, for novices and experienced researchers alike. This Handbook meets that need, providing a comprehensive, up-to-date overview of the field, written by a stellar line-up of leading international experts. Chapters are divided into eight thematic areas, and as well as covering theory, also contain case studies to show how TBLT can be implemented in practice, in a range of global contexts, as well as questions for discussion, and suggested further reading. Comprehensive in its coverage, and written in an accessible style, it will appeal to a wide readership, not only researchers and graduate students, but also classroom teachers working in a variety of educational and cultural contexts around the world.

MOHAMMAD J. AHMADIAN is currently Head of Postgraduate Taught at the School of Education, University of Leeds. He has published widely on task-based language teaching and second-language acquisition. Recent publications include *Recent Perspectives on Task-Based Language Teaching and Learning* (co-editor, 2018).

MICHAEL H. LONG was Professor of Second Language Acquisition at University of Maryland, College Park. He was the author of well over 100 articles and book chapters. In 2017, he received a lifetime achievement award from the International Association for Task-Based Language Teaching.

CAMBRIDGE HANDBOOKS IN LANGUAGE AND LINGUISTICS

Genuinely broad in scope, each handbook in this series provides a complete state-of-the-field overview of a major sub-discipline within language study and research. Grouped into broad thematic areas, the chapters in each volume encompass the most important issues and topics within each subject, offering a coherent picture of the latest theories and findings. Together, the volumes will build into an integrated overview of the discipline in its entirety.

Published titles

The Cambridge Handbook of Phonology, edited by Paul de Lacy
The Cambridge Handbook of Linguistic Code-switching, edited by Barbara E. Bullock and Almeida Jacqueline Toribio
The Cambridge Handbook of Child Language, Second Edition, edited by Edith L. Bavin and Letitia Naigles
The Cambridge Handbook of Endangered Languages, edited by Peter K. Austin and Julia Sallabank
The Cambridge Handbook of Sociolinguistics, edited by Rajend Mesthrie
The Cambridge Handbook of Pragmatics, edited by Keith Allan and Kasia M. Jaszczolt
The Cambridge Handbook of Language Policy, edited by Bernard Spolsky
The Cambridge Handbook of Second Language Acquisition, edited by Julia Herschensohn and Martha Young-Scholten
The Cambridge Handbook of Biolinguistics, edited by Cedric Boeckx and Kleanthes K. Grohmann
The Cambridge Handbook of Generative Syntax, edited by Marcel den Dikken
The Cambridge Handbook of Communication Disorders, edited by Louise Cummings
The Cambridge Handbook of Stylistics, edited by Peter Stockwell and Sara Whiteley
The Cambridge Handbook of Linguistic Anthropology, edited by N.J. Enfield, Paul Kockelman and Jack Sidnell
The Cambridge Handbook of English Corpus Linguistics, edited by Douglas Biber and Randi Reppen
The Cambridge Handbook of Bilingual Processing, edited by John W. Schwieter
The Cambridge Handbook of Learner Corpus Research, edited by Sylviane Granger, Gaëtanelle Gilquin and Fanny Meunier
The Cambridge Handbook of Linguistic Multicompetence, edited by Li Wei and Vivian Cook
The Cambridge Handbook of English Historical Linguistics, edited by Merja Kytö and Päivi Pahta
The Cambridge Handbook of Formal Semantics, edited by Maria Aloni and Paul Dekker
The Cambridge Handbook of Morphology, edited by Andrew Hippisley and Greg Stump
The Cambridge Handbook of Historical Syntax, edited by Adam Ledgeway and Ian Roberts
The Cambridge Handbook of Linguistic Typology, edited by Alexandra Y. Aikhenvald and R. M. W. Dixon
The Cambridge Handbook of Areal Linguistics, edited by Raymond Hickey
The Cambridge Handbook of Cognitive Linguistics, edited by Barbara Dancygier
The Cambridge Handbook of Japanese Linguistics, edited by Yoko Hasegawa
The Cambridge Handbook of Spanish Linguistics, edited by Kimberly L. Geeslin

The Cambridge Handbook of Bilingualism, edited by Annick De Houwer and Lourdes Ortega

The Cambridge Handbook of Systemic Functional Linguistics, edited by Geoff Thompson, Wendy L. Bowcher, Lise Fontaine and David Schönthal

The Cambridge Handbook of African Linguistics, edited by H. Ekkehard Wolff

The Cambridge Handbook of Language Learning, edited by John W. Schwieter and Alessandro Benati

The Cambridge Handbook of World Englishes, edited by Daniel Schreier, Marianne Hundt and Edgar W. Schneider

The Cambridge Handbook of Intercultural Communication, edited by Guido Rings and Sebastian Rasinger

The Cambridge Handbook of Germanic Linguistics, edited by Michael T. Putnam and B. Richard Page

The Cambridge Handbook of Discourse Studies, edited by Anna De Fina and Alexandra Georgakopoulou

The Cambridge Handbook of Language Standardization, edited by Wendy Ayres-Bennett and John Bellamy

The Cambridge Handbook of Korean Linguistics, edited by Sungdai Cho and John Whitman

The Cambridge Handbook of Phonetics, edited by Rachael-Anne Knight and Jane Setter

The Cambridge Handbook of Corrective Feedback in Second Language Learning and Teaching, edited by Hossein Nassaji and Eva Kartchava

The Cambridge Handbook of Experimental Syntax, edited by Grant Goodall

The Cambridge Handbook of Heritage Languages and Linguistics, edited by Silvina Montrul and Maria Polinsky

The Cambridge Handbook of Arabic Linguistics, edited by Karin Ryding and David Wilmsen

The Cambridge Handbook of the Philosophy of Language, edited by Piotr Stalmaszczyk

The Cambridge Handbook of Sociopragmatics, edited by Michael Haugh, Dániel Z. Kádár and Marina Terkourafi

The Cambridge Handbook of Task-Based Language Teaching

Edited by
Mohammad J. Ahmadian
University of Leeds
Michael H. Long
University of Maryland, College Park

Shaftesbury Road, Cambridge CB2 8EA, United Kingdom

One Liberty Plaza, 20th Floor, New York, NY 10006, USA

477 Williamstown Road, Port Melbourne, VIC 3207, Australia

314–321, 3rd Floor, Plot 3, Splendor Forum, Jasola District Centre, New Delhi – 110025, India

103 Penang Road, #05–06/07, Visioncrest Commercial, Singapore 238467

Cambridge University Press is part of Cambridge University Press & Assessment, a department of the University of Cambridge.

We share the University's mission to contribute to society through the pursuit of education, learning and research at the highest international levels of excellence.

www.cambridge.org
Information on this title: www.cambridge.org/9781108811934

DOI: 10.1017/9781108868327

© Cambridge University Press & Assessment 2022

This publication is in copyright. Subject to statutory exception and to the provisions of relevant collective licensing agreements, no reproduction of any part may take place without the written permission of Cambridge University Press & Assessment.

First published 2022
First paperback edition 2024

A catalogue record for this publication is available from the British Library

Library of Congress Cataloging-in-Publication data
Names: Ahmadian, Mohammad Javad, editor. | Long, Michael H., editor.
Title: The Cambridge handbook of task-based language teaching / edited by Mohammad Javad Ahmadian, Michael H. Long.
Description: London ; New York : Cambridge University Press, 2022. | Series: Cambridge handbooks in language and linguistics | Includes bibliographical references and index.
Identifiers: LCCN 2021024734 (print) | LCCN 2021024735 (ebook) | ISBN 9781108491389 (hardback) | ISBN 9781108868327 (ebook)
Subjects: LCSH: Language and languages – Study and teaching – Methodology. | Second language acquisition. | Task analysis in education. | BISAC: LANGUAGE ARTS & DISCIPLINES / Linguistics / General | LANGUAGE ARTS & DISCIPLINES / Linguistics / General | LCGFT: Essays.
Classification: LCC P53.82 .C36 2021 (print) | LCC P53.82 (ebook) | DDC 418.0071–dc23
LC record available at https://lccn.loc.gov/2021024734
LC ebook record available at https://lccn.loc.gov/2021024735

ISBN 978-1-108-49138-9 Hardback
ISBN 978-1-108-81193-4 Paperback

Cambridge University Press & Assessment has no responsibility for the persistence or accuracy of URLs for external or third-party internet websites referred to in this publication and does not guarantee that any content on such websites is, or will remain, accurate or appropriate.

As the full manuscript of *The Cambridge Handbook of Task-Based Language Teaching* was submitted to Cambridge University Press, Professor Mike Long, co-editor of this volume and a pioneer of task-based language teaching, passed away after a brave battle with cancer. Enumerating the many contributions of Mike Long to applied linguistics, language education, and second language acquisition cannot possibly do him justice in a short piece like this. He had been professor in the School of Languages, Literatures and Cultures at the University of Maryland since 2003. Previously he had held appointments at the University of Hawai'i and the University of Pennsylvania. He published widely in applied linguistics generally, but perhaps is most well-known for his work in second language acquisition. He is the author of the highly influential Interaction Hypothesis, a theoretical framework that has stimulated a huge volume of research, advancing both second language theory-building and practice. He also made leading contributions to our understanding of age effects in second language acquisition, and to needs analysis.

His contributions to task-based learning and teaching are immense. Mike was an inaugural recipient of the International Association for Task-Based Language Teaching's Distinguished Achievement Award. He has had a profound impact on the development of TBLT both as an area of enquiry, with high empirical standards, and also as an established pedagogical framework in many parts of the world. His impact on the field of TBLT lives on, through his writings, through his personal relationships with many researchers in the field (including the contributors to this book), and through the continuing achievements of his many Master's and doctoral students.

Mike's memorial webpage can be found at: https://iatblt.wixsite.com/mikelong.

Mohammad J. Ahmadian
Leeds May 2021

Contents

List of Figures		*page* xii
List of Tables		xiv
List of Contributors		xvii
Preface Michael H. Long and Mohammad J. Ahmadian		xxv

Part I: The Rationale for Task-Based Language Teaching 1

1   The Psycholinguistics of Task-Based Performance
    Peter Skehan   3

2   A Pedagogical Rationale for Task-Based Language Teaching for the Acquisition of Real-World Language Use   *Martin Bygate, Virginia Samuda, and Kris Van den Branden*   27

Part II: Tasks and Needs Analysis   53

3   Why Task? Task as a Unit of Analysis for Language Education   *Shoko Sasayama*   55

4   Adapting and Advancing Task-Based Needs Analysis Methodology across Diverse Language Learning Contexts   *Ellen J. Serafini*   73

4A Developing a Task-Based Approach: A Case Study of a Teacher Working with Australian Aboriginal Students in Vocational Education and Training   *Rhonda Oliver*   99

4B A Task-Based Language Needs Analysis of Syrian Refugee Parents in Turkey   *Şeyma Toker and Ayşenur Sağdıç*   109

4C Task-Based Language Teaching in a Japanese University: From Needs Analysis to Evaluation   *Craig Lambert*   121

4D The Implementation of a Task-Based Spanish Language Program in Qingdao, China: A Case Study   *Melissa Baralt, Wang Fei, Zhanting Bu, Hao Chen, José Morcillo Gómez, and Xunye Luan*   135

5   The L in TBLT: Analyzing Target Discourse   *Michael H. Long*   151

5A	Blustery with an Occasional Downpour: An Analysis of Target Discourse in Media Weather Forecasts *Ryo Maie and Bradford Salen*	173
5B	"I Have a Question": A Corpus-Based Analysis of Target Discourse in Office-Hour Interactions *Ayşenur Sağdıç and Derek Reagan*	188

Part III: The Task Syllabus and Materials — 203

6	The Cognition Hypothesis, the Triadic Componential Framework and the SSARC Model: An Instructional Design Theory of Pedagogic Task Sequencing *Peter Robinson*	205
7	From Needs Analysis to Task Selection, Design, and Sequencing *Roger Gilabert and Aleksandra Malicka*	226
7A	Task-Based Telecollaborative Exchanges between US and Italian Students: A Case Study in Program Design and Implementation *Elena Nuzzo and Diego Cortés Velásquez*	250
8	Exploring the Nuts and Bolts of Task Design *Virginia Samuda and Martin Bygate*	262
8A	Designing Pedagogic Tasks for Refugees Learning English to Enter Universities in the Netherlands *Seyit Ömer Gök and Marije Michel*	290

Part IV: Methodology and Pedagogy — 303

9	A Psycholinguistically Motivated Methodology for Task-Based Language Teaching *Gisela Granena and Yucel Yilmaz*	305
10	Technology-Mediated Task-Based Language Teaching *Marta González-Lloret and Nicole Ziegler*	326
10A	Delivering Task-Based Language Teaching at Scale: A Case Study of a Needs-Based, Technology-Mediated Workplace English Program *Katharine B. Nielson*	346
10B	Task-Based Language Teaching and Indigenous Language Revitalisation *Katherine J. Riestenberg and Ari Sherris*	359
10C	Task-Based Simulations for Diplomatic Security Agents *Catherine J. Doughty and Emilio Pascal*	374

Part V: Task-Based Language Teaching with School-Age Children — 395

11	Child Interaction in Task-Supported EFL/CLIL Contexts *María del Pilar García Mayo*	397
11A	Tasks for Children: Using Mainstream Content to Learn a Language *Rhonda Oliver and Masatoshi Sato*	416
11B	A Case Study of a Task-Based Approach for School-Age Learners in China *Yafu Gong and Peter Skehan*	432

Part VI: The Teacher in Task-Based Language Teaching 445
12   Teacher Preparation and Support for Task-Based Language
      Teaching   *Martin East*   447
12A Connecting Teacher Training to Task-Based Language
      Teaching Implementation: A Case Study of Preservice Teachers
      in Honduran Bilingual Schools   *Lara Bryfonski*   463
12B Training for Tasks the Cooperative Way: An Online Tutored
      Task-Based Language Teaching Course for Teachers, Managers
      and Course Designers   *Neil McMillan and Geoff Jordan*   478

Part VII: Task-Based Assessment and Program Evaluation   505
13   Task-Based Language Assessment   *John M. Norris and Martin East*   507
14   Evaluating Task-Based Language Programs   *John M. Norris and
      John McE. Davis*   529
14A Comparing the Effectiveness of Task-Based Language Teaching
      and Presentation-Practice-Production on Second Language
      Grammar Learning: A Pilot Study with Chinese Students of
      Italian as a Second Language   *Ilaria Borro*   549
14B Examining High-School Learners' Experience of Task
      Motivation and Difficulty in a Two-Week Spanish Immersion
      Camp   *Laura Gurzynski-Weiss, Lindsay Giacomino, and Dylan
      Jarrett*   566
14C Designing a Classroom-Based Task-Based Language
      Assessment Framework for Primary Schools: Blurring
      the Lines between Teaching, Learning, and Assessment
      Koen Van Gorp   585

Part VIII: Research Needs and Future Prospects   603
15   Methodological Approaches to Investigating
      Task-Based Language Teaching: Advances and
      Challenges   *Andrea Révész*   605
16   Task-Based Language Teaching as an Innovation: A
      Task for Teachers   *Kris Van den Branden*   628
17   The Adoption of Task-Based Language Teaching in Diverse
      Contexts: Challenges and Opportunities   *Jonathan Newton*   649
      Conclusion   *Mohammad J. Ahmadian and Michael H. Long*   671

Index   676

Figures

4D.1	A visual representation of the current program	page 145
5.1	Soccer texts: genuine, simplified, elaborated, and modified elaborated versions	166
5.2	Steps in an analysis of target discourse	168
5B.1	Overall structure and flow of office-hour interactions	194
6.1	The Triadic Componential Framework for task classification – categories, criteria, analytic procedures, and design characteristics	211
6.2	An example of increasing the complexity of pedagogic task versions following the SSARC Model of task sequencing	217
7A.1	Instructions for the second task of the second round	253
7A.2	First part of the instructions for the last task of the second round	257
8.1	Overview of empirically grounded design variables	270
8A.1	Task topics and sequence	295
8A.2	Pre-task activities for real-life task (B2)	296
8A.3	Main-task activities for real-life task (B2)	297
8A.4	Post-task activities for real-life task (B2)	297
10A.1	Screenshot of learning activity using an excerpt from a MaineHealth employee orientation video	349
10B.1	Spot-the-difference texts	364
10B.2	Some conversational feedback moves	369
10C.1	Questions to the Diplomatic Security Panel	376
10C.2	Diplomatic Security agents' requests for simulations	376
10C.3	Simulation design feedback from Diplomatic Security agents assigned in the field	377
10C.4	Diplomatic Security agent feedback on distance-learning tradecraft course	377
10C.5	Simulation 1: Assess security risks at a venue	380
10C.6	Simulation 2: Prepare a protection escort	382
10C.7	Simulation 3: Conduct a security motorcade	385

10C.8	Interview with female Diplomatic Security agent	388
10C.9	Interview with male Diplomatic Security agent	389
11A.1	Frequencies of meaning-focused input across four years over three terms	421
11A.2	Frequencies of input-providing and output-prompting corrective feedback across four year levels over three terms	422
11A.3	Frequencies of form-focused episodes across four year levels over three terms	423
11A.4	Frequencies of L1 use across four years over three terms	423
11A.5	Cumulative frequencies of focused pedagogical moves per hour	424
12A.1	Training timeline	467
12B.1	Course aims	481
12B.2	Output task criteria, Session 5	490
13.1	Example prompt for an Integrated Performance Assessment	514
13.2	Portion of a rating rubric from an Integrated Performance Assessment	514
13.3	Task-based assessment template from the Georgetown University German Department	515
14A.1	GSI calculated on reaction times to spill-over segments	559
14A.2	GSI calculated on reaction times to wrap-up segments	560
14A.3	UGJT outcomes	560
14B.1	SLIC program design	569
14B.2	Task-specific motivation questions	570
14B.3	Example of a reflective journal prompt	571
14B.4	Task difficulty questions	572
14B.5	Elements of task complexity	573
14B.6	Average ratings for all students (n = 8) by domain	575
14B.7	Average ratings for all students (n = 8) by day	576
14B.8	Day 1 design (University life: "finding suitemates")	580
14B.9	Day 7 design (#Adulting: "Healthy habits plan")	580
14B.10	Day 8 design (On the job: "Carry out a job interview")	580
14B.11	Average difficulty ratings for all students (n = 8) by domain	581
14B.12	Average difficulty ratings for all students (n = 8) by day	581
14C.1	Extract from the Flemish attainment goals for reading proficiency	590
14C.2	Matching advertisements	592
14C.3	Analysis diagram for reading tasks	594
14C.4	Reading task "Family looking for a robot" – guidelines for analysis	596
14C.5	A teacher's interpretation of student A's reading development	597
17.1	The role of context in TBLT research	653

Tables

1.1	Tasks, task conditions, and explicit-implicit processes	*page* 9
4.1	Examples of methodological rigor in task-based needs analysis practice	81
4B.1	Perceived frequency and difficulty of thirty target tasks	115
4B.2	Target task types and target tasks	118
4C.1	Criticality of task-types across workplace domains	123
4C.2	Criticality of criteria of success on oral tasks	124
4C.3	Syllabus content and task-types represented	126
4C.4	Evaluation of pedagogic tasks	130
4C.5	Evaluation of focus on form activities	131
5.1	Soccer texts by the numbers	167
5A.1	Summary of the broadcast sample	174
5A.2	Radio and television subtasks	177
5A.3	Radio forecast transcript 16MAR17MR1	178
5A.4	Television forecast transcript 07APR17AV2	179
5A.5	Frequency and proportion of utterances with ellipsis	182
5A.6	Top five most frequent collocations	182
5A.7	An example of prototypical discourse for afternoon FM radio	183
5A.8	An example of prototypical discourse for Local 1 television in the morning	184
5B.1	Characteristics of MICASE office hours	191
5B.2	Distribution of MICASE office-hour types	192
5B.3	A prototypical office-hour session	197
7.1	Dimensions of needs analysis and their description	233
7A.1	A comparison of the main features of the two rounds of the program	252
7A.2	Synthesis of the tasks administered in the two rounds	255
8.1	Task typology, based on Pica et al. (1993).	267
8.2	Task typology and tasks used in Skehan and Foster (1996–99)	268

8A.1	Task design	294
10A.1	MaineHealth employees hourly engagement in months 1 and 3 of the program	351
10A.2	Units with topics related to job tasks in careers in healthcare and hospitality, as well as daily tasks	352
10A.3	Average achievement test scores by type of test	353
10A.4	Voxy levels, proficiency test scores, and CEFR levels	353
10A.5	Engagement, proficiency, and achievement test scores for learners in Cohort 1	354
10A.6	Engagement, proficiency, and achievement test scores for learners in Cohort 2	354
10B.1	Rich and elaborated input	363
10B.2	Focus on form	366
10B.3	Providing negative feedback	367
10C.1	Diplomatic simulations	378
11A.1	Demographics of Mandarin CLIL teachers	418
11A.2	Frequencies of meaning-focused input moves across four year levels over three terms	421
11A.3	Frequencies of input-providing and output-prompting corrective feedback across four year levels over three terms	422
11A.4	Frequencies of form-focused episodes across four year levels over three terms	422
11A.5	Frequencies of L1 use across four year levels over three terms	423
11A.6	Cumulative frequencies of focused pedagogical moves for each year level	424
12A.1	Teacher backgrounds	466
12A.2	TBLT training	468
12A.3	Prominent daily reflection themes	472
12B.1	Participants' working roles	484
12B.2	Participants' highest qualifications	484
12B.3	Engagement in forum tasks	485
12B.4	Completion of Output tasks	487
14A.1	Needs analysis outcome	552
14A.2	SPR test: mean reaction times (standard deviation) to consistent and inconsistent items in the three tests at the spill-over and wrap-up segments	558
14A.3	GSI values	559
14A.4	UGJT outcomes: mean scores (SD)	560
14A.5	Functional-adequacy rates (median)	561
14B.1	Average ratings (standard deviation) for all students (n = 8) by domain	573
14B.2	Average ratings (standard deviation) for all students (n = 8) by day	574
14B.3	Daily exit tasks for each domain of the immersion program	575

14B.4	Average task difficulty/mental effort ratings for all students (n = 8) by domain	578
14B.5	Average task difficulty/mental effort ratings for all students (n = 8) by day	579
14C.1	Task-specification framework for the reading task "Family looking for a robot" (TotemTaal, Grade 4, Unit 1)	591
14C.2	Assessment framework in TotemTaal	593
17.1	Dimensions of context	651

Contributors

Mohammad J. Ahmadian is Head of Postgraduate Studies at the School of Education at the University of Leeds. His research has appeared in such journals as *TESOL Quarterly*, *Language Teaching Research*, *ELT Journal*, and the *International Journal of Applied Linguistics*.

Melissa Baralt is Associate Professor of Spanish Linguistics and Applied Psycholinguistics at Florida International University in Miami. She specializes in first and second language acquisition, bilingual language development, and language teaching. Her research seeks to shed light on the cognitive, environmental, and social factors that lead to successful language outcomes.

Ilaria Borro is about to complete her PhD in Applied Linguistics at the University of Portsmouth. She is a member of GRAAL, a research group whose main interest is in TBLT experimental research and language teachers training. She carried out and published experimental studies about corrective feedback and TBLT.

Lara Bryfonski is Assistant Professor of Linguistics at Georgetown University where she conducts research on second language acquisition and TBLT, specifically: training task-based teachers, corrective feedback, materials development, language learning in study abroad, and methods for second language research.

Zhanting Bu is Associate Professor of English Linguistics at Qingdao University in Shandong, China. He specializes in systemic functional linguistics and applied linguistics. He conducts research on academic and journalism discourses, with a focus on evaluative language using a corpus linguistics approach, to include appraisal theory.

Martin Bygate has been involved with TBLT throughout his career. A recipient of the International Association for Task-Based Language Teaching's Distinguished Achievement Award and a former co-editor of the journal *Applied Linguistics* and the John Benjamins TBLT series, he has published and edited widely. He is an emeritus professor at Lancaster University, UK, and now lives in France.

Hao Chen is a lecturer of Spanish at the School of Foreign Languages at Qingdao University in Shandong, China. She conducts research on Spanish language teaching and on Latin American literature. She has published translations of works by Alejo Carpentier, Che Guevara, Jordi Llobregat, Eduardo Zalamea Borda, and Javier Cercas.

Diego Cortés Velásquez is Associate Professor of Applied Linguistics at the University of Rome 3, Italy. His main research interests are TBLT, cross-cultural pragmatics, and intercomprehension. He also serves as an assistant editor for the journal *Instructed Second Language Acquisition*.

John McE. Davis is a research scientist in the Center for English Language Learning and Assessment at Educational Testing Service (ETS). He holds a PhD in Second Language Studies from the University of Hawai'i and conducts research and product development projects in language pedagogy, teacher training, and program evaluation.

Catherine Doughty is director of the Division of Curriculum and Staff Development in the Foreign Service Institute School of Language Studies, overseeing educational technology innovation, curriculum development, learning counseling services, and staff professional development. She leads the School of Language Studies in applying principles of instructed second language acquisition in language training for diplomats.

Martin East is Professor of Language Education in the School of Cultures, Languages and Linguistics at the University of Auckland, New Zealand, and, in 2017, began a term as president of the International Association for Task-Based Language Teaching. His research focus is on innovative practices in language pedagogy and assessment.

María del Pilar García Mayo is Professor of English Language and Linguistics at the University of the Basque Country (Spain). She has published widely on the second/third language acquisition of English morphosyntax and the study of conversational interaction in EFL. She is the director of the Language and Speech research group and the editor of *Language Teaching Research*.

Lindsay Giacomino is a Lecturer in the Department of World Languages and Cultures at Iowa State University. Her research focuses on task complexity, instructed second language acquisition of second language phonology, and individual differences with a focus on language-learning strategies.

Roger Gilabert is currently an associate professor and researcher at the University of Barcelona. His research interests include second and foreign language production and acquisition, task-based needs analysis, task design and task complexity, individual differences and second language production and acquisition, multimedia learning, and game-based learning and second-language acquisition.

Seyit Ömer Gök is an EAP lecturer at Groningen University. He has a PhD in Applied Linguistics from Leicester University, and his main research area is materials design and development. He is also interested in lesson study, teaching English to young learners, curriculum development, and course and syllabus design.

Yafu Gong is a senior research fellow at the National Institute of Education Sciences of China (NIES). His interests include curriculum development, task-based language teaching, English language assessment, and teacher professional development. He has published numerous articles and books, and presented at many conferences in China, including the TESOL China Assembly.

Marta González-Lloret is a professor of Spanish Applied Linguistics at the University of Hawai'i at Manoa. She has been teaching for more than twenty-five years and her research focuses on task-based language teaching, technology-mediated language learning, and second language pragmatics. She is currently, editor of the NFLRC Pragmatics & Language Learning book series, and co-editor of the John Benjamins TBLT series. She is president of the organization CALICO and secretary of the International Association of Task-Based Language Teaching. She is currently editing the *Routledge Handbook of Second Language Acquisition and Technology* with Nicole Ziegler.

Gisela Granena is an associate professor at the Open University of Catalonia (Spain). Her research interests include the role of cognitive aptitudes in instructed and naturalistic learning contexts; corrective feedback in computer-mediated communication; task-based language teaching; age effects; and measures of implicit and explicit language knowledge.

Laura Gurzynski-Weiss is Associate Professor and Director of Undergraduate Studies in the Department of Spanish and Portuguese at Indiana University. She investigates interaction- and task-based instructed second language acquisition, the dynamicity of individual differences, feedback use and perception, teacher cognition, and emerging bilingualism in elementary-aged children.

Dylan Jarrett is a PhD candidate in Hispanic Linguistics in the Department of Spanish and Portuguese at Indiana University. His research focuses on syntactic and semantic change, experimental approaches to meaning, and task-based instructed second language acquisition with a focus on learner motivation.

Geoff Jordan studied Philosophy of Science with Popper and Lakatos at the London School of Economics in the 1960s. He moved to Spain in 1978 and has been involved in ELT ever since. Now semi-retired, he works for Leicester University as an associate tutor on their distance learning MA in TESOL and Applied Linguistics, and with Neil McMillan on a distance-learning course on TBLT.

Craig Lambert is Associate Professor of Applied Linguistics and TESOL at Curtin University, Western Australia. His published work has appeared in *Studies in Second Language Acquisition, Applied Linguistics, Modern Language Journal, TESOL Quarterly*, and *Language Teaching Research*, among other international journals and edited books. His recent books include *Referent Similarity and Nominal Syntax in Task-Based Language Teaching* (Springer, 2019), *Task-Based Language Teaching: Theory and Practice* (with Rod Ellis and Peter Skehan; Cambridge, 2020) and an edited book *Using Tasks in Second Language Teaching: Practice in Diverse Contexts* (with Rhonda Oliver; Multilingual Matters, 2020).

Michael H. Long was Professor of Second Language Acquisition at the University of Maryland. His recent publications included the *Handbook of Language Teaching* (Blackwell, 2009) and *Second language acquisition and Task-Based Language Teaching* (Wiley-Blackwell, 2015). In 2009, he was awarded a doctorate honoris causa by Stockholm University for his contributions to the field of second language acquisition. In 2017, he received a lifetime achievement award from the International Association for Task-Based Language Teaching. He passed away in 2021, shortly before the publication of this book.

Xunye Luan is a lecturer of Spanish at the School of Foreign Languages at Qingdao University in Shandong, China. He specializes in regional language policies, Spanish language teaching, and language teaching methodologies in China. He works closely with Chinese teachers to implement communicative approaches to Spanish foreign language teaching.

Ryo Maie is a PhD student in Second Language Studies at Michigan State University and holds an MA in Second Language Acquisition from the University of Maryland. His interests include cognitive psychology of second language acquisition, usage-based and cognitive linguistics approaches to language learning, and applied statistics in second language research.

Aleksandra Malicka is a member of the Open University of Catalonia TechSLA Lab research group. Her research activity focuses on second language acquisition in traditional and online contexts, learning based on pedagogical tasks, curriculum design, personalized learning, and the role of individual differences in the process of learning a second language.

Neil McMillan is a freelance English teacher, teacher-educator and materials designer based in Barcelona, Spain since 2010. He holds a doctorate in Scottish literature from the University of Glasgow (2001) and has worked in the English language teaching industry since 2002. He helped set up the cooperative SLB in 2014, and is its current president. He is currently an author and collaborating professor for the Open University of Catalonia on the Master's degree in Technology-Mediated Language Teaching and Learning.

Marije Michel is Associate Professor and the chair of Language Learning at Groningen University. Her research covers socio-cognitive aspects of second language acquisition and task-based language pedagogy, focusing on second language writing processes and alignment in digital contexts. Marije is the treasurer of the European Second Language Association (EuroSLA) and co-chair of the AILA World Congress of Applied Linguistics 2021.

Jose Morcillo Gómez is a teaching professor of Spanish for the Florida International Dual Degree in Spanish, located at Qingdao University in Shandong, China. He also serves as the program coordinator. His research encompasses TBLT in China, task-based methodology, and technology-mediated TBLT, examining teachers' cognitive load with eye-tracking technology.

Jonathan Newton is Associate Professor and Programme Director for the MA in Applied Linguistics/TESOL Programmes at the School of Linguistics and Applied Language Studies (LALS) at Victoria University of Wellington, New Zealand.

Katharine B. Nielson earned her PhD in second language acquisition from the University of Maryland in 2013. She is the founder of Voxy EnGen, a public benefit company that delivers high-quality, needs-based English instruction to immigrants and refugees, rapidly giving them the tools they need to advocate for themselves and improve their economic outcomes.

John Norris is Senior Research Director of the Center for Language Education and Assessment Research at ETS. He holds a PhD in Second Language Acquisition from the University of Hawai'i, and he conducts research on task-based language teaching, language assessment, program evaluation, and teacher development.

Elena Nuzzo is Associate Professor of Applied Linguistics at the University of Rome 3. She teaches and researches in the fields of second language acquisition and teaching, with a focus on second language Italian. Her main research interests include applications of speech act theory to second language learning and cross-cultural communication, and TBLT.

Rhonda Oliver is Head of the School of Education at Curtin University, Western Australia. She has published extensively on second language acquisition, especially in relation to child language learners, but has also conducted research on language learners in high schools and universities. Recently she has undertaken work in the area of Aboriginal education.

Emilio Pascal is the education technology specialist in the Romance Languages Division at the Foreign Service Institute School of Language Studies, where his focus is to integrate web technologies into teaching and learning, as well as to develop digital curricula. His areas of expertise include immersive simulation design and distance learning.

Derek Reagan is a doctoral student in Applied Linguistics at Georgetown University. His main research interests include task-based language teaching, second language pedagogy, technology-assisted language learning, and teacher cognition. Derek has experience teaching English and Spanish in K–12 and university settings in the United States and abroad.

Andrea Révész is Professor of Second Language Acquisition at the UCL Institute of Education, University College London. Her main research interests lie at the interface of second language acquisition and instruction, with particular emphases on the roles of task, input, interaction, and individual differences in second language acquisition. In relation to these topics, she also holds an interest in investigating the cognitive processes underlying second language performance and development using mixed-methods approaches.

Katherine J. Riestenberg is a visiting assistant professor at Haverford College. She conducts research on language teaching and learning with a focus on the revitalization of Indigenous and minoritized languages. She works closely with language teachers and activists in the United States and Mexico to teach languages and create educational materials.

Peter Robinson is Professor of Linguistics and Second Language Acquisition at Aoyama Gakuin University in Tokyo, Japan, where he teaches courses in Applied Linguistics and Second Language Acquisition, and supervises graduate student dissertation research.

Ayşenur Sağdıç is a PhD candidate in Applied Linguistics at Georgetown University. Ayşenur's research focuses primarily on second language pragmatics, task-based language teaching, and technology-assisted language learning. Her work has appeared in journals such as System, Applied Pragmatics, ITL - International Journal of Applied Linguistics as well as several edited volumes.

Bradford Salen is a PhD student in the Department of Linguistics at Georgetown University. He studied Linguistics and Second Language Acquisition at the University of Maryland. His research interests include computational approaches to second language processing, language acquisition and assessment, and psycholinguistics.

Virginia Samuda has worked in Brazil, Singapore, the United States and the United Kingdom as a language teacher, materials writer, teacher educator and classroom researcher, and has long been interested in the use of tasks in language education, pedagogic task design and the role of the teacher in TBLT. She currently lives in France.

Shoko Sasayama is Associate Research Scientist at ETS, where she specializes in task-based language teaching, language assessment, and teacher training. Her research focuses on the role of task design in learning and assessment, including her award-winning publication, "Is a 'complex' task really complex? Validating the assumption of cognitive task complexity" in *Modern Language Journal* (2016).

Masatoshi Sato is a professor at Andrés Bello University, Chile. His research interests include peer interaction, corrective feedback, learner psychology, and the research–pedagogy link. In addition to his publications in international journals and co-edited volumes (John Benjamins, 2016; Routledge, 2017, 2019; LTR: 2021), his textbook from Cambridge University Press (with Shawn Loewen) will appear in 2022.

Ellen J. Serafini is Associate Professor of Spanish Applied Linguistics at George Mason University, Virginia. Her research explores how social, pedagogical, and individual factors dynamically impact learner outcomes in diverse language learning settings. Her work appears in edited volumes and journals such as the *Modern Language Journal, Studies in Second Language Acquisition,* and the *International Journal of Bilingual Education and Bilingualism.*

Ari Sherris is Associate Professor of Bilingual Education at Texas A&M University–Kingsville. His research focuses on Indigenous communities strengthening their language and education. He supports Salish Qlispe and Safaliba wellness, activism, and self-determination. His recent work is published in the journals *Language Awareness* and *Writing and Pedagogy.*

Peter Skehan is an honorary research fellow at Birkbeck College. He has taught at universities in the United Kingdom, Hong Kong, and New Zealand. His interests include second language acquisition, particularly task-based instruction and language aptitude. He is currently researching speaking style in task-based performance.

Şeyma Toker is a doctoral candidate in Applied Linguistics at Georgetown University. Her research interests include multilingualism, migration, identity and social justice in second language acquisition. Şeyma has taught several EFL/ESL courses in Italy, Turkey and the United States and has experience mentoring pre-service teachers and volunteer tutors for adult refugee learners.

Kris Van den Branden is Professor of Linguistics and a teacher educator at the Faculty of Arts at the KU Leuven (Belgium). He is one of the series editors of the Task-Based Language Teaching: Issues, Research, and Practice series (John Benjamins) and an editor of *TASK: Journal on Task-Based Language Teaching and Learning.*

Koen Van Gorp is Assistant Professor of TESOL and Second Language Studies at Michigan State University. He is a research fellow at the Centre for Language and Education (KU Leuven, Belguim) and co-editor of *TASK: Journal on Task-Based Language Teaching and Learning.*

Fei Wang is a lecturer of Spanish at the School of Foreign Languages at Qingdao University in Shandong, China. She specializes in second-language acquisition and foreign-language teacher training. Her research seeks to elucidate the cognitive, social, political, environmental, and emotional factors that affect successful foreign-language learning.

Yucel Yilmaz is Associate Professor of Second Language Studies at Indiana University. His research focuses on second-language interaction and corrective feedback; computer-mediated communication; task-based language teaching; individual differences in second-language acquisition; and explicit and implicit learning processes.

Nicole Ziegler is Associate Professor of Second Language Studies at the University of Hawai'i at Mānoa. Her research agenda focuses on instructed second-language acquisition, including mixed method and interdisciplinary research in second language interaction, task-based language teaching, technology-mediated language learning, and task-based approaches for Maritime English.

Preface
The Origins and Growth of Task-Based Language Teaching

Michael H. Long and Mohammad J. Ahmadian

The use of various kinds of tasks to promote language development is the core component in an innovative approach to foreign and second language learning, task-based language teaching (TBLT), the focus of this volume. Tasks also occupy a central role in a thriving area of investigation in the field of second language acquisition. TBLT and second language acquisition enjoy a symbiotic relationship.

Task-based language teaching was first proposed in the 1980s and 1990s (Long, 1985; Long & Crookes, 1992, 1993; Nunan, 1989; Robinson, 1994, 1998; Skehan, 1996). Its early advocacy was initially ignored or, in some quarters, greeted with a mixture of skepticism and outright hostility, notably from textbook writers and armchair pedagogues. Criticisms continue to this day, although they tend to be more measured now. Some are rational, constructive, and serve to motivate new research and improvements to classroom practice. Others clearly reflect misunderstandings or thinly disguised commercial agendas – even though TBLT is no panacea. (For detailed deconstructions and responses, see, for example, R. Ellis [2009], Long [2016], Robinson [1994], Skehan [2002].)

After the slow start, interest in the use of tasks, both in TBLT and second language acquisition, has grown steadily over the past twenty years. This is apparent in the increasing numbers of monographs, edited volumes, articles, and special issues of major second language acquisition and language-teaching journals devoted to TBLT, as well as the creation in 2009 of a TBLT book series, published by John Benjamins. Under the stewardship of Kris Van den Branden, Martin Bygate, and John Norris, the International Association for TBLT (iatblt.org) was formed in 2005, and has held eight biannual international conferences: Leuven (2005), Hawai'i (2007), Lancaster (2009), Auckland (2011), Alberta (2013), Leuven (2015), Barcelona (2019), and Ottawa (2019). The ninth is scheduled for Innsbruck in 2022. The

IATBLT also recently launched a new journal: *TASK – Journal on Task-Based Language Teaching and Learning*.

Why the Interest?

There are at least five reasons for the growing interest in TBLT:

1. Adult learners perceive the relevance of courses that have obviously been designed to meet their real-world second language (L2) needs, not those of someone else or of no-one in particular – courses through which they can acquire a *functional command* of the L2, not merely learn *about* it.
2. Evaluations consistently show that students and teachers prefer task-based to grammar-based courses. Adult and school-age learners, alike, find working on communicative pedagogic tasks more interesting, enjoyable and motivating, and teachers respond to their students' enthusiasm. Traditional grammar-based lessons, conversely, tend to become monotonous, with no apparent purpose other than to introduce the "structure of the day" (whether or not the students concerned are developmentally ready for it), and then to practice it on the altar of "automatization," as if second language acquisition were a matter of acquiring a new set of language habits.
3. Numerous studies of various aspects of task-based language learning and teaching have appeared in books and refereed journals – far more research in forty years than on all other approaches to language teaching combined. Comparative studies at the program level consistently find that students not only prefer task-based courses, but also learn more from them (Bryfonski & Mackay, 2017). It has often been observed that TBLT is the closest the field has ever had to a researched pedagogy.
4. With its focus on incidental and implicit language learning while doing tasks, not just explicit language learning, TBLT lends itself to situations where syllabus content has to give priority, or at least equal billing, to something other than language. Such is the case with immersion, bilingual education, content-and-language-integrated learning (CLIL), and tertiary-level English medium instruction (EMI) programs, among others. It is no accident that some early adopters have included programs within economically and politically powerful countries or regions whose languages – Japanese, Korean, German, Flemish, Cantonese, Italian, Russian, Swedish, Finnish, Catalan, Basque, Polish, Urdu, Persian, etc. – have limited numbers of speakers beyond their own borders, so where the L2 is taught as an important subject or even used as a medium of instruction. Others have been government agencies, educational institutions, and occupational and vocational training programs – for groups as varied as physicians, diplomats, airline

personnel, journalists, nurses, military linguists, and tourism industry workers – in which functional L2 abilities are recognized as important. In all these cases, L2 learning and teaching are taken seriously, and TBLT is recognized as a viable option.
5. The underlying principles of TBLT are in general alignment with the results of over four decades of theory and research on second language acquisition inside and outside classrooms, which, after all, is the process language teaching is designed to facilitate. The same research findings, conversely, are not at all consistent with attempts to impose a generic, pre-set, grammatical syllabus on students, with no regard for their developmental stage, for individual differences, or for why they are learning the L2. The second language acquisition research findings are also inconsistent with the way a grammatical syllabus is typically delivered: via present – practice – produce (PPP).

If Task-Based Language Teaching Is So Good, Why Isn't It More Widely Used?

Despite the increased interest, scholarly research and writing, and successful implementation in many programs around the world, task-based course design has had less impact on what goes on in classrooms than might have been expected by now. Most language teaching continues to be based on coursebooks that adhere to a grammatical syllabus and PPP. If TBLT is really such an improvement, why should that be?

There are several reasons, six of which are listed below:

1. A major factor is the multi-billion dollar publishing industry's stranglehold on language teaching. Its most lucrative product is the coursebook, and even more lucrative, the coursebook series, whose destructive impact on any kind of communicative language teaching, not just TBLT, has long been pointed out, most perceptively by Geoffrey Jordan in journal articles (e.g., Jordan, 2019; Jordan and Gray, 2019) and in the archives of his insightful and amusing blog, *What do you think you're doing?* (https://applingtesol.wordpress.com/author/duffyjordan/). Publishers spend large amounts of money on advertising, conference sponsorships, and wining and dining people who make decisions about textbook adoptions. Perhaps this should not be surprising. Vast profits are made from harmful products in many walks of life (nuclear weapons, armaments, fossil fuels, opioids, animal products, etc.), and albeit on a smaller scale, language teaching is no exception.
2. Millions of language teachers lack adequate training (in many cases, *any* training), a problem often compounded by an inadequate command of the language they are teaching. Coursebooks are attractive to such teachers and the school systems that employ them because they

provide predigested lessons that are easy to use and do not require much expertise at all. The target language is cut up into manageable, bite-sized pieces, and typical exercise formats do not require an advanced command of the L2. Each unit follows the same familiar structure. Pedagogic decisions, however ill-conceived, have already been made for them by the textbook writer.

3. Another reason the status quo persists is washback from language testing, which, like publishing, has become a multi-billion dollar industry increasingly centralized in the hands of a few powerful corporations. Most of their products target receptive skills through a combination of discrete-point vocabulary or grammatical items and multiple-choice listening or reading comprehension questions. The tests are often machine-scorable, so cheaper to administer, thereby increasing profits for the vendors. The tests typically have high internal reliability, which, given enough items with a wide range of difficulty, and test-takers of a wide range of ability, is easy to achieve. Validity is a different matter, less talked about; suffice to say, few standardized tests can be accused of assessing communicative – much less, domain-specific, task-based – abilities.

4. A properly designed TBLT program requires expertise at both the program and classroom levels, including an initial investment of resources to conduct a learner needs analysis, followed by production or purchase of task-based materials and tests. Task banks can gradually be built by materials designers and teachers, but the absence of appropriate pedagogic materials often constitutes a bottleneck in the early days of setting up a genuine TBLT program, necessitating only gradual transition to full-fledged task-based instruction. The investment for whole programs is minor, compared with the long-term benefits, of course, but beyond the reach of most teachers, especially if they are working alone. Institutional support is crucial. The ideal settings for TBLT are countries or institutions where a functional command of an L2 is very important and where similar types of students can be predicted over time. Communicative needs will be similar, as a result, meaning that additional needs analyses for new cohorts will be unnecessary, and with some fine-tuning, materials and tests can be re-used, making the whole program more cost-effective.

5. Contrary to what has sometimes been alleged, teachers play a much more important role in TBLT than in grammar-based programs (Skehan, 2002; Long, 2016; Van den Branden, 2016). For most applied linguists, ourselves included, this is as it should be, with the teacher the appropriate decision-maker in his or her classroom, not a distant textbook writer who has never met the students concerned. However, this usually requires a better command of the L2, basic professional training, and an understanding of the rationale for TBLT. Even then, concrete models and support for teachers are very important in the early

stages (East, this volume), as documented, for example, in the histories of one of the earliest successful implementations of TBLT in over 200 primary and secondary schools in Flanders (Van den Branden, 2006).

6. The lack of sufficient concrete models of TBLT in action has often been lamented. Teachers understandably want to see real examples of task-based materials and lessons. In fact, plenty of potential models exist, but not many have been described – or better yet, videoed – and published, as few books or journals cater to such "hands-on" material. One aim of the present volume is to begin to rectify the situation through inclusion of a chapter and case studies about materials design and classroom implementation (e.g., Doughty & Pascal, this volume; Gök & Michel, this volume; Samuda & Bygate, this volume; Toker & Sağdıç, this volume) describing concrete examples of each step in the design and implementation of a TBLT program, including, again, what goes on in the classroom. The problem, of course, is that concrete examples will inevitably illustrate TBLT in use with particular populations in specific settings (e.g., programs for children or adults, for foreign or second language learners, for academic, occupational, or vocational training, for refugees or migrant workers, for struggling indigenous communities, in culturally proximate or distant settings, and so on). Populations and settings vary greatly, so most readers will still have to generalize (i.e., abstract away from those examples), when seeking ideas and guidance for their own situation.

The Present Volume

As the title indicates, *The Cambridge Handbook of Task-Based Language Teaching* concerns task-based, not task-supported, language teaching. In task-supported language teaching (TSLT), miscellaneous pedagogic tasks are employed, not because they are relevant to students' intended uses of the L2 beyond the classroom (which are unknown, because there is no needs analysis in TSLT), but to practice items in a grammatical syllabus. Thus, the psycholinguistic rationales for the two approaches are very different. Of course, needs analyses are also irrelevant when designing task-based programs for young learners, whose eventual uses of the L2 are usually unknown. Then, the designer is free to choose high-interest pedagogic tasks for them, but again, tasks whose purpose is to engage students in communicative L2 use, not to practice particular structures.

A well-known example of TSLT is the procedural syllabus, proposed by Prabhu and trialed in the Bangalore Project (Prabhu, 1987). The procedural syllabus is of historical interest, but has little in common with the task syllabus, and suffers from several major flaws and limitations. (For detailed critical analyses, see Beretta [1989, 1990], Long [2015: 216–21].) Indeed,

TSLT and hybrid TBLT and TSLT syllabuses continue to find support in some quarters (e.g., R. Ellis, 1993, 2019), but their embrace of the psycholinguistically discredited grammatical syllabus, among several other problems, makes them qualitatively different from genuine TBLT, so they are not dealt with in this book. Pedagogic tasks in TBLT are defined (for present purposes, simply) as meaning-focused, outcome-oriented activities whose (task, not linguistic) complexity gradually increases until they resemble the target tasks that students will do through the L2 outside the classroom.

This handbook is intended to serve as a comprehensive, up-to-date, scholarly survey of TBLT, of use to theorists and researchers, but most importantly, to practitioners. It should appeal to a wide readership, including the following:

1. Preservice and inservice language teachers keen to implement TBLT in their teaching context, but insufficiently familiar with the requirements, procedures, and implications of this approach to language teaching.
2. Inservice language teachers who already use TBLT, wholly or in part, but would like to brush up on or expand their knowledge of recent developments in the area.
3. Postgraduate students and experienced researchers who are keen to know more about the latest theory and research on TBLT, as well as about innovations in the ways and diverse real-world settings in which it is implemented.

Numerous aspects of tasks and TBLT are the subject of debate and merit serious further exploration: TBLT does not have all the answers. There are knowledge gaps of which we are aware, and in all probability, others of which we are blissfully ignorant. The speed with which the TBLT and task-related second language acquisition literature is expanding makes it difficult for both practitioners and researchers to find up-to-date surveys written by experts, yet produced in an accessible style and with concrete examples that make the discussions meaningful for classroom teachers.

The co-editors, Mohammad Ahmadian and Michael Long, have both taught courses on TBLT, including demonstration lessons and microteaching, to graduate students and preservice and inservice teachers in the Middle East, East Asia, the United Kingdom, continental Europe, Australia and the United States for many years now (since 1980 in Long's case), and are familiar with practical requirements. Both they and their students have been conducting original empirical studies of TBLT for many years, too. One of the most important needs for teachers and researchers is a single volume that not only introduces current debates but also presents case studies that showcase how genuine TBLT is implemented, not just in the laboratory, but via the use of technology and in the classroom, and with as wide a range of populations and in as wide a range of contexts as possible. *The Cambridge Handbook of Task-Based Language Teaching* is accompanied by a companion website which contains supplementary materials, including tasks, syllabi, and any other resources used in case studies. We are grateful to the authors of the chapters and case studies, to anonymous outside readers, and to Rebecca Taylor and Isabel Collins at Cambridge University Press, for helping to fill this need.

References

Beretta, A. (1989). Attention to form or meaning? Error treatment in the Bangalore Project. *TESOL Quarterly*, 23(2), 283–303.

Beretta, A. (1990). Implementation of the Bangalore Project. *Applied Linguistics*, 11(4), 321–37.

Bryfonski, L. and McKay, T. H. (2017). TBLT implementation and evaluation: A meta-analysis. *Language Teaching Research*, 23(5), 603–32.

Ellis, R. (1993). Second language acquisition and the structural syllabus. *TESOL Quarterly*, 27(1), 91–113.

Ellis, R. (2009). Task-based language teaching: Sorting out the misunderstandings. *International Journal of Applied Linguistics*, 16(2), 221–46.

Ellis, R. (2019). Towards a modular language curriculum for using tasks. *Language Teaching Research*, 23(4), 454–75.

Jordan, G. (2019). A response to Hughes. *ELT Journal*, 73(4), 456–58.

Jordan, G. and Gray, H. (2019). We need to talk about coursebooks. *ELT Journal*, 73(4), 438–46.

Long, M. H. (1985). A role for instruction in second language acquisition: task-based language teaching. In K. Hyltenstam and M. Pienemann, eds. *Modeling and assessing second language development*. Bristol: Multilingual Matters, pp. 77–99.

Long, M. H. (2015). *Second language acquisition and task-based language teaching*. Oxford: Wiley-Blackwell.

Long, M. H. (2016). In defense of tasks and TBLT: Non-issues and real issues. *Annual Review of Applied Linguistics*, 36, 5–33.

Long, M. H. and Crookes, G. (1992). Three approaches to task-based language teaching. *TESOL Quarterly*, 26(1), 27–56.

Long, M. H. and Crookes, G. (1993). Units of analysis in syllabus design: The case for task. In G. Crookes and S. M. Gass, eds. *Tasks in pedagogical context. Integrating theory and practice*. Bristol: Multilingual Matters, pp. 9–54.

Nunan, D. (1989). *Designing tasks for the communicative classroom*. Cambridge: Cambridge University Press.

Prabhu, N. S. (1984). Procedural syllabuses. In J. A. S. Read, ed. *Trends in Language Syllabus Design*. Singapore: SEAMEO Regional Language Centre, pp. 272–80.

Prabhu, N. S. (1987). *Second language pedagogy*. Oxford: Oxford University Press.

Robinson, P. (1994). Comments on Rod Ellis' "The structural syllabus- and second language acquisition." Implicit knowledge, second language learning and syllabus construction: motivating relationships. *TESOL Quarterly*, 28(1), 161–66.

Robinson, P. (1998). State of the art: SLA theory and second language syllabus design. *The Language Teacher*, 22(4), 7–14.

Skehan, P. (1996). A framework for the implementation of task-based instruction. *Applied Linguistics*, 17(1), 38–62.

Skehan, P. (2002). A non-marginal role for tasks. *ELT Journal*, 56(3), 289–95.

Van den Branden, K., ed. (2006). *Task-based language education: From theory to practice*. Cambridge: Cambridge University Press.

Van den Branden, K. (2016). The role of teachers in task-based language education. *Annual Review of Applied Linguistics*, 36, 164–81.

Part I

The Rationale for Task-Based Language Teaching

1

The Psycholinguistics of Task-Based Performance

Peter Skehan

1.1 Background Issues

Traditional accounts of second and foreign language learning are not learner-centred. What is to be taught is decided by the teacher, often in conjunction with textbooks or wider national or school-based policies. In such cases the units underlying teaching are usually structural, and the sequencing is based, largely, on convention – the sequence that is (collectively and unempirically) regarded to conform to a linguistic analysis of difficulty. Methodology is likely to move from presentation of (teacher-chosen, decontextualised) material, followed by controlled practice and then some freer production. All of this puts the teacher centre-stage, assumes the teacher knows best, and relegates the learner to a passive bit-part role (Skehan, 2002; Long, 2015).

In contrast, task-based approaches start from the learner and from meaning. Tasks require learners to express worthwhile and frequently personal meanings. Then, the language that is important is the language used to express those meanings, as determined by the learner. The tasks themselves may be the result of a needs analysis of how the learner will use language (Long, 2015), or the result of choosing a challenge at the right level of complexity (Willis & Willis, 2007), or even negotiated with the learners themselves (Gong & Skehan, this volume). The intention is that the task will be facilitative of the learner being able to shape language development in ways that are individual and maximise the chances that *personal* developmental paths will be followed, as opposed to paths that have been devised for everyone, and for no-one (Long, 2015; Ellis et al., 2020).

1.2 Exploring the Nature of Learning

Underlying any claims about language instruction, traditional or task-based, has to be a view of what language learning is. Broadly the major distinction is that between explicit learning and implicit learning (Ortega, 2009). The former is associated with some degree of awareness of what is being learned, a clear linguistic focus, and, possibly, metalinguistic focus. The latter, implicit learning, does not involve consciousness or metalinguistic knowledge. It is assumed to take place in response to statistical regularities within input, and so exposure to input, and the patterns it contains, are enough to lead to development.

In relation to language learning, a number of positions have been advanced that are relevant to task-based instruction. A clear starting point here is De Keyser's (2020) account of learning. He assumes that first language acquisition is largely implicit in nature, but that there is a critical period, after which language learning is essentially explicit. His account is based on work within cognitive psychology that explores consistent paths within explicit learning (Anderson, 1995). These include the fundamental stages of explicit initial learning, followed by proceduralisation and automatisation, where fluency is achieved. Key issues here are the well-established path that this sort of learning follows (cf. the power law of practice, N. Ellis, 2002), and the need for considerable opportunity to use the target item or pattern of language for the power law to come into operation. In addition, however, there is the issue of transfer-appropriate processing (De Keyser, 2020), the finding that generalisation of a specific piece of learning may not be easily accomplished, a point of some importance in a domain as complex as language.

A clear exponent of the contrasting implicit learning perspective is Paradis (2009). He accepts that explicit learning can occur in older learners, but that implicit learning is the preferable learning mode – more enduring and more robust. Ullman (2015) also considers that explicit and implicit learning are completely distinct, but is more charitable in his view of explicit learning, suggesting that the two types of learning can co-exist and that each has its strengths and weaknesses.

An additional possibility is that explicit learning and knowledge can become implicit learning and knowledge. This has been the basis for the different interface positions that exist (R. Ellis, 1994; Han & Finneran, 2013). These explore whether explicit learning can become implicit learning (the strong interface position) or whether explicit learning can facilitate subsequent implicit learning (the weak interface position) (R. Ellis, 2006). For now, it is difficult to make a clear distinction between a strong version of the explicit-to-automatisation account and the explicit-becomes-implicit account. As we will see, this turns out to be not a vital problem for task-based approaches.

These different accounts of the nature of learning and of knowledge feed into our understanding of the underlying theory of using tasks in language learning (Ellis et al., 2020). It is clear that the different accounts contrast, and so the broad question is whether task-based approaches are more consistent with any particular one of these positions, or whether it can accommodate more than one of them. To address this question, we need to engage with the details of task-based instruction.

1.3 An Overview of Task-Based Instruction Components

In this section on task components, we will first focus on tasks themselves, and then explore the relevance of task conditions. Regarding the first of these, the last thirty years has seen considerable research into how different task types and characteristics have impacted upon language development and performance. Important generalisations have emerged from this research. For example:

- Structured tasks raise accuracy (Skehan & Foster, 1999).
- Information manipulation and/or integration raise complexity (Tavakoli & Foster, 2008).
- Tasks based on familiar and/or concrete information raise fluency (Skehan & Foster, 1997).
- Tasks with more elements raise accuracy (Gilabert, 2007; Révész, 2011).
- Tasks with more support raise fluency (Malicka & Sasayama, 2017).

It is noteworthy that many of the researchers who have contributed to this literature view performance in terms of complexity, lexis, accuracy, and fluency. We will explore these areas from a performance perspective in a later section, but in terms of learning, they are consistent with a pressure towards initial development (complexity, structural, and lexical), followed by greater control, with lower error (accuracy) and then producing language more smoothly, quickly, and without repair (fluency). So these performance areas do have a developmental dynamic also.

Interesting as these findings from task research are, it has also been argued (Skehan, 2016) that there are relatively few robust and reliable generalisations associated with task characteristics. In contrast, findings from task conditions research have been more dependable and generally associated with larger effect sizes (Skehan, 2016, 2018). We need to consider what happens before a task, what happens during the task, and finally what happens after the task has been completed.

Research at the pre-task phase has been predominantly associated with planning. An extensive literature exists, with fairly consistent generalisations. For example:

- Pre-task planning is consistently associated with higher complexity and fluency (Ortega, 2005).
- Planning has more effect when tasks are more complex (Foster & Skehan, 2012).
- Speakers prioritise accuracy first, and complexity later (Mehnert, 1998).
- More time for planning leads to greater fluency (Skehan & Foster, 2005).

But the pre-task phase is not, in principle, confined to planning. There are studies exploring pre-task video monitoring (Kim, 2013; Kim & McDonough, 2011). In addition, a range of more pedagogic (and less formally researched) techniques are available (Willis & Willis, 2007) to provide relevant input pre-task, so that students can do a task more effectively.

Most pre-task research suggests that it is the ideas and organisation of the task that are emphasised (Skehan, 2018). In other words, there is pressure on the interlanguage system to grow as it is pushed to express more complex meanings. There is a consistent language complexity effect across many studies and proficiency levels (Bui et al., 2018). There is also a robust fluency effect, in this case seemingly associated with structural complexity driving larger units of production, and making pausing and repair less likely (Skehan, 2018). It has been proposed (R. Ellis, 2003) that pre-task preparation can also lead to rehearsal of what is going to be said, although accuracy effects from pre-task planning are not as consistent or large (Ortega, 2005). Pang and Skehan (2014) make some suggestions as to why this is so. Those doing a task need to remember what was planned, or attended to, earlier. If they do not, the advantages are diminished. From the qualitative study Pang and Skehan report that participants tended to have difficulty in remembering this information and so the potential gain was lost.

The task phase itself has also been the focus for considerable research, not so much for the task itself, but for the way the task is done. For example, Ellis and Yuan (2005) have argued that we need to consider on-line, as well as pre-task, planning. On-line planning is the regrouping and anticipation that occurs while a task is actually being done. They (Yuan & Ellis, 2003; Ellis & Yuan, 2004) operationalised this through giving more time for task completion. The results suggest that when tasks are done with more relaxed time conditions, there is greater accuracy. More time enables more attention to be directed to avoiding error, and to monitoring (Ahmadian, 2012a, 2012b; Ahmadian & Tavakoli, 2014). Wang (2014) reports that a combination of pre-task and on-line planning is the most effective treatment of all, since it leads to greater complexity *and* accuracy: having something to say and also the conditions to be accurate in saying it.

The other major area for research, mid-task, has been the nature of the feedback that is provided (Mackey, 2012). Learners working on completing a task are likely to encounter communicative difficulties and then potentially receive feedback on their attempts at communication that misfire (Long, 2015). Provision of feedback at this point is therefore extremely timely and personalised. The interaction hypothesis proposes that these conditions are ideal for language development: a need to mean, an indication of where there is a limitation, and then help to remedy this situation (Mackey, 2012). Feedback is being provided, in other words, at exactly the right moment (Doughty, 2001) for processing and for potential incorporation into an emerging interlanguage system. A considerable literature now exists on the major dimensions along which feedback can be located (input providing vs output prompting, and explicit vs implicit) and also which sorts of feedback are most effective. The central point here is that during the task, we have a process that can advance underlying ability to use a language (Ellis & Shintani, 2014).

Next we turn to the post-task phase, and it will be argued that there are two general possibilities here: post-task tasks, and post-task development (Skehan, 2007, 2013). Post-task tasks themselves are of two sorts. First of all, there is the opportunity to repeat a task. The literature in this area has grown rapidly in recent years (Bygate, 2001, 2018). A range of alternative approaches to implementing repetition have indicated that, cleverly done, learners are happy to see the advantages of doing a task more than once. Lynch and Maclean (2001), for example, show how the use of a poster carousel worked well with a group of oncologists where one of a pair presented a poster to a changing audience. The findings from the literature suggest that a repeated performance is very clearly superior to the original (Wang, 2009); that if there is more than one repetition, there is some degree of sequence in what is emphasised. Lambert et al. (2016) report that early repetitions focus on complexity, then fluency comes more into prominence, followed eventually by a concern for accuracy.

An alternative post-task condition is to give learners a task to do after the task proper in an attempt to modify the way they did the actual task. There is the danger that learners may concentrate excessively on getting a task done and bypass form. Clearly a teacher cannot interfere while a task is being done, so it is difficult to insinuate pedagogic norms into the task itself. Following suggestions by Lynch (2007), Skehan and collaborators (Skehan & Foster, 1997; Foster & Skehan, 2013; Li, 2014) have explored whether anticipation of a post-task condition can change how the original task was done. Specifically, they wanted to achieve a greater prioritisation of accuracy. Broadly the studies were consistent with this claim. Interestingly, of two post-task operationalisations, requiring speakers to transcribe their performance had a stronger influence on accuracy than telling speakers that they might be required to re-do a task publicly. So it appears that foreknowledge of what is to come can change the nature of attention allocation within a task.

More ambitiously, though, the post-task phase can be used to develop the language that has been made salient by an actual task – in other words, to exploit the task performance for purposes of instruction (Willis & Willis, 2007). Tasks themselves emphasise meaning, and so something additional may be needed to bring form into focus. But if a task has been successful in creating a need to mean (Samuda, 2001), the possibilities created by a task can be vital, provided that they are capitalised upon. In other words, if there is noticing within the task, or a record of what has happened during the task (through a cell phone recording possibly or through teacher monitoring) then the need to mean from the task itself can be responded to and developed in the post-task phase.

To return to points made at the beginning of the chapter, what we have here is a learner-centred basis for acquisition. And the range of possibilities at this stage is extensive and will depend on the nature of the language that has emerged as problematic. Included in the possibilities are:

- further communicative development, including repetition through parallel tasks
- carefully devised practice activities, which develop hesitant performance
- consciousness-raising activities designed to extend insights about the developing interlanguage
- explanation for any difficulties
- extension activities.

As Willis and Willis (2007) have observed, teaching is compatible with a task-based approach, but the key is its location. It is more appropriately done *after* the task and needs to be based on an agenda that is the result of learner, not teacher, focus. The teaching, or organised presentation, or practice, then capitalises on what has been made salient by the task. Above all, what this achieves is that potentially fleeting insights from the task itself are consolidated and extended. This is the point at which teachers can draw on their expertise effectively.

1.4 Task-Based Instruction and Psycholinguistic Accounts of Development

Table 1.1 identifies connections between psycholinguistic processes and task options. The first major column shows the task and task condition influences from the last section. Then, for each of these, sub-phases or components are shown in the second column. The subsequent three columns show the learning potential/psycholinguistic linkage; the connection with explicit and implicit processes, and finally the impact on performance in terms of measures of complexity, accuracy, lexis, and fluency (CALF).

Starting with task characteristics (the first row in the mid-task section of Table 1.1), a default approach here would assume implicit learning. Tasks

Table 1.1 *Tasks, task conditions, and explicit-implicit processes*

Phase	Attentional focus	Learning potential/ Psycholinguistic linkage	Explicit/implicit connection	Performance impact
Pre-task phase	Generating ideas	Pushing for new language Accessing less available repertoire	Largely explicit, but some implicit	Complexity
	Organising subsequent performance	Easing subsequent processing, especially Formulation	Explicit: Promotes proceduralisation	Complexity Accuracy Fluency
	Rehearsing	Easing performance Easing Formulation	Explicit: Promotes proceduralisation	Accuracy Fluency
Mid-task phase	Task characteristics	Extending performance Channelling performance Proceduralise (improve Formulation)	Explicit and implicit pattern-making Explicit and implicit proceduralisation/ learning	Complexity Accuracy Fluency
	On-line planning	Easing performance conditions Enabling better second language mental lexicon operations	Explicit and implicit through retrieval	Accuracy
	Generating feedback	Personalised feedback at right time	Implicit (and possibly slightly explicit)	Accuracy Complexity
Post-task phase	Repetition	Extending performance Polishing performance	Explicit potential and proceduralisation Implicit improvement through deeper retrieval	Complexity Accuracy Fluency
	Post-task task	Influencing attention allocation	Implicit	Accuracy
	Development	Working on newly emerging language Consolidating newly emerging language	Explicit: Declarative Explicit: Proceduralisation	Complexity or Accuracy, Fluency

would trigger the need to mean, and learners would respond by attempting to communicate. They might draw upon material that has been noticed in the input, or semi-activated interlanguage, or language offered by interlocutors. In this way, particularly with feedback, the interlanguage system could develop. If tasks are well structured, they could build in some degree of repetition and extension. In this way, the initial insight can be consolidated, and extended, particularly with task repetition. None of this need involve awareness (although this cannot be precluded) and so the view of learning would be implicit. But we also have to recognise that it is fiendishly difficult to distinguish clearly between explicit and implicit processes. It may be useful, but we can only talk about tendencies here.

All of the pre-task components in Table 1.1 have more of an explicit emphasis. The retrieval and development of ideas, the planning of how a performance will be structured and interlocutor contributions anticipated, and even the detailed preparation of language, all involve awareness and probably reliance on declarative memory. There may be some implication regarding access to implicit processes, such as of language retrieval and priming, but the emphasis is on conscious and directed attention.

Next, from Table 1.1, are the during-task stages of on-line planning and feedback. On-line planning, through relaxed performance conditions, enables some degree of re-Conceptualisation, but mainly enables more effective Formulation processes. This allows the second language mental lexicon more time for retrieval of lemmas, including greater depth of information. In this, it supports more proceduralisation, and also might enable implicit processes to operate more effectively. Feedback, too, can have implications for implicit and explicit processes, especially the former, since there may be little time to engage awareness, although there may be some explicit involvement if (lack of) time pressure permits.

The involvement of explicit processes is clearer when post-task work focusses on language made salient by the task itself. Armed with some record of what language has been made salient by the task, the post-task phase can be exploited for instruction, for extension/integration work, for practice work, or for consciousness-raising activities. Recall also that the essence of a task-based approach is that the focus is on meaning and learner-nominated language. Any post-task work will meet these two conditions. So this means declarative > procedural > automatisation sequences can be reconciled with a task-based approach. The salient language has come from the learner's attempts to express meanings. The subsequent work can then try to address issues connected with the number of repetitions of a new form that are likely to be needed for it to be established, to be used error-free, and even to be used fluently. This would recast the role of the teacher, since s/he would be able to respond to language that emerged within a task, and then to build upon that emerging language. This would mean that learners could benefit from the focus and even practice, and teachers could benefit from the 'peg' that would have been made available.

Clearly, within Table 1.1 there are uncertainties regarding the more tentative pedagogic judgements that are made for the explicit/implicit connection column. In view of this, the table brings out the flexibility of a task-based approach. The instructional choices are considerable, involving task characteristics and task conditions/phases, with a whole range of options available. Looking at these choices makes it clear that a task-based approach is not immutably linked to any particular view of acquisition or learning. It is compatible with a viewpoint such as that of De Keyser (2020), advocating a progression from declarative to procedural to automatised knowledge. It is also compatible with the view that second language learning is implicit (Paradis, 2009; N. Ellis, 2002, 2005; R. Ellis, 1994; Ullman, 2015). Then the development of greater facility would come from implicit processes being brought into operation through feedback and repeated exposure to communicative need.

Importantly, the table shows that second language development is probably a judicious combination of explicit *and* implicit processes and that the balance will depend on task choice and task condition factors. Task-based courses can be designed where implicit processes dominate and learners' development will follow from their engagement with meaning expression through tasks. Similarly, if there is emphasis on the potential of the pre-task phase to focus on new or emerging language or the post-task phase to work explicitly with language that has been made salient, explicit accounts will have the greater importance. But most of the time it is likely there will be a mixture, with one assuming greater importance some of the time, and the other predominating at other points.

An important point to recall here, following De Keyser (2020), and Faretta-Stuttenberg and Morgan-Short (2018), is that second language development is almost certainly not one unified process and system. De Keyser (2020) argues that one has to consider that different processes may dominate at different proficiency levels, with explicit processes having greater importance at lower levels and with simpler language patterns, and implicit processes at higher levels, and with more complex patterns. Faretta-Stuttenberg and Morgan-Short (2018) also argue for a context-relatedness, with explicit processes being more relevant for instructed contexts and implicit processes for acquisition-rich contexts. Individual differences may also have importance. The implication from all of these points is that any approach to language instruction has to contain considerable flexibility to adapt to these various language, context, and learner factors. The argument in this section is that a task-based approach meets this criterion. After all, a central feature of a task-based approach is that it is learner-driven. It follows that it has to have the capacity to react to the different ways individual learners wish to interpret it.

1.5 Second Language Task-Based Performance

When the field of task research developed, investigators had the problem of deciding which performance variables were most effective at detecting task effects and task condition effects. As time went on the issue of second language task performance emerged in its own right as a significant area, and different psycholinguistic accounts have been proposed for the structure and measurement of this performance. In this section we will first explore the different measures that have been proposed, and then we will examine different theoretical accounts of the patterns of results that have been found.

A wide range of measures of second language task performance have been proposed, but two general approaches account for the bulk of research. These are measures of interactional and feedback moves within task performance; and measures of complexity, lexis, accuracy, and fluency. There have been other suggestions like range of language (e.g., tenses), or effectiveness of task fulfilment, but these have not been used so much, and are, arguably, not as psycholinguistic in nature. Measures of interaction and feedback are covered elsewhere in this volume. It is sufficient to say that a view of tasks as generators of high-quality, timely, and personalised feedback highlight the importance of these measures. If particular task features or conditions provoke a greater use of such interactional moves, it is assumed that such tasks are providing, through quality of interaction, more opportunities for restructuring, development, and greater control (Long, 2015).

We will focus here on CALF measures. A major reason is simply their ubiquity, reflected in major publications (Housen et al., 2009, 2012). They were used in early studies of task-based performance, such as that of Crookes (1989) and since then, a significant proportion of task-based studies have drawn on the same areas. Partly, this is because they have been shown to have distinct statistical independence (Skehan & Foster, 1997; Tavakoli & Skehan, 2005), although this diminishes somewhat at higher proficiency levels (Bui et al., 2018). Partly, as argued earlier, the measures have been proposed as reflecting different stages of development (Skehan, 2007). More pragmatically, these measures are also used because progress has been made in refining each of them, and in addition, we now have an extensive literature reporting significant effects of task manipulations upon them.

It seems clear that structural complexity is itself complex, and needs to be measured by (at least) an index of subordination (clauses per analysis of speech (AS) unit is the most typical measure) and a measure of the number of words per clause. These two measures do not correlate highly and appear to measure different aspects of complexity, one more discourse-oriented and one more clause-oriented (Skehan, 2018). Accuracy is generally measured through the proportion of error-free clauses or number of error-free clauses per 100 words. (Other measures of accuracy, such as incorporating error gravity, tend to correlate very highly with the two commonest measures.) Lexis is generally measured text-internally, usually through a length-corrected type-token ratio, and a text-external measure, usually called lexical sophistication (Read, 2000), based on the proportion of difficult words that are used, where difficulty is generally defined in terms of frequency. Finally, fluency is the most differentiated area for measurement, subsuming speed (syllables or words-per-minute), pausing (per 100 words) and repair (standardised per 100 words for repetition, reformulation, false starts, and replacements). There are also more global measures, such as length of run and phonation time. More recently, attention has also been paid to pause location, contrasting end-of-clause with mid-clause pauses, and also pause type, exploring unfilled and filled pauses (Skehan, 2018).

With the exception of accuracy, which is largely unchanged, all other areas have seen progress in interrogating the underlying constructs, conducting empirical work, and developing subtler and more sophisticated measures of each performance dimension and sub-dimensions. These developments in measurement will feed through in coming years to the theories that are proposed to account for second language performance and its connection with acquisition and development.

For now, though, we have to consider the theoretical accounts that are available. The two that have been arguably most influential are Skehan's (1998; 2018) Limited Attention Capacity (LAC) approach and Robinson's (2011) Cognition Hypothesis, more recently associated with the SSARC Model (stabilise, simplify, automatise, restructure, and complexify) (Robinson, 2015). We will consider each briefly in turn and then compare them. Skehan (1998; 2018) has proposed a viewpoint that is grounded in the body of task research findings, but which is also based on a set of principles. These are:

Principle One: *Working memory and attention are limited*. While attention may vary somewhat (e.g., for motivational reasons), there is still a maximum that represents a significant functional constraint.

Principle Two: *The CALF framework is useful*. The claim is simply that viewing performance through these sub-dimensions is revealing about the impact of the different task and task condition influences.

Principle Three: *Tasks are analysable, but difficult to work with*. As indicated in the last section, it can be argued that the extant generalisations are limited in number and task findings are often inconsistent. There is a fundamental distinction between the intended task and the actual task

(Breen, 1984; Skehan, 2018). In addition, (and see Principle Five), task conditions are more dependable sources of influence on performance (Skehan, 2016).

Principle Four: *Linking task performance to the Levelt model of speaking is productive and a potential basis for effective predictions.* Levelt (1989), in a model of first language speaking, distinguishes between three major stages: Conceptualisation, Formulation, and Articulation. These three stages are assumed to operate in parallel, modular fashion. This first language model has been generalised to the second language case (De Bot, 1992; Kormos, 2006), although with modifications particularly at the Formulator and Articulator stages. In addition, the parallel functioning of the first language contrasts with the second language case, since Formulator difficulties (particularly limitations in the second language mental lexicon) may prevent easy parallel functioning. (See Ellis et al., 2020, chap. 3 for further discussion.)

Principle Five: *Task characteristics and task conditions influence performance separately and in combination.* The essential point here is the claim that attentional limitations are a constraint, not an inevitability. But essentially this represents a challenge – the need to overcome attentional limitations by judicious task design/choice, implementation through task conditions, and combinations of these. Task and task condition research has delivered a range of generalisations, such as structured tasks raising accuracy and pre-task planning raising complexity and fluency (and accuracy, slightly). Careful combinations of tasks and conditions (Tavakoli & Foster, 2008; Foster & Skehan, 2013) suggest that attention allocation can be manipulated, and that more than one performance area can be raised simultaneously.

Principle Six: *Task difficulty needs to be analysed distinctly for the Conceptualiser and the Formulator.* This point is relevant because of the contrast with the Cognition Hypothesis (below). Conceptualisation emphasises the ideas within a task, their accessibility, their need for manipulation, and so on. Formulation is concerned with how the second language mental lexicon is accessed, is adequate and can respond to the demands that are made upon it by the Conceptualiser. The pressures on these two areas are distinct, so difficulty in one area may not influence difficulty in the other.

The LAC approach, in itself, does not have a lot to say about acquisition. The LAC focus is more on creating useful conditions in what happens before, and then, most important of all, exploiting language made salient by the task at the post-task phase. If anything, attentional limitations suggest that it will be difficult, mid-task, to be able to focus on new language; useful though these opportunities are, the scope to attend to, *and retain* such useful input will be limited. The LAC approach is consistent with both explicit and implicit interpretations of second language development: whether material is incorporated implicitly and then processes of learning take place, or whether language is made salient, explicitly, and then worked on through tasks themselves or post-task activities, is entirely neutral. Both fit in with the approach.

The Cognition Hypothesis/SSARC Model (Robinson, 2011; 2015) takes a very different view of attention, regarding it as expandable, and likely to respond to task demands. A first, important distinction is between two classes of variable – the cognitive factors of resource-directing variables and resource-dispersing variables. The first group comprises factors like time perspective, reasoning demands (causal, spatial, intentional), number of elements, and perspective taking. These push towards engagement with language itself when the more complex value, such as more elements, is involved. An important additional point is that more complex tasks are also predicted to raise structural complexity *and* accuracy simultaneously, reflecting the push towards language engagement without constraint of attentional resources. They are also predicted to lead to more noticing, and to generate more feedback. In contrast, resource-dispersing factors are not predicted to lead to language engagement or to have a connection with task complexity, but instead are concerned with the dispersal (or focusing) of resources. Typical features here are planning time, plus or minus single task, task structure, number and independence of steps, plus or minus prior knowledge.

In addition to these cognitive factors, the Cognition Hypothesis also discusses task condition, or interactive factors, and task difficulty, or learner factors. The former sub-divides into participation variables, which are seen as making interactional demands, and participant variables, with these linking with the nature of any interaction which occurs. Task difficulty factors connect with the participants themselves, and divide into ability variables, such as working memory, and affective variables, such as motivation and anxiety. These variables have an impact on how difficult a task will be for an individual (and note the different view of task difficulty in the LAC approach).

So far, this portrayal of the Cognition Hypothesis presents it largely as a performance-oriented model, but it also connects with acquisition and task sequencing. Robinson (2015) offers two principles for this:

Task Sequencing Principle 1: Only the cognitive demands of tasks relating to intrinsic conceptual and cognitive processing complexity (i.e., resource-directing and resource-dispersing variables) are involved in task sequencing. Task condition and task difficulty variables, while important, do not influence sequencing itself.

Task Sequencing Principle 2: In sequencing tasks, resource-dispersing variables should be increased first, and only then should resource-directing variables be increased. The intention here is to guide learners from the known (SS), through the development of automaticity (A), finally to the need to develop new form-function mappings and to restructure-complexify (RC).

Three equations from the SSARC Model are relevant for this (Robinson, 2015: 94):

SS (stabilise, simplify) = i x e [('s'rdisp) + ('s'rdir)]^n (Step 1)
A (automatise) = i x e [('c'rdisp) + ('s'rdir)]^n (Step 2)
RC (restructure, complexify) = i x e [('c'rdisp) + ('c'rdir)]^n (Step 3)

Where i = current interlanguage state
    e = mental effort
    's' = simple task demands
    'c' = complex task demands
    rdisp = resource-dispersing tasks
    rdir = resource-directing tasks
    n = potential number of practice opportunities with tasks.

SS (simple, stable) keeps task demands low (with resource-directing and resource-dispersing variables). A (automatise) increases resource-dispersing demands only, to nurture speedier access to resources. RC (restructuring, complexifying) is when resource-directing demands increase and destabilise interlanguage. An example of these ideas in operation is given in Ellis et al. (2020: 83).

1.6 Comparing the Two Approaches

We will compare the two approaches under four general headings: theoretical foundations; research base; timescale and connection to real-world teaching; and relevance for acquisition.

1.6.1 Theoretical Foundations

The LAC approach draws heavily on Levelt's model of first language speaking, coupled with general views from cognitive psychology regarding working memory and attentional limitations. The focus is extending these viewpoints to the case of second language speech performance, with tasks. In this respect the functioning of the Formulator stage, drawing on a more limited second language mental lexicon, and coupled with limited attentional resources, becomes key, and the basis for accounting for many effects that have emerged with task research. The Cognition Hypothesis draws less on psycholinguistics (but see Kormos, 2011), and more on linguistics, through Givon's (1985) work and cognitive linguistics (Robinson & Ellis, 2008). There are also connections to different analyses of attention (Sanders, 1998) in cognitive psychology. These are the basis for the prediction of the joint raising of complexity and accuracy: task complexity is seen as driving both simultaneously.

1.6.2 Research Base

With the LAC approach, a large number of studies have been published (see Skehan (2018) for a review of these studies). The focus has been broadly on exploring the effects on CALF-performance of task characteristics and task conditions. Most of these studies have been supportive of (a) the impact of attentional and working memory limitations on performance, often showing evidence of trade-off between different performance areas, especially between accuracy and complexity, and (b) an account of any studies where accuracy and complexity are both raised through the conjoint effects of task and task condition combinations of influence. The first type of evidence is exemplified by Foster and Skehan (2012); the second, by Skehan and Foster (2005; 2013). Robinson (2008) has pointed out that LAC studies are often much stronger in offering post-hoc interpretations of findings rather than making falsifiable predictions. There is force to this point. However, Skehan (2018) does review some studies that pursue what may be termed mini-theories, through a discourse-based interpretation of information structure, where supported predictions are made, such as that of Wang and Skehan (2014).

The Cognition Hypothesis has generated more research than the LAC approach (Robinson, 2011). The research is of two main sorts: there are targeted studies, and there are meta-analyses. The targeted studies have mostly focused on the construct of task complexity and have probed the prediction that greater task complexity leads to increased linguistic complexity and accuracy. In general, these results have not delivered clearly confirming evidence. There are examples of each of these dependent variables being increased, but rarely both – the key prediction of the hypothesis. If one can generalise, greater task complexity tends to be associated with slightly greater accuracy (Jackson & Suethanapornkul, 2013) but not language complexity. So the central prediction of the hypothesis, that attention is expandable and that task demands lead to a simultaneous focus on complexity and accuracy, is not supported very much, although Skehan (2016; 2018) suggests higher proficiency levels may have more potential in this regard. The results of targeted studies are consistent with the results of meta-analyses. Jackson and Suethanapornkul (2013) and Malicka and Sasayama (2017) have both conducted such analyses, with slightly conflicting findings. Jackson et al. (2013) report a small effect for accuracy. In contrast, Malicka et al. (2017) report very little effect for accuracy or complexity, but small effects for lexis and fluency. As a result of these studies it seems fair to conclude that the jury is still out on this issue, but what has been published so far is not very supportive of this particularly bold prediction. The broad range of task studies does suggest that task complexity is important (as argued by both the LAC approach and the Cognition Hypothesis), but that raising accuracy and complexity simultaneously is not easily done.

1.6.3 Timescale and Extension to Teaching

Both approaches are largely performance-oriented and based on relatively brief and self-contained tasks. Each, though, does try to make a potential connection with more extended teaching. These extensions are, it has to be admitted, speculative. The LAC approach, as we have seen, addresses the issue of new language through pre-task work, and then post-task activities which feed off language made salient by the task itself. It also relates accuracy and fluency, as indicators of control, to task features (structured tasks, familiar information), as well as task condition variables, such as repetition and a post-task task intended to induce attention to accuracy. There is also the claim that teachers can adapt instruction, through knowledge of task and task condition effects, to promote complexity or accuracy or fluency selectively. In all these suggestions, the functioning of task research is towards methodology within task-based teaching. Little is proposed regarding longer term teaching sequences or syllabus-linked decisions.

The Cognition Hypothesis has much more to say in this area. First of all, there is the prediction that task complexity can drive the development of language form, increasing complexity (and potentially new language) and accuracy simultaneously. Second, there is the claim that task complexity also drives greater noticing and feedback, such that acquisitional processes are being fostered by appropriate task design and choice. But finally, the SSARC Model offers suggestions for task sequencing. In other words, there is much more in this account that links with learning and teaching. It should be said, though, that these suggestions do not link clearly to more extended teaching sequences as much as to small collections of tasks, spanning, perhaps, two or three lessons.

1.6.4 Relevance for Acquisition

The two approaches vary in how they fit with the views of acquisition described earlier. Both are broadly consistent with either an explicit or an implicit basis for development, but they contrast in their emphases. The LAC approach, with the importance it places on the post-task phase, and also with the sequence of complexity > accuracy > fluency, seems closer to an explicit-to-implicit approach, with the important qualification that language emerges from a focus on meaning and is selected by the learner. After that, the issue of development is meant to be supported (though not assured) by opportunities through tasks and task conditions for greater proceduralisation and automatisation. More importantly, though, a post-task focus on the language that has emerged can foster the development of new language. The initial consolidation/extension could then be followed by more task work or even by more practice-oriented activities. Of course, implicit processes are possible, but it is likely that these processes will be slower and less certain (although perhaps ultimately more robust).

The Cognition Hypothesis has perhaps a greater emphasis on an implicit approach to acquisition. Task complexity is again the key, and is the driver for more attention to form, more feedback and more complex language. This seems slightly more compatible with learners identifying patterns implicitly, with feedback helping them to avoid error with the pattern so found. Even so, one could also sketch out a path for explicit learning. Noticing, for example, is consistent with focused attention to facilitate implicit learning, but it could also reflect conscious attention and potential reflection on the structure of language. Perhaps the Cognition Hypothesis has less emphasis on the need for sustained work and repeated practice. The role of a more complex task in pushing the learner to use new and more complex language is clear. What is less obvious is that if learning is gradual, there needs to be continued focus and opportunity for use. This seems to be conceptualised less centrally. In that respect the functioning of the SSARC sequence is illuminating. The SSARC Model (Robinson, 2015) proposes that tasks be ordered to produce the sequence stabilise > simplify > automatise > restructure > complexify. In other words, automatisation precedes restructuring and complexifying. One assumes here that the purpose is to create a more effective, stable foundation (SSA) for the change in the interlanguage system that will then occur. The interesting question, then, is what happens after the RC stages, and whether there needs to be more automatisation at this point.

1.7 Conclusions

Psycholinguistics, by its nature should have a great deal to contribute to task-based instruction. It focuses on issues of learning, memory, processing, and models of language performance. The major conclusion we can draw is that tasks provide a very supportive and very flexible arena for learning to take place. A range of choices are available, with tasks themselves, and with what happens before, during, and after a task is done. Different choices made with each of these can predispose (though not guarantee) explicit or implicit processes and knowledge. In this way, a task-based approach to instruction can be regarded as broadly neutral in its view of learning, and adaptable according to the educational situation. Tasks themselves can promote a need to restructure and develop new language, or they can support control processes associated with proceduralisation. Pre-task activities can similarly make noticing and new language more likely, or provide organisational frames or rehearsal opportunities to push for smoother performance. Mid-task options can provide ideally-timed feedback opportunities, or more time to engage in on-line planning, or more support. Post-task activities have the potential to change attention allocation during the earlier task, or to enable repetition and more control, or, more ambitiously, to provide opportunities for considerable nurturing of the language that has been made salient by the task itself. There is no 'one' task-based approach, no 'authorised version'. It is more the case that a task-based approach offers guidance for flexible decision-making in varied circumstances.

There has also been interesting research exploring second language performance itself. There has been clear progress in developing more construct- and empirically sound measures of the different dimensions of second language task performance. But there is much more work to be done to establish the linkages between task characteristics and performance. In contrast, the generalisations that emerge with task conditions (pre-, mid-, post-) are more extensive and more robust. They also have potential linkages to learning. One approach (LAC) is more research-then-theory and descriptive in nature, and is better at accounting for extant findings, and generating new studies than it is at offering a wide range of predictions (although some, as we have seen, are possible). The other major approach, the Cognition Hypothesis/SSARC Model, is better at making predictions, has generated considerable research, and has clear things to say about links with instruction. On the other hand, the database currently available does not provide strong support: some studies do confirm aspects of the Cognition Hypothesis, but not many meet its more stringent predictions. There is considerable scope for future progress.

Further Reading

Doughty, C. (2001). Cognitive underpinnings of a focus on form. In P. Robinson, ed. *Cognition and second language instruction*. Cambridge: Cambridge University Press.

Ellis, R., Skehan, P., Li, S., Shintani, N., and Lambert, C. (2020). *Task-based language teaching*. Cambridge: Cambridge University Press.

Long, M. H. (2015). *Second language acquisition and task-based language teaching*. New York: Wiley.

Robinson, P., ed. (2011). *Second language task complexity: Researching the Cognition Hypothesis of language learning and performance*. Amsterdam: John Benjamins.

Robinson, P. (2015). The Cognition Hypothesis, second language task demands, and the SSARC model of pedagogic task sequencing. In M. Bygate, ed. *Domains and directions in the development of TBLT*. Amsterdam: John Benjamins, pp. 87–122.

Skehan, P. (2015). Limited attentional capacity and cognition: Two hypotheses regarding second language performance on tasks. In M. Bygate, ed. *Domains and directions in the development of TBLT: A decade of plenaries from the International Conference*. Amsterdam: John Benjamins, pp. 123–55.

Skehan, P. (2016). Tasks vs. conditions: Two perspectives on task research and its implications for pedagogy. In A. Mackey, ed. *Annual Review of Applied Linguistics*, 24, 34–49.

Study Questions

1. How can tasks be adapted to focus on explicit or implicit processes?
2. Do tasks need to be adapted for learners in foreign language compared to second language contexts?
3. Can the same tasks be adapted for different proficiency levels, or are different tasks needed?
4. Consider whether, as argued in the chapter, task conditions have led to more, and more robust, generalisations about performance than task characteristics. If so, how could you account for this?
5. Much task research has relied on performance measures of complexity, accuracy, lexis and fluency. How satisfactory do you think this is? Which alternative measures might be better? Do you think our understanding of tasks would be changed very much if different measures were used?
6. What evidence can you find for and against the positions advocated by Skehan (2015) and Robinson (2015)?

References

Ahmadian, M. J. (2012a). The relationship between working memory capacity and L2 oral performance under task-based careful online planning condition. *TESOL Quarterly*, 46(1), 165–75.

Ahmadian, M. J. (2012b). The effects of guided careful online planning on complexity, accuracy, and fluency in intermediate EFL learners' oral production: The case of English articles. *Language Teaching Research*, 16, 129–49.

Ahmadian, M. and Tavakoli, M. (2014). Investigating what learners do and monitor under careful online planning conditions. *Canadian Modern Language Review*, 70(1), 50–75.

Anderson, J. R. (1995). *Learning and memory*. New York: John Wiley.

Breen, M. (1984). Process syllabus for the language classroom. In C. J. Brumfit, ed. *General English syllabus design*. ELT Document 118. Oxford: Pergamon Press, pp. 47–60.

Bui, G., Skehan, P., and Wang, Z. (2018). Task condition effects on advanced-level foreign language performance. In P. Malovrh and A. Benati, eds. *Handbook of advanced proficiency in second language acquisition*. New York: Wiley, pp. 219–37.

Bygate, M. (2001). Effects of task repetition on the structure and control of oral language. In M. Bygate, P. Skehan, and M. Swain, eds. *Researching pedagogic tasks: Second language learning, teaching and testing*. Harlow: Longman, pp. 23–48.

Bygate, M. (2018). *Learning language through task repetition*. Amsterdam: John Benjamins.

Crookes, G. (1989). Planning and interlanguage variation. *Studies in Second Language Acquisition*, 11, 367–83.

De Bot, K. (1992). A bilingual production model: Levelt's "speaking" model adapted. *Applied Linguistics*, 13, 1–24.

DeKeyser, R. (2020). Skill acquisition theory. In B. VanPatten, G. D. Keating, and S. Wulff, eds. *Theories in second language acquisition*. New York: Routledge, pp. 83–104.

Doughty, C. (2001). Cognitive underpinnings of a focus on form. In P. Robinson, ed. *Cognition and second language instruction*. Cambridge: Cambridge University Press, pp. 206–57.

Ellis, N. (2002). Frequency effects in language processing: A review with implications for theories of implicit and explicit language acquisition. *Studies in Second Language Acquisition*, 24(2), 143–88.

Ellis, N. (2005). At the Interface: Dynamic interactions of explicit and implicit language knowledge. *Studies in Second Language Acquisition*, 27(2), 305–52.

Ellis, R. (1994). *The study of second language acquisition*. Oxford: Oxford University Press.

Ellis, R. (2003). *Task-based language learning and teaching*. Oxford: Oxford University Press.

Ellis, R., ed. (2005a). *Planning and task performance in a second language*. Amsterdam: John Benjamins.

Ellis, R. (2005b). Planning and task-based performance: Theory and research. In R. Ellis, ed. *Planning and task performance in a second language*. Amsterdam: John Benjamins, pp. 3–36.

Ellis, R. (2006). Modelling learning difficulty and second language proficiency: The differential contributions of implicit and explicit knowledge. *Applied Linguistics*, 27(3), 431–63.

Ellis, R. and Shintani, N. (2014). *Exploring language pedagogy through second language acquisition research*. London: Routledge.

Ellis, R., Skehan, P., Li, S., Shintani, N., and Lambert, C. (2020). *Task-based language teaching*. Cambridge: Cambridge University Press

Ellis, R. and Yuan, F. (2004). The effects of planning on fluency, complexity, and accuracy on second language narrative writing. *Studies in Second Language Acquisition*, 26(1), 59–84.

Ellis, R. and Yuan, F. (2005). The effect of careful within-task planning on oral and written task performance. In R. Ellis, ed. *Planning and task performance in a second language*. Amsterdam: John Benjamins, pp. 167–92.

Faretta-Stuttenberg, M. and Morgan-Short, K. (2018). The interplay of individual differences and context of learning in behavioural and neurocognitive second language development. *Second Language Research*, 34(1), 67–101.

Foster, P. and Skehan, P. (2012). Complexity, accuracy, fluency and lexis in task-based performance: A synthesis of the Ealing research. In A. Housen, F. Kuiken, and I. Vedder, eds. *Dimensions of L2 performance and proficiency: Complexity, accuracy, and fluency in SLA*. Amsterdam: John Benjamins, pp. 199–220.

Foster, P. and Skehan, P. (2013) The effects of post-task activities on the accuracy of language during task performance. *Canadian Modern Language Review*, 69, 249–73.

Gilabert, R. (2007). The simultaneous manipulation of task complexity along planning time and [+/- here-and-now] effects on L2 performance. In M. d. P. Garcia-Mayo, ed. *Investigating tasks in formal language learning*. Bristol: Multilingual Matters, pp. 44–68.

Givon, T. (1985). Function, structure, and language acquisition. In D. Slobin, ed. *The crosslinguistic study of language acquisition*. Vol. 1. Hillsdale, NJ: Lawrence Erlbaum Associates, pp. 1008–25.

Han, Z. and Finneran, R. (2013). Re-engaging the interface debate: Strong, weak, or none at all? *International Journal of Applied Linguistics*, 24(3), 370–89.

Housen, A. and Kuiken, F. (2009). Complexity, accuracy, and fluency in second language acquisition. *Applied Linguistics*, 30(4), 461–73.

Housen, F., Kuiken, F., and Vedder, I. (2012). *Dimensions of L2 performance and proficiency: Investigating complexity, accuracy, and fluency in SLA*. Amsterdam: John Benjamins.

Jackson, D. O. and Suethanapornkul, S. (2013). The Cognition Hypothesis: A synthesis and meta-analysis of research on second language task complexity. *Language Learning*, 63(2), 330–67.

Kim, Y. (2013). Effects of pre-task modelling on attention to form and question development. *TESOL Quarterly*, 47(1), 8–35.

Kim, Y. and McDonough, K. (2011). Using pretask modelling to encourage collaborative learning opportunities. *Language Teaching Research*, 15(2), 183–99.

Kormos, J. (2006). *Speech production and second language acquisition*. Mahwah, NJ: Lawrence Erlbaum.

Kormos, J. (2011). Speech production and the Cognition Hypothesis. In P. Robinson, ed. *Second language task complexity: Researching the Cognition Hypothesis of language learning and performance*. Amsterdam: John Benjamins, pp. 39–60.

Lambert, C., Kormos, J., and Minn, D. (2016). Task repetition and second language speech processing. *Studies in Second Language Acquisition*, 38, 1–30.

Levelt, W. J. (1989). *Speaking: From intention to articulation*. Cambridge: Cambridge University Press.

Li, Q. (2014). Get it right in the end: The effects of post-task transcribing on learners' oral performance. In P. Skehan, ed. *Processing perspectives on task performance*. Amsterdam: John Benjamins, pp. 129–54.

Long, M. H. (2015). *Second language acquisition and task-based language teaching*. New York: Wiley.

Lynch, T. (2001). Seeing what they meant: Transcribing as a route to noticing. *English Language Teaching Journal*, 55, 124–32.

Lynch, T. (2007). Learning from the transcripts of an oral communication task. *English Language Teaching Journal*, 61, 311–20.

Lynch, T. and Maclean, J. (2001). A case of exercising: Effects of immediate task repetition on learners' performance. In M. Bygate, P. Skehan, and M. Swain, eds. *Researching pedagogic tasks: Second language learning, teaching and testing*. Abingdon: Routledge, pp. 141–62.

Mackey, A. (2012). *Input, interaction, and corrective feedback in L2 learning*. Oxford: Oxford University Press.

Malicka, A. and Sasayama, S. (April, 2017). The importance of learning from the accumulated knowledge: Findings from a research synthesis on task complexity. Paper presented at the 7th Biennial International Conference on Task-Based Language Teaching, Barcelona, Spain.

Mehnert, U. (1998). The effects of different lengths of time for planning on second language performance. *Studies in Second Language Acquisition*, 20: 52–83.

Ortega, L. (2005). What do learners plan? Learner-driven attention to form during pre-task planning. In R. Ellis, ed. *Planning and task performance in a second language*. Amsterdam: John Benjamins, pp. 77–109.

Ortega, L. (2009). *Understanding second language acquisition*. London: Hodder Education.

Pang, F. and Skehan, P. (2014). Self-reported planning behaviour and second language performance in narrative retelling. In P. Skehan, ed. *Processing perspectives on task performance*. Amsterdam: John Benjamins, pp. 95–128.

Paradis, M. (2009). *Declarative and procedural determinants of second languages*. Amsterdam: John Benjamins.

Read, J. (2000). *Assessing vocabulary*. Cambridge: Cambridge University Press.

Révész, A. (2011). Task complexity, focus on L2 constructions, and individual differences: A classroom-based study. *Modern Language Journal*, 95, 162–81.

Robinson, P. (2008). The Cognition Hypothesis. Presentation at the Task-Based Learning and Teaching Conference, Honolulu, Hawaii.

Robinson, P. (2011a), ed. *Second language task complexity: Researching the Cognition Hypothesis of language learning and performance*. Amsterdam: John Benjamins.

Robinson, P. (2011b). Second language task complexity, the Cognition Hypothesis, language learning, and performance. In P. Robinson, ed. *Second language task complexity: Researching the Cognition Hypothesis of language learning and performance*. Amsterdam: John Benjamins, pp. 3–38.

Robinson, P. (2015). The Cognition Hypothesis, second language task demands, and the SSARC model of pedagogic task sequencing. In M. Bygate, ed. *Domains and directions in the development of TBLT*. Amsterdam: John Benjamins, pp. 87–122.

Robinson, P. and Ellis, N. (2008). *Handbook of cognitive linguistics and second language acquisition*. London: Routledge.

Samuda, V. (2001). Guiding relationships between form and meaning during task performance: The role of the teacher. In M. Bygate, P. Skehan, and M. Swain, eds. *Researching pedagogic tasks: Second language learning, teaching and testing*. Harlow: Longman, pp. 119–40.

Sanders, A. (1998). *Elements of human performance*. Mahway, NJ: Lawrence Erlbaum.

Skehan, P. (1998). *A cognitive approach to language learning*. Oxford: Oxford University Press.

Skehan, P. (2002). A non-marginal role for tasks: A response to bruton. *English Language Teaching Journal*, 35(3), 289–95.

Skehan P. (2007). Task research and language teaching: Reciprocal relationships. In S. Fotos, ed. *Form-meaning relationships in language pedagogy: Essays in honour of Rod Ellis*, Oxford: Oxford University Press, pp. 289–301.

Skehan, P. (2013). Nurturing noticing. In J. Bergsleithner, S. N. Frota, and J. K. Yoshioka, eds. *Noticing and second language acquisition: Studies in honor of*

Richard Schmidt. Honolulu: National Foreign Language Center, pp. 169–80.

Skehan, P. (2015). Limited attentional capacity and cognition: Two hypotheses regarding second language performance on tasks. In M. Bygate, ed. *Domains and directions in the development of TBLT: A decade of plenaries from the International Conference*. Amsterdam: John Benjamins, pp. 123–55.

Skehan, P. (2016). Tasks vs. conditions: Two perspectives on task research and its implications for pedagogy. *Annual Review of Applied Linguistics*, 24, 34–49.

Skehan P. (2018). *Second language task-based performance: Theory, research, and assessment*. New York: Routledge.

Skehan, P. and Foster, P. (1997). The influence of planning and post-task activities on accuracy and complexity in task based learning. *Language Teaching Research*, 1, 185–211.

Skehan, P. and Foster, P. (1999). Task structure and processing conditions in narrative retellings. *Language Learning*, 49(1), 93–120.

Skehan, P. and Foster, P. (2005). Strategic and on-line planning: The influence of surprise information and task time on second language performance. In N. Ellis, ed. *Planning and task performance in a second language*. Amsterdam: John Benjamins, pp. 193–216.

Tavakoli, P. and Foster, P. (2008). Task design and second language performance: The effect of narrative type on learner output. *Language Learning*, 58(2), 439–73.

Tavakoli, P. and Skehan, P. (2005). Planning, task structure, and performance testing. In R. Ellis, ed. *Planning and task performance in a second language*. Amsterdam: John Benjamins, pp. 239–76.

Ullmann, M. T. (2015). The declarative/procedural model. In B. Van Patten and J. Williams, eds. *Theories in second language acquisition: An introduction*. 2nd ed. Abingdon: Routledge, pp. 135–58.

Wang, Z. (2009). *Modelling speech production and performance: Evidence from five types of planning and two task structures*. Unpublished PhD thesis, Chinese University of Hong Kong.

Wang, Z. (2014). On-line time pressure manipulations: L2 speaking performance under five types of planning and repetition conditions. In P. Skehan, ed. *Processing perspectives on task performance*. Amsterdam: John Benjamins, pp. 27–62.

Wang, Z. and Skehan P. (2014). Structure, lexis, and time perspective: Influences on task performance. In P. Skehan, ed. *Processing perspectives on task performance*. Amsterdam: John Benjamins, pp. 155–86.

Willis, D. and Willis, J. (2007). *Doing task-based teaching*. Oxford: Oxford University Press.

Yuan, F. and Ellis, R. (2003). The effects of pre-task and online planning on fluency, complexity, and accuracy in L2 monologic oral production. *Applied Linguistics*, 24, 1–27.

2

A Pedagogical Rationale for Task-Based Language Teaching for the Acquisition of Real-World Language Use

Martin Bygate, Virginia Samuda, and Kris Van den Branden

2.1 Introduction

This chapter considers what task-based language teaching (TBLT) can offer for classroom language learning. The use of tasks can enrich learners' language learning experience in many ways. For instance, using tasks can make it easier for learners to understand the meaning, use and relevance of the formal features of the target language. As learners engage with the meanings and uses of language for achieving the outcomes of the task, tasks become an invaluable context for the teacher and learners to focus on formal features of the language. But, while it is true that tasks can be used to help improve the fluency, accuracy and complexity of learners' language (e.g., Skehan, 2014), in addition we will be exploring how TBLT can also help learners engage with a wide range of different aspects of the target language.

2.2 Background

In essence, TBLT is a simple proposition (Van den Branden, Bygate & Norris, 2009) namely, instead of organising instruction by first presenting discrete items of the new language, learners then practising them, before being primed to use the language in free communication (a sequence widely known as PPP), the cycle is inverted. The learners start by trying to use language receptively or productively while responding to the demands of an initial task. A focus on form is gradually introduced where students need it, within the context of the task. Additional follow-up practice is provided where this might be helpful. Students then return to communicating on the same task, or on a follow-up task. In this perspective on TBLT, instead of being an 'add-on' at the end of the PPP sequence, tasks are the starting- and end-point of a cycle of work, and often they are the mid-point as well. This is really a simple 'technological innovation': simple, but far-reaching. (Floud (2019) offers a lucid account of technological development in a way that relates well to the development of TBLT, see appendix at the end of this chapter.)

Used in this way, tasks become the pedagogic thread and reference point for teaching. This means that a unit within a TBLT programme typically reflects answers to a small number of key questions:

- Is this a useful task for the students involved?
- Can students do the task?
- Can students usefully extend their language repertoire by doing it?
- Have students extended their language repertoire and control on the task?

The task, then, serves as reference point for encountering and exploring new language, and for assessing learning outcomes.

However, on observing task performance, the teacher may well sense that while the on-task work has effectively launched the agenda, valuable potential aspects of language are not being grasped, and on-task work could be usefully supported by some off-task focusing. As Van den Branden (2016: 166) points out,

> Learning often involves overcoming obstacles, correcting errors or misconceptions, refining behavior, building up new understandings, and revising commonly held beliefs. For this to occur, the (interactional) support of another person will often be helpful, decisive, and even crucial.... In classrooms, support may come from peers..., but in many cases, the help of a more competent partner will be necessary. In second language classrooms, the teacher clearly stands out as the most competent partner of the learners involved.

This consideration gives rise to a further key question: Would learning and task performance be effectively enhanced by additional intervention by the teacher, focusing on new language? Adding this question introduces the possibility that various other types of learning activities can cluster around the task to provide additional practice and support. The revised set of key questions then is:

- Is this a useful task?
- Can students do the task?
- Can students usefully extend their language repertoire by doing it?

- Would learning and task performance be effectively enhanced by additional intervention by the teacher, focusing on-task or off-task on new language?
- Have students extended their repertoire and control of language on the task?

As can be seen, our form-focusing question, even if the form focus is off-task (in the sense that it interrupts or follows the performance of a particular task), is embedded within the task-based sequence, ensuring that the task remains the defining context both before and after any form-focused work. In this respect the account we will be proposing in this chapter uses the task as the starting- and end-point of a unit of work, with various types of intervention arising in the course of the scheme of work.

This perspective can be usefully related to the two kinds of approach to TBLT outlined in Ellis (2019). For us, form-focusing preferably arises from tasks, rather than being introduced before students work on a task. That is, we do not see tasks as an opportunity for learners to display correct use of an explicitly taught language feature while trying to achieve a communicative outcome. Rather in our account tasks aim 'to provide opportunities for using language naturally in order to achieve a communicative outcome' (Ellis, 2019: 456), so that the task is the context for learners to engage with meanings to be expressed through the target language, and with the forms that can be used to communicate them. A task can be thought of as a sort of workbench for grappling with language and learning how to use it – like a carpenter learning to work with wood; a painter experimenting with paints on the paper or canvas; or the laboratory for an apprentice chemist or biologist. People learning carpentry or painting or chemistry on the workbench will also seek help from a teacher. In TBLT once the students have started grappling with the problem in the context of the task, the teacher can then interact with the students and help to shape their understandings of the language options and provide feedback on the ways they are handling the task. In other words, the task is the context both for learning and for teaching.

Three assumptions underpin this perspective. The first is the very well-known one that the overall purpose of second language teaching (and thus of TBLT) is to foster the ability to *use* the target language (rather than to describe aspects of it, translate to or from the target language, or apply the rules). Importantly, as many others before us have said, using language provides a special opportunity for developing that ability (e.g., Brown, 2007; de Bot, Lowie & Verspoor, 2008; Ellis, 2009, 2015; Johnson, 1996; Long, 2015; Skehan, 1998, 2014; Widdowson, 1983).

Our second assumption, which by implication also applies to TBLT, is that in order to develop the ability to use a second language, learners also need to know *about* the language, the kind of knowledge referred to as 'declarative knowledge'. Declarative knowledge can be particularly important for many second language learners for whom the time available to learn the language, and the amount of exposure to it, are limited. It is also widely seen as crucial for the acquisition of particularly problematic linguistic features (DeKeyser, 2005; Dörnyei, 2009; Ellis, 2017). This assumption is widely accepted, although in TBLT there are disagreements over the relative importance, timing, and handling of that focus.

The use of declarative knowledge is also important because there is general agreement that learners differ in terms of the individual aptitudes they bring to learning (DeKeyser, 2019; Ranta, 2002; Skehan, 1989; Van den Branden, 2016; Wen, Biedron & Skehan, 2017). For example, they can differ in terms of their ability to perceive and memorise new material, and in terms of their ability to analyse the patterns of the language implicitly, whether during 'on-line' oral communication, during relatively unpressured reading, or when presented with more or less pre-structured samples of language. More generally (and this applies to all learners), the implicit analysis of linguistic patterns can take a lot of time and a lot of data, and both time and data may be lacking in many contexts associated with second/foreign language learning (Lightbown & Spada, 2013). Finally, some learners will have to perform tasks that demand a high degree of accuracy, and their ability to achieve this would be enhanced by providing them with declarative knowledge of language items, rules or patterns that they might otherwise fail to notice implicitly. All these reasons point to the importance of complementing task-based work with the use of form-focused activities – activities that draw learners' attention to formal features of the language that are relevant for the task. In this chapter we consider how this might work within a TBLT approach.

A final assumption is that if we recognise the importance for language teaching of both the ability to use the target language, and the valuable role of declarative knowledge, then this sets a pedagogical problem for *any* systematic approach to language pedagogy, including for TBLT. Spada (2019) has neatly encapsulated this as a question of how to 'integrate' activities focusing on developing use (the tasks) with activities focusing on form. We take 'integration' to refer firstly to the way declarative knowledge is made relevant and comprehensible to learners in relation to particular task demands, and secondly how that knowledge is subsequently reactivated during communication. In other words, to maximally foster language learning, TBLT requires a well-considered synthesis of focus on meaning and focus on form.

We explore implications from these three assumptions in the remainder of this chapter. Our first section considers ways in which the use of tasks can contribute directly to learning through what we will call the meaningfulness principle. The second section focuses on the recognition of the place of conscious awareness of language in second language learning. We see this partly in term of focusing on form during communication, and partly in terms of the many ways of raising learners' awareness outside of the context of ongoing communication. We refer to this as the accessibility principle. In the final section we discuss some responses to Spada's integration issue – that is, how to integrate on-task communication and conscious awareness of language.

2.3 The Meaningfulness Principle

The central feature of tasks is that they set an objective (to play a game, to design something, to agree something, to prepare a report, to read, write or perform a story, to buy something, to make something work, or perhaps to create something, such as a model or a meal). In trying to achieve the objective, learners have to use language to communicate or understand meanings. This need to use language brings with it a number of valuable advantages. A basic advantage is that engagement with meanings requires learners to form personal and interpersonal understandings through the use of language (Croft & Cruise, 2004). That is, learners have to relate the language they are using to what they themselves mean during the task. To do this they also need to relate what they say to what they think the speaker or writer means, and to their and their interlocutors' knowledge. This will sometimes involve them in relating what they say to their or their interlocutors' values and beliefs. All this means that task-based language will inevitably take on interpersonal social and cultural significance, along with layers of personal meanings.

Studies have shown how this can happen. For instance, Aubrey (2017) found that intercultural factors can pervade interaction at a very broad level: he found significant differences in the flow of talk between native speaker–second language (L2) learner dyads, compared with L2 learner–learner dyads. Tasks can also mediate interpersonal relationships. Barnes (1976) showed this in data taken from first language (L1) classroom tasks. In one instance as they get involved with the task, two students gradually come to take on complementary dialogic roles as they attempt to solve a science puzzle: one of the students gets into the role of formulating a series of enabling questions, while his friend takes on the role of trying to answer them, thinking aloud until they are both satisfied with their answers. Language here has a heuristic function, but as the students attempt to crack the problem, they also use the language to mediate their own relationship. In other words, the language used between students will often take on personal or group meanings, often leading to laughter, joking and the development of group identity. Second language learners can sometimes play with language; for instance, Bygate (1988) showed how a group identifying lines of rivers or roads on a map, compared a curve to the 'belly of a C', alluding in passing to the fact that Celia, one of the participants, was pregnant . In contrast, in other groups students might use the target language to variously express amusement or irritation with the way the activity unfolded.

Furthermore, and this is of course part and parcel of TBLT, the language used can also be oriented towards significant social contexts (such as social events, cultural activities, service encounters, professional needs, or academic purposes) for the meaningful use of the target language outside the classroom. Van den Branden (2016) for example reported a task carried out by low-educated adult L2 students and their teacher in the context of local shops and services. Here, the language was used to communicate genuine material needs of the students (what they wanted to buy), but also to relate them as non-native speakers to the shop staff. In another study, Andon, Dewey, and Leung (2018) analysed tasks carried out as an element in a Masters-level programme, in which students use language not only to find things out and to articulate ideas, but also to relate to each other and to the teaching staff.

Samuda (2001) provides several extracts showing students relating to each other through talk. In a task in which they were asked to speculate about a person's possible identity and leisure activities on the basis of the contents of their pockets, they also created a rapport by sharing jokes, or points of view, or even disagreeing. Canto, de Graaff, and Jauregi (2014) report on on-line tasks involving groups of students in the Netherlands and Spain. Even less socially contextualised tasks at much lower levels of proficiency can involve the participants in using the target language to mediate relations between learners and between learners and the teacher. For instance, Shintani's (2016) study of a series of variations of a task used with six-year old Japanese learners of English shows how the teacher and learners gradually use more and more English to manage their behaviour and negotiate their identities in the classroom. Kobayashi and Kobayashi (2018) report how during a poster-presentation task, groups of students used English between one presentation and the next to mediate reviews of their performance and plan their next presentation. They used language to ask and offer advice, check the language they had used, and review the way their talk had been interpreted. Sometimes they incorporated into their presentations words and concepts used in questions asked by members of the audience. At other times, the speaker ploughed on despite the audience's questions, creating a less positive interpersonal vibe. Tasks, then, are a place where language becomes embedded in personal and interpersonal values and identities.

Studies have also focused on the specific question of whether tasks can engage the use of pragmatic features of language. Reagan and Payant (2018) report the use of tasks that positively affected learners' production of L2 requests in terms of the ways they handled the pragmatic moves. Verheyden et al. (2016) show how the written L2 output of young Turkish learners of Dutch as a second language gets better over the course of a single school year with regard to six measures of writing quality (including lexical richness, complexity, content, and accuracy, and pragmatic genre conventions) as a result of repeated practice at writing meaningful narrative stories. Levkina (2018) analyses the impact of email tasks on students handling of apologies, justifications, and thanks, and finds clear evidence of an increase in pragmatic awareness in the written data. Gomez-Laich and Taguchi (2018) showed how the design of a task can help to focus learners' attention on pragmatic features relevant to successful performance of the task in question, notably the elements needed to write a persuasive text. In addition, the design of the tasks was shown to affect the nature of the interaction between the students. Similarly, Alcón-Soler (2018) provides evidence that the use of tasks can influence the use of pragmatic markers (here, request mitigators, etc.) as well as the patterns of interaction between the students. Taking these studies together, there is little doubt that a major function for tasks is to bring about the socially situated use of language.

By doing so, task performance can engage the complex mental processes involved in authentic, meaningful language behaviour outside the classroom. Task performance in the classrooms mirrors and elicits holistic language use. L2 reading, listening, speaking and writing are all hugely complex challenges because so many aspects of performance need to be attended to at the same time, and this is the kind of practice that TBLT elicits. This is the exact reason why strongly form-focused approaches concentrating on the presentation and practice of discrete items are often associated with transfer problems, or carry-over problems (Lightbown & Spada, 2013; Long, 2015; Larsen-Freeman, 2009). The meaningful focus of task-based language has therefore an essential contribution to make to second language learning and development through TBLT.

However, the task-based focus on meaning has another rather different role to play in language learning: it can provide invaluable clues to help enable learners to interpret and decipher the language system (Hatch, 1983; Long, 2015). Knowing that a piece of language is meaningful provides clues that can help learners not only work out what it means, but what the parts of the utterance or sentence might be. Dakin (1973) demonstrated this many years ago in an exercise designed to lead learners to work out the meaning and functioning of a series of unique grammatical categories in an invented language, which he called Novish. Working with nothing but meaningful sentences, by using a process of inductive learning, learners were able to infer the entire series of grammatical categories that they had never seen before, all without any explicit instruction. Context provided the clues.

Unlocking how the language works through meaningful communication has been shown to operate just as powerfully in TBLT classes both for young second language learners and in adult second language classes. Shintani's (2015) detailed study referred to earlier reveals how six-year old Japanese learners of English as a foreign language were able to interpret the language used in listening-based tasks and work out what the parts of the utterances meant and how they functioned grammatically. Gradually they came to internalise it, and eventually voluntarily use elements themselves.

One of the most pervasive problems in teaching and learning language is how to enable learners to grasp the contextual meanings of new features, some of which may be quite abstract. How, for example, to convey the meaning and use of features such as the indefinite and definite articles, the simple past, or the different modals and their various meanings. Samples of recorded data suggest how this can happen. In Bruner (1983) a mother and very young child playing a game of 'peekaboo'. A doll or furry toy animal is first shown to the child, and then hidden behind a screen or piece of furniture. The adult asks the child 'Where has it gone? Where has it gone?' and then gradually moves it along behind the screen saying 'It's coming, it's coming, it's coming back . . . here it is! It's come back to you!' In the talk accompanying the game, the adult is perfectly illustrating the use of the present perfect and the progressive forms. Our point here is that the use of language is directly accessible when it occurs in the context of ongoing activities, such as tasks. No explanation is needed here of the use of the progressive or perfect: context makes it clear.

Samuda's (2001) study shows how a task can set up the basis for inductive learning: by requiring students to *speculate* (here, about the identity of the person whose coat the things were taken from), they get involved in expressing degrees of certainty or uncertainty – the meanings conveyed in English by 'epistemic' modals, without anybody talking *about* modality or epistemic meanings. The task enables them to induce the meanings directly, from which they can then focus on finding appropriate forms, whether we are using input- or output-based tasks (Ellis, 2017).

Studies that have shown the power of tasks to facilitate the learning of new language include those using input-based tasks (Ellis, 2001; Shintani, 2016), and those involving interactive tasks (Verhelst, Jaspaert, and Van den Branden, 2012). In the latter study, two-and-a-half-year-old beginner learners of Dutch as a second language were found to pick up the meaning of new words if they were firmly embedded in concrete play, particularly the play that the children were personally interested in. The concrete physical context of the play allowed the children to derive the meaning of new words from their link to specific objects and movements; at the same time, the children were eager to decipher the meaning of the new words *because* it was linked to their personal interests, ambitions, and goals.

To summarise, then, the fact that tasks require learners to engage with meaning-making provides opportunities for them to experience and explore the functional uses of language. In the process, learners also find themselves using the language to mediate social relationships, enabling it to become personally meaningful. In the process, the meaningful dimensions of tasks also provide a gateway for learners to understand and identify the various elements of the language, and infer how they work.

2.4 The Accessibility Principle

Tasks, then, are an invaluable resource for language learning in lots of different ways. However, there are reasons why simply doing tasks will not ensure the learning of all aspects of a language.

One challenge can derive from the fact that communicative discourse contains considerable redundancy. By 'redundancy', we refer to language or language features that are not needed to understand the broad gist of the discourse, or to make oneself understood. The fact that language features can be redundant means that they can be ignored – and consequently not learned. Matters are made harder for learners by the fact that many grammatical features lack prominence and are therefore difficult– sometimes impossible – to notice: features like certain verb endings, noun and adjective endings, verb auxiliaries, pronouns, articles, and some conjunctions (see, for example, Long, 2015: 301–4). They are particularly hard to notice if they are unstressed or elided, as many are. It is true that some, such as *-ing*, or the prominent fricative *-s* ending in English, are generally clearly perceptible. But even they are usually unnecessary for communication to function. For instance, a story can be told without using past tense verb inflections, and by the same token, we can understand another person's story without noticing them even if they have been pronounced.

There are other challenges in a TBLT approach. One is the challenge of focusing simultaneously on meaning and form. Performing a task involves complex demands on attention (Johnson, 1996; Skehan, 1998; VanPatten, 1996). We are all familiar with the problems of 'multi-tasking' – attending to several things at once: planning, keeping track of what we have done in the task and what we are trying to achieve; taking care that we are getting our message across; and dealing with problems as they arise. A significant amount of attention is devoted to handling communication rather than to spotting, and managing new language. Also, importantly, communicative discourse is transitory so that remembering material can also be difficult. So, there is a good chance that some new features encountered during a particular task will be forgotten. How often, for instance, do we ask for help with a word (or look it up in the dictionary) while talking or writing, and then afterwards find ourselves unable to recall it?

In any case, even if we *have* noticed a new feature, highlighting it in some way and showing how it works is usually helpful. During the task, learners are largely focused on the sequential links in the chain of discourse, and in any case the sequence of words alone does not give information about language patterns and options, unless as noted above you have a huge amount of it, as in L1 acquisition. (In L2 acquisition the time available to learn the language is usually much shorter.) Thus, for many it is helpful to have some kind of summary, or an explanation of targeted features, at some point in the lesson cycle, and to have some additional examples of the feature apart from the one that occurred in the task.

In addition to these issues, we already noted that, in any case, learners differ. No class can be entirely homogeneous, whether in terms of level, in terms of previous language learning experience, in terms of aptitudes for learning, in terms of their needs and interests, or indeed in terms of the basic alertness of different learners at a particular time on a particular day (DeKeyser, 2019; Skehan, 1989; Van den Branden, 2016). Some learners will find some material easy to notice, understand, analyse, or remember, and others not.

No responsible approach to TBLT (or indeed to any form of language teaching) can ignore these issues (Dörnyei, 2009). As Skehan (this volume) has argued, the careful design and implementation of tasks can help to shift learners' attention to formal features during task performance. However, this can be complemented by the use of techniques for promoting language accessibility during on-task work. At the same time, it is *also* clear that TBLT must find ways of complementing 'on-task work' to address some of the problems that we have just been discussing. And, indeed, the literature has proposed a rich range of pedagogic strategies for making language features accessible to learners. In what follows we group techniques and strategies of implicit and then explicit form focus.

2.5 Implicit Form Focus

Implicit techniques of form focus are techniques used during communication to make language features more prominent and more perceptible. They work by adjusting aspects of the discourse during delivery so as to make the features more noticeable to learners (Ellis, 2019; Long, 2015). Considerable research has shown the value of these techniques. Some are based on studies of adult–child talk in L1 acquisition, which have shown how adults can adjust their speech to make it more accessible to the child (Bruner, 1983; Hatch, 1983; Wells, 1981, 1985). But other studies have explored talk between non-native speakers, or between native and non-native speakers (Hatch, 1983; Long, 1983). The kind of techniques identified include the use of stress, the use of heightened intonation patterns, and slowing down the speed of speech. Speakers will also break down utterances to isolate the target feature, repeat the target feature, and rebuild the utterance around the target feature. Sometimes whole utterances are repeated (Ellis, 1984). In writing, features can be repeated, highlighted, or italicised. Similar features are often used in books for children, including the use of rhyme, and spacing of the text on the page. Each of these techniques helps to make 'target' features of the language more accessible, making them more easily perceptible, or drawing learners' attention to the features. They can be especially valuable in teacher talk – both generally while managing lessons, but also in relation specifically to task work: for example, when teachers are working with students on and around tasks and task outcomes (Van den Branden, 2016).

A second type of implicit form focus occurs when meanings and understandings are negotiated interactively during communication. 'Negotiation for meaning' occurs when there is a communication problem between interlocutors, and the listener asks for clarification of what the other is saying, the speaker seeks help, or the speaker or listener provide clarification (Gass & Varonis, 1994; Long, 1983; Pica, 1994; Varonis & Gass 1985). Negotiation for meaning therefore involves breaking down the problem utterances interactively to highlight the segment that needs negotiation, rather than allowing the flow of language to carry on uninterrupted. This has been shown to aid both L2 learners' comprehension of target language input (Van den Branden, 2000) and production of output (Van den Branden, 1997).

One important element of negotiation for meaning sequences is the use of 'communication strategies' (Yule and Tarone, 1991), which are strategies people use to find alternative ways of getting their meaning across when a previous attempt seems to have failed (Kasper and Kellerman, 1997). Communication strategies are used by speakers to compensate for limitations in their repertoire. But they are also used to compensate for potential limitations in listeners' repertoires, and more generally to make communication accessible to readers or listeners. This means they are also useful for teachers (Sarab, 2003; Van den Branden, 2016). A meta-analysis by Mackey and Goo (2007) showed that implicit types of negative feedback (including recasts, clarification requests and confirmation checks that are embedded in negotiation routines) have a positive impact on L2 acquisition. They reported stronger effects on vocabulary acquisition as compared to grammar acquisition, but found that the effects for the latter were more enduring.

All these various types of implicit form focus have been clearly shown to be valuable tools for making language accessible during communication, are therefore potentially helpful for learning, and will certainly be exploited by attentive learners. However, for reasons outlined earlier, implicit form focus is not always sufficient for all learners. In the next section we therefore consider the role of explicit form focus.

2.6 Explicit Form Focus

While tasks provide a fertile environment for learning language directly from use, it cannot be expected to carry the entire load of language learning. Often, learners also benefit from standing back from their on-line engagement with the message and considering patterns in the language they are using, or patterns they could be using, to perform the task (Ellis, 2017).

Samuda (2001), for instance, showed a teacher getting a class to pause in their work and feed back to her the opinions and ideas they had been sharing in the task they were engaged in up to that point in the lesson. This kind of interaction is clearly a kind of on-task exchange between students and teacher. During the exchange, the teacher writes ideas from the students on the board, and then jointly they pool words and expressions they can use to express their degrees of certainty about their ideas, expressing degrees of certainty being the central point of the task. Students go back to working on the task in groups. Then, when they have finished, the teacher carries out a further review, and once again the students' responses are written up on the board. The material on the board can then be used to systematise the students' awareness of the language features. This can then be used as a resource for any follow-up phase of the task, such as writing up their ideas or producing a poster. It is important to stress that the language material written on the board is not decontextualised: it is clearly central to the communicative focus of the task and that of any further task phases. At the same time, it is somewhat removed from the students' on-line communication.

This is perhaps best seen as a kind of 'within task' procedure, since the material is gathered onto the board before the task has been completed. Van den Branden (2016: 170–71) identifies a number of techniques that a teacher can employ within the context of task-based work:

- The teacher should produce a wide variety of *questions, cues, and prompts* to elicit learner output.
- The teacher should provide *feedback* on the students' written and oral output. Feedback may come in different shapes, including explicit corrections, recasts, confirmation and clarification requests, metalinguistic comments, extensions, and elaborations . . .
- The teacher should incorporate a *focus on form* in the meaning-oriented work the students are doing.
- The teacher should provide ample *input* and should *model*, or practice the performance of a task or the use of a certain strategy.

The reader will have noticed that these techniques and procedures all depend on the teacher's involvement. All use the task as the context for the form focus while it is in progress.

Others (e.g., d'Ely, Mota & Bygate, 2019; Hawkes, 2012; Sheppard & Ellis, 2018) have investigated the impact of carrying out some kind of task review before students perform a repeated version of the task. In one study (Kobayashi & Kobayashi 2018), students carried out a sequence of poster presentations to different groups, and reviewed their performance independently between each presentation. These studies all show that reviewing the task before a second iteration (usually with different partners) has the effect of improving aspects of learners' language on the second performance. This suggests the potential value of carrying out some kind of interim 'debriefing', whether before continuing with the task or before re-doing the task with a different interlocutor. In these examples, form focus is introduced after the task has been attempted, and prior to a fresh attempt.

Focusing on the language is also possible after the task has been completed (although in the final section of this chapter, we will return to the limitations of post-task focus on form). Lynch (2018b) explores what happens when students transcribe their own speech. Self-transcription becomes a form of self-correction, and in Lynch's study, doing this helps the students to adjust their talk. Self-correction has also been shown to be valuable in task-based writing lessons (Bitchener & Ferris, 2011; Bitchener & Storch, 2016), as is 'other-transcription' or 'other-correction'. One way of doing this that integrates correction into the task itself is when students jointly prepare a text, poster, a web or email message (Canto et al., 2014), or an oral presentation (Kobayashi & Kobayashi, 2018). In these cases, the form focus is built into the iterative and collaborative design of the task.

So far, we have been considering form focus arising out of learners' task-based work. Johnson (1996), however, remarks that observing skilled performance can also be helpful to the learner, especially when the learners have already attempted to do the task themselves. As we have noted earlier, doing a task oneself can alert one to the various challenges it poses; observing someone else do it afterwards can enable us to notice ways of dealing with those challenges that neither teacher nor learner might have spotted: the choice of words or phrases, ways of opening or closing the discourse, the use of small talk, the manner of delivery, the choice of grammatical features, and so on. Van den Branden's (2016) account of the tasks in local shops provides a context for this kind of form-focus activity.

Before moving to our last section, we should note the importance of the final debriefing phase of a task cycle in drawing learners' attention to language. Among a set of seven principles Van den Branden draws from educational research (2016: 166), two are particularly relevant at this point:

> Challenge: The teacher tries to make sure that the students learn a lot and expects full effort from the students. The teacher asks the students to explain about the answers they give. The teacher doesn't let students give up when the work gets hard. The teacher wants the students to learn from their mistakes.

Consolidate: The teacher checks to make sure the students understand what she or he is teaching. The teacher gives feedback and useful comments on students' work and helps the students understand how they improve their work and correct their mistakes. At the end of the day or lesson, the teacher summarizes what the students have learned.

These two principles help to underline the importance of the final review phase. The principle of *challenging* the students carries through from the start to the end of the task: this principle reminds us that the teacher should be holding the students accountable, and requiring outcomes from their work on the task. The principle of *consolidating* brings closure to the task: here the teacher ensures understanding, provides correction where needed, the closing summary acting as a reminder of what they have been focusing on.

The final review phase is frequently emphasised as a key point in a lesson, since it helps to underline central learning points, and reinforce the importance of those points in a way that might help learners' recall. For example, discussing task-based science lessons in mother tongue classes, Barnes (1976) reports a teacher in plenary mode reviewing with the students what they had been studying in their various groups. This turns out to be a crucial phase in the lesson. It requires everyone to share with each other across the class what they had been doing, the thought processes they had followed and why, and their conclusions. Doing this also enables the teacher to mediate the work of the different groups and make it available to everyone. Crucially for us, this phase also enables the teacher to review terminology that the students needed to do the task, the meanings of the terms, and the concepts central to the task. This review phase then helps bring together concepts and language from across the groups that are likely to be useful on another occasion.

Another important function is that by requiring the students to report back in plenary mode reinforces their accountability: when doing the task, students will be aware that they will be expected to talk about what they thought, what they said, what they did, and why. At the same time, carrying out a review like this also reminds the students what purpose the task served. Working with students of English as an additional/second language in the UK, Cameron, Moon, and Bygate (1996) found numerous examples of precisely this kind of phase in lessons across the curriculum. They also (personal communication with participating teachers) found cases where the absence of this review phase undermined what had otherwise been quite valuable task-based work earlier in the lesson. Indeed, also in Samuda's (2001) study, a final review phase was a crucial point in the lesson: it brought together the substantive ideas of the groups, gathered up valuable relevant language, and served to prepare for the subsequent writing phase. Similar plenary review phases are reported in Shintani

(2016, 2018) and Lynch (2018a), and Toth (2008) analyses a lesson in which the teacher handled an entire task in plenary mode, comparing this with what happened when students did the same task in pair-work mode.

These studies help to show that, in addition to the more implicit types of focus on form considered earlier, some form of explicit work following the task can usefully complement on-task work. This can be led by the teacher, but equally, it can be negotiated by the students themselves. Crucial, though, for a TBLT approach is that any form focus occurs in response to issues arising in the task itself: the aim is for reflection on language form to be always grounded in the particular context of a given task, and in the learners' needs and purposes. We prioritise this over the use of explicit instruction prior to the task, or 'pre-emptive focus on form', as discussed for instance in Ellis (2017). In the final section of this chapter we consider some of the broader issues in interrelating form focus and on-task work.

2.7 Integrating Task and Form Focus in Task-Based Language Teaching

We have seen that from the perspective of the meaningfulness principle, tasks are a remarkably rich resource for the learning of language. The use of tasks is not sufficient on its own, however – we also need to deploy strategies to make the language accessible for learning. Over the past fifty years, there has been widespread agreement that reconciling these two aspects of language pedagogy is a major challenge (see, e.g., Brumfit, 1984; DeKeyser, 2005; Ellis, 2019; Lightbown & Spada, 2013; Long, 1983, 2015; Widdowson, 1983). Over-emphasising accessibility (generally with a focus on accuracy) usually fails to carry over into fluent use. Equally, concentrating on the task to the exclusion of focusing on language could result in a lack of accurate language development. Spada (2019) has called this 'the problem of integration' (a problem she suggests applies to all approaches to language pedagogy). The question for TBLT then is how to integrate the meaningfulness principle and the accessibility principle.

Our first step is to place tasks (the meaningfulness principle) at the starting- and end-points of the teaching cycle throughout the programme. Thus, tasks have a major role in focusing learning. Firstly, they define the agenda and contextualise the focus for each scheme of work, for each unit or chapter. Secondly, they constitute the reference point for assessing progress and outcomes throughout. Any focus on formal features of the language (the accessibility principle) then arises within a context established by the choice of task.

Although some (notably Brumfit, 1984), and more recently Ellis (2019), have argued for separating task-type work and form-focus activities, it is fundamental to TBLT that the two facets must be related. There seem to be two aspects to this. The first is that any knowledge about a language (the focus on form) needs to be related to how it is used: it has to be stored in memory in terms of how it is used in discourse. Widdowson (1983) referred to this as 'readiness for use', Lightbown & Spada (2013) as requiring 'transfer-appropriate practice' (see also Spada & Lightbown, 2008) – practice designed in such a way that learners can transfer it from the learning environment into real life. The aim is to ensure that the language practised is accessible during communication, and not just archived in dictionary-like lists in a separate memory store to be consulted at leisure (Bruner, 1966).

The learning cycle begins, then, by firstly requiring learners to work with meanings (the 'meaningfulness principle'). Tasks can be used to create a kind of 'space' for language. This 'space' takes the form of the contexts and the communication needs that emerge in the tasks. These contexts and communication needs shape the learners' use of language. Not all language is relevant for all tasks. Learners and teacher can narrow down the language that is useful both for the task and for the learners' development – the relevant concepts and forms. Whether an input (comprehension-based) task or an output task, it is the task that is the starting point for learners to mobilise their prior knowledge and their existing language resources and try to put them to use. Doing this inevitably involves stumbles, errors, and the use of various types of non-target forms. This is a crucial phase because it is the point when students and teacher can identify language useful for the task. This naturally leads to a focus-on-form phase in which students and teacher review familiar options, possibly homing in on the details of some of the forms, checking on meanings, exploring paradigms, considering other examples, or asking for support. Language work of this kind constitutes a kind of workshop activity, supporting the main task.

The transfer-appropriate-practice principle also has implications for what happens after form-focus activities. Clearly, it needs to be transferred into use. This is partly to embed the forms that have been focused on back into the context of the task; it is also partly because acquiring language as a skill requires the learner to be able to monitor their use of the material – say, in terms of choice of vocabulary, genre, discourse style, grammatical choice in relation to context and meaning, and so on – the kinds of monitoring that native speakers also use (Levelt, 1989).

Integration then becomes a two-way phenomenon. To stop at the form-focus phase would not ensure integration and would leave the learning cycle incomplete. Merely *exploring* useful language patterns risks leaving the new language in a memory store unconnected with the task. It would also mean that teacher and learners would not be able to assess the learning of the new language in the context of the task. We need to know, 'Can they use it?' Furthermore, if we do not go beyond a focus-on-form phase, we would risk undermining the task-based nature of the overall programme.

So, to avoid these problems, and to complete the learning cycle, a second integration phase is needed: the language needs integrating *back* into the task. This implies returning to the task. This might be the unfinished task, or else a follow-up version of the task, in which the new material would be activated. Language that had been explored during the form-focus phase can now be put back into circulation in the context of task-based use. Doing this creates opportunities for further checking of the new material, for transferring the material to other discourse modes (from written to oral, or from oral to written), as well as the opportunity for interim assessment.

The strength of this approach is amply illustrated in studies by Samuda (2001), Van den Branden (2016), and Lynch (2018b). Lynch reviews a series of different studies that he had undertaken with different students over a period of time, each of which explored a different way of involving the learners in *recycling* an initial performance in later task cycles. The recycling he refers to involved the learners in 'adapting and modifying their previous output, rather than merely doing the same thing again' (2018b: 193). Each study employed a different type of recycling. For instance, in one task working in threes, students were asked to explain to partners a topic they would be interested in researching. They were 'to monitor how understandable their language was for their two partners' (197) before the students then formed new groups of three and told their new partners their topic of interest, bearing in mind the problems of understanding raised the first time around. In a second activity, students presented a poster to a series of different colleagues: the feedback, including questions for clarification, from each colleague fed into a gradual improvement on subsequent presentations of the poster. In a third task, again with a different cohort of students, participants rehearsed a conference presentation. Each rehearsal involved some kind of form-focus: an audio-recording by the tutor of problems words; short recordings of oral summaries by the participants; and video-recordings of group presentations. Analysis of the data (both language data and students' self-report questionnaires) on each of the studies showed consistent support for the use of form focus within some kind of a cycle, starting and ending with a version of the target task.

The value of this kind of cyclical approach is also clearly borne out in a number of meta-analyses of the impact of task-based interaction on the acquisition of grammar (Bryfonsky & McKay, 2019; Cobb, 2010; Keck et al., 2006). They show that the acquisition of grammar rules is positively impacted by task-based interaction, when students are given the opportunity to use the grammar rule that they were explicitly taught in communicative interaction.

Further empirical evidence supporting the crucial importance of the integration of explicit instruction and meaningful language use can be found in the research base on the effects of strategy instruction on language development (Bimmel, Van den Bergh & Oostdam, 2001; Field, 2009; Friesen and Haigh, 2018; Maeng, 2014; Park, 2010; Plonsky, 2011; Vandergrift and Goh, 2009, 2012). Whether with regard to listening skills, reading skills, or writing skills, explicit strategy instruction has been found to have a substantial impact on task performance and skills development, at least if the strategy instruction is skilfully embedded in the actual use of the strategies when students are performing meaningful language tasks. The research also suggests that in the first stages of instruction, the modelling of a specific strategy by the teacher in the context of a meaningful task has clear benefits, but in subsequent task performances, modelling and explicit instruction should gradually be replaced by scaffolding and the teacher delegating the autonomy to select and deploy appropriate strategies to the learners.

To sum up, 'integration' means firstly working from the meaningfulness principle and grounding the new language work in preliminary encounters with a task; secondly, using the accessibility principle, ensuring that relevant language focus is provided both within and off task; and thirdly, that any form focus is integrated back into the task in subsequent task-based work. It is from this perspective that the task can provide a firm base for sustainable and effective language learning and teaching.

2.8 Conclusion

In this chapter, we have seen that, to exploit its learning potential, TBLT depends on two things: the meaningfulness principle – work on tasks, with all the rich range of learning potential that they offer; and the accessibility principle – form-focused work on language, anchored in, and arising out of, the task to ensure that language forms and patterns are noticed, understood and have some initial uptake. Neither of these principles is sufficient, each being supported by the other.

For these two principles to work, the integration principle is crucial. Consider just for a moment other fields of learning. No one would disagree that in order to learn to play tennis, the learner needs to do more than 'hit a ball against a wall'. We need to play actual games of tennis. Just as in learning to play the piano, a learner has to play actual pieces of music, such as Bach preludes, Scarlatti sonatas, or jazz classics. It is never going to be enough just to play scales, arpeggios, and exercises, or just to hit a ball against a wall. But equally, no one would expect to be able to play the various kinds of music or become a competent tennis player just by playing. We also need help to understand what the difficulties are and how to overcome them. And we need practice activities to help to prepare us. So, task-based work and form-focused work depend on each other. Task-based work needs the support of form-focused activities. Form focus, on the other hand, needs to be anchored to relevant tasks. To be viable, TBLT needs both, but to support each other they need integrating.

We said at the beginning of this chapter that TBLT reconfigures classroom learning. The reason it does so is that it starts, works through, and ends cycles of learning with a focus on tasks. The task is like the laboratory or sports field in which learners try things out 'in action'. The form-focus work then reflects on the action that took place on the sports field or in the laboratory – before returning to the action. This is not a complicated change, but it re-*centres* learning on tasks. In that sense, it reconfigures classroom learning.

The approach we have been describing in this chapter is grounded in reflection, in practice, and in research studies. However, approaches to language teaching are in constant development, particularly in light of experience, findings from teacher development and research projects. Writing on a completely different topic (innovation in gardening technology) Floud (2019: 185) writes:

> On occasion, an innovation is disruptive and sweeps all before it; much more often, it makes a bit of a difference but needs to be rethought and altered before being widely adopted. People need to be trained in the new ways; suppliers have to be found for the components of a new machine; money has to be borrowed to cover the cost of experimentation to get it right.

This chapter suggests some re-thinking which the future development of TBLT might benefit from. Hopefully, this re-thinking will include projects to investigate how different types of form-focused activities can be used to complement task-based work, so as to effectively integrate form focus into use.

Further Reading

Bygate, M. (2018). Creating and using the space for speaking within the foreign language classroom. What, why and how? In R. Alonso Alonso, ed. *Speaking in a second language*. Amsterdam: John Benjamins, pp. 153–74.

Samuda, V. (2001). Guiding relationships between form and meaning during task performance: The role of the teacher. In M. Bygate, P. Skehan, and M. Swain, eds. *Researching pedagogic tasks: Second language learning, teaching and testing*. Harlow: Longman, pp. 119–40.

Shintani, N. (2015). The incidental grammar acquisition in focus on form and focus on forms instruction for young, beginner learners. *TESOL Quarterly*, 49(1), 115–40.

Toth, P. D. (2008). Teacher- and learner-led discourse in task-based grammar instruction: Providing procedural assistance for L2 morphosyntactic development. *Language Learning*, 58(2), 237–83.

Van den Branden, K. (2016). The role of teachers in task-based language education. *Annual Review of Applied Linguistics*, 36, 164–81.

Study Questions

1. Evaluate the view presented in this chapter that input as well as output tasks are a valuable tool for engaging learners with a wide range of aspects of a target language.
2. What do you think are the main ways in which tasks can be used to help make new language accessible to learners? How far can tasks be expected to do this on their own? How far is support likely to be needed from the teacher, and why?
3. What in your view is the importance of the notion of 'integration' for language teaching in general, and for TBLT in particular? What do you see as the main implications for the use of TBLT in the classroom?
4. How would you react to the suggestion that the meaningfulness, accessibility and integration principles apply equally to courses addressing beginners and courses addressing more advanced second language learners?

References

Alcon-Soler, E. (2018). Effects of task-supported language teaching on learners' use and knowledge of email request mitigators. In N. Taguchi and Y. Kim, eds. *Task-based approaches to teaching and assessing pragmatics*. Amsterdam: John Benjamins, pp. 55–81.

Andon, N., Dewey, M., and Leung, C. (2018). Tasks in the pedagogic space: Using online discussion forum tasks and formative feedback to develop academic discourse skills at Masters level. In V. Samuda, K. Van den Branden, and M. Bygate, eds. *TBLT as a researched pedagogy*. Amsterdam: John Benjamins, pp. 235–63.

Aubrey, S. (2017). Inter-cultural contact and flow in a task-based Japanese EFL classroom. *Language Teaching Research*, 21(6), 717–34.

Barnes, D. (1976). *From Communication to Curriculum*. Harmondsworth: Penguin.

Bimmel, P. E., van den Bergh, H., and Oostdam, R. J. (2001). Effects of strategy training on reading comprehension in first and foreign language. *European Journal of Psychology of Education*, 16, 509–29.

Bitchener, J. and Ferris, D. R. (2011). *Written corrective feedback in second language acquisition and writing.* London: Routledge.

Bitchener, J. and Storch, N. (2016). *Written corrective feedback for L2 development.* Bristol: Multilingual Matters.

Brown, H. D. (2007). *Teaching by principles: An interactive approach to language Pedagogy.* White Plains, NY: Pearson Education.

Brumfit, C. J. (1984). *Communicative methodology in language teaching.* Cambridge: Cambridge University Press.

Bruner, J. S. (1966). *Toward a theory of instruction.* Cambridge, MA: Harvard University Press.

Bruner, J. S. (1983). *Child's talk.* Cambridge: Cambridge University Press.

Bryfonski, L. and McKay, T. (2019). TBLT implementation and evaluation: A meta-analysis. *Language Teaching Research,* 23, 603–32.

Bygate, M. (1988). Linguistic and strategic features of the language of learners working in oral communication exercises. Unpublished PhD thesis. Institute of Education, University of London.

Cameron, L. J., Moon, J. P. and Bygate, M. (1996). Language development in the mainstream: How do teachers and pupils use language? *Language and Education,* 10(4), 221–36.

Canto, S., de Graaff, R., and Jauregi, K. (2014). Collaborative tasks for negotiation of intercultural meaning in virtual worlds and video-web communication. In L. Ortega and M. González-Lloret, eds. *Technology-mediated TBLT: researching technology and tasks.* Amsterdam: John Benjamins, pp. 183–212.

Cobb, M. (2010). Meta-analysis of the Effectiveness of Task-Based Interaction in Form-Focused Instruction of Adult Learners in Foreign and Second Language Teaching. San Francisco: University of San Francisco. Unpublished Doctoral Dissertation. Retrieved from: https://repository.usfca.edu/diss/389.

Croft, W. and Cruise, D. A. (2004). *Cognitive linguistics.* Cambridge: Cambridge University Press.

Dakin, J. (1973). *The language laboratory and language learning.* Harlow: Longman.

de Bot, K., Lowie, W., and Verspoor, M. (2005). *Second language acquisition: An advanced resource book.* London and New York: Routledge.

D'Ely, R., Mota, M.B., and Bygate, M. (2019). Strategic planning and repetition as metacognitive processes in task performance: Implications for EFL learners' speech production. In Z. Wen, and M. J. Ahmadian, eds. *Researching L2 task performance and pedagogy.* Amsterdam: John Benjamins, pp. 199–228.

DeKeyser, R. (2005). What makes second-language grammar difficult? A review of issues. *Language Learning,* 55(S1), 1–25.

DeKeyser, R. (2018). Task repetition for language learning: A perspective from skill acquisition theory. In M. Bygate, ed. *Learning language through task repetition* Amsterdam: John Benjamins, pp. 27–42.

DeKeyser, R. (2019). The future of aptitude research. In Z. Wen, P. Skehan, A. Biedron, S. Li, and R. L. Sparks, eds. *Language aptitude. Advancing theory, testing, research, and practice.* London: Routledge, pp. 317–29.

Dörnyei, Z. (2009). *The psychology of second language acquisition.* Oxford: Oxford University Press.

Ellis, R. (1984). *Classroom second language development.* Oxford: Pergamon.

Ellis, R. (2009). Task-based language teaching: Sorting out the misunderstandings. *International Journal of Applied Linguistics*, 19(3), 221–46.

Ellis, R. J. (2016). Anniversary article focus on form: A critical review. *Language Teaching Research*, 20(3), 405–28.

Ellis, R. (2017). Position paper: Moving task-based language teaching forward. *Language Teaching*, 50(4), 507–26.

Ellis, R. (2019). Towards a modular language curriculum for using tasks. *Language Teaching Research*, 23(4), 454–75.

Field, J. (2009). *Listening in the language classroom.* Cambridge: Cambridge University Press.

Floud, R. (2019). *An economic history of the English garden.* London: Allen Lane.

Friesen, D. C. and Haigh, C. A. (2018). How and why strategy instruction can improve second language reading comprehension: A review. *Reading Matrix: An International Online Journal*, 18(1), 1–18.

Gass, S. and Varonis, E. M. (1994). Input, interaction, and second language production. *Studies in Second Language Acquisition*, 16, 283–302.

Gomez-Laich, M. P. and Taguchi, N. (2018). Task complexity effects on interaction during a collaborative persuasive writing task: A conversation analytic perspective. In N. Taguchi and Y. Kim, eds. *Task-based approaches to teaching and assessing pragmatics.* Amsterdam: John Benjamins, pp. 83–109.

Graham, S. and Perin, D. (2007) What we know, what we still need to know: Teaching adolescents to write. *Scientific Studies of Reading*, 11(4), 313–35.

Hatch, E. M. (1983). *Psycholinguistics: A Second Language Perspective.* Rowley, MA: Newbury House.

Hawkes, M. (2012). Using task repetition to direct learner attention and focus on form. *ELT Journal*, 66(3), 327–36.

Johnson, K. (1996). *Language teaching and skill learning.* Oxford: Blackwell.

Kasper, G., and Kellerman, E., (1997), eds. *Communication strategies: Psycholinguistic and sociolinguistic perspectives.* London: Longman.

Keck, C., Iberri-Shea, G., Tracy-Ventura, N. and Wa-Mbaleka, S. (2006). Investigating the empirical link between task-based interaction and acquisition: A meta-analysis. In L. Ortega and J. Norris, eds. *Synthesizing research on language learning and teaching.* Amsterdam: John Benjamins, pp. 91–131.

Kobayashi, E. and Kobayashi, M. (2018). Second language learning through repeated engagement in a poster presentation task. In M. Bygate, ed.

Learning language through task repetition. Amsterdam: John Benjamins, pp. 223–54.

Larsen-Freeman, D. (2009). Teaching and testing grammar. In M. Long and C. Doughty eds. *The handbook of language teaching.* West Sussex: Wiley-Blackwell, pp. 518–42.

Levelt, W. J. M. (1989). *Speaking: From intention to articulation.* Cambridge, MA: The MIT Press.

Levkina, M. (2018). Developing pragmatic competence through tasks in EFL contexts: does proficiency play a role? N. Taguchi and Y. Kim, eds. *Task-based approaches to teaching and assessing pragmatics.* Amsterdam: John Benjamins, pp. 137–57.

Lightbown, P. and Spada, N. (2013). *How Languages Are Learned.* Oxford: Oxford University Press.

Long, M. H. (1981). Input, interaction and second language acquisition. *Annals of the New York Academy of Sciences*, 379, 259–78.

Long, M. H. (1983). Native-speaker/non-native speaker conversation and the negotiation of comprehensible input. *Applied Linguistics*, 4(2), 126–41.

Long, M. H. (2015). *Second language acquisition and task-based language teaching.* Chichester: John Wiley & Sons.

Lynch, A. (2018a). Promoting learning from second language speaking tasks: Exploring learner attitudes to the use of comparators and oral feedback. In V. Samuda, K. Van den Branden, and M. Bygate, eds. *TBLT as a researched pedagogy.* Amsterdam: John Benjamins, pp. 213–34.

Lynch, A. (2018b). Perform, reflect, recycle: enhancing task repetition in second language speaking classes. In M. Bygate, ed. *Learning language through task repetition.* Amsterdam: John Benjamins, pp. 193–222.

Mackey, A. and Goo, J. (2007). Interaction research in SLA: A meta-analysis and research synthesis. In A. Mackey, ed. *Conversational interaction in second language acquisition.* Oxford: Oxford University Press, pp. 407–52.

Maeng, U. (2014). The effectiveness of reading strategy instruction: A meta-analysis. *English Teaching*, 69, 105–27.

Park, Y. H. (2010). A relationship between reading comprehension and reading strategy use: Meta-analysis. *English Teaching*, 65(3), 3–22.

Pica, T. (1994). Research on negotiation: What does it reveal about second language learning conditions, processes and outcomes? *Language Learning*, 44, 439–527.

Plonsky, L. (2011). The effectiveness of second language strategy instruction: A meta-analysis. *Language Learning*, 61, 993–1038.

Ranta, L. (2002). The role of learners' language analytic ability in the communicative classroom. In P. Robinson, ed. *Individual differences and instructed language learning.* Amsterdam: John Benjamin, pp. 159–80.

Reagan, D. and Payant, C. (2018). Task modality effects on Spanish learners' interlanguage pragmatic development. In N. Taguchi and Y. Kim, eds. *Task-based approaches to teaching and assessing pragmatics.* Amsterdam: John Benjamins, pp. 113–36.

Samuda, V. (2001). Guiding relationships between form and meaning during task performance: The role of the teacher. In M. Bygate, P. Skehan, and M. Swain, eds. *Researching pedagogic tasks: Second language learning, teaching and testing*. Harlow: Longman, pp. 119–40.

Sarab, A. R. (2003). A study of the communication strategies of second language teachers. Unpublished PhD thesis. University of Leeds.

Sheppard, C. and Ellis, R. (2018). The effects of awareness-raising through stimulated recall on the repeated performance of the same task and on a new task of the same type. In M. Bygate, ed. *Learning language through task repetition*. Amsterdam: John Benjamins, pp. 171–92.

Shintani, N. (2016). *Input-based tasks in foreign language instruction for young learners*. Amsterdam: John Benjamins.

Shintani, N. (2018). Mediating input-based tasks for beginner learners through task repetition: A socio-cultural perspective. In M. Bygate, ed. *Learning language through task repetition*. Amsterdam: John Benjamins. pp. 255–78.

Skehan, P. (1989). *Individual differences in second language learning*. London: Edward Arnold.

Skehan, P. (1998). *A cognitive approach to language learning*. Oxford: Oxford University Press.

Skehan, P. (2014). The context for researching a processing perspective on task performance. In P. Skehan, ed. *Processing perspectives on task performance*. Amsterdam: John Benjamins, pp. 1–26.

Spada, N. (2019). Plenary address, 8th International TBLT Conference, Ottawa, August 2019.

Spada, N. and Lightbown, P. M. (2008). Form-focused instruction: Isolated or integrated? *TESOL Quarterly*, 42(2), 181–207.

Toth, P. D. (2008). Teacher- and learner-led discourse in task-based grammar instruction: Providing procedural assistance for L2 morphosyntactic development. *Language Learning*, 58(2), 237–83.

Van den Branden, K. (1997). Effects of negotiation on language learners' output. *Language Learning*, 47(4), 589–636.

Van den Branden, K. (2000). Does negotiation of meaning promote reading comprehension? A study of primary school classes. *Reading Research Quarterly*, 35(3), 426–43.

Van den Branden, K. (2016). The role of teachers in task-based language education. *Annual Review of Applied Linguistics*, 36, 164–81.

Van den Branden, K., Bygate, M. and Norris, J. (2009). Task-based language teaching: Introducing the reader. In K. Van den Branden, M. Bygate, and J. Norris, eds. *Task-based language teaching: A reader*. Amsterdam: John Benjamins, pp. 1–13.

Vandergrift, L. and Goh, C. (2009). Teaching and testing listening comprehension. In M. Long and C. Doughty eds. *The handbook of language teaching*. Sussex: Wiley Blackwell, pp. 395–411.

VanPatten, B. (1996). *Input processing and grammar instruction.* New York: Ablex.
Varonis, E. M. and Gass, S. M. (1985). Non-native/non-native conversations: A model for negotiation of meaning. *Applied Linguistics,* 6(1), 71–90.
Verheyden, L., Van den Branden, K., Rijlaarsdam, G., van den Bergh, H., and De Maeyer, S. (2010). Written narrations by 8 to 10-year old Turkish pupils of Flemish primary education: A follow-up of seven text features. *Journal of Research in Reading,* 33(1), 20–38.
Verhelst, M., Jaspaert, K., and Van den Branden, K. (2012). The impact of input on early second language vocabulary acquisition. *ITL International Journal of Applied Linguistics,* 163, 21–42.
Wells, G. (1981). *Learning through interaction.* Cambridge: Cambridge University Press.
Wells, G. (1985). *Language development in the pre-school years.* Cambridge: Cambridge University Press.
Wen, Z., Biedron, A., and Skehan, P. (2017). Foreign language aptitudetheory: yesterday, today and tomorrow. *Language Teaching,* 50 (1), 1–31.
Widdowson H. G. (1983). *Learning purpose and language use.* Oxford: Oxford University Press.
Yule, G. and Tarone, E. (1991). The other side of the page: Integrating the study of communication strategies and negotiated input in SLA. In R. Phillipson, E. Kellerman, L. Selinker, M. Sharwood-Smith, and M. Swain, eds. *Foreign/second language pedagogy research.* Bristol: Multilingual Matters, pp. 162–71.

Appendix On Technological Change

'Technology' means 'how we do things'. For an economist, it refers to the whole complex of ways in which the economy operates. It is not only about machines ...; it also describes the working methods used in every form of economic activity, from architecture to zoos. It encompasses bookkeeping, ploughing the soil, digging canals. Technology changes because someone somewhere has a bright idea about doing things better and manages to convince others to adopt the newfangled notion. We usually call the idea an 'invention' and the process of putting it into practice 'innovation'.

Invention is often very difficult to explain; it's a creative act and as difficult to understand as the genius of Mozart or Jane Austen. It's sometimes just a tweak, such as altering the shape of a spade, sometimes as epoch-making as the steam engine. Quite often it borrows something that works in another context in order to solve a different problem ... . Innovation, on the other hand, usually occurs because it pays; it makes it possible to do something better than before and to do it more cheaply. . . . On occasion, an innovation is disruptive and sweeps all before it; much more often, it makes a bit of a difference but needs to be rethought and altered before being widely adopted. People need to be trained in the new ways; suppliers have to be found for the components of a new machine; money has to be borrowed to cover the cost of experimentation to get it right (Floud, 2019: 185).

Part II

Tasks and Needs Analysis

3

Why Task? Task as a Unit of Analysis for Language Education

Shoko Sasayama

3.1 Introduction

Why use task as a unit of analysis for second language (L2) education? Before we consider this fundamental question in task-based language teaching (TBLT), it will be worthwhile to make the goal of this chapter explicit: To survey how researchers and educators in different disciplines have conceived of the role of tasks in language acquisition and instruction, and to consider associated implications for L2 education. It is *not* the purpose of this chapter to argue that the use of tasks is the only "correct" way to organize a language program, nor that TBLT is the only "right" approach to language education. What approach one adopts as a language educator depends on a number of factors, including local educational cultures, as well as societal pressures of various kinds (e.g., Butler, 2011; Hu, 2002, 2005), availability of teacher training and support (e.g., Butler, 2011, 2016, Carless, 2004), plausibility of identifying learner needs (e.g., Cameron, 2001; Ellis, 2017), and the potentially overriding influence of government-mandated curricula and high-stakes examinations (e.g., Butler, 2016, 2011; Carless, 2007; Luo & Xing, 2015). Teachers and learners have to do what they can within the educational environments they encounter. Nevertheless, despite this reality, a variety of educational theories and research findings seem to converge in suggesting that the use of task as a unit of analysis offers a number of benefits in organizing and executing effective language programs. I will first provide a brief overview of the origin of "task" in education, explore definitions of a task in the TBLT literature, and consider the roles played by tasks in language programs, before discussing the core question, "Why task?"

3.2 Where Does the Idea of Task Originate in Relation to Education?

The idea of a task in TBLT is largely influenced by John Dewey's (1938) notion of experiential education (e.g., Norris, 2015), as well as TBLT's specific language educational predecessor, communicative language teaching (CLT). Neither antecedent called a task by its name, but their notions of effective practices in education/teaching shared several of the core characteristics of a task in TBLT. In one of Dewey's (1938) classic works of the early twentieth century, "Experience and education," he cast doubt on traditional education, where knowledge was simply transmitted from the knowledge holder (i.e., teachers) to the less knowledgeable (i.e., students). Instead, Dewey underscored the importance of learning or knowledge generation through experience. In essence, he valued learning that resulted from educative experiences that involved interactions with peers, teachers, and the surrounding environment. Knowledge was thus viewed to be generated out of experience, rather than something that should be transmitted from one to the other. Importantly, in Dewey's view, it was practical, hands-on activities, or tasks, that made this *learning by doing* possible, by providing a platform for students to interact with others and co-construct knowledge.

Dewey's theory of education also points to the critical role played by real-world tasks, in addition to those pedagogic tasks used in the classroom. He saw education as an opportunity to prepare students for the real world and valued the use and application of knowledge (acquired through pedagogic tasks) to real-world problems. Thus, tasks were considered not only as an instrument to elicit interaction and collaboration among students (i.e., the means to promote learning), but also as a medium that provided learners with opportunities to apply the knowledge acquired and practice dealing with real-world tasks (i.e., the ultimate goal of learning).

A similar notion also emerged in language education in the late 1960s, with the rise of CLT. Around that time, language education experienced a shift –similar to changes inspired by Dewey and others in the field of education in general – in its approach to L2 instruction (Littlewood, 1981). Dissatisfaction with the traditional knowledge transmission type of structure-based approaches to language teaching (e.g., the grammar-translation method, audiolingualism) grew as the needs for communication among people from different linguistic backgrounds became more urgent. Language educators began looking for an alternative way of teaching foreign languages that focused more on functional and communicative, rather than merely structural, aspects of the language. In CLT, the focus of teaching shifted from a focus on discrete linguistic knowledge and instead emphasized communication and doing tangible hands-on activities. With CLT, the emphasis was on the development of learners' ability to communicate with others in the L2. Its underlying theory of learning assumed that activities, which are authentic, meaning- (rather than form-) oriented, and meaningful to the learners, promote language learning (Richards & Rogers, 2001). Interestingly, in contrast to Dewey's experiential education, communication activities or what we might call tasks were seen simply as the means to help L2 learners develop their ability to communicate, rather than as activities that they might actually need to deal with in the real world (i.e., the goal of learning).

Task-based language teaching emerged during the 1980s as a derivative of, and alternative to, CLT (Long, 1985). Although they share some common characteristics, TBLT is distinct from CLT, especially in how it considers the role of tasks. Unlike CLT, TBLT uses task as a unit of analysis – the most basic element (Long, 2004) of a language program – for a variety of purposes, ranging from identifying what learners in a TBLT program should eventually be able to do, to designing a program curriculum and course syllabi, to planning what happens in the classroom (e.g., lessons, activities), and including the assessment of learners' progress and achievement. Reflecting fundamental influences from Dewey's experiential education, TBLT treats tasks as both the means and the goals of learning – another difference from CLT. In a nutshell, TBLT revolves around developing L2 learners' ability to engage in and accomplish real-world tasks (i.e., educational goals) through the use of carefully designed tasks in the classroom (i.e., educational means). Here, the idea is that if we want our learners to be able to do well on the kinds of tasks they will encounter in the real world, we need to structure our teaching *around* and teach *toward* those real-world tasks.

It is important to note that, in the L2 pedagogy literature, the terms, "task-based language teaching" and "TBLT," have oftentimes been used loosely to include any approach to L2 education that includes the use of communication tasks in the classroom (e.g., Willis, 1996; Willis & Willis, 2007). Strictly speaking, those approaches should be treated distinctly from TBLT because they are fundamentally different from it in their educational principles. Unlike TBLT, they do *not* emphasize real-world tasks, and they use task as a unit of analysis for designing lessons but *not* for the other aspects of a language program, such as needs analysis, curriculum and syllabus design, and assessment. In other words, they may use tasks as a pedagogic device, but *not* as the goal of education. In the TBLT literature, these approaches that utilize communication tasks in the classroom are often called "task-supported language teaching" or "TSLT" (Ellis, 2003). To clearly distinguish TBLT from TSLT, some scholars have used the term "task-based language *education*" to emphasize the use of task as a unit of analysis for all aspects of L2 education, rather than solely to design classroom activities (e.g., Norris, 2015; Van den Branden, 2006). In this chapter, however, for consistency, I will use the term, "task-based language teaching" or "TBLT," to refer to an approach to language education that uses task as a unit of analysis for any and all aspects of a language program.

3.3 What Is a Task?

So, what do we mean by a task in TBLT? The word "task" is multifaceted, and it is in fact used to refer to different types of activities. Indeed, in the relatively short history of TBLT, task has been characterized in many different ways, and its definition sometimes varies from one scholar to the next. One dimension of task that everyone seems to agree on has to do with its focus on the *use* of the language for some communication purpose. Thus, what is being referred to as a task in TBLT requires active participation or engagement by the learner, whether the task is productive or receptive in nature, and its primary communicative focus is meaning, not language forms. Task-based learning, then, emphasizes meaning-oriented, active use of the language to get something done, rather than a focus on discrete and isolated knowledge of language forms.

However, beyond this emphasis on the use of language for communication purposes, it is fair to say that there is no agreed-upon single definition of task. From some perspectives, tasks are the real-world activities that people do with language (e.g., Crookes, 1986; Long, 1985, 2015a), and thus they define the target and the goal of learning. In TBLT, this notion of tasks is closely related to the learners' needs and what they (will eventually) have to be able to do in the L2 outside the classroom in the real world. These tasks are often referred to as *target tasks* (Long, 2015a: 109). Other researchers, however, have conceived of tasks differently and portray them primarily as classroom learning activities (e.g., Bygate & Samuda, 2008; Ellis, 2003; Nunan, 2004; Skehan, 1998). From this perspective, tasks are seen as the means, rather than goals, of learning, providing learners with critical opportunities to acquire knowledge and skills in their L2. These tasks are typically contrasted with target tasks and called *pedagogic tasks* or "communicative activities learners do in instructional settings" (Bygate, Norris & Van den Branden, 2015: 1).

As the theory and practice of TBLT has continued to grow and evolve (Long, 2015b), some have sought to call out what they perceive to be uncertainties in definitions of task and to question what qualifies as a task (e.g., Widdowson's [2003] critique of Skehan's [1998] definition of a task; Ellis's [2017] more recent paper calling for a debate to come to a consensus about the definition of a task in TBLT). But "what qualifies as a task?" is really the wrong question to be asking. There is not much value in debating if a given activity can be considered a (pedagogic) task or not because what is important is *how* that activity is being used to achieve *what goals*, rather than whether it can be qualified as a task in some abstract sense.

An editing activity, where learners are asked to find grammatical errors in a given passage and correct them, can serve as a good illustration. Is this activity a task or not a task? The answer may seem straightforward – it seems like a typical form-focused grammar activity that can be completed successfully without much attention to the meaning of the passage. If that is the case, this activity should probably not be considered a task in the traditional sense, because it does not require learners to focus on meaning. But, what if the passage that the learners are editing is a transcript of a model conversation between a customer and a café clerk that they are working on as the first step toward their own performance of ordering something at a café? What if this activity is being used to draw learners' attention to grammatical accuracy as a way of helping them communicate successfully when they have to deal with this kind of a task (i.e., ordering at a café) in the real world? From this perspective, the nature of the same activity changes from a mere grammar-correction exercise to a meaning-focused endeavor where learners are also paying attention to form.

On the one hand, then, it probably suffices to define a task by the core dimension that all agree on – a task is some sort of a hands-on activity whose focus is on meaning. At the same time, rather than trying to decide whether a given activity qualifies as a task or not in some abstract sense, perhaps it is more important to think carefully about how a given activity fits within the larger context of a lesson or course, as well as what learners might gain from engaging in it. In thinking about this relationship between individual tasks and the larger instructional context in which they are embedded, it is critical to understand the roles played by target tasks and pedagogic tasks in TBLT.

3.4 What Tasks for What Purposes?

So, what roles do target tasks and pedagogic tasks play in TBLT? In TBLT, target tasks – identified on the basis of learners' real-world needs – provide the core unit of analysis for language education as a whole (see Chapters 4 and 5 and the case studies in Chapters 4A to 4D for more details on task-based needs analysis). Everything from what is taught in the classroom to what is assessed derives from those target tasks. The goal of language education in TBLT is to help L2 learners acquire linguistic and other related knowledge and skills to be able to deal with the target tasks that are critical to them in the real world. Pedagogic tasks, on the other hand, are designed to help learners gradually accomplish the target tasks that are important for them. Pedagogic tasks can take a variety of forms and may include activities that ask learners to (a) watch/listen to/read a model performance of a target task, (b) analyze the nature of language use in the model, (c) practice using the language for communication purposes, and (d) reflect on their own language use.

To better illustrate this relationship between a target task and a pedagogic task in TBLT, let's take ordering food as an example of a target task (see also Long, this volume). What do learners need to be equipped with to be able to successfully order coffee and snacks at a café? They need to be familiar with interactional patterns that a customer and a café clerk typically engage in; they need to know words, grammar, and pragmatics associated with ordering food at a café; they need to experience ordering in a safe, low-stakes environment to develop the requisite abilities; and so on. Pedagogic tasks to this end may be designed to include a variety of activities, such as watching model conversations between a customer and a café clerk, analyzing these models to identify what is being said by whom and in what order, practicing ordering a few items with a partner, practicing placing an order for more items and perhaps with rather complicated food restrictions (which often happens in the real world), and reflecting on their own performance and thinking about how they might improve their next performance. In TBLT, all of these pedagogic tasks are designed sequentially to help learners perform the specified target task well, and ultimately in the real world.

It is worth acknowledging that tasks are used, and may even play important roles, in approaches to language education other than TBLT, often referred to under the cover term of TSLT. In TSLT, tasks are used *in support of* otherwise form-focused instruction; thus, the notion of target tasks is largely irrelevant, and pedagogic tasks are designed and utilized differently from their role in TBLT. In TSLT, pedagogic tasks do not derive from target tasks, but are, to a great extent, determined by the kinds of linguistic knowledge and skills that the learners need to acquire (e.g., certain linguistic forms, ability to read/listen to a short passage, ability to express opinions orally/in writing). In other words, pedagogic tasks in TSLT still prioritize the use of the language for communication purposes, but they are *not* specifically designed to help learners deal with well-defined target tasks in the real world. A spot-the-difference task is a good example. The teacher may prepare two similar pictures with some differences and ask learners to describe their pictures to each other and find what information they do not share. The teacher may have chosen such a task not because learners will need to be able to describe a picture and spot the differences in the real world, but because it will encourage them to use a particular aspect of the target language (e.g., question formation, grammar related to description, vocabulary related to what is depicted in the pictures) for communication purposes.

In summary, target tasks refer to the real-world activities that L2 learners need to be able to successfully engage in, and in TBLT, they serve as the goal of learning and determine what gets taught in the classroom. Pedagogic tasks, on the other hand, refer to those activities that learners do in the classroom. They may or may not resemble the kinds of activities people do in the real world, but they are intended to develop learners' abilities toward specific target tasks. In TSLT, pedagogic tasks are meaning-oriented activities used in the classroom, and they derive from the kinds of linguistic knowledge and skills that learners need to develop, rather than from the kinds of tangible tasks they will need to be able to handle in the real world (i.e., target tasks). Thus, while TSLT may accrue the benefits of using communication tasks in language classrooms (see the next section), it is distinct from TBLT in its core approach to language education.

3.5 Why Task?

What benefits does the use of task as a unit of analysis in L2 education provide? Theories and research findings in diverse educational domains seem to converge and suggest that the use of tasks is critical in promoting any learning, and L2 learning in particular. Below, I will answer the question of "Why task?" from different points of view, including perspectives related to (a) TBLT as a researched pedagogy, (b) motivation and engagement, (c) assessment, and (d) program design.

3.5.1 Task-Based Language Teaching as a Researched Pedagogy

As discussed in Chapters 1 and 2 in greater detail, principles of TBLT are argued to be compatible with empirical findings in the field of L2 acquisition. Effective L2 instruction can be designed only by taking into account learning theories, and it cannot be based solely on teachers' intuitions or students' desires. This notion of evidence-based pedagogy or *researched pedagogy* is at the heart of TBLT (e.g., Samuda, Bygate & Van den Branden, 2018), with L2 acquisition theories providing key sources of evidence that underpin task-based instructional approaches. Accumulated research evidence emphasizes the importance of input, output, and interaction in L2 acquisition, and tasks (of both the target and pedagogic types) can provide an ideal platform for these important conditions.

In his input hypothesis, Krashen (1985) emphasized the importance of comprehensible input in acquiring the second language. Comprehensible input is a particular type of input that is slightly above the current level of the learners but is made comprehensible to them, for instance, by the use of contextual cues (e.g., gesture, realia, other aspects of context) or elaboration (e.g., paraphrasing, repetition). Comprehensible input provides L2 learners with opportunities to be exposed to and experience the language as a whole. It also allows them to analyze unconsciously (Krashen, 1985) or consciously (Schmidt, 1990) how language is used in context and develop understandings of important form-meaning relationships.

Tasks, then, can play an important role in providing L2 learners with a critical opportunity to be exposed to meaningful, comprehensible input. Let's return to our example target task of ordering coffee at a café. To help learners perform this target task, the teacher may design a series of pedagogic tasks. As the first pedagogic task of this sort, the teacher may ask learners to watch a video of a handful of people ordering different items at a café. This input, made comprehensible by the use of visuals and other contextual cues (and potentially by the use of captions, repeated viewing of the video, or activation of learners' prior knowledge/schema about the situation prior to the video viewing), helps learners to see what successful communication in this particular situation looks like. It also provides them with an opportunity to be exposed to and learn new language forms associated with the situation (e.g., how to open and close this type of transaction, words related to ordering food, pragmatics).

Although input is a necessary condition for second language acquisition, it is by no means a sufficient condition. Learners need to be given opportunities to produce output and use the language for communication purposes in order to fully acquire it (output hypothesis; Swain, 1985). In other words, output provides benefits that input alone cannot bring about. Output allows L2 learners to notice the gap between what they can receptively understand and what they can productively express. Output also enables them to realize that what they want to express in the L2 may not equal what they are able to say. This noticing of the gap (Schmidt, 1990), in turn, helps L2 learners and the teacher alike to identify what they can and cannot express in the target language and decide what learning needs to happen next. Additionally, by producing L2 output, learners are also able to practice using the language and develop fluency.

Using the same example target task of ordering food at a café, following the input-based pedagogic task, the teacher might then have learners practice ordering one or two items. During this pedagogic task, learners are encouraged to realize that they can indeed communicate in their L2, or they may notice that they do not know some language forms that they need to successfully complete the task. By repeating the task and practicing ordering items with different partners, learners can also work on building up their fluency.

Interaction offers all the benefits that input and output provide and some additional advantages. According to the interaction hypothesis (Long, 1981, 1996, 2015a), one important aspect of interaction that helps promote L2 acquisition is *negotiation for meaning*. During interaction, L2 learners may encounter language forms in the input that are not familiar to them or experience failure in making themselves understood. As a result, learners may engage in negotiation with their interlocutor to make each other understood in many ways, including through requesting clarification, asking questions, checking their understanding, elaborating their ideas, and circumlocuting. This negotiation for meaning helps L2 learners (a) get input that is more comprehensible and is appropriate for their current level of proficiency, (b) draw attention to particular language forms that are essential in the context of communication, and (c) acquire communication strategies.

Smith (2003) illustrated how this negotiation for meaning can be elicited through the use of pedagogic tasks in a synchronous computer-mediated communication environment. Intermediate-level English language learners were assigned to pairs to work on different tasks, including a picture-based jigsaw task. In this task, one learner in each pair was given a half of a picture set, and the other learner received the other half. To encourage negotiation for meaning, the picture set included items that required the use of low-frequency vocabulary for their description (e.g., an ax, a rake, a snow shovel). Only one of the dyad was given those low-frequency words in their task input. Their task was to (a) carefully describe the pictures they each had and (b) collaboratively sequence the pictures in the correct order. To successfully complete this task, the learners engaged in a number of instances of negotiation for meaning. As seen in the excerpt below, for example, one learner initiated the negotiation by asking questions about the word he did not know (i.e., ax), which then encouraged the other learner to explain the meaning of the word "ax."

J: There are Ax, Rake, and so on.
J: He hold ax in a clean garage, and everything is in order in everywhere.
B: ax mean is hammer?
J: no
J: That's different
B: what is it?
J: Ax is used to cut tree
J: or wood

(Smith, 2003: 48)

Another important role played by interaction has to do with feedback. Interaction offers an ideal platform for L2 learners to engage in meaning-making activities and receive positive or negative feedback. During interaction, L2 learners can test hypotheses about how the L2 might work and get feedback from their interlocutor about whether they were indeed correct. For instance, an L2 Japanese speaker might hypothesize from overheard input at an art museum that the word for a work of art in Japanese is "*sakuhin.*" They might then use this word in a conversation with an artist: "*Kotoshi no sakuhin sugoi ii desune!*" [Your work this year is very nice!] The artist might then reply: "*Arigatou. Kotoshi no sakuhin wa tokubetsu dene.*" [Thank you. This year's work is special to me.] This positive feedback from the interlocutor – received during the target task of interacting with an artist in Japanese – serves to confirm the L2 learner's hypothesis about Japanese and contributes to solidifying their L2 learning.

What might negative, but useful, feedback look like? Take, for example, a group of L2 learners of Spanish engaging in a pedagogic task to discuss what students from Chile should do when they visit the United States

(Annenberg Learner, n.d.). As seen in the excerpt below, when reporting on what his group had discussed, a learner mistakenly said four *and* five days to answer the question of how many days the students from Chile might need to visit New York. In response, the teacher gave negative feedback in the form of a comprehension check with an emphasis on the problematic expression ("Cuatro *y* cinco?"). This negative feedback during interaction is shown to draw learners' attention to form in the context of communication, and it is argued to help them develop or revisit their understandings of the important form-meaning relationships (Long, 2015a).

> TEACHER: ¿Cuántos días más o menos recomienden ustededes? [How many days more or less do you recommend?]
> LEARNER: Um, cuatro y cinco días. [Um, four and five days.]
> TEACHER: Cuatro *y* cinco? Nueve? [Four and five? Nine?]
> LEARNER: Oh no no no no! Cuatro o cinco días. [Oh no no no no! Four or five days.]
> TEACHER: Cuatro o cinco. Entiendo. [Four or five. I see.]
> (Annenberg Learner, n.d.)

What all of these examples show is that tasks of both the target and pedagogic types provide L2 learners with opportunities to be exposed to input, produce output, and engage in meaningful interaction with others. Tasks, thus, serve as an ideal locus and platform for pedagogic interventions that are grounded in second language acquisition theories and findings, and that are likely to foster L2 learning.

3.5.2 Motivation and Engagement

Another perspective featuring noteworthy support for tasks can be found in theory and research on learner motivation. It should be clear that not all tasks are equally engaging, and that tasks need to be carefully designed to increase learner engagement in them and their associated motivation for learning. Having said that, fundamentally, tasks – both target and pedagogic tasks – are likely to offer more possibilities to be meaningful and engaging for L2 learners than other activities that do not require their active engagement (e.g., working on multiple-choice or fill-in-the-blanks grammar questions). Indeed, tasks or hands-on activities have been found to increase task-doers' motivation and engagement in education in the area of L1 reading (e.g., Guthrie & Wigfield, 2000), STEM education (e.g., Liu, Toprac & Yuen, 2009), language instruction (e.g., Long & Porter, 1985), game theory (e.g., Coleman, 1968; Klein & Freitag, 1991), social work (e.g., Fortune, Lee & Cavazos, 2005), and other applied domains. Multiple theories of motivation have been proposed both in educational psychology in general, and more specifically in second language acquisition, in relation to L2 learning (see Dornyei, 2001 for a summary). Keller (1983), for example, argued in his education-oriented theory of motivation that (a) interest,

(b) relevance, (c) expectancy, and (d) outcomes determine the level of students' motivation for learning in educational settings. According to Keller, students are more likely to be engaged in the instruction if it (a) is designed around students' inherent and genuine interests, (b) is perceived to be relevant not only to their instructional needs but also to their personal needs (e.g., desire to be connected with others, to be in control of activities), (c) entails activities that students feel can be achieved successfully, and (d) offers some sort of reward or punishment depending on the outcomes of their performance or learning.

It can be argued, then, that tasks (especially when designed appropriately) have a clear potential to fulfill all of these determinants of motivation. In TBLT, target tasks (and related pedagogic tasks) derive from learners' needs in the real world and therefore are more likely to be congruent with their interests and relevant to their goals for learning. This aspect of TBLT can be clearly contrasted with other more form-focused approaches (e.g., the grammar-translation method, audiolingualism, and even TSLT), where what is to be presented to learners is determined externally to them regardless of their needs, interests, or readiness for acquiring the particular language forms. Crookes and Schmidt (1991) also pointed out that collaborative tasks offer L2 learners better possibilities for meeting their desire to be part of a community and to feel connected with others. Tasks can be designed to include learner choice (e.g., learners can work on pedagogic tasks in the order that makes sense to them as long as they all reach the final, expected outcome), which will help them feel in charge of their learning. Pedagogic tasks can also be designed to be at just the right level for a specific group of learners (which again is difficult with the grammar-translation method), so that they feel they have a high likelihood of success in doing the tasks. When it comes to outcomes, the advantage of tasks is quite clear – outcomes of tasks are much more transparent and potentially more powerful than other classroom activities. Good outcomes can be a successfully-ordered pizza or an affirmative, positive message from the interlocutor (e.g., "Yeah, I know what you mean"), while bad outcomes may be an ice cream in a flavor the learner did not want (e.g., a banana flavor instead of vanilla). Looking at these characteristics of tasks, we can see how advantageous they are in motivating L2 learners to engage in their learning and thus serve to promote their language acquisition.

3.5.3 Assessment

Tasks also offer a number of benefits from an assessment perspective, especially when predicting test-takers' knowledge and skills to be able to handle real-world, target tasks (see Norris & East, this volume, for a full discussion of the different uses of task-based language assessment). Through the use of assessment, if one wishes to make a claim about what learners can *do* in the real world, a more accurate prediction can be made by having them do the kinds of target tasks that they will likely encounter in the real world, rather than other types of assessment activities. For example, the TOEFL iBT® task is designed deliberately to replicate the kinds of tasks that target test-takers (i.e., students who wish to engage in tertiary education in English) will most likely need to be able to do on a campus where English is used as a medium of instruction and for other activities. Among various items on TOEFL iBT®, an integrated task type asks test-takers to read a passage on an academic topic, listen to a lecture on the same topic, and summarize the main points of the reading and the lecture in writing. The extrapolation to be made here is that if a test-taker does well on this test item that replicates a common real-world academic task (along with other items included in the TOEFL iBT® test), it is more likely for them to be able to handle similar types of tasks in the real world. This kind of argument is harder to make if the item that is being extrapolated from does not resemble a real-world target task. If someone does well on form-focused activities, like fill-in-the-blanks questions or identifying English words from non-English words, can it be argued convincingly that they will be able to do the kinds of real-world tasks required of them once at a university? These kinds of decontextualized, form-focused assessment items do not directly measure test-takers' skills to this end, and it is hard to argue for their ability to handle real-world tasks based on their performance on such assessment items (although some tests attempt to argue precisely that; see Norris, 2018 for more details on this issue).

Task-based criterion-referenced performance assessment also offers a number of benefits in communication-oriented language programs and makes meaningful outcomes assessment possible (Long, 2015b; Long & Crookes, 1993; Long & Norris, 2000; Norris, 2009). From this perspective, tangible performance tasks help us gauge what learners have become able to *do* in the target language as a result of instruction. In a TBLT program in particular, where learners have undertaken a series of pedagogic tasks carefully designed to help them achieve a specified target task, task-based assessment provides a meaningful indicator of learners' ability to deal with the target task and thus their progress in the course or program. To return to our example target task of ordering coffee at a café, having learners actually go to a café and order a predetermined set of items (or simulating that experience) would give us considerably more information about their ability to perform that target task, compared to an activity to fill in the blanks for grammar and vocabulary items within a transcribed conversation between a customer and a clerk. Thus, the use of tasks for assessment purposes is critical in understanding what learners can do with the language and what they still need to work on, in reference to the types of target tasks that are crucial to their success in the real world.

3.5.4 Program Design

One last response to the question of "Why task?" has to do with the design of a language education program. Simply put, the use of tasks facilitates the application of backward design (Wiggins & McTighe, 1998) of instructional programs and thus helps make program design more logical and effective. In this approach, the desired goals and learning outcomes are determined first, and the smaller pieces of curriculum – course syllabi, units, lessons, and activities – are designed so as to meet those specified goals and outcomes (hence, the name "backward" design). In explaining the benefits of backward design, Wiggins and McTighe argued that effective learning happens when a curriculum derives from the end-state or the goal, rather than it being determined by what happens in the classroom. "In short, the best designs derive backward from the learnings sought" (Wiggins & McTighe, 1998: 14).

Applying this idea of backward design in a TBLT program, it is straightforward to determine the "learnings sought" (Wiggins & McTighe, 1998: 14) by analyzing learners' real-world needs and identifying the kinds of target tasks that they (will) need to be able to do outside the classroom. This use of target tasks, in turn, helps establish clear and meaningful learning outcomes that are in turn observable and measurable. Here, learning outcomes function as a means of demonstrating that learners have indeed achieved the specified learning goals, or in the case of a TBLT program, have become able to do the specified target tasks (see Norris & Davis [this volume] for more on learning outcomes assessment in TBLT programs). In backward design, once learning outcomes are specified, syllabi and lessons are designed to help learners achieve those learning outcomes. Here, too, the use of tasks provides language teachers with a concrete unit of analysis for syllabus design and lesson planning.

Take the example of developing a TBLT course for students who will need English in their future workplaces. Based on a careful needs analysis, we might identify target tasks to be successful participation in a variety of activities in a typical workplace (Benevides & Valvona, 2018). Focusing on part of one possible target task – giving a business presentation – we might specify learning outcomes, such as being able to (a) understand the questions asked in English, (b) answer questions without pausing much after the questions are asked, (c) use appropriate language in answering the questions, and (d) elaborate on their answers sufficiently. To help learners achieve these outcomes, they might engage in a variety of pedagogic tasks, including: (a) practicing comprehending the types of questions typical of a Q&A session following a business presentation; (b) writing down answers to the questions provided about a product that they will be presenting later, paying attention to their use of grammar, vocabulary, and elaboration; (c) practicing asking and answering the questions in pairs; and (d) participating in a simulated Q&A (see Sasayama [2018] for more detailed descriptions of these pedagogic tasks). This example illustrates how the logical progression from desired goals and learning outcomes back to syllabus design and lesson planning can be achieved quite easily when the unit of analysis is a tangible task. In a nutshell, in designing L2 programs, target tasks help us determine meaningful targets (i.e., goals and learning outcomes) that are appropriate for a specified group of L2 learners, and pedagogic tasks allow us to design instruction that would help learners achieve the targets by serving as an efficient unit of instruction.

3.6 Conclusion

There are lots of answers to the question "Why task?" As explained above, tasks offer a number of benefits in language education. They provide an ideal platform for pedagogic interventions that are grounded in second language acquisition theories and findings. Tasks, especially when derived from learners' real-world needs in the case of TBLT, are meaningful and engaging for L2 learners. When used as an assessment tool, they allow predictions as to what learners can *do* in the L2 in the real world, and show in concrete terms what abilities learners have developed through instruction. Tasks also help make instructional program design more logical and effective by using target tasks as the goal of learning and designing series of pedagogic tasks to achieve those specified target tasks. Given these benefits, perhaps the more appropriate question to be asking of language education at this stage is "Why *not* task?"

I have also argued throughout this chapter that, in order to take full advantage of all the benefits tasks have to offer, it makes a lot of sense to embrace the idea of TBLT, where pedagogic tasks are designed based on target tasks (i.e., the goal of learning) identified through learner needs analysis, rather than TSLT or CLT. Certainly, it is true that the use of pedagogic tasks, even when not designed to help achieve specified target tasks, can still provide a number of benefits in terms of second language acquisition. Tasks give L2 learners opportunities to use the language for communication purposes, engage in collaboration and interaction with others, and take an active part in their learning in general. However, the (typically occasional) use of tasks in the classroom that have no obvious relevance to real-world target tasks does not allow for the fullest and arguably most effective use of tasks as a guide for program design or as an indicator of what learners can actually do in the real world.

To reiterate, TBLT is not a one-size-fits-all approach to language teaching and learning, and it may not be appropriate for all language programs in all educational settings. Having acknowledged that, I would still like to challenge my fellow educators and ask "Why not TBLT?" in hopes of eliciting both individual reflection and healthy debate about the purpose and goals for language teaching, as well as the means for achieving them. As we go about designing language programs and teaching language courses, and otherwise seeking to enable meaningful and effective language learning, it is important for each of us to carefully consider this question and find reasonable answers for ourselves and others interested in the outcomes of our efforts.

Further Reading

Dewey, J. (1938). *Experience and education*. New York: Macmillan.

Long, M. H. (2015). TBLT: Building the road as we travel. In M. Bygate, ed. *Domains and directions in the development of TBLT: A decade of plenaries from the international conference*. Amsterdam: John Benjamins, pp. 1–26.

Long, M. H. and Norris, J. M. (2000). Task-based teaching and assessment. In M. Byram, ed. *Encyclopedia of language teaching*. London: Routledge, pp. 597–603.

Norris, J. M. (2015). Thinking and acting programmatically in task-based language teaching: Essential roles for program evaluation. In M. Bygate, ed. *Domains and directions in the development of TBLT: A decade of plenaries from the international conference*. Amsterdam: John Benjamins, pp. 27–57.

Samuda, V., Van den Branden, K., and Bygate, M. (2018). *TBLT as a researched pedagogy*. Amsterdam: John Benjamins.

Study Questions

1. Think of your language learning or teaching experiences. How does the use of tasks or a lack of it explain how well you or your students learned the second language(s)?
2. What are some challenges that the use of tasks may present to language teachers in your context? How can those challenges be mitigated to allow for an effective use of tasks as a unit of analysis for language education?
3. "Why not TBLT?" What factors may make it difficult to introduce TBLT in your teaching context? How can these factors be addressed to allow for the benefits of TBLT?

References

Annenberg Learner. (n.d.). *Teaching foreign languages K-12: A library if classroom practices*. Retrieved from: https://www.learner.org/series/teaching-foreign-languages-k-12-a-library-of-classroom-practices/creating-travel-advice/view-analyze-video/.

Benevides, M. and Valvona, C. (2018). *Widgets Inc: A task-based course in workplace English*. 2nd ed. Tokyo: Atama-ii Books.

Butler, Y. G. (2011). The implementation of communicative and task-based language teaching in the Asia-Pacific region. *Annual Review of Applied Linguistics*, 31, 36–57.

Butler, Y. G. (2016). Communicative and task-based language teaching in the Asia-Pacific region. In N. Van Deusen-Scholl and S. May, eds. *Second and foreign language education, encyclopedia of language and education*. 3rd ed. New York: Springer, pp. 327–38.

Bygate, M., Norris, J. M., and Van den Branden, K. (2015). Task-based language teaching. In C. A. Chapelle, ed. *The encyclopedia of applied linguistics*. Malden, MA: Wiley-Blackwell, pp. 1–8.

Bygate, M. and Samuda, V. (2008). *Tasks in second language learning*. Basingstoke: Palgrave.

Cameron, L. (2001). *Teaching languages to young children*. Cambridge: Cambridge University Press.

Carless, D. (2004). Issues in teachers' re-interpretation of a task-based innovation in primary schools. *TESOL Quarterly*, 38, 639–62.

Carless, D. (2007). The suitability of task-based approaches for secondary schools: Perspectives from Hong Kong. *System*, 35, 595–608.

Coleman, J. S. (1968). Social processes and social simulation games. In S. S. Boocock and E. O. Schild, eds. *Simulation games in learning*. Beverly Hills: Sage, pp. 29–51.

Crookes, G. (1986). *Task classification: A cross disciplinary review* (Technical Report No. 4). Honolulu: Center for Second Language Classroom Research, Social Science Research Institute, University of Hawai'i at Manoa.

Crookes, G. and Schmidt, R. W. (1991). Motivation: Reopening the research agenda. *Language Learning*, 41(4), 469–512.

Dewey, J. (1938). *Experience and education*. New York: Macmillan.

Dornyei, Z. (2001). *Teaching and researching motivation*. Harlow: Pearson Education.

Ellis, R. (2003). *Task-based language learning and teaching*. Oxford: Oxford University Press.

Ellis, R. (2017). Position paper: Moving task-based language teaching forward. *Language Teaching*, 50(4), 507–26.

Fortune, A. E., Lee, M., and Cavazos, A. (2005). Achievement motivation and outcome in social work field education. *Journal of Social Work Education*, 41(1), 115–30.

Guthrie, J. T. and Wigfield, A. (2000). Engagement and motivation in reading. In M. L. Kamil, P. B. Mosenthal, P. D. Pearson and R. Barr, eds. *Reading research handbook*. Vol. III. Mahwah, NJ: Erlbaum, pp. 403–24.

Hu, G. W. (2002). Potential cultural resistance to pedagogical imports: The case of communicative language teaching in China. *Language, Culture and Curriculum*, 15, 93–105.

Hu, G. W. (2005). Contextual influences on instructional practices: A Chinese case for an ecological approach to ELT. *TESOL Quarterly*, 39, 635–60.

Keller, J. M. (1983). Motivational design of instruction. In C. M. Reigelruth, ed. *Instructional design theories and models: An overview of their current status* Hillsdale, NJ: Lawrence Erlbaum, pp. 383–434.

Klein, J. D. and Freitag, E. (1991). Effects of using an instructional game on motivation and performance. *The Journal of Educational Research*, 84(5), 303–8.

Krashen, S. (1985). *The input hypothesis: Issues and implications.* New York: Longman.

Littlewood, W. (1981). *Communicative language teaching: An introduction.* Cambridge: Cambridge University Press.

Liu, M., Toprac, P., and Yuen, T. T. (2009). What factors make a multimedia learning environment engaging: A case study. In R. Z. Zheng, ed. *Cognitive effects of multimedia learning.* Hershey, PA: IGI Global, pp. 173–92.

Long, K. J. (2004). Unit of analysis. In M. S. Lewis-Beck, A. Bryman, and T. Futing Liao, eds. *The SAGE encyclopedia of social science research methods.* Thousand Oaks, CA: Sage, pp. 1157–58.

Long, M. H. (1981). Input, interaction and second language acquisition. *Annals of the New York Academy of Sciences*, 379, 259–78.

Long, M. H. (1985). A role for instruction in second language acquisition: Task-based language teaching. In K. Hyltenstam and M. Pienemann, eds. *Modelling and assessing second language acquisition.* Bristol: Multilingual Matters, pp. 77–99.

Long, M. H. (1996). The role of the linguistic environment in second language acquisition. In W. C. Ritchie and T. K. Bahtia, eds. *Handbook of second language acquisition.* New York: Academic Press, pp. 413–68.

Long, M. H. (2015a). *Second language acquisition and task-based language teaching.* Malden, MA: Wiley Blackwell.

Long, M. H. (2015b). TBLT: Building the road as we travel. In M. Bygate, ed. *Domains and directions in the development of TBLT: A decade of plenaries from the international conference.* Amsterdam: John Benjamins, pp. 1–26.

Long, M. H. and Crookes G. (1993). Units of analysis in syllabus design: The case for task. In G. Crookes and S. Gass, eds. *Tasks in language learning.* Bristol: Multilingual Matters, pp. 9–54.

Long, M. H. and Norris, J. M. (2000). Task-based teaching and assessment. In M. Byram, ed. *Encyclopedia of language teaching.* London: Routledge, pp. 597–603.

Long, M. H. and Porter, P. (1985). Group work, interlanguage talk, and second language acquisition. *TESOL Quarterly*, 19(2), 207–27.

Luo, S. and Xing, J. (2015). Teachers' perceived difficulty in implementing TBLT in China. In M. Thomas and H. Reinders, eds. *Contemporary Task-based language teaching in Asia: Contemporary studies in linguistics.* London: Bloomsbury Academic, pp. 139–55.

Norris, J. M. (2009). Task-based teaching and testing. In M. Long and C. Doughty, eds. *Handbook of language teaching*. Cambridge, MA: Blackwell, pp. 578–94.

Norris, J. M. (2015). Thinking and acting programmatically in task-based language teaching: Essential roles for program evaluation. In M. Bygate, ed. *Domains and directions in the development of TBLT: A decade of plenaries from the international conference*. Amsterdam: John Benjamins, pp. 27–57.

Norris, J. M. (2018). Task-based language assessment: Aligning designs with intended uses and consequences. *Japan Language Testing Association (JLTA) Journal*, 21, 3–20.

Nunan, D. (2004). *Task-based language teaching*. Cambridge: Cambridge University Press.

Richards, J. C. and Rogers, T. S. (2001). *Approaches and methods in language teaching*. Cambridge: Cambridge University Press.

Samuda, V., Van den Branden, K., and Bygate, M. (2018). *TBLT as a research pedagogy*. Amsterdam: John Benjamins.

Sasayama, S. (2018). An evidence-based approach to L2 task design. *Taking it to Task*, 3(1), 3–15.

Schmidt, R. W. (1990). The role of consciousness in second language learning. *Applied Linguistics*, 11(2), 129–58.

Skehan, P. (1998). *A cognitive approach to language learning*. Oxford: Oxford University Press.

Smith, B. (2003). Computer-mediated negotiated interaction: An expanded model. *The Modern Language Journal*, 87, 38–57.

Swain, M. (1985). Communicative competence: Some roles of comprehensible input and comprehensible output in its development. In S. Gass and C. Madden, eds. *Input in second language acquisition*. Rowley, MA: Newbury House, pp. 235–53.

Van den Branden, K. (2006), ed. *Task-based language education: From theory to practice*. Cambridge: Cambridge University Press.

Widdowson, H. (2003). *Defining issues in English language teaching*. Oxford: Oxford University Press.

Wiggins, G. and McTighe, J. (1998). *Understanding by design*. Alexandria, VA: Association for Supervision and Curriculum Development.

Willis, J. (1996). *A framework for task-based learning*. Harlow: Longman.

Willis, D. and Willis, J. (2007). *Doing task-based teaching*. Oxford: Oxford University Press.

4

Adapting and Advancing Task-Based Needs Analysis Methodology across Diverse Language Learning Contexts

Ellen J. Serafini

4.1 Introduction

All people learning another language, by choice or by necessity, have different reasons, desires, or goals for using that language, whether inside or outside of a classroom. For instance, a university student in Japan studying English may need to be able to listen to a lecture and take notes in English. An international student majoring in nursing in a US university likely needs to learn how to take and interpret a patient's vital signs. Aboriginal speakers in Australia may seek to develop vocational skills in English to improve their economic chances while Indigenous speakers in Mexico may desire to maintain their language and reverse language shift in their communities. On the other hand, political refugees from war-torn countries like Syria likely have more immediate needs, like securing food, clothing, and shelter, with the eventual goal of fully integrating into society (e.g., applying for a job; registering their child for school).

As these situations illustrate, language learners and their needs and goals are not only diverse, but can also be characterized as "voluntary" or "involuntary," due to forces that are both internal and external in nature (Long, 2015a). As Long observes, millions of involuntary language learners have sought refuge in countries in which their first language (L1) is not spoken, or minimally valued. In addition to global and regional wars and conflicts, this continual social upheaval is caused by "famine, disease, poverty, 'ethnic cleansing,' deforestation, religious persecution, and government oppression" (89).

Learners who voluntarily choose to gain proficiency in another language is also on the rise due to the increasing demand for bi/multilingual forms of education, diplomatic government and international relations opportunities, and occupations like healthcare, where providers need a functional command of a language to better serve their patients (Long, 2015a). Voluntary learners also include immigrants who desire to maintain their ancestral, heritage, or community language through heritage language and bilingual education (Flores & García, 2017) and Indigenous speakers who desire to revitalize their languages and cultures through grassroots efforts (Riestenberg & Sherris, 2018, this volume; Skutnabb-Kangas & Cummins, 1988).

This vast and ever-increasing diversity of language learners around the globe demands that language educators charged with meeting communicative needs do so in a way that is relevant and accountable, which is a central tenet underlying the theoretical and pedagogical framework of task-based language teaching (TBLT; Long, 1985, 2005a, 2015a). Task-based language teaching rejects a one-size-fits-all approach to language learning and has been implemented by language program designers, researchers, and practitioners across the globe, with positive effects on learning outcomes and stakeholder perceptions (Bryfonski & McKay, 2019).

The current chapter details the first step in designing relevant courses that directly respond to learners' specific communicative needs in the real world – a needs analysis (NA). An NA not only provides answers to *what* language learners should learn, but also considers the key, yet often overlooked, question of *why* (Van Avermaet & Gysen, 2006).

First, the theoretical principles underlying a task-based NA are laid out, as are desirable standards of methodological rigor for identifying *target tasks,* or the things students need, or will need, to be able to *do* in the target language beyond the classroom. Next, a critical synthesis of research reporting on the design and implementation of a task-based NA in educational and social contexts around the globe is provided. Considering advances, innovations, and gaps over the last thirty years, this chapter identifies two priority areas for research and practice: (i) the need to expand the geographical and methodological scope of NA practice, particularly in novel settings where languages other than English (LOTEs) are under study, and (ii) the need to consider different dimensions of context in task-based NA and how they impact language teaching, learning, and learner needs. In light of these priorities, this chapter argues that community-based, or service-learning, settings are "optimal" contexts for TBLT adoption and emphasizes the need to secure sustainable support and resources for task-based researchers to employ rigorous, socially informed, and culturally sensitive methods in order to effectively meet the diverse needs of diverse learners.

4.2 Foundations of Task-Based Needs Analysis: The Two Ps

One fundamental belief that unites TBLT scholars and practitioners is that a one-size-fits-all approach to language learning and teaching like that espoused in commercial textbooks serves no one, and can be particularly detrimental for learners who need to acquire another language for social survival. For this reason, an orientation to learner needs is primary, and TBLT aims to ensure that learning outcomes are not only optimal, but ethical, guided by both psycholinguistic and philosophical considerations (Crookes, 2009; Long, 2009, 2015a). Together, the sound psycholinguistic rationale based on cumulative research findings in second language acquisition, as well as the socially progressive origins rooted in revolutionary movements in education (e.g., Dewey, 1938; Freire, 1970/2000; Kolb, 1984), constitute a solid theoretical base from which to motivate and investigate questions about TBLT's effectiveness.

To date, the first P, or the psycholinguistic dimension of TBLT (e.g., "respect learner syllabuses") underpins "much of the research in task-based language pedagogy" (Leung, Harris & Rampton, 2004: 244), which has demonstrated positive effects on L2 development (for a recent meta-analysis, see Bryfonski & McKay, 2019). However, the theory behind TBLT also draws heavily on the second P, or its philosophical foundations (e.g., "learner-centeredness"; "learning by doing"). For example, the core tenet of "individual freedom" maintains that "individuals should be free to pursue their goals and live their lives as they see fit" (Long, 2015a: 69), which enables possibilities of "Emancipation" for teachers and learners, focusing on promoting not *what* to think, but *how*. Such an approach to language teaching is more likely to lead to a "Participatory democracy" in which teachers' and students' voices share equal weight. In contrast to more traditional, teacher-centered classrooms, this environment also lends itself to creating "Egalitarian teacher–student relationships" that "will not only improve classroom climate but also create advantageous psycholinguistic conditions for language learning" (Long, 2015a: 77), which illustrates the potential synergies between the two Ps underlying TBLT.

These two dimensions also clearly converge in motivating the first step in the design, implementation, and evaluation of the "strong version" of a task-based curriculum: learner needs identification (for overviews of differences between task-*based* and task-*supported* language teaching, see discussions in Bygate [2016: 387–88], and Samuda, Bygate, & Van den Branden [2018: 12]). The following section briefly reviews the origins and evolution of task-based NA, with a focus on methodological principles, advances, and gaps over the years.

4.3 Evolution of Task-Based Needs Analysis and Principles of Methodological Rigor

Task-based NA owes much to language researchers and practitioners who first recognized the limited outcomes of purely structural approaches to language teaching and aimed to implement communicative language teaching in large-scale initiatives like the Bangalore Project (Prabhu, 1987) and that funded by the Council of Europe (Richterich & Chancerel, 1987). They challenged traditional ways of teaching language by centralizing the actual real-world purposes for which learners are studying a non-primary language, including their *wants, desires, demands, expectations, motivations, lacks, constraints,* and *requirements* (Brindley, 1984: 28).

Target situation analysis or Munby's Communication Needs Processor (CNP) (Munby, 1978) arguably represents the first model of NA, which involves a set of procedures and questions about key variables for communication like topic, participants, medium, etc. that are then used to construct the target language needs profiles of a group of learners (Hutchison & Waters, 1987). Other models of NA have since emerged, like present situation analysis, mainly within English for specific purposes (ESP) and English for academic purposes (EAP) (e.g., Dudley-Evans & St. John, 1998; Hutchison & Waters, 1987; Swales, 1990). However, although these early efforts represented a vast improvement over TENOR, or teaching English for no reason (West, 1994, c.f., Lambert, 2010), they were based solely on introspection about learner needs and did not involve designing and implementing an actual NA.

In the context of ESP, Brown (2016) builds on previous work to provide a useful overview of different approaches to defining needs (12–17) and different strategies for analyzing them (18–27). For example, while a democratic approach to needs is based on whatever the majority wants, a discrepancy view centers on whatever is missing, and a diagnostic view on whatever will do the most harm if missing. Such needs can be analyzed through classroom-learning and teaching analysis, individual differences analysis, rights analyses, means analysis, or language audits. Ideally, Brown argues that the approach to defining and analyzing needs should reflect the original purposes of the NA: "the needs viewpoints and analysis strategies must be carefully related to the purposes of the NA because the outcomes of the NA itself may be predetermined to some extent by how the needs are conceived of at the outset and how the analysis strategies are initially selected by the needs analysts" (28).

These precursors set the stage for the development of task-based NA, which centralizes the concept of task as the unit of organization and analysis in all phases of curriculum design and evaluation (Long, 1985, 2005a, 2013; Norris, 2009; Van den Branden, 2006; Van den Branden,

Bygate & Norris, 2009). In task-based NA, identifying *target tasks* based on learner needs is the main goal, wherein a task is intended to represent the relationship between what happens in the classroom and beyond, or "the purposes for which people are learning a language, i.e., the tasks that learners will need to be able to perform" (Van den Branden, 2006: 3). The definition of task employed in the current chapter encompasses the many things "people *do* in everyday life, at work, at play, and in between" (Long, 1985: 89), from making an airline reservation to going grocery shopping. Defined in this way, the notion of task is separate from the language needed to realize it, which contrasts the language-focused view of task in task-*supported* language teaching as a communicative activity or vehicle to practice linguistic forms (Ellis, 2003). In other words, task-based curriculum design does not predetermine which linguistic structures, words, notions, or functions will inform syllabus design (Long & Crookes, 1992); rather, it follows a more nonlinear process, similar to how language learning is thought to occur.

All NAs require significant thought, planning, and support, and ideally, specialized training in task-based curriculum design and instruction. The first key questions a needs analyst must consider are who to consult and how, and these decisions can lead to more or less methodologically robust NAs. A considerable body of work now exists that discusses and establishes desired standards in task-based NA methodology (e.g., Berwick, 1989; Brown, 2009, 2016; Long, 2005a, 2015a; Serafini, Lake & Long, 2015), which has contributed significantly to raising awareness among language researchers and educators and strengthening overall validity and reliability in NA practice. This work collectively emphasizes the importance of collecting data from multiple sources via multiple methods, in order to allow for data triangulation, or consulting the same source via different methods and using the same method to tap different sources. Source by method interactions are a "gold" standard because they increase the chances that the target tasks derived from the NA reflect the functional capacities that learners actually need to develop. Nonetheless, a disappointing minority of studies meet this standard (Serafini, Lake & Long, 2015), which can be attributed to the constraints imposed by practical feasibility (e.g., time, resources, access) and to a lack of studies conducting NA in the first place (Bryfonski & McKay, 2019). Overall, NA researchers do not prescribe *one* right way to conduct NA but recommend evaluating different sources and methods and selecting "those procedures that best fit the purpose, scale, focus, approaches, syllabuses, and constraints of the particular NA" (Brown, 2009: 277).

4.3.1 Sources and Sampling

There are several sources to evaluate, based on the likely reliability of their judgments or intuitions about learner needs beyond the classroom. Needs analysts must consider factors such as content and language expertise, relative subjectivity or objectivity, preservice vs. inservice learner status, and target language status (e.g., monolingual or bilingual native speakers, heritage, L2, etc.). To know *what* learners must do to successfully function within a specialized domain, insider sources, or experts within the academic, occupational, or vocational domain of interest (e.g., engineers, domestic workers, interpreters, or healthcare workers) are the most likely to provide accurate, reliable, and objective information about essential target tasks (e.g., writing a lab report, applying for a social security number, or explaining a diagnostic exam). Though they may be outsiders to the specialized domain, consulting applied linguists and sociolinguists is also key given their expertise in language learning and teaching and related research methods, which is especially valuable in the second major phase of a NA: analyzing task-relevant target discourse, or genuine examples of target language use in specialized discourse domains (see Long, 2015: 169–204, this volume).

Along with domain insiders and outsiders, learners can also be a valuable source of information, particularly inservice learners who are already working or functioning in the domain of interest on a daily basis. After all, learners are the reason the NA is being carried out in the first place, and whose language development (and lives) will be affected by its results (Benesch, 1996). However, when interpreting results, one should consider that learners' perceptions about their needs are likely to be more subjective in nature and also influenced by factors like level of proficiency and relationship to the target language and culture. For example, an L2 speaker at low or intermediate proficiency may view and articulate their needs differently from a more fluent, heritage or native (monolingual or bilingual) speaker from a distinct linguistic and cultural background. Finally, relevant published and unpublished literature, like job announcements or training manuals, as well as samples of learner performance, such as placement exams, can also provide valuable sources of information.

Ultimately, an NA should strive to include as many sources as possible (minimally two), which facilitates triangulation and the ability to resolve any discrepancies across sources. Additionally, it is best practice to report sample size and employ a stratified random sample whenever possible. Such a sample, compared to one of convenience, increases confidence that findings accurately reflect the communicative needs of the larger target population.

4.3.2 Methods and Sequences

Like sources, methods used are equally important to evaluate in the planning and design phase. Brown (2009: 281) clearly articulates a few factors to keep in mind when selecting among the many quantitative and qualitative methods available:

> Research can vary from quantitative to qualitative on a number of dimensions: the quantitative research approach tends to use quantitative (data) and be experimental, statistical, highly intervening, highly selective, variable operationalizing, hypothesis testing, deductive, controlled, cross-sectional, large sample, and etic, while the qualitative research approach tends to use qualitative (data) and be non-experimental, interpretive, non-intervening, non-selective, variable defining, hypothesis forming, inductive, natural, longitudinal, small sample, and emic.

Quantitative methods might include online questionnaires, surveys, and language proficiency and competency measures and are best used with large samples of respondents for whom large amounts of data can be processed efficiently. Qualitative methods such as focus groups, interviews, (non)participant observation, ethnographic methods, and journals are intended for smaller samples of participants and produce rich, complex data that quantitative methods are not likely to reveal. Most researchers would agree that employing a mixed-methods approach is ideal for obtaining robust NA results because qualitative and quantitative methods tend to be complementary to one another. Qualitative data add depth while quantitative data give breadth, and can verify the representativeness of qualitative findings for the wider population.

The sequence, or order of implementing methods, also matters greatly. In general, it is best practice to implement qualitative methods, an inductive procedure, before quantitative methods, which are deductive in nature (Berwick, 1989), which allows categories of needs to emerge in a bottom-up, rather than top-down, fashion, and ensure that the needs analyst discovers learner needs that may not have surfaced otherwise. Further, data collected in the open-ended phase of the NA should be used to inform the closed-ended phase. For example, themes that emerge in semi-structured interviews should directly inform the items and wording used in questionnaires and surveys, particularly insofar as they reflect domain-insider knowledge. Further, pilot-testing methods is imperative to reveal and resolve any issues related to timing, clarity, redundancy, ambiguity, or technology that may threaten validity and reliability.

When reporting NA results, it is important to include basic details about the number and nature of survey or questionnaire items (e.g., multiple-choice, type of rating or ranking scale used, close-ended vs. open-ended, etc. (See Dörnyei & Taguchi, 2010 for further discussion on questionnaire design in L2 research). A representative sample of questions used in focus groups or interviews, or ideally the full protocol, should also be included as an appendix. This level of detailed methodological reporting will help the reader independently interpret and evaluate the data, not to mention facilitate replication.

4.3.3 Source x Method Interactions: The Goal

The sources, methods, sampling, and procedures discussed thus far each contribute to determining methodological rigor in task-based NA practice. However, needs analysts must strive to ensure that each step in the NA planning and design process facilitates the broader goal of achieving source by method interactions, as described at the beginning of this section. In practice, most task-based NAs do not actually meet this "gold standard," given constraints of feasibility, little to no specialized training, poorly informed designs, methodological underreporting, and the overall lack of NAs conducted in the first place. For example, in the only TBLT meta-analysis to date (Bryfonski & McKay, 2019), only four studies reported carrying out an NA (in a sample of fifty-two).

Another issue is that few systematic reviews of NA methodology exist. One exception is Serafini, Lake, and Long (2015) who conducted a critical methodological overview of NA practice in ESP and EAP contexts around the globe over a thirty-year time period (1984–2014). Methodological aspects of NAs were reviewed, including the target learner population, context (English as a foreign language [EFL] or English as a second language [ESL]; ESP or EAP), sources, methods, and source and/or method triangulation. A majority of studies conducted in earlier (1984–1999, $n = 10$) and later (2000–2014, $n = 23$) time periods were carried out in EFL (e.g., the Middle East) vs. ESL contexts (e.g., the United States), and in specialized occupational domains (e.g., engineering, journalism) rather than generalized academic domains. In the earlier studies, methodological reporting varied, but several studies triangulated information from multiple sources while holding method constant. For example, Svendsen and Krebs (1984) conducted interviews with three different sources (director, supervisor, entry-level workers) in a US healthcare setting. Other studies also triangulated methods across various sources, such as Jasso-Aguilar (1999/2005), who used participant observation, interviews, and a questionnaire to collect data from hotel staff on the communicative needs of hotel housekeepers. However, less than half of studies reported source x method interactions. For an exception, see Table 4.1 for a summary of Cumaranatunge (1988), who investigated the communicative needs of Sri Lankan domestic aids in Kuwait.

The later studies revealed certain changes and similarities with those published earlier. A major improvement was that a majority employed a mixed-methods approach and provided more methodological detail (e.g., number of items, sample size, pilot-testing). More studies also followed recommended sequencing procedures with inductive methods preceding deductive ones (e.g., Gilabert, 2005). However, while a majority reported source OR method triangulation, less than half, or 39 percent, reported source x method interactions, indicating a persistent and critical gap.

Table 4.1 *Examples of methodological rigor in task-based needs analysis practice*

	Cumaranatunge (1988) Sri Lankan domestic aids in Kuwait	
Triangulation of sources	Domestic aids	Questionnaires Structured interviews Participant observation
Triangulation of methods	Structured/informal interviews	Domestic aids Agencies/employers Government officials
Source x method interaction	Domestic aids Agencies/employers Government officials	Questionnaires Structured interviews Participant observation
	Gilabert (2005) Journalists in Catalonia, Spain	
Triangulation of sources	Journalists	Structured interviews Questionnaires Nonparticipant observation
Triangulation of methods	Structured/unstructured interviews	Journalists Journalism company reps Scholars
Source x method interaction	Journalists Journalism company reps Scholars	Structured/unstructured interviews Questionnaires Nonparticipant observation

Gilabert (2005), who investigated the needs of journalists in Catalonia in Spain, is an exception, as seen in Table 4.1.

In addition to identifying advances and shortcomings in NA practice, Serafini, Lake, and Long (2015) illustrated desirable methodological standards by detailing a large-scale NA carried out to meet the linguistic and cultural needs of nonnative English-speaking trainees, including international postdocs, visiting fellows, research fellows, and clinical fellows at an international scientific research institution in the United States. The focus of the NA was to identify what learners needed to be able to do to function successfully during a typical day or week at work, as well as survival skill tasks outside the workplace (e.g., choosing a cell phone plan). Semi-structured interviews were first carried out with a small convenience sample of domain experts (e.g., principal investigators, or PIs, and US and international graduate students and postdocs), the results of which informed three online questionnaires asking respondents to rate the difficulty, frequency, and criticality of target tasks (e.g., write a formal email). Following three cycles of piloting and revision, three different groups of domain experts in varied specialty areas (e.g., biochemistry and genetics, neuroscience, biophysics, immunology/infectious diseases) responded, including postdocs and PIs who were native and nonnative English speakers. Two additional procedures were carried out to enhance data interpretation and elucidate findings: nonparticipant observation in the lab, with a focus on a key communicative event, the weekly "lab meeting," and analysis of recorded language use during lab meetings. For further detail and guidance, the reader is referred to a step-by-step NA procedure (Serafini, Lake & Long, 2015: 22) and a contextually adaptable methodological checklist (25).

In sum, over time there has been increased awareness among task-based researchers, leading to more NAs that consult multiple sources and use multiple quantitative and qualitative methods to do so, which strengthens the validity and reliability of NA practice in general. However, there is still a long way to go, especially in terms of consistent implementation and reporting practices. Equally important to consider, if not more so, are the contexts in which NAs have been conducted and reported, given that "so far the discussion of NA appears to be all about English" (Brown, 2009: 274). Though it is a global lingua franca and the most studied second/foreign language in the world (Jenkins, 2006; Phillipson, 1992), it is essential to survey NAs conducted for LOTEs and to consider the historical, cultural, social, and political factors within LOTE contexts that impact learner needs in ways that are unique and different from those of English learners. Not doing so not only precludes knowledge about the diversity of learner needs in second, foreign, heritage, Indigenous, and bi/multilingual settings, but also limits possibilities for contextual adaptation and methodological innovation.

In this light, the following section first considers the general geographical expansion of TBLT in various educational and social contexts. Then, a review of task-based studies reporting on NAs in diverse ESL/EFL and LOTE settings is provided with a focus on identifying recent trends and innovations in NA methodology in research published in the last five years.

4.4 Task-Based Needs Analysis Practice in Diverse Educational and Social Contexts

Since TBLT was first introduced in the field of teaching and learning second and foreign languages over thirty years ago (Long, 1985), it has slowly, but steadily, spread geographically to many regions around the world, including East Asia, Asia-Pacific, the Middle East, Europe, North America, and Latin America. This growth is particularly notable in east Asian EFL contexts, where English is not a dominant language but where governments have often mandated it as the foreign language to be taught and learned in school (Adams & Newton, 2009), for example, in China (e.g., Li & Ni, 2013), Taiwan (e.g., Lin & Wu, 2012), Vietnam (e.g., Phuong et al., 2015), South Korea (e.g., Park, 2012), and Japan (e.g., Lambert, 2010, this volume).

In these contexts, the implementation of TBLT is met with variable perceptions, interpretations, resistance, and success, which has been attributed to dominant cultural norms and preferences for traditional grammar-focused, teacher-centered language instruction (e.g., Adams & Newton, 2009; Carless, 2007, 2012; Littlewood, 2007; Tinker Sachs, 2009). Many scholars have discussed these contextual challenges in terms of factors that are institution-related (e.g., focused exams and assessments, large class sizes), teacher-related (e.g., preference for traditional, teacher-centered instruction), and student-related (e.g., traditional views and beliefs about effective language teaching) (see Shehadeh, 2012: 6–8). To overcome these challenges, Carless (2012) and others have argued that TBLT must be adapted to the prevailing educational culture, which would imply a "weak" version of TBLT, or a task-*supported* approach, while other scholars have argued that the real problem lies with "'appropriate' traditional approaches" themselves (Shehadeh, 2012: 8), which often produce international students entering US higher education who struggle to communicate in English.

Regardless of whether or not a school system's culture, policies, or practices align with effective language pedagogy, these barriers must be addressed for successful adaptation. While thoughtfully discussed in relation to Asia and other EFL contexts (e.g., Shehadeh & Coombe, 2012), far less is known about adapting TBLT in other social and educational contexts, and what that means for identifying learner needs. Below, NA research is surveyed in language for specific and academic purposes contexts where TBLT is commonly practiced, followed by social survival and language revitalization settings, where it has recently seen encouraging growth.

4.4.1 Language for Specific and Academic Purposes

Adults learning language within a specific occupational domain, such as engineering or nursing, are likely to share a uniform set of communicative needs and thus, it is unsurprising that it is in this context where "strong" versions of TBLT are thought to be most readily applied (Bygate, 2016) and where the majority of task-based NAs are conducted and reported (Serafini, Lake & Long, 2015). However, more questions arise in academic settings where learner needs are more generalized, and thus more difficult to define.

Lambert (2010, this volume) offers insight into addressing these questions by detailing a task-based, two-year program based on the needs of English majors at a Japanese university. Prior to the researcher's TBLT intervention, which was funded by the university, English was taught without any consideration of communicative needs, as in many EFL contexts around the world. To identify critical tasks following graduation, Lambert and his colleagues began by analyzing job-placement records for the five years preceding the study, and determined business and education to be the most relevant workplace domains. The researchers then conducted semi-structured interviews with domain experts and used that information to create open-ended surveys, which asked English majors who had graduated within the previous five years to describe their use of English in the workplace. Finally, from the 150 tasks identified via these methods, 14 target task types (e.g., translating documents) informed items in a closed-ended survey that asked English majors graduating within the past 25 years to rate the criticality of identified tasks. Of particular importance in this context was the finding that pragmatic skills, like cultural awareness and politeness, were considered more important in oral tasks than pronunciation, grammatical accuracy, and fluency. By following methodological best practices, this work provides a valuable model for curricular development in similar academic settings.

In western Europe, where the prevailing educational culture is more aligned with communicative teaching styles, task-based ESP research in Spain has focused on specialized occupational domains (e.g., Gilabert, 2005; Malicka, Gilabert & Norris, 2019). For example, Malicka, Gilabert, and Norris (2019) utilized NA information to design and organize tasks in a syllabus created for hotel receptionists working in a bilingual region of Spain (Catalonia). They employed ten semi-structured interviews and three workplace observations with domain experts (hotel receptionists) and domain novices (tourism interns) which rendered fifty target tasks categorized into eight target task types; for example, making recommendations, giving directions, etc. (For more detail, see Malicka et al., 2019: 86.) Importantly, participants provided insight into what made tasks more or less difficult in both cognitive and linguistic terms, which information the researchers used to grade and sequence pedagogic tasks. Researchers also reported collecting discourse samples of authentic tasks based on workplace observations. These aspects make this study a valuable contribution in both theoretical and practical terms, though a mixed-methods approach could strengthen the validity of NA findings, as noted by the authors (Malicka et al., 2019: 94).

In the United States and Canada, there has been an increase in task-based curriculum design for L2s other than English, like Korean (Chaudron et al., 2005), French (Liakina & Michaud, 2018), and, most notably, Spanish (González-Lloret & Nielsen, 2015; Martin & Adrada-Rafael, 2017; Serafini & Torres, 2015), which is likely linked to a rising demand for specialized courses and programs (Abbott & Martínez, 2018; Long & Uscinski, 2012; Sánchez-López, 2013). For example, González-Lloret and Nielsen (2015) detailed the development and evaluation of a rigorous task-based Spanish course for training in the US Border Patrol Academy. In light of the poor proficiency outcomes of the previous grammar-based program, this course was intended to improve agents' ability to understand and communicate in Spanish in order to be effective at their job, which requires functioning in "high-stakes and high-stress" situations and being able to "assist injured people, communicate with immigrants who have been abandoned by smugglers, calm detained families, explain legal rights and immigration procedures, reunite parents with children, and resolve conflicts with minimal risk and damage" (528). To design an eight-week program, an NA based on interviews with domain experts (agents, supervisors, and trainers) and document analysis of tactical training procedures for new agents rendered seven target tasks in Spanish (e.g., offering and providing first aid, inspecting vehicles at a checkpoint). Formative target task assessments, oral proficiency measures, and perceptions from preservice and inservice agents demonstrated TBLT's effectiveness in this setting.

Serafini and Torres (2015) also took a task-based approach to designing a 15-week Business Spanish course taught at two medium-size public universities in the northeastern United States (for a replication of this study, see Martin & Adrada-Rafael, 2017, and for a report of learner task-specific motivation, see Torres & Serafini, 2016). Rather than relying on their own nonexpert intuitions, the researchers employed two data-gathering stages, starting with an online open-ended questionnaire administered to domain experts (business instructors, business graduates, and an accountant) that identified forty target tasks, such as understanding a business case study or writing a memo. In the second phase, university business majors rated the frequency and difficulty of each task in a Likert-scale closed item questionnaire. In a third phase, questionnaire data were analyzed according to learner ratings to determine task relevance and identify task-based course objectives. This resulted in fourteen target tasks, which were classified into five target task types (e.g., writing formal correspondence) that served as the exit tasks through which learners' performance was evaluated. Though small-scale in nature, this NA demonstrates the practical value of TBLT for language practitioners who are nonexperts in the domain of interest and who are operating with little to no institutional support.

4.4.2 Language as Social Survival: Refugee and Humanitarian Aid

Thus far, this chapter has detailed NAs for voluntary learner populations who are seeking to gain linguistic and cultural competence in another language for their own personal, academic, or professional reasons. But, as argued previously, TBLT is particularly relevant for learners who, for historical, political, social, or economic reasons usually beyond their control, *must* acquire language skills to survive in a new society. Here I highlight two examples of NAs conducted for adult L2 learners of Dutch in Flanders, Belgium (Van Avermaet & Gysen, 2006) and Syrian refugees seeking humanitarian aid in Turkey (Toker & Sağdıç, this volume).

Van Avermaet and Gysen (2006) reported two large-scale NAs in Belgium conducted for adult immigrants (1993) and FL learners (1999), which was supported by the Flemish Ministry of Education. Along with reporting an exceptional level of methodological detail, this work stands out for situating the broader sociopolitical circumstances surrounding the needs of immigrant language learners in Flanders, which were linked to "European unification, leading to a greater mobility and exchange of workforce, the waves of migration from Northern Africa (e.g., Morocco, Algeria) and Turkey, as a result of the economic reconstruction of Europe after the Second World War, and the recent influx of political refugees" (22). Following a postwar migration in the 1980s, this situation changed from "a temporary phenomenon [...] to a more permanent one" (23), spurring the demand for L2 Dutch courses for immigrant learners with both social survival and professional communicative needs. To determine relevant domains and language use situations, Dutch native and nonnative speakers and L2 Dutch teachers were consulted via interview. A large sample of L2 Dutch learners also completed an open-ended and closed-ended questionnaire, in which they rated the importance of thirty language use situations pertaining to five needs domains (work/business; education/training; informal social contacts; formal social contacts; children's education). In addition to discussing the interrelated problems of specification, complexity, and extrapolation in deriving and organizing target tasks and task types based on NA results, the researchers offer a step-by-step practical model for needs research (Van Avermaet & Gysen, 2006:44 [Figure 10]) and argue that L2 teaching, even at an elementary proficiency level, should be based on relevant societal language use domains.

Amid the backdrop of increasing global displacement, recent work by Toker and Sağdıç (this volume) report a task-based approach to identify the communicative needs of Syrian refugee parents in Turkey displaced by war. To identify the most critical communicative needs of the Syrian refugee population, who in Turkey number well over three million, the study triangulates data from three insider sources, including teachers, administrators, and parents in K–12 Turkish schools utilizing three methods, sequenced from open-ended to closed-ended procedures: semi-structured interviews (conducted through Skype), a questionnaire, and nonparticipant observation. In the interviews, participants were asked "what they typically do on a school day and events and situations that require them to interact with (other) parents" while the questionnaires asked parents to rate task frequency and difficulty. Nonparticipant observation focused on a report card ceremony on the last day of the semester. Results showed that the most frequent tasks were technology-mediated, while the most difficult involved communication with other parents about school-related topics. Results of an NA informed a task-based Turkish language curriculum for refugee parents who must integrate (temporarily or permanently) into society, representing a valuable social innovation in TBLT practice that is clearly motivated and situated within a broader sociopolitical context.

4.4.3 Language as Human Right: Indigenous Contexts

A growing number of innovative task-based NA studies have also been conducted for Indigenous speakers of socially marginalized or stigmatized minority languages or dialects who are either acquiring the dominant societal language (Oliver, Grote, Rochecouste & Exell, 2012, 2013a, 2013b) or aiming to maintain and revitalize their maternal language (Riestenberg & Sherris, 2018). Long-term work by Oliver and colleagues reports on the outcomes of a task-based NA for Australian Aboriginal adolescent students enrolled in a vocational education and training (VET) boarding school. The goal of the VET school curriculum is not only to prepare students to be successful in a vocation, but also to develop their written and oral proficiency in Standard Australian English learned as an L2 or a second dialect, depending on whether they speak a traditional Aboriginal language (e.g., Ngariyin, Kija), a creole, or Aboriginal English as a primary language.

To create a task-based syllabus in response to a request from the school, the researchers conducted an NA utilizing qualitative methods, including unstructured interviews conducted with the school principal and leadership team, the teachers, workplace staff, and Aboriginal students, non-participant observations of interactions at various workplace sites, and document analysis of vocational materials. This triangulation of sources and methods revealed key needs and target tasks that were work-oriented (e.g., knowing tool names, like 'wrench'; understanding safety procedures), socially-oriented (e.g., filling out a form; communicating with healthcare providers), and, crucially for this population coming from remote rural communities, needs related to cross-cultural communication and behavior, such as using appropriate gestures to express agreement, verbalize enthusiasm, greet colleagues, ask for clarification, and understand humor. To further understand cultural constraints in this setting, Oliver (this volume) offers a rich case study of a teacher's perceptions and experiences using tasks in the VET program.

Recent task-based work has also been carried out in Latin American Indigenous and US native American contexts where local grassroots efforts, and less frequently, government-supported language policy, have aimed to revitalize minority languages within a framework of language as a human right (Hult & Hornberger, 2016; Ruíz, 1984; Skutnabb-Kangas & Cummins, 1988). Riestenberg and Sherris (2018) report a ground-breaking example of a task-based NA adapted in the service of revitalizing two critically endangered languages in two distinct contexts: Macuiltianguis Zapotec in Oaxaca, Mexico, and Salish Qlipse in the northwestern United States (Montana). Informed by a keen understanding of the unique sociohistorical factors at play and the dynamics of power, ethnicity, identity, and language ideologies, the authors argue successful adaption of TBLT not only depends on learner investment in the target language, but on teacher and community investment, as well, which is particularly salient in Indigenous settings where there may be "few tasks that learners authentically need to do in the language" (440).

> Because TBLT aims to foster learners' ability to communicate in the real world, there must be an active speech community on which to base authentic and useful communicative tasks for the learners. Speakers must be using the language in at least some social domains, and these domains must be accessible to learners, at least in principle. This presents a dilemma in Indigenous language contexts if language loss has resulted in an overall decrease in language use across social domains and a social divide between older and younger generations.
> (Riestenberg & Sherris, 2018: 439)

In the Zapotec setting, the researchers aimed to identify *plausible* target tasks through structured interviews with students, semi-structured focus groups with parents and community language activists, and meetings with community leaders and members of the wider community. Based on daily interaction with Zapotec speakers, three target speaking tasks – salutations, small talk, and making purchases – informed the after-school task-based lessons offered over the course of a year. In the Salish Qlispe setting, tasks were tied to school life and the academic curriculum (e.g., school routines; peer interaction) within the Nkwusm immersion school on the Flathead Reservation. The NA involved gathering iterative input from community Elders, parents, teachers, and school administrators to develop a task-based oral proficiency assessment. Riestenberg and Sherris conclude that the positive outcomes observed were contingent on successful collaboration with teachers, students and community members and call for more TBLT work in Indigenous language settings, "as long as there is community interest" (456).

4.5 Innovations, Gaps, and Future Directions in Task-Based Needs Analysis

As seen in the previous sections, flexibility is a key strength of TBLT, as the process of identifying learners' communicative needs can be adapted to a range of local contexts. The studies highlighted have illustrated the variable ways NA can be put into practice and suggested answers to outstanding questions, such as how applicable TBLT is in academic settings where learner needs are less specialized (Lambert, 2010, this volume), and how to confront challenges in deriving target tasks from NA results in occupational and social survival settings (Malicka, Gilabert & Norris, 2019; Van Avermaet & Gysen, 2006). Further, studies have demonstrated the effectiveness of TBLT in identifying and assessing high-stakes tasks in specialized L2 settings (González-Lloret & Nielsen, 2015), as well as its practical value for teachers who are outsiders to the domain of interest and who have little institutional support (Serafini & Torres, 2015). Though not reviewed here, interested readers should consult other task-based NAs conducted in novel settings with L2 learners of Afrikaans in South Africa (Adendorff, 2014), beginning FL learners of Chinese in Denmark (Bao & Du, 2015), and Japanese L2 learners in a study abroad program in Japan (Iizuka, 2019).

Importantly, this work has also revealed valuable examples of methodological innovation in NA practice, specifically in vocational, social survival, and Indigenous language contexts (Oliver, Grote, Rochecouste & Exell, 2012, 2013a, 2013b; Riestenberg & Sherris, 2018; Toker & Sağdıç, this volume). These studies exemplify the adaptability of TBLT without necessarily achieving the desirable, yet often unattainable, standard of source by method interactions. However, they provide a valuable model for situating learner needs within a broader sociohistorical and sociopolitical context which responds to the call to explore "how language teaching contexts are affected by the larger social, political, and educational setting in which the teaching takes place" and to better understand "how the linguistic features of interactions, both inside and outside of the classroom, are affected by the social context in which the interaction takes place" (McKay & Rubdy, 2009: 9).

Contextually situating NA practice requires task-based needs analysts to understand fundamental sociolinguistic concepts, like language variation (e.g., how language use varies over time, space, context, and across social groups); the relationship between language and identity (i.e., ways that people construct their identities through language); and language attitudes and ideologies, or the often unanalyzed beliefs about language, language varieties and language practices that intersect with one's beliefs about other social and political categories (Woolard & Schieffelin, 1994). Learners are impacted differently by these ideologies, depending on the context they are in. For instance, when working with heritage learners of minority languages in the United States, knowing about the history of multilingualism and linguistic diversity, as well as US language policy and the ideologies it embodies, is key for language educators (and students themselves) to understand and critically reflect on how these factors shape individual students' linguistic and affective experiences, as well as language shift on a societal level (Leeman & Serafini, 2016).

4.5.1 Optimal Setting for Adoption of Task-Based Language Teaching: Service-Learning and Community-Based Context

In addition to heritage settings, community-based or service-learning settings require an understanding of the connection between the social and the individual. While task-based research in this setting is scarce, it would arguably be optimal (Serafini, 2021) given several shared underlying philosophical principles with TBLT (Long, 2015a), including learning by doing, learner-centeredness, egalitarian relationships, and mutual aid and cooperation. In fact, the very notion of task arguably originates in John Dewey's "seminal concept of education as an introduction to the activities of the community" (Leung, Harris & Rampton, 2004: 243). This focus on community reflects the aims of service-learning pedagogy, which seeks to address student needs and community needs through (i) formal instruction, (ii) learning outside the classroom, and (iii) critical reflection (National Service-Learning Clearinghouse, 2008). This approach aligns with the principle underlying TBLT that learning is experiential (Dewey, 1938) and we learn new skills, including language skills, by doing things, which also embodies learner-centeredness. Service-learning also presupposes a mutually beneficial experience for students and community partners, which requires building egalitarian relationships and mutual aid and cooperation among all stakeholders.

However, there is a distinction between traditional and critical orientations to service learning; the former tends to prioritize students' learning gains and frame service learning as a sort of volunteerism, whereas the latter emphasizes building students' critical consciousness of the root or historical precedents of social problems and reflection on their role in maintaining or transforming them (Mitchell, 2008; Rabin, 2015). Thus, a critical approach to service learning echoes the philosophical origins of TBLT, which rest on the assumption, that "education, of *all kinds, not just TBLT, serves to either preserve or challenge the status quo, and so is a political act*, whether teachers and learners realize it or not" (Long, 2015a: 63). Thus, critical service-learning, particularly for US heritage speakers, aims to build critical language awareness and agency in challenging the status quo, if desired (Leeman, Rabin & Román-Mendoza, 2011).

In light of these considerations, a mutually beneficial and critically oriented service-learning curriculum would require carrying out a collaborative NA that positions community members as domain experts and consults them and seeks their input and evaluation in all phases of a TBLT program, from NA to assessment (Serafini, 2021). Riestenberg and Sherris's (2018) study provides a valuable example by prioritizing the needs, desires, attitudes, and perceptions of the community and recognizing their expertise in determining learner needs. Other critically oriented work that incorporates notions of power into NA practice can also serve as useful models (e.g., Benesch, 1996, 1999; Flowerdew, 2005; Konoeda & Watanabe, 2008).

4.6 Conclusions

Task-based language teaching is always enacted "on the ground" (Samuda, Bygate & Van den Branden, 2018) in contexts that are specific and local.

While a dominant focus on ESL/EFL contexts in diverse specialized occupational and academic domains has fostered key insights into the contextual constraints confronting TBLT, particularly in East Asia, more recent work conducted in vocational, social survival, and Indigenous settings across the world, particularly those focusing on LOTEs, have revealed novel adaptations of task-based principles. It is argued here that task-based NAs must incorporate a more robust focus on the role of context when identifying and analyzing learner needs, with attention to historical, cultural, social, and political factors at play and a critical awareness of how these intersect with the needs and identities of diverse (voluntary and involuntary) learners. Future research must also explore potentially optimal contexts for TBLT adoption, such as (critical) service-learning settings, which requires identifying and prioritizing both learner and community needs.

To account for the link between the social and the individual, we need multi-faceted methods that include, but are not limited to, ethnographic methods, media analysis, conversation analysis, and especially, critical discourse analysis (e.g., Fairclough, 1995, 2001) with attention to the ways that social inequities are "enacted, reproduced and resisted by text and talk in the social and political context" (van Dijk, 2015: 466). This requires going beyond the identification of target tasks to collect and analyze samples of target discourse (Long, this volume) through nonparticipant observation. These collective efforts will reveal more complex, situated, and critical insights about learner needs.

Ultimately, the continued vitality, innovation, and effectiveness of TBLT hinges on TBLT practitioners having the knowledge, support, and resources to employ methods that are not only rigorous and practically feasible, but also sociolinguistically informed and culturally relevant. As a scholarly field and community of practice, it is important to find sustainable ways to support achieving these ends. One approach is to identify potential public and private funding bodies (e.g., international/national professional organizations) and advocate for funding initiatives that support teacher-led, action-based research projects implementing TBLT in local contexts, as well as creating academic-community partnerships to foster the design of task-based service-learning curricula. Moreover, institutions should incentivize interdisciplinary collaboration among faculty in different disciplines to foster cross-fertilization of methods in task-based NA practice.

Further Reading

Berwick, R. (1989). Needs assessment in language programming: From theory to practice. In R. K. Johnson, ed. *The second language curriculum*. Cambridge: Cambridge University Press, pp. 48–62.

Brown, J. D. (2009). Foreign and second language needs analysis. In M. H. Long and C. Doughty, eds. *The handbook of language teaching*. Oxford: Blackwell, pp. 269–293.

Lambert, C. (2010). A task-based needs analysis: Putting principles into practice. *Language Teaching Research*, 14(1), 99–112.

Long, M. H. (2005). Methodological issues in learner needs analysis. In M. H. Long, ed. *Second language needs analysis*. Cambridge: Cambridge University Press, pp. 19–76.

Long, M. H. (2015). Identifying target tasks. In M. H. Long, ed. *Second language acquisition and task-based language teaching*. Oxford: Wiley-Blackwell, pp. 117–68.

Oliver, R., Grote, E., Rochecouste, J., and Exell, M. (2013). Needs analysis for task-based language teaching: A case study of Indigenous vocational education and training students who speak EAL/EAD. *TESOL in Context*, 22(2), 36–50.

Riestenberg, K. and Sherris, A. (2018). Task-based teaching of indigenous languages: Investment and methodological principles in Macuiltianguis Zapotec and Salish Qlispe revitalization. *Canadian Modern Language Review*, 74(3), 434–59.

Serafini, E. J., Lake, J., and Long, M. H. (2015). Needs analysis for specialized learner populations: Essential methodological improvements. *English for Specific Purposes*, 40, 11–26.

Shehadeh, A. (2012). Introduction: Broadening the perspective of task-based language teaching scholarship: The contribution of research in foreign language contexts. In A. Shehadeh and C. A. Coombe, eds. *Task-based language teaching in foreign language contexts*. Amsterdam: John Benjamins, pp. 1–22.

Van Avermaet, P. and Gysen, S. (2006). From needs to tasks: Language learning needs in a task-based approach. In K. Van den Branden, ed., *Task-based language teaching in practice*. Cambridge: Cambridge University Press, pp. 17–46.

Study Questions

1. What are examples of cultural, social, and practical constraints on conducting methodologically rigorous NAs? Can you think of ways to overcome those constraints?
2. Some researchers assert that strong versions of TBLT are not suitable for younger learners or for novice instructed second/foreign language learners whose needs are not necessarily specified or uniform. Do you share this perception? Why or why not?
3. What are potential sources of financial support for task-based language practitioners on both a large- and small-scale?
4. How can task-based programs build sustainability and continuity in the long term? What role might NA replication play in this endeavor?

References

Abbott, A. and Martínez, G. (2018). Spanish for the professions and community service learning: Applications with heritage learners. In K. Potowski, ed. *The Routledge handbook of Spanish as a heritage language*. London and New York: Routledge, pp. 389–402.

Adams, R. and Newton, J. (2009). TBLT in Asia: Constraints and opportunities. *Asian Journal of English Language Teaching*, 19, 1–17.

Adendorff, E. (2014). A task-based approach to improving the communicative skills of university students learning Afrikaans as an additional language. *Stellenbosch Papers in Linguistics Plus*, 43, 1–16.

Bao, R. and Du, X. (2015). Implementation of task-based language teaching in Chinese as a foreign language: Benefits and challenges. *Language, Culture and Curriculum*, 28(3), 291–310.

Benesch, S. (1996). Needs analysis and curriculum development in EAP: An example of a critical approach. *TESOL Quarterly*, 30, 723–38.

Benesch, S. (1999). Rights analysis: studying power relations in an academic setting. *English for Specific Purposes*, 18(4), 313–27.

Berwick, R. (1989). Needs assessment in language programming: From theory to practice. In R. K. Johnson, ed. *The second language curriculum*. Cambridge: Cambridge University Press, pp. 48–62.

Brown, J. D. (2009). Foreign and second language needs analysis. In M. H. Long and C. Doughty, eds. *The handbook of language teaching*. Oxford: Blackwell, pp. 269–93.

Brown, J. D. (2016). *Introducing needs analysis and English for specific purposes*. Abingdon: Routledge.

Brindley, G. (1984). *Needs analysis and objective setting in the Adult Migrant Education Program*. Sydney: Adult Migrant Education Service.

Bryfonski, L. and McKay, T. H. (2019). TBLT implementation and evaluation: A meta-analysis. *Language Teaching Research*, 23(5), 603–32.

Bygate, M. (2016). Sources, developments and directions of task-based language teaching. *Language Learning Journal*, 44(4), 381–400.

Carless, D. (2007). The suitability of task-based approaches for secondary schools: Perspectives from Hong Kong. *System*, 35, 595–608.

Carless, D. (2012). TBLT in EFL settings: Looking back and moving forward. In A. Shehadeh and C. A. Coombe, eds. *Task-based language teaching in foreign language contexts: Research and implementation*. Amsterdam: John Benjamins, pp. 345–58.

Chaudron, C., Doughty, C., Kim, Y., Kong, D., Lee, J., Lee, Y., Long, M. H., Rivers, R., and Urano, K. (2005). A task-based needs analysis of a tertiary Korean as a foreign language program. In M. H. Long, ed. *Second language needs analysis*. Cambridge: Cambridge University Press, pp. 105–24.

Crookes, G. (2009). Radical language teaching. In M. H. Long and C. Doughty, eds. *The handbook of language teaching*. Oxford: Blackwell, pp. 595–609.

Cumaranatunge, L. K. (1988). An EOP case study: Domestic aids in West Asia. In D. Chamberlain, and R. J. Baumgardener, eds. *ESP in the classroom: Practice and evaluation*. ELT document 129. London: Modern English Publications/The British Council, pp. 127–33.

Dewey, J. (1938). *Experience and education*. New York: Macmillan Company.

Dörnyei, Z. with Taguchi, T. (2010). *Questionnaires in second language research: Construction, administration, and processing*. New York: Routledge.

Dudley-Evans, T. and St. John, M. J. (1998). *Developments in English for Specific Purposes: A multi-disciplinary approach*. Cambridge: Cambridge University Press.

Ellis, R. (2003). *Task-based language learning and teaching*. Oxford: Oxford University Press.

Fairclough, N. (1995). *Critical discourse analysis: The critical study of language*. London: Longman.

Fairclough, N. (2001). Critical discourse analysis. In A. McHoul and M. Rapley, eds. *How to analyze talk in institutional settings: A casebook of methods*. London and New York: Continuum, pp. 25–28.

Flores, N. and García, O. (2017). A critical review of bilingual education in the United States: From basements and pride to boutiques and profit. *Annual Review of Applied Linguistics*, 37, 14–29.

Flowerdew, L. (2005). Integrating traditional and critical approaches to syllabus design: The 'what', the 'how' and the 'why'. *Journal of English for Academic Purposes*, 4, 135–47.

Freire, P. (1970/2005). *The pedagogy of the oppressed*. New York: Herder and Herder/Continuum.

Gilabert, R. (2005). Evaluating the use of multiple sources and methods in needs analysis: A case study of journalists in the Autonomous Community of Catalonia (Spain). In M. H. Long, ed. *Second language needs analysis*. Cambridge: Cambridge University Press, pp. 182–99.

González-Lloret, M. and Nielson, K. B. (2015). Evaluating TBLT: The case of a task-based Spanish program. *Language Teaching Research*, 19, 525–49.

Hult, F. M. and Hornberger, N. H. (2016). Revisiting orientations in language planning: Problem, right, and resource as an analytical heuristic. *Bilingual Review/Revista Bilingüe*, 33, 30–49.

Hutchison, T., and Waters, A. (1987). *English for specific purposes*. Cambridge: Cambridge University Press.

Iizuka, T. (2019). Task-based needs analysis:Identifying communicative needs for study abroad students in Japan. *System*, 80, 134–42.

Jasso-Aguilar, R. (1999) Sources, methods and triangulation in needs analysis:A critical perspective in a case study of Waikiki hotel maids. *English for Specific Purposes*, 18(1), 27–46.

Jasso-Aguilar, R. (2005). Sources, methods and triangulation in needs analysis: A critical perspective in a case study of Waikiki hotel maids. In M. H. Long, ed. *Second language needs analysis*. Cambridge: Cambridge University Press, pp. 127–58.

Jenkins, J. (2006). Current perspectives on teaching world Englishes and English as a lingua franca. *TESOL Quarterly*, 40, 157–81.

Kolb, D. A. (1984). *Experiential learning: Experience as a source of learning and development*. New Jersey: Prentice Hall.

Konoeda, K. and Watanabe, Y. (2008). Task-based critical pedagogy in Japanese EFL classrooms: Rationale, principles, and examples. In M. Mantero, C. P. Miller and J. L. Watzke, eds. *Readings in language studies*. Vol. 1. St. Louis: International Society for Language Studies.

Lambert, C. (2010). A task-based needs analysis:Putting principles into practice. *Language Teaching Research*, 14(1), 99–112.

Leeman, J., Rabin, L., and Román-Mendoza, E. (2011). Identity and activism in heritage language education. *The Modern Language Journal*, 95, 481–95.

Leeman, J. and Serafini, E. J. (2016). *Sociolinguistics in heritage language education: Promoting critical translingual competence*. In S. Beaudrie and M. Fairclough, eds. *Innovative approaches in heritage language pedagogy: From research to practice*. Washington DC: Georgetown University Press, pp. 56–79.

Leung, C., Harris, R., and Rampton, B. (2004). Living with inelegance in qualitative research on task-based learning. In B. Norton and K. Toohey, eds. *Critical pedagogies and language learning*. Cambridge: Cambridge University Press, pp. 242–68.

Li, G. and Ni, X. (2013). Effects of a technology-enriched, task-based language teaching curriculum on Chinese elementary students' achievement in English as a foreign language. *International Journal of Computer-Assisted Language Learning and Teaching*, 3, 33–49.

Liakina, N. and Michaud, G. (2018). Needs analysis for task-based curriculum design: How useful can it be for general purpose L2 courses? *Nouvelle Revue Synergies Canada*, 11.

Lin, T. and Wu, C. (2012). Teachers' perceptions of task-based language teaching in English classrooms in Taiwanese junior high schools. *TESOL Journal*, 3, 586–609.

Littlewood, W. (2007). Communicative and task-based language teaching in East Asian classrooms. *Language Teaching*, 40, 243–49.

Long, M. H. (1985). A role for instruction in second language acquisition: Task-based language teaching. In K. Hyltenstam and M. Pienemann, eds. *Modeling and assessing second language development*. Bristol: Multilingual Matters, pp. 77–99.

Long, M. H. (2005a) *Second language needs analysis*. Cambridge: Cambridge University Press.

Long, M. H. (2005b). A rationale for needs analysis and needs analysis research. In M. H. Long, ed. *Second language needs analysis*. Cambridge: Cambridge University Press, pp. 1–16.

Long, M. H. (2005c). Methodological issues in learner needs analysis. In M. H. Long, ed. *Second language needs analysis*. Cambridge: Cambridge University Press, pp. 19–76.

Long, M. H. (2009). Methodological principles for language teaching. In M. H. Long and C. Doughty, eds. *The handbook of language teaching*. Oxford: Blackwell, pp. 373–94.

Long, M. H. (2013). Needs analysis. In C. A. Chapelle, ed. *The encyclopedia of applied linguistics*. Oxford: Wiley-Blackwell.

Long, M. H. (2015a). *Second language acquisition and task-based language teaching*. Oxford: Wiley-Blackwell.

Long, M. K. and Uscinski, I. (2012). Evolution of languages for specific purposes programs in the United States: 1990–2011. *Modern Language Journal*, 96, 173–89.

Malicka, A., Gilabert, R., and Norris, J. M. (2019). *From needs analysis to task design:Insights from an English for specific purposes context*, 23(1), 78–106.

Martin, A. and Adrada-Rafael, S. (2017). Business Spanish in the real world: A task-based needs analysis. *L2 Journal*, 9(1), 39–61.

McKay, S. L. and Rubdy, R. (2009). The social and sociolinguistic contexts of language learning and teaching. In M. H. Long and C. Doughty, eds. *The handbook of language teaching*. Oxford: Blackwell, pp. 10–25.

Mitchell, T. D. (2008). Traditional vs. critical service-learning: Engaging the literature to differentiate two models. *Michigan Journal of Community Service Learning*, Spring, 50–65.

Munby, J. (1978). *Communicative syllabus design*. Cambridge: Cambridge University Press.

National Service-Learning Clearinghouse. (2008). *History of service-learning in higher education*. New York: National Service-Learning Clearinghouse.

Norris, J. (2009). Task-based teaching and testing. In M. H. Long and C. J. Doughty, eds. *The handbook of language teaching*. Oxford: Wiley-Blackwell, pp. 578–94.

Oliver, R., Grote, E., Rochecouste, J., and Exell, M. (2012). Addressing the language and literacy needs of Aboriginal high school VET students who speak SAE as an additional language. *Australian Journal of Indigenous Education*, 41(2), 1–11.

Oliver, R., Grote, E., Rochecouste, J., and Exell, M. (2013a). A task-based needs analysis for Australian Aboriginal students: Going beyond the target situation to address cultural issues. *International Journal of Training Research*, 11(3), 246–59.

Oliver, R., Grote, E., Rochecouste, J., and Exell, M. (2013b). Needs analysis for task-based language teaching: A case study of Indigenous vocational education and training students who speak EAL/EAD. *TESOL in Context*, 22 (2), 36–50.

Park, M. (2012). Implementing computer-assisted task-based language teaching in the Korean secondary EFL context. In A. Shehadeh and C. A. Coombe, eds. *Task-based language teaching in foreign language contexts: Research and implementation*. Amsterdam: John Benjamins, pp. 215–40.

Phillipson, R. (1992). *Linguistic imperialism*. Oxford: Oxford University Press.

Phuong, H. Y., Van den Branden, K., Van Steendamn, E., and Sercu, L. (2015). The impact of PPP and TBLT on Vietnamese students' writing performance and self-regulatory writing strategies. *International Journal of Applied Linguistics*, 116, 37–93.

Prabhu, N. S. (1987). *Second language pedagogy*. Oxford: Oxford University Press.

Rabin, L. (2015). Service-learning/Aprendizaje-servicio as a global practice in Spanish. In M. LaCorte, ed. *The Routledge handbook of Hispanic applied linguistics*. New York: Routledge, pp. 168–83.

Richterich, R. and Chancerel, J.-L. (1987). *Identifying the needs of adults learning a foreign language*. Oxford: Prentice Hall.

Riestenberg, K. and Sherris, A. (2018). Task-based teaching of indigenous languages: Investment and methodological principles in Macuiltianguis Zapotec and SalishQlispe revitalization. *Canadian Modern Language Review*, 74(3), 434–59.

Ruíz, R. (1984). Orientations in language planning. *NABE Journal*, 8, 15–34.

Samuda, V., Bygate, M., and Van den Branden, K. (2018). Introduction: Towards a researched pedagogy for TBLT. In V. Samuda, K. Van den Branden, and M. Bygate eds. *TBLT as a researched pedagogy*. Amsterdam: John Benjamins, pp. 1–22.

Sánchez-López, L. (2013). Spanish for specific purposes. In C. A. Chapelle ed. *The encyclopedia of applied linguistics*. Oxford: Wiley-Blackwell.

Serafini, E. J. (2021). Service learning in heritage language education: A critical overview of motivation, design, and outcomes. In J. R. Torres and D. Pascual y Cabo, eds. *El español como lengua de herencia (Advances in Spanish Language Teaching Series)*. London and New York: Routledge Press.

Serafini, E. J., Lake, J., and Long, M. H. (2015). Needs analysis for specialized learner populations: Essential methodological improvements. *English for Specific Purposes*, 40, 11–26.

Serafini, E. J. and Torres, J. (2015). The utility of needs analysis for non-domain expert teachers in designing task-based Spanish for the Professions curricula. *Foreign Language Annals*, 48, 447–72.

Shehadeh, A. (2012). Broadening the perspective of task-based language teaching scholarship: The contribution of research in foreign language contexts. In A. Shehadeh and C.A. Coombe, eds. *Task-based language teaching in foreign language contexts: Research and implementation*. Amsterdam: John Benjamins, pp. 1–20.

Shehadeh, A. and Coombe, C. A. (2012). *Task-based language teaching in foreign language contexts: Research and implementation*. Amsterdam: John Benjamins.

Skutnabb-Kangas, T. and Cummins, J. (1988). Language for empowerment. In T. Skutnabb-Kangas and J. Cummins, eds. *Minority education: From shame to struggle*. Bristol: Multilingual Matters, pp. 390–95.

Svendsen, C. and Krebs, K. (1984). Identifying English for the job: Examples from healthcare occupations. *The ESP Journal*, 3, 153–64.

Swales, J. (1990). *Genre analysis English in academic and research settings*. Cambridge: Cambridge University Press.

Tinker Sachs, G. (2009). Taking risks in task-based teaching and learning. *Asian Journal of English Language Teaching*, 19, 91–112.

Torres, J. and Serafini, E. J. (2016). Micro-evaluating learners' task-specific motivation in a task-based business Spanish course. *Hispania*, 99, 289–304.

Van Avermaet, P. and Gysen, S. (2006). From needs to tasks: Language learning needs in a task-based approach. In K. Van den Branden, ed. *Task-based language teaching in practice*. Cambridge: Cambridge University Press, pp. 17–46.

Van den Branden, K. (2006). *Task-based language teaching: From theory to practice*. Cambridge: Cambridge University Press.

Van den Branden, K., Bygate, M., and Norris, J. M. (2009). Task-based language teaching: Introducing the reader. In K. Van den Branden, M. Bygate, and J. M. Norris, eds. *Task-based language teaching: A reader*. Cambridge: Cambridge University Press, pp. 1–13.

Van Dijk, T. A. (2015). Critical discourse analysis. In D. Tannen, H. Hamilton, and D. Schiffrin, eds. *The handbook of discourse analysis*. 2nd ed. Oxford: Wiley Blackwell, pp. 466–85.

West, R. (1994). Needs analysis in language teaching. *Language Teaching*, 27, 1–19.

Woolard, K. A. and Schieffelin, B. B. (1994). Language ideology. *Annual Review of Anthropology*, 23, 55–82.

4A

Developing a Task-Based Approach

A Case Study of a Teacher Working with Australian Aboriginal Students in Vocational Education and Training

Rhonda Oliver

4A.1 Introduction

This case study documents the development and use of tasks, based on a previously conducted needs analysis (see Oliver, Grote, Rochecouste & Exell (2012, 2013a, 2013b) for a description of this), by one teacher working in a unique school context – an independent vocational education and training (VET) boarding school for older adolescent (aged between 15 and 19 years) Australian Aboriginal students. To maintain anonymity, in this chapter the school is referred to as Kutja School – a pseudonym selected by the local elder as in his language, Nintirringkutja, Kutja means learning to speak.

Kutja School is located in the great southern area of Western Australia, and is located about 715 kilometres from the capital city, Perth. It is an independently run school governed by a board made up mostly of Aboriginal community members who oversee the operation of this and two 'sister' schools, which are located 400 and 460 kilometres away. It is located within an operational farm that consists of approximately 1,000 acres of land. The school caters for up to seventy Aboriginal students at any one time. The students may choose to stay for up to four years, but some leave after only a short period of time because they find separation from family, community and their 'country' (i.e., their traditional lands) too difficult.

The goal of Kutja School is to prepare the students for a successful transition to life beyond the classroom, with the school motto being 'training for life'. The primary aims of the curriculum are to develop the students' vocational skills and their proficiency in standard

Australian English (SAE), including their written and oral competence. In this way the teachers at the school help address the 'long-term disadvantage' (Commonwealth of Australia, 2016: 7.14) that Aboriginal people continue to experience in Australia. This is especially the case for those living in regional and remote areas where their quality of life, in terms of economic, physical, social and emotional wellbeing remains exceedingly low (Australian Bureau of Statistics [ABS], 2016a; 2016b).

Prior to their enrolment at Kutja School a large proportion of the students have attained only low levels of educational achievement, something that is not unusual in many Indigenous populations across the globe. Because this school has a VET rather than academic focus, it is attractive to such students. Furthermore, many students have connections to the school because of relatives who had previously attended the school. With their families' support, the students choose this boarding school as the one in which to enrol – a school that is widely known by various Aboriginal communities for its vocational training and culturally sensitive approach.

The students travel many thousands of kilometres to attend Kutja School, coming from a range of areas including the far north, north-west and central desert areas of Western Australia, with more than half coming from small, remote communities. Unlike in many urban and large regional locations, in such communities Aboriginal culture and language remain strong. Even for others coming from regional towns, they tend to live lives more culturally and linguistically connected to the Aboriginal heritage than those who live in larger regional and urban areas. As noted by Oliver (in press), 'the languages spoken by the students include traditional languages (e.g., Ngariyin, Kija, Jaru, Walmarjarri) but also Kriol (a particularly type of creole spoken in northern Australia), Aboriginal English (as distinct dialect of Australian English) and, generally with less proficiency, Standard Australian English'.

In fact, it was because of the challenges the students were experiencing with SAE that the principal of the school reached out and a research relationship began. It is on the basis of this relationship that the current study and previous investigations were undertaken at the school. The initial requests received from the school leadership centred on the students' difficulties with SAE, particularly for those students who were acquiring it as a second language, rather than dialect. In response to this a large-scale needs analysis was undertaken (the outcomes of which are described next), a task-based approach introduced at the school, and ongoing contact maintained – for more than a decade – between the staff at the school and the research team from Curtin University. As part of this relationship the research team has provided regular professional learning opportunities for the teachers (e.g., on Aboriginal students' language needs and task-based approaches).

4A.2 Needs Analysis

As indicated, a thorough needs analysis was undertaken at Kutja School to empirically document the language and vocational needs of the students, particularly with regard to encouraging full and appropriate participation in the workplace. As recommended by Long (2005), data were collected from various sources: interviews with stakeholders (i.e., the school leadership team, the VET and other teachers at the school, staff in workplaces where students do work place experience, and the students themselves), observations of workplace interactions and the interrogation of vocational documentation (Oliver et al., 2012, 2013a, 2013b). In this way, we were able to consider the actual environment where the students would use language and, thereby, overcome the shortcomings of traditional needs analyses, which are often based simply on teacher intuitions (Gilabert, 2005; Long, 2005). It also meant that an appropriate task-based syllabus informed by this evidence could be developed (Long, 2005). Specifically, the teachers could select and use tasks (a term that aligned with their conceptual understanding of what could be 'done' in class) to address their students' needs. Although the student body has changed since the original needs analysis was undertaken, ongoing interactions with the teachers and students for other research at the school suggest that many of the needs identified seven years ago remain current for those students now enrolled at the school.

The identified needs were wide ranging and, although mostly addressing vocational and behavioural requirements, they involved the students developing associated communicative skills. For example, it was recognised by the employer group and VET teachers that the students needed to develop an understanding around workplace duties and the language aligned with these, which included knowing tool names and procedures, both in oral and written form (e.g., a wrench, spanner, 'screwing off' [attaching] boards, tethering fencing wires, etc.). It also involved being familiar with safety procedures and being able to comprehend product warnings such as the need to wear protective gear when using particular equipment. Various stakeholders also described the interactive needs of the students such as understanding instructions given about different workplace tasks, and importantly the ability to ask for clarification when unsure. To be able to do this, however, requires the students to develop a level of resilience to overcome what the students themselves described as 'getting shame' (i.e., an Aboriginal English phrase that equates to an overwhelming feeling of embarrassment, especially when singled out for doing something poorly or too well (Grote & Rochecouste, 2012).

The workplace stakeholders, VET teachers, as well as the English and mathematics teachers at the school suggested the students needed to be able to use the type of language and behaviour that demonstrated they had a 'strong work ethic'. By this they meant that students should use the type of language that indicated their enthusiasm for being employed and their enjoyment at achieving well in the workplace. For example, instead of using gestures to signify agreement, such as an almost indiscernible nod of the head (as happens in their communities) – they needed to learn to say loudly and clearly something like 'yes, sure' when asked to perform a task at work. Related to this the stakeholders identified the need for the students to develop communicative skills required for socialising at work. For instance, they described the students' need to develop the linguistic skills and confidence to greet workmates warmly in the morning by saying 'hello' or 'good morning' and not just gesturing their greeting (in remote Aboriginal communities this is often done by raising and flicking your index finger and thumb in a very subtle way). It also involved developing the language skills so they could engage appropriately when asked to talk about such things as where they come from, what they did on the weekend or last night, and which 'footy' (Australian rules football) team they support. In addition, some employers felt that what was most important was for the students to develop the confidence to understand and use humour in the workplace – something that is a common expectation in many 'trade' workplaces in Australia. At that same time, the mainstream teachers, community members and the students recognised the need of the students to 'hold strong' to their culture and language – so that they can maintain a positive self-identity, but also to continue to make use of their important communicative links with family and other community members.

Another key area of need identified by the stakeholders was developing the students' language skills in order for them to satisfy their personal and functional needs. This was identified particularly in relation to those skills that foster their successful transition to life beyond the classroom, and more than just in the workplace (e.g., doing banking, filling in forms, communicating with health care professionals, engaging in positive and proactive ways with people in authority – police, hospital workers, and government workers who often manage their communities). It should be noted that those who come from remote communities often have had little exposure to the type of language and behaviours considered everyday communicative events in urban and regional areas. The importance of developing such skills cannot be underestimated – they enable Aboriginal people to overcome the 'long-term disadvantage', as described previously. It is these areas of language need that are addressed in the current case study.

4A.3 Case Study – Background

The data for this case study came from regular, but non-participant observations made over the course of one year in one classroom at Kutja School.

The class enrolment fluctuated, but generally there between twelve and sixteen students in attendance, which is typical at the school. With permission, classroom observations were supplemented with information provided by the teacher (Jamie), who shared his perceptions about and experiences with using tasks. Through regular and often informal discussions, he also articulated what he did and provided a rationale for how he selected and/or developed the tasks he used. Field notes were made about the classroom observations and the discussions as soon possible after each visit. Photographs were taken as a visual record of the tasks that were used in Jamie's classroom. As required, and because of the distances involved and the time between visits, further questions were asked and answered by way of email exchanges.

At the time of the data collection, Jamie was relatively new to teaching, having previously been a butcher for thirty years, then a youth worker and school chaplain, before retraining to become teacher at the age of fifty. During his teacher education post-graduate course, he specialised in teaching Aboriginal students and he uses this to inform his classroom practices. He has brought his wealth of 'outside' school experience into the classroom, too. In fact, this outside experience goes some way in explaining his development of tasks that, wherever possible, mirror 'real-life'. During post-observation discussions he described how his own learning preference 'is to see and do' and described how 'this naturally aligns with a task-based learning approach'. He also indicated that teaching this way is 'more enjoyable' for him. During the course of the data collection he taught English, mathematics, health, work readiness, and driver training, including a programme called Keys4life. After-school he was also instrumental in running the Bushrangers cadet programme. This is a youth-based conservation and community development programme aligned to Western Australian Department of Parks and Wildlife.

Regardless of which subject Jamie was teaching, it was clear that he adopted an approach underpinned by the promotion of interaction, which was often task-based. This was reflected in the way he organised the students to actively engage with each other and with the tasks he developed by having them work interactively in groups and pairs. The advantage of this is that not only could he develop the students' awareness and language related to the content he was covering, but by having them engage in unscripted talk during the tasks he was also preparing them 'for the dynamics of the communicative encounters' they would have outside school (Oliver et al., 2013: 247).

Although such a communicative approach is common in English as a second language classrooms, it is quite an unusual approach to take when teaching Aboriginal students. This is because they are often naturally very quiet and, in fact, can be quite non-communicative in class, especially those who come from remote communities. Additionally, organising task-based interaction can be complicated in Aboriginal contexts because of various cultural constraints that occur within Aboriginal society (e.g., genders tend to interact separately, some individuals are deemed to have seniority even when aged the same because of their position in the family or because they have been through traditional 'law' – something akin to initiation in other societies). This complex situation was made even more difficult in Jamie's classroom because of the ever-changing student enrolment, and therefore, the class dynamics were often in a state of flux. Despite all this, he was able to achieve high levels of interactional engagement amongst his students because he gave them the autonomy to organise their groups in ways that they deemed were culturally and socially appropriate. Furthermore, the students were willing to engage because Jamie designed tasks that were motivating to them and clearly aligned to their real-life needs post-school. Examples of such tasks are described next.

4A.4 The Tasks

According to Nunan (2004: 4), a task is 'a piece of classroom work that involves learners in comprehending, manipulating, producing or interacting in the target language while their attention is focused on mobilising their grammatical knowledge in order to express meaning'.

Such a 'meaning focus' was particularly evident in Jamie's classroom possibly because he developed and selected tasks with real functional goals. As well as providing considerable opportunities for meaningful language use and development, the tasks had an authentic focus. In addition, the tasks involved the students working together collaboratively to understand and/or resolve real-life problems, to address relevant moral dilemmas or emotional issues using their own language resources. The examples selected for this case study include those around the functional need of 'getting a driver's licence' and 'budgeting and managing money'. By ensuring such relevance, the tasks Jamie's students used in class were able to address their diverse range of needs (East, 2017).

4A.4.1 Getting a Driver's Licence

In the original needs analysis, workplace and community member stakeholders identified the need for the students to have a driver's licence, and to understand the responsibilities and consequences of having this. For example, as identified in Oliver et al. (2003: 256), the students' need to understand that when asked by someone (especially in the workplace) the question: 'Can you drive?' it is not just one about ability, but also about the legality of doing so. This area of need has been a key focus of the school for a number of years and multiple staff members are engaged in the practical task of helping the students to obtain their driver's licence. For Jamie, however, addressing the need goes beyond the practicalities of driving and involves being able to understand the language related to driving. In the initial stages, this involves developing an understanding of the road rules – content the students (and everyone else) attempting to get their learner's permit are tested on (in SAE). It also requires the students to be able to give and to follow oral directions when driving or when navigating for someone else. As noted previously those living in remote communities use a lot of gestures and when driving, they have been observed asking a question and giving directions without a spoken word being uttered. For example, during the data collection stage, one student was observed letting go of the steering wheel to ask which way to turn (using gestures alone), which would have been an immediate fail in a practical driving test.

To address these practical driving needs, and to do so in the safety of the classroom, Jamie developed a number of tasks where students moved toy cars on a road map following directions given by a fellow student or giving an oral description of a route followed by a car 'driven' by another. To begin, these directional tasks were modelled by Jamie and then by different members of the class, and as the students developed confidence with giving and receiving oral directions, they did so independently as one-way information gap tasks in groups and pairs. Jamie also used information from the permit test (written at a level beyond the literacy level of most of the students in his class) to design quizzes, and had the students work collaboratively to determine what the particular road rule was and how it manifests when driving – again using the road map and toy cars to determine the correct answer. In this way, the actual 'doing' of moving the cars and negotiating in pairs or groups, supported the students understanding of the written English road rules, but also served to develop their oral communicative skills and their abilities to work collaboratively with others.

Sadly, there is a disproportionate number of Aboriginal people, particularly in remote communities, who are injured or who lose their lives in road accidents, with many being young people. To draw attention to the impact of road accidents and the consequence of things such as not wearing seat belts (or helmets on motor bikes), driving after drinking or doing drugs, not only to those involved, but also on their family and friends, Jamie organised open-ended group discussion tasks. He said he did this to 'get them on board emotionally to start with' and because he had observed that this was an area of need for his students. He would often select newspaper articles reporting accidents as a stimulus for these tasks. He would then provide task directions and assign roles to different members of the group (group leader, secretary, person who reports to the class). Then by working together, they could make links to their various personal experiences, record these in a table, and then determine ways to counter some of the issues. As a result, the students went on to make road safety posters, and write poems or personal reflections in their journals, and these pieces of work were also shared with other members of the class.

4A.4.2 Budgeting and Managing Money

Another functional need that was addressed by Jamie, and done so using repeated pedagogical tasks over the course of the whole year, was related to the topic of budgeting and managing money. As indicated, one of Jamie's roles was teaching mathematics to his class. He used this as an opportunity to teach about money and how to spend it wisely. Although budgeting was not identified in the original needs analysis, it was a need identified by Jamie based on his discussion with his students, and his observations from interacting with families of the students. This highlights how needs analyses should not remain static, but should be evolving, current and responsive.

Each of the students were paid a set salary each week. Amounts were deducted because of behavioural misdemeanours (e.g., leaving class without permission, swearing in class) or bonuses paid because of classroom achievements (e.g., attending class, completing assignments). Each week each individual student's salary was added to a virtual bank balance. When amounts were spent, including 10 per cent be given to a charity of their choice (which evolved from a decision-making task), this was deducted from the total. In addition, 10 per cent bank interest was added on a monthly basis (a concept that was initially new and difficult for the students to grasp). As part of their mathematics course, the equations surrounding these additions and subtractions were calculated first by the students and then checked for accuracy by the teacher.

Next, this bank balance was a key resource for a set of tasks concerned with budgeting and managing money in a virtual world that Jamie designed. At the beginning of the year, the students had things they could choose to buy from a display of goods – cars, laptops, etc. Group tasks were organised to help the students prioritise their spending, but each student had to work collaboratively to determine their personal goals – a task designed to help them to consider what they really wanted. For example, a number of the male students wanted cars, whereas the girls were less interested in this as it would mean an added responsibility of becoming the driver for older members of their communities. Many wanted the latest mobile phone so they could stay in touch with family and friends, and some wanted laptops to help them with their vocational goals. Once they had made their choices the groups justified their decisions: first they presented to another group and, if willing, to the whole class. This also gave them the opportunity to practice speaking – talking about things that were of interest to them. Although an authentic task in that it simulated real life (budgeting), it also had a real pedagogical purpose – in this case providing opportunities for the students to speak with confidence, in SAE, and to a larger audience.

As the year progressed, additional requirements were added to the larger budgeting task. For instance, after yet another change to the class enrolment, Jamie observed a diminishing willingness for the students to collaborate with each other. In response, he added a new goal which was for the class to form 'shared house' groups. As a first step they had to decide who they would share a house with, and then in this group they had to decide on the household budget – how they would spend their money for bills, food, etc. They also had to decide who would buy the different items of furniture for their home. This required considerable cooperation and members of the class, and some groups in particular were observed to initially struggle with coming to a consensus around their goals in a timely way. This led Jamie to include more group goal-setting tasks – for instance, in his health class he had the shared houses develop house rules and set goals for healthy living (e.g., drink more water). In this way, the tasks were cumulative with each pedagogic tasks contributing to addressing a larger functional need.

4A.5 Conclusion

In all the tasks Jamie designed, the students were required to use their own linguistic resources to negotiate to achieve understanding, but with a focus that reflected very real-life tasks. In this way he was able to use a task-based approach to develop his students' communicative and SAE skills, but also those skills that they would need as they transitioned to life beyond the classroom. Because of the way he designed the tasks, their purpose was transparently relevant to his students. Consequently, the students were highly motivated and were observed to enthusiastically engage with the tasks. Importantly for this cohort, they could do so in ways that were culturally and socially appropriate to them. Although Jamie mostly addressed the needs identified in the original needs analysis, he also determined other needs based on his vast experience of life 'outside' the classroom, and from the evidence he heard in interactions with his students and the actions he observed.

Over the course of the year, the students' oral language confidence increased, both in speaking to each other in pairs and small groups, but also to larger groups of students. They also displayed increasing willingness to use SAE and did so in ways that suggested their understanding and proficiency had increased. It was also evident that the students were aware of consequences of their actions, related to both safe driving and careful budgeting, but also to how they interacted with each other.

References

Australian Bureau of Statistics [ABS] (2016a). National Aboriginal and Torres Strait Islander social survey. Retrieved from www.abs.gov.au

Australian Bureau of Statistics [ABS] (2016b). *Schools, Australia*. Retrieved from www.abs.gov.au

Commonwealth of Australia (2016) Finance and Public Administration References Committee: Aboriginal and Torres Strait Islander experience of law enforcement and justice services. Canberra, Commonwealth of Australia.

East, M. (2017). Task-based teaching and learning: Pedagogical implications. In N. Van Deusen-Scholl and S. May, eds. *Second and foreign language education*. Cham, Switzerland: Springer International Publishing.

Gilabert, R. (2005). Task complexity and L2 narrative oral production. Unpublished doctoral dissertation, University of Barcelona, Spain.

Grote, E. and Rochecouste, J. (2012). Language and the classroom setting. In Q. Beresford and G. Partington, eds. *Reform and resistance in Aboriginal education*. Crawley, WA: UWA Press.

Long, M. H. (2005), *Second language needs analysis*. Cambridge: Cambridge University Press.

Nunan, D. (2004). *Task-based language teaching*. Cambridge: Cambridge University Press.

Oliver, R. (2020). Developing authentic tasks for the workplace using needs analysis: A case study of Australian Aboriginal vocational students. In C. Lambert and R. Oliver, eds. *Using tasks in diverse contexts*. Bristol: Multilingual Matters.

Oliver, R., Grote, E., Rochecouste, J., and Exell, M. (2012). Addressing the language and literacy needs of Aboriginal high School VET students who speak SAE as an additional language. *Australian Journal of Indigenous Education*, 41(2), 1–11.

Oliver, R., Grote, E., Rochecouste, J., and Exell, M. (2013a). Needs analysis for task-based language teaching: A case study of Indigenous vocational education and training students who speak EAL/EAD. *TESOL in Context*, 22(2), 36–50.

Oliver, R., Grote, E., Rochecouste, J., and Exell, M. (2013b). A task-based needs analysis for Australian Aboriginal students: Going beyond the target situation to address cultural issues. *International Journal of Training Research*, 11(3), 246–59.

4B

A Task-Based Language Needs Analysis of Syrian Refugee Parents in Turkey

Şeyma Toker and Ayşenur Sağdıç

4B.1 Introduction

Today, we are witnessing the highest level of global displacement of human populations on record. By the end of 2018, 70.8 million people worldwide had been forcibly displaced due to natural disasters and political conflicts. 25.9 million of this population are refugees, the majority of whom come from countries such as Syria, Afghanistan, and Sudan and reside in neighboring countries (UNHCR, 2018). As a neighbor of Syria, Turkey is currently hosting 3,676,288 Syrian refugees under Temporary Protection Regulation, based on Article 91 of the Law on Foreigners, approximately half of whom are school-aged children, with the other half consisting of the adults responsible for them (UNHRC, 2019).

To expand the educational opportunities for school-aged children beyond the refugee camps, Turkey made public schools accessible to refugee children in 2014. Since then, refugee children and their parents have been members of school communities in Turkey. Yet, studies on Syrian refugee students in Turkish schools have revealed that teachers harbor serious concerns about communicating with refugee students and their parents (Aykırı, 2017; Er & Bayındır, 2015; Kiremit, Akpınar & Akçan, 2018). These issues are partly attributable to refugee parents' limited involvement in Turkish schools (Ergen & Şahin, 2019; Olgun-Baytaş & Toker, 2019). Teachers have great difficulty communicating with refugee parents due to the latter's lack of language proficiency in Turkish (Uzun & Bütün, 2016), the sole official language of the Turkish Republic.

While these studies point to the communication challenges in general, we take a step beyond that and identify the communicative tasks most critical for refugee parents seeking to interact with the target speech community in the

K–12 context (kindergarten through to twelfth grade). Using task-based language teaching (TBLT), a learner-centered language-learning approach that supports learning by doing, we conducted a needs analysis (NA) with domain experts (namely, first language [L1] Turkish-speaking parents, teachers, and school administrators) to identify target tasks that could inform a task-based Turkish language course for refugee parents.

4B.2 Present Study: A Needs Analysis for Refugee Parents in the K–12 Context in Turkey

This study explores the language-learning needs of refugee parents by examining (1) the tasks those with children enrolled in K–12 Turkish schools are expected to perform within this domain, (2) the perceived difficulty and frequency of the tasks, and (3) the sequence in which these tasks should be presented to the parents in a task-based Turkish language course.

The target second language (L2) learners are refugee parents who have children enrolled in public or private K–12 schools in Turkey. The target language for them is Turkish. The NA was conducted with L1 Turkish-speaking domain experts (parents, teachers, and administrators) from various K–12 school settings in Turkey, including kindergarten, elementary, middle, and high schools. At least one city from each region of Turkey is represented in the interviews and questionnaire data. Nonparticipant observation was conducted at an elementary school in western Turkey. The elementary school setting was selected because it is where parents are most engaged in schooling in Turkey.

4B.3 Needs Analysis Criteria and Sources

The NA utilized triangulation of data from different insider sources obtained through interviews, a questionnaire, and nonparticipant observation. As Long (2005) states, domain insiders are valid sources of information, due to their familiarity with the target tasks; therefore, in our study, we relied on the information provided by domain experts, who are, in this case, L1 Turkish-speaking parents, teachers, and administrators from varying K–12 school contexts. Several of the domain experts reported having worked and interacted with Syrian refugee students and parents. We used convenience sampling to recruit participants for interview and observation and snowball sampling to recruit participants for the questionnaire.

4B.3.1 Method
Three methods of data collection were employed and sequenced: from more open (observation and interview) to closed (questionnaire). The

first author conducted nonparticipant observation in an elementary school at *karne töreni* (a report card ceremony) on the last day of the academic semester, when parents are expected to socialize with the other parents and watch the ceremony of children receiving report cards from the teacher. The purpose of the observation was to triangulate the data obtained from the interviews and obtain further insight into the tasks parents engage in on site and the nature of the language associated with those tasks. Then, both researchers conducted semi-structured interviews with nine domain experts (L1 Turkish-speaking parents, teachers, and administrators) to identify the tasks refugee parents are expected to perform in K–12 school context. We asked each group customized questions about what they typically do during a school day and events and situations that require them to interact with other parents. The needs and tasks identified in the insider interviews and triangulated through observation informed the design of the questionnaire. The questionnaire included thirty closed items about various target tasks' frequency and difficulty, and it was completed by fifty-three parents.

4B.3.2 Design and Procedure

In this study, we adapted the NA procedure recommended by Serafini, Lake, and Long (2015), with some slight changes:

Step 0 Review literature on communication problems of Syrian refugees in Turkey.
Step 1 Collect and analyze data from domain insiders to identify target tasks.
    1A Conduct nonparticipant school observation.
    1B Conduct semi-structured interviews with domain experts (parents, teachers, administrators).
Step 2 Assess the generalizability of target tasks for the target population.
    2A Create questionnaire items based on observation and interview data.
    2B Pilot the questionnaire.
    2C Administer the questionnaire.
Step 3 Triangulate findings from all sources of data to identify high-frequency and potentially problematic target tasks for Syrian refugee parents.

Step 0 was informed by previous research on the education of Syrian refugee learners in Turkey, which suggested the necessity for refugee parents' more active involvement in Turkish schools (Aykırı, 2017; Er & Bayındır, 2015; Ergen & Şahin, 2019; Kiremit et al., 2018; Olgun-Baytaş & Toker, 2019; Uzun & Bütün, 2016).

In Step 1, following Serafini et al. (2015), we used an open procedure to identify the target tasks for refugee parents in Turkish schools. The only change we made in our study was to conduct the classroom observation in Step 1, instead of in Step 3, so that we could use multiple sources of data obtained through open-ended methods to inform the questionnaire. Nonparticipant observation (Step 1A) was conducted on the last day of the semester in a public elementary (K–4) school in western Turkey. The school had 704 students and 33 teachers. As in all public K–12 schools in Turkey, the medium of instruction was Turkish. Based on the report of the teacher whose class was observed, almost all parents and students came from households where Turkish was the only L1. The observation took place in the classroom of a second-grade teacher, with the permission of the school director and the teacher. The first author attended classes all day to observe, and took field notes during *karne töreni*. This event is one of the opportunities for parents to socialize with other parents and talk to teachers and school administrators. For Step 1B, we first created three sets of open-ended interview questions for the domain experts. Each set began with background questions about the educational context and participants' background. Subsequent questions attempted to elicit information about the target tasks refugee parents are expected to perform in the school context. We piloted the interview questions in Turkish using a think-aloud protocol with one participant from each group and revised the questions based on the results. We then recruited parents, teachers, and administrators for the semi-structured interview. We interviewed nine domain experts in total (eight women and one man); four teachers, one school administrator, one school counselor, three parents with children at kindergarten, elementary-, middle-, and high-school level. Two of the teachers, the school administrator, and the counselor were also parents. Therefore, we were able to get more input from them regarding their dual role as parents and teachers/administrators. Interviews were conducted in Turkish, through Skype, and took approximately fifteen minutes. They were then partially transcribed to identify a list of target tasks, their perceived frequency, and difficulty. This, together with the observation notes, informed the questionnaire items in Step 2.

Based on the analysis of the data from Step 1, in Step 2 we designed and administered an online questionnaire with thirty closed items to a larger population of L1 Turkish-speaking parents to identify the target tasks that would be most important and problematic for refugee parents. The questionnaire consisted of four main sections: (1) target tasks in parent–administrator interaction (twelve items); (2) target tasks in parent–teacher interaction (ten items); (3) target tasks in parent–parent interaction (four items); and (4) other tasks (four items). The objective of each section was to elicit information with respect to the perceived frequency and difficulty of target tasks. Each target task item asked parents to rate the frequency and difficulty of the task using a four-point Likert scale, for frequency from 1 (never) to 4 (very frequent) and for difficulty from 1 (very easy) to 4 (very difficult). The questionnaire was piloted (Step 2B) with two Turkish parents using a think-aloud protocol. Participants were asked to complete each section of the questionnaire on their mobile phone while thinking aloud for each item. They were then asked to pause at the end of each section to share their opinions about the content, clarity, and format of the questions. Based on the think-aloud data from pilot participants, we revised the language and design of the questionnaire to make it more user-friendly. In Step 2C, researchers shared the questionnaire with the parents of students in Turkish schools among their social media circles, and participants were requested to share the questionnaire with other parents. Out of 101 participants who started the questionnaire, 53 completed it (41 women, 9 men, and 3 other). If a participant did not respond to more than half of the items, they were excluded from the analysis. Participants' ages ranged from 32 to 55. Thirty-five parents had only one school-aged child, while seventeen parents had two, and one had three. Eight parents provided input for students at a kindergarten level, twenty-three at elementary-school level, eighteen at middle-school level, and nineteen at high-school level.

In Step 3, data from the school observation, interviews, and questionnaire were triangulated and analyzed to identify the most frequent and most challenging tasks for refugee parents in Turkish schools. Content analysis was conducted on the observation notes and interview data. Questionnaire findings were analyzed using descriptive statistics, as well as Cronbach's alpha, to calculate the internal reliability of the frequency (0.84) and difficulty (0.90) data, which was acceptably high in both cases.

4B.4 Findings

4B.4.1 Identifying Target Tasks: Findings from Observation and Interviews

Classroom observation on the last day of the semester included three main target tasks performed by all parents: (1) small talk with other parents before the report card ceremony on topics such as weather, work, and vacation plans; (2) reading students' report card; and (3) having one-on-one short conversations with the teacher regarding their children's academic progress and study plan for the semester break. Before the report card ceremony, an unforeseen emergency arose when a student injured his head during a classroom activity. The teacher called the student's parents to take him to the hospital, but since the parents were not available, the teacher herself took the student to the hospital and updated the parents on the phone regularly. The teacher indicated that at least once a month, they would encounter such emergencies, which required them to call the injured student's parents promptly.

Interviews with parents, teachers, and school administrators offered further insights into different types of target tasks for refugee parents in the K–12 school context. Parents, especially from the K–4 level, indicated that dropping off/picking up the student, communicating with the teacher and other parents on *WhatsApp* chat groups, and helping the student with daily homework were among the most frequent tasks they performed daily. Most of the reported tasks were performed by mothers across all grade levels. Teachers reported that they use *WhatsApp* chat or text-messages (i.e., SMS) to send announcements ranging from last-minute requests for classroom materials to parent–teacher meeting invitations. School administrators also agreed that technology-mediated communication is key to their interaction with parents. Schools have been moving away from traditional communication platforms (e.g., written official letters) toward digital media, such as text-messages and e-okul, an online learning information and management platform provided by the Turkish Ministry of National Education (MoNE), to communicate with parents. Parents receive regular text-messages and reminders from school officials about teacher–parent meetings, and workshops organized by the school counselor, as well as automated texts from e-okul about their children's grades and absenteeism reports. Classroom observation and interviews with three groups of insiders suggested thirty target tasks in total, which informed the questionnaire administered to a larger population of parents across K–12.

4B.4.2 Findings from the Questionnaire: Frequency and Difficulty of Target Tasks

Table 4B.1 shows the perceived frequency and difficulty of the thirty target tasks. In terms of frequency, technology-mediated receptive reading tasks, such as reading text-messages sent by the teacher, other parents, and/or the school, and using e-okul to monitor student's progress, ranked highest on the list. These tasks require a smartphone with Internet access. Two of the most frequent interactional tasks, dropping off/picking up the student and helping the student with homework, were daily tasks performed by parents. Other interactional tasks included communicating with the room parent, reading and responding to text-messages in parent–parent and teacher–parent *WhatsApp* chat groups, and attending parent–teacher meetings.

Several interactional tasks were generally classified as more challenging. These included collaboration and communication with other parents and the room parent regarding class activities, responding to *WhatsApp* messages on teacher–parent and parent–parent chat groups, and having phone or face-to-face conversations with the teacher, other parents, and/or school administrators. Information on the perceived difficulty of target tasks by L1 Turkish-speaking parents is important to gather, as it shows that

Table 4B.1 *Perceived frequency and difficulty of thirty target tasks*

Questionnaire Item	N	Frequency* Mean	SD	Rank***	Difficulty** Mean	SD	Rank***
A. Parent–administrator communication							
1. Enrolling the student in school	53	2.32	0.89	15	1.98	0.63	16
2. Filling out documents related to school registration	53	2.11	0.67	18	1.85	0.57	21
3. Having a face-to-face conversation with school administrators	53	2.15	0.53	17	2.02	0.57	14
4. Having a phone conversation with school administrators	53	1.79	0.57	23	2.17	0.53	7
5. Signing a school field trip permission slip	53	2.43	0.69	13	1.79	0.79	23
6. Calling the administration in the event of an emergency	53	2.00	0.78	22	1.92	0.79	18
7. Submitting a doctor's note to the school administration	53	2.07	0.65	19	1.81	0.73	22
8. Attending parent workshops held by the school	53	2.28	0.70	16	2.00	0.65	15
9. Reading text-messages sent by the school	53	2.84	0.99	4	1.87	1.02	20
10. Reading official documents sent by the school	53	2.73	0.81	8	1.85	0.91	21
11. Attending meetings held by the school counselor	53	2.43	0.93	13	2.06	0.95	13
12. Having a face-to-face meeting with the school counselor	53	2.02	0.80	21	2.09	1.04	11
B. Parent–teacher communication							
13. Dropping off and picking up the student	53	2.96	1.07	2	2.21	1.01	5
14. Engaging in small talk with the teacher(s)	53	2.43	0.77	13	1.89	0.80	19
15. Having a face-to-face meeting with the teacher about the student's academic standing	53	2.40	0.60	14	1.94	0.77	17
16. Having a phone conversation with the teacher about the student's academic standing	53	2.04	0.81	20	2.11	0.89	10
17. Attending parent–teacher meetings	53	2.70	0.75	9	1.92	0.70	18
18. Reading text-messages on teacher–parent WhatsApp groups	53	3.04	1.18	1	2.07	1.36	12
19. Responding to text-messages on teacher–parent WhatsApp groups	53	2.57	1.26	10	2.40	1.38	3
20. Reading text-messages sent by the teacher	53	2.96	1.24	2	2.19	1.40	6
21. Reading official documents sent by the teacher	53	2.81	0.79	6	1.68	0.73	25
22. Informing the teacher via phone in the event of an emergency	53	2.51	0.90	11	1.89	0.93	19
C. Parent–parent communication							
23. Having a face-to-face conversation with other parents	50	2.28	0.70	16	2.14	0.89	8
24. Reading and responding to text-messages on parent–parent WhatsApp groups	50	2.80	1.12	7	2.22	1.17	4

Table 4B.1 (cont.)

Questionnaire Item	N	Frequency Mean	SD	Rank	Difficulty Mean	SD	Rank
25. Communicating with the room parent about class activities	50	2.82	1.35	5	2.52	1.46	2
26. Collaborating with other parents about class activities	50	2.48	1.09	12	2.58	1.20	1
D. Other tasks							
27. Helping the student with homework	50	2.94	0.98	3	2.40	1.01	3
28. Monitoring the student's academic progress through an online information management system (e.g., e-okul)	50	3.04	0.95	1	1.72	0.78	24
29. Shopping for school supplies requested by the teacher/ school	50	2.82	0.80	5	2.12	0.80	9
30. Reading the student's report card	50	2.82	0.85	5	1.68	0.68	25

Notes:
* Frequency scale: 1 – never, 2 – sometimes, 3 – frequent, 4 – very frequent;
** Difficulty scale: 1 – very easy, 2 – easy, 3 – difficult, 4 – very difficult
*** Rank ordered based on the mean score

interpersonal tasks might also be more challenging for refugee parents; however, these findings should be interpreted carefully. Parents who speak Turkish as an L1 might have found certain tasks more difficult for reasons other than task and language-related factors. For instance, some working mothers we interviewed reported that keeping up with messages on *WhatsApp* chat groups was especially difficult for them, since they hardly had time for it after a busy day. One limitation of our study is that we were unable to collect data from Syrian refugee parents as we did not speak Arabic. Nevertheless, we predict that these tasks are also challenging for refugee parents given that successful completion of these tasks would involve a number of steps. We take the difficulty findings into consideration when sequencing target task types and target tasks, as well as observation and interview findings with regard to the communicative nature of these tasks.

4B.5 Developing a Task-Based Curriculum Based on the Needs Analysis

We adapted Serafini and Torres's (2015) task-selection procedure to suggest a sequence of target tasks for a beginner-to-elementary level course for refugee parents in Turkey. First, based on the mean scores,[1] we categorized target tasks as

---
[1] Mean of 2.50 was used as a threshold for categorization as it is the middle point on the 1 to 4 Likert scale of the questionnaire.

- high frequency (M ≥ 2.50)
- low frequency (M < 2.50)
- high difficulty (M ≥ 2.50)
- low difficulty (M < 2.50).

We mostly focused on high-frequency tasks for curriculum development, since refugee parents would be expected to perform these tasks daily or weekly. Sixteen tasks were categorized as high-frequency. Fifteen of them fell into the intersection of the high-frequency and low-difficulty categories, and one task was in the high-frequency and high-difficulty categories. The remaining fourteen low-frequency tasks were discarded, except "engaging in small talk with the teacher(s)" and "having a face-to-face meeting with the teacher about the student's academic standing," because most parents and teachers at the K–4 level we interviewed reported these two tasks to be a part of their frequent communicative practice. This procedure led to eighteen target tasks in total, which we grouped into four target task types, taking into consideration the perceived difficulty and insight gained from observation and interview findings with regard to task complexity. Table 4B.2 demonstrates the four target task types and target tasks that can inform a Turkish language course specific to refugee parents.

Proposed target task types are sequenced to progress from more frequently performed, less complex tasks, to tasks that require more collaboration and familiarity with formal Turkish. It is important to note that a robust investigation of the cognitive complexity of tasks (Robinson, 2001), including collection and analysis of target discourse samples, is needed to determine the most optimal sequence for a task-based curriculum.

4B.6 Conclusion

This study is the first to conduct a NA to uncover the Turkish language needs of refugee parents in Turkey, an understudied learner population. The triangulated findings from insider sources (parents, teachers, and administrators) through nonparticipant observation, interviews, and a questionnaire, revealed that technology-mediated receptive tasks, such as reading text/*WhatsApp* messages sent by the teacher, other parents, and/or the school and using e-okul to monitor student's progress, as well as interactional tasks, including dropping off/picking up the student and helping the student with homework, were among the most frequent tasks. Communicating and collaborating with other parents about school-related tasks was perceived to be most difficult. Using the NA findings, we then proposed a sequence of target task types and target tasks for a task-based curriculum that can be implemented by the MoNE to address the real-life needs of Syrian refugees, who are responsible for their children

Table 4B.2 *Target task types and target tasks*

Target task types	Target tasks
1. Following and responding to announcements and requests	Reading text-messages on teacher–parent WhatsApp groups
	Responding to text-messages on teacher–parent WhatsApp groups
	Reading and responding to text-messages on parent–parent WhatsApp groups
2. Monitoring the student	Dropping off and picking up the student
	Monitoring the student's academic progress through an online information management system (e.g., e-okul)
	Helping the student with homework
	Attending parent–teacher meetings
	Reading a student's report card
	Informing the teacher in the event of an emergency via phone
	Having a face-to-face meeting with the teacher about the student's academic standing
3. Reading official texts	Reading text-messages sent by the school
	Reading official documents sent by the school
	Reading text-messages sent by the teacher
	Reading official documents sent by the teacher
4. Collaborating on class activities	Engaging in small talk with the teacher(s)
	Communicating with the room parent about class activities
	Collaborating with other parents about class activities
	Shopping for school supplies requested by the teacher/school

enrolled in Turkish schools and therefore need to complete various communicative tasks in Turkish. Currently, there are MoNE-funded Turkish language courses offered free for refugees in public education centers in fifty-two cities in Turkey; however, the curricula for these language courses do not reflect the genuine communicative needs of refugee learners. Using a task-based curriculum built on a systematic NA such as the one reported in this study will ultimately be most helpful to this population, given how critical it is for refugee parents to complete target tasks to participate effectively in their school community in the host country. Findings of this NA can be a springboard for the MoNE to develop a Turkish language course specific to refugee parents. The next steps toward implementing a TBLT course in this context are conducting analysis of target discourse and developing pedagogic tasks and appropriate task-based assessment. We hope that this study motivates further research on the next steps and encourages language programs with adult refugee populations in other contexts to carry out their own language NA.

Further Reading

Long, M. H. (2005), ed. *Second language needs analysis*. Cambridge: Cambridge University Press.
Serafini, E. J., Lake, J. B., and Long, M. H. (2015). Needs analysis for specialized learner populations: Essential methodological improvements. *English for Specific Purposes*, 40, 11–26.
Loewen, S. (2004). Second language concerns for refugee children. In R. Hamilton and D. Moore, eds. *Educational interventions for refugee children: Theoretical perspectives and implementing best practice*. London: Routledge, pp. 35–52.
Miller, J., Austin Windle, J., and Yazdanpanah, L. K. (2014). Planning lessons for refugee-background students: Challenges and strategies. *International Journal of Pedagogies and Learning*, 9(1), 38–48.
Calvert, M. and Sheen, Y. (2015). Task-based language learning and teaching: An action-research study. *Language Teaching Research*, 19(2), 226–44.

Study Questions

1. This NA relied on data from insider sources. What other sources could be included in a language NA for adult refugee learners, for instance, for vocational or other purposes?
2. Considering our NA findings, discuss possible factors that may influence task sequencing in a TBLT curriculum.
3. After identification of target tasks, the next stage in a task-based NA is an analysis of target discourse, analyzing genuine language samples that are produced during the completion of those tasks. Based on these NA findings, what target discourse samples (written texts, written, and/or oral interactions) could be analyzed for developing pedagogic tasks?

References

Aykırı, K. (2017). Sınıf öğretmenlerinin sınıflarındaki Suriyeli öğrencilerin eğitim durumlarına ilişkin görüşleri. *Turkish Journal of Primary Education*, 2, 44–56.
Er, A. R. and Bayındır, N. (2015). İlkokula giden mülteci çocuklara yönelik sınıf öğretmenlerinin pedagojik yaklaşımları. *Uluslararası Sosyal ve Eğitim Bilimleri Dergisi*, 2(4), 175–85.
Ergen, H. and Şahin, E. (2019). Sınıf öğretmenlerinin Suriyeli öğrencilerin eğitimi ile ilgili yaşadıkları problemler. *Mustafa Kemal Üniversitesi Sosyal Bilimler Enstitüsü Dergisi*, 19(44), 377–405.

Kiremit, R. F., Akpınar, Ü., and Akcan, A. T. (2018). Suriyeli öğrencilerin okula uyumları hakkında öğretmen görüşleri. *Kastamonu Eğitim Dergisi*, 26(6), 2139–49.

Long, M. H. (2005), ed. *Second language needs analysis*. Cambridge: Cambridge University Press.

Olgun-Baytaş, M. and Toker, Ş. (2019). *Translanguaging as a pedagogical approach with Syrian refugee learners in Turkey: Lessons learned from a collaborative inquiry*. Individual paper presentation at the American Association for Applied Linguistics, Atlanta, Georgia.

Robinson, P. (2001). Task complexity, task difficulty, and task production: Exploring interactions in a componential framework. *Applied Linguistics*, 22, 27–57.

Serafini, E. J., Lake, J. B., and Long, M. H. (2015). Needs analysis for specialized learner populations: Essential methodological improvements. *English for Specific Purposes*, 40, 11–26.

Serafini, E. J. and Torres, J. (2015). The utility of needs analysis for non-domain expert instructors in designing task-based Spanish for the professions curricula. *Foreign Language Annals*, 48(3), 447–72.

UNHRC. (2018). Global trends: Forced displacement in 2018. Retrieved from: https://www.unhcr.org/5d08d7ee7.pdf.

UNHRC. (2019). Syria regional refugee response. Retrieved from: https://data2.unhcr.org/en/situations/syria/location/113.

Uzun, E. M. and Bütün, E. (2016). Okul öncesi eğitim kurumlarındaki suriyeli sığınmacı çocukların karşılaştıkları sorunlar hakkında öğretmen görüşleri. *Uluslararası Erken Çocukluk Eğitimi Çalışmaları Dergisi*, 1(1), 72–83.

4C

Task-Based Language Teaching in a Japanese University

From Needs Analysis to Evaluation

Craig Lambert

4C.1 Context

The project took place at a municipal university in southern Japan between April 2001 and February 2006. The university was rated highly in the region for its foreign language department, and it attracted learners each year from as far away as Hiroshima in the north and Okinawa in the south. Cohorts of 125–150 English majors entered the program each year, and more than 500 English majors were enrolled in the four-year program at any given time.

The vast majority of English majors at the university were at the intermediate level (TOEIC [Test of English for International Communication] C-Level, 470–730; CEFR [Common European Framework of Reference for Languages] B1–B2), which means that they had "sufficient knowledge for daily activities and conducting business within certain limits" (Educational Testing Service, 2008). Exceptions were a subpopulation of students who had returned from living or studying abroad. This created a positively skewed distribution of proficiency scores in the population, with the upper tail extending to TOEIC B-Level (730–860, CEFR C1) and even A-Level (860–990, CEFR C2).

The English program could be characterized as one in which "teaching is defined in terms which exclude any concept of need" (West, 1994). Learners often majored in English because their secondary school English scores made them competitive, and they needed a university degree to obtain stable employment. Japanese companies typically trained their employees after hiring, and university background demonstrated capacity rather than meeting specific job requirements. In fact, English majors often received positions that did not require English at all.

In the first two years of the program, learners completed basic studies courses. In the third and fourth years, they specialized in areas such as translation, interpretation, literature, drama, business English, and English teaching. The basic studies classes consisted of grammar, history, and culture, together with taster courses in translation, interpretation, business English, literature, and teaching English as a foreign language (TEFL). Japanese was typically the medium of instruction. The oral English strand was added to the basic studies curriculum. These four semester-long courses met once a week for ninety minutes over fifteen-week semesters. The entire strand consisted of approximately ninety contact hours of instruction.

In April 2000, the author was hired with tenure and asked to coordinate the oral English strand. Teaching loads were reallocated, so that the author and two full-time contract teachers taught the new courses. One was a new hire who had an MA in TESOL (teaching English to speakers of other languages), and the other had an MA in English literature with several years of full-time English as a foreign language (EFL) teaching experience at the university. Both teachers were committed to helping the author develop the new program and given reasonable teaching loads to allow them the time to do so. The university also provided funding to conduct a task-based needs analysis.

4C.2 Needs Analysis

In order to identify English majors' future needs, it was necessary to draw on the experiences of in-service graduates and managers in target workplace domains (Long, 2005). Previous research had shown that reliable dimensions of Japanese English majors' opinions regarding their second language needs were too general to serve as input for second language course design (Lambert, 2001).

The needs analysis took place concurrently with the early stages of writing and piloting instructional materials. It involved an iterative approach to building consensus among graduates and experts on the critical tasks English majors faced after graduation (see Lambert [2010] for details). Following Long (2005), multiple data sources and methods of data collecting were combined and triangulated. The needs analysis began with a document analysis of the job-placement records available in the Office of Student Affairs. This served to identify the workplace domains into which English majors had been placed over the five years preceding the study. Business and education accounted for 93 percent of job placements. Next, semi-structured ethnographic interviews were conducted with experienced informants in these two workplace domains. The interviews provided a sense of how informants conceptualized their duties as a basis for designing an open-ended survey. The survey was sent to all

English majors who had graduated over the five-year period preceding the study, requesting descriptive information on their use of English. The results were summarized and recirculated to respondents for modifications, in order to identify patterns. Approximately 150 target tasks were mentioned in the interviews and questionnaires, but it was possible to categorize these into 14 task-types that were common to both workplace domains. This list provided a basis for a final closed-item survey to all English majors who had graduated over the twenty-five-year period preceding the study. The questionnaire asked them to rate the fourteen task-types and eight criteria for success that had emerged in terms of criticality within their workplace domains.

Of the 198 informants who responded to the final questionnaire, 49 percent were in business and 44 percent in education. Of the 98 respondents in business, 58 percent had more than ten years' experience in the field, 29 percent had three to ten years, and 13 percent had less than three years. At least 20 percent held positions at the managerial level. The primary subcategories of business were civil service (city hall, post office, public welfare, and nonprofit organizations), the travel industry (airlines, travel agencies, and hotels), planning (advertising, graphic design, and printing), manufacturing (electronics appliances and precision instruments), retail sales, and clerical work. Of the eighty-seven respondents in education, 72 percent had more than ten years' experience, 15 percent had between three and ten years', and 13 percent had less than three years. At least 17 percent worked at the level of principal or program coordinator, and 36 percent as classroom teachers. Table 4C.1 summarizes the fourteen task-types in terms of criticality.

Table 4C.1 *Criticality of task-types across workplace domains (n=198)*

1	Locating information from English sources	2.97
2	Translating documents from English to Japanese	2.78
3	Summarizing English information in Japanese	2.74
4	Creating and editing official English documents	2.72
5	Interpreting between Japanese and English speakers	2.58
6	Sending/receiving official communications by email	2.46
7	Asking for/giving advice	2.43
8	Making/taking telephone inquiries	2.42
9	Discussing socially	2.36
10	Explaining procedures/arrangements	2.35
11	Negotiating terms and conditions	2.33
12	Assisting English-speaking customers	2.17
13	Solving problems in groups	2.11
14	Promoting products	1.75

Values for each task-type indicate mean criticality on a scale of 1–4, from unimportant to essential.

Table 4C.2 *Criticality of criteria of success on oral tasks (n=198)**

1	Being able to communicate the meaning sufficiently	3.28
2	Using an appropriate range of vocabulary	2.92
3	Demonstrating cultural awareness	2.92
4	Speaking politely	2.89
5	Responding naturally while listening	2.78
6	Speaking with good pronunciation	2.61
7	Speaking fluently without too many pauses and repetitions	2.41
8	Speaking accurately without too many grammatical errors	2.29

*Values for each criterion indicate mean criticality on a scale of 1–4, from unimportant to essential

The most critical tasks for English majors (Tasks 1–6 in Table 4C.1) involved written rather than oral English skills. These tasks included searching for needed information from sources, such as the Internet and the news. They also involved translating, summarizing, and editing written English documents, such as teaching materials, company catalogs, and contracts. Interpreting from Japanese to English when foreign guests visited schools or companies was also critical. Task-types involving interactive oral English skills (Tasks 7–14 in Table 4C.1) were of lesser importance.

Table 4C.2 summarizes the results for the criticality of criteria for success on oral English tasks across the workplace domains. When speaking English in the Japanese workplace, pragmatics was more important than fluency or grammatical accuracy (Lambert & Kormos, 2014). Following effective task completion (Criterion 1 in Table 4C.2), appropriateness in terms of lexical choice, cultural awareness, politeness, and language of listening (e.g., backchannels) were considered more important than pronunciation, grammatical accuracy, and fluency.

4C.3 Goals and Objectives

The results of the needs analysis indicated that oral English skills were a secondary priority for English majors in terms of immediate future need. Furthermore, separate courses in the English curriculum were devoted to translation, simultaneous interpretation, business English and advanced English grammar (Tasks 1–6 in Table 4C.1). Japanese specialists with years of work experience in these areas before entering academia taught these courses.

Meetings were set up with senior academic and administrative staff to discuss the results and build a consensus on goals and objectives for the program. Three goals emerged from these discussions. First, adding devoted oral English courses to the basic studies curriculum had not been a matter of immediate need, but rather of capacity-building. Need can drive capacity, but capacity can also drive need. A second consensus was that oral English classes would increase Japanese learners' interest and motivation across the English curriculum. As the capacity to interact in English developed, learners might develop interests and corresponding desires to pursue them. Finally, a third consensus was that graduates who could speak English would increase the accountability of the university's English program in the eyes of primary employers. Discussion thus resulted in three goals for the oral English course:

- build the interactive and pragmatic competence of English majors
- increase interest and motivation across the English program
- increase the accountability of the program with employers.

Eight task-types (Tasks 7–14 in Table 4C.1) involving oral interaction skills had been identified that could function as objectives for the course. A task-based syllabus could be organized around these tasks, and pedagogic tasks relevant to learners' needs could be developed based on them.

Finally, the needs analysis provided a foundation for criterion-based measures of assessing task performance. Assessment would focus primarily on task completion and pragmatics rather than accuracy and fluency (Table 4C.2).

4C.4 Syllabus Design

Table 4C.3 summarizes the syllabuses created for the four semesters of the program. These provided coverage of the oral task-types and target tasks identified in the needs analysis. Several parallel versions of pedagogic tasks were created for each module to allow adequate practice, and progressively more challenging versions of these pedagogic tasks were created for subsequent lessons in each module, based on reasoning demands, the amount of information required, and the learners' role in generating task content. Reasoning demands typically involved the need to incorporate contingencies, account for multiple perspectives (Lambert & Robinson, 2014; Robinson, 2010), or compare options explicitly (Lambert, 2019; Lambert & Nakamura, 2019). Information load typically involved incorporating more information, multiple types of information, or completing a larger number of sub-tasks connected with the information (Robinson, 2010). Finally, task content involved moving from initial pedagogic tasks in which fictitious content was supplied by the materials writers to authentic content supplied by the learners' based on their personal experiences (Lambert, 1998, 2017; Ellis, Skehan, Li, Shintani & Lambert, 2020, chap. 6).

Table 4C.3 *Syllabus content and task-types represented*

Module	Content	Task-types
Semester 1		
Schedule module	Organize events	Negotiate terms
	Plan and organize events	Negotiate terms
	Organize contingent events	Solve problems
Map and instruction module	Give directions indoors	Explain procedures
	Give directions round town	Explain procedures
	Teach recipes	Explain procedures
Social module	Whodunit?	Solve problems
	Relate short anecdotes	Discuss socially
	Create and relate anecdotes	Discuss socially
Semester 2		
Travel industry module	Explain itineraries	Telephone inquires
	Explain tours	Explain arrangements
	Compare tours	Assist customers
	Promote tours	Promote products
Problem-solving scenario module	Express and support opinions	Give advice
	Clarify and elaborate opinions	Ask for advice
	Compare multiple perspectives	Negotiate terms
	Make informed decisions	Solve problems
Electronics industry module	Promote electronic products	Promote products
	Explain how to use office equipment	Explain procedures
	Respond to and log customer complaints	Assist customers
	Propose and evaluate business ideas	Solve problems
Semester 3		
Dear Abby module	Summarize and give advice on problems	Give advice
	Multiple perspectives	Solve problems
Job search module	Select the best people for jobs	Solve problems
	Interview simulations	Solve problems
Delivery routes module	Optimize work procedures	Negotiate terms
	Relate plans to others	Explain procedures
Customer service module	Travel agency	Telephone inquires
	Restaurant	Assist customers
	Travel agency	Negotiate conditions
Real estate industry module	Describe apartments	Promote products
	Compare apartments	Give advice
	Outline accommodation options	Solve problems
Semester 4		
International travel module	Negotiate a ten-day travel itinerary to UK	Negotiate terms
	Negotiate a ten-day travel itinerary to USA	Explain procedures
	Plan a thirty-day trip combining transport	Solve problems
Social module	Interpret symbolic value of pictures	Discuss socially
	Interpret English haiku poems	Discuss socially
	Interpret news stories	Discuss socially
	Odd one out	Solve problems
Economic problems module	Summarize and give advice on problems	Give/ask for advice
	Develop company strategies as a team	Solve problems

4C.4.1 Assessment

Criterion-referenced assessments incorporated five performance criteria (task completion, negotiation of meaning, lexical range, politeness, and language of listening). At the end of each semester, instructors assessed learners' oral performance on each criterion on a scale of one to four (inadequate, in need of improvement, sufficient, or exceptional). Criterion-level performance was three on each of the criteria. Weekly written conversations prepared as homework were also assessed.

Time constraints made it impossible to assess learners on all task-types within a given semester. Instead, they received three to five pedagogic tasks representing the types covered, and a copy of the assessment criteria, for practice. Pairs of students then performed one of these tasks chosen at random for the final assessment. All were two-way interactive tasks (Long, 1990), so learners simultaneously performed as speaker and listener.

4C.5 Materials

Based on concurrent piloting of task sequences during the needs analysis, some key facets of instructional material suited to the program were identified:

1. A simple and clear pedagogic structure to the units would establish expectations and procedures on the part of teacher and learners and optimize learners' time on task and teachers' autonomy.
2. Alternative practice opportunities in each module would keep learners more interested and engaged (rather than repetition of parallel pedagogic tasks each week).
3. In addition to interactive pedagogic tasks, receptive pedagogic tasks (listening and reading) within each unit would provide a means of introducing new task-relevant language and drawing learners' attention to forms related to the assessment criteria within the context of communication (Long, 2000). The most effective way to do this was to sequence tasks so that learners: (1) attempted interactive versions of a task-type, (2) performed receptive versions based on native speakers performing the same pedagogic tasks, and (3) performed alternate versions of the interactive pedagogic tasks. This approach seemed to best sensitize each learner to gaps in his or her linguistic repertoire and provide opportunities to fill them.
4. Opportunities for personal investment in terms of learner-generated content helped optimize learners' task performance (Lambert, 2002; Lambert & Minn, 2007; Lambert, Philp & Nakamura, 2017; Lambert & Zhang, 2019). Two points in the task sequences provided opportunities to achieve this. Before completing the first interactive task sequence, learners completed a discussion task in which they shared previous

task-relevant experiences. The aim was to generate a richer range of task-relevant lexis and content on the interactive tasks and facilitate the noticing of developmentally relevant gaps in second language resources. The second intervention point came after each lesson. As homework, learners' generated authentic content for the pedagogic tasks in the next lesson, based on personal experience. Thus, each module typically began with teacher-generated content in the first lesson and moved to learner-generated content in subsequent lessons.

Each ninety-minute lesson incorporated pedagogic tasks with five foci: (1) prior knowledge activation, (2) interaction to activate current second language resources, (3) receptive tasks to provide meaningful exposure to new and various task-relevant second language forms, (4) interaction to incorporate new ways to do the task, and (5) conversation writing and content generation as revision and planning for the subsequent lesson. The framework of the lessons was as follows (see Lambert, 2020, for details):

Step 1 – *Warm-up (five minutes):* Brief receptive tasks familiarized learners with the objective of the unit and task-relevant pragmalinguistic features. These tasks frequently involved matching or ordering sentences in task-based monologues or dialogues and identifying forms used for different pragmatic functions.

Step 2 – *Share your own ideas (ten minutes):* This step consisted of an interactive discussion task to activate task-relevant personal experiences and lexis. Questions were provided or learner-generated content prepared as homework for this step.

Step 3 – *See how well you can do the task (twenty-five minutes):* This step alternated two formats. The first involved three parallel pedagogic tasks to activate and automatize current task-relevant linguistic resources (Lambert, Kormos & Minn, 2017; Lambert & Robinson, 2014). Based on individual differences, the teacher could provide pre-task planning-time of some sort before this stage, require learners to repeat one of the tasks with different partners each time, or require them to complete all three tasks with the same partners. Teachers could also impose increasing time pressure on task performance. The second format consisted of a sequence of tasks in which the output from one task provided essential input to the next (Lambert, 2004).

Step 4 – *Learn new ways to do the task (twenty-five minutes):* Audio samples of task performances were developed, based on the performances of eight native speakers of English of different gender and ethnic backgrounds. They performed the same tasks that learners performed in Stage 3 of the lesson. The key functions and forms in each speaker's approach to the task were preserved and included in more condensed scripts that were rerecorded in the university's recording studio. After performing each receptive task with a focus on meaning, form-focused activities drew learners' attention to forms relevant to the criteria of assessment. Activities used to focus learners' attention in this way were listening to find the mistakes in printed versions, identifying multiple forms to accomplish specific functions, guessing answers to cloze passages and listening to check them, and dictation of passages of the performances.

Step 5 – *Try the task again (twenty-five minutes):* The two formats used were the same as Step 3 above. Groups received pre-task planning-time, if necessary, to incorporate new forms from Step 4.

Step 6 – *Homework:* Learners reviewed the transcripts for Step 4 and prepared a written version of a task performance that improved on their performance in class. They also developed authentic task content based on personal experience.

4C.6 Evaluation

In January 2006, the 275 English majors enrolled in the first two years of the English major course completed a survey eliciting their responses to the pedagogic tasks and supporting activities. They rated each in terms of perceived usefulness for improving their oral English on a four-point scale (not useful, sufficient, effective, or ideal). Table 4C.4 summarizes the results for the tasks.

The two most popular tasks (travel and electronics) covered four task-types, including assisting English-speaking customers, receiving telephone inquiries, explaining procedures and arrangements, and promoting products. The second two (anecdotes and problem scenarios) covered the remaining four task-types (solving problems as groups, negotiating terms and conditions, giving advice, and discussing socially). Task-based language teaching thus provided a means of designing highly popular tasks, based on identified learner needs, in a context in which generalist approaches to instruction were the norm.

On the other hand, the least popular pedagogic tasks (interpreting haiku poems) were not directly related to learners' future needs. This unit was written by one of the teachers in the program using the six-step instructional framework developed for the project. After writing many units together, the teachers were capable of writing units on their own using the instructional framework. The clear pedagogic structure resulted a sense of ownership of the program as well as high levels of motivation. This unit was connected to the teacher's interests. As Table 4C.4 indicates, the unit was not evaluated highly, but this was an important

Table 4C.4 *Evaluation of pedagogic tasks*

Pedagogic Tasks	n*	Evaluation				Mean
		ideal	effective	sufficient	not useful	
Travel customer service tasks	151	38	87	25	1	3.07
Electronics customer service tasks	117	39	48	26	4	3.04
Anecdote tasks	116	36	47	30	3	3.00
Problem-scenario tasks	119	39	45	31	4	3.00
Map tasks	118	31	58	24	5	2.98
Apartment customer service tasks	117	39	42	27	9	2.95
News interpretation tasks	131	33	56	37	3	2.92
Restaurant customer service tasks	150	34	74	38	4	2.92
Job search tasks	117	26	57	27	7	2.87
Dear Abby tasks	150	19	90	39	2	2.84
Picture interpretation tasks	155	29	70	48	8	2.77
Economic problem-solving tasks	129	22	62	37	8	2.76
Schedule problem-solving tasks	118	18	54	42	4	2.73
Haiku interpretation tasks	131	18	45	55	13	2.52

* Values represent those who completed/responded to each task on the questionnaire

learning experience for the teacher, and the autonomy and motivation fostered was important to the success of the program overall.

Table 4C.5 summarizes the results for the activities used to draw learners' attention to specific language and content within each lesson.

Learners found form-focused activities most helpful in conjunction with receptive pedagogic task performance, and as homework. The three activities learners felt most useful related to receptive pedagogic tasks. In addition to listening to someone do the tasks that they had just completed and performing the task as listener, learners found dictation of key passages and listening to find errors very helpful. They also found revisiting transcripts as homework, and writing improved conversations, helpful. Likewise, working with learner-generated content as homework and in class was helpful. Finally, learners valued identifying different forms used to achieve task-relevant functions. Cloze passages and sentence-matching were rated as the least helpful.

4C.7 Conclusions

This case study has described an example of how the principles of task-based language teaching as argued by Long (2000) were employed successfully in a context in which TENOR (teaching English for no obvious reason) was the norm. Some observations on what contributed to this success might provide input for projects in similar contexts:

Table 4C.5 *Evaluation of focus on form activities*

Processing stage	Activity	n	ideal	effective	sufficient	Not useful	Mean
Receptive task stage	Dictation	270	106	113	46	5	3.19
Receptive task stage	Listen for meaning	270	97	127	43	3	3.18
Receptive task stage	Find mistakes	271	80	138	47	6	3.08
Homework stage	Write conversations	272	65	139	59	9	2.96
Homework stage	Generate task content	272	44	151	72	5	2.86
Receptive task stage	Label forms for function	270	51	132	80	7	2.84
Prior knowledge stage	Question boxes	275	55	130	75	15	2.82
Receptive task stage	Guess and check cloze passages	270	60	97	98	15	2.75
Warm-up step in lesson	Match sentences	272	32	144	82	14	2.71

1. Ensure that the institution and academic staff recognize the need for the project. This is essential in acquiring funding, as well as securing workload reductions, access to university facilities and local introductions. In the present study, the author spent a year making the case for the project and securing support before initiating any work on it.
2. It is essential to have cooperative and motivated teachers on the project. Teachers' workloads should allow them to make a meaningful contribution. In the present case study, the author fostered a sense of ownership over the project in the teachers, and this enthusiasm transferred to their students.
3. If another project were conducted, an attempt would be made to expand the needs analysis to include an analysis of discourse stage (Hillman & Long, 2020; Long, this volume). In the present study, discourse samples were created based on pedagogic task performances rather than target task performances.
4. Likewise, if another project were conducted, the evaluation would seek to document learning on tasks. In the present study, evaluation was limited to learners' subjective responses to the program.

Instruction in many EFL contexts around the world is similar to what was faced in the present study, in that instruction is often "defined in terms which exclude any concept of need" (West, 1994). This case study demonstrates that task-based language teaching might provide a means of defining needs with enough precision to avoid TENOR in such educational contexts.

Further Reading

Ellis, R., Skehan, P., Li, S., Shintani, N., and Lambert, C. (2020). *Task-based language teaching: Theory and practice*. Cambridge: Cambridge University Press, Chapters 6–7.

Lambert, C. (2004). Reverse-engineering communication tasks. *ELT Journal*, 58(1), 18–27.

Lambert, C. (2020). Instructional frameworks for using tasks in task-based instruction. In C. Lambert and R. Oliver, eds. *Using tasks in second language teaching: Practice in diverse contexts*. Bristol: Multilingual Matters, pp. 13–32.

Lambert, C. and Robinson, P. (2014). Learning to perform a narrative task: A semester long study of task sequencing effects. In M. Baralt, R. Gilabert, and P. Robinson, eds. *Task sequencing and instructed second language learning*. London: Bloomsbury, pp. 207–30.

Study Questions

1. What were the future needs of the learners in pursuing the target language in this program?
2. What were the desires and interests of learners?
3. What constraints were involved in the educational and cultural context of the program?
4. What resources were available in terms of time and personnel for developing the program?

References

Educational Testing Service (2008). *TOEIC test data and analysis 2007: Number of examinees and scores in FY2007*. The Institute for International Business Corporation, TOEIC Steering Committee.

Ellis, R., Skehan, P., Li, S., Shintani, N., and Lambert, C. (2020). *Task-based language teaching: Theory and practice* Cambridge: Cambridge University Press, Chapters 6–7.

Hillman, K. and Long, M. (2020). A task-based needs analysis for US Foreign Service officers: The challenge of the Japanese celebration speech. In C. Lambert and R. Oliver, eds. *Using tasks in diverse contexts*. Bristol: Multilingual Matters.

Lambert, C. (1998). The role of the learner in classroom task performance. *Journal of Nanzan Junior College*, 26, 85–101.

Lambert, C. (2001). The viability of learner' beliefs and opinions as input for L2 course design. *RELC Journal*, 32(1), 1–15.

Lambert, C. (2002). Task sequencing and affective performance variables. *Kitakyushu University Faculty of Foreign Studies Bulletin*, 103, 97–175.

Lambert, C. (2004). Reverse-engineering communication tasks. *ELT Journal*, 58(1), 18–27.

Lambert, C. (2010). Task-based needs analysis: Putting principles into practice. *Language Teaching Research*, 14(1), 99–112.

Lambert, C. (2017). Tasks, affect and second language performance. *Language Teaching Research*, 21(6), 657–64.

Lambert, C. (2019). *Referent similarity and nominal syntax in task-based language teaching*. Singapore: Springer.

Lambert, C. (2020). Instructional frameworks for using tasks in task-based instruction. In C. Lambert, and R. Oliver, eds. *Using tasks in diverse contexts*. Bristol: Multilingual Matters.

Lambert, C. and Kormos, J. (2014). Complexity, accuracy and fluency in task-based research: Toward more developmentally-based measures of second language acquisition. *Applied Linguistics*, 35(5), 607–14.

Lambert, C., Kormos, J., and Minn, D. (2017). Task repetition and second language speech processing. *Studies in Second Language Acquisition*, 39, 167–96.

Lambert, C. and Nakamura, S. (2019). Proficiency-related variation in syntactic complexity: A study of English L1 and L2 oral descriptive discourse. *International Journal of Applied Linguistics*, 29, 248–64.

Lambert, C. and Minn, D. (2007). Personal investment in L2 task design and learning: A study of two Japanese learners of English. *ELIA: Estudios de Lingüística Inglesa Aplicada*, 7, 127–48.

Lambert, C., Philp, J., and Nakamura, S. (2017). Learner-generated content and engagement in L2 task performance. *Language Teaching Research*, 21 (6), 665–80.

Lambert, C. and Robinson, P. (2014). Learning to perform narrative tasks: A semester-long study of task sequencing effects. In M. Baralt, R. Gilabert, and P. Robinson, eds. *Task sequencing and instructed second language learning*. London: Bloomsbury, pp. 207–30.

Lambert, C. and Zhang, G. (2019). Engagement in the use of English and Chinese as second languages: The role of learner-generated content in instructional task design. *Modern Language Journal*, 103(2), 391–411.

Long, M. H. (1990). Task, group and task-group interactions. In S. Anivan, ed. *Language teaching methodology for the nineties*. Singapore: Regional English Language Centre, pp. 31–50.

Long, M. (2000). Focus on form in task-based language teaching. In R. D. Lambert and E. Shohamy, eds. *Language policy and pedagogy*. Amsterdam: John Benjamins, pp. 191–96.

Long, M. (2005). Methodological issues in learner needs analysis. In M. Long, ed. *Second language needs analysis*. Cambridge: Cambridge University Press, pp. 19–76.

Robinson, P. (2010). Situating and distributing cognition across task demands: The SSARC model of pedagogic task sequencing. In M. Putz and L. Sicola, eds. *Inside the learner's mind: Cognitive processing in second language acquisition*. Amsterdam: John Benjamins, pp. 243–68.

West, R. (1994). Needs analysis in language teaching. *Language Teaching*, 27 (1), 1–19.

4D

The Implementation of a Task-Based Spanish-Language Program in Qingdao, China

A Case Study

Melissa Baralt, Wang Fei, Zhanting Bu, Hao Chen,
José Morcillo Gómez, and Xunye Luan

4D.1 Introduction

This case study reports on the development, implementation, and evaluation of China's first university-level, fully task-based Spanish foreign-language program. The Spanish dual degree program at Qingdao University (QU) is the result of an international partnership between QU in Qingdao, China and Florida International University (FIU) in Miami, Florida. The collaboration has taken almost a decade to develop, with the universities' shared goals of (1) cultivating multilingual, globally aware citizens, (2) strengthening the educational relationship between China, the United States, and Latin America, and (3) developing a top-tier Spanish-language teacher-training program. In this chapter, we report on how we developed the program, describing our needs analysis study, program, team-based approaches to overcoming challenges, teacher training, community engagement, and ongoing evaluation process. A key aspect of our program is the direct link between task-based outcomes and real-world community outreach (e.g., presenting a final business plan to a local corporation; running the reading club; doing an interview with a radio station; teaching a lesson at a local school). We conclude with implications for task-based language teaching (TBLT) applications and for the teaching of Spanish as a foreign language in China.

4D.2 Background: Spanish-Language Study in China

China has seen a significant increase in Spanish foreign-language study in the past twenty years. In 1999, approximately 500 undergraduate students were studying Spanish; by 2016, this number had increased to almost 20,000 undergraduate students (Phillips, 2018). The increased interest in Spanish has been driven by China's expanded global business and trading ventures in Latin America and also, by growing job opportunities worldwide that require Spanish-language proficiency. This includes economic partnerships with Spain. China's Prime Minister, Li Keqiang, for example, stated that the China–Spain partnership is "the most strategic partnership for China in Europe," highlighting the Spanish-speaking country as the key to China's relationship with Europe (Esteban, 2016). A quick internet search of "Spanish" (in Chinese) provides several page results related to online course offerings for Spanish-language learning in China. Before 2005, Spanish classes were barely taught in private academies; now, it is easy to find private language centers that offer Spanish as a foreign language in every major city in China (González Puy, 2012). This shows that Spanish-language offerings are growing in public and private spaces in China, both in the traditional and online modalities.

Foreign-language education in China is considered a significant cultural resource and is also part of a "Chinese Culture Going Global" strategy to foster cross-cultural learning. Foreign-language education development in China has gone hand-in-hand with the nation's socioeconomic changes since the foundation of the People's Republic of China in 1949. At present, there are over 900 English-, 400 Japanese-, 100 Russian-, and 50 Spanish-language teaching faculty members across China's 1,200 universities and colleges. While China's Ministry of Education promotes a unified approach and publishes standards on the teaching of foreign languages (e.g., curriculum standards, shared syllabuses for foreign-language majors, and national exams), their implementation varies greatly in practice. For example, for Spanish-language teaching, all universities receive the Teaching Program for Basic and Advanced Spanish Language Majors in Chinese Superior Schools (*Programa de Enseñanza para Cursos Básicos y Superiores de las Especialidades de la Lengua Española en Escuelas Superiores Chinas*).

University-level Spanish-language teachers are expected to use this program to prepare students for the national exam. The Ministry is also working to expand foreign-language study opportunities at the K–12 level. A national curriculum for Spanish-language teaching at the high-school level was recently released; however, a shortage of qualified Spanish-language teachers has prevented this from being widespread. According to Fuliang Chang, Vice Dean at the Foreign Studies University of Beijing, Spanish-language professors (Chinese or foreign) must have at least a Master's degree in linguistics, literature or pedagogy of Spanish as a foreign language (*Español como Lengua Extranjera*) in order to work at Chinese universities. That said, China continues to rely heavily on native speakers of Spanish who teach in China. This is undergirded by the ideological trope in China that "native speaker status is better"; there is also a tendency to prefer peninsular native speakers (Wang, 2019).

4D.3 Needs Analysis and Outcome

With this as our sociocultural and historical backdrop, the vision upon inception of the FIU–QU program was to create a fully task-based Spanish foreign-language program. Once the university partnership was finalized, we began with a detailed needs analysis. Literature in applied linguistics shows that a careful analysis of learner needs for the targeted language is critical for foreign-language teaching and teacher training (Long, 2005). The purpose of the needs analysis was to inform the design of QU's Spanish-language and teacher-training programs. The first stage of our needs analysis included interviewing the following stakeholders:

- the QU vice provost
- twenty undergraduate students who were currently majoring in Spanish at QU (five from each year level)
- two QU graduates who were working for Chinese companies with clients in Latin America
- the QU vice chair of the Spanish program
- the QU director of international programs
- the QU vice dean for international programs
- QU Spanish-language teachers.

From this, we obtained insights into administrators' vision and goals for the students, and learned about Ministry of Education-mandated requirements, students' learning and career goals, sample real-world tasks that Chinese businesses do with the Spanish language, and teachers' perspectives on Spanish-language teaching.

Data from these interviews were used to create a bilingual questionnaire that we then sent out to all of the Spanish-language students at QU, with 118 students responding. We also observed classes and shadowed graduates of the program in their workplace. We additionally spoke with companies in Qingdao who require Spanish-language proficiency for various jobs. Our needs analysis thus employed multiple methods, including interviews, observations, and questionnaires, as well as multiple sources, such as administrators, teachers, students, graduates, workers, and job descriptions. While a detailed report on the needs analysis is beyond the scope of this chapter, key outcomes can be summarized in the areas of tasks, and then student, administrator, and teacher perspectives.

4D.3.1 Tasks

Several real-world tasks were generated from our needs analysis study, which we then organized into target task types and then into larger categories. For example, in the larger category of *Business*, an example of a target task type is *Communicating with a Client*. Within this task type we organized the tasks, which including skyping with a client, giving a factory tour via video, answering questions about a product, reporting an update via phone, reporting an update via email, listening to a client's concerns, and creating solutions for a client's concerns. The tasks were then organized across our different courses and sequenced into course syllabuses according to psycholinguistic research recommendations (Baralt, Gilabert & Robinson, 2014).

4D.3.2 Student Perspective

We learned from the needs analysis that Chinese undergraduate students at QU were keenly interested in achieving communicative competence in the Spanish language. While most wanted to engage in business with Latin America or Spain, many wanted to teach Spanish in China, work in the tourism industry for Spanish speakers, or serve in government. Several were interested in pursuing a graduate degree in Spanish abroad. QU students emphasized their desire to have more opportunities to practice oral conversation and to learn more about different Spanish linguistic varieties.

4D.3.3 Administrator Perspective

QU administrators wanted to prepare their students for the future job market. They expressed goals for their students in the Spanish language, such as engaging in business and commerce (with a focus on Latin America), becoming future teachers of Spanish, going abroad to continue Spanish-language studies, and working in the government in foreign trade. At the time of the needs analysis, four QU Spanish graduates were pursuing a Master's degree in Spain and one in Shanghai. Administrators wanted to broaden this group and their geographical reach. Administrators expressed the opinion that students should be able to do tasks such as write a resume and a cover letter in Spanish, and simultaneously interpret a video-based conference between a Chinese company and a client in Latin America. A challenge that administrators acknowledged was the desire to help students communicate better in Spanish while at the same time preparing them for the Chinese National Standards Test in Spanish that is mandated by the Ministry of Education.

4D.3.4 Teacher Perspective

Teachers were excited at the prospect of professional development opportunities and to be part of the program's creation. They expressed reservations about how to implement TBLT while also fulfilling the Foreign Language Teaching Advisory Board under China's Ministry of Education. Many of the teachers were taught Spanish themselves in a classroom where Chinese was used as the medium of instruction, and so they would need ongoing teacher support. We also learned from the teachers and from the coordinator about the value of the national standards tests. Teachers expressed a keen desire to help students communicate better and improve their oral proficiency, while at the same time prepare them for the national standards tests. We learned that these tests, the 4/8 national standards test bands, are organized by the Foreign Language Teaching Advisory Board. Board members comprise language professors and foreign language experts from Chinese universities across the country. The board members establish the national standards that guide teaching for their designated languages. All universities in China are required to register their foreign-language majors and to test them in bands 4 (basic level) and 8 (advanced level). Only students majoring in a foreign language may take these tests. The 4/8 test bands are widely recognized and highly esteemed in Chinese society – more so than the TOEFL (Test of English as a Foreign Language), DELE (*Diplomas de Español como Lengua Extranjera*), or TEF (*Test d'Evaluation de Français*). We learned that Chinese companies that require foreign-language proficiency for a job require band 4 or band 8 certification. Students' performance on the 4/8 test bands is also used nationally as an indication of the university's caliber for foreign-language teaching and learning. Teachers recognized the testing environment in China and acknowledged the challenges that it poses for the implementation of a TBLT-based program. However, preparing students for these tests, and administering these tests, would be mandatory alongside our TBLT program.

4D.4 Program Structure and Goals

At the onset, it was evident that implementing our program while also continuing with the Ministry of Education-mandated tests would be our greatest challenge. After several discussions, we decided to structure our program as follows. Students who declared a Spanish major at QU would do the QU, Ministry of Education curriculum in their first two years (completing China's basic level). They would then take the Spanish test band 4. In their second year, they would apply to the FIU–QU fully task-based Spanish program. We created a task-based assessment for this application process, as well as a criterion-referenced guide to assess students' performance for the tasks. If they passed, they could enter the program. Students would then begin the fully task-based program, which takes two years. The task-based program equips students with opportunities to do every task that emerged from the needs analysis (across various courses). In their fourth year, these students also take the Spanish test band 8; however, preparation for the test is their responsibility.

As part of the program, FIU sent two permanent Spanish teachers to live and teach at QU. These teachers both hold a PhD in Spanish and have had extensive training in Spanish applied linguistics and in TBLT. These teachers would implement the new task-based courses, teaching them at QU, as well as work with QU Spanish teachers. Every summer, another FIU faculty member would go to QU to teach an upper-level course, such as Spanish linguistics or a course that students voted for (e.g., Spanish-language linguistic varieties; culture in Spanish-speaking Caribbean countries). Course sizes could not be larger than thirty students. The instructors would also work closely with the QU Chinese Spanish-language teaching staff to gradually implement TBLT into their practice at the basic level, and, to generate team-based ideas for professional development. To diversify the program, QU also hired two teachers from Latin America to join the staff. In addition, Spanish teaching staff and the students would work to create extensive community outreach and engagement activities, as well as internships with companies in Shandong province and abroad. We would align these with the task-based assessments in the TBLT program. Finally, FIU assigned a teacher online, based in Miami, who provides online tutoring to students via virtual video meetings, online chat, or asynchronous exchanges.

4D.5 Challenges and Team-Based Solutions

Once we began to implement the task-based program with the first student cohort, we encountered several challenges. The first was a need to better connect the QU basic Spanish program (years 1–2) to the fully task-based program (years 3–4) – for both teachers *and* students. The basic Spanish program, which is designed by the Ministry of Education, provides students with courses in basic Spanish, Spanish listening, Spanish conversation, Spanish reading, Spanish grammar, Spanish interpretation and translation, as well as peninsular literature and Chinese culture in Spanish. To provide a brief example of what these courses look like, basic Spanish utilizes the textbook published by the Foreign Language Teaching and Research Press of China. The methodology is grammar-translation: students are told the meanings of words and phrases in Chinese and are then expected to memorize and translate sentences. The courses are informed by "hierarchical Confucianism" (Zhou & Li, 2015), which emphasizes the transmission of language knowledge by the teacher and does not cultivate communicative competence. Teachers stated that this approach is energy-consuming for them, and everyone agreed that it is less effective for students (students were facing difficulties in real communicative contexts). Coupled with this is the fact that TBLT training for Chinese teachers is rare to begin with (Orton, 2011; Scrimgeour, 2010); thus the teachers had no prior exposure to task-based training. Our solution was to acknowledge this and brainstorm ways as a team to slowly implement TBLT. We recognized that there *is* flexibility in implementing the Spanish basic-level courses, and that gradually implementing tasks into teachers' practice would assist us with this. Research shows that teachers are reluctant to change, for various reasons (East, 2012; Orton, 2010; Scrimgeour, 2010); however, the excitement about creating China's first fully task-based program for Spanish foreign language has been a driving motivation for all of us. Additionally, the average age of Spanish teachers at QU is thirty-four; we are a young program overall that is still accruing years of experience (see Gurzynski-Weiss, 2017, on the role of teachers' years of experience as a moderator of how TBLT is implemented). A gradual approach to TBLT has required extensive teacher training and support, as well as practice opportunities. So far, we have done this via teacher workshops, sharing a repertoire of tasks that are accessible to all in a task bank, and modeling of task-based methodology to implement the tasks. Our strategy, which we agreed upon as a team, has been first for everyone to introduce at least one task into their teaching practice per *unit*, and gradually, per *week* of teaching. So far, this has been an acceptable way to introduce "doing" TBLT in our contexts. It has also helped us to better connect the QU program with the fully task-based program that students begin in year 3. In this way, both students and teachers have felt better prepared to do tasks (measured by questionnaires). Nevertheless, we continue to experiment as based on teachers' needs.

A gradual approach to introducing TBLT has gone hand-in-hand with our second main challenge: the belief in China that "native speaker status is better." This ideology results in teachers doubting their proficiency level or not believing in themselves, which can lead to minimal exposure to, and use of, the target language. It also fosters a feeling of a tiered system of native and nonnative teachers in the same department, which is not productive for morale or team-based work. We have tackled this challenge by emphasizing that teachers do not have to have perfect proficiency in order to be excellent teachers. In fact, in his book on TBLT, Ellis (2003: 333) highlighted the benefits of nonnative speaking teachers:

> Medgyes (1994) points to several advantages of teachers being nonnative speakers – they provide good models for their students, they know what learning strategies can be usefully taught, they can supply information about the [target] language, they can anticipate and

prevent difficulties, they are good at showing empathy, and, most obviously, they can exploit the use of the students' [first language]. TBLT, however, may not be the most obvious vehicle for maximizing these strengths.

This research base is emphasized at all of our workshops and trainings. Explicit conversations about the issue, as well as practicing together at trainings, has helped us to combat the ideology, and we continue to work on it. We also have explicit conversations about attitudes toward peninsular linguistic varieties versus Latin American linguistic varieties. Additionally, our needs analysis brought to light the mismatch between QU administrators' goals for students – a focus on business with Latin America – and the unconscious preference for peninsular Spanish. We discuss this mismatch and brainstorm ways to address it. The recent hire of two Spanish teachers from Cuba at FIU and QU has helped to foster these conversations significantly.

The third challenge we faced is the foreign-language teaching context of Spanish in China. There is a lack of authentic communicative contexts for *both* teachers and students to use Spanish outside the classroom. Our solution to this – very much informed by our needs analysis – was to create various programs throughout our community, and to link these programs to students' task-based assessments. The following section provides some examples. These programs and task outcomes have created diverse and rich ways to use the language for real-world tasks outside the classroom. A team-based approach to overcoming these challenges has been critical in our implementation.

4D.6 Task-Based Language Teaching via Community Outreach and Community Service

The creation of community engagements in Spanish in Qingdao has helped to spearhead the success of our program. So far, our main components have been:

1. *Presenting business plans to real companies in Qingdao.* For our Spanish business class, we invite multinational Chinese companies to attend students' final presentations of their business plans. In some cases, students are assigned a company for whom they must come up with an idea, and students must go and present it to that company (e.g., Hisense). All of the pedagogic tasks that students worked on together in the classroom were sequenced and led up to these final presentations as their final exit task. The authenticity of this task has been exceptionally motivating and also, engages community partners with QU. Companies provide our students with feedback in addition to students' task-based assessment from their Spanish teacher.

2. *El Cine Club en Español*. (Spanish-language cinema club). To (1) foster cultural exchange, (2) serve the community of Qingdao, and (3) give our students and staff more opportunities to use Spanish in authentic contexts, we have also created a cinema club. Every month in the city of Qingdao, our TBLT program shows a movie in Spanish with Chinese subtitles. Before and after each showing, our students and teachers give a presentation on the film in Spanish. Students are entirely responsible for running the program, including creating posters in both Spanish and Chinese to promote the screenings to the community. They also advertise all Cine Club events in a Spanish-language WeChat group. The city of Qingdao has been very involved in supporting our Cine Club, hosting the movie showings at the 1907 Cinema Museum of Qingdao, the Mofeimo Art Gallery, and different movie theaters throughout the city. We have recently paired with the city's Bayou Cinema Club (a well-attended cinema club in Chinese in Qingdao) to further engage the community and encourage them to see Spanish-language films.
4. *National dubbing contest*. This interest and excitement about the Cine Club has also garnered participation in the Chinese National Dubbing in Spanish Contest, sponsored by the Foreign Studies University of Beijing. For this, teams of students from around the country "dub" movies into Spanish. Dubbing is the addition of a simultaneous translation audio overlap onto a movie in filmmaking. In 2018, QU Spanish-language students won second place in the nation. This was the first time in history that a university from Shandong province won a foreign-language national award.
5. *Club de lectura* (Spanish-language reading club). Based on students' needs, another program goal was to create an open space in the city of Qingdao to learn about and share Hispanic literature. Not only does this serve our own students and teachers by providing additional settings in which to use the language, it also serves our community. The aim of this club is to facilitate knowledge about Latin American and Spanish authors. The club meetings are hosted by Crown Plaza Hotel in Qingdao and are open to the public. A few months before each meeting, a novel in Spanish is chosen by our students and announced on social media. During the club meetings, students and teachers do a brief introduction and presentation on the author and the novel. Everyone is then invited to read aloud a brief section of the book, and this is followed by a group discussion on the plot and the historical context of the novel. All reading club meetings are entirely run by QU students. Some community members who do not speak Spanish have read translated books in Chinese and attended our meetings, contributing what they can in Chinese, with a student helping to interpret the community member's ideas. Spanish speakers living in Qingdao have also attended this club.

6. *Se Habla Español Radio Podcast*. Another community outreach program that created with our students is a Spanish-language podcast, housed within the Netease app. For this podcast, our students interview in Spanish (1) Hispanic people living in Qingdao or other cities in China, (2) Spanish-language academics from QU, FIU, and the Foreign Studies University in Beijing, and (3) Chinese citizens who speak Spanish, work in Chinese or multinational companies, and utilize Spanish often for work. So far, we have podcast participants from China, Colombia, Argentina, Costa Rica, Nicaragua, Ecuador, Perú, Chile, and Spain. Students from QU are fully responsible for conducting and editing the interviews. The podcast has served as an excellent tool not only for our students and teachers, but also for Spanish-language teachers throughout China. Teachers have access to the recordings in Spanish and thus have exposure to multiple varieties of Spanish. As of last year, the *Se Habla Español Radio Podcast* had 700 subscribers and continues to grow. Like the other initiatives, students' activities for the podcasts are tied to their exit tasks in the TBLT program.

Our community outreach projects have provided authentic spaces for students, teachers, and community members to use Spanish in an authentic way. We continue to develop more opportunities based on students' career goals. These include teaching Spanish lessons at local elementary schools, participating in interviews with Spanish radio stations, and extensive teacher-training efforts in the Shandong province community and throughout China and abroad. Each project involves completing a task that we have directly tied to our courses in the Spanish TBLT program.

4D.7 The Current Program and Evaluation Processes

Figure 4D.1 visually demonstrates how the program currently operates. It shows how we have implemented a fully task-based program while addressing the main challenges of preparing students for the Chinese national tests, teacher training and language ideology awareness, the gradual increase of tasks in the QU basic Spanish-language program, and creating more opportunities to use the target language in authentic contexts. Our program is still a work in progress, and we continue to consciously reflect as teachers together to keep improving it (Phipps & Borg, 2009; Zheng & Borg, 2014). One observation that has emerged is the presence of extensive translanguaging in our classrooms (Mazzaferro, 2018). The QU students strategically use Chinese as a first language, English as a second language, and Spanish as a third language – relying on all of their linguistic resources – in both the oral and written mode. We have engaged with recent literature on translanguaging to consider this practice by students and reflect on how to teach students its value as an interactional strategy. Using "task" as a lens through which we

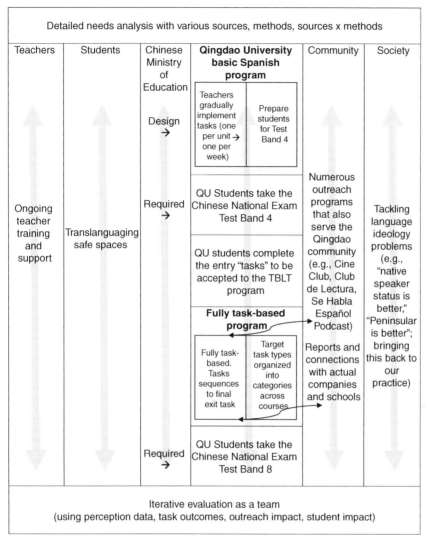

Figure 4D.1 A visual representation of the current program

consider course content synergies and assessment tasks has also helped us, reflecting on the task and task work-plan (Baralt, 2018; Samuda 2015). As Van den Branden (2006) has reported, it has been imperative in our context that the teachers are the ones generating ideas for incorporating more task-based approaches. Revisiting students' needs with each new student cohort has also contributed to ideas for tasks both inside and outside of the QU classrooms.

4D.8 Program Evaluation

Evaluation of our program is being conducted using various methods and triangulation. We rely on student task outcomes, number of student graduates from the program, number of students' places in Spanish-speaking internships and/or jobs, number of attendees at our community outreach programs, as well as student and teacher perception data. So far, over 200 students have graduated. Fifty percent have been placed in internships, all with Chinese companies, and where Spanish-language proficiency is needed. Several students have obtained jobs working abroad in Latin America and the Caribbean. One student graduate moved to work in Equatorial Guinea, a Spanish-speaking country in Africa. Forty-five percent of student graduates have obtained jobs in China in which they need to use Spanish daily for their work. Thousands of people have been reached with our community outreach events. Nine hundred have attended our cinema club events. A couple thousand people have listened to our students' *Se Habla Español Radio Podcast*. In 2019, 100 attended the reading club. Based on our feedback questionnaires, our community outreach has been very positive. Student and teacher perception data, also measured by questionnaires, indicate that they are accepting of, and pleased with, the program. Finally, several of our students have gone on to pursue a Master's or PhD in Spanish in Spain, Latin America, or China, which is indicative of continued efforts with the Spanish language. These evaluation data points provide us with continued insight into the progress and adaptations we make to the program.

4D.9 Conclusion

Creating a fully task-based, Spanish foreign-language program at QU in China has been incredibly challenging, but also, exceptionally rewarding. The partnership between FIU and QU took years to finalize, and we had excellent administrative support to conduct a detailed and lengthy needs analysis. A rigorous needs analysis with various sources, methods, and sources x method triangulations (Long, 2015) was imperative for the design and implementation of the program. As we began to plan its design, we encountered significant challenges, such as how to implement a task-based program while fulfilling the requirement to prepare students for the Chinese National Standards Test in Spanish; student and teacher acceptance of TBLT; unconscious ideological beliefs about native-speaker status (and peninsular varieties of Spanish); and a lack of authentic opportunities for both students and teachers to use the language. A team-based approach has been vital to addressing these challenges. A gradual approach to TBLT at the lower level, leading up to a two-year, fully task-based program, has so far worked for us. Extensive teacher training, ideology myth-busting, and support has also been essential; this has worked best by affirming *teachers* as the "change agents" (Van den Branden, 2016). Finally, the creation of multiple community outreach programs has been essential to provide more opportunities in which students, teachers, and community members can do real-world tasks in

Spanish. These programs simultaneously serve the Qingdao community. Based on our lessons learned, we would like to conclude with recommendations for implementing a TBLT program:

1. The needs analysis is critical. Data from the needs analysis is the basis on which the entire program is created.
2. Take a gradualist approach to TBLT. At the lower level, teachers had the idea of incorporating one task in their practice per unit, and then gradually moving to doing so each week. This has worked well for us and is supported by TBLT research (Van den Branden, 2006).
3. Honor cultural contexts. It is important to consider how TBLT truly fits in Chinese contexts. This is in regard to a Confucian context in terms of cultural and philosophical approaches to teaching, but also, in respecting national mandates. We have tried to do this to the best of our ability by running our program alongside the national exams and also, by honoring natural translanguaging spaces as students navigate the differences between contexts.
4. Explicitly acknowledge language ideology. This should take three forms: (1) explicitly talking about the unfortunate trope that native speaker status is better, (2) brainstorming ways that this negatively impacts students and how we can all tackle it, and (3) engaging in more collaborations with Chinese- and American-trained Spanish-language teachers. Eastern and Western approaches to teaching are different, and teachers from both backgrounds need to understand and appreciate each others' perspectives. Workshops in which teachers practice together can facilitate these talks; doing so will prepare participants to serve students better.
5. Ongoing, extensive teacher support is key. A series of TBLT teacher-trainings, professional development opportunities, practice sessions, and task banks are necessary in order to facilitate teachers' transitioning from a more grammar-based to a task-based approach.
6. Community outreach programs create authentic learning opportunities. Community outreach programs such as movie clubs, reading clubs, podcasts, school service visits, and interactions with real community stakeholders can be a fantastic way to create opportunities for students to use the language in real-world ways. Tie these to students' task-based assessments. This has been enormously successful in our contexts.

Our program is still a work in progress, and we continue to learn together. A fully task-based approach to the teaching of Spanish as a foreign language is very viable in China, but it requires a team effort, ongoing discussions, support and collaboration, and evaluation data that are reflected on iteratively and often. We view our program as a service to our students and to the QU community; this vision has been a foundation of its success. We hope that this case study can provide insight to others who are looking to implement a fully task-based program in other contexts.

Further reading

Baralt, M. and López-Bravo, M. (2016). Teaching Chinese as a foreign language: A classroom study on the timing of grammar around a task. *Chinese as a Second Language Research*, 5, 27–61.

East, M. (2012). *Task-based learning from the teachers' perspective*. Amsterdam: John Benjamins.

McDonough, K. and Chaitmongkol, W. (2007). Teachers' and learners' reactions to a task-based EFL course in Thailand. *TESOL Quarterly*, 41(1), 107–32.

Orton, J. (2011). Educating Chinese language teachers: Some fundamentals. In L. Tsung and K. Cruickshank, eds. *Teaching and learning Chinese in global contexts*. London: Continuum, 151–64.

Zheng, X. and Borg, S. (2014). Task-based learning and teaching in China: Secondary school teachers' beliefs and practices. *Language Teaching Research*, 18, 205–21.

Zhang, E. Y. (2007). TBLT-innovation in primary school English language teaching in mainland China. In K. Van den Branden, K. Van Gorp, and M. Verhelst, eds. *Tasks in action: Education from a classroom-based perspective*. Newcastle: Cambridge University Press, pp. 68–91.

Study Questions

1. What different sources and methods did the FIU-Qingdao TBLT team use to conduct the needs analysis?
2. What were three of the main challenges that the team encountered when they began to plan the implementation of the program? How did they address those challenges?
3. When conducting the needs analysis, the researchers discovered a mismatch in terms of QU administrators' goals for students and teachers' attitudes toward a geographical variety of Spanish. What was the discrepancy? What other ways could this mismatch be addressed?
4. Why was creating community outreach and service projects so instrumental for the Qingdao Spanish TBLT program?

References

Baralt, M. (2018). Becoming a task-based teacher educator. TBLT as a researched pedagogy. V. Samuda K. Van den Branden, and M. Bygate, eds. *TBLT as a Researched Pedagogy*. Abingdon: Routledge.

Baralt, M., Gilabert, R., and Robinson, P. (2014). *Task sequencing and instructed second language learning*. London: Bloomsbury.

Baralt, M. and López-Bravo, M. (2016). Teaching Chinese as a foreign language: A classroom study on the timing of grammar around a task. *Chinese as a Second Language Research*, 5, 27–61.

Bygate, M., Samuda, V., and Van den Branden, K., (2018), eds. *Task-based Language Teaching as a researched pedagogy*. Amsterdam: John Benjamins.

Carless, D. (2004). Issues in teachers' reinterpretation of a task-based innovation in primary schools. *TESOL Quarterly*, 38(4), 639–62.

East, M. (2012). *Task-based learning from the teachers' perspective*. Amsterdam: John Benjamins.

Ellis, R. (2003). *Task-based language teaching and learning*. Oxford: Oxford University Press.

Esteban, M. (2016). Spain's relations with China: Friends but not partners. *Chinese Political Science Review*, 1, 373–86.

González Puy, I. (2012). El español en China. In VV. AA., *El español en el mundo. Anuario del Instituto Cervantes, capítulo dos*. Madrid: Instituto Cervantes.

Gurzynski-Weiss, L. (2017). *Expanding individual difference research in the interaction approach: Investigating learners, instructors, and other interlocutors*. Amsterdam: John Benjamins.

Long, M. (2005). *Second language needs analysis*. Cambridge: Cambridge University Press.

Long, M. (2015). *Second language acquisition and task-based language teaching*. Malden, MA: Wiley Blackwell.

Markee, N. (2007). *Managing curricular innovation*. Cambridge: Cambridge University Press.

Mazzaferro, G. (2018). *Translanguaging as everyday practice*. Cham, Switzerland: Springer.

Medgyes, P. (1994). *The non-native teacher*. London: Macmillan.

McDonough, K. and Chaitmongkol, W. (2007). Teachers' and learners' reactions to a task-based EFL course in Thailand. *TESOL Quarterly*, 41(1), 107–32.

Phillips, T. (2018). Study of Portuguese and Spanish explodes as China expands role in Latin America. *The Guardian*. Retrieved on October 10, 2019 from: https://www.theguardian.com/world/2018/sep/02/study-of-portuguese-and-spanish-explodes-as-china-expands-role-in-latin-america

Phipps, S. and Borg, S. (2009). Exploring tensions between teachers' grammar teaching beliefs and practices. *System*, 37, 380–90.

Sachs, G. T. (2007). The challenges of adopting and adapting task-based cooperative teaching and learning in an EFL context. In K. Van den Branden, K. Van Gorp, and M. Verhelst, eds. *Tasks in action: Education from a classroom-based perspective*. Newcastle: Cambridge University Press, pp. 235–64.

Samuda, V. (2015). Tasks, design, and the architecture of pedagogical spaces. In M. Bygate, ed. *Domains and directions in the development of TBLT: A decade of plenaries from the international conference*. Amsterdam: John Benjamins, pp. 271–301.

Scrimgeour, A. (2010). The yin-yang of Chinese language teaching in Australia: The challenges native speaker trainee teachers face in the Chinese classroom. In A. J. Liddicoat, ed. *Languages in Australian education: Problems, prospects and future directions*. Newcastle upon Tyne: Cambridge Scholars, pp. 127–44.

Wang, F. (2019). *The status of Spanish language teachers in China*. Paper presented at Qingdao University, June, 2019.

Willis, D. and Willis, J. (2007). *Doing task-based teaching*. Oxford: Oxford University Press.

Van den Branden, K. (2006), ed. *Task-based language education: From theory to practice*. Cambridge: Cambridge University Press.

Van den Branden, K. (2016). The role of teachers in task-based language education. *Annual Review of Applied Linguistics*, 36, 164–81.

Van den Branden, K., Bygate, M., and Norris, J. (2009), eds, *Task-based language teaching: A reader*. Amsterdam: John Benjamins.

Zheng, X. and Borg, S. (2014). Task-based learning and teaching in China: Secondary school teachers' beliefs and practices. *Language Teaching Research*, 18, 205–21.

Zhang, E. Y. (2007). TBLT-innovation in primary school English language teaching in mainland China. In K. Van den Branden, K. Van Gorp, and M. Verhelst, eds. *Tasks in action: Education from a classroom-based perspective*. Newcastle: Cambridge University Press, pp. 68–91.

Zhou, W. and Li, G. (2015). Chinese language teachers' expectations and perceptions of American students' behavior: Exploring the nexus of cultural differences and classroom management. *System*, 49, 17–27.

5

The L in TBLT

Analyzing Target Discourse

Michael H. Long

5.1 Introduction

One of the many positive features of task-based language teaching (TBLT) is its potential for providing learners with the *functional* second language (L2) abilities required to meet their real-world communicative needs. Identified via a needs analysis, the target tasks for specific groups or specific types of learners – what they need to be able to *do* in and through the new language – are the starting-point for task-based course design, for task-based materials writing, and eventually, for task-based, criterion-referenced, performance assessment. (For a recent overview, see Long, Lee & Hillman, 2019.) The striking growth in the number and methodological sophistication of NAs in recent years (Serafini et al., 2015, this volume) testifies to the increasing recognition of their importance if language teaching programs are to be relevant for learners and built on solid foundations.

A task-based needs analysis comprises two equally important parts. In the first part, using a variety of sources of information, of methods of obtaining that information, and triangulation of methods and sources, *target tasks* are identified for a particular group or type of learner. The process has been described in detail by Brown (2009, 2016), Long (2005, 2015: 85–168, 2018), Malicka et al. (2017), Serafini (this volume), and Serafini et al. (2015), among others, so will not be dealt with here. The second part involves the collection of genuine samples of the spoken or written language use (discourse) to perform the target tasks successfully, and analysis of the samples, known as analysis of target discourse, to produce one or more archetypal models. This process, by which linguistic input is selected and graded for incorporation into task-based materials (i.e., into so-called pedagogic tasks), and then learned, and to the extent possible, taught – has received less attention in the TBLT literature (but see Long, 2015: 169–204). The collection, selection, modification, learning, and teaching of task-relevant language – the L in TBLT – is the focus of this chapter.

5.2 Why Is the Second Part of a Needs Analysis Necessary?

It is rare for applied linguists or language teachers to be familiar with insider-to-insider communication in the academic disciplines, occupations, or vocational training fields of interest to their students. Their expertise lies in applied linguistics and language teaching, after all, not in such fields as law, criminology, political science, architecture, medicine, engineering, computer science, nursing, cooking, or automobile mechanics, much less in the way language is used to socialize novitiates into each domain. Research has shown their intuitions can even be faulty about the language used to accomplish everyday social survival tasks with which they *are* familiar, such as ordering a cup of coffee (Bartlett, 2005) or making a restaurant reservation (Granena, 2008), and that the models presented in textbooks, based on their writers' intuition, are often wildly unrealistic.

The situation can be ameliorated to some extent when programs repeatedly cater to the same types of learners. For example, an increasingly common situation in many parts of the world involves students working toward a bachelor's degree in science, engineering, computer science, economics, political science, business, tourism, etc., at an English-medium university in their home country and/or, when they graduate, intending to study for a masters or doctorate at an English-medium university overseas in one of those fields. When either the domestic or the overseas university has language programs for students in the same areas year after year, and most universities do, then a thorough needs analysis is called for. It can identify target tasks for those *types* of students (not merely for particular groups of students), making development of subject-specific or occupation-specific task-based materials and tests a worthwhile long-term investment.

If a program is delivered by a stable (ideally, permanent), full-time, trained faculty, teachers can gradually become knowledgeable about their students' occupation or major field of study, perhaps initially in part by collaborating with subject matter specialists from the area concerned. To take a common example in the occupational sphere, large-scale government English as a second language and foreign language programs (e.g., for law enforcement personnel, diplomats, diplomatic security staff, military linguists, and intelligence personnel) also have the same types of learners year after year. Over time, therefore, their teachers, too, can become very knowledgeable about their students' work.

The same is true of L2 programs for school-age children. A foreign language needs analysis for elementary and secondary pupils is unnecessary, as most parents have little or no idea about their children's future needs in the language, if any, or why they are being obliged to study a foreign language at all. However, the *second* language needs of immigrant and other minority language-speaking children soon to be moved into mainstream classrooms with native speakers are real to them and to their teachers. Second language programs for them should be based on a needs analysis of the tasks such children will face when mainstreamed, and knowledge of the content areas is readily available from other teachers within the same school building.

Last, but by no means least, even in what unfortunately tend to be unstable, poorly resourced programs for migrant workers and refugees, teachers quickly grow familiar with the typical social survival tasks the students and their parents confront during their first weeks and months in the new country (see Toker & Sağdıç, this volume). Many, such as using public transport, following street directions, renting an apartment, visiting a doctor, applying for a credit card, or interviewing for a job, are tasks with which the teachers themselves are already familiar, although some may present additional challenges for new arrivals, who may lack a credit history or documentation concerning their education, health status, prior employment, etc., and for some of whom attempting even apparently "simple" target tasks may be to tread delicately through what for them is a cultural minefield.

Those three examples are best-case scenarios, where teachers can gradually develop content expertise by dealing with the same types of students over time. Content expertise, however, does not necessarily equate to insights about language use. Absent insider knowledge, with the exception of occasional corpus-based materials, the models that learners encounter in many commercially published language teaching textbooks are usually based on the intuitions of a materials writer as unfamiliar as the classroom teacher with genuine language use in the target discourse domain. And outsiders' intuitions have repeatedly been found unreliable, sometimes risibly so. Major discrepancies are observed between textbook dialogs and discourse samples collected in several daily situations – for example, at the gas station, the restaurant, the train station, the post office, and elsewhere (Taborn, 1983). That is why the second part of a needs analysis is necessary.

Even for everyday "social survival" tasks, studies have often revealed embarrassing discrepancies between authentic language use and the language modeled in coursebooks. That includes tasks that applied linguists may have witnessed and performed many times themselves, such as giving street directions (Scotton and Bernsten, 1988), purchasing a train ticket (Long, 2015: 188–191), attending a doctor's appointment (Cathcart, 1989), or attending a business meeting (Williams, 1988). Given such findings, even with relatively simple, high-frequency, publicly visible tasks, it is obviously incumbent upon materials writers to obtain genuine examples of target language use in specialized discourse domains of which they have little personal experience or none whatsoever. Commercially published coursebooks usually rely on the textbook writer's intuitions and employ oversimplified lexis, collocations, grammatical functions, topics, and discourse structure. Dialogs purporting to represent ordering food in a restaurant, buying something in a shop, or interviewing for a job are often wholly unrealistic, and little more than thinly disguised vehicles for more practice of the grammatical *structure du jour* (structure of the day).

For all these reasons, designers of genuine task-based materials base pedagogic tasks on careful study of the target tasks identified in the first part of the needs analysis, and then of samples of genuine language use surrounding successful performance of those tasks – i.e., authentic target discourse (TD). In an analysis of target discourse (ATD), the typical internal structure of the TD, and the recurring patterns in the linguistic features that co-occur with obligatory and optional elements in that structure, are distilled to produce archetypal, or prototypical, models. The models are then elaborated (see below), not linguistically simplified, to match students' current L2 abilities, and integrated into pedagogic tasks. These tasks of gradually increasing complexity (task complexity, not linguistic complexity) constitute the single most important source (not the only source) of new language for both teachers and learners, especially of task-specific and domain-specific language.

5.3 Collecting Genuine Target Discourse Samples

The first step in the second part of a needs analysis is to collect TD samples. These can take many forms, from written documents (textbooks, journal articles, prescription drug labels, email messages, job application forms, cell phone contracts, car rental agreements, repair manuals, etc.) to audio or video recordings of all sorts of spoken discourse (university lectures, office-hour appointments, job interviews, service encounters, sales presentations, weekly research laboratory meetings, conference presentations, doctors' visits, street directions, restaurant orders, shopping purchases, etc.). When collecting data, care must be taken to observe any legal restrictions, which can vary from one country or location within a country to another, on the use of certain kinds of written documents or on recording certain kinds of public or private spoken transactions. Some recordings may require the parties' written consent.

Once legal matters have been taken care of, it is important to obtain multiple examples of the same kind of TD. This is, first, in order to be able to identify, and where appropriate, subsequently remove, any idiosyncratic features pertaining to particular examples of written documents or to individual speakers, and second, and more importantly, to note variations due to such factors as workplace size, time of day, and location.

Two workers may share the same *occupation*, but their *jobs* may be very different.

Differences in workplace *size* have fairly predictable effects. In a large hotel, for example, receptionists may predominantly deal with checking guests in and out, whereas their counterparts in smaller establishments may work alone much of the time and have to deal with every aspect of a guest's stay. As a rule of thumb, solitary workers in large versions of almost any workplace (hotels, railway stations, airports, shops, museums, government offices, etc.) tend to be specialists, responsible for a narrower range of duties. Those in nominally the same occupation (receptionist, ticket clerk, shop assistant, museum guide, etc.) in smaller workplaces, tend to be generalists, with a wider range of duties. To take two extreme examples, compare the *job* of a teacher in a one-room rural schoolhouse with that of a teacher in a large urban high school, or again, of a surgeon tending to civilian victims of air strikes with that of a surgeon in a large modern hospital in Frankfurt, Tel Aviv, or New York.

Where *time* is concerned, the frequency and importance of target tasks for a hotel receptionist, for example, can vary depending on the shift being worked. More check-ins, requests for information and room changes occur in the afternoon, evening, and overnight, more provision of tourism information to guests, more check-outs, and more resolution of payment issues in the morning.

Where *location* is concerned, the names of everyday items can vary from one country, or region within a country, to another, most obviously, but not only, as a function of the variety of the target language involved. Compare, for example, the names for different types of bus and train tickets (day-tripper, cheap day return, round-trip, easy rider, etc.) in the United Kingdom, Australia and the United States, the increasingly impenetrable lexicons required in many countries for such a mundane task as ordering coffee, the names for parts of a car (boot/trunk, bonnet/hood, etc.) in the United Kingdom and United States, for "bread" in Saudi/MSA: خبز (khubz, χʊbəz) and ECA: عيش(ayesh, ʕeɪʃ), or for "computer": *jisuanji* (computing machine) in Mandarin, and *diannao* (electronic brain) in Taiwan. Of course, if as the result of a detailed needs analysis, it is known exactly where, for what purpose, and with whom, a group of learners will be using the L2, far from removing such variants, the syllabus designer will ensure they are preserved in the resulting teaching materials. This will include everything from the appropriacy or not of a whole variety of English, French, Spanish, Chinese, Arabic, etc., to appropriate pronunciation and local usage of T/V forms (e.g., in Spain vs. El Salvador), and of lexical items and collocations.

In light of these and other potential sources of variability, it is easy to see why it is important to collect as many samples of (especially spoken) TD as it is feasible for the analyst to handle. His or her job is to compare the samples, remove idiosyncrasies, and identify commonalities at the level of internal discourse structure, along with corresponding linguistic features at the level of grammar, lexis, collocations, formulaic utterances, phonology, and pragmatics.

5.4 Analysis of Target Discourse

Analysis of target discourse – analysis of language use surrounding the successful performance of target tasks – differs from a true discourse analysis. A discourse analysis must meet certain requirements, and is predictive; it sets out to produce a generative model capable of handling new instances of the performance of a particular task or speech event, like a shopping purchase, a traffic stop (O'Connell, 2014), hotel reservation, job interview, weather forecast (Maie & Salen, this volume), office-hour appointment (Sağdıç & Reagan, this volume), or classroom lesson.

Sinclair and Coulthard (1975: 15–17) listed four requirements for an adequate discourse analysis:

1. The analysis must employ a finite set of categories; if new categories can be added each time the existing set is found unable to handle the data, the analysis is merely an illusion.
2. Categories must be transparent and operationally defined, so as to preempt fudging if problematic (non-fitting) data are encountered.
3. The system must be comprehensive, capable of handling all the data without recourse to a "miscellaneous" or "other" category.
4. The system must have two or more levels, with each level entering into a "consists of" relationship with units at the level below it, and at least one impossible combination.

Sinclair and Coulthard's analysis of classroom lessons had five levels: lesson, transaction, exchange, move, and act. Exchanges, for example, consisted of initiations, responses, and (optional) feedback moves (i.e., the infamous I-R-F sequence so prevalent in language teaching classrooms, most notoriously during audio-lingual and presentation, practice, and production lessons). The requirement that there be one or more impossible, or "ungrammatical," combinations of categories (e.g., I-F-R) is because without such constraints, any structure would be possible, meaning in effect that the TD would have no structure, and the analysis, therefore, no predictive power.

An ATD (see Long, 2015: 180–87) is less ambitious and simpler. Only the second requirement applies. To guarantee that an analyst is not simply "making up" the findings, categories must still be transparent and operationally defined, so as to allow independent analysis of a subset of the same data by one or more raters and calculation of inter-rater reliability. The other three requirements, 1, 3 and 4, do not apply. There is no requirement 1, that an ATD employ a finite set of categories, because there is also no requirement 3, that an ATD be exhaustive. An analysis of relationships among types of teacher questions and types of student responses, for example, may not need to involve an account of everything, or anything, else in a lesson.

As for requirement 4, that of a hierarchical system, an ATD is "flatter" and, depending on the research question, the structure linear and not necessarily hierarchical at all; there may be an interest in just one level of analysis, and not necessarily in "consists of" relationships with units at other possible levels. For example, conditions on the provision of negative feedback and learner uptake in teacher–student interaction may exclusively involve moves at a single level of analysis, (e.g., with type of error affecting type of feedback, and type of feedback in turn affecting the likelihood of uptake). It is obviously possible to relate items in a sequence to units at another level in the I-R-F exchange structure (e.g., types of error to the "response" move, and prompts, elicits, and recasts to the "feedback" move), but that would not necessarily provide additional relevant information for an investigation whose focus is sequential relationships among errors, different types of feedback, and learner uptake. Unlike most discourse analyses, an ATD may also focus on more than one dimension of language use (although with care taken not to mix units from different dimensions). For example, some responses to learner error may be types of negative feedback in a pedagogically oriented ATD, but simultaneously examples of models, repetitions, recasts, and extensions, in a more psycholinguistically oriented analysis.

An ATD is a micro-scale exercise in data-mining. Samples of task performance are compared and distilled to reveal their typical internal structure. Once identified, sometimes in the form of a flowchart showing a sequence of obligatory and optional subtasks or moves (see, e.g., Hillman & Long, 2020; O'Connell, 2014), the analyst searches for the critical and/or most frequent linguistic correlates of those components. Lists are drawn up of the items commonly used to perform each of them. Formulaic expressions, lexical items, collocations, morphology, syntax and pragmatics are all of potential interest, some more so, some less so, as a function of the L2, target task, and type of TD being analyzed. Depending on how much variation is found in the way the task is typically performed, one or more prototypical models are produced. These models, along with the internal structure of the TD and the list of linguistic correlates, will constitute the core ingredients for the materials writer when producing a series of pedagogic tasks of gradually increasing complexity that teachers and learners will work on in the classroom.

5.5 Target Discourse Structure

A number of ATDs have been carried out in recent years, but few have appeared in the published literature. Based on his nonparticipant observation during a ride-along program, and subsequent analysis of the transcripts of conversations during eight US police traffic stops, O'Connell (2014) summarized the typical pattern police officers followed, yielding the following TD structure:

- Greet the vehicle's occupant(s) and introduce themselves (probably).
- Ask for a driver's license and registration (always).
- Ask for identification cards from passengers (possibly).
- Ask about ownership of the car (possibly).
- Explain why the driver had been stopped (always).
- Ask where the driver was going (possibly).
- Tell the driver to stay in the car while the information the driver provided is checked on the computer in the officer's patrol car (always).
- "Lecture" the driver about their violation(s) (probably).
- Issue a warning, a repair order, or a citation (always).
- Explain any action required of the driver or options regarding payment of the fine or court appearance (always).
- Return the license (always).
- Bid farewell (always).

O'Connell provided a flowchart representation of the structure, complete with alternative segments (not mentioned above) according to whether the office issues a warning, repair order, or citation, plus examples of the language used at each juncture, and prototypical models of conversations between police officers and motorists.

In a very different occupational domain, Hillman and Long (2020) provide an analysis of formal celebration speeches often required of US diplomats at meetings of Japanese–US associations and a variety of other ceremonial events, such as launches of new collaborative binational projects. The target task, delivering a celebration speech, presents a serious challenge for diplomats stationed in Japan, in part due to the importance of maintaining the appropriate register in Japanese for such occasions throughout, with the right levels of formality, deference, and politeness, often expressed via use of particular formulae and grammatical markers. (For the use of TBLT in teaching a morphologically complex language, see Gilabert & Castellvi, 2019.) Obligatory and optional components of the typical structure of celebration speeches – introduce self, congratulate organizers, thank organization, comment on the occasion, explain organization's importance, express respect to organization, recognize other important guests, pray for future success, congratulate organizers again, thank organizers – are presented as a flowchart, with important and/or high-frequency Japanese lexical items, collocations, and formulaic utterances listed for each component, culminating in a prototypical celebration speech.

5.6 An Example: Buying/Selling a Cup of Coffee

One of the earliest published ATDs, a study by Bartlett (2005), involved a much simpler target task – buying/selling a cup of coffee – which will serve as an illustration of the process. Aside from English being the L2 in that case, the advantages are that (i) most readers will already be familiar with the task – in some cases, very familiar, (ii) interactions between customers and baristas are usually quite short, making provision of at least a few examples from the original study compatible with current space constraints, and (iii) model dialogs for similar tasks frequently appear in commercial language-teaching coursebooks.

Bartlett recorded a total of 248 conversations at three locations, two commercial coffee shop chains and a campus coffee cart, involving the task of buying and selling a drink item (usually a cup of coffee) and/or a sundry. Of these, 168 were transcribed. (That is far more than would be required for materials writing, of course. Bartlett was conducting a demonstration research project, as were Maie & Salen [this volume]) Bartlett (2005: 314) found:

> a generalizable pattern of elements ... It typically involved the sub-tasks of either greeting the server or responding to the service bid (*Can I help you?*), specifying the order, possibly confirming the order and options, sometimes asking for additional information about a menu item, responding to the server-initiated *Anything else?*, and finally, the predictable sub-task of paying and closing (which was sometimes non-verbal).

She provided transcriptions of numerous samples of genuine TD. The two examples below (1 and 2) were typical.

Transcription 1
S: Can I help you ma'am?
C: Can I try an iced macadamia latte?
S: Did you want that blended or on the rocks?
C: Blended
S: OK. Did you want whipped cream on that?
C: Yes
S: Anything else for you?
C: (non-verbal response)
S: OK. That'll be 4.48
C: (hands over money)
S: Thank you. 50 cents is your change. Would you like your receipt?

C: (non-verbal response)
S: OK. It'll be ready for you in just one minute.

(Bartlett, 2005: 314)

Transcription 2
S: May I help you?
C: Hi. Can I get a double iced chai?
S: 2%?
C: 2%
S: Double iced chai 2%. Do you have a stamp card?
C: Yes
S: (stamps card) There you go. Alright (hands over change). Thank you.

(Bartlett, 2005: 315)

As noted earlier, it is important to obtain multiple TD samples (perhaps five to ten, depending on the target task and how much variation is found in the first few examples), as language use for the same target task can vary for a number of reasons. In this case, for example, baristas reported some differences (confirmed in Bartlett's data) according to time of day. Morning and lunchtime "rush hour" customers were mostly regulars, performing the task through shorter interactions, less phatic talk, and more non-verbal confirmation of need and price. Regulars knew what they wanted and how to order it succinctly, allowing for more ellipsis on both the server's and customer's part. Interactions could be longer when customers were novices, or when problems arose, for example, because customers had forgotten their frequent-user card, specific names and sizes of drinks were unclear, an item had run out, or non-task-specific small talk occurred. Compare transcription 3, involving a novice customer, confused by the many options listed in the menu on the wall above the counter, and transcription 4, involving a regular:

Transcription 3 (novice)
C: All the different names and (3) Hey
S: Oh what are you looking for?
C: XXX the frappuccino?
S: Frio. We have like a chocolate one which says the mocha cappuccino
C: (3) Where?
S: Third from the bottom is the iced mocha (that's the) mocha frappuccino. The regular frappuccino is the XXX and cream
C: Oh right. What's the difference between a regular one and a (.) mocha one?
S: That's it one has chocolate in it and the other one doesn't
C: Let me try the: e:r mocha
S: Mo[cha? OK]
C: [Yeah]
S: OK (40) three forty-eight please
C: Three of 'em?
S: Forty-eight (said louder)

C: er XXX (blender noise)
S: Yeah (2) There you go (.) Thank you very much. You have a great day

(Bartlett, 2005: 317–318)

Transcription 4 (regular customer)
S: How about for you, sir?
C: A double latte
S: Hot? 2%?
C: (non-verbal)
S: (relays order to drink maker) Double hot latte 2%. Out of three. And your card (hands over card and gives change) We'll see you next time after the Spring Break for your free drink
C: Alright
S: OK. Thank you.

(Bartlett, 2005: 316)

Many of Bartlett's findings, notably those concerning ellipsis and intertextuality, paralleled those from an earlier study of conversations between passengers and the ticket clerk in a one-man operation (the same person served as ticket clerk, porter, platform announcer, flagger, and kiosk seller) at a small railway station in rural Pennsylvania (subsequently reported in Long, 2015: 188–91). "Due to shared background knowledge," Bartlett writes (2005: 322), "there is a high degree of implicitness and ellipsis in the server and customer turns," as in transcription 5:

Transcription 5
S: What can I get for this morning?
C: Regular (XXX). Right to the top.

(Bartlett, 2005: 322)

The customer indicates he wants a regular coffee, with the cup filled right to the top, and no room left for milk or cream. No polite form is used, and both customer and server understand the meaning of "right to the top." Bartlett continues, "Ellipsis is a time-saver when people are in a hurry or when there is a line. Moreover, to serve a customer or to order without a polite request form (*Would you like XX? May I have a XX, please?*) was not impolite, but pragmatically appropriate in this context" (2005: 322).

In both settings, railway station and coffee shop, the context-embedded nature of the interactions allowed use of pronouns and deictics (*those, the big one, this one/that one, here/over there*), and intertextuality (e.g., referring to the menu on the wall, *third from the bottom*):

Transcription 6
S: Hi. Can I help you ma'am?
C: Yeah. Can I get- [MHL Note: not *May I have*] (Pointing through the glass display cabinet) Are those the scones?
S: Yuh huh

> C: The big ones?
> S: Yeah, We have blueberry or cranberry
>
> (Bartlett, 2005: 324)

Although often used in commercial textbooks, generic terms are typically absent in genuine transactions. Just as the uninformative *ticket* was used just once in twenty-one conversations at the railway station (perhaps significantly, by the only nonnative speaker among the passengers), *mesa* (*table*) only once in making a restaurant reservation in Spanish (Granena, 2008), again by a nonnative speaker, and *coffee* sparingly in Bartlett's data – and then not with its everyday generic meaning, but the domain-specific sense of a brewed or drip coffee of the day. In the real world, the seller/server already understands by their mere presence that the customer in each case wants a ticket, a table, or a coffee. Generic nouns are of little use in most such service encounters. The issue is, what *kind* of ticket, table, or coffee? Technical and subtechnical lexical items are the accepted currency and what learners need to know. In this case, that potentially means the names for a large variety of types of coffee (*espresso, latte, frappuccino, frio, americano, machiatto, regular, 2%, skinny, non-fat, vanilla, on the rocks, blended, iced*), and sizes (*double, triple, quad, tall, short, medium, grande, skinny, venti*), as well as toppings, other add-ons, and loyalty cards (*frequent-user card, stamp card, coffee card*), terms for some of which vary from one location to another.

Although an ATD can generally be performed by hand, Bartlett used concordancing software to identify the most frequent linguistic realizations of subtasks. For example, the most frequent linguistic realizations of customer requests were "*Can I get* …?" (forty-two tokens), "*Can I have* ..?" (thirty-two tokens), "*I'll have* …" and "*I'd like*…" (seven tokens each). Conversely, despite frequently being a major focus of textbook models, few polite request forms, such as *please* and (only six instances of) "*Could I* …?," were observed in the 168 transcripts. Authentic TD contained ellipsis, implicitness, intertextuality, deixis, different uses of grammatical structures, e.g., *did* ("*Did you want X?*"), and non-fluencies (fillers and incomplete utterances), features "all too often absent from models presented in textbooks" (Bartlett, 2005: 329).

5.7 From Genuine Discourse Samples to Prototypical Models of Spoken or Written Target Discourse

An ATD is conducted to identify the typical internal structure of task performance, the typical sequence of its component parts (subtasks), and their linguistic correlates. (For an excellent example of the whole process for "Making a restaurant reservation in Spanish," see Granena, 2008.) As noted earlier, variations due to workplace size, location, time of day, or other factors, are also of interest if frequent enough. The next step is to create one or more prototypical examples of the TD – in the present case, dialogs pertaining to a spoken service encounter. The models will serve as the basis for task-based pedagogic materials (i.e., pedagogic tasks).

Following the linear structure established for the TD, models should reflect the most commonly observed sequences of obligatory and optional moves, with any unwanted or unhelpful idiosyncrasies peculiar to individual speakers or locations removed. Retained are the grammatical form-function relationships; for example, *did* as a mitigation device, not a past tense marker (*Did you want whipped cream with that?*) and the specific "technical" lexical items and collocations used in the domain of interest, along with other typical features of the TD, including appropriate levels of colloquial and idiomatic usage, and of ellipsis and intertextuality. If common enough, examples of communication breakdowns (e.g., in this case, over the names of types of coffee) and their resolution should also be included. In the interest of naturalness and genuineness, the prototypical models should draw extensively on the language observed in the genuine samples. Important items, even if seemingly difficult, are *not* removed from the models as part of the usual *simplification* process. How will learners ever acquire them if they never appear in the input? Rather, they are retained and made comprehensible through input *elaboration* (see below). Needless to say, while based on examination of genuine samples of TD, and not simply products of a commercial materials writer's data-free intuitions and imagination, judgment and creativity are still required.

Based on the findings of her ATD, Bartlett presented a prototypical encounter for a customer (not a regular) who orders one drink (a coffee) and a sundry (a scone). The dialog reflects features found in the genuine samples: use of domain-specific lexical items (*grande latte, blended, on the rocks, 2%, skimmed,* not the generic *coffee*), ellipsis (*Anything else? Here or to go?*), and pronouns and deictics resulting from implicitness, intertextuality and the context-embedded nature of the conversation (*one of those, the one in the back*), colloquial language when stating a price (*That'll be X*) and handing over an item (*There you go*), *did* as a mitigating device, and even a false start by the customer (line 12). Idiosyncrasies were removed, in this case, for example, the term *skinny*, used only by employees at one of the three locations. Bartlett offers the following prototypical dialog:

Transcription 7
S: Hi. Can I help you?
C: Can I get a grande latte with vanilla?
S: Did you want that blended or on the rocks?
C: Blended, I guess
S: 2% or skimmed?
C: Uhm 2%

S: 2% OK. Any whipped cream?
C: Sorry?
S: Did you want whipped cream on that?
C: Yes
S: Anything else?
C: No, thanks. That's it. Oh no. Can I get- are those scones?
S: Yeah we have cranberry and blueberry
C: (pointing) I think I'll have one of those
S: A blueberry scone?
C: Yeah. The one in the back
S: This one
C: Yeah that's it
S: OK. For here or to go?
C: To go
S: OK. That'll be 3.48
C: (hands over money)
S: How about a frequent user card?
C: Oh sure
S: Thank you. 52 cents is your change (hands over change). And your card. OK. It'll be ready for you in just one minute.
C: Thank you
S: (hands over drink) There you go. Have a nice day
C: You, too.

(Bartlett 2005: 338)

Bartlett (2005: 330–336) surveyed several EFL/ESL textbooks that included dialogs supposedly showing how to order food in restaurants or canteens (the nearest thing in the books to ordering coffee). Even though the authors often claimed their sample dialogs were modeled on real-life conversations, this seemed doubtful. They were in fact frequently oversimplified, obviously contained inauthentic communicative structure and unrealistic situational content, and could mislead learners (330). Most customer requests, for example, focused on "*Could I ...,*" "*I would like ...,*" "*I'll have ...*" and "*May I ...,*" with no instances of the most frequently used in real life, "*Can I get ....*" Dialogs in some books were little more than thinly disguised pattern drills practicing polite requests in repetitive question-and-answer sequences. One customer even made what Bartlett's data had shown is an unlikely request for "*a cup of coffee.*" Typical features of context-embedded talk, such as ellipsis, open-endedness, intertextuality and inexplicitness, were absent, as, in most cases, were pre-closings and closings. Textbook dialogs needed to be contextualized, Bartlett concluded, and to reflect genuine native speaker use. There is a bigger question, however. If the intuitions of textbook writers are so faulty when treating such a simple, familiar task, how reliable will they be about language use in domains about which the writers have no direct experience and about which they know little or nothing?

5.8 Linguistic Input in Pedagogic Tasks: Genuine, Simplified, Elaborated, or Modified Elaborated?

Buying/selling a cup of coffee was used to illustrate the second part of a needs analysis, the ATD process, which ends with production of prototypical dialogs or other spoken or written texts for subsequent use in pedagogic tasks. These tasks constitute a major source of new language in the classroom, especially, but not only, of new domain-specific language. Once prototypical models of TD are available, the job of the analyst or materials writer (often the same person) is to incorporate variants of them into the design of pedagogic tasks for classroom use or computer-based instruction. Classroom experience shows that it is usually a good idea to expose students to one or two examples of successful native speaker performance of the full spoken or written target task first, just so they can see what they are aiming to achieve. Then, if the students for whom the pedagogic tasks are intended are sufficiently advanced, the models may be usable as they stand. If not, parts may need to be *elaborated* (not simplified) in various ways. The task, not the language, is simplified, thereby preserving the genuine target language use that learners will encounter and need to be able to handle when performing the target task outside the classroom. Sequences of pedagogic tasks are then gradually made more complex.

Ordering a cup of coffee is, of course, a very simple, everyday "social survival" task. Things can get much harder. The following example concerns the opening paragraph of a written text about the role of soccer in society. Figure 5.1 shows four versions of the same text (again, a very short text, due to space limitations). Version A is the *genuine* version, originally written by and for native speakers, not for language teaching. Version B shows a traditionally *simplified* version of the same text, where what is lost through simplification is immediately apparent. Gone are the examples (bolded in version A for easy identification) of idiomatic, native-like L2 use in the original, including lexis and collocations, and with them, some of the genuine passage's meaning (see Long & Ross, 1993) as a result of substituting "groups" for "masses," "each week" for "on a regular basis," "with other people" for "with one another," and so on. Each change entails a slight loss of information. Moreover, in version B, the easy flow of the natural-sounding genuine version has become a series of short, stilted-sounding, staccato-like sentences.

Version C, the *elaborated* version, preserves all the original bolded items, maintains roughly the same level of comprehensibility, and sounds closer to natural English usage, but at a price. As shown in Table 5.1, version C is considerably longer overall than both versions A and B, with a higher average number of words per sentence than both of them (triple the average for version B, and as measured by an approximation to s-nodes

> **A Genuine**
>
> Professional soccer brings larger **masses of** people together, and **on a regular basis**, than just about anything except wars. Matches **at whatever level** are one of the **few remaining occasions** when people express themselves passionately and publicly, and interact **with one another** instead of with anti-social computer screens and **hand-held electronic devices**.
>
> **B Simplified**
>
> Large groups of people meet each week for professional soccer games. The groups for soccer are larger than groups for anything except wars. Soccer games are one of the few times when people are still passionate in public. People communicate with other people at games. Games are social, not anti-social, like computers and cellphones.
>
> **C Elaborated**
>
> Professional soccer matches are regular times when large crowds, large **masses of** people, meet together **on a regular basis**, usually once a week. The crowds at soccer matches are bigger than for almost anything except wars. Matches **at whatever level** of soccer, from the highest level to the lowest, are one of the only times, one of the **few remaining occasions**, when people still show strong emotions, express themselves passionately, in public, singing and shouting, and interacting with one another socially, communicating **with one another**, with other people in the crowd, instead of with anti-social computer screens and **hand-held electronic devices**, like tablets and cellphones.
>
> **D Modified elaborated**
>
> Professional soccer matches are times when large crowds, large **masses of** people, meet together. The matches bring people together **on a regular basis**, usually once a week. The crowds for soccer are bigger than for almost anything except wars. Matches **at whatever level** of soccer, from the highest level to the lowest, are one of the **few remaining occasions**, one of the only times, when people still show strong emotions, express themselves passionately, in public. They sing and shout, and interact with one another socially. They communicate **with one another**, with other people in the crowd, instead of with anti-social computer screens and **hand-held electronic devices**, like tablets and cellphones.

Figure 5.1 Soccer texts: genuine, simplified, elaborated, and modified elaborated versions

per sentence,[1] nearly twice its syntactic complexity). Nevertheless, studies have shown that despite these potentially serious disadvantages, the redundancy that elaboration provides can render spoken or written input almost as comprehensible to learners as simplified input, and without the negative consequences of linguistic simplification for acquisition (Yano et al., 1994).

Elaboration can be achieved through a variety of devices, some illustrated here, including (but not only) the use of synonyms, appositional phrases, defining/restrictive relative clauses, rephrasing, repetition,

---

[1] Here, tensed verbs and modals.

Table 5.1 *Soccer texts by the numbers*

	Words	Sentences	Words/ Sentence	S-nodes	S-nodes/ Sentence
Genuine (A)	52	2	26	4	2
Simplified (B)	54	5	10.8	6	1.2
Elaborated (C)	106	3	35.3	6	2
Modified elaborated (D)	111	6	18.5	11	1.8

matching chronological order and order of mention, and a variety of prosodic changes, such as increased stress and brief one-beat pauses before and/or after key information-bearing items. All of these devices add *redundancy* to the input, increasing its comprehensibility without removing unknown items. Echoing similar first language acquisition findings for caretaker talk with young children, they were among the strategies and tactics found by research on foreigner talk discourse (FTD) in the 1970s and 1980s to be common ways in which native speakers modified their speech and the *interactional structure of conversation* with low proficiency nonnative speakers to establish and maintain comprehensibility, and to repair breakdowns in communication (Chaudron, 1982; Long, 1983a, b).

Finally, version D shows a *modified elaborated* version of the same text. While still much longer overall than versions A and B, simply breaking up the rather unwieldy sentences of the elaborated version has restored sentence length and syntactic complexity to normal levels, while further increasing comprehensibility and preserving the meaning of the original text *and* the new language to which students must be exposed if they are to progress. (For illustrative studies, reviews of research findings, and additional comparisons and discussions of genuine, simplified, elaborated, and modified elaborated texts, see Farshi & Tavakoli [2019], Hillman [2021], Long [2015: 250–59], Long [2020], Oh [2001], and Yano, et al. [1994].)

5.9 Learning and Teaching New Language in Task-Based Language Teaching

To this point, we have described the role of the second part of a needs analysis, the ATD, in identifying and selecting new language to be taught in a task-based course. The steps (the subtasks) in conducting an ATD are summarized in Figure 5.2.

Selection of both target tasks and language in TBLT is data-based and systematic, and unlike the world of commercial coursebook publishing (languages for no particular purpose), does not rely on a textbook writer's intuitions. Intuitions are highly problematic even where simple tasks like

> 1. Collect spoken and/or written samples of the language used (i.e., the TD), to perform the target task(s) successfully.
> 2. Identify TD segments corresponding to subtasks.
> 3. Determine which subtasks or moves are obligatory, and which are optional.
> 4. Draw a flowchart showing the sequence of subtasks or moves. (For two examples, see the flowcharts for police traffic stops and celebration speeches described above.)
> 5. List the linguistic items (grammar, vocabulary, collocations, formulaic sequences) that frequently co-occur with each move or subtask.
> 6. Use the results of steps 3–5 to create models of the TD of interest. (The models will serve as the basis for pedagogic tasks.)
> 7. Depending on student proficiency, elaborate the input as necessary.

Figure 5.2 Steps in an analysis of target discourse

ordering a coffee are concerned, and much more so when, as is often the case, target tasks and TD domains are less familiar or wholly unfamiliar to the materials writer. The L in TBLT must be *relevant* to meet learners' communicative needs, and ATD is a way of ensuring that.

In the case of Bartlett's model, domain-specific lexical items might seem the area of most potential difficulty. However, names and descriptors of coffee items are easy enough to teach using pictures or, better, a trip to a coffee shop (see Van den Branden, 2016, for a task-based field trip of that sort), and most students will only need to learn how to order the two or three types of coffee they prefer. In fact, it is not the coffees per se, but how to negotiate their purchase that is the problem. Solving that will entail the need to understand, use, and respond to colloquial language, deictics, ellipsis, multimodality and intertextuality (in Bartlett's prototypical dialog, concerning the location of scones and final payment), and rapid-fire fragments rather than the laborious and unnatural complete sentences common in textbook models. Depending on students' cultural backgrounds and (lack of) familiarity with the society where the L2 is spoken, some may also need to learn how purchases are organized, for example in the USA as opposed to parts of the Arab world. Several chapters and case studies in this volume (particularly but not only, those in Parts III, IV, and V), address various aspects of task-based classroom language learning and teaching in detail.

Things that native speakers and "cultural natives" no longer notice because they are so familiar (and often because they have never experienced another culture), may be as much a challenge for some learners as the language involved in doing a task. For example, some recent arrivals in the United States whose vehicle is stopped by police may assume they should get out of their car and offer the officer money, as they would have to do in their country of origin. Suffice to say, neither is a good idea in the United States. In the case of a shopping purchase, it may be such things as power relationships between server and customer, whether bargaining is allowed, the level of formality and politeness expected or accepted, who initiates sales talk, when, where and how payment is performed, and so on. Some of this may eventually be learnable by observation of natives at play, but TBLT can speed up the process.

5.10 Conclusion

In sum, the first part of a task-based needs analysis involves the identification of target tasks for particular types or groups of learners. The second part consists of an ATD. Representative samples of the typical subtasks and genuine language use involved in successful performance of those target tasks are examined for common patterns and the essential and/or frequent linguistic items employed to perform them. Based on the observed patterns, one or more prototypical models of spoken or written discourse are produced. These become the basis for the development of TBLT materials and constitute a major source of *relevant* new language for students and teachers. Depending on the level of students' L2 proficiency, modified (elaborated, not simplified) versions of language in the models may be required. Guided by ten general methodological principles (for a detailed rationale and illustrations of their implementation, see Long, 2009, 2015: 300–28.), teachers implement them via pedagogic procedures they choose because they are appropriate for local conditions (the current pedagogic focus, learner characteristics, etc.) to facilitate students' acquisition of the new language, in context, as they work on initially simple, progressively more complex pedagogic tasks – gradual approximations to the full target tasks identified in the first part of the needs analysis.

Further Reading

Granena, G. (2008). Elaboration and simplification in scripted and genuine telephone service encounters. *International Review of Applied Linguistics*, 46 (2), 137–66.

Long, M. H. (2015). Analyzing target discourse. In M. H. Long, *Second language acquisition and task-based language teaching*. Oxford: Wiley Blackwell, pp. 169–204.

Long, M. H. (2020). Optimal input for language learning: genuine, simplified, elaborated, or modified elaborated? *Language Teaching*, 53(2), 169–82.

O'Connell, S. P. (2014). A task-based language teaching approach to the police traffic stop. *TESL Canada*, 31(8), 116–31.

Oh, S.-Y. (2001). Two types of input modification and EFL reading comprehension: simplification versus elaboration. *TESOL Quarterly*, 35(1), 69–96.

Study Questions

1. What are the pros and cons of input elaboration?
2. How, if at all, could the first and/or second part(s) of needs analyses differ for *groups* of learners and *types* of learners?
3. Are there cases where native speaker intuitions could constitute a valid basis for materials writing?
4. Would an algorithm for input elaboration be desirable, and if so, can you sketch one?

References

Bartlett, N. D. (2005). A double shot 2% mocha latte, please, with whip: Service encounters in two coffee shops and at a coffee cart. In M. H. Long, ed. *Second language needs analysis*. Cambridge: Cambridge University Press, pp. 305–43.

Borro, I. (2020). Enhanced incidental learning of formulaic sequences by Chinese learners of Italian. Ph.D. dissertation. University of Portsmouth.

Brown, J. D. (2009). Foreign and second language needs analysis. In M. H. Long and C. J. Doughty, eds. *Handbook of language teaching*. Oxford: Wiley-Blackwell, pp. 269–93.

Brown, J. D. (2016). *Introducing needs analysis and English for specific purposes*. New York and London: Routledge.

Cathcart, R. (1989). Authentic discourse and the survival English curriculum. *TESOL Quarterly*, 23(1), 105–26.

Chaudron, C. (1982). Vocabulary elaboration in teachers' speech to L2 learners. *Studies in Second Language Acquisition*, 4(2), 170–80.

Farshi, N. and Tavakoli, M. (2019). Effects of differences in language aptitude on learning grammatical collocations under elaborated input conditions. *Language Teaching Research*. DOI: 10.1177/1362168819858443

Gilabert, R. and Castellvi, J (2019). Task and syllabus design for morphologically complex languages. In J. W. Schwieter and A. Benati, eds. *Cambridge handbook of language learning*. Cambridge: Cambridge University Press, pp. 527–49.

Granena, G. (2008). Elaboration and simplification in scripted and genuine telephone service encounters. *International Review of Applied Linguistics*, 46(2), 137–66.

Hillman, K. (2021). Effects of different types of auditory input on incidental vocabulary learning by L2 Japanese learners. Unpublished PhD dissertation in second language acquisition. College Park, MD: University of Maryland.

Hillman, K. and Long, M. H. (2020). A task-based needs analysisfor US Foreign Service Officers, and the challenge of the Japanese celebration speech. InC. Lambert and, R. Oliver, eds. *Using tasks in diverse contexts*. Bristol: Multilingual Matters, pp. 123–45.

Long, M. H. (1983a). Linguistic and conversational adjustments to non-native speakers. *Studies in Second Language Acquisition*, 5(2), 177–93.

Long, M. H. (1983b). Native speaker/non-native speaker conversation and the negotiation of comprehensible input. *Applied Linguistics*, 4(2), 126–41.

Long, M. H. (2005). Methodological issues in learner needsanalysis. In M. H. Long, ed. *Second language needs analysis*. Cambridge: Cambridge University Press, pp. 19–76.

Long, M. H. (2009). Methodological principles in language teaching. InM. H. Long and C. J. Doughty, eds. *Handbook of language teaching*. Oxford: Blackwell, pp. 373–94.

Long, M. H. (2015). Analyzing target discourse. InM. H. Long, *Second language acquisition and task-based language teaching*. Oxford: Wiley Blackwell, pp. 169–204.

Long, M. H. (2018). Needs analysis. InC. Chapelle, ed. *The concise encyclopedia of applied linguistics*. 2nd ed. Oxford: Wiley-Blackwell.

Long, M. H. (2020). Optimal input for language learning: genuine, simplified, elaborated, or modified elaborated? *Language Teaching*, 53(2), 169–82.

Long, M. H., Lee, J., and Hillman, K. (2019). Task-based language learning. InJ. W. Schwieter and A. Benati, eds. *Cambridge handbook of language learning*. Cambridge: Cambridge University Press, pp. 500–26.

Long, M. H. and Ross, S. (1993). Modifications that preserve language and content. In Tickoo, M., ed. *Simplification: Theory and application*. Singapore: SEAMEO Regional Language Centre, pp. 29–52.

Malicka, A., Gilabert Guerrero, R., and Norris, J. M. (2019).From needs analysisto task design:Insights from an English for specific purposes context. *Language Teaching Research*, 23(1), 78–106.

O'Connell, S. P. (2014). A task-based language teaching approach to the police traffic stop. *TESL Canada*, 31(8), 116–31.

Oh, S.-Y. (2001). Two types of input modification and EFL reading comprehension: simplification versus elaboration. *TESOL Quarterly*, 35(1), 69–96.

Scotton, C. M. and Bernsten, J. (1988). Natural conversations as a model for textbook dialogue. *Applied Linguistics*, 9, 372–84.

Serafini, E. J., Lake, J. B., and Long, M. H. (2015). Needs analysis for specialized learner populations: Essential methodological improvements. *English for Specific Purposes*, 40, 11–26.

Sinclair, J. H. and Coulthard, M. (1975). *The English used by teachers and pupils*. Oxford: Oxford University Press.

Taborn, S. (1983). The transactional dialogue: Misjudged, misused, misunderstood. *ELT Journal*, 37(3), 207–12.

Van den Branden, K. (2016). The role of teachers in task-based language education. *Annual Review of Applied Linguistics*, 36, 164–81.

White, L. (1989). Against comprehensible input. The Input Hypothesis and the development of L2 competence. *Applied Linguistics*, 8(1), 95–110.

Williams, M. (1988). Language taught for meetings and language used in meetings: Is there anything in common? *Applied Linguistics*, 1(1), 45–58.

Yano, Y., Long, M. H., and Ross, S. (1994). The effects of simplified and elaborated texts on foreign language reading comprehension. *Language Learning*, 44(2), 189–219.

5A

Blustery with an Occasional Downpour

An Analysis of Target Discourse in Media Weather Forecasts

Ryo Maie and Bradford Salen

5A.1 Introduction

Weather is so quotidian in our daily lives that its criticality is easily overlooked. When immigrating into countries with different climates and not knowing what is possible, even such mundane matters as the high/low temperature of the day can have significant, and occasionally even lethal, consequences (see National Research Council, 2010, for such cases). There is evidence that a well-educated first-language-speaking public's interpretation of weather terminologies is subject to wide variation, often deviating from how professional meteorologists understand and use terms (Murphy & Brown, 1983a, 1983b). It is not hard to predict, then, that understanding weather forecasts, and the language employed to deliver them, can be even more variable for second-language speakers. Language teaching materials dealing with forecasts thus need be based on careful analysis of genuine target language use.

The ubiquity and practical importance of weather forecasts and the fact that they have to date not been a target discourse domain in the task-based language teaching (TBLT) literature motivated us to carry out the study reported here. Although we recognize that target tasks must usually be identified during the first stage in a needs analysis before collecting samples of language use in the target discourse domains (see Long [2005, 2015] and Serafini [this volume] for guidelines), we deemed *understanding a weather report* an obvious one even without formally identifying it as a target task through a detailed needs analysis. In this case study, we outline the methods and procedures that were followed to collect and analyze samples of target discourse in media weather forecasts, and then compare the results with those of previous studies (see Long [this volume] for a review).

5A.2 Methods

5A.2.1 Sampling

For analysis, we collected recordings of 302 radio and television weather forecasts from the Washington DC area over a roughly one-month period (March 8–April 21, 2017). See Table 5A.1 for the breakdown of the recordings. We collected all data from three time periods each day, morning (6:00–11:59 a.m.), afternoon (12:00–5:59 p.m.), and evening (6:00–11:59 p.m.), and did not focus on the hours after midnight (12:00–5:59 a.m.) due to lower listenership (Pew Research Center, 2018). All were live broadcasts in English, sound- or video-recorded by the authors and stored on a shared Google Drive. Radio forecasts were recorded on a Samsung Notebook 305E, and television forecasts on a MacBook Pro laptop.

We sampled radio broadcasts from one station on the AM band and one on the FM dial. Although AM band listenership in the United States has been in steady decline since the 1980s (Keith, 1993), growth in FM listenership has powered an overall increase in audience (Pew Research Center, 2018). In the United States in 2017, the combined broadcast radio reach was roughly 290 million people who reported listening to terrestrial (non-Internet) radio at least once per week across both bands (Pew Research Center, 2018). The fact that broadcast radio is a free consumer medium and enjoys high availability and reach made commercial broadcast radio an ideal target for an analysis of target discourse. For television forecasts, our sample came from one national and two local broadcasts. We expected that the use of multiple radio/television sources would allow us to investigate commonalities and disparities among stations in how weather reports were presented. Note that we were not able to include any

Table 5A.1 *Summary of the broadcast sample*

	Radio		TV			Total
	AM	FM	Local 1	Local 2	National	
Morning	25	23	28	27	–	103
Afternoon	23	24	18	20	25	85
Evening	22	21	23	23	–	89
Total	70	68	69	70	25	302

national-level radio broadcast due to the lack of any comparable national forecasts online.[1]

5A.2.2 Transcription and Coding

We first transcribed the radio and television forecasts separately and independently. The first author transcribed the television, and the second author the radio, broadcasts. Then we combined all transcripts and reviewed them together. Any errors and discrepancies in transcription were discussed until a consensus was reached. Our discussions primarily concerned (a) whether a transcript had any transcription errors, (b) where utterances began and ended, (c) pause length, and (d) suprasegmental features. We drew upon a modified version of Winn's (2005) study for transcription conventions, originally adapted from Gumperz and Berenz (1993). Examples of the transcript and coding sheet are available on demand.

We identified subtasks at the utterance-level. After all transcriptions were complete, we selected approximately 10 percent of the total dataset for analysis to develop a broad overview of how weather forecasts were structured. The limited sample consisted of 15 radio and 15 television broadcasts, both randomly selected ($n = 30$). Our initial observations provided us with a basic framework from which to differentiate among the utterances that pertained to different subtasks. It must be noted that not every utterance in a given broadcast segment was coded as part of a subtask. For example, banter among meteorologists and journalists, common in the vast majority of broadcasts, was not coded for subtask because of irrelevance to the overarching task of understanding a weather report. After the baseline framework was established, we re-coded each broadcast segment concurrently, for common subtasks in the corpus. Specifically, each subtask was directly related to the information relayed in a given utterance. For example, the subtask "determining current weather" was identified by being language specific to current conditions (e.g., *right now it's sunny, we have showers across the region*). The subtask included data on temperature, precipitation, wind gusts, and weather advisories.

5A.2.3 Language Analysis

Due to space constraints, we restrict our discussion here to the analysis of linguistic features already found relevant in the TBLT literature: structural ellipsis, use of technical and subtechnical vocabulary, and collocations.

---

[1] Although the National Weather Service (NWS) and the National Oceanic and Atmospheric Administration (NOAA) offer continuous weather reports over radio, their computer-generated speech is not at all comparable in listenership or form to live-broadcast human meteorologists and reporters.

We first manually coded the instance and type (i.e., noun phrase [NP] or verb phrase [VP]) of structural ellipsis on an utterance-by-utterance basis, and counted the number of forecasts whose utterances at least had one instance of structural ellipsis, and also the proportion within a segment represented by elided utterances. We modeled our annotation scheme after best-practices in creating gold-annotated corpora (see Wissler, Almashraee, Díaz & Paschke [2014] for a brief overview of annotating corpora for Natural Language Processing).

We identified technical and subtechnical vocabulary by examining all transcripts, and then obtained raw frequencies using the concordance software, *AntConc* (version 3.5.2, Anthony, 2017). Although the definition of technical vocabulary seems straightforward (i.e., items that bear a specialized meaning and usage in a discipline), there is no consensus as to what subtechnical terms really mean (Baker, 1988). In our study, we defined them as "items which have a specialized meaning in one or more disciplines, in addition to a different meaning in general language" (Baker, 1988: 92). It is also important to note that even when the same subtechnical terms appear in two or more disciplines, they usually have discipline-specific usage (Hyland & Tse, 2007). One aim here was to capture usage of subtechnical vocabulary items specific to media weather broadcasts. We also conducted a more fine-grained bigram search of the corpus to identify the most frequent two-word collocations. Bigrams are units made of any two words. We then looked for the most frequent bigrams in general and also for collocations that included weather-related words or technical and subtechnical vocabulary items.

5A.2.4 Developing Prototypical Discourse Samples

Producing prototypical discourse samples is the goal of an analysis of target discourse. In this study, we adopted a quantitative approach wherein numerical results on the proportion of subtasks and frequencies of linguistic features (e.g., structural ellipsis and technical and subtechnical vocabulary) were directly translated into prototypical samples. If a given subtask, for instance, occupied 45 percent of utterances in the discourse, we modeled our prototypical samples to have them reflect that proportion. Furthermore, although we observed some patterns in the distribution of subtasks across time blocks and broadcast stations, we found that their distributions were varied. We thus opted to create samples of weather forecasts for a specific broadcast station in a specific time period, rather than making unwarranted generalizations.

One important principle of analyses of target discourse is to "obtain multiple examples of the same kind of target discourse ... to identify, and *where appropriate*, subsequently remove, any idiosyncratic features" (Long, this volume; our emphasis). We deemed generalizing over such variability was spurious in our case because it would be to ignore particular characteristics of, say, a broadcast station that should not be overlooked. Rather, we preferred to capture that uncertainty by collecting sufficient examples and reflect it in our prototypical samples. Of course, this assumes that one knows (from the first part of the needs analysis) which specific broadcast station students usually tune in to.

5A.3 Results

5A.3.1 Subtasks and Discourse Structures

We identified two recurrent subtasks for radio and five for television forecasts. Table 5A.2 below lists the radio and television subtasks. Unexpectedly, there were no observable patterns in the order in which the subtasks were carried out in both media, although they together accounted for a majority of the utterances (i.e., around 80–90 percent). Rather, their order seemed contingent on what was of immediate importance, such as incoming storms, strong winds, and weather advisories (e.g., flash floods, thunderstorms, and heavy snow accumulations). Hence, we cannot present any generalized sequence in subtasks, as was done in previous studies (e.g., Bartlett, 2005; O'Connell, 2014), but to present their relative proportion in a given forecast. Pedagogically speaking, however, this means that learners cannot be trained on one prototypical sequence of the subtasks, but rather need to be exposed to diverse combinations in order to handle the variation within the target task flexibly. See the appendix for detailed results on the subtask proportion in a tabular format.

Radio forecasts consisted of the subtasks "determining the current weather" (CW) and "understanding an outlook of expected weather

Table 5A.2 *Radio and television subtasks*

	Coding notation	Full subtask name
Radio		
Current weather	CW	Determining the current weather
Outlook	O	Understanding a summary of expected weather conditions
Television		
Current weather	CW	Determining the current weather in maps
Future weather	FW	Understanding future weather conditions in maps
Headlines	H	Understanding weather headlines
Outlook	O	Understanding a summary of expected weather conditions
Extended outlook	EO	Understanding an extended summary of expected weather conditions

conditions" (O). Primarily, CW involved a general overview of ongoing weather with occasional instances of weather advisories, while O was a summary of future weather projected for the rest of the day or the next day. We found that the proportion of CW slightly decreased as the time of day progressed (from 23.63 percent in the morning to 12.59 percent in the evening), while that of O increased (from 57.6 percent to 71.89 percent). This may reflect the change in their relative importance in radio forecasts, such that in the evening, there is less need to attend to ongoing weather but rather to discuss a summary of future weather conditions to prepare for the coming day and beyond. Table 5A.3 provides an example of a transcript of a radio forecast from AM radio in the afternoon of March 16, 2017. In this example, the meteorologist began by presenting an overview of current weather, providing information on temperatures and wind gusts in the area (lines 1–4). He then proceeded to an outlook of future conditions, discussing what to expect in the evening of the same day and the next day (lines 5–10). The floor was then returned to the host of the radio station, who reported temperatures and wind gusts of specific places that were of particular interest to the majority of the audience (lines 11–13).

Television forecasts, on the other hand, were more detailed and extensive (see the transcript in Table 5A.4 from the afternoon of April 7, 2019). This was due to the fact that they were generally longer (31.21 to 13.68 utterances) and that they afforded visual materials to aid comprehension (see Maie & Salen, 2018 for the visual materials). Here, the meteorologist began by discussing weather headlines (understanding weather headlines: lines 2–6), the critical points to be taken about the forecasts. She then proceeded to an overview of current weather conditions depicted

Table 5A.3 *Radio forecast transcript 16MAR17MR1*

Line	Speaker	Subtask	Utterance
1	M	CW	Temperatures right now close to 20 degrees below average
2	M	CW	Another extremely cold day out there on our Thursday
3	M	CW	However at least it's a little bit better than yesterday
4	M	CW	Still seein' winds gusting 20 to 30 miles per hour and our wind chills are in the 20s
5	M	O	Overnight tonight gonna be a cold night
6	M	O	Back into the mid to upper 20s for the most part
7	M	O	As we move into the day tomorrow remember that refreeze so give yourself some extra time tomorrow morning
8	M	O	Watch out for slick spots
9	M	O	Highs tomorrow back into the mid to upper 40s
10	M	O	I'm a WXYZ meteorologist Jane Doe
11	H	CW	39 degrees at Reagan National
12	H	CW	Winds still gusting to 31 and it feels like 30
13	H	CW	Here in Northwest, we have a temperature of 33 degrees

Note. M = Meteorologist. H = Host.

Table 5A.4 *Television forecast transcript 07APR17AV2*

Line	Speaker	Subtask	Utterance
1	M	–	I'm meteorologist Jane Doe
2	M	H	It is going to be a blustery day
3	M	H	Not the most comfortable day
4	M	H	And in fact, it's going to feel, like March
5	M	H	Cloudy, blustery, some showers out there, even through the higher elevations, a little snow mixed on in
6	M	H	Especially in the morning
7	M	CW	Now as we head through the afternoon, I put the feels-like temperatures here, because the winds are going to be such an impact that it's gonna feel into the upper 30s and low 40s for much of the day
8	M	CW	This is about as warm as it's gonna feel today
9	M	CW	This is 3 o'clock, 38 for Frederick, 39 for Leesburg, 42 for Washington
10	M	CW	You might have to break out the winter jacket today.
11	M	CW	It's going to feel like March
12	M	FW	Now as we head through the evening hours, 8 o'clock, if you have evening plans, yeah, hang onto that winter jacket
13	M	FW	It's gonna be cold tonight, feeling 31 for Martinsburg
14	M	FW	Still breezy tonight and actually we're gonna stay breezy for tomorrow as well
15	M	FW	By 7 o'clock in the morning, it will feel, below freezing across the board into the 20s and the actual temperature will drop below freezing as you head west of 95 with those clear skies in place
16	M	FW	So, pretty cold, first thing in the morning
17	M	FW	In fact, there is a freeze watch in place for areas west of 95, in some of our colder spots
18	M	FW	So if you got a little, uh, early going on the planting, you might wanna protect some of that vegetation or, uh, plants and flowers that you do have out there
19	M	O	Ok, so for Saturday
20	M	O	We're looking at temperatures into the low 60s
21	M	O	Just breezy instead of windy, but look at all the sunshine out there
22	M	O	It's going to be a gorgeous day on Saturday
23	M	O	As we head to Sunday, more comfortable
24	M	O	72 degrees
25	M	EO	How about some, more typical spring weather?
26	M	EO	Yeah, it's gonna be nice next week
27	M	EO	We're actually reaching near 80
28	M	EO	A little above average but we'll take it
29	M	EO	Nationals are back in town and, 80s are here for Monday and Tuesday
30	M	EO	A stray shower overnight Tuesday into Wednesday morning but only a little bit of a cool down Wednesday at 68

Note. M = Meteorologist.

on an interactive map (lines 7–11) and subsequently followed up with future weather, which was a prediction for the immediate future, especially for the rest of the day or early morning of the following day (lines 12–18). The CW and FW sections often dealt with estimates of temperatures, precipitation, and weather advisories. Later, they were summarized in panels as weather outlooks, each presented on its own (lines 19–24). Finally, the meteorologist presented an extended outlook (understanding an extended outlook of expected weather conditions: lines 25–30), with a short-term forecast (2–3 days) preceding a long-term one (7–10 days).

We found that the proportions of the subtasks varied dramatically for television forecasts, depending on the time of day, broadcast stations, and whether they were region-specific or nation-wide (see appendix). First, the proportion of FW decreased with the time of day (from 31.74 percent in the morning to 20.87 percent in the evening), while that of EO increased (from 17.37 to 25.41 percent). Like the radio forecasts, there became less need to address FW in the evening because it has already been covered earlier in the day, but to discuss predictions of weather conditions in the further future. Second, the two local broadcast stations differed in the proportion of the subtasks they most frequently covered, with Local 1 preferring CW (25.49 percent) and with Local 2, FW (38.73 percent). Lastly, while the local broadcasts covered all five subtasks with roughly the same frequency, the national forecasts mostly handled FW (85.82 percent). This may be because (a) the national forecasts were much shorter in length (13.44 sentences) and (b) they had to discuss weather across the nation and were thus only able to present it on a national map, which was a feature of FW (and CW). In this light, local meteorologists tended to be "generalists," compared to national forecasters who only performed a limited but specialized number of the tasks (see Long, 2005, 2015 for similar results). In sum, we found that the internal structure of weather forecast discourse depended on time and locality, and this highlighted the importance of conducting analyses of target discourse *in situ*. This also meant that separate prototypical discourse samples need be developed for different time periods of day and for different broadcast stations.

5A.3.2 Analysis of Linguistic Features

Ellipsis

Previous analyses of target discourse have demonstrated that communicative uses of language are full of structural ellipses, which are intricately situated in a given discourse (e.g., Bartlett, 2005; Long, 2005, 2015). We found this to be the case in our data, as well, summarized in Table 5A.5. The table lists the number of forecasts whose sentences had at least one instance of structural ellipsis, and the proportion of the entire discourse sample that the elided utterances occupied. NP ellipsis was often an elision of the subject of a sentence. VP ellipsis was an omission of copula or auxiliary verbs (i.e., be and have). NP+VP ellipses were an amalgamation of the two. *None* of the 138 radio forecasts were completely without ellipses, and the result was very similar for the television forecasts (ellipses in 159/164), underscoring the pervasive nature of structural ellipsis in the weather forecast discourse there, too. Below, is an example of three types of ellipsis that we identified in the data.

a. NP+VP
   34 degrees, light snow mainly to the west and northeast of Baltimore
   [It will be] 34 degrees [and we'll see] light snow mainly to the west and northeast of Baltimore.
b. NP
   Well, still is the morning rush tomorrow
   Well, [there] still is the morning rush tomorrow.
c. VP
   Tuesday's high about 36
   Tuesday's high [is] about 36.

Technical and Subtechnical Vocabulary

Technical vocabulary items frequently observed in our samples included *thunderstorm*, *wind-chill*, *sleet*, *gust* (verb), *blustery* and *Nor'easter*. At first glance, these terms seem straightforward. However, difficulties immediately arise when considering, for example, different types of precipitation like *sleet* or *wintry mix*, as most people cannot reliably describe the difference between sleet, freezing rain, wet snow, and a wintry mix. Instances of subtechnical vocabulary included *accumulation*, *chance* (adjective), *front* (noun), *freezing* (adjective), *system*, *pressure* (noun), *sprinkle*, *showers*. Note that all of these examples are either low-frequency lexical items in general (*accumulation*), or the lower frequency form if the words had more than one part of speech (Davies, 2008) – e.g., "those could gust to twenty miles per hour" or "we'll see a chance shower this afternoon." At minimum, this suggests that novice second-language listeners would not be familiar with these terms.

Collocations

Prior to analyzing the data, we predicted that weather reporting would be replete with frequent collocations unique to this genre. Additionally, our predictions included the use of unique compound noun phrases (e.g., *rain showers* and *cold front*) as well as descriptive collocations (e.g., *heavy rains* and *low pressure*). These predictions were confirmed in the data. Our analysis found a surprisingly high frequency of verb collocations (e.g., *get to*, *look at*, and *moving through*). It is also interesting to note that the top verb collocations all refer to movement or action of some kind, reflecting the constantly changing state of weather. Other high-frequency verb collocations include *look/looking to; looking good; move/moves into, move/moving in; go*

Table 5A.5 *Frequency and proportion of utterances with ellipsis*

	Radio (n = 138)		TV (n = 164)	
Ellipsis	Frequency	Proportion %	Frequency	Proportion %
Total	138	48.97	159	38.39
NP+VP	137	8.65	159	26.58
NP	53	14.65	64	5.10
VP	102	35.06	135	11.65

Table 5A.6 *Top five most frequent collocations*

Word	Top collocation	Unique collocations	Tokens
showers		260	801
	some showers		117
	snow showers		68
	rain showers		54
	few showers		38
	showers around		30
rain		197	579
	some rain		65
	rain showers		54
	heavy rain		49
	light rain		34
	more rain		25
look		111	479
	look at		128
	looking at		47
	looks like		37
	looking good		20
	look to		12
get		170	433
	get into		34
	get to		20
degrees		143	417
	degrees in		27
	degrees outside		26
	degrees at		24
	degrees for		23
	degrees by		18

through, and *go into*. This fact is not realized in existing teaching materials that characterize weather as static, nondynamic events. For example, the language teaching video that serves as a model of weather reporting in English that is currently available from the British Council free website does not resemble our sample in speech pattern/rate, discourse structure, nor lexical content. Table 5A.6 summarizes examples of the five most frequent collocations identified in the corpus.

Table 5A.7 *An example of prototypical discourse for afternoon FM radio*

	Subtask	Utterance
1	CW	We have clear skies right now
2	CW	Temperatures in the upper 40s, wind gusts up to 30 miles per hour
3	O	Clouds increase, snow showers possible later tonight
4	O	Lows around 30 with wind-chills dropping into the 20s
5	O	Watch out for slick spots
6	O	Tomorrow morning, highs back up to mid 30s
7	O	Still chilly, with rain mixed in with some sleet
8	CW	Right now, 39 degrees at Reagan National, 40 at Dulles
9	–	I'm meteorologist Jane Doe from WXYZ weather

5A.3.3 Prototypical Discourse Samples

Table 5A.7 and 5A.8 each provide an example of a prototypical forecast for afternoon FM radio, and morning Local 1 television forecast, respectively. In principle, the same can be done to develop any other prototypical models. These samples can be used as classroom materials, with necessary elaboration of any lexical items that may be unfamiliar to learners, especially (sub) technical items (e.g., *snow showers*, *wind-chills*, and *sleet*; see Long [this volume] for details of the input elaboration process). When creating more samples, one recommended strategy is to base them on the prototype(s) by moving the order of the subtasks to reflect variation or by changing words and phrases that describe weather conditions. For instance, we can derive another example from Table 5A.7 by changing *snow showers* to *rain showers*, *upper 40s* to *mid 60s*, and changing information about precipitation to wind gusts. This may be useful for language teachers who often do not have time to produce multiple examples from square one.

5A.4 Conclusion

In this chapter, we reported results of our case study on three aspects of conducting an analysis of target discourse: identifying recurrent subtasks to understand the internal structure of weather forecast discourse, analyzing linguistic features that frequently co-occur with the subtasks, and developing samples of prototypical discourse that can be used as the basis for task-based materials for classroom teaching. Although we found some general patterns and variability that characterized the target discourse we sampled, we would not predict that our results would be directly transferable to broadcasts in other areas. Rather, future researchers/practitioners need to conduct their own analyses of target discourse so they can learn the specifics of the target domain. This means that through the first part of the needs analysis it is necessary to know which radio or television stations students often listen to (or watch) and in which time period(s).

Table 5A.8 *An example of prototypical discourse for Local 1 television in the morning*

	Subtask	Utterance
1	–	I'm sensitive when it comes to ice cream and cold weather
2		I mean, it's gonna feel like upper 20s
3	–	You might not ever be able to eat an ice cream again
4	–	It's gonna be tough
5	CW	Not a big wind out there this morning, but a little bit of a breeze with wind-chills feeling 5 or 6 degrees cooler than actual temperatures
6	O	But a very nice afternoon coming
7	O	We'll be in and out of the sunshine, but clouds will gradually thicken later on, but not until we get into the upper 50s to around 60
8	O	Clouds will eventually lead to a little chance for rain showers but probably not until 9 or 10 o'clock tonight
9	CW	So, here are the current temperatures, which are in the low and mid 30s but they feel cooler because of the winds
10	CW	So, close to 30 degrees for those wind-chills this morning
	CW	Here's the rain trends for tonight
12	CW	It's moving on the west sides of the Cleveland up towards Detroit now, which will gradually move in our direction
13	FW	So here's future weather to help you plan that out
14	FW	Mainly dry, through 4 or 5 o'clock by 9 o'clock tonight
15	FW	But a chance for showers coming in from the west
16	FW	Here is 1AM, uh, so this is a very late evening into a very early morning rain chance for tomorrow
17	FW	But I think that's out of here before the sun comes up and we'll have a dry start tomorrow
18	FW	Then later on in the day tomorrow, another chance of a passing shower
19	EO	(0.5) Extended outlook here
20	EO	Tomorrow, mostly clear skies, with temperatures around 50
21	EO	Chance of another shower on Saturday but then we go into Sunday, highs around 70 degrees, looking really nice
22	–	Let's check the roadways on this Thursday morning

Once such information is collected, the sample broadcast weather reports can be transcribed and analyzed so as to distill commonalities (or dissimilarities) in order to develop prototypical models. In the case study reported here, the aim was to be as transparent as possible in reporting methods and procedures used in in data collection and analysis, such that that the results can serve as a model for future research and language teaching.

Further Reading

Chaudron, C. J., Doughty, C. J., Kim, Y., Kong, D.-K, Lee, J., Lee, Y.-G., Long, M. H., Rivers, R., and Urano, K. (2005). A task-based needs analysisof a tertiary Korean as a foreign language program. In M. H. Long, ed. *Second language needs analysis*. Cambridge: Cambridge University Press, pp. 225–61.

Bartlett, N. D. (2005). A double shot 2% mocha latte, please, with whip: Service encounters in two coffee shops and at a coffee cart. In M. H. Long, ed. *Second language needs analysis*. Cambridge: Cambridge University Press, pp. 305–43.

Hillman, K. and Long, M. H. (2020). A task-based needs analysis for US Foreign Service Officers, and the challenge of the Japanese celebration speech. In C. Lambert, and R. Oliver, eds. *Using tasks in diverse contexts*. Bristol: Multilingual Matters, pp. 123–145

Long, M. H. (2005). Methodological issues in learner needs analysis. In M. H. Long, ed. *Second language needs analysis*. Cambridge: Cambridge University Press, pp. 19–76.

Long, M. H. (2015). Analyzing target discourse. In M. H. Long, ed. *Second language acquisition and task-based language teaching*. Oxford: Wiley Blackwell, pp. 169–204.

O'Connell, S. P. (2014). A task-based language teaching approach to the police traffic stop, *TESL Canada*, 31(8), 116–31.

Study Questions

1. We discussed that technical and subtechnical vocabulary are not well-defined in our field. Would you classify the following words as technical, subtechnical, or just weather-related words? *showers, frigid, slick spots, icing, system,* and *stray.* How would you explain your classification?
2. In our data, NP and VP ellipses were found to be prevalent. Let's say you are teaching a group of adult learners. How would you explain to them if they ask you why these sentences often lack the subject of the sentence or auxiliary verbs, and how would you justify their use when they apparently look ungrammatical to them?
3. The prototypical sample in Table 5A.7 may not be difficult to comprehend for first-language speakers, but it may be for second-language speakers, especially those with lower proficiency or no experience with listening to weather forecasts in English. What elaborations would you make to the sample in order to make it more accessible to lower proficiency learners? On what aspects?

References

Anthony, L. (2017). AntConc (Version 3.5.2) [Windows]. Tokyo, Japan: Waseda University. Retrieved from: http://www.laurenceanthony.net/software.html.

Baker, M. (1988). Sub-technical vocabulary and the ESP teacher: An analysis of some rhetorical items in medical journal articles. *Reading in a Foreign Language*, 4, 91–105.

Davies, M. (2008-) *The Corpus of Contemporary American English (COCA): 600 million words, 1990-present*. Retrieved from: https://www.english-corpora.org/coca/.

Gumperz, J. and Berenz, N. (1993). Transcribing conversational exchanges. In J. A. Edwards and M. D. Lampert, eds. *Talking data: Transcription and coding in discourse research*. Hillsdale, NJ: Lawrence Erlbaum Associates, pp. 91–121.

Hyland, K. and Tse, P. (2007). Is there an "academic vocabulary"? *TESOL Quarterly*, 41, 235–54.

Keith, M. C. (1993). AM radio: The status and struggle. *Journal of Radio Studies*, 2, 1–10.

Long, M. H. (2015). *Second language acquisition and task-based language teaching*. Oxford: Wiley Blackwell.

Long, M. H. (2019). Optimal input for language learning: Genuine, simplified, elaborated, or modified elaborated? *Language Teaching*, 53(2) 169–82.

Maie, R. and Salen, B. (2018, March). Task-based analysis of target discourse in media weather forecasts. Paper presented for the TESOL 2018 International Convention & English Language Expo, Chicago: IL.

Murphy, A. H. and Brown, B. G. (1983a). Forecast terminology: Composition and interpretation of public weather forecasts. *Bulletin of the American Meteorological Society*, 64, 13–22.

Murphy, A. H. and Brown, B. G. (1983b). Interpretation of some terms and phrases in public weather forecasts. *Bulletin of the American Meteorological Society*, 64, 1283–89.

National Research Council. (2010). *When weather matters: Science and services to meet critical societal needs*. Washington DC: National Academies Press.

Pew Research Center (2018). Audio and podcasting fact sheet. Retrieved from: https://www.pewresearch.org/wp-content/uploads/sites/8/2018/07/State-of-the-News-Media_2017-Archive.pdf.

Winn, M. (2005). Collecting target discourse:The case of the US naturalization interview. In M. H. Long, ed. *Second language needs analysis*. Cambridge: Cambridge University Press, pp. 265–304.

Wissler, L., Almashraee, M., Díaz, D. M., and Paschke, A. (2014, June). The gold standard in corpus annotation. Paper presented for the IEEE German Student Conference, University of Passau, Germany.

Appendix

Summary of subtasks in radio forecasts (AM/FM)

Subtask	Overall (%)	Morning (%)	Afternoon (%)	Evening (%)
CW	22.63/17.44	25.30/21.96	23.39/22.57	18.81/6.38
Outlook	68.88/61.55	66.05/49.15	68.83/64.27	72.16/71.63

Summary of subtasks in television forecasts (Local 1/Local 2/National or Local 1/Local 2)

Subtask	Overall (%)	Morning (%)	Afternoon (%)	Evening (%)
Headlines	10.95/13.10/4.89	6.59/9.99	13.26/14.00	14.56/15.98
CW	25.49/7.79/7.87	24.20/5.55	24.67/11.59	27.72/6.92
FW	16.24/38.73/85.82	20.15/43.34	20.05/38.81	8.48/33.26
O	14.99/14.77/0.00	14.88/14.82	13.82/11.55	16.04/17.09
EO	19.93/20.16/1.41	14.79/19.95	19.38/19.32	28.95/21.87

5B

"I Have a Question"

A Corpus-Based Analysis of Target Discourse in Office-Hour Interactions

Ayşenur Sağdıç and Derek Reagan

5B.1 Introduction

Office-hour interactions, a speech event that may involve several speech acts and discoursal moves (Hymes, 1974), are omnipresent in academic contexts. Universities in the United States are increasingly multilingual spaces in which English is often used as the lingua franca between instructors, students, staff, and administrators. During office hours, English for academic purposes (EAP) students meet with instructors, most of whom do not share a language other than English with their EAP students. Navigating such interactions can be a challenging task for all students for several reasons. In the context of the university, a student assumes a position of subordinate status to their instructor, and a successful communication involves recognizing this difference in status and encoding and decoding the necessary illocution in an appropriate manner. Additionally, due to their semi-private nature, the pragmatic norms surrounding office hours may seem unclear. These challenges increase when students need to manage such interactions in their second language (L2) in a speech community in which they are novices. Learners of an L2 need not only attend to the linguistic communication norms of the academic community around them, but also to the preferred pragmatic patterns to accomplish vital tasks, such as attending office-hour sessions. The latter requires L2 pragmatic competence, the capacity to comprehend and use language appropriately in its social context (Culpeper, Mackey & Taguchi, 2018). In what follows, we will briefly review previous research findings on EAP learners' pragmatic needs during one-on-one academic encounters and introduce the present study. We will then describe the data and methods and report our findings on types of office hours, subtasks, and frequent pragmatic and interactional features. In the final section, we provide a prototypical sequence of an office-hour session based on the analysis and discuss the implications for task-based L2 pragmatic instruction.

In a needs analysis of L2 pragmatics conducted with 180 graduate and undergraduate US-based EAP students, Youn (2018) observed that attending office hours was a task that was perceived by instructors, students, and administrators to be not only important, but challenging, requiring strong pragmatic abilities. The interviews with the instructors and administrators revealed that students were at times perceived as too polite, awkward, direct, or rude. The importance of office hours has also been observed by Skyrme (2010) in a longitudinal study. She mentioned that international undergraduates found office-hour appointments important, as these sessions provided opportunities for resolving misunderstandings about academic content and building relationships with instructors that are otherwise difficult in large classes. However, attending office hours proved difficult for the students, due to cross-cultural differences in pragmatic expectations. Turning to research on advising sessions, speech events in which students meet with their advisor to plan out their academic schedule, Bardovi-Harlig and Hartford (1993) longitudinally examined the pragmatic patterns of first language (L1) and L2 speakers of English during face-to-face advising sessions in a US university. Their findings showed that over time, L2 users improved their pragmatic skills by appropriately using the speech acts of suggestions and rejections. However, their speech diverged from that of L1 English speakers in terms of the frequency with which they employed mitigators and upgraders, even after a lengthy stay in the target language community.

Overall, research has revealed various pragmatic challenges EAP students may experience during non-classroom academic encounters, such as office hours, while underscoring the need to provide learners with pragmatic instruction through data-driven genuine materials. Task-based pragmatics studies (e.g., González-Lloret, 2008; Reagan & Payant, 2018; Taguchi & Kim, 2018) have continuously shown that interactive pedagogic tasks that include authentic linguistic input facilitate learners' pragmatic development. However, developing effective pedagogic tasks requires a systematic analysis of target discourse (ATD), a crucial step in task design, which involves the collection and analysis of genuine speech samples produced while completing target tasks (Long, 2015; Long, this volume). A proper ATD is essential, as pragmatics research (e.g., Ren & Han, 2016; Vellenga, 2004) has shown that commercial textbooks, and the language activities they contain, lack the authentic pragmatic input needed to complete communicative tasks requiring high pragmatic skills and metapragmatic awareness.

Due to the ubiquity of office hours and the obstacles they present for learners, research is warranted on attending office hours as a target task-type. Although under-utilized in task-based language teaching research and practice, a corpus, a principled collection of language data, can help in providing researchers and instructors with authentic linguistic input for an ATD. Corpora's stratified random sampling makes the language representative, which Biber (1993: 243) defines as "the extent to which a sample includes the full range of variability in a population." Therefore, corpus-based ATD findings can be argued to be generalizable to other instances of linguistic patterns found in the same speech event. Additionally, using an existing corpus eliminates the need to collect new language samples, easing the data-collection process. The Michigan Corpus of Academic Spoken English (MICASE) is particularly valuable for EAP researchers and instructors because it provides not only genuine, consequential interactions that have unfolded in real life, but also transcriptions of the interactions for research and teaching purposes. The pedagogic tasks that are developed based on this study can be used to promote L2 pragmatic development in various EAP contexts where attending office hours is a target task-type.

5B.2 The Study

This study reports an ATD of the MICASE instances of face-to-face office-hour interactions between English-speaking students and instructors in a US university setting. The office hours were coded for office-hour types, subtasks, and pragmatic and interactional features. Based on the analysis, a prototypical example was produced which can offer a model for data-driven task-based pragmatic instruction in EAP contexts. The following research questions guided the study:

1. What types of face-to-face office hours are there?
2. What are the subtasks involved in attending face-to-face office hours?
3. What pragmatic and interactional utterances are most frequent in face-to-face office-hour interactions?

5B.3 Data and Method

5B.3.1 The Corpus: MICASE
Our language data come from MICASE, which is a freely available specialized corpus of 1.8 million words of English academic speech. The corpus involves approximately 200 hours of recordings and 152 speech events (e.g., office hours, lectures, dissertation defenses) that took place on the University of Michigan campus between 1997 and 2001 (Simpson, Briggs, Ovens & Swales, 2002). As shown in Table 5B.1, MICASE has fourteen instances of office-hour sessions, covering a variety of academic disciplines from the humanities to the sciences. The recorded interactions range in

Table 5B.1 *Characteristics of MICASE office hours*

Office-hour sessions	Speakers	Total words	Male %	Female %	L1 %	L2 %
14	106	171,188	41	59	90.57	9.43

length from 25 to 178 minutes, with a mean length of 79 minutes, and involve a total of 106 interactants. Among the 106 speakers, 96 are native English speakers and 10 are either near native or nonnative speakers.

5B.3.2 Data Analysis and Coding

We used both qualitative and quantitative data analysis processes to identify the different types of office hours and the representative target discourse for each type. As part of the analysis, we completed the following seven steps:

1. Download the fourteen instances of office-hour transcripts and organize the data.
2. Read, record, and code emergent linguistic (e.g., modal verbs), pragmatic (e.g., requests, suggestions, recommendations), and interactional patterns (e.g., discourse markers) that occurred in the office-hour transcripts.
3. Create a coding book based on recurring patterns across cases.
4. Describe and classify individual codes into themes.
5. Further refine and evaluate our codes and subsequent themes.
6. Calculate frequency of occurrence of target discourse items and rank them.
7. Visualize the findings, following Hillman and Long's (2020) ATD procedure.

Throughout the analysis, each step was conducted by both researchers in tandem. During Steps 3 and 4, we met several times to develop and revise the coding book. We then coded the occurrence of representative discourse themes and the frequency of their occurrence across all office-hour interactions on MICASE. A subset of fourteen transcripts was coded by both researchers to estimate interrater reliability for the coding process. The overall percentage of interrater agreement in coding the interactions using the coding book was 92 percent. Inconsistencies were resolved by consensus. A trained external rater, an L1 English speaker, also coded four randomly selected transcripts using the updated coding scheme. Overall, the percent agreement was 94.4 percent. The first author then recoded the inconsistencies, leading to a reliable dataset. Next, all coded expressions were compiled and organized in a Microsoft Excel sheet. The coded expressions were organized by subtask, which was defined as "a differentiated process which, while having a number of steps and an outcome, is dependent on or part of another major target task" (Gilabert, 2005: 184), and ranked according to their respective frequency of occurrence in the MICASE transcripts.

5B.4 Findings

5B.4.1 Types of Office Hours

Our first research question aimed to explore different types of office hours in MICASE. Our findings indicated that office hours took the form of either prearranged appointments or drop-in sessions. While the former were more common for humanities and social science courses, the latter were more common for science and engineering classes. The prearranged office hours were meetings in which the student(s) and the instructor met in a designated place at a designated time and discussed coursework (e.g., final project, research paper topic, or thesis). In drop-in sessions, on the other hand, the instructor, often a graduate student instructor, met with one or more students and answered questions with respect to coursework (e.g., problem sets or homework exercises). The sessions also varied in terms of whether or not the session length was predetermined, regardless of type (i.e., by appointment or drop-in). There were office hours where the instructor allotted a specific amount of time per student, and there were others where the session's length was not predetermined, lasting as long as it needed to take. Table 5B.2 shows the distribution of the office-hour types.

The most frequent office-hour type was drop-in sessions where the length of the session was not predetermined. This was followed by prearranged sessions whose length was also not predetermined. These findings indicate that it might be more common for EAP students to have office hours where there is no predetermined length, which requires students to be mindful of the time and to recognize and produce moves such as pre-closing (e.g., okay) and closing (e.g., bye) while managing to achieve their communicative goals by the end of the session. This can be especially challenging when there are several students attending the same appointment, which was common in the corpus. Only four out of fourteen took place between a single student and an instructor. As for the descriptive analysis of all office-hour appointments, we found that the interlocutors' speech was often informal, informational, and highly interactive. While

Table 5B.2 *Distribution of MICASE office-hour types*

Length/session type	Prearranged sessions	Drop-in sessions
Predetermined	3	0
Not predetermined	4	7

both interlocutors contributed to the interaction equally, they differed in their linguistic and pragmatic patterns, which we will discuss next.

5B.4.2 Office-Hour Subtasks and Frequency of Subtask Utterances

The second research question addressed the subtasks involved in attending office-hour sessions. The third question focused on the most frequent pragmatic and interactional utterances in the MICASE data. Figure 5B.1 illustrates the overall structure and flow and the seven subtasks that occurred in the target task-type of attending office hours. All subtasks were frequently used in the interactions; however, while the subtasks *Requesting* and *Informing and recommending* were obligatory, *Greeting*, *Initiation to subject matter*, *Justifying request*, *Wrapping up*, and *Leave-taking* were optional, depending on the office-hour type. In the following, we will discuss the subtasks and present the most frequently used expressions that occurred in each. The raw frequency of the expressions (i.e., how many times the expression occurred across all fourteen office-hour sessions) will appear in parentheses following each expression.

5B.4.3 Overall Structure and Flow of Office-Hour Interactions

Greeting

As seen in the figure, *Greeting* is the first subtask. While it was frequently employed by both interlocutors in prearranged office-hour sessions, this subtask was optional in drop-in sessions. The most frequently used greeting utterances were "hi" (29) and "hey" (19), reflecting the informal nature of the exchange. Questions – "how are you?" (11) and "what's up?" (3) – followed initial greetings. Answers to the questions varied, with "pretty good" (13) being one of the few frequently occurring expressions.

Initiation to Subject Matter

The first subtask, *Greeting*, is followed by *Initiation to subject matter*, in which the student or the instructor introduce the topic of the meeting by asking questions. Frequently, the student sets the scene by saying that they are going to make a request or by introducing a topic relevant to their question. Students' utterances often started with the stance-taking devices "I think" (357), "I think that" (89), or "I thought" (55), signaling to the instructor that the student is about to share their personal opinion or experience. Additionally, as Fraser (2010) indicates, these lexical expressions allow speakers to maintain face through hedging, a pragmatic strategy that diminishes the force of an utterance. The phrases "okay, so" (217) and "alright, so" (31) were used at the beginning of sentences by both students and instructors to introduce a new topic or to provide an explanation;

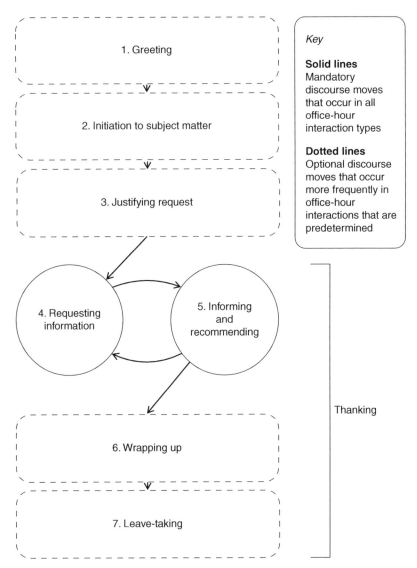

Figure 5B.1 Overall structure and flow of office-hour interactions

however, their use was not exclusive to this subtask. Both utterances also frequently appear in *Requesting information* and *Informing and recommending*.

Justifying Request

Although not used by all students in this subtask, some justified their office-hour appointment request by providing reason(s) for their confusion about the course-related content. This subtask, which often occurred in the middle of the meeting, made the interaction efficient, as instructors could easily identify where students were experiencing difficulties. Based on our analysis, we determined that employing this subtask was an effective politeness strategy because it helped students mitigate the face-threatening nature of making a request to an instructor. Students employed the following utterances, indicating that it is frequent and pragmatically preferred for them to acknowledge their confusion or lack of understanding of the subject matter: "I don't know" (161), "I still don't know" (1), "I don't understand" (13), "I don't remember" (10), "I don't get" (3), "I didn't get" (2), "I'm confused" (2), "I was confused" (6), "I get confused" (4), "I'm getting confused" (1), "that confuses me" (1). Upon hearing these utterances, instructors either addressed students' confusion (e.g., "okay, so+[sentence]") or asked further clarification questions (e.g., "can you+[verb]").

Requesting Information

The majority of the office-hour sessions consist of a cyclical pattern of communication, in which a student makes a request for information and an instructor makes an attempt to provide information and/or recommendations. Based on the MICASE data, this cycle can be limited to a single question and answer, or it may involve an exchange containing several questions and answers. In this obligatory subtask, students often used interrogative sentences to solicit: a) (further) information, b) feedback, c) recommendations, and/or d) clarification from the instructor. These sentences often included the following utterances: "can you+[verb]?" (56) and "do you know" (30). Students also explicitly stated that they have a question for their instructors using the following utterances: "I have a question" (13), "I had a question" (2), "I have another question" (1). In turn, instructors employed utterances starting with "how do you+[verb]" (39), "do you think" (26), "what do you think" (8), "why do you think" (6). They also used "does that make sense?" (17) to check students' comprehension and "do you have a question?" (2), "do you have questions?" (2), "you have a question?" (1), "did you have another question?" (1) to elicit further questions from students. For questions, such as "did you have another question?", the auxiliary "did" is not a past tense marker. Instead, it is a syntactic mitigation device used by the instructor to create interpersonal distance.

Informing and Recommending

Throughout this obligatory subtask, instructors used declarative sentences to a) give recommendations, b) evaluate students' work with compliments or criticism, and/or c) answer students' questions. Instructors asked questions to start a conversation about a new, but related, topic, and to elicit (further) information from the student(s). They used the following utterances when sharing information and making recommendations to students: "you wanna+[verb]" (149), "you want to+[verb]" (55), "you might wanna" (31), "you might want to" (5), "you have to+[verb]" (105), "you could+[verb]" (100), "you need to" (75), "you should" (64). Understanding the pragmatic meaning of modals in instructor recommendations is key for learners, and should be highlighted through pragmatics instruction. Moreover, "I don't think+[sentence]" (37), "I don't think so" (7), "I don't think that" (6) were used by instructors to politely disagree with students without explicitly stating that they were wrong. Finally, we observed that predetermined office hours include more questions and answers among the interlocutors than the ones that are not predetermined.

Wrapping Up

This optional subtask was used by the interlocutors to signal that the office-hour session was about to end shortly, either because all questions had been answered, or because the allotted time was about to end. Both students and instructors, in this subtask, frequently used expressions "see you" (4) or "see you," followed by a phrase indicating a specific time frame: "tomorrow" (5), "next week" (1) "tomorrow morning" (1), "tomorrow in class" (1), "in class" (1), "in the lecture" (1), [a day of the week] (2), "later today" (1), or [specific time of the day] (1). Students and instructors also used "okay, sounds good" (2) and "yep, sounds good" (1) to indicate mutual agreement on the topic being discussed. Finally, students used "thank you" (54) and "thanks" (26) to show appreciation for their instructors' time and assistance, and instructors responded with "you're very welcome" (2). As in *Informing and recommending*, the utterances in this subtask occurred more frequently in the predetermined office hours than in those that were not predetermined. Additionally, we observed instances of student- or instructor-initiated small talk during this subtask, which functioned as a pre-closing move and a tool for building rapport.

Leave-Taking

This is the final possible subtask, marking the end of an office-hour session. Interlocutors used "bye" (10), "bye bye" (4), "have a good day" (1), "take it easy" (1), and "you, too" (2). Most of these utterances appeared as adjacency pairs, as shown in the following excerpt:

> STUDENT 1: Yeah, see you Wednesday. Bye!
> STUDENT 2: Take it easy.
> STUDENT 1: You, too.

In sum, based on our ATD, office-hour attendees are expected to navigate more communicative subtasks when the office-hour session is predetermined. When the session is not predetermined, the office-hour attendee may treat the interaction as more transactional, in which case they are only expected to ask direct questions that the instructor is expected to answer.

Based on the ATD findings, we used frequent patterns in the data to develop a short, prototypical drop-in office-hour session of predetermined length. The model, as shown in Table 5B.3, includes the most frequent subtasks and pragmatic and interactional utterances, and is assumed to take place between an undergraduate student, Sarah, and an instructor for an entry-level Linguistics course at a US university. Erroneous utterances and other idiosyncrasies were removed, while the linguistic complexity of the utterances was retained. In the table, "I" denotes instructor and "S" denotes student.

In terms of pedagogic implications, EAP instructors, especially those teaching advanced learners, can use the prototypical office-hour interaction to design a pedagogic task in which students role-play attending office hours. Learners may be provided with a scenario similar to the one

Table 5B.3 *A prototypical office-hour session*

Function	Speech
Greetings	I: Hi, Sarah. Are you here for office hours?
	S: Um, hi, yeah.
	I: How are you?
	S: I'm okay. How about you?
	I: I'm pretty good. Feel free to sit down.
Initiation to subject matter and Justifying request	S: Okay, so, I have a question about writing the IPA symbols. When we're writing them, do we need to put them in the brackets or the forward slashes? I don't understand, like, when I'm supposed to use which.
Requesting information and Informing and recommending	I: That's a good question. Um, so remember we talked about this in class.
	S: Oh okay.
	I: So you should use the brackets when you're describing what was actually pronounced.
	S: Mkay.
	I: And you should use the forward slashes to describe how something is supposed to be pronounced.
	S: Oh so it's forward slashes for how it is supposed to sound, but the brackets for how someone said it?
	I: Basically.
	S: Okay, great. Yeah, that's the only question I had so far about the quiz. Oh wait, could I ask one more quick question?
	I: Yes.
	S: What's gonna be covered on the quiz? Like, chapter one through?
	I: Well, it could be anything. Chapters 1, 2, 3, or 4, which is what we've covered the last two weeks.
	S: So, it can be pretty much anything we've done so far. [Laughter]
	I: That's right. [Laughter]
Wrapping up	S: Alright, thank you. I'll see you in class.
	I: Uh huh, see you in class.
Leave-taking	S: Okay, bye.
	I: Bye.

described for the prototypical office-hour dialogue. Then, students could be instructed to ask questions about a specific topic with which students are familiar. The task is successfully completed when the student is able to get their questions answered by the instructor. Additionally, during the interaction, instructors could employ focus on form practices, such as recasts, depending on learners' needs. They could also use Figure 5B.1 and Table 5B.3 to create a formative assessment checklist, which could be developed based on frequently occurring subtasks and expressions. Upon completion of the task, instructors can then share the checklist with their students and provide feedback on how pragmatically successful students were. Another task would be to ask students to judge the task performance of a classmate by filling in the checklist. The findings can also be used to create pedagogic tasks for learners with lower proficiency. Tasks, not the language, may be simplified (e.g., only completing one subtask, such as *Greeting*) or sections of the model dialogue could be elaborated while retaining the genuine language use to ease comprehension.

5B.5 Conclusion

The present study conducted an ATD of office-hour interactions at a US university, so that the findings can serve as a basis for developing pedagogic tasks for teaching students the necessary pragmatics for navigating office hours. Additionally, we aimed to demonstrate how a spoken corpus such as MICASE can be used for task-based research and instruction. Data-driven tasks taking students' personal or professional communicative needs into consideration provide optimal learning opportunities (e.g., González-Lloret & Nielson 2014; Sağdıç, 2019). Although this is the first study to conduct an ATD on office hours, the findings have several limitations that should be acknowledged. As mentioned, the MICASE data come from naturally occurring office-hour sessions at a large US public university. Therefore, the data may not be fully representative of the pragmatic patterns observed in non-US English-speaking academic contexts. There is also inevitable pragmatic variation among English-speaking academics in the United States, depending on their age, gender, level of education, field, and social identity. Nevertheless, we observed clear and distinct patterns across all office hours. Due to the nature of the MICASE data collection, some of the recordings appeared to start after the office-hour session began or stopped before the conclusion of the interaction. This may have affected our findings, in that some subtasks were seen as optional (i.e., *Greeting* and *Leave-taking*), which might have proved obligatory with documentation of the entire exchange. Another limitation is that because the MICASE data only included spoken language samples produced during office hours, it was not possible to examine any possible pre-task interactions, such as scheduling an appointment, which might be required for prearranged office-hour appointments. Students would benefit from practicing with pedagogic tasks that will prepare them to complete this step. Another future area of investigation is the use of computer-mediated communication tools, such as Skype and Zoom, in academic encounters. Future research can analyze virtual office hours to identify the pragmatic speech patterns involved in such interactions, given that virtual meetings are becoming increasingly frequent, resulting in different challenges for learners.

Further Reading

Biber, D. (2006). *University language: A corpus-based study of spoken and written registers*. Amsterdam: John Benjamins.

Gonzalez-Lloret, M. (2019). TBLT and L2 pragmatics. In N. Taguchi, ed. *The Routledge handbook of SLA and pragmatics*. New York: Routledge.

Long, M. H., ed. (2005). *Second language needs analysis*. Cambridge: Cambridge University Press.

Simpson-Vlach, R. C. and Leicher, S. (2006). *The MICASE handbook: A resource for users of the Michigan corpus of academic spoken English*. Ann Arbor: The Regents of the University of Michigan.

Taguchi, N. and Kim, Y. (2018), eds. *Task-based approaches to teaching and assessing pragmatics*. Amsterdam: John Benjamins.

Youn, S. J. (2018). Task-based needs analysis of L2 pragmatics in an EAP context. *Journal of English for Academic Purposes*, 36, 86–98.

Study Questions

1. Go to the MICASE corpus website;[1] choose "search MICASE" and then "office hours" under the "speech event type" section. Search for the modal verbs "could," "should," and "might" using the "find" function. Based on your analysis of the concordance lines, discuss their frequency of occurrence relative to each other and the speech acts in which each modal verb occurs the most.
2. Besides office hours, there are other speech events in which L2 learners are likely to participate in academic contexts. Go to the MICASE corpus website; choose "browse MICASE" and choose "advising session" and "discussion sections" under the "speech event type" section. Based on reviewing some of the transcripts, to what extent do you think they differ from one another and from office hours? Why?

---

[1] https://quod.lib.umich.edu/cgi/c/corpus/corpus?page=home;c=micase;cc=micase

3. What types of linguistic, academic, and social factors can account for pragmatic variation in office-hour interactions?
4. Based on the ATD findings discussed in this case study, what kind of task-based pedagogic tasks can be designed to prepare L2 learners to attend face-to-face office hours?
5. Considering the subtasks and the frequent pragmatic expressions displayed in Table 5B.3, to what extent would they differ in computer-mediated office-hour interactions? Why?

References

Bardovi-Harlig, K. and Hartford, B. S. (1993). Learning the rules of academic talk: A longitudinal study of pragmatic change. *Studies in Second Language Acquisition*, 15, 279–304.

Biber, D. (1993). Representativeness in corpus design. *Literary and Linguistic Computing*, 8(4), 243–57.

Culpeper, J., Mackey, A., and Taguchi, N. (2018). *Second language pragmatics: From theory to research*. New York: Routledge.

Fraser, B. (2010). Pragmatic competence: The case of hedging. In G. Kaltenböck, W. Mihatsch, and S. Schneider, eds. *New approaches to hedging*. Bingley: Emerald, pp. 15–34.

Gilabert, R. (2005). Evaluation the use of multiple sources and methods in needs analysis: A case study of journalists in the Autonomous Community of Catalonia (Spain). In M. H. Long, ed. *Second language needs analysis* Cambridge: Cambridge University Press, pp. 182–99.

González-Lloret, M. (2008). "No me llames de usted, tratame de tu": L2 address behavior development through synchronous computer-mediated communication Unpublished PhD dissertation. University of Hawai'i at Mānoa.

González-Lloret, M. and Nielson, K. B. (2014). Evaluating TBLT: The case of a task-based Spanish program. *Language Teaching Research*, 19(5), 525–49.

Hillman, K. K. and Long, M. H. (2020). Target tasks for US foreign service officers: The challenge for TBLT of the Japanese celebration speech. In C. Lambert and R. Oliver, eds. *Using tasks in diverse contexts*. Bristol: Multilingual Matters, pp. 123–145.

Hymes, D. (1974). *Foundations in sociolinguistics: An ethnographic approach*. Philadelphia: University of Pennsylvania Press.

Long, M. H. (2015). *Second language acquisition and task-based language teaching*. Malden, MA: Wiley-Blackwell.

Reagan, D. and Payant, C. (2018). Task modality effects on Spanish learners' interlanguage pragmatic development. In N. Taguchi and Y. Kim, eds. *Task-based approaches to teaching and assessing pragmatics*. Amsterdam/Philadelphia: John Benjamins

Ren, W. and Han, Z. (2016). The representation of pragmatic knowledge in recent ELT textbooks. *ELT Journal*, 70(4), 424–34.

Sağdıç, A. (2019). From researchers to L2 classrooms: Teaching pragmatics through collaborative tasks. In S. Anwaruddin, ed. *Knowledge mobilization in TESOL: Connecting research and practice*. Leiden: Brill Publishing, pp. 113–27.

Simpson, R. C., Briggs, S. L., Ovens, J., and Swales, J. M. (2002). *The Michigan corpus of academic spoken English (MICASE)*. Ann Arbor: The Regents of the University of Michigan.

Skyrme, G. (2010). Is this a stupid question? International undergraduate students seeking help from teachers during office hours. *Journal of English for Academic Purposes*, 9(3), 211–21.

Taguchi, N. and Kim, Y. (2018), eds. *Task-based approaches to teaching and assessing pragmatics*. Amsterdam/Philadelphia: John Benjamins.

Vellenga, H. (2004). Learning pragmatics from ESL & EFL textbooks: How likely? *TESL-EJ*, 8(2).

Youn, S. J. (2018). Task-based needs analysis of L2 pragmatics in an EAP context. *Journal of English for Academic Purposes*, 36, 86–98.

Part III

The Task Syllabus and Materials

6

The Cognition Hypothesis, the Triadic Componential Framework and the SSARC Model

An Instructional Design Theory of Pedagogic Task Sequencing

Peter Robinson

6.1 Introduction

In this paper I summarize the instructional design theory I have proposed (cf. Reigeluth & Carr-Chelmann, 2009) which aims to provide theoretically motivated, operationally feasible, and empirically researchable criteria for grading and sequencing tasks in a task-based syllabus. There are three related components of this instructional design theory. The Cognition Hypothesis (Robinson, 2001b, 2003a), which has been the basis of an increasing amount of empirical research in recent years, provides the *theoretical motivation* for the task sequencing claims I will describe. The Triadic Componential Framework (Robinson, 2001a, 2005, 2007a) houses these claims in an *operationally feasible* taxonomy of task design features, and the SSARC Model (Robinson, 2010, 2015) provides a stepwise guide for how to combine task design features (specified in the Triadic Componential Framework) so as to progressively increase the cognitive complexity of pedagogic tasks in ways that are currently being *empirically researched* for their effects on second language (L2) learning, and also for their effects on improvements in success in achieving task outcomes on real-world target tasks requiring use of the L2 (see e.g., Allaw & McDonough, 2019; Baralt, Gilabert & Robinson, 2014a; Benson, 2016; Jingo, 2018; Levkina, 2014; Long, 2015; Long & Crookes, 1992; Malicka, 2018; Malicka, Gilabert & Norris, 2017; Steenkamp & Visser, 2011). I begin by summarizing basic issues involved in – and some historical context for – the Cognition Hypothesis and SSARC Model of task sequencing.

6.2 Time, Acquisition Orders and the Structural Syllabus

A syllabus is the result of decisions about how language teachers and learners can make the best use of their time together. It specifies the *units* of instruction, and the order or *sequence* in which they are presented to learners. Theoretically, a decision about L2 syllabus design should be based on research into what the units of language acquisition are, and how they are learned under various psycholinguistic processing conditions, by learners with differing abilities for language processing (Robinson, 2009, 2010, 2015). In purely operational terms, a syllabus is a *schedule* for learning. It specifies the 'what' of learning, and the 'when', or sequence, in which it is to be learned. It also specifies 'how long', or how many times, various learning sequences should be presented to learners in instructional programmes.

Answers to these critical questions for how to operationally *deliver* instruction – 'what' to teach, 'when' to teach it, and for 'how long' – are provided every time a teacher (of any subject matter) conducts a class, for five minutes, an hour, a semester, or longer. Individual *teachers* often answer them, drawing on their own intuitions about the best solution, or on their memory for previously effective solutions. And L2 learning *programme designers* often provide teachers with operational answers to them, in the form of a syllabus, which aims to co-ordinate teacher and learner activities within and across classes, and across levels of a language learning programme.

Second language acquisition (SLA) research is concerned with much more than decision-making about classroom instruction, materials design and assessment. But many areas of SLA research do have theoretical implications for each of these, and so for complementary operational decisions about L2 syllabus design which co-ordinates and articulates them all. For example, a common answer to the question 'what' to teach has been to teach 'units' of language, most often the *grammatical structures* or *patterns* of a language (see Ellis, 1993, 2019). There are other ways of describing the units of language for instruction. One can identify a list of *words* that need to be learned (Willis, 1990). Or one can identify a list of *expressions* that are typically used to *do* things in a language (Munby, 1978), such as 'apologize', 'invite' or 'disagree'.

The decision to base units of instruction on language thus depends on how we divide up the language to be learned. There is no one, acknowledged best way to divide language up as 'units' for this purpose. And so language-based syllabuses differ in what they present to learners, and in what sequence. For example, a structural syllabus presents a series of examples that illustrate grammatical rules, such as, in English, the rule for third person subject-verb agreement. Examples illustrating this would be '*I go*', '*You go*', '*He/She goes*'. That can be learned, in a sense, almost instantaneously. It is often presented to learners at the very beginning of English language instruction. But SLA research has shown (see, e.g., DeKeyser, 2005) that however easy it is to understand and apply a rule like this in classroom contexts, it is one of the most difficult things about English to control and produce accurately in everyday English conversation. In fact, of the rather small number of grammatical morphemes in English, it appears to be one of the most difficult to learn. Here are some other grammatical morphemes of English.

1. I *ate* the cake yesterday. (Irregular past tense).
2. There are two book*s* on the table (Plural *S*).
3. That is Mary*'s* book (Possessive *S*).
4. He is runn*ing* to the shop (Progressive *ing*).
5. I walk*ed* to school (Regular past tense).

Research into SLA in the 1970s (see Dulay & Burt, 1974; Dulay, Burt, & Krashen, 1982) showed that the order in which they are successfully produced, with consistent accuracy in L2 English speech is 4 and 2 together, followed by 1, followed by 5 and 3 together. This is what has been called an *accuracy order* for L2 English, which was claimed to be followed by learners of many different first languages. The evidence for these early claims about morpheme accuracy orders has been revisited and re-evaluated (see Hulstijn, Ellis & Eskildson, 2015), and there is evidence for a much stronger role of the first language in determining the order in which morphemes are acquired than was concluded by the earlier morpheme studies (Murakami & Alexopoulou, 2016), but the basic claim that developmental sequences characterize both first and second language acquisition still receives contemporary support (see, e.g., Ellis, 2015). However, the order in which these developmentally emergent aspects of the structure of English (such as the grammatical morphemes referred to above) are presented in any textbooks used to learn English, or to teach English from, is very often different from the order in which SLA research has shown they are likely to be acquired. There are many other examples that we know of, concerning the order in which structures of English are learned, such as negation, or question formation (see Abrahamsson, 2013; Larsen-Freeman & Long, 1991; Meisel, 2013). But very few of these orders of acquisition are accommodated in structural syllabuses, or textbooks that adopt them. So the third person S example is just one indication of a basic problem with structural syllabuses for L2 language learning. They are based on 'third person' (the linguist, or teacher's) intuitions about what is difficult for the learner. And these are not always right, as SLA research has often shown.

6.3 Towards Task-Based Syllabus Design

But there are alternatives to structural, grammatical syllabuses (Baralt, Gilabert & Robinson, 2014; Long, 2015; Long & Crookes, 1992; Robinson, 1994, 2007a, 2009, 2013a), and much recent SLA research has implications for these task-based approaches to syllabus design, too. I will describe these task-based alternatives to structure-based syllabuses, and the very recent SLA research that is relevant to them. Before this, some precursors to contemporary proposals for syllabus design are acknowledged.

In a wide-ranging and insightful chapter called 'The problems and principles of syllabus design', Henry Widdowson talked about two constraints on a language teaching syllabus. On the one hand, he said, a syllabus 'is concerned with both the selection and ordering of what is to be taught' (1990: 127). Following this partial definition, a *structural* syllabus is clearly the result of selecting grammatical forms to be taught and then sequencing them in an order that is most effective for instructed L2 learning. In this way the structural syllabus is a means for teachers to set 'goals' for learners, assessed in terms of mastery or successful use of grammatical forms. But Widdowson argued that a syllabus 'is also an instrument of educational policy' (1990: 127) and that this reflects 'ideological positions concerning the nature of education in general' (1990: 127). He distinguished educational policies that focus on future social role, occupational abilities and 'societal needs', from those that focus on the individual, within any society, and personal 'self-realization'. An example of the former is an educational policy that promotes and invests in the teaching of English for specific purposes (ESP). This enables people to learn and use English (or any language) to do jobs in a society, like learning English for health-care and nursing purposes, and the many specific occupational tasks they entail, as identified via a needs analysis (Long, 2005). An example of the latter is an educational policy that promotes and invests in the teaching of a language so that the learner may better understand cultural and communicative, as well as purely linguistic differences between themselves and people from other first language communities. Widdowson's reason for raising this distinction is to make the broad point that proposals for syllabus design 'have always to be referred to socio-cultural factors in particular educational settings' (1990: 129). Educational systems may differ in whichever focus they promote, and so one choice of syllabus, in one setting, may be different from another choice in a different setting, for these ideological reasons. Widdowson was talking about external constraints on syllabus implementation, whereas I have been more concerned with psycholinguistic and other cognitive constraints on learning, and their implications for, in particular, task-based syllabus design.

At about the same time as Henry Widdowson was writing the chapter referred to above, Christopher Candlin (1987) was writing another influential chapter, 'Towards task-based language learning', with implications for the selection and ordering of classroom content, and so for syllabus design. In this chapter, Candlin (1987: 5) argues for:

> the introduction of *tasks* as the basis for classroom action .... They serve as a compelling and appropriate means for realizing certain characteristic principles of communicative language teaching and learning, as well as serving as a testing-ground for hypotheses in pragmatics and SLA ... task-based language learning is not only a means to enhancing classroom communication and acquisition but also the means to the development of classroom syllabuses.

Candlin was arguing for the adoption of 'tasks' as the 'units' of syllabus design, rather than linguistic units such as grammatical structures, functional phrases, or vocabulary lists (as Long, 2005, 2015; Long & Crookes, 1992, has also consistently, and constructively argued). And since this early and stimulating paper, many other proposals for task-based language teaching have been made, and a growing amount of SLA research has been done into task-based learning. A task, Candlin (1987: 10) said, is 'one of a set of differentiated, sequenceable, problem-posing activities involving learners and teachers'. In the following section I describe current SLA research into task-based teaching and the 'sequenceable' aspect of tasks Candlin identified, and their implications for task-based syllabus design.

6.4 Task Complexity, Task Characteristics and Task Sequencing

The ability to perform complex tasks, in any domain of thought and endeavour, such as mathematics, music or aviation, is inevitably grounded in attempts to perform simple tasks (adding single digit numbers, doing two- or five-finger exercises or acknowledging a call from ground crew to confirm cargo doors have been checked). In both unschooled, schooled and training programme settings performance on these tasks is supported by caregivers, peers, teachers and occupational trainers. Over time, and courses of instruction, from these simple beginnings, tasks are staged to increase in complexity for learners in what are judged to be manageable ways. So after years of instruction, and practice, learners come to be able to do calculus, or play a piano piece by Chopin, or negotiate with air-traffic control about changes of flight plan given unexpected on-board, or other, emergencies. These increases in the complexity of learning tasks are of course informed, as much as is possible, by mathematics or music learning theory, or ergonomics research into effective pilot training. Efforts are now under way to similarly inform decisions about increasing L2 task complexity in classrooms, drawing on SLA theory (e.g., Baralt, Gilabert &

Robinson, 2014; Robinson, 2011a, 2011b, 2015; Robinson & Gilabert, 2007, 2020).

In tandem with theoretical claims about the effects of task complexity on L2 learning and performance, recent studies are also adopting an increasingly diverse range of measures to confirm the differentials in cognitive demands that more versus less complex tasks are traditionally hypothesized to make (Tsang & Wilson, 1997). Such measures supplement subjective questionnaire responses that have been used to elicit participants' ratings of task demands (Robinson, 2001a, 2001b). These measures include time estimation (Baralt, 2013), since cognitively demanding tasks have been shown to lead to less accurate judgments of time on task (e.g., Smith, 1969), and dual-task performance (Révész, Michel & Gilabert, 2016), since performance on cognitively demanding tasks has long been known to be more susceptible to disruption by a secondary task than performance on a simpler task version (e.g., Heuer, 1996). Physiological indices of mental effort, such as galvanic skin response and heart rate are also likely to be used in future to help confirm differences in the cognitive demands simple versus complex task versions are hypothesized to make (Charles & Nixon, 2019).

Some dimensions of task complexity being studied for their possible effects on language performance and learning are described below, all of which are accommodated in the Triadic Componential Framework (see Figure 6.1).

6.4.1 Planning Time

There have been many studies of how tasks can be made easier for learners by giving them time to plan what they will do or say in the L2 (see e.g., Ellis, 2005; Skehan, 2014). This is perhaps the area that has received the most attention by SLA researchers interested in tasks, and it has clear implications for effective pedagogic decision-making. However, the influence of planning time needs to be evaluated with respect to other task characteristics, which can differentiate its effects on learner performance and learning. So, having time to plan a task that requires causal reasoning can be expected to lead to different language, and learning opportunities than having time to plan a task that requires spatial reasoning. The Triadic Componential Framework places planning time in the context of these and other task characteristics that it may be expected to have effects in combination with. In general, the studies of planning time that have been done to date seem to show that having time to plan a task increases the accuracy, fluency and complexity of learner language. In the Triadic Componential Framework, providing planning time (which simplifies task demands) versus not providing it (which complexifies task demands) is classified as a 'resource-dispersing' dimension of task complexity.

Task Complexity (cognitive factors)	Task Condition (interactive factors)	Task Difficulty (learner factors)
(Classification criteria: cognitive demands)	(Classification criteria: interactional demands)	(Classification criteria: ability requirements)
(Classification procedure: information-theoretic analyses)	(Classification procedure: behaviour-descriptive analyses)	(Classification procedure: ability assessment analyses)
a) **Resource-directing variables** making cognitive/conceptual demands	a) **Participation variables** making interactional demands	a) **Ability variables** and task-relevant resource differentials
+/− here and now	+/− open solution	h/l working memory
+/− few elements	+/− one-way flow	h/l reasoning
−/+ spatial reasoning	+/− convergent solution	h/l task-switching
−/+ causal reasoning	+/− few participants	h/l aptitude
−/+ intentional reasoning	+/− few contributions needed	h/l field independence
−/+ perspective-taking	+/− negotiation not needed	h/l mind/intention-reading
b) **Resource-dispersing variables** making performative/procedural demands	b) **Participant variables** making interactant demands	b) **Affective variables** and task-relevant state-trait differentials
+/− planning time	+/− same proficiency	h/l openness to experience
+/− single task	+/− same gender	h/l control of emotion
+/− task structure	+/− familiar	h/l task motivation
+/− few steps	+/− shared content knowledge	h/l processing anxiety
+/− independence of steps	+/− equal status and role	h/l willingness to communicate
+/− prior knowledge	+/− shared cultural knowledge	h/l self-efficacy

Figure 6.1 The Triadic Componential Framework for task classification – categories, criteria, analytic procedures, and design characteristics (from Robinson, 2007a).

6.4.2 Single/Dual Tasks

Another dimension of task complexity that is similar to this is the single-dual task dimension. It is much less complex to answer a phone call in the L2 than it is to answer a phone call and monitor a TV screen at the same time, to check the weather, or changes in exchange rates, for example (see e.g., Damos, 1991). The latter, a dual task, disperses learner attention and memory resources over a number of L2 and other stimuli but does not direct them to any specific aspect of language that can be useful in helping the learner to fulfil task demands. As with +/– planning time, I have therefore called +/– single tasks a resource-dispersing dimension of task demands (e.g., Robinson 2001a, 2003b, 2005, 2007a, 2011a). In general, tasks made complex on these resource-dispersing dimensions all lead to poorer accuracy, fluency and complexity of performance.

6.4.3 Intentional Reasoning

In contrast, I think there are dimensions of task complexity which direct learners' attention to the language needed to meet task demands. On these 'resource-directing' dimensions I have argued that increasing task complexity should lead to more accurate and complex learner language, over time. However, complex tasks on these dimensions also negatively affect fluency. For example, in L2 English, tasks which require complex reasoning about the intentional states that motivate others to perform actions can be expected to draw heavily on the use of cognitive state terms for reference to other minds – *she suspected, realized,* etc. – and in so doing orient learner attention to the complement constructions accompanying them – *suspected that, wonders whether,* etc. – so promoting awareness of, and effort at, complex L2 English syntax (see Ishikawa, 2008; Lee & Rescorla, 2002; Nixon, 2005; Robinson, 2007b, 2012b; Tomasello, 2010). I call this the –/+ intentional reasoning demands dimension of complexity.

6.4.4 Spatial Reasoning

Another example of resource-directing task demands are those tasks that require complex spatial reasoning, and articulation of this in describing how to move, and in what manner, from point A to point E, by way of intermediary landmark points B, C and D, etc. (see Levkina & Gilabert, 2014). These can be expected to draw heavily on the use of constructions for describing motion events (Berman & Slobin, 1994). Such tasks therefore have the potential to promote awareness of lexicalization patterns in L2 English for describing these motion events, in which motion and manner are typically conflated on verbs (e.g., *rushed*) and paths are expressed outside the verb in satellites that conflate a number of motion events (e.g., *rushed out of the house, down the street and into the post office*).

English lexicalization patterns are different from those in Japanese, where motion and path tend to be conflated on verbs, and manner encoded separately (e.g., *isoide haitta*). Consequently, Japanese makes much less use of event conflation in reference to motion than English does. So a task requiring complex spatial reasoning (giving directions from a large map of an unknown area) may prompt Japanese L2 learners of English to revise their preferred ways of referring to motion, in line with English lexicalization patterns (see Cadierno & Robinson, 2009; Robinson, Cadierno & Shirai, 2009). This is one example of how the increasingly complex efforts to encode conceptualisations in the L2, along resource-directing dimensions of task complexity, can prompt what I have called – adapting Slobin's (1996) thinking-for-speaking hypothesis to SLA – 're-thinking for speaking' in a second language (Robinson, 2007d; Robinson & Ellis, 2008).

6.4.5 Here and Now/There and Then

In yet a different conceptual domain, tasks requiring reference to events happening now, in a shared context (here and now) orient learner attention to morphology for conveying tense and aspect in the present, compared to events requiring much more cognitively demanding reference to events happening elsewhere in time and space (there and then). There-and-then tasks require greater effort at conceptualization (since events are not visually available in a shared context) and make greater demands on memory (see Gilabert, 2007; Ishikawa, 2007; Robinson, 1995a).

One effect of performing tasks on this dimension is to draw learners' attention to the morphological forms and phrases that can be used to refer to the present and the past in English, and these are needed to help them perform the tasks (Robinson, 1995a; Robinson, Cadierno & Shirai, 2009). The morphology for referring to the past in English is much later acquired by L2 learners than the morphology for referring to the present (Meisel, 1987), so complex tasks may promote learner attention to, and use of it. That is, in this and other cases of increasing the complexity of resource-directing demands of tasks, what I have called the 'Cognition Hypothesis' predicts more attention to and 'noticing' of L2 forms in the input available during task performance, or in recasts of learners' own output (Robinson, 1995b, 2017; Schmidt, 1990, 2001), and more uptake and incorporation of them (Loewen, 2004; Robinson, 2007b), as well as increasing accuracy and complexity of production on complex compared to simpler task versions.

6.5 The Cognition Hypothesis of Task-Based Language Learning

Expanding on the ideas described above, for some years now I have been developing and researching the predictions that fall within the scope of what I call the Cognition Hypothesis of task-based learning (e.g., Robinson, 2001b, 2005, 2011a), which claims tasks should be sequenced for learners on the basis of increases in their cognitive complexity alone, and not on linguistic grading, as in traditional structural syllabuses. The fundamental pedagogic claim of the Cognition Hypothesis is that pedagogic tasks should be designed and sequenced to increasingly approximate the complex cognitive demands of real-world target tasks. For example, one target task may be to give directions using an authentic street map to another person while driving quickly through an unknown city. If so, then cognitively simple tasks are designed and performed first in the L2, in which learners have planning time, and use a small map of an already known area. Subsequently, incrementally more complex versions are performed, by first taking away planning time, then by making the map a larger one, and finally by using an authentic map of an unknown area. The idea is basically the same as the procedures guiding educational decision-making and training in many areas of instruction, such as pilot training or mathematics education, where simple tasks and simulations are performed before more complex ones.

So the Cognition Hypothesis is a *pedagogic claim* about the criteria to be adopted for classifying and sequencing tasks for learners. The Triadic Componential Framework (e.g., Robinson, 2001b, 2007a) describes a taxonomy of task characteristics that can be used to examine the implications of the Cognition Hypothesis for classroom practice and syllabus design. This taxonomy distinguishes between the cognitive demands of pedagogic tasks contributing to differences in their intrinsic *complexity* (e.g., whether the task requires a single step to be performed, or dual, or multiple simultaneous steps, or whether reasoning demands are low or absent, versus high), from the learners' perceptions of task *difficulty*, which are a result of the abilities they bring to the task (e.g., working memory capacity) as well as affective responses (e.g., anxiety). I distinguish both of these from task *conditions*, which are specified in terms of information flow in classroom participation (e.g., one- versus two-way tasks), and in terms of the grouping of participants (e.g., same versus different gender). This Triadic Componential Framework enables the complex classroom learning situation to be analysed in a manageable way, allowing interactions among these three broad groups of complexity, difficulty and condition factors to be researched and charted. It is also intended to be used to operationally guide the design and sequencing of pedagogic tasks in language programmes (e.g., as shown in Malicka, Gilabert & Norris, 2017; Steenkamp & Visser, 2011). Underpinning the pedagogic claim of the Cognition Hypothesis are five ancillary theoretical claims (described in Robinson 2001b, 2003a, 2005, 2011a).

6.5.1 Output

The first of these claims concerns the effects of task complexity on accuracy, fluency and complexity of language production. Increasing the cognitive demands of *monologic tasks* contributing to their relative complexity along *resource-directing dimensions* described in the Triadic Componential Framework will push learners to greater accuracy, and also complexity of L2 production in order to meet the consequently greater functional/communicative demands they place on the learner. That is, greater effort at conceptualization will lead learners to develop the L2 linguistic resources they have for expressing such conceptualizations. Along resource-directing interactive tasks, only accuracy will be prompted by greater task complexity, since the greater amounts of interaction complex interactive tasks entail will mitigate efforts at complex turns and so syntax. However, along resource-directing dimension of both monologic and interactive tasks, fluency will be negatively affected as tasks increase in complexity (see Robinson (2001b: 307; Figure 4) for a schematic illustration of these claims). In contrast to these claims about the effects of resource-directing dimensions of task complexity, along resource-dispersing dimensions of complexity, on both monologic and interactive tasks, then increasing task complexity will cause accuracy, complexity and also fluency of production to decrease.

6.5.2 Interaction, Uptake and Incorporation

The second claim is that cognitively complex tasks promote more interaction (as shown in Kim (2009); Robinson (2001a, 2007b) and also heightened attention to, and memory for input provided during interaction, so increasing learning from the input, and incorporation of forms made salient in the input (as well as more Language Related Episodes on complex tasks, see Gilabert, Baron & Llanes (2009); Kim (2012); Solon Long & Gurzynski-Weiss (2017)). So, for example, there should be more uptake of oral recasts on complex, compared to simpler, tasks, or more use of written input provided to help learners perform complex tasks.

6.5.3 Memory

Related to this, the third claim is that on complex tasks there will be greater depth of processing and elaborative rehearsal (Craik & Tulving, 1975; Robinson, 1995b, 2003b), encouraged by the task demands, leading to longer-term retention of input provided (written prompts, oral feedback, etc.) than on simpler tasks.

6.5.4 Automaticity

Fourthly, the inherent repetition involved in performing simple to complex sequences will also lead to automaticity and efficient scheduling of the components of complex L2 task performance.

6.5.5 Aptitudes

Fifthly, and importantly, individual differences in affective and cognitive abilities contributing to perceptions of task difficulty will increasingly differentiate learning and performance as tasks increase in complexity. That is, we know that individual differences in, say, aptitude for mathematics, aren't reflected in performance on doing very simple addition problems (e.g., adding 2 and 6). However, they are reflected in success at doing complex maths problems, like calculus, or quadratic equations (see, e.g., Snow, Kyllonen & Marshalek, 1984). Similarly, aptitudes for second language task performance will matter most on complex versions of pedagogic L2 tasks. So, for example, learners with higher pattern-recognition abilities, and greater phonological working memory capacity will learn better from interaction (demonstrate more uptake and long term retention of information provided in recasts) occurring during complex L2 task performance than counterpart learners, lower in pattern-recognition and working memory capacity. This example illustrates what I have called an aptitude complex for task-based learning (see Robinson, 2001c, 2007b, 2012a, 2013b, 2015), in this case from recasts provided during oral task-based interaction (cf. Kim, Payant & Pearson, 2015; Trofimovich, Ammar & Gatbonton, 2007).

6.6 The SSARC Model of Pedagogic Task Sequencing

Based on the Cognition Hypothesis, and the Triadic Componential Framework for taxonomising task demands, the SSARC Model (Simplify, Stabilize/Automatize/Restructure, Complexify) provides a guide to how pedagogic tasks can be designed and sequenced, so as to progressively increase in their cognitive demands and gradually approximate the demands of real-world target tasks. The SSARC Model (Robinson 2007a, 2009, 2010, 2015; and see Long, 2015, for discussion) proposes that pedagogic versions of target tasks are first performed (and designed for learners) in such a way that they are simple on both resource-directing and dispersing dimensions specified in the Triadic Componential Framework (SS/simplify tasks, stabilize the developing interlanguage system). On a subsequent version of a pedagogic task, resource-dispersing dimensions of task demands are increased in complexity (but not resource-directing dimensions), for example by removing planning time, so as to automatize (A/automatize) by requiring faster access to learners' current knowledge of the L2 during task performance. Finally, the third step involves increasing complexity of versions of pedagogic tasks along both resource-directing dimensions, as well as resource-dispersing dimensions, for example, by increasing reasoning demands on pedagogic versions of tasks performed without planning time. This promotes restructuring of the current interlanguage system, and the development of new form-function/concept mappings along resource-directing dimensions of task demands (cf. Robinson & Ellis, 2008) (RC/restructure and complexify the interlanguage system) (see Figure 6.2). Increasing task complexity by sequencing shifts in task demands, following the steps described in the SSARC Model, induces

> Step 1. (SS) Simply, Stabilize (task versions are simple on both resource-dispersing and resource-directing dimensions of task demands specified in the Triadic Componential Framework in Figure 6.1).
>
> e.g., – intentional reasoning, + planning time
>
> Step 2. (A) Automatize (task versions are simple on resource-directing dimensions of task demands, but complex on resource-dispersing dimensions specified in the Triadic Componential Framework in Figure 6.1).
>
> e.g., – intentional reasoning, – planning time
>
> Step 3. (RC) Restructure, Complexify (task versions are complex on both resource-directing dimensions of task demands, and resource-dispersing dimensions specified in the Triadic Componential Framework in Figure 6.1).
>
> e.g., + intentional reasoning, – planning time

Figure 6.2 An example of increasing the complexity of pedagogic task versions following the SSARC Model of task sequencing

(in the theory proposed here) similar shifts in the structure of interlanguage resources used to accomplish them.

The SSARC Model describes these three stages in gradually increasing the complexity of pedagogic (classroom) versions of target (real-world) tasks, in a way that is intended to be of operational use during task-based syllabus design across a variety of language programmes and educational settings for instruction. Studies in Baralt, Gilabert and Robinson (2014), and an increasing number of other studies (e.g., Allaw & McDonough, 2019; Malicka, 2018) are currently exploring the effectiveness of sequencing decisions based on the Cognition Hypothesis, and the SSARC Model, for promoting accuracy, fluency and complexity of learner language, as well as interaction and uptake of corrective feedback provided during interaction over the course of task sequences, and the extent to which such SSARC sequences enable learners to achieve real-world target task success.

While my work on the Cognition Hypothesis, and its five ancillary theoretical claims, has had as a primary motivating goal the development of feasible sequencing criteria for classroom tasks, it is not limited to this either in explanatory scope or in potential practical application. The Cognition Hypothesis is also important to explore for those concerned to develop equivalent forms of language tests (such as versions of standardized proficiency tests, such as TOEFL, TOEIC, etc.) and for those concerned to measure gain and achievement resulting from classroom exposure during task-based language teaching instruction accurately, by using equivalent pre- and post-test measures of language use. So it also addresses fundamental issues in language assessment, within specific programmes, that measure gain from instructional task design options. More broadly, it also aims to articulate a framework for comparing and coordinating relationships across programmes of instruction in local, and international settings (for example, those that adopt Common European

Framework of Reference for Languages (CEFR) rating scales for distinguishing between learner levels of second language proficiency) that ground instructional design decisions about sequences of tasks in task-based language teaching programmes (and the levels of proficiency that success on such sequences of task can lead to) in similar ways, for diverse populations of learners.

Of particular interest is the interaction of differences between learners in the abilities and dispositions they bring to task performance that affect their perceptions of task difficulty, such as aptitude or anxiety, with the complexity factors manipulated during task design, and the effects of these task difficulty–complexity interactions on performance and learning (Kim & Tracy-Ventura, 2011; Robinson, 1997, 2001c, 2007c, 2012a, 2013b, 2015, 2020; Robinson, Mackey, Gass & Schmidt, 2012; Yang, Chang, Hwang & Zou, 2020). Understanding these interactions will be important if we are to be able to make informed decisions about how to match learners, with differing sets or profiles of strengths in abilities and dispositional tendencies, to tasks where they have the most chance of being successful. The Cognition Hypothesis, and the Triadic Componential Framework for examining its theoretical claims, makes focused, pedagogically useful research into all of these areas possible, and is prompting an increasing amount of needed empirical research into the area of task complexity, sequencing and task-based language instruction (e.g., Allaw & McDonough, 2019; Baralt, Gilabert & Robinson, 2014; Garcia-Mayo, 2007; Jingo, 2018; Levkina, 2014; Levkina & Gilabert, 2014; Malicka, 2018; Robinson, 2011b), hopefully providing, thereby, an evidentiary (non-intuitive) and theory-driven basis for task-based syllabus design, and a basis for coordinating programme-wide decisions about the assessment of task-based language learning and performance.

Further Reading

Baralt, M., Gilabert, R., and Robinson, P. (2014), eds. *Task sequencing and instructed second language learning.* London: Bloomsbury Academic Publishing.

Robinson, P. (2001). Task complexity, cognitive resources, and syllabus design: A triadic framework for examining task influences on SLA. In P. Robinson, ed. *Cognition and second language instruction.* Cambridge: Cambridge University Press, pp. 287–318.

Robinson, P. (2005). Cognitive complexity and task sequencing: Studies in a componential framework for second language task design. *International Review of Applied Linguistics* 43: 1–33.

Robinson, P. (2011), ed. *Second language task complexity: researching the cognition hypothesis of language learning and performance.* Amsterdam: John Benjamins.

Robinson, P. (2015). Second language task demands, the Cognition Hypothesis, and the SSARC model of pedagogic task sequencing. In M. Bygate, ed. *Domains and directions in the development of TBLT*. Amsterdam: John Benjamin, pp. 123–59.

Study Questions

1. Briefly describe a series of pedagogic tasks, graded from simple to complex, that would help airport staff at the passenger arrivals counter of a busy international airport practice giving information about hotel accommodation options to visitors. Which dimensions of task complexity would you operationalize in designing the series of tasks?
2. How would you design a study to see whether practicing teachers could reliably classify pedagogic tasks as making here-and-now or there-and-then demands, or −/+ spatial reasoning demands, or as single- versus dual-task demands? Do you think one of these simple/complex pedagogic task characteristics would be easier for teachers to recognize and reliably classify than others?
3 Do you think the modality of task performance, writing versus speaking, would affect the items you included in a questionnaire assessing learners' perceptions of task difficulty? Why, or why not?

References

Abrahamsson, N. (2013). Developmental sequences. In P. Robinson, ed. *The Routledge encyclopedia of second language acquisition*. New York: Routledge, pp. 173–77.

Allaw, E. and McDonough, K. (2019). The effect of task sequencing on second language written lexical complexity, accuracy and fluency. *System*, 85: 1–24.

Baralt, M. (2013). The impact of cognitive complexity on feedback efficacy during online versus face-to-face interactive tasks. *Studies in Second Language Acquisition*, 36: 1–37.

Baralt, M., Gilabert, R., and Robinson, P. (2014), eds. *Task sequencing and instructed second language learning*. London: Bloomsbury Academic Publishing.

Benson, S. D. (2016). Task-based language teaching: An empirical study of task transfer. *Language Teaching Research*, 20: 341–65.

Berman, R. and Slobin, D.I. (1994), eds. *Relating events in narrative: A cross-linguistic study*. Mahwah, NJ: Lawrence Erlbaum.

Cadierno, T. and Robinson, P. (2009). Language typology, task complexity and the development of L2 lexicalization patterns for describing motion events. *Annual Review of Cognitive Linguistics*, 6: 245–76.

Candlin, C. (1987). Towards task-based language learning. In C. Candlin and D. Murphy, eds. *Language learning tasks*. London: Prentice Hall, pp. 5–22.

Charles, R. and Nixon, J. (2019). Measuring mental workload using physiological measures: A systematic review. *Applied Ergonomics*, 74:221–32.

Craik, F. and Tulving, E. (1975). Depth of processing and the retention of words in episodic memory. *Journal of Experimental Psychology: General*, 104: 268–94.

Damos, D. (1991), ed. *Multiple task performance*. Hillsdale, NJ: Lawrence Erlbaum.

DeKeyser, R. (2005), ed. *Grammatical development in language learning*. Malden, MA: Wiley-Blackwell.

Dulay, H. and Burt, M. (1974). Natural sequences in child second language acquisition. *Language Learning*, 24: 37–54.

Dulay, H., Burt, M., and Krashen, S. (1982). *Language two*. Oxford: Oxford University Press.

Ellis, R. (1993). The structural syllabus and second language acquisition. *TESOL Quarterly*, 27: 91–113.

Ellis, R. (2005), ed. *Planning and task performance in a second language*. Amsterdam: John Benjamins.

Ellis, R. (2015). Researching acquisition sequences: Idealization and de-idealization in SLA. *Language Learning*, 65: 181–209.

Ellis, R. (2019). Towards a modular curriculum for using tasks. *Language Teaching Research*, 23: 454–74.

Garcia-Mayo, M. (2007), ed. *Investigating tasks in formal language learning*. Bristol: Multilingual Matters.

Gilabert, R. (2007). The simultaneous manipulation of task complexity along panning time and +/– Here-and-Now dimensions: Effects on Oral L2 production. In M. del Garcia-Mayo, ed. *Investigating tasks in formal language learning*. Bristol: Multilingual Matters, pp. 44–68.

Gilabert, R., Baron, J., and Llanes, M. (2009). Manipulating cognitive complexity across task types and its impact on learners' interaction during task performance. *International Review of Applied Linguistic*, 47: 367–95.

Heuer, H. (1996). Dual task performance. In O. Neumann and A. Sanders, eds. *Handbook of perception and action*. Vol. 3. New York: Elsevier, pp. 113–43.

Hulstijn, J., Ellis, R., and Eskildson, S. (2015), eds. Orders and Sequences in the Acquisition of L2 Morphosyntax: 40 Years On [special issue]. *Language Learning*, 65(1).

Ishikawa, T. (2007). The effects of increasing task complexity along the +/– Here-and-Now dimension on L2 written narrative discourse. In M. del Garcia-Mayo, ed. *Investigating tasks in formal language learning*. Bristol: Multilingual Matters, pp. 136–56.

Ishikawa, T. (2008). Task complexity, intentional reasoning demands and second language speech production. Unpublished PhD dissertation, Aoyama Gakuin University, Tokyo, Japan.

Jingo, C. (2018). Cognitive task analysis in task-based syllabus design for the teaching and learning of Kiswahili as a second language in Ugandan secondary schools. Unpublished PhD dissertation, Stellenbosch University, South Africa.

Kim, Y. (2009). The effects of task complexity on learner-learner interaction. *System*, 37: 254–68.

Kim, Y. (2012). Task complexity, learning opportunities, and Korean EFL learners' question development. *Studies in Second Language Acquisition*, 34:627–58.

Kim, Y., Payant, C., and Pearson, P. (2015). The intersection of task-based interaction, task complexity, and working memory: L2 question development through recasts in a laboratory setting. *Studies in Second Language Acquisition*, 37: 549–81.

Kim, Y. and Tracy-Ventura, N. (2011). Task complexity, language anxiety and the development of the simple past. In P. Robinson, ed. *Second language task complexity: Researching the Cognition Hypothesis of language learning and performance*. Amsterdam: John Benjamins, pp. 287–306.

Larsen-Freeman, D. and Long, M. (1991). *An introduction to second language acquisition research*. London: Longman.

Lee, E. and Rescorla, L. (2002). The use of psychological state terms by late talkers at age 3. *Applied Psycholinguistics*, 23: 623–41.

Levkina, M. (2014). The role of task sequencing in L2 development as mediated by working memory capacity. Unpublished PhD dissertation, University of Barcelona, Spain.

Levkina, M. and Gilabert, R. (2014). Task sequencing in the development of L2 spatial expressions. In M. Baralt, R. Gilabert, and P. Robinson, eds. *Task sequencing and instructed second language learning*. London: Bloomsbury Academic Publishing, pp. 37–70.

Loewen, S. (2004). Uptake in incidental focus on form in meaning focused ESL lessons. *Language Learning*, 54: 153–88.

Long, M. (2005), ed. *Second language needs analysis*. New York: Cambridge University Press.

Long, M. (2015). *Second language acquisition and task-based language teaching*. Oxford: Blackwell.

Long, M. and Crookes, G. (1992). Three approaches to task-based syllabus design. *TESOL Quarterly*, 26: 27–56.

Malicka, A. (2014). The Role of Task Complexity and Task Sequencing in L2 Oral Monologic Production. Unpublished PhD dissertation, University of Barcelona, Spain.

Malicka, A. (2018). The role of task sequencing in fluency, accuracy and complexity: Investigating the SSARC model of task sequencing. *Language Teaching Research*, 15: 1–24.

Malicka, A., Gilabert, R., and Norris, J. (2017). From needs analysis to research tasks: Insights from an English for specific purposes context. *Language Teaching Research* 21: 1–29.

Meisel, J. (1987). Reference to past events and actions in the development of natural second language acquisition. In C. Pfaff, ed. *First and second language acquisition processes*. Rowley, MA: Newbury House, pp. 206–25.

Meisel, J. (2013). Development in second language acquisition. In P. Robinson, ed. *The Routledge encyclopedia of second language acquisition*. New York: Routledge, pp. 165–73.

Munby, J. (1978). *Communicative syllabus design*. Cambridge: Cambridge University Press.

Murakami, A. and Alexopoulou, T. (2016). L1 influence on the acquisition of English grammatical morphemes: A learner corpus study. *Studies in Second Language Acquisition*, 38: 365–401.

Nixon, S. (2005). Mental state verb production and sentential complements in 4 year old children. *First Language*, 25: 19–39.

Reigeluth, C. and Carr-Chelmann, A. (2009), eds. *Instructional design theories: Building a common knowledge base*. New York: Routledge.

Révész, A., Michel, M., and Gilabert, R. (2016). Measuring cognitive task demands using dual-task methodology, subjective self-ratings, and expert judgments: A validation study. *Studies in Second Language Acquisition*, 38: 703–37.

Robinson, P. (1994). Implicit knowledge, second language learning, and syllabus construction. *TESOL Quarterly*, 28: 161–66.

Robinson, P. (1995a). Task complexity and second language narrative discourse. *Language Learning*, 45: 99–140.

Robinson, P. (1995b). Attention, memory, and the 'noticing' hypothesis. *Language Learning*, 45: 283–331.

Robinson, P. (1997). Individual differences and the fundamental similarity of implicit and explicit adult second language learning. *Language Learning*, 47: 45–99.

Robinson, P. (2001a). Task complexity, task difficulty and task production: Exploring interactions in a componential framework. *Applied Linguistics*, 22: 27–57.

Robinson, P. (2001b). Task complexity, cognitive resources, and syllabus design: A triadic framework for examining task influences on SLA. In P. Robinson, ed. *Cognition and second language instruction*. Cambridge: Cambridge University Press, pp. 287–318.

Robinson, P. (2001c). Individual differences, cognitive abilities, aptitude complexes and learning conditions in second language acquisition. *Second Language Research*, 17: 368–92.

Robinson, P. (2003a). The Cognition Hypothesis, task design, and adult task-based language learning. *Second Language Studies* 21(2): 45–105.

Robinson, P. (2003b). Attention and memory during SLA. In C. Doughty and M. Long, eds. *Handbook of second language acquisition*. Oxford: Blackwell, pp. 631–78.

Robinson, P. (2005). Cognitive complexity and task sequencing: Studies in a componential framework for second language task design. *International Review of Applied Linguistics*, 43: 1–33.

Robinson, P. (2007a). Criteria for classifying and sequencing pedagogic tasks. In M. Pilar Garcia-Mayo, ed. *Investigating tasks in formal language learning*. Bristol: Multilingual Matters, pp. 7–27.

Robinson, P. (2007b). Task complexity, theory of mind, and intentional reasoning:Effects on L2 speech production, interaction, uptake and perceptions of task difficulty. *International Review of Applied Linguistics*, 45: 191–213.

Robinson, P. (2007c). Aptitudes, abilities, contexts, and practice. In R. DeKeyser, ed. *Practice in second language learning: perspectives from applied linguistics and cognitive psychology*. New York: Cambridge University Press, pp. 256–86.

Robinson, P. (2007d). Re-thinking -for-speaking and L2 task demands: The Cognition Hypothesis, task classification, and sequencing. Plenary address presented at the Second International Conference on Task-Based Language Teaching, September, University of Hawai'i at Manoa, Honolulu, USA.

Robinson, P. (2009). Syllabus design. In M. Long and C. Doughty, eds. *Handbook of language teaching*. Oxford: Blackwell, pp. 294–310.

Robinson, P. (2010). Situating and distributing cognition across task demands: The SSARC model of pedagogic task sequencing. In M. Putz and L. Sicola, eds. *Cognitive processing in second language acquisition: Inside the learner's mind*. Amsterdam: John Benjamins, pp. 243–68.

Robinson, P. (2011a). Second language task complexity, the Cognition Hypothesis, language learning, and performance. In P. Robinson, ed. *Second language task complexity: Researching the Cognition Hypothesis of language learning and performance*. Amsterdam: John Benjamins, pp. 3–38.

Robinson, P. (2011b), ed. *Second language task complexity: Researching the Cognition Hypothesis of language learning and performance*. Amsterdam: John Benjamins.

Robinson, P. (2012a). Individual differences, aptitude complexes, SLA processes, and aptitude test development. In M. Pawlak, ed. *New perspectives on individual differences in language learning and teaching*. Oxford: Springer, pp. 57–75.

Robinson, P. (2012b). Abilities to learn: Cognitive abilities. In N. Seel, ed. *Encyclopedia of the sciences of learning*. New York: Springer, pp. 59–63.

Robinson, P. (2013a). Syllabus design. In C. Chapelle, ed. *The encyclopedia of applied linguistics*. Oxford: Wiley-Blackwell, pp. 5494–98.

Robinson, P. (2013b). Abilities and aptitudes for second language learning and performance. *Kanto JACET Journal*, 5: 1–15.

Robinson, P. (2015). Second language task demands, the Cognition Hypothesis, and the SSARC model of pedagogic task sequencing. In M.

Bygate, ed. *Domains and directions in the development of TBLT*. Amsterdam: John Benjamins, pp. 123–59.

Robinson, P. (2017). Attention and awareness. In J. Cenoz and D. Gorter, eds. *Encyclopedia of language and education: Vol. 6. language awareness and multilingualism*. New York: Springer, pp. 125–34.

Robinson, P. (2020). Aptitude in second language acquisition. In C. Chapelle, ed. *The concise encyclopedia of applied linguistics*. Oxford: Wiley-Blackwell, pp. 40–44.

Robinson, P., Cadierno, T., and Shirai, Y. (2009). Time and motion: Measuring the effects of the conceptual demands of tasks on second language speech production. *Applied Linguistics*, 38: 533–54.

Robinson, P. and Ellis, N. (2008). Conclusions: Cognitive linguistics, second language acquisition, and L2 instruction – Issues for research. In P. Robinson and N. Ellis, eds. *The handbook of cognitive linguistics and second language acquisition*. New York: Routledge, pp. 489–545.

Robinson, P. and Gilabert, R. (2007), eds. Task complexity, the Cognition Hypothesis and second language instruction [special issue]. *International Review of Applied Linguistics (IRAL)*, 45(2).

Robinson, P. and Gilabert, R. (2020). Task-based learning: Cognitive underpinnings. In C. Chapelle, ed. *The concise encyclopedia of applied linguistics*. Oxford: Wiley-Blackwell, pp. 1046–51.

Robinson, P., Mackey, A., Gass, S., and Schmidt, R. (2012). Attention and awareness in second language acquisition. In S. Gass and A. Mackey, eds. *The Routledge handbook of second language acquisition*. New York: Routledge, pp. 247–67.

Schmidt, R. (1990). The role of consciousness in second language learning. *Applied Linguistics*, 11: 129–58.

Schmidt, R. (2001). Attention. In P. Robinson, ed. *Cognition and second language instruction*. Cambridge: Cambridge University Press, pp. 1–34.

Skehan, P. (2014), ed. *Processing perspectives on second language task performance*. Amsterdam: John Benjamins.

Slobin, D. (1996). From 'thought and language' to 'thinking for speaking'. In J. Gumperz and S. Levinson, eds. *Rethinking Linguistic Relativity*. Cambridge: Cambridge University Press, pp. 70–96.

Smith, N. (1969). The effect on time estimation of increasing the complexity of a cognitive task. *The Journal of General Psychology*, 81: 231–35.

Snow, R., Kyllonen, P., and Marshalek, R. (1984). The topography of learning and ability correlations. In R. Sternberg, ed. *Advances in the psychology of human intelligence*. Vol. 2. Hillsdale, NJ: Lawrence Erlbaum, pp. 47–104.

Solon, M., Long, A. Y., and Gurzynski-Weiss, L. (2017). Task complexity, language related episodes and the production of L2 Spanish vowels. *Studies in Second Language Acquisition*, 39: 347–80.

Steenkamp, A. and Visser, M. (2011). Using cognitive complexity analysis for the grading and sequencing of Isixhosa tasks in the curriculum design of a communication course for education. *Per Linguam*, 27: 11–27.

Tomasello, M. (2010). *Origins of human communication*. Bradford, MA: MIT Press.

Trofimovich, P., Ammar, A., and Gatbonton, E. (2007). How effective are recasts: The role of attention, memory and analytic ability. In A. Mackey, ed. *Conversational interaction in second language acquisition*. Oxford: Oxford University Press, pp. 171–93.

Tsang, P. and Wilson, G. (1997). Mental workload measurement and analysis. In G. Salvendy, ed. *Handbook of human factors and ergonomics*. New York: Wiley, pp. 418–48.

Widdowson, H. (1990). *Aspects of language teaching*. Oxford: Oxford University Press.

Willis, D. (1990). *The lexical syllabus*. London: Collins.

Yang, Q., Chang S., Hwang, G., and Zou, D. (2020). Balancing cognitive complexity and gaming level: Effects of a cognitive complexity-based gaming level on EFL students English vocabulary level, anxiety, and performance. *Computers in Education*, 149: 1–20.

7

From Needs Analysis to Task Selection, Design, and Sequencing

Roger Gilabert and Aleksandra Malicka

7.1 Introduction

An ever increasing number of teachers and programmes around the world have adopted tasks as units of their teaching. While we do not have exact figures on the use of tasks as units either in task-based programmes (Long, 2015) or in task-supported ones, any quick use of library search engines or more general search engines will confirm the exponential growth of reporting on the use of tasks in programmes worldwide since the 1980s. Tasks are defined here as goal-oriented processes driven by meaning and which draw on communicative and cognitive resources in order to achieve an outcome. Tasks are susceptible to pedagogic intervention and they are sequenceable.

Motivated by an interest in providing solutions to second language use and development, it is not surprising that most of the research effort behind tasks has been geared towards task design, in order to understand and meet learners' communicative needs. When the decision to adopt a task-based approach has been made, the very first question teachers and syllabus designers are faced with is what it is that learners need to learn. One possible solution, which we embrace here, is to conduct a needs analysis (NA) in order to obtain information about learners' present and future needs. The idea of investigating and adapting to learners' needs has existed since the 19070s (Munby, 1978; Wilkins, 1976; see Long (2005) for a historical overview and a comprehensive critique), but it is only in the last two decades that it has been conducted from a theoretically task-based perspective (Long, 2005; Serafini, Lake & Long, 2015), in which task is the unit of reference around which the NA is organized. The idea of adapting instruction to the tasks learners need to carry out in real life is coherent and consistent with what a number of administrative bodies have demanded and encouraged, such as the European Centre for Modern Languages of the Council of Europe,[1] or the OECD (2012, 2015), on a wide spectrum, ranging from a focus on academic achievement (US) to a focus on personal development (EU) (Holmes, Anastopoulou, Schaumburg & Mavrikis, 2018).

However, while there has been considerable attention to both NA and to task design separately, less reflection and empirical work has been devoted to the transition from needs analysis to design (see Malicka, Gilabert & Norris (2017) for an exception), which will be the focus of this paper. This transition is about the crucial interface between what we learn about learners' needs and our macro and micro decision-making during task and syllabus design. Below, we first define NA and address relevant theoretical and methodological issues relating NA first to the issue of task selection, and how NA may aid the highly complex decision regarding how tasks may be selected into a programme. We then move on to examine how NA may directly and indirectly inform task design. Finally, we address the issue of how task sequencing may also be aided by the information obtained through task-based NA.

7.2 What Is Task-Based Needs Analysis? Challenges and Advantages

Needs analysis is defined as a professional, in-depth inquiry into what learners need to learn (Long, 2005, 2015; Serafini et al., 2015). By taking 'task' as a unit of analysis, NA identifies the specific tasks a particular community of learners needs to be able to perform in the foreign or second language. Task-based NA uses multiple sources and methods to detect, analyze, and describe the tasks and sub-tasks (Gilabert, 2005) learners will need to perform within a specific community.

Needs analysis is challenging for a number of reasons. First and foremost, while desirable, NA is not always possible, and teachers and syllabus designers are often left to their own resources to intuitively predict, try to capture, or simply imagine what their learners' needs may be. In many institutions teachers and syllabus designers often find out about their students' needs once they get to know them when teaching has started, which may be late for introducing major changes in the curriculum or even in instructional design and materials. Many contexts directly do not allow for enquiries prior to course starting. Even if institutions are willing to carry out an NA, time or economic constraints (e.g., liberating teachers to get involved in data collection) may hinder any attempts at conducting the NA. Additionally, communities of

---

[1] See, for example, Ollivier (2018) who suggests that through real-world tasks learners will be able to participate in activities beyond the classroom by taking into consideration social interactions determining action and communication.

learners may range from relatively stable, homogenous, and 'predictable' student populations to dynamic communities with changing social and language learning needs (e.g., migrants, displaced persons, and refugees). Finally, even if an NA happens, the information obtained from the NA may not always transfer to task design if it clashes with the interests of a community (i.e., students' wants – e.g., engineers may not find it interesting to learn about engineering tasks after twelve hours of working on engineering tasks, or institutional goals – e.g., implementation of task-based language teaching (TBLT) in China, Saoquian & Baoshu, 2013).

Even if those challenges are overcome and an NA does indeed happen, it is an issue whether and how information coming from an NA can be transferred to task and syllabus design. As Malicka et al. (2017) have pointed out, there exist a number of unresolved issues in this respect, such as how exactly to transfer the information obtained from an NA to actual design, how the information about the variables that confirm the tasks' internal complexity, and its perception of difficulty by users, can be used to inform pedagogically sound task design, as well as pedagogic task sequencing and grading.

7.2.1 Theoretical Underpinnings

Beyond the work of Long (2005, 2015) and Serafini et al. (2015) there has been only limited reflection on the theory and methodology behind task-based NA. At a theoretical level, suffice to say, task-based NA feeds on at least two major fields of knowledge: discourse and textual studies, and second language acquisition.

Regarding discourse and textual analysis, NA springs from the idea that language (Swales, 1990) is contingent and specific, to the point that Long (2005: 1) has suggested that every language course should be a course for specific purposes. Only an accurate description of the tasks, processes, procedures and language associated with each task will make it possible for the design to reflect the specificity of discourse. Needs analysis is consistent with second language acquisition principles in that it does not assume learners should learn in a cumulative way and actually looks at the kinds of cognitive and communicative characteristics each task will require. It integrates the idea that by performing tasks, learners will advance through developmental sequences at different paces (Pienemann, 1998; Pienemann & Kawaguchi, 2005). Also within second language acquisition, NA has fed on the tradition of syllabus design, and the very useful distinction by Wilkins (1976) that in analytical syllabi, learners analyze the language rather than synthesize it as in more traditional synthetic syllabi.

Since readers can already access an in-depth reflection on theoretical and methodological issues in the work of Long (2005) and Serafini et al. (2015), what we highlight here are a number of key concepts in task-based NA that have proven crucial for their transferability to task selection, task design, and task sequencing. First and foremost, the distinctions between target tasks, target task-types and pedagogic tasks (Long, 2005) have been crucial to our understanding of what actually ends up constituting a task-based syllabus. While target tasks are the real-life tasks we wish learners to be able to perform successfully in the second language, programmes and syllabi typically contain the pedagogic versions, approximations to real tasks that will prepare learners for the complex performance of target tasks outside the classroom. In Long's view, target task-types are the intermediate abstractions between target and pedagogic tasks that make it possible to adapt to heterogenous groups with limited time in a course. As we will see in more detail in the next sections, this distinction is important for all areas under inspection here, since it affects selection, design, and sequencing.

Secondly, the distinction between tasks (i.e., major, highly complex tasks, such as creating an advertising campaign) and sub-tasks (i.e., smaller tasks conforming the major task, such as emailing the client, organizing campaign strategic meetings, giving presentations, calling suppliers) (Gilabert, 2005) has been useful in creating task 'maps' of major complex tasks with associated sub-tasks. Based on our long experience in different task-based course design in various domains,[2] we would like to claim that when classes are heterogenous in their needs, actual sub-tasks in preparation for larger target tasks may be shared by more different domains than very specific target tasks. For example, tasks such as emailing, calling, meetings, videoconferencing, and socializing, among others, are common to a campaign in advertising and a fire extinguishing campaign. While the campaigns themselves are not comparable, some of the sub-tasks might be. Sub-tasks may be used for the generation of task prototypes from which pedagogic tasks are then derived. There is a clear scarcity of studies in this area, which would benefit from systematic research, since heterogeneous classes willing to use communicative tasks are not uncommon.

A third useful methodological concept coming out of the theoretical reflection on NA is the use of multiple sources and methods. As will be seen in Section 7.2.4., in order to capture the multidimensional nature of tasks, multiple sources and methods need to be recruited for a meaningful and successful NA to proceed. The complex and multidimensional description of tasks cannot be addressed from using a single method (e.g., surveys, as was mostly done in the 1970s with early NAs). Instead, a multiplicity of data-collection techniques need to be combined in order to guarantee an accurate description of each task. These include, for example, face-to-face

---

[2] Beyond general language courses, Gilabert has directly participated or collaborated in the creation of task-based courses in the areas of journalism, advertising, public relations, international relations, business, medicine, and tourism among others. Malicka has created or collaborated in task-based courses in the area of Business English, tourism and CLIL in both face-to-face and online modalities.

interviews (where sources verbally report task descriptions), direct observations of tasks (which sometimes confirm and sometimes contradict what sources may say about them during face-to-face interviews), or surveys (which, if done with a large enough sample, may help researchers to confirm the frequency and need for training of each of the identified tasks). As Long (2015) has pointed out, triangulating information from a variety of sources during NAs will also guarantee a more accurate and precise description of each task. This will overcome conflicting views on their description (e.g., the idealized vision of bosses/supervisors may have as to how the task is performed and what actually happens according to the domain experts directly involved in their performance). One of the outcomes of methodological reflections and actual data collection is that domain experts, who are directly involved in the performance of target tasks, tend to be the source of the most accurate informants, so should be central sources in NAs (Serafini et al., 2015).

7.2.2 Empirical Findings

The point of this section is not to provide a complete research synthesis covering all studies that have been conducted from a task-based NA perspective, but rather to point out how empirical findings may inform further NAs. Exactly like the specificity they try to capture, the outcomes of NAs are by nature also specific. Typically, what applies to one context, to a specific community of learners, does not apply to others. If well conducted, the outcomes of NAs should be contingent and highly specific. This does not mean that empirical findings are to be discarded altogether because they are not generalizable. What may allow for a higher degree of transferability and generalizability are the step-by-step decisions leading researchers from the information obtained through NA to the different aspects of task selection, task design, and task sequencing.

This was the goal of an NA reported by Malicka et al. (2017) in the tourism sector, more specifically, for a hotel receptionist's job. The objective of this study was four-fold:

1. to gain knowledge about the typical real-life tasks performed in this domain (*task selection*)
2. to use the information about perceived task difficulty to single out variables which can be manipulated in the pedagogic versions of the real-life tasks (*task difficulty*)
3. to decide on the order in which pedagogic tasks should be administered in the classroom (*task sequencing*)
4. to gain insight into the language used to perform these tasks (*analysis of discourse*).

By means of ten semi-structured interviews and three observations, both with domain experts and domain novices, fifty target tasks were identified and classified into task-types, such as 'greeting and saying goodbye to clients' or 'providing information'. Two noteworthy findings regarding the difficulty of real-life tasks were: (1) tasks that are performed on a regular basis and that have a certain routine to them, for example, if the receptionist elicits a series of pieces of information from a client, are easy (e.g., check-in and check-out), and (2) there are tasks whose difficulty depends on a number of factors. For instance, factors that render 'making a restaurant recommendation' complex are the receptionist's familiarity with the area, their familiarity with the types of restaurants, and the number of options to choose from.

The insights obtained about target tasks and their difficulty were the first step in the development of a NA-based pedagogic unit called 'Overbooking'. Made up of a sequence of three pedagogic tasks, this unit brings together the findings from a task-based NA and insights from current task complexity theorizing (the Triadic Componential Framework; Robinson, 2005; Robinson & Gilabert, 2007). Three versions of this task were developed, with differing levels of complexity. The manipulated factors were +/– reasoning demands (understood as the mental operations required to successfully perform the task), and +/– number of elements (characteristics of room and hotels). While the simple task required the receptionist to describe a few options of rooms the hotel offered, in the most complex task they had to describe multiple options, apologize for the overbooking situation, recommend the best alternative, and justify their choice[3]. Importantly, this study shed light on how the information obtained from an NA can be used for both macro decisions (task selection: which real-life tasks to build a pedagogic unit around) and micro decisions (variables subject to manipulation in an individual pedagogic task, and the order in which they are presented to learners).

Let us contrast this study with two other NA reports which were concerned with determining the difficulty of real-life tasks. Chaudron et al. (2005) carried out an NA with the objective of designing pedagogic tasks for students of Korean. The analysis of survey responses and discourse samples revealed 'giving directions' and 'shopping for clothes' as particularly relevant to this group of learners. Needs analysis was used to identify factors contributing to the complexity of these tasks. In the direction-giving task, these were the size of the area (small vs. big) and number of directions to give (few vs. many). In the shopping task the number of purchase decisions (e.g., size, design, type, colour, and price negotiation) determined complexity. In another study, Serafini and Torres (2015) carried out an NA to design a business course for students of Spanish. Forty target tasks were identified through an online survey administered to business professionals and graduates. Business majors then rated those tasks for frequency and difficulty on a five-point Likert scale.

---

[3] See Malicka et al. (2017) and Malicka (2018) for full operationalization of complexity and task instructions.

Because their focus was on NA itself, neither of these studies articulated whether, and how, the information obtained through the NAs translated into pedagogic task design. Also, neither tapped into the factors that made real-life tasks easy or difficult; in other words, they were more concerned with *between/across-task difficulty* (i.e., relative difficulty of one target task in relation to other tasks), but not *within-task difficulty* (i.e., conditions under which a task is simple vs. complex).

To our knowledge, beyond the Serafini et al. (2015) systematic research synthesis on methodological advances, no research syntheses or meta-analyses of NA have been conducted that gather and analyze empirical findings. The fact that NA has begun to emerge as an avenue of research in its own right, however, is evidenced by the amount of scholarly literature produced to date, both researchers' and language education professionals' sustained interest in NA, and improvements in the methodological literacy and rigour found in reports of empirical studies.

7.2.3 Dimensions of Needs Analysis

As target tasks are complex and holistic, an NA should aim to identify as many aspects of tasks as possible to ensure their thorough and precise description. What follows is a non-exhaustive list of dimensions of tasks that may be targeted during NA (see Table 7.1). It should be noted that not all dimensions apply to every task or sub-task, and other dimensions not included here may be necessary to describe certain particularities of tasks. These general dimensions may then be subsequently helpful at different stages of syllabus design: task selection, design, and sequencing.

The dimensions NA may uncover are divided into seven broad categories. 'General aspects of tasks' is concerned with such matters as the tasks' goal, frequency, outcome, topics, sub-/target tasks. 'Participants and interaction' deals with information exchange and communication between participants involved in a task, the rules of interaction, psycholinguistic aspects, intercultural communicative aspects, and non-verbal aspects (Boswood & Marriott, 1994; East, 2012; Pica et al., 1993). 'The physical space where tasks take place' includes factors that have to do with the spatial and psychosocial setting of tasks (Boswood & Marriott, 1994). 'Tasks' cognitive demands' is concerned with tasks' attentional and memory demands, mental processes, and perceived difficulty of tasks, as well as the recruiting of higher- and lower-order skills (Robinson, 2001, Robinson & Gilabert, 2007; Skehan, 1998, 2009; Bloom, Engelhart, Furst, Hill & Krathwohl, 1956). 'Tasks' linguistic demands' deals with the linguistic resources necessary to complete a task (Palotti, 2019; Gilabert & Castellví, 2019). 'Communication and technology' taps into the communication channels and technological tools and platforms associated with performing a task (González-Lloret 2014, González-Lloret & Ortega 2014). Finally, 'other dimensions' includes such matters as assessment, task

Table 7.1 *Dimensions of needs analysis and their description*

NA dimension	Dimension description	Example/information obtained through NA
GENERAL ASPECTS OF TASKS		
Task goal	What is the task's ultimate goal? *Associated information:* Steps involved in task performance, task length, when performed, need for training.	Solving a problem, reaching an agreement, describing a product, process or service, etc. *Associated information:* In how many steps is a task performed, when it is a performed, and whether a task requires training or not.
Task frequency	How frequently is a task performed?	Frequent versus infrequent tasks; Tasks performed on an hourly/daily/weekly/monthly/annual basis.
Task outcome	What is the final product of a task?	A written report, a public presentation, a sale, an academic paper, a satisfactory review by a client or customer, etc.
Topics or subject-matter	What general and specific topics a task may cover?	A list of potential topics which may be tackled in tasks.
Target sub-tasks/Sequence of procedures	Tasks that may be performed simultaneously or in a predetermined sequence (Gilabert, 2005), step-by-step description of the task (Long, 2015).	Whether the task is stand-alone or there are other parallel tasks accompanying it.
PARTICIPANTS AND INTERACTION		
Number of participants	How many participants are involved in a task?	Tasks performed individually, in pairs, in groups (small or large); across groups.
Participant status	What is the status relationship between task participants?	Participants in equal positions vs. different positions (low vs. high) within the organization, institution, or company.
Rules of interaction	Set of accepted behaviours during interaction; dos and don'ts.	The importance of listening, having control over the conversation, floor-taking rules, things to make sure happen, topics to avoid.
Participants' attitudinal values, concepts, and norms	Individual characteristics participants bring to a task.	Knowledge, educational training or concepts that are crucial to the successful performance of a task; being patient or sympathizing; aggressiveness, encouragement, or optimism, among others.

Table 7.1 Continued

NA dimension	Dimension description	Example/information obtained through NA
Psycholinguistic aspects	The way information is shared between participants and each participant's contribution to task (Pica et al., 1993).	One-way/two-way/multiple-way information flow, convergent or divergent goals, a single solution or multiple solutions, split or shared information.
Intercultural communicative competence aspects	Are there any intercultural components of the tasks that may be relevant to task design (East, 2012)?	Tasks can be neutral or interculturally charged. They may require competence in negotiating differences appropriately using language, as well as relating effectively to the 'other'?
PHYSICAL SPACE WHERE TASKS TAKES PLACE		
Spatial setting	The characteristics associated with the physical space in which the task takes place (Bosswood & Marriott, 1994).	Behind doors, open office space, meeting room, private online chat, an open online forum, at home, press conference room, fairgrounds, restaurant/café/bar, planes/trains/car, among others.
Psychosocial environment	Factors associated with psychosocial characteristics of the environment in which the task takes place.	Noisy vs. quiet; Familiar vs. unfamiliar physical space; culturally close vs. distant setting; relaxed vs. stressful environment.
TASKS' COGNITIVE DEMANDS		
Cognitive aspects of the task (Robinson, 2001; Robinson & Gilabert, 2007; Skehan, 1998, 2009)	Attentional and memory demands tasks place on those who perform them.	The number of simultaneous elements/items involved in task performance; whether spatial or intentional reasoning are required; whether taking a perspective is required; whether tasks are performed under time pressure; whether familiarity with the task is important.
Higher and lower (Bloom et al., 1956) required to perform the task	Mental processes necessary for successful task completion.	Sample lower-order skills: gathering, classifying, or summarizing information, etc.; sample higher-order skills: establishing relationships and associations, hypothesis-testing, judging, etc.
Degree of perceived difficulty of tasks/complexity factors	How easy or difficult is a task perceived to be by those who perform it.	Perceived mental effort, difficulty, anxiety or stakes; information about what factors or conditions make a task more or less complex (e.g., task features, available resources, time constraints, multi-tasking, interlocutors, or external factors).

TASKS' LINGUISTIC DEMANDS		
Language associated with performing a task	Linguistic resources necessary for task completion.	Skills: receptive or productive, or both; terminology: specific vocabulary items, expressions, idioms; other multi-word units; grammatical features; phonology: features related to tone or intonation; pragmatic/discursive moves (e.g., commands or requests); other features: rhetorical devices, turn-taking, style and level of formality, language variation.
COMMUNICATION AND TECHNOLOGY		
Technological/digital tools and platforms (González-Lloret, 2014; González-Lloret & Ortega, 2014)	Technology involved in performing a task and its influence on the task.	How technology is built into task performance, how it potentially transforms the task in terms of difficulty, the level of digital literacy required from task participants.
Communication channels	What means are used to perform a task.	Face-to-face vs. computer-mediated communication; verbally via videoconferencing vs. by phone, via email; conventional writing on paper or interactive online chats, among others.
OTHER DIMENSIONS		
Criteria for assessment	According to domain experts, what constitutes successful task performance?	Qualitative and quantitative indices/measures of task completion/performance.
Support during task performance (Mayer, 2009)	Documents, people and other resources one can resort to during task performance,	Internet searches, specialized literature (text book, journal, report, technical manuals, visuals), human and online translators, colleagues.
Non-verbal aspects	Aspects of task that do not have to do with language.	Dress code, body language, facial expressions, eye-gaze, gestures, distance from interlocutor, non-verbal expression of emotions.

support, and tasks' non-verbal aspects, attitudinal values, concepts, and norms, and sequence of procedures.

Before we discuss the relevance of obtaining information about these dimensions to task selection, design and sequencing, we would like to point out that target tasks are not entities that are somehow fixed by their description through NA, as in a still picture. Tasks are dynamic and susceptible to change and adaptations in ever-changing social, academic and professional environments. Ideally, NA in any institution should be able to incorporate the possibility of sustained updating of task descriptions. NA should aspire to achieve some degree of predictability as to how tasks will be performed, while keeping in mind that these may be transformed by changing conditions.

7.2.4 Needs Analysis Dimensions and Their Relevance to Task Selection, Pedagogic Task Design and Task Sequencing

The outcome of NAs is often a long list of reasonably complex task descriptions that an academic, professional, or social community needs to carry out. But what is gained from obtaining such detailed information when it comes to selection, design, and sequencing? The outcomes of NAs are raw material, in most cases possibly not quite directly usable for immediate, unprocessed task design. What we would like to highlight here is that each dimension that is relevant to a particular task will impact its selection, design, and sequencing in a reciprocal way, whereby, for example, selection decisions will depend on information from NA, as well as considerations affecting design and sequencing.

7.3 From Needs Analysis to Task Selection

7.3.1 Target Task Descriptions: Outcomes of Needs Analysis

Outcomes of NA are the basic material that will feed decision-making during task integration into a syllabus. Both macro- and micro-design decisions will be greatly facilitated by the information collected during NA. There are, however, no guidelines in the literature based on any systematic research about how tasks emerging from an NA may be selected for their inclusion in a syllabus. Consequently, task selection on the basis of an NA may depend on a number of factors. If information about tasks has been collected from a variety of sources (e.g., not only from heads and bosses, but also from domain experts) and through an array of methods (e.g., interviews, observations, and surveys, among others), task descriptions will necessarily have to go through a process of analysis, interpretation, and description by researchers and/or syllabus designers. This job may require looking ahead to task design (to check if task design will be feasible) and sequencing (to check if it will fit the syllabus in terms of distribution and time requirements) in order to be completed.

7.3.2 Target Tasks and Sub-Tasks

One of the lessons learned over the years of empirical research is that target tasks often take the form of a core overarching task with a constellation of sub-tasks, i.e., fully rounded tasks with a goal, communicative and cognitive steps, and an expected outcome, but are subsidiary to other larger and more complex tasks, leading to such a core task (Gilabert, 2005). Take as an example a journalistic interview, where the overarching and complex target task is the interview itself. But leading to it there are a number of sub-tasks making such a complex task possible (e.g., contacting the source via email, arranging a time and a place to meet, documenting the interview, preparing an initial set of questions, among others). Once what is typically a long list of tasks and their associated sub-tasks have been identified, analyzed, and described, they need to be grouped into target task-types (e.g., information to be requested over email, mobile, social media or face-to-face) that will make their inclusion into the syllabus more feasible. But how general or how narrow should the focus of those task-types be? Do we create an email task that may help learners across contexts (i.e., in a heterogeneous group of learners learning general English for various contexts) or do we choose one specific context as an example that can be generalized to others? There is probably no single right answer to this question. The course designer needs to find a balanced and reasonable match between the scope of those prototypes and the course conditions and learner characteristics (i.e., a heterogeneous interest group or a homogeneous group of students working within the same area). Based on task-types, pedagogic task design may proceed, so that specific decisions can be made about what task should look like for teaching purposes.

7.3.3 Factors for Task Selection

If the NA was well conducted (Long, 2005; Serafini et al., 2015) the long list of target tasks and sub-tasks should contain information about the frequency, difficulty, and need for training (based on their importance or priority) of each of the tasks. Frequency provides an accurate temporal picture of the tasks that the end-users of the syllabus will surely need to be able to perform in the second language. Important as it is, however, frequency cannot be the only criterion for selection since some tasks may be highly frequent and others may be infrequent yet critical, requiring some intense training. Through the use of surveys with a large enough sample, Gilabert (2005) reported validating the difference between frequency and need for training, since some tasks rated low in frequency but very high in need for training, which helped with the decision to select them as candidates for inclusion in the syllabus. As seen in Section 7.2.3 above, another important criterion may be the degree of perceived difficulty and complexity according to domain experts. Some tasks may be perceived as difficult or higher-stakes by experts and hence as requiring more mental effort. Those target tasks are better candidates for selection than simple tasks or sub-tasks that may be more frequent but which do not need so much training. Such information obtained during NA can greatly facilitate the decision-making process about which tasks should be selected for the syllabus. Again, the decision about selection cannot only be based on the outcomes of NA alone. Designers will need to consider each task or sub-task in terms of design and sequencing in the actual syllabus. To our knowledge, no systematic reporting of selection criteria exists, so this aspect of the transfer from NA to actual selection remains a subject for further investigation.

7.4 From Needs Analysis to Task Design

Of all the areas of syllabus design we have mentioned (i.e., NA, selection, design, and sequencing), task design is by far the area that has received the most attention in task-based research. While there is a lack of reflection on task design per se (see conclusions for further development of this point), the drive to empirically research the effects of design on language comprehension, production, or development has been stronger and broader than any other area.

7.4.1 Task Goals

One of the most basic and fundamental contributions of NA to task design is to identify task goals. A well-conducted NA targets not only the identification of real-life tasks (the 'raw material', mentioned before), but also an in-depth analysis of each of them. The most general, but key, objective of such an analysis is to determine task goals. By 'task goal' is meant the ultimate objective of the real-life task, and sample general task goals may include, for example, 'solving a problem', 'reaching an agreement', 'convincing someone of one's point of view', or 'selling a product'.

7.4.2 Task Design Features

In the previous section we saw how the information obtained in an NA can be used to make informed decisions about task selection. The immediate product of an NA is an ostensibly exhaustive inventory of authentic situations encountered in professional, occupational, and social domains, the conditions under which these situations take place, the steps needed to solve them, and the performance standards associated with them. However, there has been scant reflection in the NA and TBLT literature on how exactly the information obtained through NA can be translated into pedagogic task design. Here we will consider the contribution of NA to task design from three complementary perspectives: interactive, linguistic, and cognitive.

Tasks that are pedagogically sound from the interactive point of view take into account the idiosyncrasies of interactional scenarios and conditions detected via NA. In this sense, the information gathered in an NA can inform decisions about matters such as the *number of participants* in a task (individual vs. two or more people) or the *information flow* between them (one-way, two-way, multiple-way). Consequently, pedagogic task versions can fall into two broad categories: *monologic* (e.g., delivering a presentation in the business context of selling a service) or *dialogic* (e.g., multiple-way decision-making about the best launch event for a new product in the domain of advertising). Furthermore, certain NA methods, such as participant observation, can prove informative when it comes to identifying typical profiles of parties involved in professional situations, or these parties' status. These considerations can be incorporated into pedagogic versions of tasks by assigning attributes to task participants that could manifest themselves via, for example, different positions of power, psychological profiles, or personal characteristics. For example in a job interview task, the interviewer could be attributed a higher status than the interviewee. This could show via different individual attributes such as different confidence levels (high vs. low) or the way of addressing each other (informal/neutral vs. formal). If the overbooking situation described in the study by Malicka et al. (2017) were a dialogic task, the participant playing the role of the receptionist could be equipped with such characteristics as patience and staying calm under pressure. On the other hand, the role of the client, who refuses to be relocated to a different hotel, could involve a more demanding and relentless demeanour.

Of pivotal importance to task design are the linguistic demands of real-life tasks. These are determined in the second phase of NA, during the analysis of the target discourse. In the broadest sense, two implications of NA for pedagogic task design here are (1) what language is required for task completion to begin with; (2) which skills should be incorporated into pedagogic task design: productive, receptive, or both. Once these macro instructional decisions have been taken, pedagogic approximations of real-life tasks should ideally incorporate concrete language detected through NA, such as terminology specific to a sector (e.g., air traffic controllers), discourse features (e.g., pragmatics), grammatical features (e.g., asking questions), or speech acts involved in performing a task (e.g., requesting information, or apologizing for a situation).

These and other linguistic features can be built into pedagogic tasks at different stages of task design. First, they can constitute the 'pre-task' stage which offers repeated exposure to new items, for example via rich listening and reading comprehension input. These are presented by means of input processing techniques, such as input flooding or input enhancement. Second, linguistic features can also be part of the main task insofar as successful task completion is only possible using specific terminology/structures. Third, they can be implemented during the 'post-task', with students' attention geared towards novel linguistic aspects by having them reflect on non-target like forms. Finally, once tasks have been used in one or more iterations of a language course, the implementation of linguistic features can be reconceptualized during task re-design.

Regarding the cognitive perspective, a well-conducted NA should yield information about the attentional and memory demands real-life tasks place on those who perform them. Needs analysis should help us discover specific attributes of tasks, such as what mental operations are required to perform them, how many pieces of information need to be stored in working memory at the same time, or whether tasks are typically performed under time pressure or with time available to plan. These attributes of real-life tasks can then be translated into pedagogical variables that can be manipulated in task design. For example, in the academic context, the task of 'writing a summary of an article' requires relatively low reasoning compared with the more cognitively demanding task of 'writing an academic article'. While the former involves low-order skills such as understanding, gathering, and classifying information, the latter involves the higher-order skill of applying one's expertise to create something new. Very importantly for task design, NA should also tell us how these cognitive factors are perceived, in terms of their relative difficulty, by those who perform them. Establishing a continuum of levels in these mental operations is a possible point of departure when it comes to organizing tasks in a curriculum. This is covered in more depth in the next section.

7.5 From Needs Analysis to Task Sequencing

As can be seen in the chapter by Robinson (this volume), task sequencing may be based on the variables selected for task design, which are in turn based on the design needed to prepare learners for the successful performance of target tasks. Task sequencing needs to feed on the information coming both from NAs and task design decisions.

7.5.1 The Unresolved Issue of Task Sequencing

Task sequencing is indeed an unresolved issue because, like task selection or task design, it involves complex decision-making. Several proposals have been put forward to address this issue, with sequencing based on the following criteria:

- mainly (or even solely) *cognitive complexity factors* (Baralt, Gilabert & Robinson, 2014; Robinson 2005, this volume)
- dimensions of *task difficulty*: code complexity, cognitive complexity, communicative stress and learner factors (Skehan 1998, 2009)
- *linguistic difficulty* (Palotti, 2019) in combination with *task complexity* in the case of morphologically complex languages (Gilabert & Castellví, 2019).

As will be seen in Section 7.7, task sequencing could be placed on a continuum ranging from NA-based human decision-making to a fully automatized machine-driven process, in which computerized systems use learner analytics to obtain information about what is simple or complex, which is already used in both the gaming industry and in serious games. Whichever the theoretical position of the designer may be, all the information necessary for sequencing decisions can be retrieved from the different dimensions described in Section 7.2.3.

7.6 Cognitive Factors Aiding Task Sequencing Decisions

A number of dimensions can assist the decision about sequencing tasks. As we saw in Section 7.4, there are several cognitive variables that can be used to obtain simple or more complex versions of tasks. If, like Robinson (2005, this volume) or Baralt et al. (2014), the choice is to use cognitive complexity as the main criterion for sequencing, then NA can greatly assist by identifying resource-directing variables, such as the number of elements, the degree of reasoning, the amount of perspective taking (Robinson, 2001; Robinson & Gilabert, 2007), the time pressure under which the task is performed, or familiarity with it (Skehan, 1998, 2009). More cognitively demanding tasks along resource-directing variables will typically also engage higher-order skills, and if this were considered during task design, the decision could be to sequence tasks in a way that learners first deal with simple versions, which require little reasoning and lower-order skills, progressively moving toward more complex tasks requiring higher-order skills. Again, sequence length will depend on a number of factors, such as course length, goals, content, and learner population, among others, and the decision to create a shorter or longer sequence will probably benefit from feedback during and after syllabus implementation in the classroom. Two dimensions that may also may be factored in when deciding on sequencing are the perceived difficulty and factors of complexity by domain experts (e.g., mental effort required by the task, and stages or anxiety generated by the task).

7.6.1 Linguistic Factors Contributing to Difficulty

Most researchers would agree that the cognitive load of a communicative task will be determined not only by its intrinsic cognitive configuration but also by the linguistic elements required to perform the task. The linguistic dimension of tasks may be determined by the objective and measurable difficulty of different linguistic features (Palotti, 2019) or by how easy or how hard it is to process them (Peinneman, 1998; Pienemann et al., 2005). Our claim here and elsewhere (Gilabert & Castellví, 2019) is that while maintaining cognitive complexity as the main organizing principle for task sequencing, the weight of the linguistic component necessary for task completion needs to be considered, since it may affect the tasks' overall cognitive load.

Recent work by Palotti (2019) has suggested that different features of a language, as well as features across languages, may display different levels of linguistic difficulty that may contribute to overall task complexity. Certain linguistic dimensions, such as morphology, may vary considerably among languages. Since in most languages we have a partial picture of what are easy and difficult linguistic features, creating a complete map of what features are easy or difficult in absolute terms may, in fact, be a conceptual impossibility. For example, the present tense is learned earlier than the past tense in the first language, but can this be considered a sequencing criterion for adult second language acquisition? In the same vein, we only have an incomplete picture of developmental sequences (Pienemann, 1998; Pienemann, Di Biase & Kawaguchi, 2005) in the acquisition of most languages in the world, which would make sequencing decisions on the basis of the processability of each linguistic dimension a very challenging endeavour.

Since feature difficulty and developmental sequences may not serve as a point of reference for sequencing (at least at this point of our knowledge), Gilabert and Castellví (2019) have suggested the 'amount of simultaneous linguistic features' (i.e., the number of linguistic elements the learner has to resort to during task performance) as a criterion for sequencing as complementary to task complexity, especially in the case of morphologically complex languages. They have proposed that, once task complexity criteria have been applied to the sequencing of tasks and some have been described as having similar levels of cognitive complexity, then linguistic criteria may be a reference. Those tasks that require few simultaneous linguistic features to be dealt with during task performance should be taught first, to be followed by tasks requiring a greater number of linguistic features. For example, cognitively simple tasks (e.g., with few elements and low reasoning demands) requiring few high-frequency words, use of the present, and use of articles, should be placed in the curriculum before other cognitively simple tasks requiring a large number of low-frequency vocabulary items, several verb tenses, use of articles, reference to several declensions, different types of prepositions, a number of pragmatic dimensions, among others. The suggestion here is not to go back to the sequencing of items typically associated with synthetic syllabi, but rather to consider linguistic criteria as subsidiary to task complexity criteria.

Experience in task design and implementation has shown that often, after several implementations of the same task, certain linguistic features emerge as associated with it. This is typically detected through the analysis of the discourse of second language users generated by the task. This is of course not always possible with all tasks and let us not forget that tasks are dynamic and changing in nature. But iterations of the same tasks may reveal that some of them require few linguistic features to be dealt with simultaneously during task performance (with little impact on cognitive load and processing), while others require the use of many features (with a considerable impact on cognitive load and processing) (See Gilabert & Castellví (2019) for a detailed description and examples). As opposed to cognitive task complexity criteria that are 'global' in the sense that they are not language-dependent, the relevance of linguistic criteria to task sequencing will depend on the characteristics of the second language being learned as well as on the first- and second-language combination. Again, feedback during and after implementation may help evaluate the efficiency of the sequence and re-adjustments in the sequence may be called for.

7.6.2 Other Factors Contributing to Sequencing Decisions

So far, what we have seen is that task sequencing decisions may be aided by the information we obtain from NA, as well as from task design. But we have also pointed out the lack of theoretical reflection or empirical findings on what a task sequence should look like, how long it should be, and what its efficiency is in promoting second language use and development. We have suggested that feedback obtained during and after syllabus implementation may help refine task design and task sequencing decisions. This is a laborious job which will take several course implementations to complete, and quite possibly may only be successful under very stable conditions e.g., same course designers, similar groups of students with similar goals over a number of years.

Our limitations in terms of task sequencing in TBLT, however, may be approached from advances in other fields, such as educational technology. Two expanding constructs are those of personalization and adaptivity (Holmes et al., 2018). Personalized learning and its algorithmic instantiation and adaptivity, allow for adaptation to individual learners' needs and abilities (Vanbecelaere & Benton, 2020). The idea of adapting to individual student needs is not a flashy and attractive idea afforded by new technologies, but consistent with the principles of TBLT and second language acquisition findings, since we know that, in accordance with their own internal syllabi, learners take individual paths at different rates in the development of their interlanguage. The use of adaptive algorithms in technological infrastructures allows for collection of large quantities of task performance data, and such data may be indicative of task difficulty or complexity, which in turn can inform sequencing decisions (Serra & Gilabert, 2020). This, we believe, may be an interesting road for TBLT studies to take in the near future.

7.7 Conclusions and Recommendations

In this chapter we have defined NA and pointed out some of its challenges and advantages in relation to task selection, pedagogic design, and task sequencing. We have done so by first identifying what we believe are general issues in NA meriting examination, and pointing out how such areas may aid decisions about what tasks or sub-tasks to select, how to use NA information to design them, and how NA may assist sequencing of tasks in a syllabus. Task selection may be greatly facilitated by information about the frequency, difficulty, and need for training of each task. Domain experts may identify values for those dimensions, which can then be corroborated by the findings of large-scale surveys, before prioritizing the teaching of more frequent tasks or those that will require more serious training because they are reported as difficult. Additionally, course designers will need to consider which tasks will be selected into the syllabus by also considering their design and what their sequence may be. In that way, a balance may be struck between NA information and course conditions and constraints. As for pedagogic design, NA may provide information about the number and type of participants and how information may flow between them, monologically or dialogically. Also the receptive and/or productive language, together with the skills associated with task goals, can be identified by NA and incorporated into pedagogic task design. The more or less specific terminology, pragmatic, discourse, grammatical phonological, and other linguistic features can be detected by NA and inserted into tasks at different stages of pedagogic task design. The attentional and memory attributes, as well as the lower- and higher-order skills obtained through interviews and task observations that real-life tasks demand from task users, can also be factored in during task design. Finally, in terms of task sequencing, we can see that tasks and sub-tasks may be placed in a logical sequence of increasing task complexity and/or task difficulty, while also taking linguistic difficulty into consideration. Tasks may be placed on a continuum from simple tasks to progressively more complex ones, and their design does not need to be random, but well informed by NA. If the option is to consider task difficulty, which also includes code complexity, task conditions and learner factors (as per Skehan, 1998), all those pieces of information may be extracted during in-depth NA. All cognitive dimensions being similar, then linguistic demands (in terms of number of simultaneous linguistic features to manage during task performance) may also serve as a complementary criterion for organizing tasks on a continuum. Current alternative ways of having data-driven NA within technological environments have also been sketched as a potential new approach.

While advances in the domain of artificial intelligence may complement or eventually even replace NA altogether by applying algorithms and consequently gaining instant access to information about the needs of a particular learner community, NA currently offers a theoretically and methodologically solid approach to identifying such needs. The information obtained via NA can be programmatically applied to different stages of TBLT curricular design, regarding both macro and micro pedagogical decisions. This chapter has focused on the so far unexplored synergy of the opportunities provided by NA and task-based educational agenda at three levels: task selection, pedagogic task design, and task sequencing. We have seen how NA can be a useful tool in choosing which real-life tasks should be included in the curriculum, how the information gathered can be built into the pedagogic approximations of real-life tasks by converting features of observed reality into manipulable task parameters, and finally, how NA can shed light on decisions regarding sequencing tasks in a curriculum. However, the information obtained through NA may also illuminate other components of TBLT curricular design not discussed here (e.g., methodological implementation, assessment or evaluation). Substantially more theoretical reflection and empirical work targeting these aspects is necessary if TBLT programmes are to take full advantage of the potential NA holds as an approach to determining language needs of learner communities. While NAs are carried out in authentic workplace, academic, or social settings and involve gathering insights from experts in domains which do not have to do with language, we cannot stress enough the role of language teaching professionals, such as teachers and syllabus designers, in the process of doing an NA, because they will ultimately be responsible for task design. Although doing NA is a time-consuming and expensive endeavour, the resources invested in NA means considerable amounts of time gained in syllabus and task design.

Further Reading

Baralt, M., Gilabert, R., and Robinson, P. (2014), eds. *Task sequencing and instructed second language learning*. London: Bloomsbury Academic.

Gilabert, R. (2005). Evaluating the use of multiple sources and methods in needs analysis: A case study of journalists in the Autonomous Community of Catalonia (Spain). In M. H. Long, ed. *Second language needs analysis*. Cambridge: Cambridge University Press, pp. 182–99.

Gilabert, R. and Castellví, J. (2019). Task and Syllabus Design for Morphologically Complex Languages. In J. Schwieter and A. Benati, eds. *The Cambridge handbook of language learning*. Cambridge: Cambridge University Press, pp. 527–49.

González-Lloret, M. (2014). The need for needs analysis in technology-mediated TBLT. In M. González-Lloret and L. Ortega, eds. *Task-based language teaching*. Vol. 6. Amsterdam: John Benjamins, pp. 23–50.

Long, M.H. (2005). *Second language needs analysis*. Cambridge: Cambridge University Press.

Malicka, A., Gilabert, R., and Norris, J. M. (2017). From needs analysis to task design: Insights from an English for specific purposes context. *Language Teaching Research*, 23(1), 78–106.

Malicka, A. (2018). The role of task sequencing in fluency, accuracy, and complexity: Investigating the SSARC model of pedagogic task sequencing. *Language Teaching Research*, 24(5), 642–65.

Study Questions

1. Think of a professional task you remember having performed in the second language (e.g., serving drinks in a local pub, organizing an international conference, giving a business presentation, doing a job interview, etc.). How many dimensions of NA, as described in the chapter, would apply to your task description? Was the task you remember doing in the second language a stand-alone task (a target task) or was it part of a larger task (a sub-task)?
2. Do you think that NA analysis is feasible in your teaching context? How realistic is it to obtain information from and about the community of students you serve?
3. What would be your criteria for sequencing tasks in your teaching context?
4. How do you think teachers would make use of the information retrieved from a NA? How do you think they would use it for their own teaching? In your view, what would teachers achieve by bringing their teaching closer to their students' actual needs?

References

Baralt, M., Gilabert, R., and Robinson, P. (2014), eds. *Task sequencing and instructed second language learning*. London: Bloomsbury Academic.

Bloom, B. S., Engelhart, M. D., Furst, E. J., Hill, W. H., and Krathwohl, D. R. (1956). *Taxonomy of educational objectives: The classification of educational goals. Handbook I: Cognitive domain*. New York: David McKay Company.

Boswood, T. and Marriott, A. (1994). Ethnography for specific purposes: Teaching and training in parallel. *English for Specific Purposes*, 13 (1), 3–21.

Chaudron, C., Doughty, C. J., Kim, Y., Kong, D.-K., Lee, J., Lee, Y.-G., Long, M. H., Rivers, R., and Urano, K. (2005). A task-based needs analysis of a tertiary Korean as a foreign language program. In M. Long, ed. *Second language needs analysis*. Cambridge: Cambridge University Press, pp. 225–61.

Council of Europe. (2001). *Common European framework of reference for languages: Learning, teaching, assessment*. Cambridge: Press Syndicate of the University of Cambridge.

East, M. (2012). Addressing the intercultural via task-based language teaching: possibility or problem? *Language and Intercultural Communication*, 12 (1), 56–73.

Gilabert, R. (2005). Evaluating the use of multiple sources and methods in needs analysis: A case study of journalists in the Autonomous Community of Catalonia (Spain). In M. H. Long, ed. *Second language needs analysis*. Cambridge: Cambridge University Press, pp. 182–99.

Gilabert, R. and Castellví, J. (2019). Task and syllabus design for morphologically complex languages. In J. Schwieter and A. Benati, eds. *The Cambridge handbook of language learning*. Cambridge: Cambridge University Press, pp. 527–49.

González-Lloret, M. (2014). The need for needs analysis in technology-mediated TBLT. In M. González-Lloret and L. Ortega, eds. *Task-based language teaching*. Vol. 6. Amsterdam: John Benjamins, pp. 23–50.

González-Lloret, M. and Ortega, L. (2014). Towards technology-mediated TBLT: An introduction. In M. González-Lloret and L. Ortega, eds. *Technology-mediated TBLT: Researching technology and tasks*. Amsterdam: John Benjamins, pp. 1–22.

Holmes, W., Anastopoulou S., Schaumburg, H., and Mavrikis, M. (2018). *Technology-enhanced personalised learning: untangling the evidence*. Stuttgart: Robert Bosch Stiftung.

Long, M. H. (2005). *Second language needs analysis*. Cambridge: Cambridge University press.

Long, M. H. (2015). *Second language acquisition and task-based language teaching*. Hoboken, NJ: Wiley-Blackwell.

Malicka, A., Gilabert, R., and Norris, J. M. (2017). From needs analysis to task design: Insights from an English for specific purposes context. *Language Teaching Research*, 23(1), 78–106.

Malicka, A. (2018). The role of task sequencing in fluency, accuracy, and complexity: Investigating the SSARC model of pedagogic task sequencing. *Language Teaching Research*, 24(5), 642–65.

Mayer, R. (2009). *Multimedia Learning*. 2nd ed. Cambridge: Cambridge University Press.

Munby, J. (1978). *Communicative syllabus design.* Cambridge: Cambridge University Press.

OECD and OCDE. (2012). *Languages in a global world : Learning for better cultural understanding.* Éditions OCDE/OECD Publishing.

OECD (2015). *Students, computers and learning – making the connection.* Paris: OECD Publishing. Retrieved from: www.keepeek.com/Digital-Asset-Management/oecd/education/studentscomputers-and-learning_9789264239555-en#.Wm9Kh3kiFpg#page3

Ollivier, C. (2018). *Towards a socio-interactional approach to foster autonomy in language learners and users.* Strasbourg: Council of Europe Publishing/Éditions du Conseil de l'Europe.

Pallotti, G. (2019). An approach to assessing the linguistic difficulty of tasks. *Journal of the European Second Language Association*, 3, 58-70.

Pica, T., Kanagy, R., and Falodun, J. (1993). Choosing and using communication tasks for second language instruction. In G. Crookes and S. Gass, eds. *Tasks and language learning. Integrating theory and practice.* Bristol: Multilingual Matters.

Pienemann, M. (1998). *Language processing and second language development: Processability theory.* Amsterdam: John Benjamins.

Pienemann, M., Di Biase, B., and Kawaguchi, S. (2005). Extending processability theory. In M. Pienemann, ed. *Cross-linguistic aspects of processability theory.* Amsterdam: John Benjamins, pp. 199–252.

Robinson, P. (2001). Task complexity, task difficulty, and task production: Exploring interactions in a componential framework. *Applied Linguistics*, 22(1), 27–57.

Robinson, P. (2005). Cognitive complexity and task sequencing: Studies in a componential frame- work for second language task design. *IRAL – International Review of Applied Linguistics in Language Teaching*, 43, 1–32.

Robinson, P. and Gilabert, R. (2007). Task complexity, the Cognition Hypothesis and second language learning and performance. *IRAL – International Review of Applied Linguistics in Language Teaching*, 45, 161–76.

Saoquian, L. and Baoshu, Y. (2013). TBLT in China (2001–2011): the current situation, predicament and future. *Indonesian Journal of Applied Linguistics*, 2(2), 147–55.

Serafini, E. J. and Torres, J. (2015). The utility of needs analysis for non-domain expert instructors in designing task-based Spanish for the professional curricula. *Foreign Language Annals*, 48, 447–72.

Serafini, E. J., Lake, J. B., and Long, M. H. (2015) Needs analysis for specialized learner populations: Essential methodological improvements. *English for Specific Purposes*, 40, 11–26.

Serra, J. and Gilabert, R. (2020). Development of L2 reading skills in digital game-based learning: Comparing teacher and automatic adaptivity. IDC Conference: London (online).

Skehan, P. (1998). *A cognitive approach to language learning.* Oxford: Oxford University Press.

Skehan, Peter. (2009). Modelling second language performance: Integrating complexity, accuracy, fluency, and lexis. *Applied Linguistics*, 30(4), 510–32.

Swales, J. (1990). *Genre analysis*. Cambridge: Cambridge University Press.

Vanbecelaere, S. and Benton, L., (2020), eds. Technology-mediated personalized learning for younger learners: concepts, design, methods and practice. *British Journal of Educational Technology* [special issue]. IDC '20: Proceedings of the 2020 ACM Interaction Design and Children Conference: Extended Abstracts June 2020 doi.org/10.1145/3397617.3398059

Wilkins, D. (1976). *Notional syllabuses*. Oxford: Oxford University Press.

7A

Task-Based Telecollaborative Exchanges between US and Italian Students

A Case Study in Program Design and Implementation

Elena Nuzzo and Diego Cortés Velásquez[*]

7A.1 The Learning Environment of Telecollaboration

The process of working together with more people through online tools to achieve an agreed goal is widely known as telecollaboration (TC) and has been largely adopted in many fields, such as language education, medicine, and business studies, among others (O'Dowd, 2018). The online tools described in the literature vary from asynchronous tools such as email, bulletin board/online forums, blogs, to synchronous tools, such as video conferencing, texting, and computer chatting (Akiyama, 2018).

In language education, TC falls under the umbrella terms of computer-assisted language learning (CALL), network-based language teaching (NBLT), computer-mediated language learning and technology-mediated contexts. The debate about the most suitable definition for TC, as well as the type of online activities that should be included in said definition is currently ongoing (Dooley, 2017). Moreover, several terms have been proposed to name this type of learning environment, such as online international learning, e-tandem, Internet-mediated intercultural foreign language education, collaborative online international learning, and virtual exchange.

Having considered the various proposals, we have chosen the label "telecollaboration," which seems to be the most concise, transparent, and consolidated term. We define it as a "paradidactic" learning environment based on virtual communication between peers, which involves

---

[*] This chapter is the result of the close collaboration of both authors. For the specific concerns of the Italian Academy, Elena Nuzzo is responsible for Section 7A2 and Diego Cortés Velásquez for Sections 7A1 and 7A3.

various possible modes, such as mentoring, online tandem exchange and asynchronous work (email, WhatsApp messages, etc.).

As Dooley mentioned (2017), collaborative exchanges, such as pen pals and others, have been documented as far back as the nineteenth century. However, with the development of Internet technology in the early 1990s these partnerships experienced a momentous shift in language learning, notably for foreign language learners whose exposure to input, opportunities for output, and contact with meaningful cultural aspects related to the target language were rather rare in the past.

A close liaison between TC and task-based language teaching (TBLT) emerged quite naturally and much of the research on TC has been situated within the TBLT framework (Dooley, 2017). This natural connection has been additionally strengthened by several scholars working in the TBLT field who, since the early days, have called for the incorporation of technology in task-based instructional designs (Doughty & Long, 2003; González-Lloret, 2003; González-Lloret & Ortega, 2014; González-Lloret & Ziegler, this volume; Skehan, 2003).

The advantages of TC can be summarized in terms of linguistic competence, intercultural competence, pragmatic competence, learner autonomy, and digital literacies and multiliteracies.

Whereas the benefits of TC programs are undisputed, "there is also clear consensus among researchers that online exchange does not automatically provide sufficient opportunities for focus on form, negotiation of meaning, and corrective feedback" (Luo & Yang 2018). Therefore, research focuses on how to implement these programs in order to achieve valuable outcomes with reasonable efforts. Among all the aspects to be considered in the implementation of a TC task-based program, task design is one of the most important because it orients the type of exchange that can take place, and consequently its effectiveness for language development (cf. González-Lloret & Ortega 2014; O'Dowd & Ware 2009).

In this paper, following O'Dowd and Ware's (2009) call for more attention to be paid to the choice and structure of the tasks in studies on TC projects, we describe in detail the implementation of a TC program between a US and an Italian university, and provide a rationale for the choices we made on the basis of the participants' needs analysis. We then discuss the program's strengths and weaknesses in light of participants' feedback.

7A.2   A Case Study: Task-Based Telecollaborative Exchanges between US and Italian Students

During the 2018/19 fall and spring semesters, a telecollaborative program was implemented with students from the University of Rome III (Università degli Studi Roma Tre, R3) and California State University, Long Beach (CSULB). The telecollaborative program was structured using two types of collaboration, namely mentoring and exchange. These modalities correspond to those labeled by Ware and O'Dowd (2008) as e-tutoring and e-partnership. In this chapter, we focus only on the telecollaborative exchange.

The main purpose of the program was to give students more opportunities for meaningful and goal-oriented communication than they would usually have in their educational contexts. Additionally, data were collected for research purposes on peer corrective feedback and various aspects of interactional competence.

7A.2.1 Participants and Structure of the Language Exchange Program

Forty-four students (twenty-two CSULB learners of Italian paired with twenty-two R3 learners of English) took part in this program, sixteen during the fall semester of 2018, and twenty-eight during the spring semester of 2019. Only two US students and one Italian student participated in both rounds. For certain aspects, the structure of this program was rather typical, following Akiyama's analysis (2018) of sixty-five studies: the participant configuration (foreign language learner–foreign language learner), the countries of residence (United States appears in more than 50 percent or the studies), and the languages involved (English is target language in 75 percent).

The schedule changed slightly from one semester to the next (see Table 7A.1), but the basic structure was the same. The differences between the first and the second round were due either to students' needs, as emerged from their comments at the end of the semester, or to research requirements.

In both rounds, a set of tasks was designed by the organizers (the authors of this paper) and written instructions were sent to the participants. The tasks were to be completed collaboratively, but they entailed individual work, as well. Specifically, each task involved writing a text in the second language and providing corrective feedback on the partner's pieces of

Table 7A.1 *A comparison of the main features of the two rounds of the program*

Fall 2018	Spring 2019
• Three tasks	• Four tasks
• Nine videocalls (three for each task)	• Eight videocalls (two for each task)
• Three pieces of writing in the second language	• Four pieces of writing in the second language
• Written corrective feedback on three pieces of writing	• Written corrective feedback on four pieces of writing
• Discussion on written corrective feedback in the giver's first language	• Discussion on written corrective feedback in the receiver's first language
	• Reflection on difficulties in giving and explaining written corrective feedback

writing. To complete the tasks, the students met virtually on a regular basis using Zoom software, and the meetings were video-recorded for both documentation and research purposes. They also communicated via email and computer or mobile chat services, but these additional exchanges were not saved. Deadlines were provided to complete each task, but the pairs were allowed to organize their encounters autonomously. Language alternation during oral communication was dictated by instructions (see Figure 7A.1).

Task 2
Short-story review

The second task you will have to complete with your partner is the review of two short stories, one by an Italian author and one by an English-speaking author. The complete task must be carried out in sessions 3 and 4 of this Language Exchange program, and completed by March 24. The short stories – of a length between four and eight pages approximately – this should be agreed between you and your partner according to your preferences.

Once all the phases of the task have been completed you must send the final version of your text to your partner, so he/she can upload it in the OneDrive folder. The final draft must be of about 500 words, in Italian, in which you briefly describe the plot, giving personal insights about the quality and the topic of the story you have read. You can use this* review to have a better idea of how to compose your own. Bear in mind that your text should only be of about 500 words.

The phases of your work are as follows:

1. Look for English-speaking authors of short stories that might interest your partner. Make sure to include a variety of genres and different levels of linguistic difficulty.
2. Video-call session. In this phase you have to decide on the short stories with your partner, investigating your mutual preferences. In one part of the meeting you will ask your partner questions and suggest some ideas for the English-speaking authors, in Italian; in the other part, your partner will do the same with you, about the Italian authors, in English.
3. Individual drafting of the reviews. Write the review of the Italian short story you have read, in Italian, and then send it to your partner.
4. Individual correction of the text sent by your partner. Use the Word revision tool (or similar program) to correct the text produced by your partner. Do not send the revised text yet.
5. Video-call session. Report the corrections to your partner's text, without showing the corrected draft yet. Use Italian for this phase, so that he/she will easier understand you and you can have the opportunity to express yourself in the second language with the specific grammar jargon. Your partner will do the same with your text, in English. At the end of the meeting you can send the texts with the revisions, so that everyone can work on the final version. Both versions – with revisions and final – of both texts should be uploaded to your shared folder on OneDrive.
6. Fill in the individual form. Based on the conversation of the second video call, fill out this** form online.

Figure 7A.1 Instructions for the second task of the second round

* A link was provided to a website with book reviews ** See Appendix at end of subchapter

It must be emphasized that the telecollaborative work was managed autonomously by the participants. The organizers sent instructions, assisted the students if they needed clarification or faced technical problems, and made sure that the deadlines were met. Apart from that, there was no teacher intervention, only peer work. As we have mentioned above, the development of learner autonomy is one of the acknowledged positive outcomes of telecollaborative programs.

7A.2.2 From Needs Analysis to Task Design

The language exchange program was offered to students attending English/Italian courses based on synthetic syllabi. The institutions involved allowed the program to be implemented just as an additional activity, thus entailing no changes in the structure of language courses. In such a context, it was not possible to conduct a real needs analysis with the use of multiple sources and methods. Therefore, the target tasks were identified on the basis of what we knew about study programs, students' profiles, curricular objectives, etc.

The profiles of the Italian and US participants were similar. They were university students between the ages of 20 and 30. Their overall level of competence in the target[1] language was intermediate to advanced, and most of them had more than two languages in their repertoire. All of them wanted to improve their interactive skills, but there were some differences regarding their immediate goals. For the CSULB students, the language exchange was an activity added to the standard Italian course, and the final versions of the pieces of writing produced to complete the tasks were assessed by the language teacher. For the R3 participants, it was part of an extracurricular activity devoted to the analysis of spoken language in the first and second language and was organized by the teacher of second language learning and teaching.

Despite these differences, we assumed that the similarities were enough to identify common linguistic needs in the two groups of participants. For both groups, the types of language courses attended by the participants were of a very general nature, so it would be difficult to select a set of "things they [would] do in and through the [second language]" (Long 2016: 6). Ideally, at the end of those courses students are expected to be capable of doing a wide variety of things with the target language but there are no explicit expectations in terms of specific tasks. Therefore, when trying to identify the target tasks for our participants, we decided it would be worth focusing on two aspects: (i) during their university life, they had to attend courses on cultural aspects related to the target language (literature, history, etc.), and (ii) it could be assumed that they were likely to

---

[1] We refer to the target languages that are relevant to this paper, namely Italian for CSULB students and English for the R3 students, and do not consider other languages they might have been learning at the time.

become second or foreign language teachers at the end of their academic career. Based on these premises, the following target tasks were identified:

- participating in a discussion about literature, cinema, history, politics, or other topics related to culture in a broad sense;
- giving a presentation on literature, cinema, history, politics, or other topics related to culture in a broad sense;
- writing an essay;
- writing a book review;
- writing an email to university staff;
- describing and explaining a structural aspect of language;
- giving corrective feedback on a piece of writing.

Accordingly, we developed the pedagogic tasks summarized in Table 7A.2. In all tasks the expected final outcome was a written text in English for the R3 participants and in Italian for the CSULB participants.

Given the ancillary role of the language exchange program in relation to the main language courses attended by the students, we did not design

Table 7A.2 *Synthesis of the tasks administered in the two rounds*

Fall 2018	Spring 2019
Task 1: Organizing a three-day trip for the partner.	Task 1: Organizing a themed tour for a possible trip together.
Outcome	Outcome
R3: A trip itinerary in Italy.	R3: A themed tour in Italy.
CSULB: A trip itinerary in California.	CSULB: A themed tour in the United States.
Task 2: Reviewing a film.	Task 2: Reviewing a short story.
Outcome	Outcome
R3: A review of an American movie.	R3: A review of a short story by an English-speaking author.
CSULB: A review of an Italian movie.	CSULB: A review of a short story by an Italian author.
Task 3: Writing a semi-fantasy short story.	Task 3: Commenting on immigration policies.
Outcome	Outcome
R3: A short story involving the United States (living or historical) personage the student likes most.	R3: A post about immigration in Italy.
CSULB: A short story involving the Italian (living or historical) personage the student likes most.	CSULB: A post about immigration in the United States.
	Task 4: Writing an evaluation email to university staff.
	Outcome
	R3: An email to CSULB Italian language coordinator with an evaluation of the language exchange program.
	CSULB: An email to R3 internship coordinator with an evaluation of the language exchange program.

a task-based syllabus. We simply developed two sets of tasks –one for each round of the program– with a similar architecture, involving the following steps, or sub-tasks (exemplified in Figure 7A.1):

- oral discussion with the partner to investigate her/his opinions, tastes, positions on the topic addressed in the task
- individual writing in the target language
- individual correction of the partner's writing sample
- oral explanation of corrective feedback to the partner
- individual revision
- reflection on the feedback process (only in the second edition).

Pedagogic tasks[2] were sequenced according to the following criteria: their topics were increasingly less concrete and familiar, and the expected final outcome required mastering the specific features of increasingly sophisticated genres.

7A.2.3 Evaluating the Program

At the end of both rounds, panel discussions were organized with each group of participants to gather feedback on the program. In addition, the last task of the second round required the students to discuss the strengths and weaknesses of the activity, and to write an evaluation email to their partners' university staff. The first part of the instructions for CSULB participants is reported in Figure 7A.2.

Generally speaking, evaluations were extremely positive from both groups of students. Students appreciated this opportunity –quite unusual for them – to use the target language in an authentically communicative way, as shown by examples[3] 1 and 2:

1. *[…] students who take part in this program can improve their ability to communicate effectively by using a foreign language: in particular they can learn how to face communicative problems during a real face to face conversation with a person who speaks another language and they can learn how to find the best solution to express their opinion in a comprehensible way. I believe this is really important for a language student, because he or she will probably experience similar situations at work in the future.*
2. *Even if my english is still rusty and I have a lot to learn, I really appreciated this activity. I feel I'm not shy of talking in english with someone else, because I realized that I'm able to find other ways to make myself understood.*

Some of them also appreciated the fact that they could improve their teaching skills, as mentioned in examples 3 and 4:

---

[2] Excluding the last task of the second round.
[3] Examples in this section are taken from the evaluation emails of some R3 students. Similar comments were found in the CSULB evaluation emails, but as they are written in Italian we decided not to report them here.

> We've come to the end of this program. The academic coordinator of the exchange program, Dr. Name Surname, is considering whether to activate the telecollaboration program next year. To help her decide, we ask you to send her an email to provide your evaluation. In your opinion, is it worth repeating this experience next year? What do you think are the strengths of the program? What are the aspects that could be improved? The complete task must be carried out in sessions 7 and 8 of this language exchange program and completed by May 19.
>
> Once all the phases of the task have been completed, you must send an email in Italian to Dr. Name Surname (name.surname@uniroma3.it), copying prof. Name Surname (name.surname@csulb.edu), Name Surname (name.surname@csulb.edu) and Name Surname (name.surname@uniroma3.it), to provide your evaluation of the telecollaboration program. There is no limit of words, but make sure you clearly expose the arguments in favor of your position.

Figure 7A.2 First part of the instructions for the last task of the second round

3. *I believe that this kind of activity is useful if you wish to learn a foreign language since it allows you to talk with a native speaker, which is not always possible in our language lessons. Moreover, I have found this project particularly useful also for developing teaching skills.*
4. *This project can be also a starting point for a job in the future, in the sense that during these months both me and Julio have been like teachers for each other.*

A third aspect that was highly appreciated was the opportunity to get to know a different culture, as reported in examples 5 and 6:

5. *It was nice to spend time with her because I have learned a lot about english, about a different culture and lifestyle. I always wanted to know about american lifestyle and since I was little, my biggest dream was to live in Los Angeles. Talking with my partner made me think about it and I felt a little bit closer to american culture.*
6. *it was amazing to meet someone from another continent and to get to know something about his culture, his nation, and his life in general.*

Many thoughtful and constructive suggestions for improvement were provided by the participants, such as giving more "free" time at the beginning, so that the partners could break the ice before dealing with the tasks at hand:

7. *I would also suggest to add a further meeting before the first task in order to let the partners break the ice and feel more comfortable before officially starting the task.*
8. *A thing I would like to suggest is to give more time to personally know each other better before starting to work together. In fact, the first time was not not easy to start talking about the topic of the task.*

Another problematic issue was language alternation, as reported in examples 9 and 10:

9. *Consider having two meetings in English, two in Italian and the remaining four (the feedback ones) divided in two halves, each one dedicated to one language.*

10. *It could be better if speakers would speak the same language during the session. That's because, it could be easier to set the brain in just one language.*

Finally, some students suggested that participants should be allowed to decide which tasks to complete, as in example 11:

11. *I would propose a list of different themes and arguments, in order to pick one with the partner, according to their preferences.*

These suggestions have been taken into account for the planning of a new round of the program. Consequently, a "zero task" has been added to the existing four. The outcome of this additional task, to be completed in just one video-call session, is an agreed document in which the pairs indicate the tasks they would like to carry out from a list of ten options. This zero task should also help the partners get to know each other a bit before the real start of the program. As for language alternation, the participants are expected to use English in four video-call sessions and Italian in the other four, making sure that they eventually have the same number of topic-discussion and feedback-discussion sessions in both languages. In the very first session, participants are free to alternate the languages as they prefer, or even to use their own first language.

7A.3 Conclusion

In this contribution we illustrated a task-based telecollaborative program that was organized between Italian students of English and Californian students of Italian with the aim of increasing their opportunities for meaningful and goal-oriented communication. The program involved more than forty people of the two languages/cultures from October 2018 to May 2019. It was greatly appreciated by the participants, who identified a number of strengths and provided interesting suggestions for improvement, as well. After a careful evaluation of the data at our disposal – particularly the video recordings of the virtual meetings, the written outcomes, and the students' comments– we could confirm the utility of the program and revised the plan for its next implementation.

Our revised language exchange program was initially set for fall 2019 but could not be implemented before spring 2021. This postponement was due to the fact that the program was a novelty for both institutions, with all the consequences that it entails. Adopting a TBLT perspective requires a paradigm shift in the way language learning and use is seen by program coordinators, language instructors, and students. Eventually, the analysis of the data collected in the two rounds helped us persuade our partners that TC work from a TBLT perspective is a valuable resource that can always be enhanced and tailored for the students' specific needs.

Further Reading

Akiyama, Y. (2018). Synthesizing the practice of SCMC-based telecollaboration: A scoping review. *CALICO Journal*, 35(1), 49–76.

Dooley, M. (2017). Telecollaboration. In C. Chapelle and S. Sauro, eds. *The handbook of technology and second language teaching and learning*. Hoboken: John Wiley, pp. 169–83.

González-Lloret, M. and Ortega, L. (2014). Towards technology-mediated TBLT. An introduction. In M. González-Lloret and L. Ortega, eds. *Technology-mediated TBLT: Researching technology and tasks*. Amsterdam: John Benjamins, pp. 1–21.

O'Dowd, R. (2018). From telecollaboration to virtual exchange: state-of-the-art and the role of UNICollaboration in moving forward. *Journal of Virtual Exchange*, 1, 1–23.

O'Dowd, R. and Ware, P. D. (2009). Critical issues in telecollaborative task design. *Computer Assisted Language Learning*, 22(2), 37–41.

Study Questions

1. Why is the telecollaborative context particularly suitable for the implementation of TBLT?
2. Are there other tasks that you would suggest for the learners described in this study?
3. Would you make different choices with regard to task complexity and sequencing?

References

Akiyama, Y. (2018). Synthesizing the practice of SCMC-based telecollaboration: A scoping review. *CALICO Journal*, 35(1), 49–76.

Dooley, M. (2017). Telecollaboration. In C. Chapelle and S. Sauro, eds. *The handbook of technology and second language teaching and learning*. Hoboken: John Wiley, pp. 169–83.

Doughty, C. J. and Long, M.H. (2003). Optimal psycholinguistic environments for distance foreign language learning. *Language Learning & Technology*, 7(3), 50–80.

González-Lloret, M. (2003). Task-based language materials: En busca de esmeraldas. *Language Learning & Technology*, 7(1), 86–104.

González-Lloret, M. and Ortega, L. (2014). Towards technology-mediated TBLT. An introduction. In M. González-Lloret and L. Ortega, eds. *Technology-mediated TBLT: Researching technology and tasks*. Amsterdam: John Benjamins, pp. 1-21.

Long, M. (2016). In Defense of Tasks and TBLT: Nonissues and Real Issues. *Annual Review of Applied Linguistics*, 36, 5–33.

Luo, H. and Yang, C. (2018). Twenty years of telecollaborative practice : implications for teaching Chinese as a foreign language. *Computer Assisted Language Learning*, 31(5–6), 1–26.

O'Dowd, R. (2018). From telecollaboration to virtual exchange: state-of-the-art and the role of UNICollaboration in moving forward. *Journal of Virtual Exchange*, 1, 1–23.

O'Dowd, R. and Ware, P. D. (2009). Critical issues in telecollaborative task design. *Computer Assisted Language Learning*, 22(2), 37–41.

Skehan, P. (2003). Focus on form, tasks, and technology. *Computer Assisted Language Learning*, 16, 391–411.

Ware, P. and O'Dowd, R. (2008). Peer feedback on language form in telecollaboration. *Language Learning & Technology*, 12(1), 43–63.

Appendix Retrospective sheet on feedback activity

After listening to the recording of the meeting, please answer the following questions:

1. First name
2. Last name
3. Session number
   2
   4
   6
   8

4. Session date _____

5. Did you have any difficulties in giving feedback to your partner?
   Yes
   No

6. If so, on which language forms? Please indicate up to 3 elements.
   _____
   _____
   _____

7. Element 1: what kind of difficulty?
   I didn't know whether the form was right or wrong
   I knew that the form was wrong, but I didn't know which form was the right one
   I didn't know how to explain the error
   Other:

8. Element 1: How did you overcome the obstacle?
   _____
   _____

9. Element 2: what kind of difficulty?
   I didn't know whether the form was right or wrong
   I knew that the form was wrong, but I didn't know which form was the right one
   I didn't know how to explain the error
   Other:

10. Element 2: How did you overcome the obstacle?
    _____
    _____

11. Element 3: What kind of difficulty?
    I didn't know whether the form was right or wrong
    I knew that the form was wrong, but I didn't know which form was the right one
    I didn't know how to explain the error
    Other:

12. Element 3: How did you overcome the obstacle?
    _____
    _____

8

Exploring the Nuts and Bolts of Task Design

Virginia Samuda and Martin Bygate

8.1 Introduction

It is generally accepted that tasks need designing. Since the central tenet of task-based language teaching (TBLT) is that tasks have the potential to shape opportunities for language use and language processing in ways that benefit learning, we might expect the design of a task to play a role in shaping those opportunities. Yet, talking about task design is not straightforward. This is partly because the term 'task design' encompasses a very broad spectrum of distinctive practices, as reflected in the range of people who engage in design, the scope of what design actually entails, the timing of when design takes place, and how it interfaces with classroom implementation. In this chapter we focus on this range of activity and the types of knowledge that come under the umbrella of 'task design' for everyday classroom use. In what follows, we will be suggesting that the concept of task design refers partly to the form given to an activity when it is planned or written down, reflecting what is known about how interaction and language processing can be shaped, as well as the ways in which participants use input information and orient to task outcomes in working through a task. In addition, we will be proposing that task design also includes actions and interventions by teachers or learners in the classroom, and that these can significantly change, enhance or undermine a task's potential.

To begin, we consider a number of key questions about design in relation to TBLT research and TBLT practice, questions that include the extent to which tasks can in fact be 'designed', in what ways, by whom, and when.

8.2 Who Does Task Design?

A wide range of people routinely engage in task design. While this can include textbook and materials writers working at distance from the intended users of the tasks they create, in TBLT the people who do design are likely to be curriculum developers working in response to specific needs analyses, as well as teachers drawing on local knowledge of the cultural contexts and social backgrounds of the students that they work with.

8.3 What Constitutes Task Design?

The term 'task design' is not solely restricted to the creation of original tasks from scratch; it also includes the common practice of tweaking aspects of existing 'ready-made' tasks to make them more accessible to particular student groups. This can involve relatively minor changes to the surface details of a task (for instance changing names or places to make the content more relevant), but also more substantial changes to its overall structure (for instance changing the order of steps to be taken through a task or altering the format of its outcome). For some examples of how teachers change the original design of a task, see work by Andon (2018), Nguyen et al. (2018) and Samuda (2015). Although technically speaking, these kinds of adjustment might be considered 're-design' rather than design proper, they make up a very substantial part of what falls under the task design umbrella and raise a number of design issues that warrant serious consideration, as we see later in the chapter.

However, the bottom line is that all these relate to the design of *tasks*. This means that the design needs to incorporate the essential elements of a task highlighted in standard definitions (Long, 1985, Skehan, 1998, Ellis, 2003, 2009; Samuda & Bygate, 2008) by providing initial input material, require a focus on semantic and pragmatic meaning, set up the need for learners to convey or infer meanings, create conditions where learners rely on their own resources, and set a goal or outcome other than the use of language. The ways in which a goal is established, and the ways in which paths between initial input and final outcome are staged and choreographed will reflect the creativity and ingenuity of an individual designer and contribute to the distinctiveness and originality of the finished task.

Before continuing, there is one further point that should made explicit here, and this is the distinction between the design of research tasks, where the primary aim is to elicit performance data, and the design of pedagogic tasks, where the primary use is as a tool for teaching and learning. The distinction is important because in the case of pedagogic task design, the focus of this chapter, there are a number of design considerations, particularly those relating to the pedagogical framing of a task, which will often not be relevant to the design of research tasks.

8.4 When Does Task Design Take Place?

In TBLT, the classic view is that design comes into play after a needs analysis has been carried out, with information derived from that analysis shaping the design of the target tasks that students will need to be able to perform, and subsequently the pedagogic tasks that will enable them to accomplish their target goals. For example, a *target* task for a tailor prior to creating a garment would be to accurately note down client names and measurements on the basis of verbal instructions relayed by an assistant; associated *pedagogic* tasks might therefore involve (among other things) listening to and identifying the spelling of common names in the target culture, writing them down, seeking clarification where needed and verifying that the information has been accurately noted. Detailed examples of this approach to task design can be found in the study by Long (2015: chap. 9) and in accounts of projects undertaken in various contexts, including for example, those by Lambert (2010), González-Lloret and Nielson (2015) and Hillman and Long (2020).

As can be seen here, this kind of work involves two broadly different types of design decision based on different sources of knowledge. Decisions relating to target tasks will be primarily shaped by what students need or want to do outside the classroom (make a hotel reservation, call emergency services to report a workplace accident for example), and those relating to the design of pedagogic tasks will be primarily shaped by understandings of how students can be helped to approximate those target goals. Closely tied up with the latter will be questions relating to second language development: how best to provide meaningful input (Gass & Madden, 1985), activate meaningful output (Swain, 1985, 1995), give rise to different types of interaction (Mackey, 2007), and create opportunities for focusing on form (Doughty & Williams, 1998). In an ideal world, this presupposes that people involved in task design, whether curriculum developers, materials writers or teachers, have a grasp of both types of knowledge, and that this will enable them to make principled, informed decisions about the tasks they create. We come back to some implications of this presupposition later in the chapter.

The aspect of task design sketched here is essentially prospective, in that it is usually undertaken as part of course development prior to classroom use. But another key aspect of task design takes place much closer to point of use, for instance by teachers as they plan lessons, or even closer to point of use, via the reactive on-line adjustments that teachers make to tasks in response to what seems to be happening (or not) as a task unfolds in the classroom. Samuda (2015) gives some examples of how teachers make changes to tasks as they plan lessons and as they work with tasks in the classroom. Of course, it is not always teachers who make changes to task design; students play a role here too (Breen,

1987), and we return to some of the issues raised by this dimension of design later in the chapter.

Another important aspect of design is essentially retrospective in that it comes into play during the evaluation of what 'worked' and what did not, either after an individual lesson, a sequence of lessons, or an entire course. Although initially retrospective in nature, this type of design also feeds forward into future use, via the revision of existing tasks and/or the design of new ones. A significant body of evaluation work of this type has been carried out by John Norris in relation to a diverse range of TBLT projects (see Norris (2015); other examples can be found in Van den Branden (2006); González-Lloret & Nielson (2015), and Shintani (2018)).

From what we have seen so far, task design is emerging as an ongoing process that does not occur at any one fixed point in time. It includes work that takes place *prospectively* as part of curriculum development and lesson planning, work that takes place *reactively* in the classroom itself, and work that take place *retrospectively* as part of lesson and/or course evaluation. As noted above, task design covers a wide range of practices, from full-scale creation of novel tasks to minor adjustments to existing ones, with those who engage in it bringing different types of knowledge to bear on different aspects of the process. This can include knowledge about student needs, knowledge about cultural and social context, knowledge about pedagogy, knowledge about language learning in relation to TBLT, as well as knowledge about different types of task and their impacts on various aspects of student performance. All of this falls under the umbrella 'task design', and forms a dynamic cycle proceeding from initial creation to final evaluation, and looping back to shape the development of future designs.

8.5 Task Design as a Bridge between Task-Based Language Teaching Theory and Classroom Practice

Task design can be seen as one way of bridging TBLT principles and classroom practices. To some extent this is reflected in the strand of second language acquisition research that has focused on the impact of different aspects of task design on different aspects of language processing, generally attempting to tease apart relationships between clusters of design features and the ways that students work with tasks. For instance, tasks where information is divided between participants have been shown to encourage shared responsibility on the part of both speaker and listener for the communication of information, leading to more collaborative negotiation of meaning. One of the eventual goals of this work has been to provide practitioners with the tools to design tasks that, all things being equal, will maximise processing conditions likely to promote learning. Since this implies a smooth transition between empirical research and classroom practice, the fruits of this kind of work are of considerable interest to practitioners, who naturally want to know what kinds of task are likely to be best suited to the needs of the students they work with. To this end, research has led to the development of a number of empirically researched task design frameworks that aim to guide practitioners in their own design decisions by highlighting what could happen when various task design features are combined and manipulated. The approach most widely adopted has been to compare the language (interaction or monologue) produced by students on pairs of tasks that differed in terms of the presence or absence of a particular design feature. To give a flavour of this kind of work, we will take a brief look at three frameworks that have been particularly influential for task design. The first, Pica et al. (1993), is closely associated with the Input/Interaction/Output Hypothesis (Long, 1981; Gass, 1997; Mackey, 2012); the second, Skehan (1998, 2001), is closely associated with the Trade-Off Hypothesis (Skehan, 1996; 1998; 2015), and the third, Robinson (2007), closely associated with the Cognition Hypothesis (Robinson, 2003, 2007, 2015).

8.6 A Framework for Task Design Based on Pica et al. (1993)

The Pica et al. framework grew out of a number of studies of language learners working on tasks typically used in language classrooms, investigating how participants negotiate for meaning, particularly when communication breaks down. This is in line with the Interaction Hypothesis, according to which specific types of negotiation 'work' enhance learning by providing opportunities for negotiating input, for receiving feedback on output through recasts, for form focusing, for noticing gaps in current interlanguage repertoire and for modifying output (Long, 1981, 1985; Pica & Doughty, 1985; Pica, 1987, 1994; Gass, 1997; Mackey & Philp, 1998; Swain, 1985, 1995; Mackey, 1999, 2007, 2012).

The Pica et al. design framework builds on this work and on an earlier proposal made by Long that certain task types (two-way tasks with closed outcomes, that is tasks that oblige participants to exchange information equally leading to one verifiable outcome, as for example a spot-the-difference task) are likely to promote more negotiation for meaning and, by inference, more opportunities for learning than other task types (one-way tasks with open outcomes, for example, 'listen to the travel agent's range of holidays on offer, and choose the one you would prefer, explaining why').

Bringing together findings from a range of studies, Pica et al. developed a task typology that classified tasks in terms of their potential for creating opportunities for negotiation work. The typology itself highlights relationships between what Pica et al. term 'the interactional activity' of a task and its 'communication goal'. The term 'interactional activity' refers to the structure of the information flow between participants carrying out a task

Table 8.1 *Task typology, based on Pica et al. (1993).*

Task type	Information flow	Interaction requirement	Goal orientation	Outcome options
Jigsaw	Two-way	Required	Convergent	1
Information Gap	One-way	Required	Convergent	1
Problem-Solving	One-way/two-way	Optional	Convergent	1
Decision-Making	One-way/two-way	Optional	Convergent	Several
Opinion Exchange	One-way/two-way	Optional	Divergent	1/Several

(one-way or two-way) and to the interaction requirements of the task (required or optional information exchange). The term 'communication goal' refers to goal orientation (convergent or divergent, that is, whether participants have to reach agreement at the end of the task), and to outcome options (one single, or many possible outcomes permitted). Pica et al. argue that different clusters of these parameters may be combined to form five distinctive task types: Jigsaw, Information Gap, Decision-Making, Problem-Solving, Opinion Exchange. Of these, it is claimed that Jigsaw is the task type most likely to maximise opportunities for second language acquisition.

Numerous pedagogical recommendations have been subsequently derived from this (Pica, 1987, and elsewhere; Mackey, 1994, among others), often with exemplars of prototypical tasks. For example, a typical Jigsaw task involves a speaker following a plan of a garden to give instructions to a partner about how to arrange the plants to conform to the layout in the plan; the partner arranges the 'plants' on a felt board according to her understanding of the instructions given; success is measured by the degree of approximation to the original plan.

Clearly the features identified here go a long way towards summarising the likely nature of the interaction. However, as we will see shortly, questions arise about what these features tell us about how the tasks might unfold, the extent to which the students have options in navigating the tasks, and how the tasks mesh with the overall lesson.

8.7 A Framework for Task Design Based on Skehan (1998, 2001)

Skehan's framework initially derived from a set of six studies carried out from an information-processing perspective by Skehan and Foster from 1996 to 1999, and which were instrumental in the development of the Trade-Off Hypothesis (Skehan, 2015, this volume). Underlying those studies was the hypothesis that learners' attentional capacities are limited. Thus, when learners are engaged in carrying out a task where the focus is on communicating meaning in real time, attentional resources may be forced into competition with each other. This competition for limited resources may lead to a trade-off in the amount of attention available to focus on accuracy of message, the amount of attention available to focus on complexity of message and the capacity available to focus on fluency of message during task performance. Skehan has argued that certain task demands and certain task conditions may predispose learners to prioritise attention to fluency over accuracy and complexity in their language production, while other task demands and/or conditions may predispose learners to prioritise complexity or accuracy.

One goal of the Skehan and Foster studies, then, was to identify a set of task types that might have an effect on different aspects of performance, on the basis that the more demanding the task, the more likely it is that attentional resources will be directed towards task completion, and away from language form. To this end, Skehan and Foster explored the effects of planning time and differential processing load on the performance of three task types initially characterised as 'personal information', 'narrative' and 'decision-making'. To give a flavour of the kinds of tasks involved, we summarise those used in these studies here:

Table 8.2 *Task typology and tasks used in Skehan and Foster (1996–99)*

Task type	Tasks		
Personal information	Instruct someone how to get to your house and turn off the oven (Foster & Skehan, 1996)	Compare surprising aspects of life in the UK (Skehan & Foster, 1997)	–
Narrative	Create a story based on pictures (no obvious story-line) (Foster & Skehan, 1996)	Tell a story based on cartoon strip (clear story-line) (Skehan & Foster, 1997)	Retell *Mr Bean* video (random events) Retell *Mr Bean* video (typical restaurant script) (Skehan & Foster, 1999)
Decision-making	Decide on appropriate punishment for crime (Foster & Skehan, 1996)	Agree on advice to give in an Agony Aunt column (Skehan & Foster, 1997)	Decide who to throw out of sinking balloon (Foster & Skehan, 1999)

To tease out ambiguities in the results of these studies, Skehan (2001) carried out a meta-analysis in which he identified five 'finer grained' characteristics which he claimed may be more powerful than task type in their potential to impinge on task performance. Reframed slightly in Skehan (2003), these are: familiarity of information, interactive vs. monologic, degree of structure, outcomes requiring justifications, and transformations of task material.

As with the Pica framework, we note that the features listed here all describe overall attributes of tasks rather than focusing on the task seen from outside, rather than the students' eye view (that is, what the students might be trying to do during a task), and the trajectory they might follow as they work their ways through it. We return to this issue later.

8.8 A Framework for Task Design Based on Robinson (2007)

Robinson's proposals for task design were originally motivated by a practical interest in task sequencing. They aimed to provide practitioners with a basis for making decisions about how to select and order tasks in such a way that they build on each other in terms of the degree of cognitive challenge they are likely to contain, thereby enabling students to gradually approximate the increased cognitive demands of the target tasks they will engage with outside the classroom. Like Skehan, Robinson approaches task design from an information-processing perspective, but one that differs significantly. In developing the Cognition Hypothesis (Robinson, 2003, 2007, 2015, this volume), Robinson has argued that when working on tasks, learners do not have a limited attention capacity as posited by Skehan, but instead have access to multiple reservoirs of attention that enable them to attend to both form and content at the same time. This means that form and content are not necessarily in competition with each other during task performance but can in fact work together, without pushing learners to prioritise one over the other; accuracy over complexity, for example.

To this end, Robinson's framework highlights the various dimensions of a task that can be manipulated in order to increase or decrease the complexity of its cognitive challenge, potentially permitting practitioners to fine-tune the tasks they use so that they match the cognitive needs of their students. The framework distinguishes between dimensions of tasks that designers can manipulate in order to help learners gain access to second language knowledge during task performance (this could include building planning time into the design of a task, for example), and dimensions that can be manipulated to promote grammaticisation of language that learners currently have at their disposal. Robinson posits that increasing the cognitive demands of tasks along this latter dimension will push students to greater accuracy and complexity in the language they produce. He also argues that manipulating task features along this dimension can promote interaction and increase attention to language input. He proposes that variants of a task can be used cyclically, first to enhance learners' fluency and overall schematic understanding of a task, then to target more complex language, and finally to integrate the more complex language into fluent performance. Another aspect of Robinson's approach is the role of individual differences among learners (particularly those relating to cognitive factors), which he argues will differentially affect performance and learning as the cognitive complexity of tasks gradually increases. Note, however, that as with the Pica et al. and Skehan frameworks, Robinson's approach concentrates on identifying overall features of tasks that are assumed to apply from beginning to end of each design. Once again, the impression is that the primary concern is to give rise to a certain type of language processing.

To summarise, here is an overview of the main design variables highlighted by each of the three frameworks.

After Pica et al. (1993)

Interactional activity

- Information flow
- Interaction requirement

Communication goal

- Goal orientation
- Outcome options

After Skehan (1998, 2001)

Task characteristics

- Familiarity
- Interactive/monologic
- Degree of structure
- Outcomes + justifications
- Transformation of task materials

After Robinson (2003, 2007)

Task difficulty

- Ability variables
- Affective variables

Task condition

- Participation variables
- Participant variables

Task complexity

- Resource-directing
- Resource-dispersing

Figure 8.1 Overview of empirically grounded design variables

Overall, the three design frameworks highlight (albeit from different theoretical perspectives) ways that different combinations of design features can give rise to different patterns of interaction, encourage students to share and exchange information in different ways, or manipulate attention to different aspects of language use. Implicit in all three is a distinction between the *topic* of a task and its design, in which the topic could be characterised in terms of the topic as the 'meat' of a task and the design as the 'skeleton' that gives it shape. This is a useful distinction because it allows us to disentangle issues relating to topic/content and the way a task is designed. Since many of the design features highlighted here (particularly those relating to how information is shared among participants and how the outcome is structured) have played a significant role in translating TBLT principles into practice, it is likely that many teachers will have encountered them in some form or other, whether explicitly in preservice and in-service professional development courses and workshops, or implicitly through exposure to tasks that embody them. Thus, these features are clearly important reference points in developing an approach to the overall design of tasks. Nevertheless the frameworks all have the significant limitation that, a little like describing meals in terms of their calories, vitamins, protein and mineral content, they tend to abstract qualities from tasks, and in the process give limited attention to what tasks consist of, what it takes to work through them, and what students might learn from them. Thus, we suggest there are other aspects of task design that are crucial in a balanced approach. The first of these is the relationship between task design and language form.

8.9 Relationships between Task Design and Focus on Form

As we have seen, according to the frameworks described above, the primary purpose of task design is to influence what are considered to be key elements of language processing (for example, whether the task provides opportunities for learners to negotiate input, directs attention to more or less complex arrays of information, enables greater levels of fluency, or pushes attention to accuracy). From this perspective, then, task design has no role to play in predetermining the occurrence of specific linguistic features (pace possibly Robinson's 'attention directing' feature of task design). Indeed, importantly, any attempt at pre-seeding tasks at the design stage with particular language features or specifying features to be targeted has been dismissed as 'structure trapping' (Skehan, 1998), and in line with Long's distinction between focus on form and focus on forms (Long, 1991, and elsewhere), to be avoided. This suggests that if as consistently argued by Long, focus on form in TBLT is to be handled by teachers reactively as problems arise, then issues relating to language form belong with implementation and not design.

However, this touches on a central preoccupation for many teachers, particularly those transitioning to TBLT. While guidance about the potential effects of design features on how students work with tasks is obviously welcome, for teachers seeking ways to integrate focus on form within tasks, lack of guidance about aspects of language that different tasks might engender remains a stumbling block (Müller-Hartmann & Shocker, 2018). Although this is a controversial area within TBLT, from the perspective of task design, one way to respond to practitioner concerns without resorting to 'structure trapping' may be found in studies that support generally predictive relationships between task design and *areas* of language use while remaining neutral about the occurrence of specific linguistic instantiations. We will take a brief look at some of these and their implications for design.

8.10 Relationships between Task Design and Areas of Language Use

Several studies have suggested that under certain conditions, certain clusters and constellations of task features can give rise to certain clusters and constellations of linguistic features, including: types of discourse feature, (Bygate, 1999), morpho-syntactic markers (Nobuyoshi & Ellis, 1993; Mackey, 1999; Shintani, 2016; Takashima & Ellis, 1999), lexical items (Ellis & He, 1999; Shintani, 2016), grammatical relationships (Newton & Kennedy, 1996), and certain semantic features (Samuda, 2001). The implication from studies such as these is that tasks can be designed to activate broad areas of language use (rather than simply attempting to channel learners into using specific linguistic structures), and this can go some way towards giving teachers and designers a sense of *domains* of language use that are likely to come into play when certain design configurations are in place.

From a design perspective, a useful resource in this regard has been the set of criteria developed by Loschky & Bley-Vroman (1993) to probe relationships between task design and areas of language likely to be mobilised. To this end they distinguish between language that might be considered *natural*, *useful* or *essential* in carrying out a task. For example the first criterion, task naturalness, refers to language that may not be essential (that it is to say, you could complete the task without necessarily using it) but that might arise naturally while carrying it out (as, for example, in a task based around a travel itinerary or a bus timetable). The second relates to language that would be *useful*, but not necessarily essential (for example, the use of prepositions in a spot-the-difference task, or a map task), and the third refers to language that is essential to carrying out the task and cannot be avoided.

One way that designers can make use of these criteria is by piloting tasks with native speakers and highly proficient non-native speakers prior to classroom use to gauge domains of language likely to be natural, useful or essential; examples can be found in McDonough & Mackey (2000), Samuda (2001), and Robinson (2003). This practice is not intended as a covert form of pre-emptive structure trapping, nor a means of predetermining language to be targeted by teachers at the pre-task stage, but rather a way of highlighting areas of meaning at the design stage, and forming a basis for building an element of implicit form focus into the overall design of a task if so desired.

One example can be found in Samuda (2001), which describes a task designed around a semantic 'space' (in this case the expression of probability and possibility) without determining in advance any of the linguistic features that could be used to fill it. The design sought to create a 'need to mean'. so that as students became involved in carrying out the task, they found themselves engaging with meanings that they needed to convey, even if at that point they did not fully possess the linguistic means to express them. By highlighting areas of meaning brought into play by the task, the design aimed to involve students in inducting meaning before gradually focusing attention on areas of language that could be useful, first implicitly and then more explicitly. In Samuda's (2001) study this was done with the support of the teacher, who, working in tandem with the design, 'led from behind' the task at points of need to highlight relationships between meanings the students wanted to convey and potentially useful language. The notion of the teacher 'working in tandem with the design' opens up for consideration a further, aspect of task design that we come back to in the next section.

Despite differences in their theoretical underpinnings, the proposals reviewed so far share the general view that aspects of design can positively influence ways that students engage with tasks from start to finish and might thus be instrumental in creating conditions for learning. There are, however, a number of reasons to be cautious here. One stems from the distinction made by Breen (1987) between the 'task-as-workplan' (reflecting the designer's intentions) and the 'task-in-process' (reflecting the fact that learners interpret and reinterpret the task in ways possibly unintended by the designer), a distinction that has divided task designers and TBLT researchers alike.

8.11 The 'Problem' of Task Design

The task-as-workplan/task-in-process distinction raises fundamental questions about the extent to which tasks can actually be 'designed'. For example, second language researchers working from the perspective of Sociocultural Theory have argued that TBLT pays a disproportionate amount of attention to the task-as-workplan and too little to what actually happens in the classroom. The nub of their argument is that learners re-shape the workplan to suit their own ends, and so it is not possible to predict relationships between task design and task performance (see, for example, Coughlan & Duff, 1994) On this basis, a number of critics of TBLT have argued that tasks should not be viewed as design blueprints imposed on learners in advance (implied, they claim, by TBLT), but rather as emergent interactions, socially constructed by those who engage with them (see, for example, Lantolf, 2000; Donato, 2000; Lantolf & Thorne, 2006; Seedhouse, 2005; Slimani-Rolls, 2005, among others.

Hence the 'problem' of task design: on the one hand, we find the Sociocultural Theory view that design is of limited value because learners will re-design and change tasks as they work with them, and on the other, the cognitive perspective that task design plays a key role in creating conditions that positively influence performance, and by extension, learning. For a while, the tension between these two theoretical positions appeared to create an impasse in talking about task design. And yet, from a classroom perspective (and recalling the notion of the 'teacher working in tandem with the design' highlighted above), it could be argued that neither position in itself fully captures the complexity of designing tasks for pedagogic purposes, and that, for TBLT to evolve as a pedagogical initiative, some degree of balance between the two positions needs to be achieved.

To this end, the classroom-oriented work of Van den Branden and colleagues in Flanders has been instrumental highlighting ways of moving the debate forward. Starting from the view that the 'task on paper' is simply a starting-point, they propose that from a pedagogical perspective, it is more fruitful to conceptualise a task as a 'highly flexible and kneadable material that can take on different existential guises as it passes through the minds, mouths and hands of different persons making use of it' (Berben et al., 2007: 56). This perspective reminds us that like any tool, rather than deterministically shaping behaviour, a task offers the potential to be used in ways which users (i.e., teachers and learners) find interesting or valuable. In other words, the task-as-workplan cannot entirely determine the processes of use. What is interesting here from a design perspective is that drawing attention to the malleability of tasks does not imply that we abandon design on the grounds that it is futile, but rather that we embrace it as a continuing and dynamic process that begins, but does not end, with the task on paper.

8.12 Task Design as Process

As noted earlier, when people talk about design in TBLT, the conventional association has often been with the task on paper, whether as a specific task type ('Describe and Draw', 'Picture Differences'), or in terms of a design feature ('Jigsaw', 'Information Gap') or discourse genre ('Personal Task', 'Map Task'). Although this is a rational starting-point, it is far from the whole picture. A more comprehensive approach to task design would be one that characterises it as a cyclical process, comprising prospective, reactive and retrospective elements at different points in time, across which the initial workplan may be subject to change. How much it changes and in what ways, however, can only be gauged by observing what happens to the workplan as it unfolds in action, as suggested in Ellis (2009), Samuda (2015). To this end, Samuda (2015) proposes the term 'task-as-workplan**s**' as an alternative to 'task-as-workplan' on the grounds that it comes closer to capturing the dynamic, multidimensional nature of pedagogic task design that we have highlighted thus far, and helps us to move away from a fixation on the idea of tasks as static entities.

For Samuda, the task-as-workplans is made up of four successive phases: *the designer's original workplan* (the task on paper*), the teacher's prospective workplan* (what the teacher intends to do with the task, as reflected in their lesson planning), *the dynamic workplan* (reflecting changes that the teacher might make as the task unfolds in the classroom), and finally, *the retrospective workplan* (changes that are made after the task has been enacted). The term 'task-as-workplans' therefore offers a window on design at different points in time, as well as reflecting the overall life-cycle of a task from conception through its various incarnations.

Conceptualising task design as a series of workplans rather than a one-off event enables us to address the 'problem' of design raised earlier. First, it normalises the view that workplans change, and rather than treating this as the stumbling block evoked by critics of TBLT, it opens up the possibility of inspecting ways that tasks actually do change in use, while still keeping the broad content material and structure of the original design as a reference point. Samuda (2015) illustrates this with reference to a case study of different teachers handling the same task. Through a combination of pre-lesson interview and post-lesson stimulated recall data, the study charts intentional and unintentional changes that the teachers make to the original design, with varying degrees of success. For example one inadvertently 'de-tasks' the design (i.e., undermines key features of the design that qualify it as a task) by removing the outcome and closing down opportunities for engagement, while another intentionally 're-tasks' the design, first of all prospectively while planning the lesson by changing the focus of the topic to align with the cultural background of the students, and then dynamically in the classroom, in response to unexpected logistical problems, by changing the way in which the outcome would be reported and shared. Samuda describes how changes made by the teachers to one aspect of the task had cumulative impacts on other aspects of its design, some positive, some negative. For example, in one class, students interacted really quite substantially in carrying out the task, and generated outcomes which led into extended language use, and offered significant opportunities for the teacher to provide feedback on their use of language. In contrast, students in the other class performed the task quite superficially, and because there was no longer any 'outcome' from the task itself, the teacher simply moved on to another activity without providing the students with any reflection on their language or the way they had been working. In this latter case, de-tasking the original design effectively turned it into an exercise, whereas in the former, re-tasking the original design provided a basis for significant language work.

In reflecting on what enabled these different degrees of success, Samuda suggests that it may have been some element of task design 'awareness' that helped one teacher successfully re-task the original design by enabling him to keep track of the design implications of changes that he made to the original workplan, including those planned before using the task and those that he made on-line in the classroom. Since this implies that some degree of task design awareness on the part of a teacher could play a role in how tasks are enacted in the classroom (again echoing the way in which the teacher worked in harmony with the task in the earlier Samuda (2001) study), it once again brings us back to questions about how we interpret the boundaries between design and implementation in classroom practice. It also raises questions about the nature of task design awareness itself, what it comprises, and how it is acquired. In other words, an understanding of task design is likely to be not just for materials designers, but also for teachers. We come back to both sets of questions later in the chapter, but before then turn to an aspect of design that has received less attention in the TBLT literature: the types of knowledge, skills and processes that underpin the act of task design.

While a considerable amount of attention in TBLT has been paid to the *outcome* of design in terms of the task-as-workplan, much less has been paid to what goes into its creation. Thus, although we know quite a lot about the various design features that make up a task and the various impacts these might have on learners' language, we know comparatively little about what goes into creating and assembling those features. Bridging this gap could be important because, as we have seen, in TBLT there has been a significant move towards context-responsive, locally driven task design handled by practitioner designers on site (Long, 2015), and understanding more about the processes underlying the act of task design could be beneficial for practitioners new to task design. To this end Johnson's (2003) study of the working practices of experienced and less experienced task designers offers a window on what designers actually do as they develop tasks for classroom use.

8.13 The Working Practices of Pedagogic Task Designers

Johnson's study focused on two groups of designers 'thinking aloud' as they developed a task from a specific design brief: one group of 'specialist designers' with considerable professional experience as task designers, materials writers and teacher educators, and one group of 'non-specialist teacher designers' with at least five years' experience as classroom teachers, who, although familiar with the use of tasks, had limited experience with design itself. Johnson was interested in seeing whether there would be differences in the ways that the two groups of designers approached the 'task' of task design, and whether this would uncover underlying aspects of the design process normally hidden from view that could be useful in supporting the professional development of teachers new to design. This is of interest to TBLT because, as we have seen, an increasing amount of task design is in the hands of practitioners with similar professional profiles to those of the non-specialist teacher designers, and so exploring their practices in relation to those of experienced designers might yield insights that could usefully contribute to their development as designers and teachers.

Johnson found a number of differences between the ways the two groups of designers developed their tasks, which he summarised as a set of hypotheses about the 'good' designer (Johnson, 2003: chap. 7). Overall, he found task design to be a messy, recursive process involving the designers in numerous false starts and constant monitoring that required them to hold in mind a wide range of task variables relating to the evolving design. Strikingly, the specialist designers appeared to 'work' much harder at their tasks and to be less satisfied with the results, exploring a wide range of options before embarking on an overall design. These they developed gradually, constantly exploring alternatives as they went, willing to abandon those that did not appear to pan out, even at an advanced stage of development. In contrast, the non-specialist teachers were more inclined to settle quickly on an initial idea, often one that was already familiar to them, then to proceed in a more linear fashion, with less inclination to take alternatives into account, and paying less attention to the consequences of design decisions that could have an impact on the task as a whole. This appears to be in line with studies of expertise in other domains, where experts have been found to be more willing to push themselves in the pursuit of more complex solutions. While non-experts are more likely to approach problems as a matter of finding a match with existing knowledge and are more quickly satisfied with the first 'fit' made, whether fully appropriate or not, characterised as 'satisficing' (Simon, 1981). Thus, the first set of findings suggested a greater willingness to try out alternatives, and consider the impact of aspects of the design on the overall structure of the task.

Related to this, Johnson's study also noted the considerable amount of time that the specialist designers devoted to visualising and rehearsing how the task might unfold at various points in the classroom, and using this as a basis for troubleshooting design flaws. This suggests that for these designers the development of the task-as-workplan is intimately bound up with projections of the task-as-process, as if the designers were developing their tasks with one eye on the task on paper and one eye on the task in the classroom. This brings to mind the work of Donald Norman on the design of everyday objects. Norman (2013) argues that all too often designers of essential objects such as doors, coffee pots and light switches privilege aesthetic appeal over intended use, and citing numerous examples of beautiful coffee pots that don't pour properly, or doors that are visually impressive, but hard to actually open, makes the case for 'user-friendly' design that marries form and function by keeping the users' perspectives at its heart. A similar case may be made for tasks that look good on the surface, but do not really work in the classroom; likewise, tasks that perform well when designed for use in a research context are not necessarily suited to the needs of the classroom (Samuda, 2015). Thus, anticipating the users' perspective and how the task would likely unfold seemed typical of the specialist designers.

A follow-up study to Johnson (2003), reported in Samuda (2005), focused on the tasks produced by the two sets of designers to see if any of the differences in the design process found by Johnson were reflected in the tasks finally produced. This study found a number of surface-level differences (task topic and content), as well as differences in the internal architecture of the tasks (the underlying design 'skeleton'). At the surface level, the tasks designed by the specialist designers showed greater range and variety in terms of the topics and content areas they were based on. This might be expected, given the more extensive design repertoires the specialist designers were likely to have at their disposal, or else as a reflection of the tendency to satisfice on the part of the non-specialist teacher designers found in Johnson's (2003) study. In addition, in terms of the internal architecture of the tasks, while all the designers incorporated features associated with TBLT (information gaps, two-way information exchange, outcomes requiring consensus and so on), there were differences in the degree of detail with which these were realised, again not particularly surprising given differences in professional experience.

Of particular interest were a number of features found across the specialist-designed tasks that were not readily captured by the design parameters highlighted in the TBLT literature. Although these features were relatively trivial in themselves, when taken together, they had the cumulative effect of giving shape to the task, and creating a sense of flow and momentum across it. This was reflected in various ways, particularly in how the openings and closings of the tasks were delineated, and how paths between them were framed. Examples of task 'beginnings' include the use of a descriptive name or title for the task ('Casting a Play;' 'Ideal People'), and some form of whole task overview that encapsulated purpose, goals and outcomes (although not the language to be used), and which preceded the instructions/rubrics for carrying it out. Movement through the tasks was chunked by marking out distinct stages, with transitions between stages corresponding to anticipated shifts in attentional focus (moving from information gathering to information synthesis, for example) and/or shifts in activity (individual work feeding into pairwork, for example), with the 'outcome' of one stage creating 'input' for the next. Final closure was clearly marked by ending the task in plenary mode, regardless of outcome type (open or closed, convergent or divergent). Many (if not all) these features can be seen as reflecting the ways in which the designers were anticipating and helping structure the unfolding of the tasks in action.

Once again in contrast, these framing features were considerably less marked in the tasks designed by the non-specialist teachers, which tended to launch directly into action, without title or overview, with movement from one part of the task to the next not necessarily marked or reflecting relevant transition points. Most striking however was the lack of attention to closure. So, for example, in a task requiring consensus as part of its outcome, it was not made clear what should happen after consensus had been reached, or whether the task had actually ended.

It is possible, of course, that these differences in design reflect differences in professional orientation. As teachers, the non-specialist designers may have been more likely to associate such features with implementation, part of what teachers would do anyway and thus for them beyond the scope of design, bringing back into view the blurred boundaries between design and implementation. Nevertheless, one striking aspect of the specialist-designed tasks was their strong pedagogic orientation. For example, the features highlighted above are all widely associated with markers of 'good' classroom practice: the activation of schemata, the use of advance organisers, variation in pacing and interaction, the marking of closure, and as such familiar to teachers as things to consider when planning lessons. However, when transposed to the context of TBLT, these markers of good practice also have a part to play in giving shape and direction to tasks *qua* tasks. In particular by delineating shape and flow, features such as these appear to prefigure the task in action, possibly reflecting the extensive amount of rehearsal and visualisation that Johnson found their designers to engage in as they developed them, and to this extent, observable design correlates of underlying processes – the tip of the design iceberg, as it were. Given this, we could also consider them examples of Norman's 'user-friendly' design.

Research, then, shows how the work of skilled designers can complement the insights from earlier socio-cognitive research (Pica et al., Skehan, Robinson) by typically building many other features into the designs of tasks that reflect the stages learners are likely to go through in working towards the task outcomes. Yet in spite of the potential value of these aspects of design, there is an important caveat to note here: no matter how user-friendly the underlying intention or how pedagogic in orientation, design features such as these are still part of the task on paper, which means they will be open to reinterpretation and adjustment as the task passes through the hands of its eventual users. That is, however carefully designed a task might be, it can still be 'de-tasked' or, indeed, advantageously 're-tasked'. However, in terms of the workplan itself, pedagogically oriented design features such as these could be seen as contributing an additional layer of design – the pedagogic framing of the task, as it were – to complement the psycholinguistic orientation of the design features normally highlighted in the TBLT literature. It would therefore be interesting to explore the interplay between design features that anticipate various types of internal processing (such as those proposed in the Pica et al., Skehan and Robinson models) and those that anticipate various types of classroom processes. In an ideal design world, these would form two mutually supportive strands: one based on design principles accruing from studies of task performance and the other on design principles accruing from studies of classroom pedagogy, not in terms of 'either/or' but in terms of 'both – and'. The development of a design relationship such as this, however, would require a more extensive database of classroom-based studies of teachers working with tasks than we currently have at our disposal, although work reported in Vandommele et al. (2018), Hartmann and Shocker (2018), Shintani (2016, 2018), and Lynch (2018) offers promising ways forward.

8.14 How Do Designers Become Designers?

As noted above, tasks are subject to reinterpretation and adjustment once in the hands of the users, and this then leads to a consideration of the role of the teacher in task design. Until recently pedagogic task design was considered something teachers would normally pick up on the side, rather than a specialist area in its own right, or indeed part of the teacher's job description. However, the advent of TBLT has refocused how we think about design, and with responsibility for the good functioning of tasks and their developing design increasingly seen as being in the hands of local teachers rather than distant experts, the question as to how designers become designers is highly relevant.

As part of their professional development, teachers are now often introduced to task design as a bridge between TBLT theory and TBLT practice. This is likely to include a grounding in the theoretical principles underpinning TBLT, exposure to empirical studies that have contributed to those principles, ways that findings from those studies might be applied to principled design, and a range of exemplar tasks. Alongside this, there are opportunities to design tasks to try out in the classroom, and to subject these to critique, evaluation and review, as documented in Calvert & Sheen (2014), Ellis (2015), East (2012, 2018), Erlam (2016), Ogilvie and Dunn (2010), among others. All this suggests that task design in some form or other has now secured a niche as a component in professional training and development, and this is highly encouraging. However it is not clear how far in itself this would provide a sufficient basis for those practitioners increasingly responsible for dealing with complex design demands that that can require them to go well beyond their comfort zone of just tweaking or adapting existing tasks and instead coping with the challenge of developing new tasks from scratch. In this regard, attention to some of the dimensions of task design touched on earlier in this chapter could help round out their development not only as TBLT teachers, but also as designers. Johnson's work on the process of design, although often overlooked in professional development, could be particularly relevant, as it suggests that, as well as acquiring knowledge about design, a key element in becoming a designer involves fostering the development of design as a skill.

The matter of 'growing' design skills for TBLT is not straightforward however. For one thing, it is likely to require significantly more time than most professional development programmes can currently afford. One finding consistent across studies of expertise and skill theory in a range of domains is the considerable amount of time it takes expertise to develop and grow (Ericsson & Smith, 1991). Thus, it would be naïve, if not misguided, to expect teachers to emerge as fully-fledged designers on the basis of brief encounters with design principles and some opportunities to apply them – not easy for contexts where TBLT has been launched as a major educational initiative and where large-scale task development is urgently required. An interim way forward however could be to foster 'designer-like' behaviour, recalling Bruner's observation that 'the schoolboy learning physics *is* a physicist, and it is easier for him to learn physics behaving like a physicist than doing something else' (Bruner, 1960/1977: 14). This implies that developing as a task designer may involve not only learning about design, but also learning how to think and act like a designer, and so raising awareness of what designers do as they create tasks could be one way of approaching this. For example, Johnson observed the experienced designers in his study juggling an extensive array of design variables, exploring alternatives, envisaging outcomes, rehearsing options, troubleshooting design flaws, drawing on an extensive repertoire of tasks and task types and exercising a considerable amount of pedagogical imagination. The key question here, then, is how to foster this type of designer-like behaviour, and through this, to activate and refine practitioners' design 'antennae'?

A possible starting-point is sustained task critique. The aim here would be to provide multiple opportunities for practitioners to engage with a broad range of tasks, not just exemplar tasks that embody key design principles, but also ones that are deeply flawed, not just the mono-episodic tasks widely used by researchers but also the multi-episodic 'extendable' tasks widely preferred by teachers (Ribé & Vidal, 1993, Skehan, 1998), and going beyond the design of individual tasks to explore how tasks might relate to each other across extended sequences. This would entail not only focusing on ways that the design creates access to meaningful input, conditions for meaningful output, provides for appropriate feedback and opportunities for focusing on form, and so on, but it would also help to encourage 'designer-like' behaviour by visualising different ways those design considerations might play out in the classroom, as we saw the designers in Johnson's study doing. From those designers we might also draw some useful critiquing rules of thumb, for example, attending to the ways tasks open, and especially to how they close (Andon (2018) for example found teachers consistently neglecting the way tasks end), tracking the ways that trajectories between openings and closings are managed and exploring the ways the task sets up a purpose for engaging with it. Actively critiquing an extensive array of tasks in this way can provide a solid foundation for design skills to develop from. We would not expect novice architects to start designing houses without first having the opportunity to explore a wide range of possibilities. Similarly, we should not expect teachers to plunge into designing tasks without prior exposure to a wide range of options. This, of course, implies open access to banks of pedagogic (not research) tasks, but promising ways forward can be found in the resources developed by Gurzynski-Weiss and colleagues at Indiana University in the United States, and posted on their TBLT Support Site (TBLT@IU). Other resources include those developed collaboratively by Müller-Hartmann and Schocker with teachers in Germany, those developed by Van den Branden and colleagues in Flanders, as well as projects posted on the IATBLT website (www.iatblt.org).

By offering practitioners a means for developing and refining their design 'antennae', sustained critique can be seen as creating the bedrock from which design skills develop, and in the process, teaching skills, too. Once this foundation has been laid, practitioners would be invited to engage with a range of design problems at increasing levels of complexity in which they would re-design existing tasks and create tasks of their own. In this, they would be encouraged to continue to think like designers by working with one eye on the developing workplan and the other on how it might unfold in the classroom. It is to be hoped that nurturing designer-like behaviour would not only play a role in supporting the ways practitioners evaluate the strengths and weaknesses of the tasks they create themselves and those they are expected to use, but that it might also feed into the development of the kind of design awareness we noted earlier in the chapter as a factor enabling teachers to successfully re-task the workplan prospectively at the planning stage, dynamically in the classroom itself and retrospectively after the event. At the present time however, this remains a research agenda waiting to be implemented.

8.15 Conclusion

At the beginning of this chapter we suggested that there is more to task design than initially meets the eye, and that the 'product' of design, what we see on paper, is merely the tip of the iceberg – hence a well-rounded understanding of what is involved in task design entails probing what lies hidden from view. We also suggested that as a bridge between TBLT theory and TBLT practice, task design involves both an element of specialist knowledge, and an element of specialist skill. Factors contributing to task design as specialist knowledge include insights from the empirical study of task performance, such as those that have informed the development of design frameworks grounded in second language acquisition. Other key factors contributing to specialist design knowledge include pedagogical understandings, drawn from empirical research into the process of task design, and insights from studies of education more broadly (Bygate et al., this volume). We have suggested that accumulated insights from a range of empirically grounded sources can form a multi-layered approach to task design, with the pedagogic supporting the socio-cognitive, and vice versa. Factors contributing to task design as a specialist skill entail reciprocal harnessing of elements of specialist knowledge by teachers, teacher educators and researchers. All this needs to be taken into account in the preparation that practitioners receive.

We have also highlighted ways that the boundaries between what constitutes 'design' and what constitutes 'implementation' are complex, and that no matter how carefully designed the task on paper may be, it is still liable to change and reinterpretation, and that how it changes and how it is reinterpreted will be shaped by the perceptions of its users. We suggest that in comparison with non-specialist designs, skilled task design is more likely to anticipate and facilitate how users will engage with a task.

By proposing a view of design that is not simply a one-off event, but a dynamic collaborative process that continues over time, we hope to have captured something of its complexity. We also hope to have provided some ways of addressing this complexity by finding ways of reconciling issues arising from the 'creative' freedom teachers and learners need if they are to bring tasks to life, with the need for systematic management of pedagogic processes. Perhaps this might enable pedagogic planning that is 'flexible enough to permit free play for individuality of experience and yet firm enough to give direction toward continuous development of power' (Dewey, 1938: 58).

Further Reading

Erlam, R. (2016). I'm still not sure what a task is: Teachers designing language tasks. *Language Teaching Research*, 20(3), 279–99.

González-Lloret, M. and Nielson, K. B. (2015). Evaluating TBLT: The case of a task-based Spanish program. *Language Teaching Research*, 19, 525–49.

Johnson, K. (2003). *Designing language teaching tasks*. Basingstoke: Palgrave Macmillan, Chapter 7.

Nguyen, B. T., Newton, J., and Crabbe, D. (2018). Teacher transformation of textbook tasks in Vietnamese EFL high school classrooms. In V. Samuda, K. Van den Branden and M. Bygate, eds. *TBLT as a researched pedagogy*. Amsterdam/Philadelphia: John Benjamins, pp. 51–70.

Samuda. V. (2015). Tasks, design, and the architecture of pedagogical spaces. In M. Bygate, ed. *Domains and directions in the development of TBLT: A decade of plenaries from the international conference.* Amsterdam/ Philadelphia: John Benjamins, pp. 271–302.

Study Questions

1. For pedagogic task design, what in your view is the importance of the types of design feature identified in the three frameworks reported in this chapter, and why?
2. In what ways can the workplan change? How far do you see this as a problem for TBLT?
3. In your view, how could 'thinking like a designer' help teachers in making their own design decisions?
4. How far should designers accommodate the perspectives of users, and what are the implications?

Acknowledgments

Our gratitude to Mike Long for his constructive comments on this chapter, and for his tireless commitment to TBLT.

References

Andon, N. (2018). Optimal conditions for TBLT? A case study of teachers' orientations to TBLT in the commercial EFL for adults sector in the UK. In V. Samuda, K. Van den Branden and M. Bygate, eds. *In TBLT as a researched pedagogy.* Amsterdam/ Philadelphia: John Benjamins, pp. 131–64.

Berben, M., Van den Branden, K., and Van Gorp, K. (2007). 'We'll see what happens': Tasks on paper and tasks in a multilingual classroom. In K. Van den Branden and M. Verhelst, eds. *Tasks in action: task-based language education from a classroom-based perspective.* Cambridge: Cambridge Scholars Publishing, pp. 32–67.

Breen, M. (1987). Learner contributions to task design. In C. Candlin and D. Murphy, eds. *Language learning tasks.* London: Prentice Hall, pp. 23–46.

Bruner, J. (1960/1977). *The process of education.* Cambridge, MA: Harvard University Press.

Bygate, M. (1999). Quality of language and purpose of task: Patterns of learners' language on two oral communication tasks. *Language Teaching Research* 3(3) 185–214

Calvert, M. and Sheen, Y. (2014). Task-based language learning and teaching: An action-research study. *Language Teaching Research*, 19(2), 226–44.

Coughlan, P. and Duff, P. (1994). Same task, different activities: analysis of SLA from an activity theory perspective. In J. Lantolf and G. Appel, eds. *Vygotskian approaches to second language research*. Oxford: Oxford University Press, pp. 173–94.

Dewey, J. (1938). *Experience and education: The Kappa Delta Phi lecture series*. Reprinted 1963. Toronto: Collier Books.

Donato, R. (2000). Sociocultural contributions to understanding the foreign and second language classroom. In J. P. Lantolf, ed. *Sociocultural theory and second language learning*. Oxford: Oxford University Press, pp. 27–50.

Doughty, C. and Pica, T. (1986). Information gap tasks: Do they facilitate second language acquisition? *TESOL Quarterly* 10(2), 305–25

Doughty, C. and Williams, J. (1998). *Focus on form in classroom second language acquisition*. Cambridge: Cambridge University Press.

East, M. (2012). *Task-based language teaching from the teachers' perspective*. Amsterdam/Philadelphia: John Benjamins.

East, M. (2018). How do beginning teachers conceptualise and enact tasks in school foreign language classrooms? In V. Samuda, K. Van den Branden, and M. Bygate, eds. *TBLT as a researched pedagogy*. Amsterdam/Philadelphia: John Benjamins, pp. 23–50.

Ellis, R. (2003). *Task-based language learning and teaching*. Oxford: Oxford University Press.

Ellis, R. (2009). Task-based language teaching: Sorting out the misunderstandings. *International Journal of Applied Linguistics*, 19(3), 221–46.

Ellis, R. (2015). Teachers evaluating tasks. In M. Bygate, ed. *Domains and directions in the development of TBLT: A decade of plenaries from the international conference*. Amsterdam/ Philadelphia: John Benjamins, pp. 247–70.

Ellis, R. (2017). Position paper: Moving task-based language teaching forward. *Language Teaching*, 50(4), 507–26.

Ellis, R. and He, X. (1999). The roles of modified input and output in the incidental acquisition of word meanings. *Studies in Second Language Acquisition*, 21(2), 285–301.

Ellis, R. and Shintani, N. (2013). *Exploring language pedagogy through second language acquisition research*. London: Routledge.

Erlam, R. (2016). I'm still not sure what a task is: Teachers designing language tasks. *Language Teaching Research*, 20(3), 279–99.

Ericsson, K. A. and Smith, J. (1991), eds. *Toward a general theory of expertise: Prospects and limits*. New York: Cambridge University Press.

Foster, P. and Skehan, P. (1996). The influence of planning and task type on second language performance. *Studies in second language acquisition*, 18(3), 299–323

Foster, P. and Skehan, P. (1999). The influence of source of planning and focus of planning on task-based performance. *Language Teaching Research,*, 3(3), 215–47

Gass, S.M. (1997). *Input, interaction and the development of second languages*. Mahwah, NJ: Erlbaum

Gass, S. M. and Madden, C. (1985), eds. *Input and second language acquisition.* Rowley, MA: Newbury House

González-Lloret, M. and Nielson, K. B. (2015). Evaluating TBLT: The case of a task-based Spanish program. *Language Teaching Research*, 19(5), 525–49.

Gurzynski-Weiss, L. (n.d.). The TBLT Language Learning Task Bank. https://tblt.indiana.edu.

Hillman, K. K. and Long, M. H. (2020). A task-based needs analysis for U.S. Foreign Service Officers, and the challenge of the Japanese celebration speech. In C. Lambert and R. Oliver, eds. *Using tasks in diverse contexts.* Bristol: Multilingual Matters, pp. 123–45.

Johnson, K. (2003). *Designing language teaching tasks.* Basingstoke: Palgrave Macmillan

Lambert, C. (2010). A task-based needs analysis: Putting principles into practice. *Language Teaching Research*, 14(1) 99–112.

Lantolf, J. P. (2000). Introducing sociocultural theory. In J. P. Lantolf, ed. *Sociocultural theory and second language learning.* Oxford: Oxford University Press, pp. 1–26.

Lantolf, J. P. and Thorne, S. (2006). *Sociocultural theory and the genesis of second language development.* Oxford: Oxford University Press.

Long, M. H. (1981). Input, interaction and second language acquisition. *Annals of the New York Academy of Sciences*, 379, 259–78.

Long, M. H. (1985). A role for instruction in second language acquisition: Task-based language training. In K. Hyltenstam and M. Pienemann, eds. *Modelling and assessing second language acquisition.* Bristol: Multilingual Matters, pp. 77–99

Long, M. H. (1991). Focus on form: A design feature in language teaching methodology. In K. de Bot, R. B. Ginsberg, and C. Kramsch, eds. *Foreign language research in cross-cultural perspective.* Amsterdam/ Philadelphia: John Benjamins, pp. 39–52.

Long, M. H. (2015). *Second language acquisition and task-based language teaching.* Oxford: Wiley-Blackwell.

Loschky, L. and Bley-Vroman, R. (1993). Grammar and task-based methodology. In G. Crookes and S. M. Gass, eds. *Tasks in language learning.* Bristol: Multilingual Matters, pp. 123–67.

Lynch, T. (2018). Perform, reflect, recycle: Enhancing task repetition in second language speaking tasks. In M. Bygate, ed. *Learning language through repetition,* Amsterdam/Philadelphia: John Benjamins, pp. 193–222.

Mackey, A. (1994). *Communicative tasks: Handbook and tasks.* Sydney: University of Sydney Language Acquisition Research Centre.

Mackey, A. (1999). Input, interaction and second language development: an empirical study of question formation in ESL. *Studies in Second Language Acquisition*. 21(4), 557–87.

Mackey, A. (2007), ed. *Conversational interaction in second language acquisition.* Oxford: Oxford University Press

Mackey, A. (2012). *Input, interaction and corrective feedback in L2 learning.* Oxford: Oxford University Press.

Mackey, A. and Philp, J. (1998). Conversational interaction and second language development: recasts, responses and red herrings. *Modern Language Journal.* 82(3): 338–56.

McDonough, K. and Mackey, A. (2000). Communicative tasks, conversational interaction and linguistic form: an empirical study of Thai. *Foreign Language Annals* 33: 82–92

Müller-Hartmann, A. and Schocker, M. (2011). *Teaching English: Task-supported language learning.* Paderborn, Germany: Verlag Ferdinand Schöningh.

Müller-Hartmann, A. and Schocker, M. (2018). The challenge of integrating focus on form in tasks: Findings from a classroom research project in secondary EFL classrooms. In V. Samuda, K. Van den Branden, and M. Bygate, eds. *TBLT as a researched pedagogy.* Amsterdam/Philadelphia: John Benjamins, pp. 97–130.

Newton, J. and Kennedy, G. (1996). Effects of communication tasks on the grammatical relations marked by second language learners. *System*, 24 (3), 309–22.

Nguyen, B.T., Newton, J., and Crabbe, D. (2018). Teacher transformation of textbook tasks in Vietnamese EFL high school classrooms. In V. Samuda, K. Van den Branden, and M. Bygate, eds. *TBLT as a researched pedagogy.* Amsterdam/Philadelphia: John Benjamins, pp. 51–70.

Nobuyoshi, J. and Ellis, R. (1993). Focussed communication tasks. *ELT Journal.* 47(3) 203–10.

Norman, D. A. (2013). *The design of everyday things: Revised and expanded edition.* New York: Basic Books.

Norris, J. M. (2015). Thinking and acting programmatically in task-based language teaching: Essential roles for program evaluation. In M. Bygate, ed. *Domains and directions in the development of TBLT: A decade of plenaries from the international conference.* Amsterdam/Philadelphia: John Benjamins, pp. 27–58.

Ogilvie, G. and Dunn, W. (2010). Taking teacher education to task: Exploring the role of teacher education in promoting the utilization of task-based language teaching. *Language Teaching Research*, 14(2), 161–81.

Pica, T. (1987). Second language acquisition, social interaction and the classroom. *Applied Linguistics*, 8, 3–21.

Pica, T. (1994). Research on negotiation: What does it reveal about second language learning conditions, processes and outcomes? *Language Learning*, 44(4), 493–527.

Pica, T. and Doughty, C. J. (1985). Input and interaction in communicative language classrooms: A comparison of teacher-fronted and group activities. In S. M. Gass and C. Madden, eds. *Input and second language acquisition.* Rowley, MA: Newbury House, pp. 115–32.

Pica, T., Kanagy, R., and Falodun, J. (1993). Choosing and using communication tasks for second language instruction. In G. Crookes and S. Gass, eds. *Tasks and language learning: integrating theory and practice*. Bristol: Multilingual Matters, pp. 9–34.

Ribé, R. and Vidal, N. (1993). *Project work step by step*. Oxford: Macmillan Heineman.

Robinson, P. (2003). The Cognition Hypothesis, task design, and adult task-based language learning. *Second Language Studies*, 21(2), 45–105.

Robinson, P. (2007). Criteria for classifying and sequencing pedagogic tasks. In M. P. Garcia Mayo, ed. *Investigating tasks in formal language learning*. Bristol: Multilingual Matters, pp. 7–26.

Robinson, P. (2015). The Cognition Hypothesis, second language task demands and the SSARC model of pedagogic task sequencing. In M. Bygate, ed. *Domains and directions in the development of TBLT: A decade of plenaries from the international conference*. Amsterdam/Philadelphia: John Benjamins, 87–122.

Samuda, V. (2001). Guiding relationships between form and meaning during task performance: The role of the teacher. In M. Bygate, P. Skehan, and M. Swain., eds. *Researching pedagogic tasks: Second language learning, teaching and testing*. Harlow: Pearson Education, pp. 119–40.

Samuda, V. (2005). Expertise in second language pedagogic task design. In K. Johnson, ed. *Expertise in language teaching*. Basingstoke: Palgrave Macmillan, pp. 230–54.

Samuda. V. (2015). Tasks, design, and the architecture of pedagogical spaces. In M. Bygate, ed. *Domains and directions in the development of TBLT: A decade of plenaries from the international conference*. Amsterdam/Philadelphia: John Benjamins, pp. 271–302.

Samuda, V. and Bygate, M. (2008). *Tasks in second language learning*. Basingstoke: Palgrave Macmillan.

Seedhouse, P. (2005). Task as research construct. *Language Learning*, 55 (3),533–70.

Shintani, N. (2016). *Input-based tasks in foreign language instruction for young learners*. Amsterdam/Philadelphia: John Benjamins.

Shintani, N. (2018). Researching TBLT for young beginner learners in Japan. In V. Samuda, K. Van den Branden, and M. Bygate, eds. *In TBLT as a researched pedagogy*. Amsterdam/ Philadelphia: John Benjamins, pp. 199–212.

Simon, H. A. (1981). *The sciences of the artificial*. Cambridge, MA: MIT Press

Skehan, P. (1996). A framework for the implementation of task-based instruction. *Applied Linguistics*, 17(1), 36–82.

Skehan, P. (1998). *A cognitive approach to language learning*. Oxford: Oxford University Press.

Skehan, P. (2001). Tasks and language performance assessment. In M. Bygate, P. Skehan, and M. Swain, eds. *Researching pedagogic tasks: Second language learning, teaching and testing.* Harlow: Pearson Education, pp. 167–85.

Skehan, P. (2003). Task-based instruction. *Language Teaching* 36, 1–14

Skehan, P. (2015). Limited attention capacity and cognition: Two hypotheses regarding second language performance on tasks. In M. Bygate, ed. *Domains and directions in the development of TBLT: A decade of plenaries from the international conference.* Amsterdam/Philadelphia: John Benjamins, pp. 123–56.

Skehan, P. and Foster, P. (1997). Task type and task processing conditions as influences on foreign language performance. *Language teaching research*, 1(3),185–211

Skehan, P. and Foster, P. (1999). The influence of task structure and processing conditions on narrative retellings. *Language Learning*, 49(1), 93–120

Skehan, P. and Foster, P. (2005). Strategic and on-line planning: the influence of surprise information and task time on second language performance. In R. Ellis, ed. *Planning and task performance in a second language.* Amsterdam/Philadelphia: John Benjamins, pp. 193–216.

Slimani-Rolls, A. (2005). Practitioner research: Rethinking task-based language learning: what we can learn from the learners. *Language Teaching Research* 9(2), 195–218

Swain, M. (1985). Communicative competence: Some roles of comprehensible input and comprehensible output in its development. In S. Gass and C. Madden, eds. *Input and second language acquisition.* Rowley, MA: Newbury House, pp. 235–53.

Swain, M. (1995). Three functions of output in second language learning. In G. Cook and B. Seidlhofer, eds. *Principles and practice in applied linguistics.* Cambridge: Cambridge University Press, pp. 125–44.

Takashima, H. and Ellis, R. (1999). Output enhancement and the acquisition of the past tense. In R. Ellis *Learning a second language through interaction.* Amsterdam/Philadelphia: John Benjamins, pp. 173–88.

Van den Branden, K. (2006), ed. *Task-based language teaching: From theory to practice.* Cambridge: Cambridge University Press.

Van den Branden, K. (2015). Task-based language education: From theory to practice ... and back again. In M. Bygate, ed. *Domains and directions in the development of TBLT: A decade of plenaries from the international conference.* Amsterdam/Philadelphia: John Benjamins, pp. 303–20.

Vandommele,G., Van den Branden, K., and Van Gorp, K. (2018). Task-based language teaching: How task-based is it really? In V. Samuda, K. Van den Branden, and M. Bygate, eds. *TBLT as a researched pedagogy.* Amsterdam/Philadelphia: John Benjamins, pp. 165–98.

8A

Designing Pedagogic Tasks for Refugees Learning English to Enter Universities in the Netherlands

Seyit Ömer Gök and Marije Michel

8A.1 Introduction

Global political, economic and environmental crises have caused people to flee their home countries in search of a safe land where they can live, work and raise their children. Consequently, many countries across the world have granted protection for refugees, often on the condition that they will return home at some point. This has, however, resulted in the growth of 'involuntary' (Long, 2015: 3) language learners at all ages. It is widely acknowledged, however, that 'the knowledge of the 'host' language is seen as a barometer of migrants' integration in a particular society' (Ros i Sole, 2014: 57). As Long (2005: 1) puts it: 'successful language learning is vital for refugees' and acquiring the national language has become one of the most fundamental elements of the European Union's integration policy (Ros i Sole, 2014).

In some cases, however, prioritising high levels of English over the national language could be more beneficial, especially for educated refugees. Improving their English might not only be more achievable and shorten the duration of their integration process, but also potentially enables them to start participating in the host society, as English gives them access to higher education, as well as the job market. For instance, in the Netherlands – the context of the current case study – virtually all university programmes require high levels of English (at least B2 according

---

We thank all learners and teachers of the English Academy for Newcomers for their participation and cooperation. In particular, we would like to name Kinan Alajak for his support and dedication to this project. Our thanks also go to Tu ba Gök for her creative and critical contributions to task design.

to the Common European Framework of Reference for Languages, CEFR) and several BA and most MA programmes are taught entirely in English (VSNU, 2012). Consequently, educated refugees with some level of English-language knowledge could be substantially supported by English for academic purposes (EAP) courses, so that they can be admitted to higher education programmes. Yet, refugees' pre- and post-migration factors are known to distinguish them significantly from other groups of learners (e.g., Ćatibušić, Gallagher & Karazi, 2019; Toker & Sağdıç, this volume), such that existing EAP programmes geared towards 'regular' international students often fail to address the needs of refugee students. This case study illustrates a task-based EAP programme that was designed for, and implemented at, an NGO of volunteers teaching English to refugees in the Netherlands.

8A.2 Context

The context of this case study is an NGO offering English-language courses for refugees who wish to pursue their studies in Dutch higher education or take the next step in their professional career. The English-language learning programme, which runs on a trimester basis, follows a modular system based on the CEFR and currently offers three entry levels: A2, B1 and B2. In each three-month trimester period, students are expected to attend forty-eight hours of face-to-face classes (four hours per week) and complete up to one hundred hours of self-study, including the weekly assignments. The ultimate goal of the programme is to help students attain the required score in the IELTS exam that gives them access to higher education; for example, 6.0 overall for most BA programmes. The curriculum has predominantly been designed to achieve this objective, and both in-class and self-study materials have been selected and developed accordingly. The syllabus follows a mainly synthetic focus on forms approach as it draws on the coursebooks selected for each level.

Recently, Middleton (2019) performed a small-scale needs analysis (NA) within the same organisation as part of his MA thesis supervised by the second author of this chapter. The NA identified a variety of additional needs for this specific group of refugee learners. In this chapter, we will present a series of one-hour lessons following a task-based approach (Bygate, Samuda & Van den Branden, this volume; Skehan, this volume) that complement each module in the existing curriculum addressing the identified needs. It should be noted, however, that the topics and language focus of the task-based strand follow the central syllabus described above. As such, students work with a 'hybrid syllabus' in which two different types are employed simultaneously (Long, 2015). To provide further context for this case study, the following section summarises Middleton's (2019) NA.

8A.3 Needs Analysis

Teaching English for No Obvious Reason (TENOR) is not very effective, as it often results in irrelevant content, low learner motivation and little awareness of what has been acquired or the inability to use the language in a functional and purposeful way (Lambert, 2010). A systematic NA should therefore be the departure point for any curriculum development, course design and/or materials development project to be effective and accountable (Jordan, 1997; Long, 2005). Nevertheless, few studies report on the NA conducted with educated refugee language learners, even though those learners are quite a distinctive group in several ways (Toker & Sağdıç, this volume). Different pre- and post-migration factors are likely to influence the language acquisition process of refugees. Pre-migration factors, such as level and progress of formal education and health and mental state, including trauma, can impact refugees' learning trajectories in the host country (Chiswick & Miller, 2001). Typically, newcomers with a higher educational background tend to have more developed learning strategies and metalinguistic skills, as well as higher motivation than regular learners (Middleton, 2019; VluchtelingenWerk, 2018). As post-migration factors, Van Tubergen (2010) identifies the level of personal investment (e.g., a refugee's commitment to stay in the host country) and the resources available to the learner. That is, if relevant resources are available, this potentially increases a refugee's desire to invest in language training to find better job opportunities.

For his NA, Middleton (2019) administered a survey and semi-structured interviews with both learners (n = 16) and teachers (n = 4) of the NGO the current case study describes. Findings revealed that the most important perceived needs were to improve: (1) English test score results (IELTS); (2) work/study vocabulary; (3) writing; and (4) listening. The specific areas in which learners identified their needs were:

1. Speaking: Taking part in classroom activities and meetings
2. Listening: Conversations with teachers/instructors or colleagues
3. Listening: Understanding teacher instructions in class
4. Writing academic texts: reports/reviews/articles
5. Writing: Formal letters/emails.

Notably, many student respondents criticised the coursebooks, as they found the topics irrelevant, boring and lacking real-life application. To quote one of the students: 'Why should I learn about Scotland? Give me something that I can use in my life.' (Middleton, 2019: 22). Also the (volunteer) teachers asked for adjustments to the material and curriculum. Specifically, they experienced a lack of structure in the programme as a whole and longed for clear objectives for individual courses, including the timeframe allowed to cover the content of the coursebooks.

All these comments suggested a compelling need for a customised curriculum, as well as the development of a series of pedagogic and real-life tasks based on the needs of the learners in this context. In general, the data support recent calls for local (instead of global) materials because these potentially meet the needs, interests and wants of specific audiences (Gök, 2019; Harwood, 2010; Tomlinson & Masuhara, 2017). For commercial purposes, publishers tend to address as wide an audience as possible, which means that 'it is rare to find a perfect fit between learner needs and course requirements, on the one hand, and what the coursebook contains, on the other hand' (Cunningsworth, 1995: 136).

For the case study at hand, the task types, topics, and sequencing were primarily determined according to Middleton's (2019) findings. The authors' experiences in (Dutch) higher education and the situations in which learners were most likely to use English in the future were also taken into account. The following sections provide details about the process of task development and implementation.

8A.4 Task Design and Methodology

From the various definitions of 'task' available in the literature (cf. Sasayama, this volume) we use the one by Bygate, Skehan and Swain (2001: 11): 'A task is an activity which requires learners to use language, with emphasis on meaning, to attain an objective.' While creating our task-based syllabus, we followed Ellis (2009) when deciding on task design and methodology. That is, we discussed until agreement was reached about the content (i.e., the 'what'), as well as the structure, of a lesson and procedures (i.e., the 'how') of teaching.

As an illustration, Table 8A.1 shows two task cycles, each of which consists of three pedagogic tasks followed by a final real-life task, which were created for the A2, B1 and B2 modules, respectively. The pedagogic tasks build on the target tasks identified by the NA and are graded according to their intrinsic complexity, as well as their themes. Each of the cycles was then planned to cover four weeks – one task per week.

The aim of the pedagogic tasks is to gradually lay the groundwork for the real-life target task at the end of a cycle. For this purpose, target tasks were first broken down into thematically linked sub-tasks before we sequenced those pedagogic tasks. The 'rational sequencing of pedagogic tasks' (Long, 2015: 227), followed criteria of frequency, criticality, learnability, complexity and difficulty. Scholars agree that task sequencing remains problematic, given that intuitions about task complexity and difficulty differ from person to person (Widdowson, 1990). The field has called for more objective measures (Révész, 2014), yet, recent empirical work suggests that subjective ratings of perceived task complexity are a suitable way to establish relative difficulty (Révész, Michel & Gilabert, 2016). Therefore,

Table 8A.1 Task design

CEFR	Cycle 1				Cycle 2			
	Week 1	Week 2	Week 3	Week 4	Week 1	Week 2	Week 3	Week 4
	Pedagogic Task 1	Pedagogic Task 2	Pedagogic Task 3	Real-life/target Task	Pedagogic Task 1	Pedagogic Task 2	Pedagogic Task 3	Real-life/target Task
A2	Why do you want/need to learn English?	How to become a good language learner	Setting short-term and long-term goals	Setting realistic future goals	Finding the university library and other facilities on the campus map	Comparing university libraries	Inside a university library	Booking a study room in the university library
B1	Making excuses and giving reasons	Asking for a deadline extension orally	Asking for a deadline extension via email	Filling out a deadline extension form	Important changes in life	What is 'culture' made up of?	Change and culture shock	Integration into a new culture
B2	Understanding the levels of CEFR and how they work	Exploring the modes of instruction delivery in Dutch higher education	Choosing courses from the university programme for refugee students	Writing a motivation letter to attend a course of the university refugee programme	Understanding 'volunteering'?	Applying for a job (the steps)	Writing a cover letter for a job position	Applying for a job and preparing for a job interview

Figure 8A.1 Task topics and sequence

we trusted our informed, but subjective, assessment when sequencing the tasks. Accordingly, we sequenced themes, from general to specific and from known to unknown, and we ensured that each pedagogic task within a cycle added cognitive load and/or performative stress (e.g., time pressure) to the former activities to progressively reach target task performance (Baralt, Gilabert & Robinson, 2014; Gilabert & Malicka, this volume; Long, 2015).

Figure 8A.1 illustrates one of the task cycles with thematically linked pedagogic tasks developed for the B1 module that focuses on 'integration'.

8A.5 Example Task Cycle

Each pedagogic and real-life task was divided into a pre-task, (main) task and post-task stage (Ellis, 2009; Willis & Willis, 2001), which in turn consisted of several activities. Typically, during the pre-task stage, the topic of the lesson was introduced to activate learners' schemata and their prior knowledge and experience. Often, this stage consisted of relevant YouTube videos to attract learners' attention, make the content more appealing, and expose them to authentic language (vocabulary, phrases and grammatical structures), in order to increase learners' readiness for the main task. Following the fundamental principles of task-based language teaching (Willis & Willis, 2001), at all times students were given the flexibility to use any linguistic feature they might want during task completion. Figure 8A.2 illustrates the activities of the pre-task stage for a real-life task at B2 level.

The specific refugee programme gives newcomers with an academic background and appropriate levels of English the opportunity to attend undergraduate or postgraduate courses without having to pay any fees. The main aim of the programme is to help newcomers continue their education and integrate into society rather than waiting 'on hold' at

> 1. Ask students whether they are aware of the specific refugee programme at their university.
> 2. Tell students that you are going to play a video introducing this programme www.youtube.com/watch?v=tkGXyqoZUQY.
> 3. Ask them to find answers for the questions below and discuss the answers in pairs after watching the video:
>   a. What is the rationale for the programme?
>   b. How was the idea first conceived?
>   c. What are the steps in the intake procedure?
> 4. Ask students whether they would like to join the programme. Why/Why not?

Figure 8A.2 Pre-task activities for real-life task (B2)

refugee centres or in their new homes. The students in this study were all potential applicants for those courses. Therefore, we included this as a central topic of one of the task-based lessons.

Following the pre-task stage, students were engaged in a series of tasks that needed to be completed either individually, in pairs or small groups during the main-task stage. The focus was on task completion and outcome rather than linguistic accuracy; however, teachers were encouraged to monitor and scaffold learners' performance whenever linguistic needs emerged, using the principle of 'leading from behind' (Gibbons, 1998), that is, providing support to students, as they are engaged in tasks, without interrupting task performance. Figure 8A.3, an example of the main-task stage, lets students rehearse the actual application procedures for the refugee programme using authentic materials.

Main tasks are designed to be integrative, that is, they are both 'input-providing' and 'output prompting' (Ellis, 2009: 224), as they involve two or more of the receptive (reading and listening) and productive (speaking and writing) skills. We aimed for input material to be authentic, for example, directly taken from relevant websites and used without any adaptation. We incorporated the input material into activities in such a way that learners would perceive them as meaningful because they were essential for successful task completion (Long, 2015).

During the post-task stage (see Figure 8A.4), students were actively encouraged to 'notice' (Schmidt, 1990; i.e., consciously recognise) the language that they and their partners had been using during task completion. In addition, teachers asked them to reflect on their overall performance. At this stage, teachers were invited to focus on form, as they could highlight useful language and provide alternatives for incorrect language that had emerged during task performance.

Finally, students were given a homework assignment that would elaborate their in-class experience.

> 1. Give students the information from the webpage about the refugee programme: www.uu.nl/en/education/incluusion/apply-for-incluusion-courses-as-refugee. Ask them to read it and find out whether they are eligible to apply for a course. Why/Why not?
> 2. Explain to students that from the list of the courses offered as part of the refugee programme, they are asked to find two/three courses that they are interested in.
> 3. In pairs, each student tells their partner what courses he/she would like to take and why. The partner then gives advice about what course would be the better option – again providing justification for the advice.
> 4. Once students have settled on the course they would like to study, give *Handout 8* and tell them to complete the course application/registration form.

Figure 8A.3 Main-task activities for real-life task (B2)

> 1. Tell students to swap their application/registration forms and comment on their partners' responses.
> 2. Explain any useful/incorrect language you, as a teacher, have noticed during the task-completion process.
> 3. Ask students to talk with their partners to discuss the questions about the lesson below.
>   a. What did I learn?
>   b. What is important about what we did today?
>   c. How can I apply what we did in real life?
>   d. Are there patterns of language I recognise?
>   e. How well did I do? How can I improve?
> 4. Homework: Tell students to find similar courses for newcomers online and ask them to share the information with the class during the next lesson.

Figure 8A.4 Post-task activities for real-life task (B2)

8A5.1 Implementation

Teaching a task-based syllabus might be perceived as more challenging than following a traditional textbook approach, because spontaneous classroom interaction and providing emergent focus on form can be daunting (Long, 2015). In particular, novice teachers could be in need of support when implementing a task-based approach (cf. East, this volume). This was also true for the context of the study presented here, as our cohort of teachers consists of volunteers within the NGO supporting refugees. Many of them had only limited teacher training and even our experienced teachers were relatively unfamiliar with task-based language teaching. At the beginning of the 2019–20 academic year, we delivered a series of training sessions on task-based language teaching prior to the actual implementation of the task syllabus. The training focused on its origin and principles, the definition of 'task' (in particular how it differs from an exercise), and after modelling sample task implementations, teachers were asked to design their own task cycles with the aim of guiding students towards successful target task performance.

In addition, teachers received a step-by-step teacher guide for each task-based lesson detailing all teacher and student actions, as well as providing handouts and links to the complete set of materials with clear instructions. Still, as task developers we were aware of the gap between 'task-as-workplan' and 'task-in-process' (Breen, 1987), which acknowledges that tasks on paper cannot and should not determine what will actually happen when they are used inside the classroom. Hence, both the learners' reinterpretation of the tasks in use and adaptations to the tasks by teachers were expected to lead to changes during classroom implementation (Duff, 1993). Accordingly, teachers were informed that they should not feel obliged to follow the instructions to the letter, but instead had the flexibility to make any necessary adjustments to better meet their students' needs and interests.

Finally, as we worked with a hybrid syllabus, to date, the task-based lessons have not become part of the regular formal assessment practices of the curriculum. Formative assessment and evaluation are embedded in the post-task stage, during which learners were encouraged to engage in self- and/or peer-assessment supported by teacher feedback (cf. Norris & East, this volume). One major aim of this approach was to raise students' consciousness towards their linguistic as well as task performance and guide them towards autonomy, taking charge of their own language learning (Benson, 2013).

8A5.2 Evaluation

With regard to the evaluation of the task-based lessons, feedback and support channels between the teachers and task designers were kept open before, during, and after the implementation process to ensure mutual understanding and to maximise the effectiveness of the task-based approach. Additionally, a feedback form solicited information about teachers' experiences after executing each task in their classroom, asking the following questions:

1. Do you think the content/topic of the task was relevant to your students' needs, interests and wants? Why/why not?
2. Do you think the language level of the task was appropriate for your students? If not, please give specific examples from your lesson.
3. Can you please evaluate the difficulty of the task from your students' perspective?
4. How was student participation during the task implementation?

5. What were the challenges you faced during the task implementation, if any?
6. What part(s) do you think need to be revised to make them more effective?

At present, we have not received sufficient feedback to systematically evaluate the classroom implementation. As mentioned before, the task-based lessons only covered one hour of the four hours of face-to-face weekly contact teachers had with students. They admitted that it was challenging to implement the tasks on top of the weekly coursework prescribed by the base syllabus. Moreover, many students were not used to tasks requiring group interaction, problem-solving and productivity in both writing and speaking, so the task-based activities required additional time and support and teachers chose to omit or minimise parts of the task-based lessons or assigned them as homework. As lead educators of the NGO, we are currently debating how to react to these experiences, pondering the options: (i) revise and shorten the task-based activities so they fit within the one hour; (ii) increase the number of face-to-face classes to six hours a week to open up more space for task-based lessons; (iii) abandon part of the base syllabus. This last option might results new challenges, because the students' priority is their short-term goal, that is, to enter university, and therefore deem IELTS preparation more relevant than the task-based activities.

In future, we aim to provide not only the teachers but also the learners with training about task-based instruction to highlight how they will benefit from these activities in the long run. Before doing, so, it seems necessary, however, to conduct a more systematic in-use and post-use evaluation of the task-based lessons, triangulating multiple data sources (e.g., questionnaires, interviews) to further calibrate and improve the task cycles in our programme.

8A.6 Conclusion

This case study explored the design and development of a series of tasks targeting a group of educated refugees learning English and their volunteer teachers at an NGO in the Netherlands. It showcases an original context that has received little attention in the literature to date: refugees learning English as a *foreign* language for academic and professional purposes. We have shown how to incorporate a task-based syllabus based on a systematic NA in an existing language programme that is geared towards learners' short-term goal to pass the IELTS test. We present a hybrid syllabus that addressed both students' IELTS goal, as well as their immediate needs and interests as identified by the NA.

Specifically, we drew on the findings of a small-scale NA within the same context performed by Middleton (2019), that informed us about the refugee learners' perceived needs in speaking, listening, and writing in academic contexts. Following a task-based language teaching approach (Bygate, Samuda, & van den Branden, this volume; Skehan, this volume), we developed a series of task-based lessons targeting these needs at the CEFR levels A2, B1 and B2, for which the NGO offered classes to refugees. One task cycle covers four one-hour lessons, to be taught across four weeks, and consists of three pedagogic tasks plus one real-life (target) task that are thematically related and sequenced according to principles of task complexity. Each task-based lesson involves the three stages of pre-task, (main) task and post-task. Learners and teachers were provided with all materials, and step-by-step guidance for each lesson was available for teachers, even though they were free to adapt the teaching according to their students' needs.

The informal evaluation of this initial implementation of our task-based activities reveals that we need to pay more attention to the in-use and post-use stages of the task-based lessons. In particular, the timing and the priority that learners and teachers currently (can) give to the task-based activities within the hybrid syllabus need to be reconsidered. We wish to provide more training and clearer instructions for both teachers and learners to enhance their adoption of the task-based approach. In addition, we aim to perform classroom observations and interviews to gain more insights into the effectiveness of the tasks and their classroom implementation. This would allow us to fine-tune the tasks such that they meet the learners' needs and interests more accurately. It might also enable us to identify further needs and continue developing other task cycles for the target group of our study: educated refugee learners of English in the Netherlands.

Further Reading

Ćatibušić, B., Gallagher, F., and Karazi, S. (2019). Syrian voices: An exploration of the language learning needs and integration supports for adult Syrian refugees in Ireland. *International Journal of Inclusive Education*, 25(1), 22–39.

Gurzynski-Weiss, L. and IATBLT (n.d.). The TBLT Language Learning Task Bank. https://tblt.indiana.edu.

Long, M. H. (2015). *Second language acquisition and task-based language teaching*. West Sussex: Wiley-Blackwell.

Samuda, V. (2001). Guiding relationships between form and meaning during task performance: The role of the teacher. In M. Bygate, P. Skehan, and M. Swain, eds. *Researching pedagogic tasks: Second language learning, teaching, and testing*. Abingdon and New York: Routledge, pp. 119–40.

Study Questions

1. In what ways are educated refugee language learners different from other learners?
2. What could be the benefits of developing a task-based syllabus to meet the needs of this specific group of learners?
3. What changes would you make to the example task cycles and tasks presented in this chapter? Explain why.
4. How would you evaluate the effectiveness of the task-based lessons? What could be the advantages of such an evaluation?

References

Baralt, M., Gilabert, R., and Robinson, P. (2014), eds. *Task sequencing and instructed second language learning*. London: Bloomsbury Academic.

Benson, P. (2013). Learner autonomy. *TESOL Quarterly*, 47(4), 839–43.

Breen, M.P. (1987). Learner contributions to task design. In C. N. Candlin and D. Murphy, eds. *Language learning tasks. Lancaster Practical Papers in English Language Education*. Vol. 7. Englewood Cliffs, NJ: Prentice-Hall, pp. 23–46.

Ćatibušić, B., Gallagher, F., and Karazi, S. (2019). Syrian voices: An exploration of the language learning needs and integration supports for adult Syrian refugees in Ireland. *International Journal of Inclusive Education*, 1, 18.

Chiswick, B. R. and Miller, P. W. (2001). A model of destination-language acquisition: application to male immigrants in Canada. *Demography*, 38(3), 391–409.

Cunningsworth, A. (1995). *Choosing your coursebook*. London: Macmillan.

Duff, P. A. (1993). Language socialization in Hungarian-English schools. Doctoral dissertation. University of California, Los Angeles.

Ellis, R. (2009).Task-based language teaching: Sorting out the misunderstandings. *International Journal of Applied Linguistics*, 19, 221–46.

Gibbons, P. (1998). Classroom talk and the learning of new registers in a second language, *Language and Education*, 12(2), 99–118.

Gök, S. O. (2019). *How are materials actually used in classrooms? Towards a systematic evaluation of a locally published coursebook series for young learners in Turkey*. Unpublished PhD thesis. Leicester University, UK.

Harwood, N. (2010), ed. *English language teaching materials: Theory and practice*. New York: Cambridge University Press.

Jordan, R. R. (1997) *English for academic purposes: A guide and resource book for teachers*. Cambridge: Cambridge University Press.

Lambert, C. (2010). Task-based analysis: Putting principles into practice. *Language Teaching Research*, 14(1), 99–112.

Long, M. H. (2005). *Second language needs analysis*. Cambridge: Cambridge University Press.

Long, M. H. (2015). *Second language acquisition and task-based language teaching*. West Sussex: Wiley-Blackwell.

Middleton, T. (2019). The L2 motivational self system and language needs of educated refugees learning English in the Netherlands. Unpublished MA thesis. Utrecht University, the Netherlands.

Révész, A. (2014). Towards a fuller assessment of cognitive models of task-based learning: Investigating task-generated cognitive demands and processes. *Applied Linguistics*, 35(1), 87–92.

Révész, A., Michel, M., and Gilabert, R. (2016). Measuring cognitive task demands using dual-task methodology, subjective self-ratings, and expert judgments: A validation study. *Studies in Second Language Acquisition*, 38(4), 703–37.

Ros i Sole, C. (2014). The paradoxes of language learning and integration in the European context. In D. Mallows, ed. *Language issues in migration and integration: perspectives from teachers and learners*. London: British Council, pp. 55–78.

Schmidt, R. (1990). The role of consciousness in second language learning. *Applied Linguistics*, 11, 129–58.

Tomlinson, B. and Masuhara, H. (2017) *A complete guide to the theory and practice of materials development for language learning*. Hoboken, NJ: Wiley.

Van Tubergen, F. (2010). Determinants of second language proficiency among refugees in the Netherlands. *Social Forces*, 89(2), 515–34.

VluchtelingenWerk Nederland (2018). VluchtelingenWerk Integratie Barometer 2018: Eenonderzoek naar de ervaringen van vluchtelingen met inburgering. [Barometer of integration 2018: An investigation into the experiences of refugees]. Retrieved from: https://www.vluchtelingen werk.nl/sites/default/files/u640/VWN_Integratiebarometer_2018_aangepastDEF_%20LR.pdf.

VSNU (Vereniging Samenwerkende Nederlandse Universiteiten) (2012). *Prestaties in perspectief. Trendrapportage universiteiten 2000–2020*. [Achievements in perspective. Trend report of [Dutch] universities 2000 to 2010]. Den Haag. Retrieved from: https://www.vsnu.nl/files/doc umenten/Publicaties/Trendrapportage_DEF.pdf.

Widdowson, H. G. (1990). *Aspects of language teaching*. Oxford: Oxford University Press

Willis, D. and Willis, J. (2001). Task-based language learning. In R. Carter and D. Nunan, eds. *The Cambridge guide to teaching English to speakers of other languages*. Cambridge: Cambridge University Press, pp. 173–79.

Part IV

Methodology and Pedagogy

9

A Psycholinguistically Motivated Methodology for Task-Based Language Teaching

Gisela Granena and Yucel Yilmaz

9.1 Theoretical Underpinnings

Methods in second language (L2) teaching come and go in a variety of sizes, shapes, and flavors: Grammar Translation, Audio-Lingual, Natural, Communicative, Silent Way, and Suggestopedia, just to name a few. Although methods may be many, one of the main differences among them is whether they follow a synthetic or an analytical approach to course design (Wilkins, 1976). These two main approaches to the design of a language course, or to syllabus design, differ in whether they see acquisition as a gradual process of accumulation of different parts that the learner is expected to integrate (i.e., a synthetic syllabus), or as a holistic process where the learner is expected to infer the parts inductively from exposure to input (i.e., an analytic syllabus).

Synthetic syllabi are external to the learner and other-directed. They are linguistic in nature and rely on the analysis of the target language provided by grammar books or textbooks. The language to be taught becomes the object of instruction, and it is broken down into linguistic units, such as grammatical structures, morphemes, functions, words, and phonemes. These parts are taught by means of pre-selected models and presented independently of one another following a sequence that is determined by vague criteria, based on course designers' intuitions about how learning takes place, rather than on theoretically or empirically motivated principles. Methods such as Grammar Translation, Audio-Lingual, Silent Way, and Total Physical Response rely on synthetic syllabi that can be structural, if organized around grammatical structures, lexical, if organized around words, and notional/functional, if organized around semantic units, like time, space, duration or probability, or communicative function, like requesting, apologizing or complimenting, or a combination of those. The synthetic syllabus is the most common in classrooms all over the world, particularly the structural syllabus, organized around grammar points.

Analytic syllabi, on the other hand, are internal to the learner in the sense that they do not try to impose an external linguistic syllabus. They focus on the learner, the learning process, and the language as a medium. Learners are presented with samples of communicative L2 use, larger textual units, or tasks that may be interesting or relevant for learners and have not been controlled for the grammar or vocabulary involved. Learners are encouraged to induce the lower-level language units, such as structures, functions, or vocabulary items. Methods such as the Natural Approach or immersion programs rely on analytic syllabi.

Both synthetic and analytic syllabi have problems and limitations (see, for example, Long [1991, 2000, 2009]; Long & Robinson, [1998]). Long (1991, 2000) viewed them as two extremes on a continuum. Synthetic syllabi are characterized by an interventionist focus on forms (FonFS), while analytic syllabi are characterized by a noninterventionist focus on meaning (FonM). Typically, FonFS relies on explicit grammar teaching, memorization of language materials, and simplified pedagogical materials to practice the linguistic structures that will be graded. It approaches the learning process sequentially, expecting learners to master language features intentionally, one by one, in the order they were taught. Information about the L2 is provided in three stages (presentation, practice, and production), with information presented either inductively, via examples that help learners notice patterns and work out rules for themselves before practicing the language, or deductively, via rules, then examples, then practice. On the other hand, FonM does not view language learning as intentional, but mostly as incidental (i.e., as taking place while the learner is processing language for meaning) and implicit (i.e., as taking place without awareness). As a result, lessons tend to be communicative and to include holistic language samples, richer and more realistic, from which learners are expected to induce grammar rules.

Long (1991, 2000; Long & Robinson, 1998) advocated a third option in language teaching, focus on form (FonF), that was able to overcome the limitations of FonM, and analytic syllabi, while capturing its strengths. The analytic syllabus from a FonF perspective employs a nonlinguistic unit of analysis, e.g., tasks. In Long's (1985, 2015) proposal for task-based language teaching (TBLT), target tasks the learner needs to complete are broken down into successively more complex approximations called pedagogical tasks. These target tasks should not be confused with communication tasks that are used to practice or support the learning of particular target structures and vocabulary and that are found in covert synthetic syllabi. Like analytic syllabi, FonF relies on a focus on meaning, but with the difference that learners' attention is systematically drawn to linguistic code features as comprehension or production problems arise incidentally while completing meaning-based tasks. This approach is partly based on Long's Interaction Hypothesis (Long, 1981, 1983, 1996) and the idea that interaction creates optimal conditions for language development by drawing learners' attention briefly to linguistic features in context, and reactively, as these features arise incidentally in L2 comprehension or production. FonF may be achieved in a variety of ways, and not only through interaction between learners or between learners and other speakers. For example, learners' attention may occasionally shift to linguistic features when completing a task that involves synthesizing information from written texts that have been elaborated or where lexical items or structures have been highlighted to make them more salient. Or a teacher may attempt to draw learners' attention to a learning problem identified while observing or assessing learners' group work using more explicit techniques, such as explicit correction.

By increasing input comprehensibility through elaboration (see Long, this volume), by highlighting and/or repeatedly using a particular item, or by providing a correction that shows a mismatch between input and output, FonF aims at inducing the noticing of linguistic features in the context of a task. In other words, FonF aims at leading learners to selectively attend to forms in the input, detect them and store them in memory (i.e., low-level awareness), but without necessarily being aware of any metalinguistic information associated with them and without necessarily understanding their meaning or function (i.e., high-level awareness), an idea based on Schmidt's (1990) Noticing Hypothesis.

An analytic approach to course design from a FonF perspective is the option in language teaching that characterizes TBLT methodology. It is an option that relies on instructional features that can be justified by theory and research findings in the field of second language acquisition and related fields (e.g., cognitive and educational psychology) as features that are necessary for, or facilitative of, L2 learning, and, therefore, as features that make language teaching more efficient by increasing the rate, or speed, of the L2 learning process. The theoretical rationale for TBLT was summarized by Long (2015) in his cognitive-interactionist theory of instructed second language acquisition (ISLA). The theory identifies problems in ISLA and offers some explanations, which form the theoretical basis of a psycholinguistically defensible methodology for TBLT.

The first problem the theory addresses is that adult L2 acquisition is highly variable and largely unsuccessful. Adult L2 acquisition is maturationally (i.e., biologically) constrained, which explains why adult L2 learners cannot reach across-the-board native-like attainment. Maturational constraints affect phonology, lexis and collocation, and morphology and syntax as early as age 4 in the case of phonology, age 6 in the case of lexis and collocation, and the mid-teens in the case of morphology and syntax

(DeKeyser, 2000; DeKeyser & Larson-Hall, 2005; Granena & Long, 2013; Hyltenstam & Abrahamsson, 2003; Meisel, 2011). The benefits of an early L2 acquisition experience are not lost, despite age-related declines in processing speed and cognitive abilities, such as the capacity for implicit learning. In the case of adult L2 learners, the capacity for implicit learning is weaker. As a result, implicit learning mechanisms, such as chunking and instance-based learning (i.e., learning that takes place through the accumulation of input, experienced events, or examples) are less efficient. One of the consequences of the decline in implicit learning capacity is, for example, that adult L2 learners will need exposure to more repetitions of a particular item and that they will be less sensitive to detecting language features that co-vary or that co-occur, such as grammatical agreement.

Age-related declines in processing speed and in the efficiency of some implicit learning mechanisms may explain why some linguistic features prove more difficult for L2 learners. These are typically nonsalient features that are harder to notice, for example, in inflectional morphology, or ambiguous, optional rules, especially when the learners' first language relies on a very different system. At the same time, the fact that the capacity for implicit learning weakens with age makes it possible for individual differences in cognitive aptitudes for implicit learning to compensate for the loss in efficiency of implicit learning mechanisms and to explain part of the variability in language-learning success. Cognitive language aptitude, not only for implicit, but also for explicit learning, is considered an inherent capacity to reach high levels of L2 proficiency, holding equal such factors as L2 exposure, motivation, and other individual differences.

Long's (2015: 30–62) cognitive-interactionist theory sees incidental and implicit learning as the default learning processes, even in adulthood, and despite age-related declines in efficiency. This view is shared by many experts in cognitive psychology (e.g., Reber & Allen, 2000) and supported by findings of experimental studies that have focused on adult learners' implicit learning of semi-artificial grammars (e.g., Rebuschat, 2008; Rebuschat & Williams, 2006, 2009; Williams, 1999, 2005). Learning that is incidental happens without the learner's intention to learn, and while the learner's attention is focused on something else. Learning that is implicit happens without the learner being aware of what is learned, even though awareness may be initially necessary, as Robinson (2003) and Schmidt (1990) argue, to notice a new form or structure, an issue that is still unclear in the field (see Long, 2015).

Learners can learn without intending to do so, and without being aware of what they learn, which results in implicit language knowledge, and they can also learn without intending to do so, but aware of what they learned, which results in more explicit knowledge. Learners can also learn intentionally and explicitly, and, usually, both implicit and explicit learning processes are at work in L2 learning. Long's (2015) theory, in fact, embraces intentional and explicit learning opportunities and considers them helpful in speeding up learning in instructed settings and necessary to make teaching more efficient. Specifically, they can facilitate initial noticing of nonsalient linguistic features and of mismatches between input and output, and help make learners aware of the cues they need to pay attention to in the language. These are all examples of explicit language processing that may facilitate subsequent implicit language processing. However, explicit learning and the resulting declarative knowledge have limitations. They work best with simple material, but may be of limited help to improve performance when the system to be learned is complex (see Doughty, 2003), or in spontaneous language use. Similarly, more explicit FonF techniques may help by bringing items to learners' attention, but those items have to be within learners' processing range and at the right developmental stage for learning to happen.

Long (2015) refers to his Interaction Hypothesis (Long, 1981, 1983, 1996) as the way to combine implicit and explicit learning in the language classroom. This facilitates L2 development by bringing learners' attention to language, for example, but not only, when there is a communication problem, and while the learner is engaged in a meaning-based task. Negative feedback, or the reactions language learners receive indicating that their language production is not target-like, plays a crucial role in the Interaction Hypothesis, and especially, but not only, through implicit negative feedback in the form of recasts. Recasts provide information about the L2 implicitly and reactively. From a psycholinguistic perspective, the information is provided in the context of a meaning-based task, which means that the learner has prior comprehension of the message that will help mapping form, meaning, and function. The learner is vested in the exchange, trying to produce or to understand language, and will be paying attention, which facilitates noticing. The recast reformulates the learner's production and, therefore, allows the learner to allocate attentional resources to linguistic code features. Finally, the fact that the learner's deviant utterance and the reformulation are juxtaposed facilitates their comparison by allowing the learner to hold both in working memory. Research shows that recasts work (e.g., Mackey & Goo, 2007; Russell & Spada, 2006), but there are also findings indicating that they may not work for all the linguistic targets in the same way (e.g., Ortega & Long, 1997) and that a greater degree of explicitness in the feedback may be necessary, depending on the saliency of the target.

The last problem that Long's (2015) cognitive-interactionist theory addresses is that of variation in between-learner and within-learner achievement. Adults' L2 attainment shows variability among individuals and within individuals, in how successfully they learn different language features. The theory sees cognitive variables as the second most powerful predictors of language achievement. Unlike affect variables such as motivation or attitude, which only have marginal influence, cognitive variables such as language aptitude typically correlate in the 0.40–0.50 range with L2 attainment. Cognitive abilities are able to explain variation among learners, as well as differential achievement of language features within learners if considered, as Long argues, in combination with particular features of the structures, such as perceptual saliency, which may interact differently with different cognitive abilities. For example, cognitive aptitudes for implicit learning may be more relevant for structures that involve co-occurrence patterns, such as grammatical agreement (Granena, 2013a).

Long's (2015) cognitive-interactionist theory of ISLA provides a coherent theoretical rationale for TBLT, outlining its psycholinguistic underpinnings and underlying assumptions. The methodology of TBLT is also motivated by research findings in instructed L2 learning. The next part of this chapter will provide a review of major research findings on variables in instructed L2 learning that have been identified as having an impact on L2 learning: attention to form, negative feedback, and cognitive individual differences. At the end of each section, we will provide suggestions that teachers can follow when implementing TBLT, and discuss the problems the findings pose for traditional options in language teaching.

9.2 Research Findings

9.2.1 Attention to Form

The findings of classroom research in French immersion programs (Swain & Lapkin, 1991) and other meaning-focused, content classrooms (Pica, 2005) indicate that even after years of meaning-focused language education, learners continue being inaccurate with linguistic phenomena that are highly frequent in the input (e.g., French gender). This evidence suggests that FonM does not suffice and that some kind of attention to form is needed in language teaching. However, it does not say much as to whether this attention to form should be at the expense of, or with the involvement of, a meaning focus, FonFS and FonF, respectively. Norris and Ortega's (2000) meta-analysis summarizing the results of instructional effects studies published between 1980 and 1998 was not able to throw much light on this issue. The results of their meta-analysis showed that FonF studies led to slightly higher effect sizes than FonFS studies ($d = 1.0$ vs. $d = .93$), but, because the observed difference was not statistically trustworthy, they concluded that their results suggested "no differences in effectiveness between FonF and FonFS instruction (as currently operationalized) and equivalent overall instructional effectiveness for both" (Norris & Ortega, 2000: 482). Norris and Ortega's results were largely based on studies that did not directly compare FonF and FonFS conditions.

Only a few studies carried out after Norris and Ortega's (2000) meta-analysis did compare FonF and FonFS directly by including groups representing each condition. Most of these focused on vocabulary acquisition. Laufer (2006), for example, targeted the acquisition of new English vocabulary by Grade 11 students in Israel. The FonF treatment involved reading a text and answering comprehension questions using a bilingual dictionary, as needed. The learners in the FonFS condition were provided with written translations and explanations of a list of vocabulary items, and additional information by the teacher if needed. Then, the learners worked on multiple-choice and fill-in-the-blanks type of exercises. The results showed that the FonFS group outperformed the FonF group, as measured by a surprise discrete-item test, where the students had to provide the meaning of the target words in English or in their first language (L1).

De la Fuente's (2006) study produced the opposite result. The study compared the relative effects of FonF and FonFS in vocabulary acquisition by university students in an elementary Spanish class. One of the treatment groups, which can be considered a FonFS condition, followed the presentation-practice-production model. The learners in this group received explanations of the new words at the presentation stage, performed controlled oral and written production tasks at the practice stage, and carried out role-plays in pairs at the production stage. The study also included two TBLT groups, but only one of them teased apart the features of FonF from the features FonFS. This FonF group first read a dialog, in which the salience of the target words was increased by bolding, and then carried out a role-play task that required students to negotiate the meanings of the target words, and finally performed free role-plays in pairs. The results showed that the two conditions were equally effective in the immediate posttest, but that the FonF group outperformed the FonFS group on the delayed posttest. After a follow-up qualitative analysis of the interactions between learners in each group, De la Fuente (2006) found that the FonF condition provided more opportunities for negotiation of meaning, concluding that FonF allowed for "deeper processing of the L2 words by helping learners to establish more productive meaning–form connections through multiple opportunities for output production (of target words) during negotiation" (282). Despite their conflicting findings, Laufer (2006) and De la Fuente (2006) had one thing in common: they both measured the effects of instruction through discrete-item tests that are likely to fall short of demonstrating what learners can do with the knowledge they gained from the treatment under the communicative pressure of a real-life situation.

Shintani's (2013, 2015) studies addressed this measurement problem by including tests assessing learners' knowledge in a communicative situation. Shintani (2015) also extended the scope of the research to grammatical targets. In Shintani (2013), six-year-olds participated in nine lessons of thirty minutes. Twenty-four nouns and twelve adjectives constituted the target vocabulary items. The FonFS group was exposed to different sets of words each time and followed the presentation-practice-production method. At the presentation stage, learners said the words individually; at the practice stage, learners said the words shown on each flashcard chorally and individually; and at the production stage, learners went on producing the words in the context of game-like tasks. In the FonF condition, all the target words occurred incidentally in every lesson, and the teacher and learners played a game where learners put the cards with the picture of items in their correct places on a map based on the teacher's directions. The control group continued with their regular lessons, which involved other communicative and game-like activities that did not involve the use of the target words. Two tests were administered at three different times: a pretest (one-week before the treatment), a one-week delayed posttest, and a four-week delayed posttest. The instruments included a discrete-item test asking learners to name the words on a flashcard and a communicative test requiring learners to use the target words in context while interacting with the teacher in a game-like activity. The results showed that the performance of the two experimental groups was equivalent in the acquisition of nouns. The FonF group, however, outperformed the FonFS group in the acquisition of adjectives.

In a follow-up paper, Shintani (2015) compared these two treatments in the extent to which they promoted incidental learning (i.e., learning that takes place in the absence of intention) of the plural -s and the copula be. Although neither treatment condition was designed to promote the acquisition of the above-mentioned forms, in a post-hoc analysis, Shintani reported that the treatment conditions provided opportunities for the acquisition of these forms, which in some cases, briefly became the focus of instruction. For example, in the FonF condition, the teacher clarified the difference between singular and plural forms in meaning, and, in the FonFS condition, the teacher provided feedback correcting learners' errors with the forms. A multiple-choice comprehension test and a controlled oral production test were administered at three times: a pretest (one-week before the treatment), posttest 1 (one-week after the treatment), and posttest 2 (six-weeks after the treatment). The comprehension test revealed that the FonF group performed better than the FonFS group on the plural -s (there was no comprehension test targeting the copula because the presence or absence of the copula does not change the meaning of a sentence). The production test results, however, did not reveal any differences between the groups.

One can argue that the limitation of the measurement tools used in Laufer (2006) and De la Fuente (2006) reduces the credibility of the evidence provided by those studies. The results of the two more recent studies (Shintani, 2013, 2015) can be considered more credible in this regard because of the relative validity of the assessment tools used. Taken together, there seems to be some evidence indicating that FonF is more effective than FonFS, especially when one weighs the existing evidence according to the limitations of the assessment methods. What was interesting is that this advantage was not limited to targets (i.e., vocabulary items) for which the treatment systematically created learning opportunities, but was extended to other linguistic phenomena for which the treatment did not offer consistent learning opportunities. FonFS leads to some success in achieving the goal that it sets out to achieve (i.e., teaching the target forms), but does not lead to a comparable amount of learning when the incidental acquisition of forms not targeted by the treatment is considered.

Admittedly, more research is necessary that can provide more conclusive findings on the relative effectiveness of FonF and FonFS. Yet, there are theoretical reasons, discussed in various publications by Long (e.g., Long, 2015), to support the implementation of FonF. One of the advantages of FonF is that it relies on a syllabus composed of meaning-based units (i.e., pedagogic tasks), whereas FonFS relies on a syllabus composed of language-based units, such as grammar structures. What this means for FonF is that, in addition to more interesting lessons, more obvious relevance to learners' needs, and more realistic target language input, both the type and quantity of language that learners are exposed to is determined by the content of the pedagogic task. For example, a lesson based on a unit focusing on a doctor's visit in a task-based syllabus will create contexts for the use of, and exposure to, multiple linguistic phenomena, rather than a single linguistic phenomenon. When implementing FonFS, however, material designers preselect target structures and proceed sequentially with target structures being taught one at a time. This approach should prove inefficient, given the time constraints language courses are subject to. Unlike FonFS, FonF provides opportunities for the incidental learning of other forms not targeted by the FonF technique. We believe that if research studies included a more comprehensive evaluation of all possible learning outcomes, this would allow them to capture the strengths of FonF, and findings would clearly favor FonF.

9.2.2 Negative Feedback

Negative feedback, also called corrective feedback (CF), is one of many techniques (see Doughty & Williams [1998] for other FonF techniques) that teachers can use to implement FonF. However, CF has a special place among other FonF techniques because the Interaction Hypothesis (Long, 1981, 1983, 1996), which inspired the idea of FonF, values it as a tool for bringing attention to language during conversational interaction, an ideal context for determining learners' linguistic needs. Two approaches have been taken toward the existing CF literature to evaluate the role of CF in L2 acquisition. The first approach aims at determining the theoretical importance of CF in L2 acquisition without considering factors that can make a difference in the effectiveness of feedback, whereas the second approach focuses on the identification of those factors. Evaluations following the first approach have generally been made by answering the guiding questions asked by Pinker (1989), which were about the extent to which CF is a) available, b) noticed, c) associated with linguistic improvement, and d) necessary for L2 acquisition. Regarding the availability of CF, the literature reviewed by Yilmaz (2016b) revealed that CF is not only available in traditional face-to-face L2 classrooms (e.g., Lyster & Ranta, 1997), but also in non-classroom contexts in which interaction takes places between native speakers and nonnative speakers either orally (e.g., Braidi, 2002) or through text-chat tools (e.g., Iwasaki & Oliver, 2003). Studies reported that between 48 and 62 percent of all learner errors attracted feedback. Regarding the noticeability of CF, studies have examined two indicators, mainly whether learners can recognize the corrective potential of the feedback and whether they can identify the linguistic source of the error. Yilmaz (2016b) showed that learners in both text-based computer-mediated communication and face-to-face instructed contexts perceive the corrective nature of 60 to 71 percent of all feedback instances. In addition, learners were able to identify the source of the linguistic problem (morphosyntax, phonology, lexis) roughly 50 percent of the time. However, they were less successful in recognizing morphosyntactic errors (ranging from 13 to 48 percent of the time) than lexical (ranging from 66 to 83 percent) and phonological errors (ranging from 21 to 60 percent). Regarding whether CF leads to linguistic improvement, the strongest evidence comes from experimental studies comparing the performance of feedback groups versus no-feedback groups (e.g., Yilmaz, 2012), which showed a strong tendency for feedback groups to outperform no-feedback groups. Meta-analyses (e.g., Li, 2010; Lyster & Saito, 2010; Goo et al., 2015) synthesizing the results of this experimental research have shown that the magnitude of the difference between feedback and no-feedback groups ranged from medium to large. Finally, regarding whether CF is necessary for L2 acquisition, Long (1996, 2015) has proposed that the role of CF changes depending on the nature of the target form: CF is necessary for certain forms and facilitative for others. Building on White's (1991) ideas, Long claimed that when learning certain L2 features, learners' knowledge about how a similar feature works in their L1 would turn against them, leading them to generate incorrect hypotheses about the target L2 feature. In these special cases, CF is necessary; that is, learners must receive CF in order to retreat from their L1-based hypotheses. Although there is some support for this position in the literature (e.g., White, 1991), more research is necessary to determine the areas of L2 that should be prioritized when providing CF.

The second approach to CF relies on research investigating the relationship between learner-external and learner-internal factors (i.e., individual differences) and CF effectiveness. We will only review the literature on learner-external factors in the remaining part of this section because learner-internal factors will be reviewed in the following section. Learner-external factors are related to how a particular type of CF is delivered or to the nature of the linguistic feature targeted by CF. The factor that has attracted the greatest amount of attention in research is feedback type. Some researchers (Carroll, 2001) argue that the most effective feedback type is the most explicit, which provides both (a) metalinguistic information in the form clues or rules to help learners detect the source of their error (e.g., metalinguistic feedback), and (b) information indicating that the learner has made an error (e.g., explicit correction). Many researchers (e.g., Sheen, 2007; Goo, 2012) have considered a feedback move explicit even if it includes only (a) or (b). Other researchers favor feedback types that push learners to correct their non-target-like production in the turn following the feedback (i.e., repair). Such feedback types (e.g., elicitation, metalinguistic feedback, clarification request, and repetition) are referred to as prompts (Ranta & Lyster, 2007) and contrasted with reformulations (e.g., explicit correction, recasts), which do not push learners to repair their errors. A third group of researchers (Doughty, 2001; Long, 2007), however, argues that explicit feedback and prompts are time-consuming and face-threatening. Also, Doughty (2001) has claimed that explicit feedback disrupts learners' language learning processing, as it interrupts their language production. These researchers advocate for the provision of implicit reformulations, or recasts, which, according to Long (2007), offer considerable potential because of their immediate contingency on the erroneous learner output, allowing learners to contrast the two forms.

Empirical studies comparing the relative effectiveness of explicit feedback or prompts versus recasts have produced mixed results, with some studies finding an advantage for prompts (e.g., Lyster, 2004) or explicit feedback (e.g., Ellis, Loewen & Erlam, 2006; Yilmaz, 2012), and some finding no difference between the feedback groups (explicit feedback vs. recasts, e.g., Loewen & Nabei, 2007; prompts vs. recasts, e.g., Lyster & Izquierdo, 2009). However, meta-analyses (Li, 2010; Lyster & Saito, 2010) also pointed to an overall trend toward the relative effectiveness of explicit feedback and prompts over recasts. One major limitation of the above literature is that it does not provide much guidance to teachers about how to mitigate some of the potential negative side effects associated with explicit feedback and prompts, such as the fact that they are time-consuming and face-threatening. One study that addressed this concern was Yilmaz (2013), which showed that receiving a few instances of explicit feedback first, and then recasts, until the end of a task was as effective as receiving only explicit feedback throughout the task. This finding means that it is not necessary to correct each error with explicit feedback in order to obtain the desired level of effectiveness. A mixed feedback treatment would be not only as effective, but also less likely to have the negative side effects associated with the explicit feedback treatment.

Not all researchers are in favor of comparing feedback types to find the most effective. For example, Goo and Mackey (2013) held that comparative corrective feedback studies are not a fruitful line of research because of the methodological problems that are almost inevitable in such comparisons. They advocated that researchers select one feedback type and explore the conditions under which it is more or less effective. In fact, some research studies had already been conducted to identify conditions favorable for a specific feedback type. Recasts were the type that attracted the most attention from researchers, a tendency that can be partly attributed to the research finding that recasts are the most frequently used feedback type in classrooms (e.g., Sheen, 2004). This research has shown that recasts bearing stress, recasts that contained only one change, recasts that involve the substitution (rather than reordering, addition, or deletion) of elements in the learner's non-target-like utterance, and short recasts, produced higher rates of noticing, as shown by their responses to feedback or individualized posttest items (Loewen & Philp, 2006; Sheen, 2006).

There is also a more experimental line of research investigating factors that impact the extent to which a specific type of feedback leads to linguistic development. The scope of this research has not been restricted to recasts. However, the findings should be taken as suggestive because only a few studies have investigated each of the factors mentioned. First, saliency, defined as the degree to which a linguistic form can be perceived and linked to an underlying meaning (Goldschneider & DeKeyser, 2001), can change the effectiveness of feedback. Corrective feedback(recasts and explicit feedback) is more effective when provided on salient forms than when provided on nonsalient forms (Yilmaz, 2012; 2016a). Second, Révész and Han (2006) showed that when learners are familiar with the content of the task, through repeating it, they are more likely to take advantage of recasts. Other studies (e.g., Révész, 2009) have shown that learners benefit more from recasts provided during a more complex task (e.g., describing a crime scene with the aid of a photograph) than from recasts provided during less complex tasks (e.g., describing a crime scene without the opportunity to look at a photograph). Third, explicit feedback and recasts are more effective when provided through text-chat tools than orally (Yilmaz, 2012). Fourth, CF (corrective recasting and recasts) is more effective when provided immediately after learners' errors, usually during a communicative task, than at the end of a task or lesson (Henderson, 2021; Arroyo & Yilmaz, 2018). Finally, explicit feedback is more effective when provided on learners' own errors than when learners overhear feedback provided to other learners' errors (Yilmaz, 2016a).

The review above shows that CF, in general, is a good investment on the teacher's part, because it is likely to aid L2 development. However, the way feedback is delivered has implications. When there is little concern about the negative consequences of CF, relatively more obtrusive feedback types, such as explicit feedback, can be a good option. However, obtrusive feedback types should be used sparingly if there are concerns about negative effects. It may also be possible for teachers to make CF more effective by providing it at the right time and under the right conditions. For example, teachers can prioritize more salient target forms over less salient ones or give written CF through chat tools, especially if the task lends itself to the possibility of being carried out online (e.g., interacting with a customer service representative using a web-based chat tool). In addition, instead of providing CF the first time learners perform a pedagogical task, teachers can ask learners to repeat the task and provide CF during the second or third iteration, when learners are already familiar with the content of the task.

The review of research findings revealed two additional observations with important implications for classroom methodology: CF is most effective when it is immediate, and CF is most effective when provided on learners' own errors. These observations, if confirmed by future research, suggest that instruction should maximize learners' production opportunities to improve their chances of receiving feedback on their own errors immediately after making an error. While this requirement is likely to be satisfied in classes following TBLT (Long, 2015), it constitutes a challenge for instruction organized around linguistic units (i.e., FonFS). As previously noted (De la Fuente, 2006; Shintani, 2013, 2015), FonFS instruction rarely leads to meaningful interaction between learners or learners and teachers, which could serve as a background for feedback provision. In addition, Long, Lee, and Hillman (2019) argue that the quantity of speaking opportunities in FonFS classes is always limited. They state that, across the world, it is typical to have three sixty-minute language classes per week, barely enough to produce four short utterances weekly if one deducts the time spent on classroom management and activities that involve no oral production from total class time.

9.2.3 Cognitive Individual Differences

Another important factor in instructional effectiveness is the role played by learner individual differences. A particular type of instruction can be better than another, but it is never the case that the effects of instruction will be the same for all learners. To put it differently, learners' response to an instructional treatment differs from one individual to another. The research paradigm called Aptitude-Treatment Interaction or ATI (Cronbach & Snow, 1977) evaluates the effectiveness of a treatment by taking individual differences systematically into account. The expectation is that the effect of different instructional interventions will be different depending on the characteristics of the learners. The long-term goal of ATI research is to obtain the best possible learning outcome by matching learners' specific aptitudes, or strengths, and instruction. Aptitude in this paradigm refers to any measurable person characteristics, such as motivation, personality, learning style, and beliefs.

In the L2 individual differences literature, except for a few studies that have focused on noncognitive variables, like anxiety (Rassei, 2015), the bulk of research has been conducted on cognitive individual differences, specifically, on cognitive language aptitude, considered the second most powerful predictor of L2 learning success (Long, 2015). Researchers have investigated the interaction between various cognitive variables, such as language analytic ability (e.g., Sheen, 2007), working memory capacity (e.g., Goo, 2012), attention control (Trofimovich et al., 2007), phonetic coding ability (Yilmaz & Koylu, 2016), and inhibitory control (e.g., Yilmaz & Sagdic, 2019), and the extent to which learners benefit from different types of instruction. While this research has produced important insights about how learning takes place under a specific instructional condition, many of these studies included a single type of instruction, which limits the utility of their results in determining the differential relationship between cognitive factors and the effectiveness of different instructional conditions.

An ideal ATI design would have to include at least two treatments. In addition, research to date has looked at a variety of cognitive individual differences and instructional interventions, making it difficult to reach conclusions that are educationally meaningful. The field (and language educators) would benefit from a joint effort to unify methodological criteria in order to investigate comparable cognitive aptitudes and comparable instructional interventions. A starting point could be a classification of cognitive aptitudes and instructional types into broader categories. In a synthetic review summarizing the results of studies that included cognitive aptitudes, Granena and Yilmaz (2018) classified cognitive variables into two categories: explicit language aptitude and implicit language aptitude (Granena, 2013b; Yilmaz & Granena, 2016). Explicit language aptitude was defined as those cognitive abilities that are more relevant to learning a language intentionally, through reasoning, deliberate hypothesis testing, and memorization. Examples of such abilities would be language analytic ability, explicit inductive learning, and rote memory ability. Implicit language aptitude was defined as cognitive abilities that are more relevant for implicit language learning and processing, that is, more relevant for acquiring patterns in the input unintentionally, through exposure. Examples of such abilities would be sequence learning ability and priming ability. The two general instructional types used to classify the instructional conditions in the published literature were explicit (i.e., instructional interventions, including presentation of rules or instructions directly asking learners to attend to forms) and implicit (i.e., interventions including neither presentation of rules nor instructions to attend to forms).

The goal of Granena and Yilmaz's (2018) review was to determine whether implicit and explicit cognitive abilities were differentially related to L2 acquisition under explicit and implicit instructional conditions. The literature search revealed a total of nine studies that included both an implicit and explicit treatment condition and measured a cognitive variable that could be categorized as falling under either explicit language aptitude or implicit language aptitude. The most important finding of the study was that explicit language aptitude facilitated learning under explicit instructed conditions to a greater extent than under implicit instructed conditions. Implicit language aptitude did not facilitate learning under either instructional type, but this result was not considered trustworthy, due to the fact that there were only two studies in the sample that included an implicit aptitude measure.

Task-based language teaching, as defended by Long (2015), is learner-centered in two ways: the content of the course is determined through the assessment of learners' future needs and L2 learning, and the nature and order of language phenomena to be learned is not predetermined. Long argues that TBLT is open to further individualization as research evidence emerges and as long as situational factors (e.g., expertise, time) allow for such adaptations. Although further research in second language acquisition is needed, some interesting findings are emerging, such as the fact that explicit language aptitude is more relevant under explicit teaching conditions. These findings can be used by TBLT practitioners to tailor instruction to cater to learners' individual differences. Differentiation as an educational practice is difficult to implement, but technology-mediated language learning is nowadays making individualization more manageable. For example, online adaptive language learning could be used to systematically match learners to specific instructional modules after determining their cognitive strengths.

9.3 Conclusions and Pedagogical Implications

Unlike grammar-based language learning and teaching, TBLT is psycholinguistically motivated by theory and research findings in second language acquisition and in neighboring fields, such as educational psychology. As a result, TBLT is a language teaching option that creates a psycholinguistically optimal learning environment. This chapter has presented evidence from research that supports features of TBLT methodology, such as the use of FonF, incidental and implicit language learning, and the importance of individualizing instruction. These are features, among many others, that grammar-based language teaching lacks, thus conflicting with theory and research in second language acquisition. The synthetic syllabus grammar-based teaching uses segments the L2 into structures, pre-selects them, and presents and practices them one at a time. From a psycholinguistic perspective, this is inefficient. We provided some evidence showing that TBLT, by virtue of relying on meaning-based units (i.e., pedagogic tasks) and FonF, lets tasks determine the type and quantity of language learners are exposed to, providing opportunities for the incidental learning of multiple linguistic phenomena within the context of a single task. In turn, the quality and quantity of language and the learning opportunities learners receive encourage incidental learning and facilitate the development and internalization of implicit language knowledge, the type of knowledge learners will need for a functional command of the L2 in spontaneous communication. Finally, TBLT is a learner-centered approach, which makes it compatible with the individualization of instruction, according to communicative needs and also psycholinguistically, by taking into account individual differences, such as cognitive aptitudes, to develop tailored instructional modules that match learners' cognitive profiles.

Further Reading

Doughty, C. J. and Long, M. H. (2003). Optimal psycholinguistic environments for distance foreign language learning. *Language Learning & Technology*, 7(3), 50–80.

Granena, G. (2016). Individual versus interactive task-based performance through voice-based computer-mediated communication. *Language Learning & Technology*, 20(3), 40–59.

Long, M. H. (2015). *Second language acquisition and task-based language teaching*. New York: Wiley.

Long, M. H., Lee, J., and Hillman, K. K. (2019). Task-based language learning. In J. W. Schwieter and A. Benati, eds. *The Cambridge handbook of language learning*. Cambridge: Cambridge University Press, pp. 500–26.

Robinson, P., Mackey, A., Gass, S. M., and Schmidt, R. W. (2012). Attention and awareness in second language acquisition. In S. M. Gass and A. Mackey, eds. *The Routledge handbook of second language acquisition*. Abingdon: Routledge, pp. 247–67.

Yilmaz, Y. (2013). The relative effectiveness of mixed, explicit and implicit feedback. *System*, 41, 691–705.

Study Questions

1. Examine the units and activities in a language teaching textbook. Can you determine whether the approach taken by the textbook writer is focus on form, focus on forms, or focus meaning? If not, what else do you need to know to be able to make a decision?
2. Does your provision of feedback change, depending on the language feature or on the learner who made the error? Which factors play a role in your decision?

3. Look for a language textbook that teaches your first language. Then, look for sample dialogs in the textbook and list any features that you would not expect to find if those conversations took place between native speakers of the language.

References

Arroyo, D. and Yilmaz, Y. (2018). An open for replication study: The role of feedback timing in synchronous computer-mediatedcommunication. *Language Learning*, 68(1), 942–72.

Braidi, S. M. (2002). Reexamining the role of recasts in native-speaker/ nonnative-speaker interactions. *Language Learning*, 52(1), 194–211.

Carroll, S. (2001). *Input and evidence: The raw material of second language acquisition* Philadelphia: John Benjamins.

Cronbach, L. J. and Snow, R. E. (1977). *Aptitudes and instructional methods: A handbook for research on interactions*. New York: Irvington.

DeKeyser, R. M. (2000). The robustness of critical period effects in second language acquisition. *Studies in Second Language Acquisition*, 22(4), 499–533.

DeKeyser, R. M. and Larson-Hall, J. (2005). What does the critical period really mean? In J. F. Kroll and A. M. B. de Groot, eds. *Handbook of bilingualism: Psycholinguistic approaches*. Oxford: Oxford University Press, pp. 89–108.

De la Fuente, M. J. (2006). Classroom L2 vocabulary acquisition: Investigating the role of pedagogical tasks and form-focused instruction. *Language Teaching Research*, 10(3), 263–95.

Doughty, C. J. (2001). Cognitive underpinnings of focus on form. In P. Robinson, ed. *Cognition and second language instruction*. Cambridge: Cambridge University Press, pp. 206–57.

Doughty, C. J. (2003). Instructed SLA: Constraints, compensation, and enhancement. In C. J. Doughty and M. H. Long, eds. *Handbook of second language acquisition*. New York: Basil Blackwell, pp. 256–310.

Doughty, C. J. and Williams, J. (1998), eds. *Focus on form in second language acquisition*. Cambridge: Cambridge University Press,

Ellis, R., Loewen, S., and Erlam, R. (2006). Implicit and explicit corrective feedback and the acquisition of L2 grammar. *Studies in Second Language Acquisition*, 28(2), 339–68.

Goldschneider, J. M. and DeKeyser, R. (2001). Explaining the 'natural order of L2 morpheme acquisition' in English: A meta-analysis of multiple determinants. *Language Learning*, 51, 1–50.

Goo, J. (2012). Corrective feedback and working memory capacity in interaction-driven L2 learning. *Studies in Second Language Acquisition*, 34(3), 445–74.

Goo, J., Granena, G., Yilmaz, Y., and Novella, M. (2015). Implicit and explicit instruction in L2 learning: Norris & Ortega (2000) revisited and updated.

In P. Rebuschat, ed. *Implicit and explicit learning of languages*. Amsterdam: John Benjamins, pp. 443–83.

Goo, J., and Mackey, A. (2013). The case against the case against recasts. *Studies in Second Language Acquisition*, 35(1), 127–65.

Granena, G. (2013a). Individual differences in sequence learning ability and second language acquisition in early childhood and adulthood. *Language Learning*, 63(4), 665–703.

Granena, G. (2013b). Cognitive aptitudes for second language learning and the LLAMA Language Aptitude Test. In G. Granena and M. H. Long, eds. *Sensitive periods, language aptitude, and ultimate L2 attainment*. Amsterdam: John Benjamins, pp. 105–29.

Granena, G. and Long, M. H. (2013). Age of onset, length of residence, aptitude and ultimate L2 attainment in three linguistic domains. *Second Language Research*, 29(3), 311–43.

Granena, G. and Yilmaz, Y. (2018). Aptitude-treatment interaction in L2 learning: A research synthesis. *Studies in English Education*, 4, 803–30.

Henderson, C. (2021). The effect of feedback timing on L2 Spanish vocabulary acquisition in synchronous computer-mediated communication. *Language Teaching Research*, 25(2), 185–208.

Hyltenstam, K. and Abrahamsson, N. (2003). Maturational constraints in SLA. In C. J. Doughty and M. H. Long, eds. *The handbook of second language acquisition*. Oxford: Blackwell, pp. 539–88.

Iwasaki, J. and Oliver, R. (2003). Chat-line interaction and negative feedback. *Australian Review of Applied Linguistics*, 17, 60–73.

Laufer, B. (2006). Comparing focus on form and focus on forms in second-language vocabulary learning. *Canadian Modern Language Review*, 63, 149–66.

Li, S. (2010). The effectiveness of corrective feedback in SLA: A meta-analysis. *Language Learning*, 60, 309–65.

Loewen, S. and Nabei, T. (2007). Measuring the effects of oral corrective feedback on L2 knowledge. In A. Mackey, ed. *Conversational interaction in second language acquisition*. Oxford: Oxford University Press, pp. 361–77.

Loewen, S. and Philp, J. (2006). Recasts in the adult L2 classroom: Characteristics, explicitness and effectiveness. *The Modern Language Journal*, 90, 536–56.

Long, M. H. (1981). Input, interaction and second language acquisition. *Annals of the New York Academy of Sciences*, 379, 259–78.

Long, M. H. (1983). Native speaker/non-native speaker conversation and the negotiation of comprehensible input. *Applied Linguistics*, 4, 126–41.

Long, M. H. (1985). Input and second language acquisition theory. In S. Gass and C. Madden, eds. *Input in second language acquisition*. Rowley: Newbury House, pp. 377–93.

Long, M. H. (1991). Focus on form: A design feature in language teaching methodology. In K. de Bot, R. B. Ginsberg, and C. Kramsch, eds. *Foreign language research in cross-cultural perspective*. Amsterdam: John Benjamins, pp. 39–52.

Long, M. H. (1996). The role of the linguistic environment in second language acquisition. In W. Ritchie and T. K. Bhatia, eds. *Handbook of second language acquisition*. New York: Academic Press, pp. 413–68.

Long, M. H. (2000). Focus on form in task-based language teaching. In R. L. Lambert and E. Shohamy, eds. *Language policy and pedagogy*. Philadelphia: John Benjamins, pp. 179–92.

Long, M. H. (2007). *Problems in SLA*. Mahwah, NJ: Lawrence Erlbaum.

Long, M. H. (2009). Methodological principles in language teaching. In M. H. Long and C. J. Doughty, eds. *Handbook of language teaching*. Oxford: Blackwell, pp. 373–94.

Long, M. H. (2015). *Second language acquisition and task-based language teaching*. New York: Wiley.

Long, M. H. and Robinson, P. (1998). Focus on form: Theory, research and practice. In C. J. Doughty and J. Williams, eds. *Focus on form in second language acquisition*. Cambridge: Cambridge University Press, pp. 15–41.

Long, M. H., Lee, J., and Hillman, K. K. (2019). Task-based language learning. In. J. W. Schwieter and A. Benati, eds. *The Cambridge handbook of language learning*. Cambridge: Cambridge University Press, pp. 500–26.

Lyster, R. (2004). Differential effects of prompts and recasts in form-focused instruction. *Studies in Second Language Acquisition*, 26, 399–432.

Lyster, R. and Izquierdo, J. (2009). Prompts versus recasts in dyadic interaction. *Language Learning*, 59, 453–98.

Lyster, R. and Ranta, L. (1997). Corrective feedback and learner uptake. *Studies in Second Language Acquisition*, 19, 37–66.

Lyster, R. and Saito, K. (2010). Oral feedback in classroom SLA: A meta-analysis. *Studies in Second Language Acquisition*, 32, 265–302.

Mackey, A. and Goo, J. (2007). Interaction research in SLA: A meta-analysis and research synthesis. In A. Mackey, ed. *Conversational interaction in SLA: A collection of empirical studies*. Oxford: Oxford University Press, pp. 408–52.

Meisel, J. M. (2011). Bilingual language acquisition and theories of diachronic change: Bilingualism as cause and effect of grammatical change. *Bilingualism: Language and Cognition*, 14, 121–45.

Norris, J. M. and Ortega, L. (2000). Effectiveness of instruction: A research synthesis and quantitative meta-analysis. *Language Learning*, 50, 417–528.

Ortega, L. and Long, M. H. (1997). The effects of models and recasts on object topicalization and adverb placement in L2 Spanish. *Spanish Applied Linguistics*, 1, 65–86.

Pica, T. (2005). Classroom learning, teaching, and research: A task-based perspective. *The Modern Language Journal*, 89(3), 339–52.

Pinker, S. (1989). *Learnability and cognition*. Cambridge, MA: Massachusetts Institute of Technology Press.

Ranta, L. and Lyster, R. (2007). A cognitive approach to improving immersion students' oral language abilities: The awareness-practice-feedback sequence. In R. DeKeyser, ed. *Practice in a second language: Perspectives from applied linguistics and cognitive psychology*. New York: Cambridge University Press, pp. 141–60.

Rassei, E. (2015). Oral corrective feedback, language anxiety and L2 development. *System*, 49, 98–109.

Reber, A. S. and Allen, R. (2000). Individual differences in implicit learning: Implications for the evolution of consciousness. In R. G. Kunzendorf and B. Wallace, eds, *Individual differences in conscious experience*. Amsterdam: Benjamins, pp. 227–47.

Rebuschat, P. (2008). *Implicit learning of natural language syntax*. Unpublished PhD Dissertation. University of Cambridge, UK.

Rebuschat, P. and Williams, J. N. (2006). Dissociating implicit and explicit learning of natural language syntax. Paper presented at the Conference of the Cognitive Science Society.

Rebuschat, P. and Williams, J. (2009). Implicit learning of word order. In N. A. Taatgen and H. van Rijn, eds. *Proceedings of the Annual Meeting of the Cognitive Science Society*, 31, 425–430

Révész, A. (2009). Task complexity, focus on form, and second language development. *Studies in Second Language Acquisition*, 31, 437–70.

Révész, A. and Han, Z. (2006). Task content familiarity, task type, and efficacy of recasts. *Language Awareness*, 15, 160–79.

Robinson, P. (2003). Attention and memory during SLA. In C. J. Doughty and M. H. Long, eds. *Handbook of second language acquisition*. Oxford: Blackwell, pp. 630–78.

Russell, J. and Spada, N. (2006). The effectiveness of corrective feedback for the acquisition of L2 grammar. In J. D. Norris and L. Ortega, eds. *Synthesizing research on language learning and teaching*. Philadelphia: John Benjamins, pp. 133–64.

Schmidt, R. W. (1990). The role of consciousness in second language learning. *Applied Linguistics*, 11, pp. 129–58.

Sheen, Y., (2004). Corrective feedback and learners' uptake in communicative classrooms across instructional settings. *Language Teaching Research*, 8, 263–300.

Sheen, Y. (2006). Exploring the relationship between characteristics of recasts and learner uptake. *Language Teaching Research*, 10, 361–92.

Sheen, Y. (2007). The effects of corrective feedback, language aptitude, and learner attitudes on the acquisition of English articles. In A. Mackey, ed. *Conversational interaction in second language acquisition*. Oxford: Oxford University Press, pp. 301–22.

Sheen, Y. (2007). The effects of corrective feedback, language aptitude, and learner attitudes on the acquisition of English articles. In A. Mackey, ed. *Conversational interaction in second language acquisition*. Oxford: Oxford University Press, pp. 301–22.

Shintani, N. (2013). The effect of focus on form and focus on forms instruction on the acquisition of productive knowledge of L2 vocabulary by young beginning-level learners. *TESOL Quarterly*, 47, 16–62.

Shintani, N. (2015). The incidental grammar acquisition in focus on form and focus on forms instruction for young beginner learners. *TESOL Quarterly*, 49, 115–40.

Swain, M. and Lapkin, S. (1991). Additive bilingualism and French immersion education: The roles of language proficiency and literacy. In A. G. Reynolds, ed. *Bilingualism, multiculturalism, and second language learning: The McGill conference in honour of Wallace E. Lambert*. Hillsdale, NJ: Erlbaum, pp. 203–16.

Trofimovich, P., Ammar, A., and Gatbonton, E. (2007). How effective are recasts? The role of attention, memory, and analytical ability. In A. Mackey, ed. *Conversational interaction in second language acquisition*. Oxford: Oxford University Press, pp. 144–71.

White, L. (1991). Adverb placement in second language acquisition: Some positive and negative evidence in the classroom. *Second Language Research*, 7, 133–61.

Wilkins, D. A. (1976). *Notional syllabuses*. Oxford: Oxford University Press.

Williams, J. (1999). Memory, attention, and inductive learning. *Studies in Second Language Acquisition*, 21, 1–48.

Williams, J. N. (2005). Learning without awareness. *Studies in Second Language Acquisition*, 27, 269–304.

Yilmaz, Y. (2012). The relative effects of explicit correction and recasts on two target structures via two communication modes. *Language Learning*, 62, 1134–69.

Yilmaz, Y. (2013). The relative effectiveness of mixed, explicit and implicit feedback. *System*, 41, 691–705.

Yilmaz, Y. (2016a). The effectiveness of explicit correction under two different feedback exposure conditions. *Studies in Second Language Acquisition*, 38, 65–96.

Yilmaz, Y. (2016b). The linguistic environment, interaction and negative feedback. *Brill Research Perspectives in Multilingualism and Second Language Acquisition*, 1, 45–86.

Yilmaz, Y. and Granena, G. (2016). The role of cognitive aptitudes for explicit language learning in the relative effects of explicit and implicit feedback. *Bilingualism: Language and Cognition*, 19, 147–61.

Yilmaz, Y. and Koylu, Y. (2016). The interaction between feedback exposure condition and phonetic coding ability. In G. Granena, D. O. Jackson, and Y. Yilmaz, eds. *Cognitive individual differences in second language processing and acquisition*. Amsterdam: John Benjamins, pp. 303–26.

Yilmaz, Y. and Sagdic, A. (2019). The interaction between inhibitory control and corrective feedback timing. *International Journal of Applied Linguistics*, 170, 204–27.

10
Technology-Mediated Task-Based Language Teaching

Marta González-Lloret and Nicole Ziegler

10.1 Introduction

The use of technology has grown exponentially during the last few decades, with technology having been increasingly incorporated into the second language (L2) learning classroom and curriculum (see Grgurovic, Chapelle & Shelley [2013] for a meta-analysis). Today's world includes the almost seamless integration of technology into nearly all aspects of our lives, with many learners having come of age using mobile phone applications, text messaging, social media, gaming, and augmented and virtual reality for everyday tasks. Thorne and Payne (2005) point out how the ubiquitous use of technology for everyday cognitive activity is likely to affect learners' development through childhood and well into adulthood, as these evolving patterns of technology in daily use have undoubtedly influenced how learners view and interact with learning environments. Considering that many of the technologies in use today have become a nearly universal aspect of our lives, it is necessary to consider how the tasks these technologies facilitate, as well as their mediating effects on L2 learning and teaching, have evolved because of them.

10.2 Tools That Connect Us with Others

As Wang and Vásquez (2012) point out, Web 2.0 technologies exploit the collaborative and participatory potential of the web, highlighting their potential to be used as a context for interaction-supported language learning. These include tools that allow us to connect to other speakers of the language synchronously (text-based, audio-based and video computer-mediated communication tools (such as Skype, Google Hangouts,

Facetime, Line, etc.) via desktop or mobile tools. These tools may also be used asynchronously (YouTube, blogs, groups, fandoms, email, Twitter, etc.), or using a combination of both synchronous and asynchronous capabilities (social networks, WhatsApp, etc.). These technologies offer learners' opportunities for increased student interaction, including negotiation and feedback provision, as well as opportunities to produce output in the target language (Peterson, 2006). Web 2.0 technologies offer researchers fertile grounds for examining interaction and L2 development, particularly regarding collaborative and community-based learning, and since many of these tools are already an indispensable aspect of many learners' daily lives, educators may find students more receptive or enthusiastic about L2 instruction situated within these contexts.

The main advantage of these technologies is that they allow students to engage in authentic, rich interaction with other speakers of the language. This is especially important in places where there may be a lack of access to speakers of the target language, such as in foreign-language-learning environments, where learners may only have the opportunity to interact with speakers of the target language within their classroom. In addition, social, economic, political, or other societal barriers may hinder available opportunities for face-to-face interaction with other speakers of the target language. Opportunities for interaction are not only beneficial for L2 linguistic and communicative growth, but also for pragmatic development, as interaction allows learners to engage in sociopragmatic practices that are essential for the development of communicative competence (González-Lloret, 2019a), and that may otherwise be absent from traditional language-learning classrooms (e.g., flirting, disagreeing or going off topic). In addition, connecting to other learners, as well as native speakers, through social networks, fandoms, and other organized groups, may support learners' development of a sense of community, an important component of language learning, as well as provide them with power to take ownership of their learning, which, in turn, promotes language development (Duff, 2012). Furthermore, learners' engagement in these interactions and communities promotes digital literacies (Thorne & Black, 2008) and identity formation, resulting in increased motivation for language learning (Black, 2005).

10.3 Everyday Tasks in the Second Language

Many learners, especially adults, already connect to the Internet to conduct a variety of tasks, including buying goods and materials, such as books, clothing, and gadgets; banking; reading customer reviews of a restaurant, hotel, travel agency, contractor, or even a teacher; navigating with an online map; and checking the weather. This is clearly not an exhaustive list, as the Internet has nearly limitless applications in terms of serving as a source of authentic tasks that can be performed in the L2. These Internet-based tasks have the potential to be more representative and potentially more relevant for learners than the tasks found in more traditional language textbooks. By drawing on technology-mediated resources, educators have the ability to create tasks that promote learning by doing, are learner-centered, provide real input and the possibility of producing more relevant output for a real audience outside the walls of the classroom (Doughty, this volume). The accompanying case study by Nielson illustrates how a course can incorporate real-world, relevant content and engage students in their own search for authentic real-world tasks.

For example, rather than asking a learner to write a book report for a language-learning class, a scenario in which the teacher is the intended audience, learners have the opportunity to explore what other readers of the same book have posted online, as well as study the structure and content of online book reviews, thus enhancing their knowledge of the genre and conventions. This also offers learners the opportunity to write their own review for the benefit of other readers, thus providing learners with an authentic, real-world audience beyond the physical boundaries of their classroom. The production of such a book review would be the combined result of sequenced pedagogic tasks, as well as numerous opportunities for focus on form, receiving and responding to feedback, and experiencing the revision process, ultimately resulting in an authentic learning outcome that learners are proud to share.

In a similar way, learners of varying levels of proficiency might engage with restaurant reviews (or hotel, tourist attraction, or movie reviews, etc.). Beginner learners can engage in reading the reviews of known restaurants and agree or disagree with the comments, provide stars, and become familiar with the vocabulary associated with restaurants. Intermediate learners might extend beyond a receptive approach to visiting restaurants in their city to write their own reviews, while advanced students can engage with other patrons and the comments they have left.

Navigating a city is a task that can greatly benefit from being more authentic and technology-mediated. Beginner students can find their way from point A to point B through the Google street 3D map. Intermediate learners can help someone find a certain business, identify and describe historical landmarks in the L2, while advanced learners can create (and record) a full tour of a city with Google Earth, including historical information, activities, places to eat, etc. These technology-mediated adaptations provide opportunities for real-world tasks, highlighting the potential developmental and performance benefits offered by the use of technology in task-based contexts. See Doughty (this volume) for the idea that learners of different proficiency level can engage with the same materials.

10.4 Spaces for Learning by Doing

In order to approximate real-world interactions, teachers have often used variations on role-play tasks. The available advantages of technology have the ability to substantially enhance how students might experience these situations. Synthetic and virtual environments, which have been identified as fertile contexts for "immersion in linguistic, cultural, and task-based settings," (Thorne, 2008: 316), provide opportunities for learners to engage in social action, perform a multitude of tasks, or pursue quests with others (in gaming). Examples of synthetic immersive environments – defined as engineered digital spaces that draw on goal-directed, collaborative gameplay "to produce explicit, educationally related outcomes in simulated, relevant interactional contexts" (Sykes, 2008: 10–11) – that incorporate tasks are:

- Julie Syke's *Croquelandia* (Sykes, 2008, 2014), where students take the role of a new college student and need to perform several tasks (requiring learners to apologize and refuse in Spanish)
- Karina Collentine's 3D island (Collentine, 2011), in which learners of Spanish had to investigate a missing persons case and solve a murder
- McGraw Hill's game accompanying their beginner Spanish Program, which places the learner in a study abroad context in Colombia (González-Lloret & Diez-Ortega, 2020)
- Jauregui and colleagues' Second Life tasks, such as renting an apartment between a student of Spanish in the Netherlands and a student in Spain (Cantó, Jauregui & De Graff, 2014).

Findings from these studies demonstrated the potential of these types of tasks for supporting negotiation and interaction, as well as increasing learners' awareness of cultural similarities and differences, highlighting the need for further research on the positive benefits of the application of task-based frameworks in synthetic immersive environments. The convergence of a social context and tasks increases learners' participation, and the consistent use of interactional strategies encourages them to stay motivated and maintain task engagement (Yeh & Wan, 2019).

Games have also been explored for their potential to facilitate interactive, experiential learning, especially multiplayer multimedia online role-playing games (MMORPGs). Games are tightly connected to the concept of tasks since, in most games, players have to accomplish a number of tasks (usually called quests) in order to advance in the game. These tasks often have all the characteristics of task-based language teaching (TBLT) tasks: they are goal-oriented, focused on meaning, require input, output and interaction, and they include feedback and are sequenced based on gaming principles of complexity, such as narrative progressive design, quest levels, feedback mechanisms, share versus divergent goals, etc.

(Reinhardt, 2019). In collaborative games, players communicate through voice and chat, and interact with game-generated text in conjunction with the visual spaces of the game. Rules and actions of play are often presented as integrated experiences, contextualizing authentic and meaningful language use, with feedback systems designed to provide targeted and scaffolded feedback (Reinhardt, 2019). Language and interaction are essential components for the success of the tasks or quests, and it is in these spaces of communication when language learning can happen. For more on games for language learning, see Cornillie, Thorne, and Desmet (2012) and Reinhardt (2019).

Other technologies that allow learners to immerse themselves in the language and learn by doing are virtual and augmented realities. Augmented reality (AR) uses printed images or text (called markers) to initiate an interaction through a mobile device, like a phone or a tablet. Virtual reality (VR) uses digital data that are "layered" over the location where the user is, allowing us to view and interact with objects. Both VR and AR have become more accessible in the field of education, in part probably because of the aggressive marketing campaigns of HoloLens and Samsung Gear VR, and the popularity of Pokemon Go. Now it is possible to learn to pilot a plane in the L2, visit far away cultural sites, or perform virtual surgery in the L2. Building on research investigating three-dimensional virtual environments, AR and VR have been highlighted for their ability to reduce distractions, potentially helping students engage more deeply with the material (Gadelha, 2018), help support students' connections between the subject matter and their own lives (Bonner & Reinders, 2018), as well as make connections between target concepts and their effects on the world (Meyer, 2016). In addition, AR draws on mobile technologies and its associated qualities, including portability (Lai, 2017), social interactivity (Reinders & Pegrum, 2017), connectivity and access (Schwienhorst, 2012), and autonomy and individuality (Benson, 2011).

For more on tasks and simulations, the accompanying case study by Catherine Doughty presents the Innovation Lab at the US Foreign Service Institute. She describes six tasks that the learners there perform (suspicious activity, inspecting a venue, check and control of visitors, crowd control, VIP protection, and motorcade security) using a 360 environment where Google Maps, Google Earth, and YouTube videos of events (e.g., riots) are projected.

10.5 Research on Technology-Mediated Tasks

As mentioned above, much of the research on technology-mediated tasks has thus far focused on computer-mediated communication (CMC) and whether this technology is effective for language learning (see Ziegler, 2016a, for a review of the effects of CMC on L2 learning outcomes). Within this line of research, findings suggest that CMC tasks support noticing. For example, research suggests that learners interacting in CMC text-chat reported noticing their errors more often than those in face-to-face (FTF) environments (Payne & Whitney, 2002). Findings also indicate that interaction in text-chat improved learners' noticing of feedback (Gurzynski-Weiss & Baralt, 2015; Lai, Fei, & Roots, 2008; Smith, 2012), attention to form (Smith & Gorsuch, 2004), and perceived salience of target forms (Ziegler, 2017). More recently, Yuksel and Inan (2014) found that learners in synchronous CMC environments noticed negotiation of meaning more than learners in FTF contexts, highlighting the positive benefits of technology for supporting noticing and the associated learning and development opportunities. Research also demonstrates that interactional features found to be beneficial in FTF, such as negotiation for meaning, modified output, and corrective feedback, can and do occur in technology-mediated contexts (e.g., Shekary & Tahririan, 2006; Ziegler & Phung, 2019), although these interactional behaviors may not always produce learning (Ortega, 2009). In addition, CMC has been shown to support the development of learner agency (i.e., control over their learning) (e.g., Sauro, 2004), as well as learners' engagement with a large variety of speech acts and discourse functions (e.g.,González-Lloret, 2019b). Finally, research has shown that CMC leads to grammatical, lexical, and modest speaking gains (Payne & Whitney, 2002; Satar & Özdener, 2008; Lin, 2014; Plonsky & Ziegler, 2016).

Within CMC, research examining social networks and writing spaces has continued to grow. These technologies allow for collaborative production (wikis, Google docs and blogs), which fosters greater creativity and content (Oskoz & Elola, 2014), as well as provides opportunities for language interaction and focus on form (Kost, 2011;). In these collaborative spaces, L2 learners increase their production (Lee, 2012) and develop more complex language and improved grammatical accuracy over time (Sauro 2014). Positive benefits have also been found for learners' intercultural competence and L2 literacy (Elola & Oskoz, 2010).

Finally, there is a growing body of research exploring the use of games as tools for language learning (Reinhardt, 2019; Sykes & Reinhardt, 2012). Games have long been considered rich environments, or "affinity spaces," as Gee (2005) termed them, for language learning, with the potential to support literacy, scientific reasoning, problem-solving skills, and leadership through the sharing of knowledge and collaboration.

L2 research on gaming suggests that multiplayer games promote learning by doing, consistently expose learners to rich textual and spoken input, and promote interaction and collaboration through extensive negotiation and repair sequences, all methodological principles of TBLT (Doughty & Long, 2003). These interactional features serve as resources for learners to maintain intersubjectivity (i.e., share understandings of the game) and develop positive, affective bonds with other players, possibly leading to a strong motivation to learn the language (e.g., Reinders & Wattana, 2012). Analysis of interactions from gaming indicate high degrees of lexical sophistication, lexical diversity, and syntactic complexity (Thorne et al., 2012), suggesting that task-based interaction in gaming contexts supports both affective as well as L2 learning outcomes such as listening, reading, and writing skills.

In addition to playing, gamers may increase their language-learning opportunities through resources outside of the game, such as related blogs and forums, and by engaging in communities of gamers. Importantly, these additional resources beyond playing the game offer learners a multiplicity of L2 input and output opportunities, supporting learners' development of reading and writing skills, and enticing learners to engage in L2 practices outside of school time (Sylvén & Sundqvist, 2012). Indeed, research by Scholz & Shulze (2017) has shown that the language used in games does actually transfer to non-game contexts, underscoring the linguistic and sociopragmatic benefits of gaming. Scenario-based games, place-based games, and simulation games have also been explored within a task-based framework, with results suggesting interesting and positive benefits. For example, Taguchi, Li, and Tang (2017) developed a scenario-based game called *Questaurant*, where the learner takes on the role of a robot that needs to perform several tasks (e.g., buying apples, withdrawing money from a bank, eating in a restaurant, making a phone call) in a Chinese-speaking community. The game targeted the learning of Chinese formulaic expressions within contextualized language practices while providing authentic language input. Results demonstrate improved learner performance in terms of formulaic expressions (as measured by pre-, post-, and delayed tests), although the receptive skills maintained through the delayed posttest and the productive skills decreased slightly over time. Although learners' perceptions indicated that they found the game helpful for learning, the authors caution that just because a game is designed with gaming and second language acquisition principles, learners may not take advantage of the language-learning opportunities available to them. Nonetheless, this research highlights how gaming has positive effects for L2 development and performance, as well as affective, social, and cultural factors.

10.6 Task Design and Learner Performance

Although most research examining how variations in task design and implementation, including complexity and planning, have been conducted in FTF contexts, a number of studies have focused on task design within CMC. For example, Blake (2008) explored how the quality of learner interaction was influenced by task design, conditions, and processes. Several other authors have explored traditional tasks, such as jigsaws, information-gap or decision-making tasks. The results of these studies remain inconclusive and even contradictory. Some researchers found jigsaw tasks to produce more negotiation (Jeong, 2011), while others have found decision-making tasks producing more negotiation (Smith, 2003) or no effect for task type (Keller-Lally, 2006). Yilmaz and Granena (2010) and Yilmaz (2011) found jigsaw tasks to elicit fewer negotiation routines than dictogloss, while jigsaw tasks had more unresolved negotiations. Granena (2016) also found that interactive information-gap tasks in voice CMC were more effective for the learning of English modals, past tense verbs, and connectors than individual ones. Given the range of results, it is difficult at this point to draw firm conclusions regarding the role of task design features in technology-mediated environments, highlighting the need for further research in these areas.

Research on the effects of pre-task planning in CMC has also yielded mixed results (Adams et al., 2014; Hsu, 2015; Ziegler, 2016b). For example, findings suggest that pre-task planning may support learners' noticing of recasts, potentially increasing opportunities for subsequent development (Lai et al., 2008), as well as benefit learners' L2 development. Hsu (2015) found immediate positive effects for complexity and delayed positive effects for complexity and accuracy across pre-task rehearsal and within-task planning conditions. However, earlier research (Hsu, 2012) found no significant differences across measures of complexity, accuracy, or fluency between learners in pre-task planning and no planning conditions. More recently, Ziegler (2018) explored differential amounts of pre-task planning time, with results indicating that three minutes of planning time resulted in greater lexical complexity when compared to no pre-task planning time or one minute of pre-task planning time. No differences were found for other measures of complexity, accuracy, or fluency. Overall, these studies demonstrate mixed results in terms of the benefits of pre-task planning, highlighting the need for further research, particularly in multimedia and oral chat, as well as text-chat conditions.

Another growing area of research is focused on understanding the effects of task complexity on L2 development in technology-mediated contexts, with a primary focus on text-based CMC (Adams & Nik, 2014; Baralt, 2014; Collentine, 2010; Nik, Adams & Newton, 2012). Much of the research on task complexity is situated within the framework of Robinson's Cognition Hypothesis (2011), whose central claim is that cognitive complexity should serve as the determining factor for the sequencing of simple and complex tasks. However, research indicates that the predictions of the role of task complexity and task sequencing may not manifest in technology-mediated contexts in the same way as in traditional FTF task-based environments. For example, the results of Nik et al. (2012) demonstrated that increasing task complexity reduced learners' interactional modification during CMC tasks, while Adams and Nik (2014) found that learners' lexical complexity and overall accuracy improved with increasing task complexity, while decreasing task complexity led to greater production. More recently, Adams, Nik, and Newton (2015) found that task complexity mediated learners' accuracy, but not the complexity of their production. Adams and Nik (2014) suggest that these results, which are contrary to the predictions of the Cognition Hypothesis, may be due to the unique characteristics of text-based CMC, in which there are more opportunities for learners to process output when compared to FTF oral interaction. The availability of additional time for planning and processing in technology-mediated tasks offers learners increased opportunities to monitor production before transmission, potentially canceling out any differences between simple and complex tasks in terms of performance, particularly complexity and accuracy (Adams & Nik, 2014). In addition, learners' cognitive load may be affected by the noncontingency of feedback episodes, as well as the amount of time between learners' initial production and the eventual transmission of the message.

This explanation seems to be supported by Baralt's (2013) study comparing reasoning demands (as a task complexity variable) in a traditional face-to-face and a CMC environment. Her results show that increased cognitive complexity in the FTF condition resulted in increased L2 development, while simple tasks in the CMC environment led to improved performance and production. These results are similar to Nik's (2010), in which simple tasks in CMC led to improved L2 accuracy, or Baralt's (2014), whose findings indicated no positive effects for complexity in the technology-mediated environment. Taken together, these results suggest that cognitive complexity may not support L2 development and performance in CMC in the same manner that they appear to do so in FTF contexts, indicating that the nature of computer-mediated learning environments seems to mediate the complexity variables and theoretical predictions of well-known frameworks (such as the Cognition Hypothesis and the Tradeoff Hypothesis) in unique ways.

As previous research has suggested (e.g., Lai & Li, 2011), task-based researchers may wish to consider the use of technology as a unique task design feature that may impact the cognitive complexity of the task simply through its implementation in a technology-mediated environment. González-Lloret and Ortega (2014) suggest that learners' digital literacies and technological familiarity are competencies unique to the context of CMC, and that these competencies may mediate how learners interact and engage with their interlocutors and the tasks themselves, highlighting the need for researchers to consider how the modality of the interaction may influence, facilitate, or constrain learners' performance and production. Overall, more research examining task design and task implementation in CMC are needed to deepen our understanding of the complexity of technology-mediated tasks.

10.7 Challenges of Technology-Mediated Task-Based Language Teaching

As research in technology-mediated environments continues to expand, it remains necessary for scholars and educators to design tasks and applications grounded in sound, empirically supported principles of second language acquisition, such as those forming the foundation of TBLT. As suggested by the studies on task complexity in CMC, two of the main challenges for incorporating technology into a task-based approach are that 1) existing frameworks may not work, which should reflect on a revision of such frameworks, and 2) the technology will modify a task and bring added layers to it. Findings suggest, as illustrated before, that the predictions of the Cognition Hypothesis, one of the most well-researched topics in FTF task-based research, are not borne out in the same ways in technology-mediated environments (e.g., Adams et al., 2015; Baralt, 2014) These similarities and differences across task design and implementation between traditional and computer-mediated contexts underscores the need for the reformulation and reapplication of framework developments for traditional oral or written task-based interaction for new and emerging technology-mediated contexts. Additional research investigating the role of modality in changing the predictions and outcomes of specific task-based frameworks is needed to help provide researchers with a better understanding of TBLT in contexts beyond the walls of the traditional language-learning classroom. These findings highlight the need for further investigation into how the use of technology mediates and modifies the nature of the task, and its subsequent possibilities for language learning, development, and performance.

Another important challenge for educators and researchers to consider is the rapid rate of innovation and change in terms of the tools available for technology-mediated TBLT. Because types of technology emerge and change relatively quickly, predicting what tools learners will need, as well as how they might use them, in the future is pure speculation. For this reason, it is essential to focus research on the uses of a tool, environment, or activity that promotes language learning (rather than the tool itself). Thus, when technology inevitably evolves and changes, it is possible to revisit whether these essential components are still intact and if TBLT principles still apply.

Finally, as technology becomes more present and permanent in the L2 curriculum, it is essential to provide educators with training for bringing TBLT to life in the classroom. This training should include supporting their digital literacies and education. As Winke (2013) points out, optimal institutional conditions, teacher training, and the support needed to include technology in their language classes are essential components for the successful incorporation of technology into the L2 classroom.

10.8 Future of the Field

Although much of the research on the efficacy of technology-mediated tasks has been conducted on written text-chat, with fewer studies examining multimodal or immersive environments, these areas of research continue to grow. These new and emerging technologies also expand the scope of contexts in which researchers and educators might broaden our understanding of how best to support and facilitate L2 learning (Wang & Vásquez, 2012). For example, mobile-assisted language learning (MALL), in which mobile devices are used for language learning, offers learners opportunities to further their development "in virtual spaces and out in the world" (Kukulska-Hulme, 2013: 2; Nielson, 2013). The centering of learners, the use of real-world contexts, and the opportunities for authentic communicative interaction make mobile learning an environment well-suited to task-based learning. In addition, the portability, connectivity, and ability of mobile devices to record and facilitate language use is well-matched to the flexibility needed for language learning beyond the classroom (Kukulska-Hulme, Lee & Norris, 2017), as mobile devices provide interactional opportunities, such as sharing information, collaborative problem solving, and authentic task completion (Lai & Zheng, 2018). Mobile learning also allows for "just in time" training for learners accessing materials in the workplace, as they are able to draw on learning opportunities and immediately apply what they learn to authentic language situations, potentially supporting high-level learning (Alley et al., 2014). Dyson's (2014) IT Careers Vodcast Project not only supported learners' improved knowledge of future careers in their field, but also learners' development of multimedia communication skills. Analysis of learners' diaries and reflections indicated task repetition, team interaction, and collaborative learning played an important role in supporting positive student outcomes. Lai and Zheng (2018) found promising trends for learners' use of social networking sites and text-chat through instant message apps, as well as positive perceptions of out-of-class learning with mobile devices. Learners indicated they perceived mobile learning as a way to enhance their interaction with other interlocutors in the target language, as well as deepen connections with peer learners and the target language community, highlighting the need for further research exploring how learners' use of mobile devices may support linguistic and sociocultural development. As Kukulska-Hulme et al. (2017) point out, mobile learning is particularly well suited to authentic, real-world tasks, highlighting the potential for investigations of this dynamic and emerging environment.

Although little research to date has examined the use of AR and VR for task-based language learning, a number of exploratory studies underscore the potential benefits of these tools for language teaching and learning (e.g., Sydorenko, Hellerman, Throne & Howe, 2019). Augmented reality is also a primary pillar for place-based games, such as Holden and Sykes' (2012) *Mentira*. *Mentira,* one of the first place-based games for language learning, set in a Spanish-speaking neighborhood in Albuquerque, New Mexico. Learners must discover information and solve quests through interactions with the game, as well as the real-world environment. Findings demonstrate that learners' motivation was positively affected by engaging in this out-of-class, real-world interaction.

Future research should consider the growing use of certain technologies, including mobile and gaming technology, as well as AR and VR, as these areas are still relatively underexplored in terms of task-based research. In addition, continued research exploring the use of new technologies in a task-based framework is needed, as this will help provide us with an improved understanding of TBLT. For example, by drawing on the methodological advantages of certain technologies, researchers may be able to enhance our knowledge surrounding critical constructs in second language acquisition, such as negotiation and noticing, as well as how technology mediates task design and implementation in terms of complexity, sequencing, repetition, and planning.

Van den Branden, Bygate, and Norris (2009:495) state that changes in education are often "responses to new technologies," and we believe that this is true for TBLT. A view in which language, culture, and pragmatic norms are a fundamental and inseparable part of communication, and, therefore, of language learning (González-Lloret, 2019a: 240), where TBLT "gives priority to activities with the goal of doing something with a language, communicating meaning with a clear objective, in an environment authentic for the learners and their context, all according to their needs." Technology-mediated TBLT offers an ideal framework in which technology and tasks provide great potential for a mutually beneficial relationship, dynamic and flexible enough to adapt to the changing needs and trends of language learning in a more globalized world. As the opportunities for L2 learning and development evolve beyond the physical constraints of a traditional classroom, with the continued integration and implementation of both classic and emerging technologies, it is necessary for our understanding of tasks, and the frameworks used to examine them, to evolve, as well.

Further Reading

Ahmadian, M. J. and García Mayo, M. del P. (2018), eds. *Recent perspectives on task-based language learning and teaching.* Boston/Berlin: De Gruyter Mouton.

Doughty, C. and Long, M. H. (2003). Optimal psycholinguistic environments for distance foreign language learning. *Language Learning and Technology*, 7, 50–80.

González-Lloret, M. (2016). *A practical guide to integrating technology into task-based language teaching*. Washington DC: Georgetown University Press.

González-Lloret, M. and Ortega, L. (2014), eds. *Technology-mediated TBLT: Researching technology and tasks*. Amsterdam: John Benjamins.

Lai, C. and Li, G. (2011). Technology and task-based language teaching: A critical review. *CALICO Journal*, 28, 498–521.

Long, M. H. (2016). In defense of tasks and TBLT: Nonissues and real issues. *Annual Review of Applied Linguistics*, 36, 5–33.

Long, M. (2015). *Second language acquisition and task-based language teaching*. 1st ed. Malden, MA: Wiley-Blackwell.

Plonsky, L. and Ziegler, N. (2016). The CALL-SLA interface: Insights from a second-order synthesis. *Language Learning & Technology*, 20, 17–37.

Van den Branden, K., Bygate, M., and Norris, J. (2009), eds. *Task-based language teaching: A reader*. Amsterdam: John Benjamins.

Ziegler, N. (2016). Taking technology to task: Technology-mediated TBLT, performance, and production. *Annual Review of Applied Linguistics*, 36, 136–63.

Study Questions

1. How can technology be used to analyze learners' language and behavior, increasing the capacity for assessment beyond individual, more traditional testing methods?
2. What are some methodological advantages to using technology for TBLT research? Are there any disadvantages?
3. What are some possible developmental advantages or disadvantages?
4. What are some possible pedagogical advantages or disadvantages?
5. How do you think technology has changed the task of making a reservation at a hotel? Has technology created any new subtasks? Have any traditional steps in this task disappeared?

References

Adams, R. and Nik, A. N. M. A. (2014). Prior knowledge and second language task production in text chat. In M. González-Lloret and L. Ortega, eds. *Technology-mediated TBLT: researching technology and tasks*. Amsterdam: John Benjamins, pp. 51–78.

Adams, R., Amani, S., Newton, J., and Nik Mohd Alwi, N. A. (2014). Planning and production in computer-mediated communication (CMC) writing. In H. Byrnes and R. M. Manchón, eds. *Task-based language teaching*. Vol. 7. Amsterdam: John Benjamins, pp. 137–61.

Adams, R., Nik, A. N. A. M., and Newton, J. (2015). Task complexity effects on the complexity and accuracy of writing via chat. *Second Language Writing*, 29, 64–81.

Alley, M., Samaka, M., Impagliazzo, J., Mohamed, A., and Robinson, M. (2014). Workplace learning using mobile technology: A case study in the Oil and Gas industry. In Y. Bayyurt, M. Kalz, and M. Specht, eds. *Communications in computer and information science*. Vol. 479. Berlin: Springer, pp. 250–57.

Baralt, M. (2013). The impact of cognitive complexity on feedback efficacy during online versus face-to-face interactive tasks. *Studies in Second Language Acquisition*, 35, 689–725.

Baralt, M. (2014). Task complexity and task sequencing in traditional versus online language classes. In M. Baralt, R. Gilabert, and P. J. Robinson, eds. *Task sequencing and instructed second language learning*. London and New York: Bloomsbury Academic, pp. 59–122.

Benson, P. (2011). *Teaching and researching: Autonomy in language learning*. Harlow: Pearson Education Limited.

Black, R. W. (2005). Access and affiliation: The literacy and composition practices of English-language learners in an online fanfiction community. *Journal of Adolescent & Adult Literacy*, 49, 118–28.

Blake, R. (2008). *Brave new digital classroom: Technology and language learning*. Washington DC: Georgetown University Press.

Blyth, C. (2018). Immersive technologies and language learning. *Foreign Language Annals*, 51, 225–32.

Bonner, E. and Reinders, H. (2018). Augmented and virtual reality in the language classroom: Practical ideas. *Teaching English with Technology*, 18(3), 33–53.

Canto, S., de Graff, R., and Jauregui, K. (2014). Collaborative tasks for negotiation of intercultural meaning in virtual worlds and video-web communication. In M. González-Lloret and L. Ortega, eds. *Technology-mediated TBLT: researching technology and tasks*. Amsterdam: John Benjamins, pp. 183–212.

Collentine, K. (2010). Measuring complexity in task-based synchronous computer-mediated communication. In M. Thomas and H. Reinders, eds. *Task-based language learning and teaching with technology*. London and New York: Continuum, pp. 105–30.

Collentine, K. (2011). Learner autonomy in a task-based 3rd world and production. *Language Learning & Technology*, 15(3), 50–67.

Cornillie, F., Thorne, S. L., and Desmet, P. (2012). ReCALL special issue: Digital games for language learning: challenges and opportunities. *ReCALL*, 24, 243–56.

Doughty, C. and Long, M. H. (2003). Optimal psycholinguistic environments for distance foreign language learning. *Language Learning and Technology*, 7, 50–80.

Duff, P. A. (2012). Identity, agency, and second language acquisition. In S. M. Gass and A. Mackey, eds. *The Routledge handbook of second language acquisition*. New York: Routledge, pp. 410–26.

Dyson, L. E. (2014). A vodcast project in the workplace: understanding students' learning processes outside the classroom. In Y. Bayyurt, M. Kalz, and M. Specht eds. *Communications in computer and information science*. Vol. 479. Berlin: Springer, pp. 258–71.

Elola, I. and Oskoz, A. (2010). Collaborative writing: Fostering foreign language and writing conventions development. *Language Learning & Technology*, 14, 30–49.

Gadelha, R. (2018). Revolutionizing education: The promise of virtual reality. *Childhood Education*, 94(1), 40–43.

Gee, J. P. (2005). Semiotic social spaces and affinity spaces: from the Age of Mythology to today's schools. In D. Barton and K. Tusting, *Beyond communities of practice: language power and social context*. Cambridge: Cambridge University Press, pp. 214–32.

González-Lloret, M. (2014). The need for needs analysis in technology-mediated TBLT. In M. González-Lloret and L. Ortega, eds. *Technology-mediated TBLT: Researching technology and tasks*. Amsterdam: John Benjamins, pp. 23–50.

González-Lloret, M. (2019a). Task-Based Language Teaching and L2 Pragmatics. In N. Taguchi, ed., *Routledge handbook of SLA and pragmatics*. London: Routledge, pp. 338–52.

González-Lloret, M. (2019b). Technology and L2 pragmatics learning. *Annual Review of Applied Linguistics*, 39, 113–27.

González-Lloret, M. and Diez-Ortega, M. (2020). Gaming alone or together: L2 beginner-level gaming practices. *Perspectiva*, 38(2), 1–21.

González-Lloret, M. and Ortega, L. (2014). Towards technology-mediated TBLT: An introduction. In M. González-Lloret and L. Ortega, eds. *Technology-mediated TBLT: researching technology and tasks*. Amsterdam: John Benjamins, pp. 1–22.

Granena, G. (2016). Individual versus interactive task-based performance through voice-based computer-mediated communication. *Language Learning & Technology*, 20, 40–59.

Grgurovic, M., Chapelle, C. A., and Shelley, M. (2013). A meta-analysis of effectiveness studies on computer technology-supported language learning. *ReCALL*, 25, 165–98.

Gurzynski-Weiss, L. and Baralt, M. (2015). Does type of modified output correspond to learner noticing of feedback? A closer look in face-to-face and computer-mediated task-based interaction. *Applied Psycholinguistics*, 36, 1393–420.

Holden, C. and Sykes, J. M. (2012). Mentira: Prototyping language-based locative gameplay. In S. Dikkers, J. Martin, and B. Coulter, eds. *Mobile media learning: amazing uses of mobile devices for teaching and learning*. Pittsburgh, PA: ETC Press, pp. 111–31.

Hsu, H. C. (2012). Investigating the effects of planning on L2 text-chat performance. *CALICO Journal*, 29, 619–38.

Hsu, H. C. (2015). The effect of task planning on L2 performance and L2 development in text-based synchronous computer-mediated communication. *Applied Linguistics*, 32, 1–28.

Jeong, N.-S. (2011). The effects of task type and group structure on meaning negotiation in synchronous computer-mediated communication. In L. Plonsky and M. Schierloh, eds. *Selected proceedings of the 2009 Second Language Research Forum*. Somerville, MA: Cascadilla Proceedings Project, pp. 51–69.

Keller-Lally, A. M. (2006). Effect of task-type and group size on foreign language learner output in synchronous computer-mediated communication. PhD dissertation. University of Texas at Austin, Ann Arbor.

Kost, C. (2011). Investigating writing strategies and revision behavior in collaborative writing projects. *CALICO Journal*, 28, 606–20.

Kukulska-Hulme, A. (2013). Re-skilling language learners for a mobile world. The International Research Foundation for English Language Education (TIRF), Monterey, USA. Retrieved from: www.tirfonline.org/english-in-the-workforce/mobile-assisted-language-learning/re-skilling-language-learners-for-a-mobile-world/.

Kukulska-Hulme, A., Lee, H., and Norris, L. (2017). Mobile learning revolution: Implications for language pedagogy. In C. A. Chapelle and S. Sauro, eds. *The handbook of technology and second language teaching and learning*. Oxford: Wiley & Sons, pp. 217–33.

Lai, C. (2017). *Autonomous language learning with technology: Beyond the classroom*. London: Bloomsbury.

Lai, C. and Li, G. (2011). Technology and task-based language teaching: A critical review. *CALICO Journal*, 28, 498–521.

Lai, C., Fei, F., and Roots, R. (2008). The contingency of recasts and noticing. *CALICO Journal*, 26, 70–90.

Lai, C. and Zheng, D. (2018). Self-directed use of mobile devices for language learning beyond the classroom. *ReCALL*, 30(3), 299–318.

Lee, L. (2012). Exploring wiki-mediated collaborative writing: A case study in an elementary Spanish course. *CALICO Journal*, 27, 260–76.

Lin, H. (2014). Establishing an empirical link between computer-mediated communication (CMC) and SLA: A meta-analysis of the research. *Language Learning & Technology*, 18, 120–47.

Meyer, L. (2016). Students explore the earth and beyond with virtual field trips. *THE Journal*, 43(3), 22–25.

Michelson, K. and Dupuy, B. (2014). Multi-storied lives: Global simulation as an approach to developing multiliteracies in an intermediate French course. *L2 Journal*, 6, 21–49.

Nielson, K. (2013). Online language learning in the workplace: Maximizing efficiency, effectiveness, and time-on-task. *Proceedings from the*

International Conference of E-Learning in the Workplace. June 12–14, New York.

Nik, A. N. A. M. (2010). Examining the language learning potential of a task-based approach to synchronous computer-mediated communication. Unpublished PhD dissertation. Victoria University of Wellington, New Zealand.

Nik, A. N. M. A., Adams, R., and Newton, J. (2012). Writing to learn via text chat: Task implementation and focus on form. *Journal of Second Language Writing*, 21, 23–39.

Ortega, L. (2009). Interaction and attention to form in L2 text-based computer-mediated communication. In A. Mackey and C. Polio, eds. *Multiple perspectives on interaction in SLA: Research in honor of Susan M. Gass*. New York: Erlbaum/Routledge/Taylor & Francis.

Oskoz, A. and Elola, I. (2014). Promoting foreign language collaborative writing through the use of Web 2.0 tools and tasks. In M. González-Lloret and L. Ortega, eds. *Technology-mediated TBLT: researching technology and tasks*. Amsterdam: John Benjamins, pp. 115–48.

Payne, S. and Whitney, P. J. (2002). Developing L2 oral proficiency through synchronous CMC: Output, working memory, and interlanguage development. *CALICO Journal*, 20, 7–32.

Peterson, M. (2006). Learner interaction management in an avatar and chat-based virtual world. *Computer Assisted Language Learning*, 19, 79–103.

Peterson, M. (2010). Massively multiplayer online role-playing games as arenas for second language learning. *Computer Assisted Language Learning*, 23, 429–39.

Plonsky, L. and Ziegler, N. (2016). The CALL-SLA interface: Insights from a second-order synthesis. *Language Learning & Technology*, 20, 17–37.

Smith, B. (2003). Computer–mediated negotiated interaction: An expanded model. *The Modern Language Journal*, 87(1), 38–57.

Rama, P. S., Black, R. W., van Es, E., and Warschauer, M. (2012). Affordances for second language learning in World of Warcraft. *ReCALL*, 24, 322–38.

Reinders, H. and Pegrum, M. (2017). Supporting language learning on the move: an evaluative framework for mobile language learning resources.' In B. Tomlinson, ed. *SLA research and materials development for language learning*. New York: Routledge, pp. 219–31.

Reinders, H. and Wattana, S. (2012). Talk to me! Games and students' willingness to communicate. In H. Reinders, ed. *Digital games in language learning and teaching*. London: Palgrave Macmillan, pp. 156–88.

Reinders, H. and Wattana, S. (2014). Can I say something? The effects of digital game play on willingness to communicate. *Language Learning & Technology*, 18, 101–123.

Reinhardt, J. (2019). *Gameful second and foreign language teaching and learning*. Basingstoke and New York: Palgrave Macmillan.

Robinson, P. (2011). Second language task complexity, the Cognition Hypothesis, language learning, and performance. In P. Robinson, ed. *Researching task complexity: Task demands, task-based language learning and performance*. Amsterdam: John Benjamins, pp. 3–38.

Satar, H. M. and Özdener, N. (2008). The effects of synchronous CMC on speaking proficiency and anxiety: Text versus voice chat. *The Modern Language Journal*, 92, 596–613.

Sauro, S. (2004). Cyberdiscursive tug-of-war: Learner repositioning in a multimodal CMC environment. *Working Papers in Educational Linguistics*, 19, 55–72.

Sauro, S. (2014). Lessons from the fandom: Technology-mediated tasks for language learning. In M. González-Lloret and L. Ortega, eds. *Technology-mediated TBLT: researching technology and tasks*. Amsterdam: John Benjamins, pp. 239–62.

Scholz, K. and Schulze, M. (2017). Digital-gaming trajectories and second language development. *Language Learning & Technology*, 21, 99–119.

Schwienhorst, K. (2012). *Learner autonomy and CALL environments*. New York: Routledge.

Shekary, M. and Tahririan, M. H. (2006). Negotiation of Meaning and Noticing in Text-Based Online Chat. *The Modern Language Journal*, 90, 557–73.

Smith, B. (2012). Eye tracking as a measure of noticing: A study of explicit recasts in SCMC. *Language Learning and Technology*, 16, 53–81.

Smith, B. and Gorsuch, G. (2004). Synchronous computer-mediated communication captured by usability lab technologies: New interpretations. *System*, 32, 553–75.

Sydorenko, T., Hellermann, J., Thorne, S. L. and Howe, V. (2019). Mobile Augmented Reality and Language-Related Episodes. *TESOL Quarterly*, 53 (3), 712–40.

Sykes, J. M. (2008). A dynamic approach to social interaction: Synthetic immersive Environments & Spanish pragmatics. PhD dissertation. University of Minnesota. ProQuest Dissertations & Theses Global. Retrieved from: http://search.proquest.com/docview/304582040?accountid=27140.

Sykes, J. M. (2014). TBLT and synthetic immersive environments: What can in-game task restarts tell us about design and implementation? In M. González-Lloret and L. Ortega, eds. *Technology-mediated TBLT*. Amsterdam: John Benjamins, pp. 149–82.

Sykes, J. M. and Reinhardt, J. (2012). *Language at play: Digital games in second and foreign language teaching and learning*. New York: Pearson-Prentice Hall.

Sylvén, L. K. and Sundqvist, P. (2012). Gaming as extramural English L2 learning and L2 proficiency among young learners. *ReCALL*, 24, 302–21.

Taguchi, N., Li, Q., and Tang, X. (2017). Learning Chinese formulaic expressions in a scenario-based interactive environment. *Foreign Language Annals*, 50(4), 641–60.

Thorne, S. L. (2008). Transcultural communication in open internet environments and massively multiplayer online games. In S. S. Magnan, ed. *Mediating discourse online*. Amsterdam: John Benjamins, pp. 305–27.

Thorne, S. L. and Black, R. (2008). Language and literacy development in computer-mediated contexts and communities. *Annual Review of Applied Linguistics*, 27, 133–60.

Thorne, S. L., Fischer, I., and Lu, X. (2012). The semiotic ecology and linguistic complexity of an online game world. *ReCALL*, 24(3), 279–301.

Thorne, S. and Payne, J. S. (2005). Evolutionary trajectories, Internet-mediated expression, and language education. *CALICO Journal*, 22, 371–97.

Van den Branden, K., Bygate, M., and Norris, J. (2009). Task-based language teaching: Introducing the reader. In K. Van den Branden, M. Bygate, and J. Norris, eds. *Task-based language teaching: A reader*. Amsterdam: John Benjamins, pp. 1–13.

Wang, S. and Vásquez, C. (2012). Web 2.0 and second language learning: What does the research tell us? *CALICO Journal*, 29, 412–30.

Winke, P. (2013, October). *Supporting teachers' efforts in implementing technology-mediated tasks*. Presented at the Task-based Language Teaching conference, Banff, Alberta, Canada.

Yeh, E. and Wan, G. (2019). The use of virtual worlds in foreign language teaching and learning. In Information Resources Management Association, ed. *Virtual reality in education: Breakthroughs in research and practice*. Hershey, PA: IGI Global, pp. 645–92.

Yilmaz, Y. (2011). Task effects on focus on form in synchronous computer-mediated communication. *The Modern Language Journal*, 95, 115–132.

Yilmaz, Y. and Granena, G. (2010). The effects of task type in synchronous computer-mediated communication. *ReCALL*, 22, 20.

Yuksel, D. and Inan, B. (2014). The effects of communication mode on negotiation of meaning and its noticing. *ReCALL*, 26(3), 333–54.

Ziegler, N. (2016a). Synchronous computer-mediated communication and interaction: A meta-analysis. *Studies in Second Language Acquisition*, 38(3), 553–86.

Ziegler, N. (2016b). Taking technology to task: Technology-mediated TBLT, performance, and production. *Annual Review of Applied Linguistics*, 36, 136–63.

Ziegler, N. (2017). The contingency of recasts, learners' noticing, and L2 development: Insights on saliency from multiple modalities. In S. Gass, P. Spinner, and J. Behney, eds. *Salience and SLA*. New York: Routledge, pp. 269–90.

Ziegler, N. (2018). Pre-task planning in L2 text-chat: Examining learners' process and performance. *Language Learning & Technology*, 22(3), 193–213.

Ziegler, N. and Phung, H. (2019) Technology-mediated task-based interactions: The role of modality. *International Journal of Applied Linguistics*, 170, 251–76.

10A

Delivering Task-Based Language Teaching at Scale

A Case Study of a Needs-Based, Technology-Mediated Workplace English Program

Katharine B. Nielson

10A.1 Introduction

Over the past thirty years, a considerable amount of empirical research has been published on various aspects of computer-assisted language learning, much of it concerning the effectiveness of various types of technology-mediated tasks. Although there have been repeated calls for evaluations and case studies of technology-mediated language courses, these remain few and far between (although see Gonzalez-Lloret and Ortega, [2014]). As Doughty and Long (2003) indicated and Gonzalez-Lloret and Ziegler point out in this volume, technology-mediated courses are ideal places to observe task-based instruction, as they often come equipped with the tools to capture large quantities of learner data. This chapter offers a glimpse into the mechanics of Voxy – a technology-mediated, task-based English course. After a brief description of the platform and general approach to language instruction, the discussion will turn to the details of a specific implementation of this course and the attendant learning outcomes.

Voxy is a web- and mobile-based language-learning platform that has been used by millions of learners around the world to improve their English skills. Voxy partners with corporations, governments, language schools, universities, and other institutions to offer needs-based, adaptive English instruction intended to help learners accomplish their real-world goals. Voxy courses are designed to leverage technology to foster the process of learning a second language, so learners are offered genuine reading and listening materials with scaffolding appropriate to their proficiency levels, a suite of learning activities that adapts in real-time to meet learners' needs, live classes that allow for interactive practice with the target tasks, and ongoing feedback.

One of the issues with delivering a task-based course to more than a few people is materials development; identifying the materials associated with real-world tasks and turning them into learning objects is time-consuming in and of itself, and when combined with the fact that even within the same course individuals are best served with differentiated instruction, the challenge becomes even greater. To address this problem, Voxy has built and patented a content-processing engine, which scans the texts or transcripts of genuine resources, identifies the features that make comprehension in English difficult for non-native speakers (e.g., the amount of coordination and subordination, the type-token ratio, the distance of pronouns from their antecedents), identifies the most important key words and phrases in each text, offers automatic glossing and/or translations of those key words and phrases, and generates a bank of potential distractors for each of the target key words or phrases. This content-processing engine produces a learning resource along with a set of data that can be combined with a suite of adaptive activities to personalize instruction in real time. For more details on how this content-processing engine works and the specific algorithms associated with text leveling, keyword extraction, and distractor generation, see Nielson (2016, 2017, 2018).

These tools enable the platform to offer hundreds of thousands of different input-focused lessons, which vary based on learners' needs and adapt based on learners' performance; these lessons are offered on desktop computers, tablets, and mobile devices, and learners can access them anywhere there is an Internet connection. The cloud-based platform does not require the installation of any specific software; however, learners are able to download lessons to complete offline when they are unable to access the Internet. In addition, the platform includes an objective measure of learner proficiency (the Voxy Proficiency Assessment, or VPA), tools for reviewing relevant target vocabulary and practicing pronunciation, an adaptive achievement test framework, and around-the-clock, instructor-mediated live instruction in both one-on-one and small group settings. All learner performance is tracked, so that stakeholders can monitor progress and improvement. Each course is evaluated according to four criteria: the time learners spend on task, mastery of language and content, stakeholder satisfaction, and evidence of success at task accomplishment. Because each implementation of Voxy is tailored to meet the needs of learners and their sponsoring organization, the course requirements, content, objectives, and target outcomes of each implementation are slightly different. To illustrate the application of the platform and approach in a real-world setting, the remainder of this chapter will address its use in the case of a large hospital in the state of Maine.

10A.2 The Case of MaineHealth

MaineHealth is the largest employer in the state of Maine, with a perpetual need to recruit and train employees for careers in healthcare-related fields. The organization has large numbers of refugee employees with limited English skills who are relegated to low-wage jobs with little room for upward mobility. The Director of Human Resources at MaineHealth sought a solution to offer these employees useful and contextually relevant English training in order to improve their performance at work and provide them with the opportunity for advancement and promotion within the MaineHealth system. To this end, she collaborated with Voxy through the Greater Portland Immigrant Welcome Center to create a workplace English program. A needs analysis with stakeholders from MaineHealth identified two important areas for these employees' development: Company Policies and Regulations, and Safety Regulations. The employees' level of English was estimated to be at the High Beginner level (approximately A1+ or A2 on the Common European Framework of Reference [CEFR]).

After identifying these critical areas for English proficiency improvement, a team of instructional designers from Voxy reviewed MaineHealth's internal employee orientation and training materials (e.g., a welcome video from the hospital's chief administrator, the employee benefits manual, and paid-time-off policy documents), as well as the hospital's safety training information (e.g., bloodborne pathogen training documents, information on how to avoid slips and falls, and recorded safety information on biohazards). Excerpts from these materials, which are delivered electronically to employees, were selected, organized into a course, and processed by Voxy's content engine.

To illustrate, one of the workplace materials reviewed by the course designers was MaineHealth's company video introducing employees to the company's values. The original video is several minutes long, and it includes an introduction to the hospital's mission and vision statements, as well as information on its core values. The Voxy team chose a forty-four second excerpt from this video, transcribed it, and submitted it to Voxy's content-processing engine to determine the keywords most relevant to understanding the meaning of the text (including, among others, ambassadors, community, values, mission, and patients), as well as the approximate difficulty level of the text. In addition, the course designers created several comprehension questions that would appear after each fifteen to twenty seconds of video to offer learners an input-focused activity to complete and to ensure that they understood the content (See Figure 10A.1 for a screenshot of this comprehension activity in progress).

After learners complete the input-focused video activity depicted in Figure 10A.1, they are offered one of many different learning activities

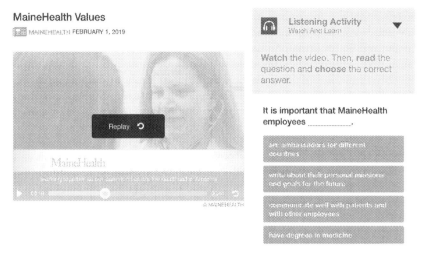

Figure 10A.1 Screenshot of learning activity using an excerpt from a MaineHealth employee orientation video

using the transcript of the text and a subset of the keywords selected during the lesson-creation process. These activities adapt in real time based on learner performance; for example, learners who are struggling with listening might need to complete a gap-fill activity using audio recordings for the blank spaces, whereas learners who are struggling with vocabulary comprehension might complete a definition-focused activity. There are thirteen different types of activities that interact with audio, video, image, and text-based sources of content. These activities are designed to give learners meaningful practice with reading and listening to authentic, job-relevant training materials in English, a task that is required for their employment. Each lesson takes learners between five and twenty minutes to complete and can be repeated as often as the learners choose.

The course includes lessons on the following topics related to employee policies and regulations: MaineHealth Values, Values in Action, The Story of MaineHealth, Tuition Assistance, Slips, Trips, and Falls, Emergency Codes and Activation, Corrective Action, HIPAA and Privacy, Computer Security, and Sexual Harassment Awareness. In addition, the course includes lessons on these workplace safety topics: Safety Tips, Personal Protective Equipment (PPE), Proper Waste Disposal, Airborne Precautions, Bloodborne Pathogens, If You Are Exposed to a Bloodborne Pathogen, Cleaning Body Fluid Spills, Chemical Safety, Cleaning Best Practices, and Injury Prevention. All of the resources used for these courses came directly from the materials that employees were expected to read and/or comprehend during their employee orientation process and/or their mandatory health and safety training. While these employees had completed this training at the beginning of their employment with MaineHealth, they did not have the English skills to understand the training materials, so they were not always complying with the policies or understanding the procedures. By creating an English course with genuine, workplace-based content that employees were obliged to understand, the course designers offered the learners meaningful, relevant English instruction.

In addition to the customized course materials developed with the hospital's content, learners in the program were also given access to the full collection of learning content in the Voxy platform, including courses related to job-specific tasks from dozens of different career sectors (e.g., Healthcare, Manufacturing, Hospitality, and Customer Service), materials for daily tasks (e.g., Filling out Forms, Applying for Social Services, Personal Financial Literacy, Citizenship Preparation), and materials for academic tasks (e.g., Understanding Academic Honesty and Preparing for the CASAS Test). All of the course content on the Voxy platform is organized into course units, with approximately twenty lessons in each. The Voxy platform recommended courses and materials based on learners' interests, career goals, and proficiency levels, and all of the course activities adapted in real-time, based on learners' performance. Finally, all learners had access to small, virtual group classes taught by trained, certified instructors 24/7. Learners were able to choose classes based on their interests, and teachers were trained to work with students to foster authentic language practice (often based on role-plays) relevant to learners' needs and goals.

At the outset, the goals of the program were to increase the English skills related to the MaineHealth job tasks of a pilot group of thirty environmental service workers who volunteered to participate. They were given paid release time from work, as well as access to a computer lab with a lab technician trained to help learners use the Voxy platform. The first cohort of eleven employees began using the platform in January 2019, and an additional cohort of fourteen began in October 2019. For various reasons, there were five employees who were not able to begin using the platform with their fellow cohort-members, so they started their usage on a rolling basis throughout the first year of the program. They are not included in the monthly, cohort-specific analyses of engagement; however, they are included in the analysis of content and proficiency gains.

10A.3 Learning Outcomes

Learners in both cohorts were encouraged to spend at least four hours per month completing lessons, taking achievement and proficiency assessments, taking small group classes, and practicing their English skills. Their time-on-task was calculated as any time spent actively completing activities, taking assessments, or participating in group classes. Time with the browser or the mobile app open but without engaging in activities was

Table 10A.1 *MaineHealth employees hourly engagement in months 1 and 3 of the program*

		Month 1 hours		Month 3 hours		
Organization	N	Mean	SD	Mean	SD	Month 3 Retention
MaineHealth (Cohort 1)	11	7.7	2.6	10.4	1.8	90%
MaineHealth (Cohort 2)	14	10.2	5.6	4.5	2.8	100%

not counted. Learner engagement was extremely high, with employees in Cohort 1 using the platform an average of nearly 8 hours a month in the first month and increasing their average usage to around 10 hours per month in the third month of the study. Learners in Cohort 2 also had quite high levels of engagement, beginning with a mean of 10.2 hours per month in the first month. Learners in Cohort 2 dropped their usage in half by the third month, completing an average of 4.5 hours of time-on-task, which was likely due to the third month of their usage falling over the December 2019 holidays, and also because they were given fewer release hours in the offsite computer lab. See Table 10A.1 for the descriptive engagement statistics for both cohorts.

Despite the drop-off in usage for Cohort 2 in the third month, the MaineHealth learners were deeply engaged with the English learning program, surpassing the monthly Voxy usage for working adults around the world (approximately two hours per month on average). But perhaps more important than the number of hours they spent engaged was the sheer diversity of the content they accessed, as well as their variable performance on the courses and units they chose to complete. As expected, all of the learners completed the units required by MaineHealth on policies and procedures and on safety. Twenty learners across both cohorts completed a unit dedicated to preparation for the CASAS Reading Exam (an English exam frequently required in government-funded workforce training programs to demonstrate outcomes for future funding). In addition to these obvious choices, though, learners completed dozens of units (each consisting of approximately twenty lessons based on genuine tasks and materials and taking three to six hours to complete) related to careers in healthcare, daily life, and careers in the hospitality industry. See Table 10A.2 for a detailed list of all of the units completed by these learners, which included topics ranging from common diseases to creating social media posts to jobs and responsibilities in the food service industries. A few learners completed units related to other industries and professions, including Architecture, Finance, and Professional Skills.

At the end of every unit, learners take an achievement test to ensure that they've understood its content, with comprehension questions, as well as

Table 10A.2 *Units with topics related to job tasks in careers in healthcare and hospitality, as well as daily tasks*

Healthcare careers	Daily life	Hospitality industry
Basic nursing skills	Accessing social services	At a hotel
Common diseases	Navigating the airport	At a restaurant
Genetics	Scheduling: calendar and time	Cooking and preparation
Gynecology	Discussing pop culture	Dining management
Health	Expressing points of view	Food
Health and wellness	Expressing preferences	Food and drink
Hospitals and nursing	Finding places in the neighborhood	Food and nutrition
Medical anatomy	Forms and personal information	Handling questions & complaints
Medicine	Getting around town	Serving at a restaurant
Optometry	Giving and following instructions	Serving food to go
Pathology and cancer	Giving recommendations	Handling money
Pediatrics	Introductions	Asking for clarification
Pharmacology	Giving personal information	Jobs and responsibilities
Review: medical news	Navigating shopping transactions	Talking about work
Surgeries and procedures	Writing social media posts	
	Understanding social media	

the opportunity to use the key words and phrases from throughout the unit in a novel context. This test is automatically scored out of 100. While learners generally did quite well on these tests, they were more successful with the units related to healthcare careers than they were other careers or academic English. This is not surprising for workers in a hospital system, some of whom had had careers in healthcare before seeking asylum in the United States. The units on TOEFL preparation and CASAS preparation had the lowest achievement test scores, with the learner average at just 53 percent. See Table 10A.3 for the complete descriptive statistics on achievement test scores by type of test.

Along with demonstrating their progress on the end-of-unit achievement tests, these employees were also encouraged to take a periodic proficiency assessment, the VPA, which considered listening skills, reading skills, and integrated reading/grammar/vocabulary competence. This assessment is not something for which learners can specifically prepare, and it consists of multiple, domain-agnostic forms and versions, in an effort to remove the potential for a test effect (see Faria et al. [2019] for a detailed description of the VPA, as well as a study of its use in a research setting). Learners are scored out of 1680 points and given an indication of their proficiency level in terms of their level on the CEFR – see Table 10A.4.

At the time of writing, learners in Cohort 1 had had one year of access to the Voxy platform and the opportunity to take up to four proficiency assessments. Twelve learners had taken at least two proficiency tests; six

Table 10A.3 *Average achievement test scores by type of test*

Course content	Mean achievement test %	Achievement test SD
Healthcare careers	83	9.57
Daily life	82	11.74
Hospitality industry	81	14.74
Employee safety	80	13.05
MaineHealth policies	75	13.58
Other careers	70	20.06
Academic English	53	22.08

Table 10A.4 *Voxy levels, proficiency test scores, and CEFR levels*

Voxy level	VPA points	CEFR
Beginner	0–50	Pre-A1
High beginner	51–210	A1
Low intermediate	211–490	A2
Intermediate	491–880	B1
High intermediate	881–1280	B2
Low advanced	1281–1670	C1
Advanced	1671–1680	C2

of them improved an entire proficiency level, while seven of them improved within their starting levels. On average, the activity level of learners who improved an entire level was very similar to those who improved within their starting levels; however, the learners who improved had an average achievement test score that was twenty percentage points higher than those who maintained their levels, indicating a relationship between mastery of language and content and proficiency improvement (see Table 10A.5).

At the time of writing, learners in Cohort 2 had had three months of engagement and proficiency data. Ten of them had taken two proficiency assessments, with five maintaining their scores, four improving, and one declining. What is striking about the three-month proficiency data is that while we see the same general pattern of learners who improved their levels having higher achievement test scores than those who maintained or declined, the overall scores are much lower. This is likely because learners in this course are able to re-take units and achievement tests as they see fit, giving them a chance to re-read and listen again to the target task materials as often as they like, with different adaptive activities and tests each time. Given that Cohort 2 had less time with the course materials, it is possible that they will also improve their scores with time (see Table 10A.6).

Table 10A.5 *Engagement, proficiency, and achievement test scores for learners in Cohort 1*

Proficiency change	N	Mean year 1 hours	Year 1 hours SD	Mean VPA change score	VPA Change score SD	Mean achievement test %
Maintain	6	53.22	14.95	67	115	67
Improve	6	52.87	16.32	199.33	101.56	87
Not tested	3	2.57	0.10	N/A	N/A	87
Total	15	**51.14**	**30.13**	**131.33**	**120.74**	**78**

Table 10A.6 *Engagement, proficiency, and achievement test scores for learners in Cohort 2*

Proficiency change	N	Mean three-month hours	Three-month hours SD	Mean VPA change score	VPA change score SD	Mean achievement test %
Maintain	5	24.56	10.80	99.00	60.45	70
Improve	4	31.31	5.77	243.50	107.06	75
Decline	1	14.75	N/A	-169.00	N/A	57
Not Tested	5	11.29	7.36	N/A	N/A	60
Total	15	**21.28**	**11.28**	**130.00**	**147.10**	**68**

The stakeholders at MaineHealth were pleased with the progress the employees made, and the workers in Cohort 1 are already participating in internal job-training programs, as well as seeking out additional training and certification in Allied Health careers, such as medical assistant and medical billing coder. Along with the human resources director, the direct managers of the program participants have commented on the increased levels of the employees' English, as well as on their increased engagement in the workplace. One supervisor reported that she had been unaware that the housekeeping staff included a midwife, a lawyer, and a former secretary at the Ministry of Foreign Affairs of the Democratic Republic of Congo. The human resources director has requested more customized units for MaineHealth employees, and a course on the English required for phlebotomy technicians is underway. The learners themselves have also given positive survey feedback on the course, stating that "The application is very user-friendly," "It was the first English course with actually good content and that I don't get tired easily," "I now understand English much more easily," "The program has helped me a lot," and "I like the group classes a lot." They also report being more confident in the workplace and interested in further education.

10A.4 Discussion and Conclusions

The intent of this chapter was to illustrate how technology can make the materials development process for task-based courses easier to accomplish, how technology-mediated courses can help document learning outcomes from task-based instruction, and how offering adult learners access to a wide variety of meaningful learning materials has benefits for engagement and language acquisition. Creating a customized content-processing engine is likely outside the scope of most language educators, but it is possible for practitioners to leverage these course design and evaluation principles and apply them in their own contexts.

First, when adult learners are given access to language-learning materials that are directly relevant to their workplaces, they are able to see the connection between what they are learning in an instructed context and their jobs, and they are also able to apply what they have learned in a genuine context right away. Starting with authentic job materials and using them to create modules of instruction for workplace training is a logical step in the materials development process. And while a tailor-made platform with built-in tools for keyword extraction, text leveling, and activity creation makes things easier and allows for learning materials to be created quickly for multiple (and different) stakeholders with various needs, it is possible to leverage off-the-shelf course-authoring tools and learning-management software to create materials. In fact, some of the techniques used by the Voxy content-authoring tool can be achieved by hand with other, free tools. Teachers and instructional designers can take genuine materials from learners' lives and jobs and use web-based programs like LexTutor Vocab Profile (https://www.lextutor.ca/vp/comp/) to identify keywords to create their own learning materials. Teachers can show clips from genuine videos required for real-world activities (e.g., training materials, lectures, and business meetings), and pause them in class for strategic comprehension questions, giving learners lists of relevant vocabulary to identify as they watch the videos.

One of the most striking findings of this implementation was the sheer volume of learning content accessed by the learners, as well as the wide range of topics they pursued. This small group of students in a workplace setting explored hundreds of different task-based topics, supporting the research on the importance of conducting a needs analysis. Learners should be consulted on their goals and interests in order to make sure that their language instruction is relevant and engaging, as one-size-fits-all approaches to instruction tend to fall short of meeting anyone's needs. While individual teachers would be hard-pressed to curate personalized learning materials for each student, it is possible to create an environment where learners are encouraged to contribute their own materials. Regardless of the context, students are generally learning a language for a reason (to get a better job, to communicate with their children's teachers, to understand media, etc.), and when they are encouraged to explore real examples of the language they are learning and collaborate with other learners and teachers on understanding those materials and producing them themselves, as suggested by Gonzalez-Lloret and Zeigler (this volume), their learning experience becomes more meaningful.

One benefit of choosing a technology-mediated course is that engagement and outcomes are generally straightforward to track. Teachers and administrators can see who is completing which learning activities, how learners are performing, and what their strengths and weaknesses might be. The group of employees at MaineHealth struggled with academic reading and writing tasks, while at the same time they excelled at tasks related to careers in healthcare and the safety requirements for their own workplace. It is unfortunate that the academic reading and writing tasks are required for government funding for adult language learners, as they are likely irrelevant to future vocational training. The stark contrast between learner performance on CASAS and TOEFL prep courses and the courses related to careers in healthcare can be used to persuade hospital administrators and grant managers that perhaps a different assessment would be better suited to this population of learners.

One of the clearest benefits for choosing a task-based approach is that course evaluation becomes straightforward; perhaps the most important measure of whether or not a task-based course is effective is whether or not learners are able to accomplish the target tasks after the course has ended. In this case study, the learners were able to speak English on the job more effectively, making them eligible for career development and economic mobility. Any task-based language teaching course that begins with a needs analysis and leverages authentic materials for learning content can include success at task accomplishment as a measure of course effectiveness. Whether these data are collected by surveys, interviews, or observation from employers, it is important to document the impact of offering learners a course based on their needs.

When implemented appropriately, a technology-mediated language course leverages technology to solve a problem (e.g., linking instructors with students who would otherwise not have access to them, offering access to real-world examples of learners accomplishing tasks in the target language, or allowing learners to work at their own pace with materials that they enjoy). In the case of MaineHealth, employees were able to access meaningful, differentiated instruction relevant to their jobs and career goals through technology. They demonstrated the ability to master the course content, and, more than that, were able to improve their communication in the workplace, better integrate themselves into the hospital community, and make themselves eligible for future training.

Further Reading

Doughty, C. and Long, M. H. (2003). Optimal psycholinguistic environments for distance foreign language learning. *Language Learning and Technology*, 7, 50–80.

Faria, A. M., Bergey, R., and Lishinski, A. (2019). Using technology to support English language learners in higher education: A study of Voxy's effect on English language proficiency. American Institutes for Research Technical Report. Retrieved from https://air.org/system/files/downloads/report/Using-Technology-to-Support-ELLs-in-Higher-Education-Voxy-January-2019.pdf.

González-Lloret, M. and Nielson, K. (2014). Evaluating TBLT: The case of a task-based Spanish program. *Language Teaching Research*, 19(5), 545-49.

González-Lloret, M. and Ortega, L. (2014). Towards technology-mediated TBLT: An introduction. In M. González-Lloret and L. Ortega, eds. *Technology-mediated TBLT: researching technology and tasks*. Amsterdam: John Benjamins, pp. 1–22.

Lai, C. and Li, G. (2011). Technology and task-based language teaching: A critical review, *CALICO Journal*, 28(2), 498–521.

Long, M. H. (2005). *Second language needs analysis*. Cambridge: Cambridge University Press.

Nielson, K. (2014). Evaluation of an online, task-based Chinese course. In M. Gonzalez-Lloret and L. Ortega, eds. *Technology-mediated TBLT: Researching technology and tasks*. Amsterdam: John Benjamins, pp. 295–321.

Van den Branden, K., Van Gorp, K., and Verhelst, M. (2007), eds. *Tasks in action: task-based language education from a classroom-based perspective*. Cambridge: Cambridge Scholars Publishing.

Study Questions

1. This case study leveraged employee training manuals and safety training materials to create meaningful, task-based learning materials. Imagine a scenario with front-line factory workers in a manufacturing plant. What are some resources that a course designer could use to develop English materials?
2. How can teachers handle intact classes with learners who have very different personal and professional goals? What are ways to incorporate personalized instruction in a traditional, face-to-face class?
3. How would you build a task-based curriculum for language learners who need to apply for jobs in the United States? What sorts of materials would you include, and how would you approach assessment?
4. On average, MaineHealth employees spent between ten and two hours per month learning English over the course of a year. This amount of

time-on-task seems relatively low compared to the in-person requirements for traditional, face-to-face language classes. Why do you think these employees were able to improve their proficiency with fewer hours than in traditional settings?

References

Doughty, C. and Long, M. H. (2003). Optimal psycholinguistic environments for distance foreign language learning. *Language Learning and Technology*, 7, 50–80.

González-Lloret, M. and Ortega, L. (2014). Towards technology-mediated TBLT: An introduction. In M. González-Lloret and L. Ortega, eds. *Technology-mediated TBLT: researching technology and tasks*. Amsterdam: John Benjamins, pp. 1–22.

Faria, A.M., Bergey, R., and Lishinski, A. (2019). Using technology to support English language learners in higher education: A study of Voxy's effect on English language proficiency. American Institutes for Research Technical Report. Retrieved from https://air.org/system/files/downloads/report/Using-Technology-to-Support-ELLs-in-Higher-Education-Voxy-January-2019.pdf.

Gonzalez-Lloret, M. and Ortega, L. (2014), eds. *Technology-mediated TBLT: Researching technology and tasks*. Amsterdam: John Benjamins

Nielson, K. (2018). Case Study: "English for Software Engineering" The conception and creation of an e-learning English-Language course tailored to learners' real-world needs. *International Journal of Advanced Corporate Learning*, 11(2), 27–29.

Nielson, K., Breen, A., Tyson, N., and Kirkham, K. (2016). *US Patent number 9,262,935*. Washington DC: US Patent and Trademark Office.

Nielson, K. Breen, A., Tyson, N., and Kirkham, K. (2017). US Patent number 9,666,098. Washington DC: US Patent and Trademark Office.

10B

Task-Based Language Teaching and Indigenous Language Revitalisation

Katherine J. Riestenberg and Ari Sherris

10B.1 Introduction

Task-based language teaching (TBLT) is purported to be malleable enough to adapt to the increasing diversity of language instruction contexts throughout the world (Ellis, 2003; Long, 2015). In Indigenous language revitalisation contexts, a task-based approach can be appealing because it does not rely on extensive language analysis or resources that may not exist, such as grammars, dictionaries, and textbooks (Hermes & King, 2007; Riestenberg & Sherris, 2018). By focusing on meaningful situations, TBLT moves away from rote, teacher-fronted practices and focuses instead on interactions among learners or between learners and teachers. Although TBLT is likely to be considered an imported pedagogical approach in many Indigenous communities, it is flexible enough for community members to realise it in the way they see fit, and, at least in principle, it lends itself to engaging with the community's own sociocultural practices while maintaining a focus on language learning. For Long (2015), the application of TBLT in diverse settings is not only empirically supported by research on second language acquisition, but it is also a philosophically-motivated, socially responsible act. This is because TBLT is 'radically learner-centered' (Long, 2015: 325) and aims to help learners meet 'present and future real-world communicative needs' (Long, 2015: 68).

However, this focus on real-world needs presents a conundrum in language revitalisation settings, where there may not be an authentic need to speak the target language, due to a lack of speakers or the widespread bilingualism associated with particular stages of language loss.

Revitalisation programmes face other specific hurdles as well. Teachers often have limited time and resources to devote to language instruction. Many are volunteers. Many are themselves learners of the language, not having learned the Indigenous language as children due to colonialist education policies, structural violence, and the compulsory assimilation practices that took place globally throughout the last two centuries and which continue to play out within and across nation states. The reflections we offer here illustrate how two groups of educators have tried to confront some of the challenges they face and make teaching more effective by adapting task-based principles so that they were more applicable, useful, and appropriate in their own programmes. Illustrative examples come from two distinct but complementary contexts: Macuiltianguis Zapotec after-school lessons in Oaxaca, Mexico, and a workshop for teachers at a Salish Qlispe immersion school in Montana in the United States. The Zapotec examples focus on teacher and learner language produced during TBLT lessons, while the Salish examples focus on how teachers began to think about creating TBLT spaces that could support language learning.

10B.2 What Is a 'Real-World Task' for an Endangered Language?

The 'tasks' of TBLT are the 'real-world communicative uses to which learners will put the [second language] beyond the classroom—the things they will *do* in and through the [second language]' (Long, 2016: 6). Grammar and word learning thus take place only in the context of their communicative objectives. On the one hand, this approach can provide an enormous advantage in language revitalisation contexts, in which it is often the case that little grammatical analysis is available in the first place. On the other hand, the authentic, 'real-world' task idealised in TBLT is at odds with the realities of language revitalisation when the target language is rarely or no longer used in day-to-day communication, making it unclear how such an approach can be implemented. This is particularly true if everyone in the community is either bilingual or only speaks the colonising language, as is the case in both the Zapotec and Salish contexts described here.

We will show how task-based methodological principles (Long, 2009, 2015) were useful for planning and teaching in these settings and helped to forge open new spaces for meaningful communication in both the Zapotec and Salish cases. Lacking an authentic communicative *need* to speak the target language, teachers sought out tasks that were functional and goal-oriented (Van den Branden, 2006), the types of interactions that take place when communication is necessary to achieve a non-linguistic objective (Ellis, 2009; Riestenberg, 2020a, 2020b). The Zapotec teachers looked for everyday communicative tasks that learners plausibly *could do* in Zapotec, focusing on encouraging students to speak Zapotec in situations in which they were already interacting with Zapotec speakers in the community but doing so in Spanish. The Salish teachers, on the other hand, focused on the school itself as a new space for meaningful and genuine language use.

10B.3   Macuiltianguis Zapotec After-School Programme

Zapotec is the term used to designate a family of 'probably twenty-some' distinct languages originating in what is now the state of Oaxaca in southern Mexico, with many speakers today living in other regions of Mexico and the United States (Beam de Azcona, 2016: 3). Although there are still speakers, all Zapotec varieties are generally considered to be endangered (Beam de Azcona, 2016). Macuiltianguis Zapotec is a variety spoken in the small municipality of San Pablo Macuiltianguis, located in the mountainous Sierra Juárez region north of Oaxaca City. The *Grupo Cultural Tagayu'* (Macuiltianguis Cultural Group) was founded in 2008 by several community members with the broad goal of preserving and revitalising the local language.

After the director of the revitalisation group attended a workshop on TBLT in multilingual contexts that Riestenberg offered in Oaxaca in 2014, they formed a collaboration to create communicative and task-based Zapotec lessons for children in the community. The group's main goal was to promote authentic spoken interaction among the learners and between learners and speakers living in the community. The reflections presented here are based on work that took place between August 2015 and June 2016, during which time Riestenberg was living in Macuiltianguis, working closely with the revitalisation group on lesson plans and language materials, and conducting research. Examples come from lesson plans and video and audio recordings of class sessions and their accompanying transcripts collected during that period (Riestenberg & Grupo Cultural Tagayu, 2019), when a fluctuating group of children (mostly ages 7–11) regularly attended a two-hour Zapotec class after school around three times per month. All learners were beginners in terms of speaking, reading, and writing, but a few had higher-level listening comprehension abilities. Class lessons were centred on speaking tasks, though pedagogical tasks involving listening, reading, and writing skills were often used to support speaking task performance.

In Macuiltianguis, the initial focus was on everyday tasks such as greeting others on the street, making small talk, and making purchases at a local store. Macuiltianguis is a small, walkable village, and many older members of the community still know Zapotec, whether or not they use it on a daily basis. The instructors decided to take advantage of this by planning opportunities for students to interact face-to-face with a variety of speakers. This included visits to speakers' homes in the community, visiting speakers at their place of work, or asking speakers to visit the Zapotec classroom.

10B.4 Salish Qlipse Teacher Education Workshop

Salish Qlispe, spoken as a first language by fewer than fifty members of the Confederated Salish and Kootenai tribes on the Flathead Reservation in northwest Montana (Sherris, Pete & Haynes, 2015; Wood, 2014), has been the focus of revitalisation efforts at the Nkwusm immersion school in Arlee, Montana since 2002. One of twenty-three Salishan languages (Kiyosawa & Donna, 2010; Thomason, 2006), Salish Qlispe (a.k.a. Selish Qlispe, Flathead or Montana Salish, or Salish Pend d'Oreille) was taught to six pre-school children who speak American English as a first language during the school's first year. By the 2009–2010 school year, twenty-seven children from pre-Kindergarten through to grade 7 were enrolled in the immersion programme, and preparations were underway for grade 8. At that time, Sherris was invited to collaborate with community members, elders, and teachers (most, save for the elders, second language speakers of Salish) to develop and facilitate a one-and-a-half-day workshop for teachers to make tasks that would 'rupture the silence', as one teacher put it, 'with Salish talk'. Funding was for the one-time workshop only and did not include follow up workshops or data collection on TBLT implementation.

10B.5 Methodological Principles

Long's (2009, 2015) ten methodological principles (MPs) for TBLT are 'universally desirable instructional design features motivated by theory and research findings' (Long, 2009: 376). These principles are described in detail in Long (2015) along with a table of references to consult for each. We describe in the following sections how educators in both the Zapotec and Salish settings identified tasks and carried out or imagined the application of task-based methodological principles (Long 2009, 2015) such as elaborating input, providing rich input, focusing on form, and providing negative feedback.

10B.5.1 Elaborate Input (MP3) and Provide Rich Input (MP4)

Task-based language teaching promotes the use of elaborated texts as opposed to simplified or genuine texts (Long, 2009, 2015). Text elaboration improves the comprehensibility of a text at the discourse level by adding redundancy (through repetition and paraphrase), ensuring regularity (through parallelism and retention of optional morphemes), and explicitly drawing learners' attention to grammatical and semantic features. In addition, TBLT calls for materials and activities that can provide learners with rich language input: target-like input that displays 'quality, quantity, variety, genuineness, and relevance' (Long, 2015: 307).

These MPs can be difficult in language revitalisation settings. Providing learners with rich written input may not be an option if there are few or no existing texts in the language, and elaborating texts can be doubly time-consuming in language revitalisation contexts because usage norms related to grammar and writing may be less well established among teachers and other authorities on the language. Exposing learners to rich spoken input can also be particularly difficult if the number of highly proficient speakers is rapidly declining. Still, providing learners with rich and elaborated input was a priority for the Zapotec and Salish teachers, and we offer examples of how these principles were realised or interpreted in the two contexts.

10B.5.2 Understanding the Uses of Traditional Tools in Zapotec

As part of the effort to provide students with rich input at the Zapotec programme, the group visited the home of a Zapotec-speaking woman in the community, Lupe, where she described different traditional tools and items in her house and their uses. Students were asked to listen and figure out the purpose of each item. The speaker knew what the tools were used for but the students did not, so there was an authentic information gap (e.g., Ellis 2009). Students demonstrated their comprehension by reiterating each item's use, which they often did by translating into Spanish. A simple transcription of one part of the interaction is given in Table 10B.1, in which Lupe is showing a woven ring that is used for setting a hot pot on so that it does not burn the table or ground below it.

We see in the example in Table 10B.1 that in order to help students understand, the speaker does not oversimplify the input or switch to Spanish but instead elaborates the Zapotec input students are receiving. She does this by adding redundancy and paraphrasing in a few different ways: 'for putting a pot on, so that it doesn't touch the ground', 'it supports a pot', 'we put a pot right here'. The example suggests that the existence of an authentic information gap led naturally to rich and elaborated input.

Table 10B.1 *Rich and elaborated input (Riestenberg, 2020a)*

Line	Speaker	Zapotec	English
1	Lupe	Para guduariu tu edhu'.	For putting a pot on.
2		Para ke' ni bittu bittu ... dhi'na	So that it doesn't doesn't ... touch
3		Bittu dhi'na la'lu pa ke' lo yu.	So that it doesn't touch the ground.
4		Lani uduariuna na ani na antusa ...	We put it here like this and a lot ...
5		Bixa te'ni antusa ruchiakana.	It supports a lot of things.
6		Ruchia ke' edhu'. Ke' edhu guduarini.	It supports a pot. We put the pot here.
7		Edhu' guduariu lo ni.	We put a pot right here.
8		Edhu' risia.	A boiling pot.
9	Student	Una olla [in Spanish].	A pot [in Spanish].

Without the elaboration, students did not understand, but with the help of paraphrasing and gestures, students began to pick up on the meaning.

10B.5.3 Elaboration of Content-Based Salish Texts

At the Salish Qlispe workshop, teachers explored the concept of input elaboration as it applied to written texts. To become familiar with textual features, teachers peer-edited elaborated texts using a technique that emphasised oral interaction through content-based information-gap tasks (e.g., Pica, Kang & Sauro, 2006). Texts were based on spot-the-difference tasks, which Sherris created based on Pica (2005) and Pica, Kang, and Sauro (2006) for science and social studies texts, as in Figure 10B.1

Teachers sat in dyads with the similar texts. Each text had several errors; these were different such that if one teacher's text had an error in one place, the other's text did not have that error; errors were not underlined as they are in Figure 10B.1. Teachers were instructed not to show each other their texts and read their texts aloud, alternating sentence-by-sentence. When they heard differences, they discussed them. Once a decision was made on who had the correct text, the teacher with the error corrected it with a pencil, in some cases asking their partner for more information, such as how to spell the correction.

Teachers then compared elaborated and unelaborated texts using sample English texts from Yano, Long, and Ross (1994). Discussion focused on the characteristics of the written text, such as repetitions, fewer pronominal references, and embedded glosses of lexical items. They identified the differences between the two types of texts and discussed how they could elaborate existing Salish texts. A few teachers commented that producing elaborated texts would not only be beneficial for students but would support their own Salish language skills by forcing them to analyse linguistic features.

Person A: Mitosis is a type of cell division necessary for sexual reproduction. It is limited to the reproductive cells in the testes, namely the sperm cells, and the reproductive cells on the ovaries, namely the eggs. Meiosis produces four reproductive cells, or gametes. These cells contain half the number (diploid) of chromosomes of the mother cell, and the chromosomes are not identical ...

Person B: Meiosis is a type of cell division necessary for asexual reproduction. It is limited to the reproductive cells in the testes, namely the sperm cells, and the reproductive cells in the ovaries, namely the eggs. Meiosis produces two reproductive cells, or gametes. These cells contain half the number (haploid) of chromosomes of the mother cell, and the chromosomes are not identical ...

Figure 10B.1 Spot-the-difference texts (Sherris, 2008: 2)

10B.5.4 Focus on Form (MP6) and Provide Negative Feedback (MP7)

Meaning, not language structure, drives lesson planning in a TBLT approach. However, instruction about language form is not entirely absent. Teachers are encouraged to 'focus on form' by briefly drawing learners' attention to language form (i.e., grammar, pronunciation) as a reactive response to communicative difficulties that arise during a lesson in which the primary focus is on meaning (Long, 2015: 317). Negative feedback is a type of focus on form that involves corrections of learner errors in a way that makes evident the difference between the correct and incorrect forms. This emphasis on feedback and contextualised correction and de-emphasis on language structure is helpful in settings with few documented grammar resources.

Further, ideologies surrounding language purity and speaking 'correctly' can lead to exclusion and prejudice in Indigenous communities (e.g., De Korne, 2016; Dorian, 1994). It may thus be particularly important in these settings to emphasise the type of supportive, rather than face-threatening, feedback that is promoted in TBLT. Hermes and King (2019: 149) found that using tasks with adult learners of Ojibwe 'created opportunities for interaction where the stakes of cultural capital were not as high and risk-taking not as daunting'. With this context in mind, we offer examples of how teachers realised or imagined feedback at the Zapotec and Salish programmes.

10B.6 Answering the Question 'Where Are You Going?' in Zapotec

One goal of the Zapotec programme was for students to be able to respond to 'small talk' questions that a Zapotec speaker might ask them when running into them on the street. Table 10B.2 shows an abbreviated transcript from a part of this pedagogical task. A student is practising answering the question, 'Where are you going?' by telling her interlocutor that she is going to buy a miscellaneous food item from the store. The student has some coins with which to buy an item that is in the imaginary store created for the task.

We see that in line 4, the learner mispronounces the word goʔo (buy). The target word contains a rearticulated vowel broken up by a glottal stop and the learner instead produces a vowel with a long dipping tone and a glottal stop at the end: gòóʔ. This dipping tone appears in the target language on a different word that is part of the sequence, the word dàá (bean). In line 6, the learner again mispronounces the word goʔo (buy). The instructors recast the mispronounced word in lines 5, 7, and 8. In line 10, the linguist (Riestenberg) offers a physical mnemonic device that corresponds sound-symbolically to the troublesome word by performing a punching motion in the air at the time of the glottal stop. In line 12, this is contrasted with a second physical motion that represents the dipping tone of dàá (bean) by

Table 10B.2 *Focus on form (Riestenberg & Sherris, 2018: 450)*

Line	Speaker	Zapotec	English	Notes
1	Instructor 1:	gani dialu?	where are you going	
2	Student:	di- dia?- diaja?	g- g- I'm going	
3	Instructor 1:	diaja?	I'm going	
4	Student:	gòó?	to buy	*mispronunciation*
5	Instructor 1:	go?o go?o	to buy to buy	*recast*
6	Student:	gô	to eat	*mispronunciation*
7	Instructor 1:	go?o	to buy	*recast*
8	Instructor 2:	go?o	to buy	*recast*
9	Student:	go?o	to buy	*repetition*
10	Linguist:	a ver a ver go?o	let's see let's see to buy	(punching motion)
11	Student:	go?o	to buy	*repetition*
12	Linguist:	dàá	beans	(swinging motion)
13	Student:	dàá	beans	(swinging motion)
14	Linguist:	go?o	to buy	(punching motion)
15	Student:	go?o dàá	to buy beans	*repetition*

swinging an arm in the air making a U-shape. In line 13, the learner mimics the swinging motion and produces a correct repetition of both words. This sequence shows how a focus on form emerged from the communicative nature of the task.

10B.7 Talking about the Weather in Zapotec

Another example of feedback comes from a task in which students were discussing the weather with one of the Zapotec co-teachers at her home. We see in the example in Table 10B.3 that the instructor often recasts or repeats the words and phrases that students offer. In line 15, the instructor asks the students if it is cold out. One student responds simply with the word '*mata*' (sweater), which at first may be taken by the instructor as a mistake. However, instead of moving on, the instructor repeats the word and expands on the production by the student, asking next, '¿Bigua rkanli dilha', gweku'li mata?' (Do you think it's cold? Are you wearing a sweater?). After a brief pause, the same student responds, '*Oo, oo*' (Yes, yes), and the interaction continues.

10B.8 Practising Offering Feedback in Salish

The workshop for Salish teachers explored approaches for offering feedback through two immersion tasks and a role-play in Hebrew, a language unfamiliar to all participants but one known as a language revitalisation success (Spolsky, 1995). The first task was greetings and introductions. Sherris shook participants' hands, greeting each person and introducing

Table 10B.3 *Providing negative feedback (Riestenberg, 2020a)*

Line	Speaker	Zapotec	English	Notes
1	Instructor	¿Bini gulha sa dilha' o si …?	What's the weather like this afternoon cold or …?	
2	Students	Rka ubaa.	It's sunny.	
3	Instructor	Dila, dila gukua ubaa?	In the morning, in the morning was it hot?	
4	Student 1	Xilaa.	Hot.	
5	Student 2	Dila rka ubaa.	In the morning it's sunny.	
6	Instructor	Na'a chunna?	And now?	
7	Student 2	Be'.	Wind.	
8	Instructor	Be'.	Wind.	repetition
9		¿Bini adika'?	What else?	
10	Student 3	Be'.	Wind.	
11	Student 2	Chi reyu'u bia [bīá?].	It's cloudy.	
12	Instructor	Chi reyu'u bia [bíá], exactamente.	It's cloudy, exactly. It's cloudy.	recast
13		Chi reyu'u bia.	It's cloudy.	repetition
14		Chi reyu'u bia.	It's cloudy.	repetition
15		Pero bini rka na'ate- bini gua rkanli dilha'?	But what's it like now- do you (all) think it's cold?	
16	Student 4	Mata.	Sweater.	
17	Instructor	¿Bigua rkanli dilha'? Abi mata.	Do you (all) think it's cold? Not sweater.	
18		¿Bigua rkanli dilha'?	Do you (all) think it's cold?	
19		¿Gwekuli mata?	Are you (all) wearing a sweater?	expansion
20	Student 4	*points to the sweater she is wearing*		
21	Instructor	¿Gwekuli mata?	Are you (all) wearing a sweater?	
22	Student 4	Oo. Oo.	Yes. Yes.	
23	Instructor	Rka dilha'. ¿Chi rka dilha'?	It's cold. Is it already cold?	
24	Student 4	*gestures 'a little' with thumb and forefinger*		
25	Instructor	Lattito.	A little bit.	takes up gesture
26	Students	Lattito.	A little bit.	

himself. Participants followed suit with relative ease. He followed this with a simple Hebrew guessing game with separate laminated illustrations of objects hung with blue tack in front of the class. Smaller illustrations of the same objects were on a table with a low screen so the small illustrations were outside of view. Sherris physically enacted the game while speaking Hebrew, providing the language necessary to play the game with each enactment.

Participants watched while Sherris selected a small illustration and dropped it into an envelope. They only saw the back of the illustration, so they did not know which one he had selected. Then he pointed to one teacher and asked them to stand by raising his hands and asked them to come towards him by gesturing towards himself. These instructions were easy to follow. Eventually, through prompts and priming, participants were leading the game too. After that, Sherris asked, 'What do I have?' as he waved the envelope and pointed to the large versions of illustrations behind him. Then he prompted and primed participants to ask, 'Do you have X?' He would respond 'Yes, I do' and nod or 'No, I don't' and shake his head as appropriate. When the selected participant pointed to an illustration and named it with rising intonation, Sherris recasted it as he had earlier prompted the participants to say, 'Do you have X?' Alternatively, Sherris simply repeated with rising intonation the name of the illustration the participant had pointed to, to elicit a nod, which he would recast with 'Yes!' If the guess was incorrect, Sherris would exclaim, 'Aww', frown, and tell the participant to return to their seat, thanking the participant by name as he moved his palms together, facing upward. Then Sherris removed from the wall the large illustration of the incorrect guess and began the game again with another participant.

If the participant guessed correctly, they began to lead the game and Sherris used prompts, priming, and recasts for support as well as gestural and verbal backchanneling to encourage output. After several turns, the participants began prompting, priming, and recasting language from their seats. With more turns, the game required fewer primes, and Sherris introduced additional language such as 'Please' and 'It's your turn'. After about fifteen to twenty minutes of the game, Sherris stopped the game and asked participants to discuss the beginner Hebrew they had learned. He organised their comments under different headings on the whiteboard: prompts/priming, recasts, repetitions, gestures, facial expressions, and actions. As the discussion developed, Sherris discussed some of the research that demonstrates that these strategies promote second language development.

Finally, participants explicitly discussed the examples of feedback in Figure 10B.2. Sherris organised participants in a grouping configuration called an inside-outside circle. Participants on the outside circle faced participants on the inside circle and vice-versa. Sherris provided role-play cards with errors in English to each participant on the outside circle and

> 1. **Clarification request (incidental focus on form)**
>   S: *Pueblos will live in specific places in the Rio Grande of New Mexico.
>   T: When you say 'will live' do you mean they don't live there now?
>   S: No. They're living there now.
> 2. **Confirmation check (incidental focus on content)**
>   S: **The UN General Assembly passed the Declaration on the Rights of Indigenous People in 2-0-7.
>   T: Do you mean 2007?
>   S: Yup, (laughs) of course.
> 3. **Recast (incidental/reactive and indirect focus on form)**
>   S: *In the late 1800s Alcatraz Island was a prison for member of the Hopi Nation resisting assimilation.
>   S: For members of the Hopi Nation.
> 4. **Recast (incidental/reactive and indirect focus on form)**
>   S: *Today there are more than 500 recognise Indigenous nations in the US.
>   T: More than 500 recognised.
> 5. **Verbal and gestural backchanneling and repetition**
>   S: Pueblo is an unwritten language that relies on talking and pride in oral tradition.
>   T: Uh-huh [nods], Pueblo is an unwritten language on talking and pride in oral tradition.

Figure 10B.2 Some conversational feedback moves (Sherris, 2010: 4)
* Ungrammatical in Standard American English
** Incorrect content

participants on the inside circle had examples of different ways to provide feedback.

With the conclusion of this task, Salish participants were keen to discuss how role-playing these forms of feedback in English, their first language, raised their awareness of how they might vary the feedback they provide in Salish Qlispe during their lessons with children. They linked some of the examples of feedback, mostly recasts, to the important role recasts played when they were using Hebrew during the guessing game. For many participants, the Hebrew guessing game and the feedback role-plays worked together to help them imagine themselves as better Salish teachers.

10.B.9 Summary and Conclusions

The Zapotec and Salish contexts represent different approaches to adapting TBLT for Indigenous language instruction. The Zapotec teachers looked for everyday communicative tasks that learners plausibly *could do* in Zapotec, focusing on encouraging students to speak Zapotec in situations in which they were already interacting with Zapotec speakers in the community but doing so in Spanish. The Salish teachers, on the other hand, focused on the school itself as a new space for meaningful language use. We hope to have shown how task-based methodological principles (Long, 2009, 2015) were useful for planning and teaching in these settings and helped to promote or imagine meaningful interaction in the target languages.

Teachers at the Zapotec programme first chose tasks by identifying potential social spaces for meaningful use of Zapotec. They chose to focus on everyday interactions such as making purchases and discussing the weather, and they took advantage of the local speaker population by making home visits. They then focused on applying task-based methodological principles such as providing rich and elaborated input, offering negative feedback, and focusing on form. A benefit of these activities as they were implemented by the Zapotec instructors is that they required very little preparation ahead of time. They did not require worksheets, audio recordings, or preparation of scripted dialogues. Some materials were required, but these were things that could be easily found in the community. The main requirement was willingness on the part of a handful of speakers in the community to interact with the children in Zapotec.

The teacher workshop on Salish TBLT generated spaces for tasks to be experienced in Hebrew, English, and Salish, discussed in debriefing sessions, and used to support the handmade (re)production of Salish tasks for content-based instruction. During the half-day conclusion to the workshop, a teacher brought in a young student. Together, they engaged in a pictorial spot-the-difference task in Salish and some additional tasks such as an information-gap crossword puzzle. Afterwards teachers discussed the prompting, priming, recasting, and repetitions they heard as the teacher and young student interacted. To Sherris, as an outsider, they had indeed 'ruptured the silence with Salish talk'.

Further Reading

Hermes, M. and King, K. (2019). Task-based language learning for Ojibwe: A case study of two intermediate adult language learners. In T. McCarty, S. E. Nicholas, and G. Wigglesworth, eds. *A world of Indigenous languages: Politics, pedagogies and prospects for language reclamation*. Blue Ridge Summit, PA: Multilingual Matters, pp. 134–52.

Henze, R. and Davis, K. (1999). Introduction to authenticity and identity: Lessons from indigenous language education. *Anthropology & Education Quarterly*, 30(1), 3–21.

Hornberger, N. H. (2008), ed. *Can schools save indigenous languages? Policy and practice on four continents*. New York: Palgrave Macmillan.

Penfield, S. D. and Tucker, B. V. (2011). From documenting to revitalizing an endangered language: Where do applied linguists fit? *Language and Education*, 25(4), 291–305.

Riestenberg, K. J. and Sherris, A. (2018). Task-based teaching of indigenous languages: Investment and methodological principles in Macuiltianguis

Zapotec and Salish Qlipse revitalization. *Canadian Modern Language Review*, 74(3), 434–59.

White, F. (2006). Rethinking Native American language revitalization. *The American Indian Quarterly*, 30(1), 91–109.

References

Beam de Azcona, R. (2016). Zapotecan languages. Oxford Research Encyclopedia of Linguistics. Oxford: Oxford University Press.

De Korne, H. (2016). Imagining convivial multilingualism: Practices, ideologies and strategies in diidxazá/Isthmus Zapotec indigenous language education. PhD dissertation. University of Pennsylvania.

Dorian, N. C. (1994). Purism vs. compromise in language revitalization and language revival. *Language in Society*, 23, 479–94.

Ellis, R. (2003). *Task-based language learning and teaching*. Oxford: Oxford University Press.

Ellis, R. (2009). Task-based language teaching: Sorting out the misunderstandings. *International Journal of Applied Linguistics*, 19(3), 221–46.

Gass, S. M. (1997). *Input, interaction and the second language learner*. Mahwah, NJ: Lawrence Erlbaum.

Gass, S. M. (2003). Input and interaction. In C. J. Doughty and M. H. Long, eds. *The handbook of second language acquisition*. Oxford: Blackwell, pp. 224–55.

Gass, S. M. and Mackey, A. (2015). Input, interaction, and output in Second Language Acquisition. In B. VanPatten and J. Williams, eds. *Theories in second language acquisition: An introduction*. New York: Routledge, pp. 180–206.

Hermes, M. and King, K. (2013). Ojibwe language revitalization, multimedia technology, and family language learning. *Language Learning & Technology*, 17(1), 125–44.

Hermes, M. and King, K. (2019). Task-Based language learning for Ojibwe: A case study of two intermediate adult language learners. In T. McCarty, S. E. Nicholas, and G. Wigglesworth, eds. *A world of Indigenous languages: Politics, pedagogies and prospects for language reclamation*. Blue Ridge Summit, PA: Multilingual Matters, pp. 134–52.

Kiyosawa, K. G. and Donna, B. (2010). *Salish applicatives*. Leiden: Brill Academic Publishers.

Long, M. H. (2009). Methodological principles in language teaching. In M. H. Long and C. J. Doughty, eds. *Handbook of language teaching*. Oxford: Blackwell, pp. 373–94.

Long, M. H. (2015). *Second language acquisition and task-based language teaching*. West Sussex: Wiley-Blackwell.

Long, M. H. (2016). In defense of tasks and TBLT: Nonissues and real issues. *Annual Review of Applied Linguistics*, 36, 5–33.

Long, M. H. (1996). The role of the linguistic environment in second language acquisition. In W. C. Ritchie and T. K. Bhatia, eds. *Handbook of research on language acquisition*. Vol. 2. New York: Academic Press, pp. 413–68.

Pica, T. (2005). Classroom learning, teaching, and research: A task-based perspective. *Modern Language Journal*, 89, 339–352

Pica, T., Kang, H., and Sauro, S. (2006). Information gap tasks: Their multiple roles and contributions to interaction research methodology. *Studies in Second Language Acquisition*, 28(2),301–38.

Riestenberg, K. (2020a). Meaningful interaction and affordances for language learning at a Zapotec revitalization program. *The Language Learning Journal*, 48(3) 316–30

Riestenberg. K. (2020b). Supporting rich input and meaningful interaction in language teaching for revitalization: Lessons from Macuiltianguis Zapotec. In W. Silva and K. Riestenberg, eds. *Collaborative approaches to the challenges of language documentation and conservation: Proceedings of the 2018 Symposium on American Indian Languages*. Language Documentation & Conservation Special Publication No. 20. Honolulu: University of Hawai'i Press, 73–88.

Riestenberg, K. J. and Grupo Cultural Tagayu' (2019). Teaching Macuiltianguis Zapotec Collection of Kate Riestenberg and Grupo Cultural Tagayu'. The Archive of the Indigenous Languages of Latin America. ailla.utexas.org.

Riestenberg, K. J. and Sherris, A. (2018). Task-based teaching of indigenous languages: Investment and methodological principles in Macuiltianguis Zapotec and Salish Qlipse revitalization. *Canadian Modern Language Review*, 74(3), 434–59.

Sherris, A. (2008). Integrated content and language instruction. Cal Digest. Washington DC: Center for Applied Linguistics. Retrieved from: http://www.cal.org/siop/pdfs/digests/integrated-contentand-language-instruction.pdf.

Sherris, A. (2010). Coaching language teachers. *Cal Digest*. Washington DC: Center for Applied Linguistics. Retrieved from: http://www.cal.org/siop/pdfs/digests/coaching-language-teachers.pdf.

Sherris, A., Pete, T., and Haynes, E. (2015). Literacy and language instruction: Flathead Salish metaphor and a task-based pedagogy for its revitalisation. In E. Piirainen and A. Sherris, eds. *Language endangerment: Disappearing metaphors and shifting conceptualizations*. Amsterdam: John Benjamins.

Sherris, A., Pete, T., Thompson, L., and Haynes, E. (2013). Task-based language teaching practices that support Salish revitalisation. In M. C. Jones and S. Ogilvie, eds. *Keeping languages alive: Documentation, pedagogy, and revitalisation*. Cambridge: Cambridge University Press, pp. 155–66.

Spolsky, B. (1995). Conditions for language revitalisation: A comparison of the cases of Hebrew and Maori. *Current Issues in Language and Society*, 2(3), 177–201.

Thomason, S. G. (2006). Salishan languages. In K. Brown, ed. *Encyclopedia of language and linguistics*. 2nd ed. Oxford: Elsevier, pp. 732–33.

Van den Branden, K. (2006). *Task based language education. From theory to practice*. Cambridge: Cambridge University Press.

Wood, R. J. (2014). Language socialization, revitalisation and ideologies in the Salish-Pend d'Oreille community. Unpublished doctoral dissertation. University of Montana, Missoula, MT.

Yano, Y., Long, M. H., and Ross, S. (1994). The effects of simplified and elaborated texts on foreign language reading comprehension. *Language Learning*, 44(2), 189–219.

10C

Task-Based Simulations for Diplomatic Security Agents

Catherine J. Doughty and Emilio Pascal

10C.1 Introduction

United States Department of State Foreign Service officers are usually required to learn a language spoken in the country of their onward diplomatic position. Their primary objective is functional ability to do their jobs using the target language. The Foreign Service Institute (FSI) trains (a) diplomats (e.g., consular affairs, public diplomacy, management, and political or economic officers) and (b) specialists (e.g., diplomatic security, information technology, financial management, and general services) in more than sixty languages. We derived this case study from FSI's Spanish tradecraft curriculum developed with and for specialists who are Diplomatic Security (DS) agents. About half of all FSI Spanish students are returning students, already experienced at their jobs, needing to learn Spanish for their next onward post. The other half typically are entry-level officers and first-time language learners, who preferably attend FSI's introductory tradecraft training in English before enrolling in Spanish.

For *ab initio* learners, Spanish training at the FSI is twenty-four to thirty-four weeks,[1] full time,[2] and includes the embedded tradecraft component.[3]

The authors gratefully acknowledge several domain experts for their support and for contributions to the design of the task-based simulations: Warren Carmichael, Karl Jonathan Kahele, Lee R. Marple, John Root, Jesse Thomas, and Robert Weitzel. In addition, we thank the following domain experts for participating in interviews, focus groups and panels, for completing surveys, and/or for piloting course content: Avetyan Avetik, Brian Brodin, Brent Brown, Maria DeLeon, Mike Escott, David Gallagher, Julia Hawley, Jonathon Jensen, Alejandro Johnson, Jason Kephart, Jason Meixner, David O. Miller, Duane Mitchell, Patrick Mitchell, Guillermo Morales, Bruce Palombo, Michael Peart, Robert Picco, Jeremy Sims, Erica Smith, Mark Thornton, Sean Waters, Kevin O'Connor, Peter Koshorn, Ryan Renuart, Heather Hix, and Steven Slupski.

The views expressed in this chapter are our own and not necessarily those of the US government.

[1] About 50 to 60 percent of students complete the Spanish training in twenty-four weeks, which is the recommended amount of time. Students may be given four- or six-week extensions, up to thirty-four weeks total, provided they continue to progress. Many factors contribute the variation in training time, such as previous language learning experience, aptitude, personal life, and health,

[2] 5.5 hours per day in class, and 2.5 hours per day of autonomous learning.

[3] Either spread out over the last nine weeks, or offered intensively for two weeks.

The Spanish all-digital curriculum is delivered via Google Suite in the secure, cloud-based Foreign Affairs Network (FAN). Students link to the DS tradecraft site in the FAN. The native-speaking mentor and the students select the simulations that best match each student's job requirements. Students prepare on their own for three to four hours in advance. The DS simulations take place in the FSI Innovation Lab, a space for learning by doing – i.e., a virtual, simulated-immersion environment (González-Lloret & Ziegler, this volume). This twenty- by thirty-foot space is surrounded by three floor-to-ceiling screens, which display images, 360-degree panoramic photos, animations, and live apps, such as Google Maps and Twitter. The Innovation Lab at the FSI is an outstanding example of an "engineered, digital space" for doing "goal-directed, collaborative" tasks (González-Lloret, this volume). One simulation leads into the next, providing opportunities for task repetition with or without increased complexity (Robinson, 2011) and intertextuality. Both the level of job expertise and the level of language proficiency determine what students accomplish in each simulation.

10C.2 Diplomatic Security Needs Analysis

Developers at the FSI have continuous access to domain experts. The Foreign Affairs Security Training Center is located in Virginia, and trainers are always willing to consult with language course developers. At the outset of developing the Spanish DS simulations (2010), the FSI sent open-ended questions to DS agents in the field (see Figure 10C.1). In 2011, the FSI hosted a DS Panel to follow up by ascertaining the importance of using the foreign language at work and solicit specific situations in which DS agents typically do so (see Figure 10C.2). The FSI also interviewed upper management officers in the DS International Programs Directorate – Western Hemisphere (located in Rosslyn, Arlington, Virginia).

In the case of Diplomatic Security, it is not possible to collect target discourse samples during the needs analysis, due to safety and security concerns. Instead, the FSI asked the domain experts to provide (in English) useful terminology and phrases for DS agents overall, and for particular situations. Native speakers rendered them into Spanish. The experts also assigned a domain category to the terminology and phrases (e.g., VIP protection, crimes and incidents, transportation, etc.). This information was entered into a spreadsheet used as the basis for developing a job aid app for smartphones, so that terms and phrases are readily available to DS agents on the job, and uploaded to online tools for vocabulary practice (e.g., Quizlet). Domain experts routinely updated the tradecraft terminology. For example, in 2019, the Consular Affairs Job Aid was reviewed and substantially updated by a consular affairs officer when posted at the FSI.

> 1. What kind of Diplomatic Security work have you done when working overseas that requires the use of foreign language?
> 2. What specific situations or interactions do you engage in where you must use your foreign language skills?
> 3. What language skills are essential for your work (specific/technical vocabulary, listening, reading, uses the phone/radio, etc.).
> 4. You are currently in basic language training. Is there anything else you would like us to know to better assist you in learning the foreign language that you need to do your job effectively?

Figure 10C.1 Questions to the Diplomatic Security Panel

> - Suspicious behavior at the hotel close to the embassy.
> - Inspecting venues and VIP protection.
> - After-hours residential break-ins (communicating with the guard on the scene).
> - After-hours vehicle accidents (communicating with local police; first responders).
> - Meeting with host government contacts to solicit assistance in response to a natural disaster or disease outbreak.

Figure 10C.2 Diplomatic Security agents' requests for simulations

She identified visa interview practices that had become obsolete and provided phrases and terminology for new practices resulting from recent changes in US immigration policy.

10C.3 Diplomatic Security Simulation Materials Development

At times, Foreign Service personnel who complete their language training must wait for some weeks before leaving for their onward post. In 2016, an experienced DS agent, who was waiting to leave for Venezuela after completing Spanish training, contributed his domain expertise to the design of the immersive simulations discussed in this case study. His collaboration with the Spanish educational technology coordinator (Pascal) resulted in the overall design shown in Appendix 1. After the materials were developed, the FSI sent them to DS agents in the field for review. Figure 10C.3 displays some feedback on the prototype simulation materials for a VIP protection simulation.

The needs analysis first led to a distance-learning course: Spanish for Diplomatic Security. Figure 10C.4 shows sample feedback from DS agents who took the online course. It is clear that students perceived the relevance of the course for their needs, documenting what Long calls the true learner-centeredness of task-based language teaching (Long 2015).

> - I like this a lot and would use it myself, I am sure. Lots of useful vocabulary.
> - The only suggestion that I would offer regards last section – Protecting a US VIP. I think it does a good job of covering the traditional advance terminology. I would think of including some basic threat and attack scenario dialogue such as:
>   - Will the intersections along the roadway be controlled by the police?
>   - Can you identify some police stations or other "safe-havens" along the route where we can evacuate to if needed?
>   - If there is a telephonic bomb threat, we plan to ...
>   - At the site, is there a secure room where we can take the protectee in case of emergency or if he/she needs to use the restroom or make a phone call?

Figure 10C.3 Simulation design feedback from Diplomatic Security agents assigned in the field

> Did you find the course content offered during the pilot relevant to your job? Was it learnable? Did the course meet expectations?
> - "Very relevant. More relevant than the regular Spanish course."
> - "Extremely relevant." "Such a particular vocabulary set and skill set." "Absolutely fantastic for day-to-day use."
> - "Very commendable."
> - "Definitive tools necessary to get straight to the point." (i.e., provided the necessary situation-specific vocabulary).
> - "This program did open your mindset ... to what type of Spanish you would need in your job."
> - "The course anticipated things I would not have thought to ask."
> - "Absolutely met my expectations."
> - Students found that the course was not difficult; the specificity of the vocabulary made it more relevant to the job.
> - Students agreed that the course was a good complement to the traditional language courses because of the specificity.
> - One student expressed that the course increased confidence in ability to complete job tasks using the language.
> - Students found the lab work helpful; the scenarios were well-structured and left enough room to develop the vocabulary.
> - This could be used outside of the course to refresh Spanish language skills, especially as many DS agents move from post to post.

Figure 10C.4 Diplomatic Security agent feedback on distance-learning tradecraft course

Subsequently, the Spanish Section developed a face-to-face, task-based tradecraft module, which includes online materials for autonomous preparation and simulations in the Innovation Lab. Students access the materials using their own personal devices (e.g., smartphone, tablet, laptop) to connect to the FAN Google Suite, and the instructors can bring up the materials in class using a Smartboard.

10C.4 Diplomatic Security Simulation Pedagogy

To prepare for each immersive simulation, students navigate to the Diplomatic Security site, where they encounter three main areas of job responsibilities that emerged from the needs analysis – facility security, VIP protection, and investigations – divided into component job responsibilities, as shown in Table 10C.1.

When students select a simulation, they link to the following elements (in Spanish):

- a statement of objectives (i.e., what they will do)
- a concise description (e.g., "The US ambassador will give a presentation at the Museum of National Art in Mexico City for an audience of approximately fifty guests, including the local and foreign press")
- a detailed statement of their particular mission in the simulation (i.e., what they should accomplish, e.g., "Assess the security of the perimeter")
- some further points they may consider or encounter, which make the simulation more complex (e.g., "You may receive some instructions via cellphone").

There are also images of the simulation venue (e.g., front and aerial views of the Museum of National Art) embedded in the descriptions, often with live links to apps, such as Google Maps, showing the locale in real time. Students can link to two apps, Quizlet[4] and the Diplomatic Security Job Aid, populated with key vocabulary and phrases as described above. The target words and phrases appear as text, and students can click on them to hear the audio. Students can program Quizlet to test themselves according to the principle of spaced repetition. They can also print out lists of useful phrases from the job aid app to use as a scaffold during the immersive simulation or access the app on their smartphones during the simulation, just as they will do in future at work.

Table 10C.1 *Diplomatic simulations*

Facility security	VIP protection	Investigations
• Monitor suspicious activity • Assess risks at a venue • Screen and control visitors • Crowd control	• Prepare a protection escort • Conduct a security motorcade	• Fugitive US criminals • International kidnapping • Passport, visa, and/or document fraud

---

[4] Quizlet is a mobile and web-based study application that allows students to study information via learning tools and games (quizlet.com).

On the day of the immersive simulation, students (either alone or with another student) meet the tradecraft mentor at the FSI Innovation Lab. The student participates in the simulation as him or herself (i.e., the DS agent in our case), and the tradecraft mentor plays the role of a local official, for instance the head of the local police or a counterpart DS agent. As González-Lloret and Ziegler (this volume) point out, "in order to approximate real-world interactions, teachers have often used variations on role play tasks"; indeed, although the technology is new, immersive simulations feel very familiar to FSI instructors. However, while the instructors are native speakers of Spanish, they are not experts in the students' jobs. Therefore, it is not possible to participate in the simulations without prior training. The mentors become familiar with the simulation components from descriptions written by domain experts and learn language identified during the needs analysis, which may not be familiar to them. Moreover, instructors at the FSI are from various Spanish-speaking countries, and they may have to learn even everyday language from the region of the student's onward post. The FSI trains mentors extensively, and they spend time observing experienced mentors before they participate in simulations with students.

The Innovation Lab staff set up in advance, so that when students and the mentor arrive, they may "enter" the simulated immersive environment. During the simulation, the mentor and/or lab staff change the displays as needed. A key point is that because the student is the domain expert, he or she always drives the action in the simulation. Each simulation is highly flexible and can be adapted to different types of security circumstances based on the experience of the DS agent. Interestingly, because the student guides the simulation, new information about the job requirements sometimes come to light, amounting to ongoing needs analysis, which the FSI captures, and adding to the knowledge base of the mentors for future iterations with other students. Moreover, student comments keep the simulations current; for instance, they may notify the FSI that a particular procedure has changed (e.g., "Oh, we don't do it that way anymore – we do this ...").

10C.5 Diplomatic Security Simulation Observations

We observed three simulations in sequence – one from facility security (assess security risks at a venue) and the two from VIP protection (prepare a protection escort; conduct a security motorcade) – that cumulatively led up to the event of the US ambassador giving a speech the National Art Museum in Mexico City.

10C.5.1 Simulation 1: Assess Security Risks at a Venue (Museo National de Artes, Mexico City)

The student accessed materials on the Diplomatic Security site to prepare for the simulation (see Figure 10C, and see Appendix 1).

The mentor, who was playing the role of the museum's security and surveillance service official, was waiting for the student "in front of the museum." In other words, the surround screen displayed the Google Maps Street View of the museum, creating the immersive environment. The student was a very experienced DS agent, and his level of Spanish was functional (ILR Speaking Level 2). He arrived without any notes or vocabulary lists, and the entire simulation took place in Spanish. The two men introduced themselves in character, and the DS-agent student immediately took the lead asking questions about the area surrounding the museum. In his preparation, the DS agent had access to Google Street View, and he clearly had done some advance reconnaissance. The museum-security mentor answered the student's questions factually, which typically led the DS agent to request a particular security measure. The mentor usually agreed to the requests, but sometimes indicated a particular measure would be too expensive, or might not be necessary. That led to alternative requests from the DS agent. This segment of the immersive simulation is a clear example of learner agency (i.e., at the initiative of the learner, rather than the instructor, as mentioned by González-Lloret and Ziegler [this volume]). In other words, the realism of

---

Objectives
After completing the simulation, you will be able to:

- discuss the terrain and perimeter of a venue, and assess outside and inside security vulnerabilities before a VIP event.
- request assistance to reinforce security measures at a venue during a VIP event.

Scenario
The US ambassador will be giving a presentation at the Museum of National Art in Mexico City for an audience of approximately fifty guests, including the local and foreign press.

Mission
- Introduce yourself appropriately to your local contact.
- Identify the security risks at the venue.
- Request assistance from local police to support the security detail of the ambassador during the drop and exit at the venue.
- Based on your inspection of the venue, request any additional support you may consider necessary.
- End your meeting with your local contact appropriately.

Figure 10C.5 Simulation 1: Assess security risks at a venue

the immersive environment triggered the student to behave as he normally does on the job.

Once the negotiations were completed, and the DS agent indicated that he was certain that the perimeter of the venue would be secured, the mentor asked if he would like to go inside the museum to continue the risk assessment. At that point, the Innovation Lab technician seamlessly switched the surround screen to display 360 panoramic photos of the interior of the museum, which the pair "walked through" with the technician navigating virtually. While inside the museum, the DS agent asked specific questions to determine security. The mentor made some suggestions regarding the flow of the event, for instance, where the ambassador could wait before his speech, a good location for him to stand while giving the speech, and a location for the "meet and greet" after the speech. The student sometimes agreed, and other times spotted a security concern, which the two then worked out to the DS-agent student's satisfaction.

Throughout the immersive simulation, the DS agent was clearly making an effort to be collegial and build rapport with his counterpart. He appropriately used polite forms in Spanish and thanked his colleague every time the museum official agreed to a security request. This is a good example of what González-Lloret and Ziegler (this volume) point out is an opportunity to develop pragmatic competence in a simulated real-world context. It was evident to observers that, in the real world, the student is confident in doing his job, resulting in learner agency throughout the simulation. Moreover, so as not to interfere with the accomplishment of the mission, the mentor did not correct any language errors overtly during the simulation, but he did recast frequently. The student often noticed the recast and repeated it, and in several cases used the correct language later in the simulation.

The simulation ended with both men agreeing that the venue would be secure for the ambassador's speech and shaking hands. The mentor then went out of character and told the student that he had done very well and that he had understood absolutely everything he had said in Spanish, but that it was his job to make the student's Spanish perfect. He spent about five minutes pointing out a few persistent errors. As such, with respect to assessment, this observation revealed task-based student self-assessment as experienced in the immersive environment, followed by the instructor's language assessment. In other words, since the simulation is untimed, the DS agent continued until he felt satisfied that he had accomplished all the tasks in his mission successfully. The mentor, who is not a domain expert, focused on assessing overall comprehensibility and provided some focus on form (Doughty & Williams, 1998; Long, 1991), but did not comment on task accomplishment.

10C.5.2 Simulation 2: Prepare a Protection Escort

We observed two students doing this simulation, one after the other (the students also observed each other). The first was a male DS agent with considerable job experience, but somewhat limited Spanish (ILR Speaking 1+). The second student, a female, also with considerable job experience – in fact, coincidentally, had contributed to the original needs analysis described above – had returned to the FSI to refresh her Spanish (back to ILR Speaking 3) after a two-year tour in Israel. She was much more proficient, offering an interesting comparison. The mentor, also female, played the role of an officer from Mexico City Ministry of Public Security, wearing a prominent police ID badge.

Figure 10C.6 displays the materials on the Diplomatic Security site that the students viewed to prepare for the protection escort simulation. (See Appendix 2 for screen shots in Spanish.) The route planning was done a week earlier in the Innovation Lab with a different instructor playing the role of a police officer. The iteration of planning we observed simulated what would occur on the day before the actual event and motorcade were supposed to take place. In other words, the students had done this task once already in the Innovation Lab, and by double-checking the route, they were repeating the task, with new information.

When we arrived to observe, the two students were seated at a table outside the surround-screen area looking over lists of useful target-language phrases and questions they had printed out from the Diplomatic Security site, and they asked the mentor a few questions (in Spanish and English). None of the three was yet in their simulation roles. When the students were ready, they "entered" the office of the police chief, and from then on, all interaction was in Spanish. The surround screen displayed

---

Objectives

After completing this activity, you will be able to:
- evaluate and discuss any potential risks along the route to the venue with your local point of contact.
- request route analysis and police escort to the venue.
- coordinate arrival of VIP to venue.

Scenario

You will be in the motorcade that is taking the US ambassador from the embassy to the National Museum of Art in Mexico City. The ambassador will be giving a presentation at the museum for an audience of approximately fifty Mexican government officials and foreign diplomatic guests. Also, the accredited local and international press will be present at the event.

Mission
- As you take the ambassador to the museum, check for any potential security risks along the way with your local security contact.
- In addition, assess the situation at the museum.

Figure 10C.6 Simulation 2: Prepare a protection escort

Google Maps, in regular map mode, with the address of the National Museum of Art already entered into the live app (real-time display).

The (lower proficiency) male DS agent volunteered to do the immersive simulation first. He brought his list with him into the surround-screen area and began by reading a question concerning what the traffic would be like the next day, fully utilizing the scaffold. The mentor clarified the precise start time of the motorcade, and then described the likely traffic conditions. The DS agent was already very familiar with the security plan reviewed before, so he focused on details, at that point no longer needing the scaffold. As readers familiar with any GPS will know, Google Maps was suggesting three routes from the US Embassy to the art museum. The mentor/police officer discussed the pros and cons of each (e.g., capacity of side roads and traffic flow) as she clicked on them from her office computer (a laptop set up inside the virtual learning space displaying on the surround screen). As González-Lloret and Ziegler (this volume) stress, the technology should be integral to the task, rather than an add-on. For this reason, the mentor controls the Google Maps display during the simulation (not the Innovation Lab technician), just as would happen in the real world. The DS-agent student and the mentor discussed details of the security plan for the motorcade. The mentor did not correct the student overtly, but a few times when his pronunciation hindered communication, she asked for clarification. For example, he said "tres tracero," and she clarified "tres atras" (three behind)? They concluded when the student was satisfied with the plan.

The second, more proficient student began confidently, speaking fluently for nearly a minute, reminding her colleague that the ambassador will be giving a talk to some invited dignitaries, and that they had already approved the security plan inside the museum and previously looked at the route. She had her prepared materials to hand, but she did not refer to these scaffolds. She explained to the police chief that her purpose was to go over the security of the route, and she could see on Google Maps that there are two suggested routes (this changed from the three suggested routes for the previous student because, in real time, the traffic conditions had changed in Mexico City). While walking over to the map on the wall, the mentor police chief said that she wanted to clear something up: "Is the ambassador going to the museum from the embassy or the airport?" The student explained that they had just gotten the news that the ambassador wants the motorcade to pick up a colleague from the airport and then go to the museum. Therefore, she explained that they will leave from the embassy, go to the airport, then go to the museum. The mentor asked if she would like to check that route on the map to see how much time it will take, and the DS agent accepted. The police chief typed "airport" into Google Maps (visible on the surround screen), and the new route came up (real-time display). As she began to say that she could show an alternate route, the DS agent interrupted to indicate that the motorcade would not need an escort to the airport, but once they picked up the dignitary, they would like to ask for the escort from the airport to the museum. The student went on to discuss details in a much more elaborate way than the lower proficiency student had. She offered a detailed plan, which she devised on the spot. The police chief concurred that the proposed plan would be possible.

While typing in the name of the closest hospital, which then appeared on the Google Map, the police chief pointed out that the hospital is strategically located halfway between the museum and the airport, which the DS agent acknowledged to be helpful in case of any kind of problem. They went on to discuss possible routes to and from the airport, including going by the hospital both times. The DS agent suggested that they decide on the absolute final route in the morning based on the traffic conditions then. The police chief concurred and asked when they needed to arrive at the airport. They discussed the precise details of timing and agreed upon the meeting time. The police chief explained that the security at the airport is handled by a private company. The DS agent said they could work with that. The DS agent then informed the police chief of new information that the dignitary will arrive with four additional people. The police chief said she would notify security at the airport. This is another clear example of a student taking initiative (learner agency), as this information is not in the simulation preparation materials.

The DS agent announced that she was satisfied with the plan. She began to say that they would see each other in the morning, but the police chief indicated that she needed to verify some details, which they discussed further. The DS agent reminded her of the specific plan, and then they thanked each other (the police chief said, "We are here to serve") and took their leave.

This extended example shows the wide-range of job-specific vocabulary use that happens during a task-based immersive simulation designed from a needs analysis. The less proficient student was able to comprehend all the vocabulary, and the more proficient student used it all effectively. Moreover, the iteration of the simulation with the more proficient student provided rich input to less proficient student, who was observing, since even observers, and particularly domain experts, experience the immersion in the simulation. As in the venue-inspection simulation, the experienced DS agents each continued until completely satisfied that they had accomplished the mission. Because the second student was very fluent and reasonably accurate, the mentor provided very little focus on form. However, she assessed that the task was not fully complete because the plan needed to include some more details about the motorcade. When prompted, the student was able to comply with that demand.

Interestingly, after the simulations, the two students and the mentor continued speaking in Spanish, further expanding the rich input. The first student wanted to know if there really are dignitaries who visit and travel along that particular road. It so happened that one of the observers (Pascal) lived in Mexico City for years, so the mentor (from Bolivia) deferred to him. He verified that because the US Embassy is centrally located, he would see motorcades frequently. The second student then quipped that she was about to go for her progress assessment. She mentioned that her colleague had suggested that she skip the simulation and focus on that. However, this DS agent explained that in addition to being fun, the immersive simulation gave her confidence, and she felt prepared for the assessment. The choice to engage in the simulation rather than "study" exemplifies how motivating technology-enhanced task-based language teaching is, which González-Lloret and Ziegler (this volume) repeatedly point out is integral to its efficacy.

10C.5.3 Simulation 3: Conduct a Security Motorcade

We observed the same two students (one less and one more proficient), who had done the protection escort simulation the week before, now conducting the security motorcade they had planned (see Figure 10C.7 for details). The Innovation Lab was set up with a driving apparatus inside the surround-screen area (i.e., a steering wheel on a long table and floor pedals that control the movement of the car on the surround screen). The FSI's Innovation Lab used Unity3d, an application for game development,

---

Objectives
After completing this activity, you will be able to:
- give directions
- discuss potential security risks
- talk over the phone to coordinate VIP arrival at the venue
- make a request for extra local security measures.

Scenario
The DS agents in the motorcade taking the ambassador to an official event receive information that there is a protest outside the museum's main entrance, which is where the event is to take place. The ambassador wants to participate in the event and does not want to cancel it.

Mission
- Look again at the map of the museum area and determine the secondary and tertiary points of entry and exit for the ambassador.
- Discuss the new entry and exit points with your local security contact.
- Ask your local contact to increase the security measures.

Additional Considerations
The conversations you will have with your local contacts to protect the ambassador could be over the phone.

Figure 10C.7 Simulation 3: Conduct a security motorcade

and a LogiTech controller driver to create the virtual driving experience. The surround screen displayed an animation of the streets of Mexico City, signs, signals, buildings, and 3D objects, all created with Autodesk Maya and synchronized with the driving apparatus.

The DS agents participated in three iterations of this simulation on the day that we observed. The same mentor was still in the role as the police chief, and the students were themselves, the DS agents responsible for leading the security motorcade. Because one student was delayed, the mentor, in role, quickly improvised and said in Spanish, "Since your colleague has not arrived, if you like, I can drive the car." The student accepted the offer, rode shotgun and navigated from a map. There were working lights at each intersection, so the driver was obliged to stop at red (all the drivers we observed automatically looked to the left and right each time before continuing!). When the mentor police chief was the driver, she did not execute the stop very well because it was her first time using the driving apparatus. She apologized and quipped in Spanish, "I am a very bad driver." Without missing a beat, the DS agent replied that she was very grateful since the ambassador would not be delayed in arriving. "Not at all. It's all part of my job," was the reply of the police chief. This kind of humorous and polite exchange occurred frequently in all of our observations, revealing opportunities for developing pragmatic competence (González-Lloret & Ziegler, this volume) as prompted by the realistic simulated immersive environment.

Street signs, building names, monuments, and other landmarks were visible *en route* to the art museum. Usually, there was some discussion between driver and navigator of how the trip was going. One of the Innovation Lab staff inserted surprise encounters along the way that the driver and navigator had to manage. Sometimes a road was blocked off by construction cones, so the navigator had to suggest an alternate route; or there was an accident, which blocked the surrounding area entirely. This resulted in extended target-language use involving directions and commands. Upon arriving at the museum, there was a protest in progress at the front entrance. The DS agent developed a plan of entry on the spot. The student then agreed to be the one to drive back to the embassy.

In the second iteration, when the two students were driving and navigating, the mentor left the Innovation Lab and later called them on a cellphone to provide messages from the pre-arranged plan (agreed upon in the previous simulation, another example of intertextuality). The student who answered the calls on her cellphone relayed the information to the driver, and together, they decided what to do. At one point, the navigator got lost (they could tell because they kept driving over the same unique stone bridge). The driver pulled over, and they discussed the map together and planned their way back to the route to the museum. In addition to straightforward direction giving, the DS agents started joking that the ambassador was going to be "really late" for his speech. This is important to note because in ongoing FSI needs analyses, students continually report that they need to be able be to converse spontaneously and collegially in daily situations.

In the third iteration of this simulation, the students switched driving and navigation roles. In this case, the less proficient student navigator had had the opportunity to hear the directions given by the more proficient student. He was also a better map-reader, thus, despite his considerably lower proficiency, he handled the incoming cellphone messages adeptly and got the ambassador to the talk on time. After completing the security motorcade immersive simulation, the students told the mentor that they especially liked that one because they were too busy driving and navigating to look at vocabulary lists. They had to remember and use directional phases ("At the next intersection, turn left;" "Go around the block.") They asked if the simulation really looks like the streets of Mexico City because they reported that it is very important to know how to get around in the city where they are working. Pascal explained that they have replicated the area from the embassy to the museum to the extent possible in the simulated software. The students also mentioned that they would not use a map but would have a GPS in the car. This is a perfect example of the need to evaluate the use of technology in task-based language teaching; as already noted (González-Lloret & Ziegler, this volume), technology should be integral to the task. As it happened, Pascal, explained to the students that he was working on a prototype which connects the driving apparatus to Google Maps Street View, so they will soon be "driving" on the actual streets. The DS agents said that would be ideal, and suggested, in the meantime, to add north and south to the map because they normally orient themselves that way when carrying out their missions.

Shortly after observing the simulations, we interviewed two students. We asked two fundamental questions, as shown in Figures 10C.8 and 10C.9, which include some extracts from the interviews that reveal DS agents' perceptions of learning processes, motivation, learner agency, and job relevance.

10C.6 Discussion

One of the most frequently asked questions about task-based language teaching is, "Could you point me to an example where it has been implemented successfully?" This extended case study offers such examples, representative of many routinely carried out in dozens of languages in the FSI's Innovation Lab, a virtual space for learning by doing. These examples show that technology enhancements in immersive simulations promote learner agency, collaborative learning, intertextuality, negotiation for meaning, pragmatic competence, and implicit learning via episodic memory. Moreover, learning by doing in a simulated immersive

DOUGHTY:	How is language learning different during the simulation compared with in class?
DS AGENT (FEMALE):	It's a different way to learn. It's fun. It reinforces vocab and grammar.
DOUGHTY:	When you say "reinforce," what do you mean?
DS AGENT (FEMALE):	In class, you look at lists and things, but in the simulation, you apply the language in what you are doing. It helps me to remember when I am acting things out. It's using new words to do your job. You have the context for using the new words. I really like the simulations. They are fun and practical. And, I want to learn everything because I know I need it. I tell other students (entry-level officers) that they are going to really need this. One time, I was working in Israel, and I had to do a hotel advance check. I did not speak Hebrew, but I noticed that the guard was Brazilian. I asked if he happened to speak Spanish, and he did, so we did the whole check in Spanish in Israel. You have FSNIs [Foreign Service National Investigators] to help, but it is much better if you know what they are talking about and what you are agreeing to.
DOUGHTY:	I noticed that you took initiative quite a lot …
DS AGENT (FEMALE):	I do that to make it more realistic. I take charge in my job. It is better if you know the particular job. For the checking the car one [not observed], I do not have to do that. I don't know how a metal detector works. For that one, it might be better if I just had to follow the directions of someone telling me how to do it. I know how to search people, but searching cars is very different.
DOUGHTY:	What do you do to prepare?
DS AGENT:	I read the scenario, and I go over the vocab list. I do the Quizlet. The night before, I review the vocab. For the Suspicious Persons scenario that we did this week, most of the vocab was already familiar to me, so I just concentrated on the new phrases like "parental kidnapping." One thing I liked about that one is that we had to create the story behind what happened.
DOUGHTY:	What do you mean by "story"?
DS AGENT (FEMALE):	We had to make hypotheses.
DOUGHTY:	Anything else?
DS AGENT (FEMALE):	Humor throughout makes it fun to learn. During driving, we were saying to each other: We should do a J-Turn [evasive driving]! We asked the designer on the way out if we could have, and he said it was programmed in!

Figure 10C.8 Interview with female Diplomatic Security agent

environment is highly motivating, as it is clear that the simulations are relevant to learners' needs.

Another frequent question is, "Is this worth all the effort?" A practical advantage of simulated-immersive-environment technology is applicability in a wide-range of simulations. The technology supports many simulations because the apps and devices are integral to the task (e.g., Google Maps menu offers seventy languages). Even FSI's in-house animations are easily modifiable to include language and cultural

DOUGHTY:	How is language learning different during the simulation compared with in class?
DS AGENT (MALE):	My brain goes into a different mode. I am forced to produce. Even with mistakes. It's nice, in a way. I'm not as vulnerable. The simulation is a distraction that takes away my nerves. During the route planning last week, we had to produce even more. It's easier to produce words when you know what you are doing.
DOUGHTY:	What do you do to prepare?
DS AGENT (MALE):	Learning the vocabulary ahead of time helps. We started using it in class. But after, in the simulation, we have to speak to people in a different way. We can use our own jargon and terminology.
DOUGHTY:	Anything else?
DS AGENT (MALE):	During the simulation, I am on the spot and forced to produce. It reinforces which words you need to focus on remembering and being able to use. When I am driving, I have to think about what is coming on the right and on the left, and just talk.

Figure 10C.9 Interview with male Diplomatic Security agent

features of various regions (e.g., signs, road layouts, and landmarks). Thus, even though considerable effort is indeed is required – from needs analysis to materials development – once the design has been completed and implemented, the simulations extend to other students who do the same target tasks. This is particularly useful at the FSI because we have a regular throughput of students with similar job requirements.

Finally, simulated immersive environments offer a potential solution to one of the thorniest issues in task-based language teaching: how to promote task complexity, hypothesized to lead to more complex language development. In these real-world contexts, students drive the action, the trained mentors participate spontaneously, and technology offers useful tools for accomplishing tasks. We observed students and mentors alike pushing the tasks toward more complex versions by adding new information, springing surprises, and striving for task completion. It remains to be determined whether complex language development ensues. For this and in general, we agree with González-Lloret and Ziegler (this volume; see also Doughty, 2015) that technology-enhanced task-based language teaching is under-researched, but indeed promising and worthy of investigation.

Further Reading

Doughty, C. J. (2015). Accountability of foreign language programs. *The Modern Language Journal*, 99(2), 412–15.

Doughty, C. J. and Long, M. H. (2003). Optimal psycholinguistic environments for distance foreign language learning. *Language Learning and Technology*, 7, 50–80.

González-Lloret, M. (2016). A practical guide to integrating technology into task-based language teaching. Washington DC: Georgetown University Press.

González-Lloret, M. and Ortega, L. (2014), eds. Technology-mediated TBLT: Researching technology and tasks. Amsterdam: John Benjamins.

Study Questions

1. In which specific ways does a simulated immersive environment engage language learning processes?
2. How can task-based needs analyses ensure that technology use in immersive simulations is integrated, not add-on?
3. What can technology-enhanced task-based language teaching designers do to ensure that materials will generalize?
4. Does a simulated immersive feel genuine (Hint: you have to try one to answer this question)? If so, how does that benefit language learners?
5. Technology has the potential to promote important aspects of task-based language teaching, such as intertextuality offering rich input and increasing task complexity levels leading to more complex language use and acquisition. Discuss.

References

Doughty, C. J. and Williams, J. (1998), eds. Focus on form in classroom second language acquisition. Cambridge: Cambridge University Press.

Long, M. H. (1991). Focus on form: A design feature in language teaching methodology. *Foreign Language Research in Cross-cultural Perspective*, 2(1), 39–52.

Long, M. H. (2005). Second language needs analysis. Cambridge: Cambridge University Press.

Long, M. H. (2015). Second language acquisition and task-based language teaching. 1st ed. Malden, MA: Wiley-Blackwell.

Robinson, P. (2011). Second language task complexity, the Cognition Hypothesis, language learning, and performance. In P. Robinson, ed. *Researching task complexity: Task demands, task-based language learning and performance*. Amsterdam: John Benjamins, pp. 3–38.

Appendix 1 Domain Expert Design: Coordinate a VIP Visit in Mexico City

General Information

Who: Ambassador
What: Conduct a walk-through with security and arrange transport with local police. Re-opening ceremony (30-minute speech); Meet and greet (30 minutes).
Maximum time: 1.5 hours

When: Date of event
Where: Museum
Why: In support of US goals in country
How: Establish your points of contact (leaders) of security teams – obtain phone numbers

- How many teams will be present and types of teams (other security teams for foreign dignitaries, local police, local security, dogs, etc.)?
    - Security leader at venue/police unit(s)/concentric circles of protection?
        - Personnel #, type of uniform, weapons, etc.
        - Languages spoken by security
    - Strategic location of security assets
    - Plan for screening pedestrians
    - Plan to control access to the event

- Route analysis and request a police escort to the venue.

Perimeter Description

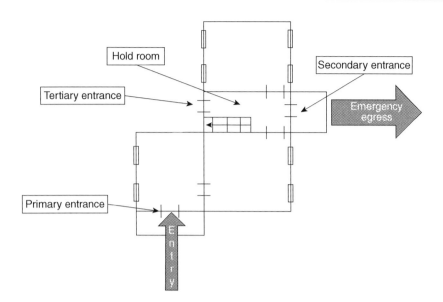

Appendix 2 VIP Protection Escort Preparation Materials

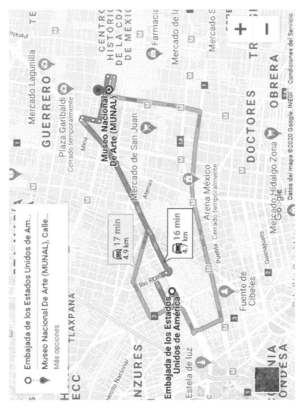

Copyright 2020 INEGI, Google Estados Unidos

Mapa del recorrido de la caravana de seguridad al lugar del evento

Haga click aquí para una vista ampliada del mapa con diferentes recorridos alternativos al lugar del evento.

Image capture: Jul 2017 Copyright 2020 Google United States

Imagery Copyright 2020 Maxar Technologies, Map Data 2020 INEGI Google

Vistas frontal y panorámica del Museo Nacional de Arte. Haga clic en las imágenes para una vista ampliada.

Part V

Task-Based Language Teaching with School-Age Children

11

Child Interaction in Task-Supported EFL/CLIL Contexts

María del Pilar García Mayo[1]

11.1 Introduction

This chapter focuses on the benefits that task-supported interaction brings for child foreign language (FL) learners, a comparatively underexplored population in the field of instructed second language acquisition. Specifically, the studies to be reviewed will consider the affordances of child–child interaction in a setting in which access to authentic input is restricted. Oliver, Nguyen and Sato (2017) consider the theoretical and methodological reasons for why child instructed second language acquisition has developed at a slower pace than research on second language (L2) acquisition by adults and, among other factors, they mention ethical issues and the potentially time-consuming nature of doing research with children (see García Mayo, 2021).

Within task-based language teaching (TBLT), defined by Ellis (2017: 111) as an instructional approach "to engage learners in natural language use and promote acquisition by having them perform a series of communicative tasks," research on L2 acquisition has recently expanded to new domains, one of them being TBLT in FL contexts (Shehadeh, 2018). As is well known, an FL context is one in which a target language is taught and learned in a setting where it is not the official language of the community (see Nikolov & Mihaljevic Djigunovic [2006] for differences between FL and L2 contexts). In an FL context, the learner has very few (three to four) hours of weekly exposure to the language and there is no access or very limited

---

[1] This work is part of the activities conducted within a program of research on child L2 task-supported interaction funded by grants FFI2016-74950-P (Spanish Ministry of Economy and Competitiveness, National Research Agency and European Regional Development Fund- AEI/FEDER/EU) and IT904-16 (Basque Government).

access to it outside the classroom. Although this situation is currently changing, due to widespread access to the Internet, which allows learners to contact native speakers at least in virtual environments (Pinter, 2011), it is of utmost importance to maximize their opportunities for learning in the classroom and to carry out research in FL contexts, in order to make informed decisions about appropriate education provision at this early stage.

Most research within TBLT in FL contexts has been carried out with adults and adolescents, mainly informed by two second language acquisition frameworks: cognitive (Long, 1996) and sociocultural (Vygotsky, 1978). The former considers learner interaction as a source of input, feedback and an opportunity to produce output, which might trigger mental processes that facilitate acquisition, such as noticing (Schmidt, 1990) and hypothesis testing (Swain, 1995). The latter sees interaction as a learning site where knowledge is co-constructed and studies how learners collaborate while completing tasks. It is that collaboration that supports their joint efforts when focusing on language problems, which Swain (2010) referred to as "languaging." It is striking, though, that given the increasing number of children who start their exposure to a FL early in life worldwide (Enever, 2018), only recently has research started to be carried out with this young population (Enever & Lindgren, 2017; García Mayo, 2017; Murphy 2014; Pinter, 2011). In fact, Collins and Muñoz (2016) have pointed out that primary FL programs are underrepresented in the second language acquisition field and that more research is clearly needed on the process of language learning in this setting.

This chapter will provide the reader with information about a selection of studies in which child participants aged 6–12 interact while completing different tasks in two FL settings, mainstream English as a foreign language (EFL) and content and language integrated learning (CLIL) (Dalton-Puffer, 2011), a teaching approach in which students learn about a subject (arts and crafts, science, history, etc.) using the language they are trying to learn. The findings of the studies will show how child–child task-supported interaction in mainstream EFL/CLIL settings is beneficial for these participants as they negotiate for meaning, focus on formal aspects of the language without the teacher's intervention, and collaborate with their peers. The children in the studies are all in the so-called middle childhood stage (Philp, Oliver & Mackey, 2008), a developmental stage characterized by children becoming more logical in their thinking. Moreover, they "can consider multiple aspects of a problem and imagine others' perspectives ... they are increasingly adept at turn-taking, topic-maintenance, and the pragmatics of speech acts such as requests ... and they already possess a highly developed L1 [first language] (or L1s)" (Philp et al., 2008: 6). Children at this stage do not hesitate to openly disagree with their partners or even try to cheat when carrying out a task (Oliver, Philp & Mackey, 2008).

An important clarification needs to be made from the outset: most studies to be considered in this chapter report data in task-supported language teaching programs rather than TBLT ones in the following sense: the tasks the researchers used were aimed at fostering communicative interaction among children in the low-input setting of FL classrooms and met the four criteria identified by Skehan (1998: 268), namely, (i) meaning is primary, (ii) there is a goal that needs to be worked toward, (iii) the activity is outcome-evaluated (i.e., successful completion), and (iv) there is a real-world relationship (i.e., "the discourse arising during task completion is intended to resemble that which occurs naturally" (Ellis, 2018: 24). However, the tasks were not integrated in the schools' curricula, as is the case in a small number of studies in FL settings, such as Shintani (2016), with Japanese children, and the case study reported by Oliver and Sato (this volume) with Chilean children. That is, the studies reported on in this chapter implement a weak version of TBLT.

In the following sections a rationale for the increasing interest in research with primary school children is provided, major findings from recent studies on children interacting in EFL settings are summarized, and lines for further research are suggested.

11.2 Learning Foreign Languages in Primary School: Interacting with Peers

Over the past three decades there has been an increasing trend for learning foreign languages in primary school. In fact, Mourão and Lourenço (2015) mention that in the European Union, over one third of countries have officially mandated FL teaching for six-year-olds (in Spain all seventeen autonomous regions mandate an early start as well) and Eurostat (September, 2018) reports that, within primary education, a clear majority of pupils (99 percent) learn English in the vast majority of European Union member states (see also Enever, 2018, for more updated figures). The learning of EFL is on the rise in East-Asian countries (China, Japan, South Korea, and Taiwan), as well (Butler, 2014), and Ellis and Knagg (2013) estimated that around half a billion primary-aged children were learning EFL around the world.

Among the reasons for this trend one can find "the younger the better" argument, which was extrapolated from successful immersion settings (Lyster, 2007) to FL contexts, where children did not clearly have the same conditions for access to input. Studies in FL contexts have shown that older starters outperformed earlier ones (García Mayo & García Lecumberri, 2003; Muñoz, 2006) and that age cannot be considered the only factor that affects FL learning. In fact, different studies have pointed to the amount and quality of input as one of the most relevant variables (Muñoz, 2019). Another reason has to do with the importance given to the knowledge of English for a person's future career and job opportunities, as the language has become a lingua franca (Jenkins, 2009) and there exists parental pressure on governments for adequate FL teaching provision. The early introduction of an FL might have benefits for children, as already pointed out in early work by Nikolov (1999): they may develop positive attitudes toward other languages and cultures and language awareness strategies (Kearney & Ahn, 2014). Language-learning opportunities could be enhanced, considering that children are able to grasp meaning drawing on paralinguistic features (intonation, gestures) and, in general, they enjoy playing and talking; in other words, they enjoy interacting with peers. In fact, Dunn (1999) notes that "What is common across so many child–child interactions ... is that they matter to the children: their emotional salience is unquestionable" (as cited in Oliver & Philp, 2014: 49).

As mentioned above, within the field of second language acquisition, there are two important frameworks that consider interaction as a key element for L2 development: the interactionist framework (Long, 1996) and sociocultural theory (Vygotsky, 1978). Research on second language acquisition has recognized the facilitative role of learner interaction in the learning process (García Mayo & Alcón Soler, 2013; Loewen & Sato, 2018; Pica, 2013). Interaction has been claimed to provide not only positive input, but also a context in which the learners are "pushed" to make their output more comprehensible (Swain, 2005) and notice (Schmidt, 1990) form-meaning connections. Input, output, and the feedback that learners may receive from their interlocutors (teachers and/or peers) play a crucial role in the language-learning process, and research has already shown a link between interaction and learning (Mackey & Goo, 2007).

Negotiation of meaning (NoM) is a particular type of interaction. It refers to the variety of conversational adjustments that interlocutors employ "to avoid conversational trouble, and tactically, to repair communication breakdowns" (Long, 1996: 418). Among those conversational adjustments, Long identified clarification requests, confirmation checks and comprehension checks, all of them illustrated in the following example, an excerpt from the interaction between two EFL children while completing a task:

1. CHI1: Where do you have the girl?
2. CHI2: What? **Clarification request**
3. CHI1: I have it in front of the door.
4. CHI2: Of the door? **Confirmation check**
5. CHI1: Is near the bench. You know? **Comprehension check**

(Lázaro Ibarrola & Hidalgo, 2017: 92)

In the example, CHI2 uses a clarification request (*what?*) to request more information about the preceding utterance, which CHI1 provides in the next turn. CHI2 then uses a confirmation check in turn 4 to make sure that he has understood the preceding utterance correctly. Finally, in turn 5,

CHI1 uses a comprehension check to determine whether CHI2 has really understood the information provided. As Oliver (2009) reported when analyzing interaction among children learning English as a second language (ESL), this is not a very common strategy at this stage of development because of children's egocentric nature and lack of interest in their partner's meaning.

To date, most research on interaction has been carried out with adult learners in ESL settings (Pica, 2013), and in a much lower proportion, with adults in EFL settings (Alcón Soler & García Mayo, 2009; Philp & Tognini, 2009; Shehadeh & Coombe, 2012. See García Mayo [2018] for references to interaction studies with adult EFL learners). As for children, except for the research in Canadian immersion programs (Lyster, 2007) and the pioneering work by Oliver (2002, 2009) with child ESL learners, little attention had been paid until recently to the process of interaction among primary school EFL children, probably under the assumption that child–child interaction would be highly unlikely in the low-input setting of an FL classroom. In previous research examining classroom observation data of languages other than English (LOTE) classes in Australia, from four primary schools and six secondary schools, Philp and Tognini (2009) suggested three main purposes of interaction in that setting: (i) interaction as practice (use of chunks or formulaic language); (ii) interaction as exchange of information, and (iii) collaborative dialogue and attention to form. The following section reports on experimental studies focused on child–child interaction in two FL settings, mainstream EFL and CLIL, and highlights the main findings derived from them.

11.3 Issues in Child–Child Interaction in Foreign Language Settings

This section considers several issues that have been reported in research in which children interact with peers while completing meaningful tasks. The following topics will be briefly considered: whether children negotiate for meaning, the type of interactional patterns they establish, their attention to language form while doing collaborative work and the role their shared L1 plays. The impact a task-implementation feature, task repetition, has on these topics will also be reviewed.

One of the first studies to be carried out in a FL setting with primary school children was Pinter (2007). She analyzed the oral interaction of one pair of ten-year old Hungarian EFL learners who had to complete a spot-the-difference task three times over a three-week period (with a different drawing each time). Pinter reported instances of peer assistance (provision of unknown words) and of the children's attention to each other's utterances. Although detailed, this study only considered one pair of children.

Within the framework of two national funded projects, García Mayo and colleagues have collected both cross-sectional and longitudinal data in several primary schools in the north of Spain. The participants were children aged 6–12 with a beginner proficiency level, as attested by standardized measures, who completed several communicative tasks designed by the researchers with the help of the teachers. Some of the children were enrolled in traditional mainstream EFL programs, in which exposure to the target language is limited to three to four hours per week, others in CLIL programs, in which exposure to the FL is usually between seven to eight hours per week because they include not only regular English language classes but also the teaching of content subjects in English. CLIL programs have been claimed to be more successful than mainstream programs because the amount of input learners are exposed to is larger and the type of input is qualitatively different (Muñoz, 2007), which has been argued to be responsible for the positive results observed in CLIL schools (Dalton-Puffer & Smit, 2007). Research to date has mainly reported overall benefits for CLIL learners in fluency and speaking confidence, a greater vocabulary and increased motivation, although the findings related to specific morphosyntactic features are hard to sustain (García Mayo & Villarreal Olaizola, 2011). In the following sections, the major findings regarding child–child interaction in FL settings will be presented, with comparisons between mainstream EFL and CLIL learners reported whenever possible.

11.3.1 Negotiation of Meaning in Child–Child EFL Interaction

García Mayo and Lázaro Ibarrola (2015) examined the oral interaction of a total of eighty third- and fifth-year primary school children (ages 8–9 and 10–11, respectively) enrolled in mainstream EFL and CLIL programs. They all had a beginner proficiency level, as attested by standardized tests. The researchers were interested in analyzing the children's NoM while they completed a picture-placement task. The children's performance (nine hours, approximately) was video-recorded after obtaining permission from the university's ethics committee, the school board, and the parents. The researchers considered conversational adjustments (clarification requests, confirmation checks and comprehension checks), repetitions (self- and other-repetitions) and L1 use. The data showed that both mainstream EFL and CLIL learners negotiated for meaning with age- and proficiency-matched peers. When matched for age (third-year CLIL vs. third-year EFL; fifth-year CLIL vs. fifth-year EFL), CLIL learners significantly doubled the number of conversational adjustments and made less use of their L1, probably due to their confidence in the use of the FL. When matched for context (third-year CLIL vs. fifth-year CLIL; third-year EFL vs. fifth-year EFL), the younger learners negotiated more, whereas the older used fewer conversational adjustments, and the L1 more frequently, probably because they considered the task too easy. In a follow-up study with the same cohorts of students but one year later, that is, when they were in fourth and sixth year of primary education, Azkarai and Imaz Agirre (2016) reported that, once again, the younger learners in both settings negotiated more often than the older ones. However, the findings regarding the impact of context were the opposite: when compared with mainstream EFL children; their CLIL counterparts were less likely to fall back on conversational adjustments. A possible explanation could be that children in the CLIL program had already gained the necessary skills to complete the task and it was not necessary for them to use conversational adjustments. In any case, the study points to the need for longitudinal studies in this type of setting, although access to schools is one of the major hurdles (see below).

Another study focusing on NoM strategies was carried out by García Mayo and Imaz Agirre (2017), who examined whether those strategies would vary depending on age and context, but also whether they would change over time. They analyzed the oral interaction of fifty-four children at Time 1 and Time 2, one year apart. The children, who were divided into four groups on the basis of their age (8–9 and 10–11) and their learning context (mainstream EFL and CLIL), completed a picture-placement and a guessing-game task (nine hours and twenty-six minutes of data were transcribed and coded). The study confirmed previous findings regarding overall tendencies: (i) the young learners used more NoM strategies and relied on their L1 to a lesser extent, (ii) children in the mainstream EFL program used their L1 more frequently and (iii) there was a decrease in the use of NoM among both groups of learners over time.

Research on NoM strategies with children in EFL settings has also shown that even very young children are able to use them. Lázaro Ibarrola and Azpilicueta Martínez (2015) identified the NoM strategies used by a group of sixteen 7–8-year-old Spanish children in a mainstream EFL program while they completed a guessing-game task. They reported that these children negotiated much less than adults and children in ESL settings, but they used all the NoM strategies except for comprehension checks. However, the lack of these checks should not mislead us into thinking that children are not interested in what their partners produce. Lázaro Ibarrola and Hidalgo (2017) analyzed the oral interaction of forty 11-year-old children in a CLIL program while they completed a picture-placement task. Besides completing the task successfully, displaying a moderate use of the L1, the children used two strategies, namely, acknowledgments and sentence completion, which revealed their willingness to cooperate with their partners. More recently, Hidalgo (2019) analyzed the oral interaction of eighty young Spanish EFL learners from two age groups (8–9 and 10–11) in a CLIL program. Although all the NoM strategies documented in the literature were used while the children completed a jigsaw task, she reported significant differences between the two groups: whereas the younger children negotiated mostly to repair communication breakdowns, using clarification requests, confirmation checks and repetitions, the older children showed a greater concern about their interlocutor's needs and negotiated to confirm that their message had been successfully conveyed. Consider the following example:

1. CHI2: a little boy?
2. CHI1: yes it have a t-shirt with many colors like ..
3. CHI2: blue   **utterance completion**
4. CHI1: blue red and black no?
5. CHI2: yes

(Hidalgo, 2019)

This example illustrates how CHI2 assists his partner by providing the word CHI1 was searching for, and shows that he is aware of the meaning his interlocutor is trying to convey.

The studies carried out so far among mainstream EFL and CLIL children have showed that they are able to negotiate for meaning with age- and proficiency-matched peers. Although to a lesser extent, they use the whole repertoire of interactional strategies attested in child and adult ESL studies, and other strategies, such as acknowledgments and sentence completion, that show that they care about their partner's production. Moreover, even though all these children have a beginner proficiency level in the FL, the older ones (10–11) use strategies that indicate a greater concern for their interlocutors' needs.

11.3.2 Repeating a Task and Its Impact on Patterns of Interaction, Attention to Form, Complexity, Accuracy and Fluency, and First Language Use

Teachers of an FL to young learners know how important it is to repeat tasks in the classroom. From a TBLT perspective, a task-implementation variable that has been researched with adults is task repetition (TR), which has recently been described as a "naturally occurring context for language learning" (Bygate, 2018: 1). The main claim in the literature is that TR offers learners the possibility of focusing their attention on formal aspects of the language that might have gone unnoticed the first time the task was carried out, when they prioritized the meaning they were trying to convey. This section summarizes studies with mainstream EFL and CLIL children repeating communicative tasks, and how that repetition had an impact on their patterns of interaction, attention to form, complexity, accuracy and fluency measures, and L1 use.

From a sociocultural perspective, the seminal work by Storch (2002) explored the relationship between learners' interactional styles and how they related to the quality of their work. She proposed a well-known model that classifies the type of interaction learners engage in into four types, based on two constructs, equality (degree of control or authority) and mutuality (level of engagement with each other's contributions). The four types of interactional patterns she proposed were: collaborative, dominant/dominant, dominant/passive and expert/novice. Storch reported that when dyads establish either collaborative or expert/novice patterns, peer interaction has a positive impact on language learning because learners pay more attention to language choice and retain knowledge that they co-construct. Collaboration among peers is analyzed by means of language-related episodes, defined as "any part of the dialogue in which students talk about the language they are producing, question their language use, or other- or self-correct" (Swain, 1998: 70). These language-related episodes have been claimed to be a sign of engagement and interest in task completion and to represent L2 learning in progress (Gass & Mackey, 2007).

As mentioned above, Pinter (2007) was probably the first study that assessed the impact of TR on learner interaction by recording a pair of Hungarian EFL learners completing a task. Her findings pointed to benefits for children at low proficiency levels. More recently, García Mayo and Imaz Agirre (2016) analyzed the oral interaction of 120 CLIL learners, 54 in their third year of primary education (mean age 7.9), and 66 in fourth year (mean age 8.98), who worked on two spot-the-difference tasks agreed upon by the teachers and the researchers. At Time 1 all children completed the same task, whereas at Time 2 twenty-one dyads repeated exactly the same task (exact TR), sixteen completed the same task-type but with different content (procedural TR), and twenty-three dyads acted as a control group, completing a guessing-game task. García Mayo and Imaz Agirre did not find any differences regarding NoM strategies at Time 1 and Time 2. However, they did find that procedural TR had a positive impact on pair dynamics. Moreover, they reported that the third-year learners fitted in the collaborative pattern, whereas fourth-year learners fitted mostly in the passive-parallel pattern identified by Butler and Zeng (2015) when studying development differences in interaction among twenty-four fourth-grade (aged 9–10) and twenty-four sixth-grade (aged 11–12) Chinese EFL learners. In both studies, it was the fourth-year learners that were characterized as passive-parallel because of their lack of engagement with each other's output. In other words, García Mayo and Imaz Agirre (2016) showed that children with the same beginner proficiency level display different collaborative patterns depending on their age range. Consider the following examples, which illustrate a collaborative and a passive-parallel pattern, respectively:

Collaborative pattern
1. Child A: and my picture it's a mountain
2. Child B: a what? **comprehension check**
3. Child A: a mountain
4. Child B: ah! Ok
5. Child A: *montaña* (mountain)
6. Child B: in my picture no, in my picture ..er ... it is .. a two ...
7. Child A: ¿*pistola*? (pistol?)
8. Child B: *la cabeza* (the head)
9. Child A: ¿*qué quieres decir*? (what do you mean?) **comprehension check**
10. Child B: *flechas* (arrows)
11. Child A: arrows, *sí* (ok)?
12. Child B: yes, arrows

(García Mayo & Imaz Agirre, 2016: 458)

Passive/parallel pattern
1. Child A: there is a snake?
2. Child B: er ..no
3. Child A: er ..there is a ... hat?
4. Child B: yes
5. Child A: there is a rock?
6. Child B: yes

(García Mayo & Imaz Agirre, 2016: 459)

Although in the first example the children use their shared L1 to move the task along, they use conversational adjustments and repetitions and are engaged with the task, unlike the children in the second example.

In recent work, Hidalgo and García Mayo (2019) report that TR has an impact on children's attention to form, operationalized as language-related episodes. They analyzed the oral interaction of forty children aged 11–12 in a CLIL program who repeated a collaborative writing task three times on a weekly basis, working with the same partner. One group (n= 20) repeated the same task (exact TR) and the other (n=20) the same task-type but with different content (procedural TR). In spite of their limited FL proficiency, these children focused on lexical and morphological aspects during collaborative writing, although most language-related episodes were form-focused in the two conditions and most were correctly resolved. The following example illustrates a form-focused language-related episode:

1. CHI2: they took
2. CHI1: take the ...
3. CHI2: took because the ..
4: CHI1: they take .took is in the past

5. CHI2: es verdad (it is true)
6. CHI1: is happening right now

(Hidalgo & García Mayo, 2019)

There is a group of studies that has considered the impact of TR on the complexity, accuracy, and fluency (CAF) of children's oral performance. Most studies on TR and CAF have been carried out with adults (Ahmadian & Tavakoli, 2011). Sample and Michel (2014) was the first one to consider CAF in the oral interaction of six Chinese EFL children (mean age 9.5), reporting that by the third TR, children were able to focus their attention on CAF simultaneously. Bret-Blasco (2017) has a much larger database of fifty Spanish-Catalan EFL children (9–10 at the onset of the study), who repeated two tasks at four points in time over a two-year period. Her findings supported Skehan and Foster's (2012) extended Trade-off Hypothesis, because the children improved the complexity and fluency of their utterances, but accuracy decreased upon TR. More recently, García Mayo, Imaz Agirre and Azkarai (2018) analyzed the oral production of 120 EFL children, 60 in third-year primary (mean age 8) and 66 in fourth-year primary (mean age 9.02) while they completed a spot-the-difference task at Time 1 and Time 2 under two conditions, namely, exact and procedural TR. They reported that procedural TR had a positive impact on fluency and accuracy at Time 2, specifically, third-year learners were more fluent, whereas learners in fourth year were more accurate, thus illustrating trade-off effects.

In FL settings, teachers are usually worried about having learners working in dyads or small groups because of potential use of their shared L1. Research with adults in FL settings (Alegría de la Colina & García Mayo, 2009; Antón & DiCamilla, 1998) has shown that balanced L1 use has positive effects on L2 learning. In general, adult learners use their L1 for metacognitive functions (to plan or organize the task), for metatalk and vocabulary searches. Pinter (2007) was probably the first to consider the impact TR had on L1 use. She reported that by repeating a task, the pair of young Hungarian EFL children's confidence increased, and they made less use of their shared L1. More recent research by Azkarai and García Mayo (2017) considered the impact of two types of TR, namely same-TR and procedural TR (i.e., the same type of task but with different content), on the L1 use of forty-two young Spanish EFL learners (9–10 years old) at T1 and T2 (three months later). The findings showed that there was a clear decrease in L1 use over time under the two TR conditions, but the number of L1 functions remained the same. The children in the study used their L1 mainly for lexical searches and borrowings, both functions connected to the need to avoid communication breakdowns.

In summary, recent research on EFL/CLIL children with a beginner proficiency level has shown that TR (i) has a positive impact on pair dynamics, fostering collaborative patterns, (ii) allows learners to focus on lexical and morphological issues and provide correct solutions for problems, (iii) has a positive effect on CAF, with trade-offs between the constructs, and, (iv) leads to a decrease in the use of the L1 that learners share.

11.4 Conclusion and Lines for Further Research

The main aim of this chapter was to show that children engaged in task-supported interaction in both mainstream EFL and CLIL settings, both low-input settings compared to second language and immersion contexts, are able to negotiate for meaning with age- and proficiency-matched peers, focus on formal aspects of language without the teacher's intervention, and solve most problems that arise. This research has also shown that a task-implementation feature, TR, becomes relevant when considering pair dynamics, attention to form, CAF, and L1 use.

There are, however, many lines of inquiry that still need to be explored in this under-researched area. For example, except for the work by García Mayo and Imaz Agirre (2019), there is no research on the impact of task modality (oral tasks vs. oral and written tasks; García Mayo & Azkarai, 2016) and pair-formation method (researcher-assigned, teacher-assigned, self-selected; Mozzafari, 2017) on pair dynamics and learning opportunities, operationalized as language-related episodes. When analyzing the oral interaction of thirty-one dyads of children aged 11–12, García Mayo and Imaz Agirre (2019) reported that most dyads were collaborative in both task modalities but the proficiency-paired group was significantly more collaborative than the other two groups. Moreover, these young learners generated more language-related episodes in the oral and written task, the lexical language-related episodes were more frequent than form-based ones in both task modalities, and at least 50 percent of the language-related episodes were correctly resolved. In addition, the pair-formation method had a clear impact on learning opportunities. Thus, researcher-assigned dyads (formed on the basis of the scores the children obtained on a standardized test) produced more language-related episodes than teacher-assigned and self-selected dyads. They also had more turns in their interaction and used the L2 more frequently (Imaz Agirre & García Mayo, 2020).

Another interesting research avenue is the study of collaborative writing tasks and attention to form among children. Collaborative writing has been claimed to be a crucial source of learning, as it is through collaboration that meaning is created and knowledge co-constructed (Swain, 2006). Dictogloss (Wajnryb, 1990) is a task that tries to draw learners' attention to formal issues in a communicative context and has been frequently used in research with adults, but not so much with children (Shak & Gardner, 2008). In a preliminary study of this topic, Calzada and García Mayo

(2020b) analyzed the effects of completing a dictogloss task on the development of the English grammatical knowledge (third person singular -*s* and articles) of 50 11–12-year-old Spanish learners. Their grammatical gains were measured by means of a grammaticality judgment test taken before and after the completion of the dictogloss. The analysis of their collaborative dialogue showed that the task allowed learners to focus on form equally, although not only on the target features.

Within the broader framework of writing-to-learn an L2 (Manchón, 2011), it is claimed that the provision of written corrective feedback activates cognitive processes that may lead to learning (Long, 1996). Studies should consider the potential of models and reformulations for children. Thus, Coyle, Cánovas Guirao and Roca de Larios (2018) reported that models attracted most of the nine- to eleven-year-old Spanish EFL children's attention to lexis, a finding in line with the study by Luquin and García Mayo (2020) with eleven- to twelve-year-old Spanish EFL children. Models appeared to boost the children's awareness and improved their writing skills, at least in relation to lexis.

Last, but not least, much more research is needed on individual differences, such as attitudes (Calzada & García Mayo, 2020a), motivation (Butler, 2017; Kopinska & Azkarai, 2020; Pladevall-Ballester, 2018), and young learners' communication strategies (Martínez Adrián, Gallardo del Puerto & Basterrechea, 2019), as they might all have an impact on these young learners' interaction.

Further Reading

Enever, J. (2018). *Policy and politics in global primary English*. Oxford: Oxford University Press.
Enever, J. and Lindgren, E. (2017), eds. *Early language learning. Complexity and mixed methods*. Bristol: Multilingual Matters.
García Mayo, M. P. (2017), ed. *Learning foreign languages in primary school. Research insights*. Bristol: Multilingual Matters.
Murphy, V. A. (2014) *Second language learning in the early school years: Trends and contexts*. Oxford: Oxford University Press.
Pinter, A. (2011). *Children learning second languages*. New York: Palgrave McMillan.

References

Ahmadian, M. A. and Tavakoli, M. (2011). The effects of simultaneous use of careful online planning and task repetition on accuracy, fluency, and complexity of EFL learners' oral production. *Language Teaching Research*, 15, 35–59.

Alcón Soler, E. and García Mayo, M.P., (2009), eds. Interaction and language learning in foreign language contexts. *International Review of Applied Linguistics (IRAL)*, 47(3). Special issue.

Alegría de la Colina, A. and García Mayo, M.P. (2009). Oral interaction in task-based EFL learning: The use of the L1 as a cognitive tool. *International Review of Applied Linguistics*, 47, 325–45.

Antón, M. and DiCamilla, F. (1998). Socio-cognitive functions of L1 collaborative interaction in the L2 classroom. *Canadian Modern Language Review*, 54, 314–42.

Azkarai, A. and García Mayo, M. P. (2017). Task repetition effects on L1 use in EFL child task-based interaction. *Language Teaching Research*, 21, 480–95.

Azkarai, A. and Imaz Agirre, A. (2016). Negotiation of meaning strategies in child EFL mainstream and CLIL settings. *TESOL Quarterly*, 50, 844–70.

Bret Blasco, A. (2017). A two-year longitudinal study of three EFL young learners' oral output: The development of syntactic complexity and accuracy. In M. P. García Mayo, ed. *Learning foreign languages in primary school. Research insights*. Bristol: Multilingual Matters, pp. 176–92.

Butler, Y. G. (2014). Current issues in English education for young learners in East Asia. *English Teaching*, 6, 3–25.

Butler, Y. G. (2017). The dynamics of motivation development among young learners of English in China. In J. Enever and E. Lindgren, eds. *Early language learning. complexity and mixed methods*. Bristol: Multilingual Matters, pp. 165–85.

Butler, Y. G. and Zheng, W. (2015). Young foreign language learners' interactional development in task-based paired assessment in their first and foreign languages. A case of English learners in China. *Education 3–13*, 44 (3), 292–321.

Bygate, M. (2018), ed. *Learning language through task repetition*. Amsterdam: John Benjamins.

Calzada, A. and García Mayo, M. P. (2020a). Child EFL learners' attitudes towards a collaborative writing task: An exploratory study. *Language Teaching for Young Learners*, 2, 52–72.

Calzada, A. and García Mayo, M.P. (2020b). Child EFL grammar learning through a collaborative task. In W. Suzuki and N. Storch, eds. *Languaging in language learning and* Amsterdam: John Benjamins, pp. 19–39.

Collins, L. and Muñoz, C. (2016). The foreign language classroom: Current perspectives and future considerations. *The Modern Language Journal*, 100, 133–47.

Coyle, Y., Cánovas Guirao J., and Roca de Larios, J. (2018). Identifying the trajectories of young EFL learners across multi-stage writing and feedback processing tasks with model texts. *Journal of Second Language Writing*, 42, 25–43.

Dalton-Puffer, C. (2011). Content-and-language integrated learning: From practice to principles? *Annual Review of Applied Linguistics*, 31, 182–204.

Dalton-Puffer, C. and Smit, U. (2007). Introduction. In C. Dalton-Puffer and U. Smit, eds. *Empirical perspectives on CLIL classroom discourse*. Frankfurt: Peter Lang, pp. 7–23.

Dunn, J. (1999). Siblings, friends, and the development of social understanding. In W. A. Collins and B. Laursen, eds. *Relationships as social contexts*. Mahwah, NJ: Lawrence Earlbaum, pp. 231–76.

Ellis, R. (2017). Task-based language teaching. In S. Loewen and M. Sato, eds. *The Routledge handbook of instructed second language acquisition*. New York: Routledge, pp. 108–25.

Ellis, R. (2018). *Reflections on task-based language teaching*. Bristol: Multilingual Matters.

Ellis, G. and Knagg, J. (2013). British Council signature event: Global issues in primary ELT. In T. Pattinson, ed. *IATEFL 2012 Glasgow conference selections*. Canterbury: IATEFL Publications, pp. 20–21.

Enever, J. (2018). *Policy and politics in global primary english*. Oxford: Oxford University Press.

Enever, J. and Lindgren, E. (2017), eds. *Early language learning. complexity and mixed methods*. Bristol: Multilingual Matters.

Eurostats (2018). Foreign language learning statistics. Document retrieved from: https://ec.europa.eu/eurostat/statistics-explained/index.php/Foreign_language_learning_statistics#Primary_education.

García Mayo, M. P. (2017), ed. *Learning foreign languages in primary education research insights*. Bristol: Multilingual Matters.

García Mayo, M. P. (2018). Child task-supported interaction in the Spanish EFL setting. Research and challenges. *International Journal of English Studies* 18, 119–43.

García Mayo, M. P. (2021) "Are you coming back? It was fun." Turning ethical and methodological challenges into opportunities in task-based research with children. In A. Pinter and K. Kuchah, eds. *Ethical and methodological issues in researching young language learning in school contexts*. Bristol: Multilingual Matters, pp .68–83.

García Mayo, M. P. and Alcón Soler, E. (2013). Negotiated input, output/interaction. In J. Herschensohn and M. Young-Scholten, eds. *The Handbook of second language acquisition*. Cambridge: Cambridge University Press, pp. 209–29.

García Mayo, M. P. and Azkarai, A. (2016). EFL task-based interaction: Does task modality impact on language-related episodes? In M. Sato and S. Ballinger, eds. *Peer interaction and second language learning: Research agenda and pedagogical potential*. Amsterdam: John Benjamins, pp. 242–66.

García Mayo, M. P. and García Lecumberri, M. L. (2003), eds. *Age and the acquisition of english as a foreign language*. Bristol: Multilingual Matters.

García Mayo, M. P. and Imaz Agirre, A. (2016). Task repetition and its impact on EFL children's negotiation of meaning strategies and pair dynamics. An exploratory study. *The Language Learning Journal*, 44, 451–66.

García Mayo, M. P. and Imaz Agirre, A. (2017). Child EFL interaction; age, instructional setting and development. In J. Enever and E. Lindgren, eds. *Researching the complexity of early language learning in instructed contexts*. Bristol: Multilingual Matters, pp. 249–68.

García Mayo, M. P. and Imaz Agirre, A. (2019). Task modality and pair formation method: their impact on patterns of interaction and attention to form among EFL primary school children. *System*, 80, 165–75.

García Mayo, M. P. and Lázaro Ibarrola, A. (2015). Do children negotiate for meaning in task-based interaction? Evidence from CLIL and EFL settings. *System*, 54, 40–54.

García Mayo, M. P. and Villarreal Olaizola, I. (2011). The development of suppletive and affixal tense and agreement morphemes in the L3 English of Basque-Spanish bilinguals. *Second Language Research* 27, 129–49.

García Mayo, M. P., Imaz Agirre, A., and Azkarai, A. (2018). Task repetition effects on CAF in EFL child task-based interaction. In M. A. Ahmadian and M. P. García Mayo, eds. *Recent perspectives on task-based language learning and teaching*. Berlin: De Gruyter, pp. 9–28.

Gass, S. M. and Mackey, A. (2007). Input, interaction and output in second language acquisition. In B. Van Patten and J. Williams, eds. *Theories in second language acquisition. An introduction*. Mahwah, NJ: Lawrence Earlbaum, pp. 175–99.

Hidalgo, M. A. (2019). Differences in the task-supported negotiations of younger and older EFL children: From repair into prevention. *International Review of Applied Linguistics*. https://doi.org/10.1515/iral-2018-0206.

Hidalgo, M. A. and García Mayo, M. P. (2019). The influence of task repetition type on young learners' attention to form. *Language Teaching Research*. DOI: 10.1177/1362168819865559.

Imaz Agirre, A. and García Mayo, M. P. (2020). The impact of agency in pair formation on the degree of participation in young learners' collaborative dialogue. In C. Lambert and R. Oliver, eds. *Using tasks in diverse contexts*. Bristol: Multilingual Matters, pp. 306–323.

Jenkins, J. (2009). English as a lingua franca: interpretations and attitudes. *Word Englishes*, 28, 200–207.

Kearney, E. and Ahn, S-Y. (2014). Preschool world language learners' engagement with language: what are the possibilities? *Language Awareness*, 23, 319–33.

Kopinska, M. and Azkarai, A. (2020). Exploring young EFL learners' motivation: individual vs. pair work on dictogloss tasks. *Studies in Second Language Learning and Teaching*, 10(3), 607–30.

Lázaro Ibarrola, A. and Azpilicueta Martínez, R. (2015). Investigating negotiation of meaning in EFL children with very low levels of proficiency. *International Journal of English Studies*, 15, 1–21.

Lázaro Ibarrola, A. and Hidalgo, M.A. (2017). Benefits and limitations of conversational interactions among young learners of English in a CLIL context. In M. P. García Mayo, ed. *Learning foreign languages in primary school. research insights*. Bristol: Multilingual Matters, pp. 86–102.

Loewen, S. and Sato, M. (2018). Interaction and instructed second language acquisition. *Language Teaching*, 51, 285–329.

Long, M. H. (1996). The role of the linguistic environment in second language acquisition. In T. K. Bhatia and W. C. Ritchie, eds. *Handbook of language acquisition* New York: Academic Press, pp. 413–68.

Luquin, M. and García Mayo, M.P. (2020). Collaborative writing and feedback: An exploratory study of the potential of models in primary EFL students' writing performance. *Language Teaching for Young Learners*, 2, 73–100.

Lyster, R. (2007). *Learning and teaching languages through content. A counterbalanced approach*. Amsterdam: John Benjamins.

Mackey, A. and Goo, J. (2007). Interaction research in SLA: A meta-analysis and research synthesis. In A. Mackey, ed. *Conversational interaction in second language acquisition: A series of empirical studies*. Oxford: Oxford University Press, pp. 407–53.

Manchón, R. M. (2011). *Learning-to-write and writing-to-learn in an additional language*. Amsterdam: John Benjamins.

Martínez Adrián, M., Gallardo del Puerto, F., and Basterrechea, M. (2019). On self-reported use of communication strategies by CLIL learners in primary education. *Language Teaching Research*, 23, 39–57.

Mourão, S. and Lourenço, M. (2015), eds. *Early years second language education. International perspectives on theory and practice*. Abingdon: Routledge.

Mozaffari, S. H. (2017). Comparing student-selected and teacher-assigned pairs on collaborative writing. *Language Teaching Research*, 21, 496–516.

Muñoz, C. (2006), ed. *Age and the rate of foreign language learning*. Bristol: Multilingual Matters.

Muñoz, C. (2007). CLIL:Some thoughts on its psycholinguistic principles. *Revista Española de Lingüística Aplicada*, 20, 17–26.

Muñoz, C. (2019). A new look at age: young and old L2 learners. In J. W. Schwieter and A. Benati, eds. *The Cambridge handbook of language learning*. Cambridge: Cambridge University Press, pp. 430–50.

Murphy, V. (2014). *Second language learning in the early school years. Trends and Contexts*. Oxford: Oxford University Press.

Nikolov, M. (1999). "Why do you learn English?" "Because the teacher is short": A study of Hungarian children's foreign language learning motivation. *Language Teaching Research*, 3, 33–65.

Nikolov, M. and Mihaljevic Djigunovic, J. (2006). Recent research on age, second language acquisition and early foreign language learning. *Annual Review of Applied Linguistics*, 26, 234–60.

Oliver, R. (2002). The patterns of negotiation for meaning in child interactions. *The Modern Language Journal*, 86, 97–111.

Oliver, R. (2009). How young is too young? Investigating negotiation of meaning and feedback in children aged five to seven years. In A. Mackey and C. Polio, eds. *Multiple perspectives on interaction*. London: Routledge, pp. 141–62.

Oliver, R. and Philp, J. (2014). *Focus on oral interaction*. Oxford: Oxford University Press.

Oliver, R., Nguyen, B., and Sato, M. (2017). Child ISLA. In S. Loewen and M. Sato, eds. *The Routledge handbook of instructed second language acquisition*. New York: Routledge, pp. 468–87.

Oliver, R., Philp, J., and Mackey, A. (2008). The impact of teacher input, guidance and feedback on ESL children's task-based interactions. In J. Philp, R. Oliver, and A. Mackey, eds. *Second language acquisition and the younger learner: Child's play?* Amsterdam: John Benjamins, pp. 131–47.

Philp, J. and Tognini, R. (2009). Language acquisition in foreign language contexts and the differential effects on interaction. *International Review of Applied Linguistics*, 47, 245–66.

Philp, J., Oliver, R., and Mackey, A. (2008). *Second language acquisition and the young learner. Child's play?* Amsterdam: John Benjamins.

Pica, T. (2013). From input, output and comprehension to negotiation, evidence, and attention. An overview of theory and research on learner interaction and SLA. In M. P. García Mayo, J. Gutierrez Mangado, and M. Martínez Adrián, eds. *Contemporary approaches to second language acquisition*. Amsterdam: John Benjamins, pp. 49–70.

Pinter, A. (2007). Some benefits of peer-peer interaction: 10-year-old children practicing with a communication task. *Language Teaching Research*, 11, 189–207.

Pinter, A. (2011). *Children learning second languages*. London: Palgrave Macmillan.

Pladevall-Ballester, E. (2018). A longitudinal study of primary school EFL learning motivation in CLIL and non-CLIL settings. *Language Teaching Research*, 23: 765–86.

Sample, E. and Michel, M. (2014). An exploratory study into trade-off effects of complexity, accuracy and fluency in young learners' oral task repetition. *TESL Canada Journal* 31, 23–46.

Schmidt, R. (1990). The role of consciousness in second language learning. *Applied Linguistics*, 11, 129–58.

Shak, J. and Gardner, S. (2008). Young learners perspectives on four focus-on-form tasks. *Language Teaching Research*, 12, 387–408.

Shehadeh, A. (2018). New frontiers in task-based language teaching research. In M. A. Ahmadian and M. P. García Mayo, eds. *Recent perspectives on task-based language learning and teaching*. Berlin: Mouton De Gruyter, pp. vii-xxi.

Shehadeh, A. and Coombe, C. A. (2012), eds. *Task-based language teaching in foreign language contexts. Research and implementation*. Amsterdam: John Benjamins.

Shintani, N. (2016). *Input-based tasks in foreign language instruction for young learners*. Amsterdam: John Benjamins.

Skehan, P. (1998). *A Cognitive approach to language learning*. Oxford: Oxford University Press.

Skehan, P. and Foster, F. (2012). Complexity, accuracy, fluency and lexis in task-based performance: A synthesis of the Ealing research. In A. Housen, F. Kuiken, and I. Vedder, eds. *Dimensions of L2 performance and proficiency. complexity, accuracy and fluency*. Amsterdam: John Benjamins, pp. 199–220.

Storch, N. (2002). Patterns of interaction in ESL pair work. *Language Learning* 52, 119–58.

Swain, M. (1995). Three functions of output in second language learning. In G. Cook and B. Seidlhofer, eds. *Principles and practice in applied linguistics*. Oxford: Oxford University Press, pp. 125–44.

Swain, M. (1998). Focus on forma through conscious reflection. In C. Doughty and J. Williams, eds. *Focus on form in classroom second language acquisition*. Cambridge: Cambridge University Press, pp. 64–81.

Swain, M. (2005). The output hypothesis: Theory and research. In E. Hinkel, ed. *Handbook on research in second language teaching and learning*. Mahwah, NJ: Lawrence Erlbaum Associates, pp. 471–83.

Swain, M. (2006). Languaging, agency and collaboration in advanced second language learning. In H. Byrnes, ed. *Advanced language learning: The contribution of Halliday and Vygotsky*. London: Continuum, pp. 95–108.

Swain, M. (2010). Talking-it-through: Languaging as a source of learning. In R. Batstone, ed. *Sociocognitive perspectives on language use and language learning*. Oxford: Oxford University Press, pp. 112–30.

Vygotsky, L. S. (1978). *Mind in society: The development of higher psychological processes*. Cambridge, MA: Harvard University Press.

Wajnryb, R. (1990). *Resource books for teachers: Grammar dictation*. Oxford: Oxford University Press.

11A

Tasks for Children
Using Mainstream Content to Learn a Language

Rhonda Oliver and Masatoshi Sato

11A.1 Introduction

This case study is based on research undertaken in a primary school in Western Australia – one that has adopted content and language integrated learning (CLIL) as an approach for teaching. The decision to use CLIL was made by the school leadership, in consultation with the school community, motivated by the seeming lack of effectiveness of previous language other than English (LOTE) programs that had been taught at the school. Because CLIL enables students to learn both content, in this case mathematics, and simultaneously a foreign language – Mandarin – its potential as an effective pedagogy has been enthusiastically embraced at the school, as it has been elsewhere. As with many CLIL programs, at this school it is underpinned by the use of content-focused pedagogic tasks, allowing us to closely examine the interface between CLIL and task-based language teaching (TBLT).

CLIL had its genesis in the successful immersion programs established in Canadian schools in the 1970s – programs that continue to current times (Cenoz, Genesee & Gorter, 2014). Like immersion, CLIL uses the target language as the language of instruction for teaching the content of mainstream subjects such as mathematics, science, social science, and the arts. A point of difference to immersion programs, however, is that in CLIL, the students' first language (L1) may also be used, as necessary, for teaching purposes. Although beginning in the 1980s (Marsh, 2002), CLIL is a relatively new language teaching approach, and teaching Mandarin to students from predominantly Australian English-speaking backgrounds is quite unusual in Australia. This is because, as in most of Australia, the majority of second languages (L2s) taught in Western Australian schools are European languages (e.g., Italian, French, and Greek) or Asian languages, such as Indonesian and Japanese. This means that the context of this case study is distinct in three ways. First, the linguistic distance between the students' L1 (English) and L2 (Mandarin) is relatively wider compared to other European languages, posing additional challenge for learners as they develop their linguistic competence of the target language (see Pasquarella, Chen, Lam, Luo & Ramirez [2011]). Second, the target language (Mandarin) is not a societal language or a language that is widely accessible outside the classroom; hence, L2 instruction in the classroom was the primary learning resource for the students (see Ballinger, Lyster, Sterzuk & Genesee, [2017]; Storch & Sato [2019]). Third, and most importantly, the target language is taught using a CLIL approach – that is, where content classes (i.e., mathematics) are taught using Mandarin as the language of instruction. As such, this provides a unique opportunity to investigate an instructional context that could potentially provide an insight into the ways in which CLIL and tasks can support L2 learning, especially for children.

As García-Mayo (this volume) notes, research on school-aged students is less prevalent in the literature than that undertaken with adults, yet teaching children a foreign language is a core part of the curriculum in many countries around the world. How to do this effectively, therefore, is an imperative for all educators concerned with teaching younger learners (see Oliver, Nguyen & Sato [2017] for a description of instructed child second language acquisition). Therefore, in this investigation we seek to explore how teachers can support their young students' L2 acquisition as they engage in pedagogic tasks connected with their CLIL. While we acknowledge that peers also provide a valuable source of data for L2 learning research (see Adams & Oliver [2019] for discussion), the complexities of data collection in real classrooms and the ethical constraints imposed in most child language research means that in this research we focused only on teacher–student interactions in Mandarin/CLIL mathematics lessons. We did this to address the following research questions:

1. What interactional moves do the CLIL teachers use when engaging their students in pedagogic tasks, and how do these differ according to the year levels they taught?
2. Do the teachers' use of interactional moves change over time?

11A.2 Method

The current study involved longitudinal classroom observation with two primary data sources: classroom observations and teacher interviews. Data were collected from four different mathematics CLIL classes for a duration of eight months, representing three school terms (the school uses a four-term system, with each term occupying approximately three months of an academic year). The participants included four CLIL teachers and their students (on average twenty-five students in each class – a total of a hundred). The students' ages ranged from six to ten years old, representing four year levels (henceforth, Year 1, Year 2, Year 3, Year 4). The first author had developed a close relationship with the school leadership team and the CLIL teachers before the current study, and they had been supportive of previous research undertaken at the school (e.g., Oliver, Sato, Ballinger & Pan, 2019). Because of its bilingual nature, the data collection and analyses were primarily conducted by a research assistant who spoke both Mandarin and English proficiently.

11A2.1 Context and Participants

As noted, the instructional context was a primary school located in Western Australia. The four individual teachers were in charge of each of the year levels. Their first language was Mandarin, although they spoke additional varieties of Chinese, as well. They were all women aged between forty-two and forty-six years old. Their overall and CLIL teaching experiences varied; however, at the time of data collection, they had had at least four years of CLIL teaching experience and had all completed workshops specifically targeting CLIL. Hence, we considered them experienced CLIL teachers. Table 11A.1 summarizes the demographic information on the teachers.

The student participants were those who were in the four CLIL classes. The majority spoke English as their first language

Table 11A.1 *Demographics of Mandarin CLIL teachers*

	Teacher			
Demographics	Year 1	Year 2	Year 3	Year 4
Gender	Female	Female	Female	Female
Age	43	46	42	42
Education	BA in education	BA in education	BA in education	BA in education
First language	Mandarin Hokkian	Mandarin Cantonese Malay	Mandarin	Mandarin Hainanese Li
Overall teaching experience (years)	8	10	10	16
CLIL teaching experience (years)	7	6	5	4

(approximately 75 percent) and approximately 25 percent were from a non-English background. Less than 10 percent of the total reported that Mandarin was either their first language or a language used in their home.

11A2.2 Data Collection and Analysis

Classroom Observation

The first source of data were classroom observations supported by recorded teacher–student interaction. Because of constraints concerning ethics approval, the recorded videos focused on the teacher-fronted activities (either pre-, post-, peer, or whole-class pedagogic tasks), although the students' utterances were audible and were included in the transcriptions. The research assistant was present during the observations and took detailed field notes. As the recorded CLIL lessons were concerned with mathematics, the pedagogic tasks included such things as working out the perimeter of a rectangle, determining the number of triangles in a pyramid, providing and following directions (e.g., moving different shapes) and using a clock to tell time.

The CLIL classes were video-recorded over three terms. In each term, two lessons were recorded for one hour in each year-level class, totaling twenty-four hours of recorded data (one hour × two classes/term × three terms × four year levels). During each of these hours, approximately twenty minutes were devoted to teacher-fronted pedagogic tasks. In order to normalize the frequencies of the focused interactional moves, these were divided by the minutes for each, yielding per-hour frequencies. In the results section, we report the total frequencies, along with the per-hour frequencies. Further, we calculated averages of two classes in each term, the frequencies for each term, which are also reported in the results section (Term 1, Term 2, and Term 3), representing the average scores.

The data were first transcribed by the chief research assistant and then verified by a second bilingual research assistant. Because of the considerable volume of data, the interactions related to personal communications and classroom management were not transcribed, although we acknowledge future CLIL research should explore this as a source of L2 use and development. Next, the focused interactional moves were coded based on what emerged from the observations and field notes, and informed by the literature.

Subsequently, 25 percent of the transcripts were coded by another Mandarin-English research assistant. Inter-rater reliability (simple agreement) was 89 percent. Inconsistencies between the two raters were discussed until agreement was reached.

Coding

The data were coded for five types of interactional moves: meaning-focused input, input-providing corrective feedback (CF), output-prompting CF, form-focused episodes, and L1 use. First, meaning-focused input included teachers' utterances that were made comprehensible for students through, for instance representation using objects, images, videos, or graphs that scaffolded the students' understanding. It also included repetition of words and phrases, whereby the teachers enhanced the input (Jensen & Vinther, 2003). As such L2 input that did not include any additional pedagogical or interactional effort on behalf of the teachers was not included in this category. Second, instances of CF were coded, with CF being information to the learners about what is and is not possible in their L2 (Mackey, Oliver & Leeman, 2003). This CF was further divided into input-providing types and output-prompting types, based on Lyster, Saito, and Sato's (2013) categorization. This was because of the differential effects that these two types of feedback can have on L2 learning (see Sato & Loewen [2018]). Third, we looked for form-focused episodes (FFEs), where the teachers explicitly drew students' attention to linguistic form (Ellis, 2016; Long, 1991). Finally, we analyzed the teachers' L1 use – when English was used in order for students to comprehend the input (Nakatsukasa & Loewen, 2015). See Oliver et al. (2019) for detailed explanations of these categories.

Teacher interviews

The second source of data were teacher interviews. Immediately following each observation, the research assistant conducted a brief interview with the teachers. Using the field notes, the interviewer reminded the teachers of specific moments when the different interactional moves were observed. The interviews were open-ended and focused on the teachers' decision-making processes. Hence, we used this information from the interviews to interpret the observational data. Examples of these will appear in the discussion section of this paper.

11A.3 Results

The first research question explored the frequency of the CLIL teachers' interactional moves and how these differed across four age groups. The second question examined changes over time.

Table 11A.2 presents the frequency of meaning-focused input moves, and Figure 11A.1 depicts the patterns graphically. The results show that the Year 1 and 2 teachers employed meaning-focused input moves more frequently than the Year 3 and 4 teachers did. However, the frequency of these moves decreased toward the end of academic year, making the

Table 11A.2 *Frequencies of meaning-focused input moves across four year levels over three terms*

Year level	Frequency		
	Term 1	Term 2	Term 3
Year 1	43.5	40.5	15.0
Year 2	42.0	18.0	9.0
Year 3	13.5	10.5	13.5
Year 4	19.5	19.5	19.5

Note: The frequencies represent the averages of the two lessons observed in each term. The frequencies have been normalized to show per-hour scores.

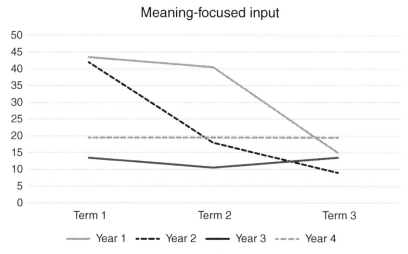

Figure 11A.1 Frequencies of meaning-focused input across four years over three terms

overall frequencies across the four year levels very similar by the end of the year.

The second move to be investigated was CF, which was further divided into two types, namely input-providing and output-prompting types, with the frequency of these shown in Table 11A.3. Figure 11A.2 presents these results visually. Although there do not seem to be any clear patterns within each feedback type, it is clear that the teachers used more output-prompting than input-providing types, regardless of the learners' age.

The third interactional move coded was FFEs. Table 11A.4 summarizes the results and Figure 11A.3 shows the results graphically. A notable pattern in this category relates to a Year 1 teacher who created a number of FFEs, yet their occurrence decreased over the course of three terms. Demonstrating individual differences, the Year 3 teacher appeared to avoid this interactional strategy altogether.

Table 11A.3 *Frequencies of input-providing and output-prompting corrective feedback across four year levels over three terms*

Year level	Term 1		Term 2		Term 3	
	IP-CF	OP-CF	IP-CF	OP-CF	IP-CF	OP-CF
Year 1	4.5	6.0	7.5	9.0	6.0	4.5
Year 2	0	6.0	1.5	3.0	0	3.0
Year 3	0	9.0	0	6.0	1.5	10.5
Year 4	0	3.0	1.5	3.0	0	0

Note: IP-CF = input-providing corrective feedback; OP-CF = output-prompting corrective feedback.

Table 11A.4 *Frequencies of form-focused episodes across four year levels over three terms*

Year level	Term 1	Term 2	Term 3
Year 1	15.0	0	4.5
Year 2	1.5	3.0	6.0
Year 3	0	0	0
Year 4	3.0	10.5	3.0

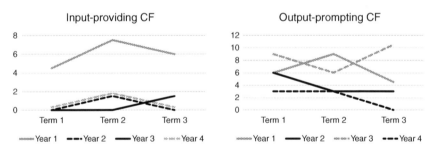

Figure 11A.2 Frequencies of input-providing and output-prompting corrective feedback across four year levels over three terms

The last interactional move to be coded was the teachers' L1 use (Table 11A.5 and Figure 11A.4). Clearly, the Year 1 teacher used much more L1 than the other teachers. Interestingly, her L1 use was comparable to that of the other teachers at Term 1, but drastically increased in Terms 2 and 3. The teachers from Years 2, 3, and 4 did not use English at all, or did so only minimally throughout the academic year.

Table 11A.6 and Figure 11A.5 report cumulative frequencies for each interactional move over the three terms.

Table 11A.5 *Frequencies of L1 use across four year levels over three terms*

Year level	Frequency		
	Term 1	Term 2	Term 3
Year 1	3.0	16.5	13.5
Year 2	0	0	0
Year 3	1.5	1.5	3.0
Year 4	0	0	0

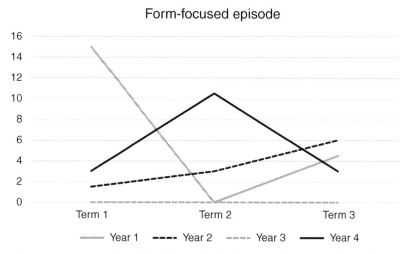

Figure 11A.3 Frequencies of form-focused episodes across four year levels over three terms

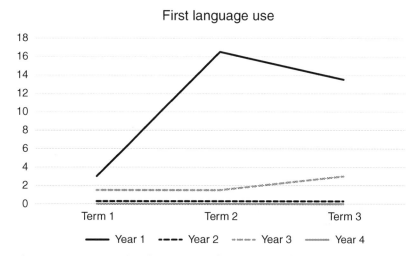

Figure 11A. 4 Frequencies of L1 use across four years over three terms

Table 11A.6 *Cumulative frequencies of focused pedagogical moves for each year level*

	Frequency				
Year level	MFI (per hour)	CF-IP (per hour)	CF-OP (per hour)	FFE (per hour)	L1 (per hour)
Year 1	66 (33.00)	10 (5.01)	13 (6.51)	13 (6.51)	22 (11.01)
Year 2	46 (23.01)	1 (2.01)	8 (3.99)	7 (3.51)	0 (0.00)
Year 3	24 (12.00)	1 (2.01)	17 (8.49)	0 (0.00)	4 (2.01)
Year 4	38 (18.99)	1 (2.01)	4 (2.01)	11 (5.49)	0 (0.00)
Total	174 (21.75)	13 (1.62)	42 (5.25)	31 (3.87)	26 (3.24)

Note: MFI = meaning-focused input; CF-IP = input-providing corrective feedback; CF-OP = output-prompting corrective feedback; FFE = form-focused episode; L1 = first language use.

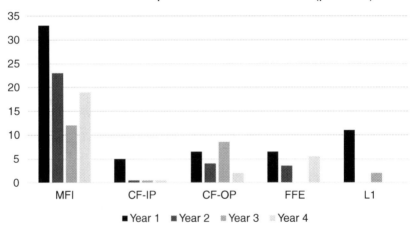

Figure 11A.5 Cumulative frequencies of focused pedagogical moves per hour
Note: MFI = meaning-focused input; CF-IP = input-providing corrective feedback; CF-OP = output-prompting corrective feedback; FFE = form-focused episode; L1 = first language use.

11A.4 Discussion

Although there was variability among the teachers and over time, it appears that when using pedagogic tasks as part of a CLIL approach, the teachers engaged in the type of interactional moves that are supportive of second language acquisition (Loewen & Sato, 2018). They provided meaning-focused input, CF (most often in the form of output-prompting feedback), provided FFEs, and used the L1 judiciously – all features purported to be facilitative of L2 acquisition. Furthermore, from the comments made during the interviews, it seems that the teachers were aware of the benefits of such interactional moves for both content and L2 learning. Further, the teachers' decision-making processes about which tasks to use to promote such interaction, and about the type of interactional strategies they selected, were informed by their awareness of the potential difficulty of the content for the particular year level they were teaching. These findings are discussed, in turn, next.

Firstly, when using pedagogic tasks, the CLIL teachers provided abundant and meaningful input to their students, and did so in various ways to scaffold their students' understanding both of the content and the L2. One of the ways they helped their students to understand was through representation using models, by drawing or using gestures and acting out the meaning. For example, the Year 4 teacher drew a rectangle on the whiteboard and pointed to each side:

TEACHER:	这是周长
	This is the perimeter.

The Year 2 teacher demonstrated the meaning of "slide" and "turn" by moving a toy chicken:

TEACHER:	以小鸡玩具为例，小鸡要平移，它可以转吗？
	Take this chicken toy as an example, if it slides to here, does it turn?
STUDENTS:	*(Silence.)*
TEACHER:	看小鸡的嘴巴在左边，如果老师把它平移到这里，它的嘴巴是在左边还是右边？
	Look, the beak of chicken is on the left. If I slide it to here, where is it, left or right?
STUDENT 1:	左边。
	Left.
TEACHER:	很好, 那小鸡的嘴巴还在左边，它有转吗？
	Good, if its beak keeps the same side (left), does it turn?
STUDENTS 2 AND 3:	没有。
	No.
TEACHER:	好，那现在老师把小鸡平移到这里，它有变大吗？
	Good. Now let me slide it to here, does it (size) grow bigger?
STUDENTS:	没有。
	No.
TEACHER:	恩，没有。我把小鸡平移到这里，它有变小吗？
	Right, it doesn't. What if I slide it to here, does it (size) become smaller?
STUDENTS:	没有。
	No.

The teachers were also observed using repetition, either repeating themselves or their students. The Year 2 teacher explained: "The content of Year 2 is more or less based on what they learned in Year 1. I give students time to think what they learned previously by repeating myself. I can tell from their faces they are recalling their knowledge and so this thinking time is worth it." Similarly, the Year 3 teacher described how she uses the same language patterns as a way to increase the amount of input she gives her students. She also suggested that this helps them "engage with the [target language] unconsciously in the long term." The Year 4 teacher, while using repetition, also challenged her students to deduce mathematical rules:

TEACHER: 长方形的长是多少厘米？
What's the length of this rectangle?

STUDENTS: 八厘米。
8 centimeters.

TEACHER: 对，宽是多少厘米？
Correct. What's the width of this rectangle?

STUDENTS: 四厘米。
4 centimeters.

TEACHER: 对了。这个长方形的周长等于什么？
Right. How to calculate its perimeter?

STUDENT 1: 这四条边加起来。
Add together all four sides.

TEACHER: 对了，我们还可以怎么算？
Right. Any other way?

The teacher provides time for the students to discuss this with each other.

TEACHER: 好，我们看这两条边(长)和这两条边宽是不是各自一样长？
All right. These two sides (length) and those two sides (width) are the same respectively, right?

STUDENT: Yes.

TEACHER: 四条边加起来就等于将长和宽相加的2倍，这样算(长方形)周长跟我们之前的结果一样吗？
Adding all four sides means the length plus the width and times by two, if we do this, is it the same result as we calculated earlier?

The teacher provides time for the students to calculate this.

STUDENTS
1 AND 2: 是一样的。
Yes.

TEACHER: 那我如果用这个方法公式算前面那个正方形，周长跟之前算的是一样的吗？
What if I calculate the perimeter of that square, is it the same result we got earlier?

Again the teacher provides time for the students to calculate this.

STUDENTS: 是的。
Yes.

She described her rationale for doing this in the following way: "I prefer to have them draw inferences about their relevant knowledge than just tell them the formula. It's a good way to help them understand what they have learned and memorise the new content." Therefore, in terms of input surrounding the content of the pedagogic tasks, the teachers' use of meaning-focused input reflected what they believed to be their students' understanding of the content and the L2.

This provision of meaning-focused input, however, changed over time and was seemingly dependent on the age of their learners and the amount of development the teachers believed occurred over the academic year. For instance, we can see how the teachers of the younger students (i.e., Year 1 and Year 2), provided more meaning-focused input than the other two teachers did. It would seem that these teachers perceived their students to need a greater level of scaffolding, both of the L2 and the content, especially at the beginning of the year, but less so as the year progressed. In contrast, the amount of meaning-focused input provided by the teachers in Year 3 and 4 remained fairly consistent throughout the year. As the Year 4 teacher explained:

> It feels like the information I need to provide stayed at the same level throughout the three terms. The content of each term is equally challenging for students, and maybe even much harder in the last term. For example, we do the calculation of perimeter in single 2D shape in term 2, and then it goes up to the calculation of area and volume in 2D and 3D shapes in the third term.

With the exception of the Year 4 teacher in Term 3, the teachers provided input-providing CF to their students. The Year 1 teacher, in particular, did so frequently explaining that for her: "It is straightforward to provide the correct form to students, especially about those 'difficult' new concepts," and that it was important to do so: "When their meaning is right, but with the incorrect form, I think it's important to give them correct linguistic form directly."

Sometimes, when the class was engaged in pedagogic tasks, she provided this feedback in the form of a recast:

STUDENT 1: 后面一步。
One step back.
TEACHER: 向后一步。
One step backward.

And at other times in the form of explicit correction:
STUDENT 1: 恩 ... 三角形。
En ... èr gè (two) triangles.
TEACHER: 对不起，没有，是。
Sorry, not èr gè, it's liǎng gè.

Generally, however, the teachers were more likely to provide output-prompting rather than input-providing CF. This included the use of confirmation checks, clarification requests, metalinguistic comments, and prompts. Decisions about the type of CF to provide seemed to be influenced by the students' content and L2 knowledge, as described by the teachers. The Year 3 teacher said: "I use more prompts and explicit correction strategies to help students produce the correct version of their meaning." For the Year 1 teacher, "Besides giving clues about the language (prompt), explaining the form of Mandarin is also needed with primary-level students." The Year 2 teacher said: "The general idea is to explain the difference between their L1 and L2 (i.e., metalinguistic comment) – it is 'dual work', but at times necessary, even for a simple word. And actually I found my students quite enjoy this process. They are hugely interested."

The results show that only three of the four teachers (Years 1, 2, and 4) engaged in FFEs during their teaching, when using pedagogic tasks, but it should be noted that in the classroom observations, all the teachers worked to draw their students' attention to linguistic form and did so in a variety of ways, just not necessarily via an FFE. They were all observed to use rising intonation, gestures and stress to show how to produce correct pronunciation, to indicate what the lexical item might be, or to model the correct grammatical form. In the following example, the Year 1 teacher uses gestures to illustrate the falling tone using her finger:

  Teacher: 现在几点了？
       What's the time?
  Student 2: 八点半。
       Half past eight.
  Teacher: 八点半。So that is "半"。
       Half past eight. It's called "bàn" (half).

From the teachers' interview comments, it did seem that they engaged in "focusing on form" quite intentionally. The Year 2 teacher, for example, said: "I know there is some basis of the [target language] among my students in Year 2, but there are many more linguistic forms they need to pay attention to." The Year 1 teacher indicated that for her: "Focus on form is a must-do strategy, based on the linguistic level of my students." Although the results did not show the Year 3 teacher using this strategy during the focused data-collection lessons, she suggested that this was because of the content and particular tasks used during the observed classes – that the pedagogic tasks that were used in the lessons at that time were more about calculation than about conceptual learning of new mathematical terms. In many ways, her response provides an explanation for the variable finding, namely, that the content being covered influenced whether or not, and how, the teachers focused on form. At the same time, there did appear to be individual differences in the interactional strategies used by the teachers, which was also the case with respect to their use of the students' L1 (English).

Only the Year 1 and Year 3 teachers were found to use the students' L1 in the observed lessons, and the Year 1 teacher's use increased over time (especially in Terms 2 and 3). This may be because she perceived her Year 1 students' L2 competence insufficient to allow them to understand the mathematics content she was addressing. In fact, both the Year 1 and Year 3 teachers indicated that their use of the L1 was because of the needs of their students and because of the content they were covering. The Year 1 teacher said: "I think using some L1 is appropriate in my class, especially when the content is complex." She also indicated that by using English, she could save time in the lessons. In contrast, the other teachers indicated that they made a conscious decision not to use the students' L1. The Year 4 teacher said: "I know they (students) can understand and are able to express their meaning with some time to think, to construct their language. Also, I don't want to spoil them. If I give the meaning of the new content in the L1 directly, they will be lazy. Although it takes time, it is a must-do thing in my class."

Hence, it can be seen that in this context, L1 use varied according to the age and ability of the students, and based on a conscious decision by the individual teachers. This finding does highlight some of the limitations of this study. Specifically, this research was undertaken in intact classes, each taught by a different teacher. So while we have described findings that may be related to age differences, the content and L2 proficiency aligned with the four year levels of the learners, these differences may well be related to the individual differences of the teachers. We also focused only on teacher-fronted pedagogic task interactions and not classroom management nor social interactions between the teachers and their students. Examining these interactions along with peer-group task interactions would furnish a more comprehensive picture of what happens in CLIL classrooms when tasks are used.

11A.5 Conclusion

This case study illustrates how pedagogic tasks used by teachers working within a CLIL context – where Mandarin is the language of instruction for children with mostly an English-speaking background – promote the type of interactional strategies that support L2 acquisition. It should be noted, however, that the tasks the teachers selected and the interactional strategies the teachers used appeared to vary according to the age of the learners and the curriculum content that had to be covered. In this way, they varied because of the teachers' perceptions about their students' abilities and needs.

Further Reading

Ellis, R. (2018). Towards a modular language curriculum for using tasks. *Language Teaching Research*, 23(4), 454–75.

García-Mayo, M. P. (2019). Pedagogical approaches and the role of the teacher. *Language Teaching Research*, 23(5), 537–40.

Oliver, R., Nguyen, B, and Sato, M. (2017). Child instructed SLA. In S. Loewen and M. Sato eds. *The Routledge handbook of instructed SLA*. New York: Routledge, pp. 468–87.

Oliver, R., Sato, M., Ballinger, S., and Pan, L. (2019). Content and Language Integrated Learning classes for child Mandarin L2 learners: A longitudinal observation study. In M. Sato and S. Loewen, eds. *Evidence-based second language pedagogy: A collection of instructed second language acquisition studies*. New York: Routledge, pp. 81–102.

Ortega, L. (2015). Researching CLIL and TBLT interfaces. *System*, 54, 103–9.

Sato, M. and Loewen, S. (2019). Towards evidence-based second language pedagogy: Research proposal and pedagogical recommendations. In M. Sato and S. Loewen, eds. *Evidence-based second language pedagogy: A collection of Instructed Second Language Acquisition studies*. New York: Routledge, pp. 1–24.

Tedick, D. and Lyster, R. (2019). *Scaffolding language development in immersion and dual language classrooms*. New York: Routledge.

Study Questions

1. Is there an interface between CLIL and TBLT?
2. If so, how does this manifest?
3. In what ways do pedagogic tasks used in CLIL align with the type of interaction that promotes second language acquisition?

References

Adams, R. and Oliver, R (2019) *Peer interaction in classrooms*. New York: Routledge.

Ballinger, S., Lyster, R., Sterzuk, A., and Genesee, F. (2017). Context-appropriate crosslinguistic pedagogy. *Journal of Immersion and Content-Based Language Education*, 5(1), 30–57.

Cenoz, J., Genesee, F., and Gorter, D. (2014). Critical analysis of CLIL:Taking stock and looking Forward. *Applied Linguistics*, 35(3), 243–62.

Ellis, R. (2016). Focus on form: A critical review. *Language Teaching Research*, 20(3), 405–28.

Jensen, E. and Vinther, T. (2003). Exact repetition as input enhancement in second language acquisition. *Language Learning*, 53(3), 373–428.

Loewen, S. and Sato, M. (2018). State-of-the-art article: Interaction and instructed second language acquisition. *Language Teaching*, 51(3), 285–329.

Long, M. H. (1991). Focus on form: A design feature in language teaching methodology. In K. De Bot, R. Ginsberg, and C. Kramsch, eds. *Foreign language research in cross-cultural perspective*. Amsterdam: John Benjamins, pp. 39–52.

Lyster, R., Saito, K., and Sato, M. (2013). State-of-the-art article: Oral corrective feedback in second language classrooms. *Language Teaching*, 46(1), 1–40.

Mackey, A., Oliver, R., and Leeman, J. (2003). Interactional input and the incorporation of feedback: An exploration of NS-NNS and NNS-NNS adult and child dyads. *Language Learning*, 35(1), 35–66.

Marsh, D. (2002), ed. *CLIL/EMILE: The European dimension – Action, trends, and foresight potential*. European Union: Public Services Contract.

Nakatsukasa, K. and Loewen, S. (2015). A teacher's first language use in form-focused episodes in Spanish as a foreign language classroom. *Language Teaching Research*, 19(2), 133–49.

Oliver, R., Nguyen, B, Sato, M. (2017). Child instructed SLA. In S. Loewen and M. Sato eds. *The Routledge handbook of instructed SLA*. New York: Routledge, pp. 468–87.

Oliver, R., Sato, M., Ballinger, S., and Pan, L. (2019). Content and Language Integrated Learning classes for child Mandarin L2 learners: A longitudinal observation study. In M. Sato and S. Loewen, eds. *Evidence-based second language pedagogy: A collection of instructed second language acquisition studies*. New York: Routledge, pp. 81–102.

Pasquarella, A., Chen, X., Lam, K., Luo, Y. C., and Ramirez, G. (2011). Cross-language transfer of morphological awareness in Chinese-English bilinguals. *Journal of Research in Reading*, 34(1), 23–42.

Sato, M. and Loewen, S. (2018). Metacognitive instruction enhances the effectiveness of corrective feedback: Variable effects of feedback types and linguistic targets. *Language Learning*, 68(2), 507–45.

Storch, N. and Sato, M. (2019). Comparing the same task in ESL vs. EFL learning contexts: An activity theory perspective. *International Journal of Applied Linguistics*, 30(1), 50–69.

11B

A Case Study of a Task-Based Approach for School-Age Learners in China

Yafu Gong and Peter Skehan

11B.1 Task-Based Language Teaching as a School Subject in China: Context and Problems

In 2000, China started an important round of curriculum innovation based on humanistic principles of education. The aim of the innovation was to change the over-emphasis on the memorization of book knowledge, and instead to encourage learners to become active and even interactive in the learning process, while developing more awareness of their social responsibilities, key character strengths, and competencies.

The Ministry of Education requires schools to offer the English program from Grade 3 (age 9) to Grade 12 (age 18) but more and more schools, particularly in cities, tend to offer it from Grade 1. The goal of the National English Curriculum is to develop students' overall ability to use the language and it has five objectives: language knowledge, language skills, learning strategies, cultural awareness, and affect. Communicative language teaching approaches are advocated, and task-based language teaching (TBLT) materials and new textbooks were developed. It has to be acknowledged, though, curriculum innovation in China has been conducted in a centralized fashion and "teachers, who are on the periphery of this decision-making process, merely implement the decisions that are handed down to them" (Markee, 1997: 63).

Most of the new textbooks in the English program were adapted from international series and have to be approved by the National Textbook Reviewing Committee. Local educational authorities then select one or two sets of approved course books for all the schools in a particular area. Originally, these textbooks were designed for the global market, so their topics mainly consist of "survival English," such as "asking the way," "ordering food in a fast-food restaurant." "Real-world" tasks are only considered "authentic" if they emulate what people do and represent the daily life of people in English-speaking countries.

In parallel to this, a number of public schools have been dissatisfied with the official coursebooks, and it is common for them to select supplementary materials. There are also many private schools not so rigidly bound to the approved set of English coursebooks. As a result, it is more open to them to experiment and select different teaching materials. Such materials, used in private and some public schools, are the focus of the current case study.

Although a TBLT ideology brought about some changes in teaching materials and methods, the authorized textbooks have provoked criticism in their adaptations and use. The criticisms include the following:

- It is difficult to distinguish a task from an activity.
- Most of the tasks are too difficult for elementary students.
- The concept of a 'task' is confusing.
- TBLT only promotes fluency, not accuracy.

As a result, many people concluded that TBLT is not suitable for the Chinese context and the National English Curriculum removed TBLT as a permissible approach in the revised version of the curriculum, published in 2011. In view of this, it is important to explore the various problems in greater depth. First, when one examines the current coursebooks, one discovers that although the National English Curriculum promoted a TBLT approach, most coursebooks are actually better characterized as following standard functional-structural approaches, not really TBLT. Second, people assumed that "real-world tasks" are those appropriate for an English-speaking environment. But these adapted books are not specially designed for students learning English in non-English-speaking environments. There is a mismatch between what learners want and what materials deliver – something which provoked complaints from students and teachers. The third problem is that, in the materials, the purpose of teaching English seems only to be used as a tool for communication. People complained that if this is the goal, most Chinese people will never have the chance to talk to an English speaker. Even when they do actually go abroad, they may use all kinds of cellphone-based translation devices to communicate for survival purposes. As a result of these problems, between 2013 and 2014, newspapers and other media launched a serious attack on English teaching.

11B.2 Wider Views on Tasks in Language Teaching

We turn next to considering whether a more international perspective can help us to propose appropriate changes to the current situation. Applied linguists and second language acquisition researchers have increasingly recognized the importance of tasks in language teaching (Long, 2015; Ellis et al., 2020). For teachers and curriculum developers, tasks can be used as means of structuring thematic content, facilitating learner–learner and learner–teacher interaction, enhancing experiential learning, and they can also be used for the internal organization of textbook content (Candlin, 2001). Graves (1996) also suggests that a major change in the selection of the content in communicative language teaching is an emphasis on the learners themselves. Learner factors, such as "attitudes, self-confidence, and motivation, and the learner's approach to learning" (24) should be taken into consideration.

Although second language acquisition researchers and curriculum designers advocate using tasks, there has not been much research on the wider use of tasks appropriate for learning. As Candlin (2001: 230) pointed out: "What is noticeable … is how little attention, proportionately speaking, has been devoted to exploring in detail the question of the role that tasks might play beyond the confines of the classroom." A key issue then becomes the meaning of the term "classroom reality," and this leads to some fundamental questions. What are the "real-world tasks" for students who are learning English in a non-English-speaking environment as a school subject? If students have no immediate use for the language outside the classrooms, how could English education be related to their life both inside and outside school?

Developing these concerns, Candlin (2001: 239) asks:

- How is the "real world" being constructed? In terms of which participants, which roles, which discursive and social relationships?
- What assumptions are being made here between some perceived identification of the social world of the classroom and the learners' social worlds outside the classroom?

These questions lead to two important issues: First, we need to be clearer about what the learners' "real world" is, both in and outside the classrooms. Second, we need to decide how appropriate content should be selected that can possibly meet these goals.

11B.2.1 A Survey of Chinese Students' Interests: The Three Worlds of Students

Crucially, therefore, empirical data are needed to provide a basis for a reflection on curriculum goals and appropriate content for language teaching materials in China, and so it was decided to conduct a study for the purpose. The guiding research questions were:

- What is the real world for Chinese students in English-language classes?
- What are the most appropriate real-world tasks for school students?

- What thematic content should be selected for students who are learning English in non-English-speaking environments?

The basic procedure was to choose a series of tasks for students to consider and then to ask why they liked certain ones and not others. The tasks were drawn from current coursebooks and from others designed by the first author. As the research study continued, student feedback led to iterative task modification and further data gathering.

The study was conducted in twenty-two schools (both urban and rural) in thirteen different provinces in China over three years. China, to state the obvious, is large and diverse and merited such extensive data collection. The target population was Grades 5–6 (age 11–12) with primary school students, and Grades 7–8 (age 13–15) with junior high-school students. In addition, teachers were interviewed. In total, 176 students and 90 teachers took part in focus groups and interviews. Given the dramatic differences between rural and urban areas in China, students and teachers in these two areas probably view the content of tasks quite differently, and all these opinions had to be collected. The students were asked to pinpoint the topics or tasks they did not like in their textbooks and to explain why not. Semi-structured interviews were carried out with both teachers and students, followed by nonparticipant observation in class. Some of the interviews were video-taped and the others were recorded. When school-teachers were interviewed, they were asked how their students reacted to the materials in the textbooks. They were also probed on students' difficulties in learning English.

Based on the interviews with both students and teachers, it was found that the thematic content of the tasks in English textbooks is a major reason for problems in the implementation of TBLT in a Chinese context. Most Chinese English-language teaching professionals (perhaps in other parts of the world, as well) assume, either explicitly or implicitly, that the most appropriate thematic content for a task should be linked to interpersonal communication situations in English-speaking countries. This is exactly what caused some serious problems for Chinese schoolteachers and students.

Both rural and urban students mentioned that they do not like the style of the textbooks, which seem to "lecture us" and "all the stories are harmonized." What they meant was that most of the texts are about "good and happy things," such as "which season do you like best," "having a birthday party," or "spring outing in a park." Characters in the textbooks share the same idea and have no conflict. However, students want to learn something more related to their real-life problems and knowledge about life skills and something "even our parents do not know." These findings were common to the vast majority of students and teachers, both rural and urban, in the study. More generally, what they actually like to talk about are their emotions, families, things that may have a connection to what might be termed their "inner world." Both rural and urban students express a need for more sophisticated ideas, reflecting the more complex and diverse realities of their living environments. They talked about their relationships with teachers, friends, and parents, and the life problems they may face in the future, as well as current political, local and international issues. They are interested in how to improve in relationships with their peers, parents, and teachers. They want readings on mental health, such as the development of positive feelings, to encourage them to deal with life problems and provide alternative solutions. Both groups of students like English songs. They do not only enjoy music, but also are interested in different ideas about the meaning of life. Many students mentioned that they are curious about how American and British high-school students live with their parents and interact with their teachers.

Moving from the responses common to both geographical areas, teachers in rural schools reported that few students really enjoyed learning English. One major problem was that certain topics in these authorized textbooks were alien to the students. The "ordering food in a fast-food restaurant," for example, is also considered unrealistic because few students in small towns and village schools have any chance to see what an actual pizza or sandwich are – these are not their daily menu in or out of schools. In the students' course books, there are tasks about the sorts of activities people do on the weekend, and according to the course book, the students are expected to talk about "visiting museums," "going to the zoo," and "watching a movie in the cinema." But these tasks are far from students' reality. When asking students in a rural area the things they themselves do at the weekend, the answers were "cooking for themselves," "going fishing in the river nearby," and "helping grandpa take care of the crops," as many rural school students have to cook for themselves on the weekend because their parents go to larger towns and big cities to earn money.

Turning to the urban context, although fourteen to sixteen year-old students like topics concerning popular music, sports, movies, food, and literature, they are also interested in what may happen in the future, in politics, friendship, love and war. Some are interested in comments about China by people from other countries. Topics on moral issues, virtues, such as violence, school bullying, and the meaning of life, are also the things they enjoy reading and discussing. They like to read articles about other countries, how people in other countries solve certain problems, their worries and concerns, and their ways of life. Urban students also want to tell stories of their own experiences when they meet English speakers from other countries. The students complain that they have soon exhausted their vocabulary and could not express more complicated ideas when they did get the opportunity to talk.

The more detailed findings lead to some interesting generalizations. The findings show that both rural and urban students have a strong need to learn something (a) more related to their own context, (b) using more challenging materials for their thinking skills and (c) leading to more knowledge about the world.

It was concluded that Chinese students' "real world" is best described in terms of "three worlds": an inner world, a knowledge world, and a future world. This interpretation of an inner world means that "giving directions" and "ordering food in a restaurant" are not "real tasks" for them. In contrast, what are "real" are their feelings, their sadness, happiness, and worries. They may have fights with schoolmates or be misunderstood by teachers. Then they feel very upset, and these feelings and emotions are genuine. A knowledge world means that they want to obtain useful knowledge for their growth through English beyond simply English-language knowledge in itself. This life-skill knowledge includes how to become successful individuals. For example, if students can learn how to cope with school bullying, they may use the skills right after class.

The future world refers to real-life problems and situations that may be encountered. Even students from rural areas want to explore the world outside their communities in the future and want to imagine their future lives. So, if the materials can reach students' hearts, activate their emotions, and teach young people to solve problems they face now, it may be considered more "authentic" than repeating what the people say in dialogues where two or three native speakers are ordering food and complaining about the British weather!

These findings have relevance for the content of a task-based approach, and they present some considerable challenges. Clearly, these students are able to articulate their viewpoints about learning in some detail. It is also clear that their views do not always (or even often) mesh with the typical views of educators and course writers. If we are to harness the motivation of these learners, we have to modify typical course content. Some of the interests that were expressed, such as school bullying, or how to grow taller, are quite surprising. Some of them also indicate a lack of realism about what can be attained in the limited amount of time available. But what they do is certainly recast the problem, the challenge, for course developers and task designers.

11B.3 Reconceptualizing the Goal of English-Language Teaching

If one takes a closer look at the "three worlds" from the previous section, it is clear that for primary and secondary school students, the goal of learning English as a foreign language is not simply communication; there are several parallel goals. It is more appropriate that the focus within each of the three worlds should be translated into a multi-goal English curriculum.

Such a multi-goal model can be broken down into three subsidiary goals: a social-cultural goal, a cognition and thinking goal, and a language use goal. These three goals are independent, yet need to be integrated in tasks and in real communication. The social-cultural goal includes mental, physical, and social well-being, with an emphasis on the development of values and attitudes. The cognition and thinking goal includes a growth mindset (Dweck, 2006) and lower- and higher-order thinking skills, as well as learning ability, including information and media literacy. The language use goal consists of language knowledge, skills, and communication strategies.

If one looks at the connection between the "worlds" from the previous section, and the different goals just described, the clearest connection is between the knowledge world and the cognition and thinking goal. Even so, the students' "knowledge world" involves not only cognitive and thinking knowledge but also social-cultural knowledge. Then, the language goal is obviously pervasive and formalizes the way other goals can be enabled through the specific language work that is necessary in any curriculum. The remaining inner and future worlds then connect with the social-cultural goal, which addresses both the personal, emotion-linked nature of the inner world, and also the wider context and worldview central to the future world. As the students mentioned, if English-language learning could stimulate logical thinking and problem-solving skills, they would love to learn English, and these needs could be perceived as the basis for their intellectual growth.

This analysis suggests that it is timely for English teaching researchers to integrate language education into whole-person development and recognize the multifunctional nature of language education. Nowadays, educators around the world talk about global competence and the survival skills that young people need in the future (Wagner & Dintersmith, 2016; Peterson & Seligman, 2004; Dweck, 2006). However, English-language teaching focuses mainly on language acquisition and language competence. We argue that successful communication does not merely involve ability for language use and cultural awareness, but is an integration of personal character strengths, thinking skills, behaviors, and world knowledge with language competence.

There are many connections with these suggestions in the literature. For example, Widdowson (1979: 16) argued that "a foreign language can be associated with ... other subjects in the school curriculum." Wesche and Skehan (2002: 220) also suggested that content-based instruction (CBI), which involves the integration of school or academic content with language teaching objectives, may be more suitable for school language teaching contexts because the "primary advantage of CBI over other communicative language teaching approaches is that using subject matter as the content for language learning maximizes learners' exposure to the second language" and it is "most effective, more motivating, also more important" (215). The multi-goal model is broadly similar to CBI or content and language integrated learning (CLIL) approaches (Nikula, 2015; Ortega, 2015), which have been gaining popularity recently. But there is a difference and it is that the tasks and thematic content focus more on issues related to children's growth. The construct of "real-world tasks" is to help students develop cognitive and thinking skills. The content is linked to the school curriculum in various subject areas (Van Gorp & Van Den Branden, 2015), but the aim of the teaching in the present context is not to teach the content knowledge itself.

11B.3.1 Selecting Thematic Content and Designing Tasks

The question we need to consider next is what content needs to be selected and tasks designed that could build task engagement (Dornyei, 2019), students' character strengths and virtues, thinking skills, and at the same time, develop students' language ability.

Seven principles of task design and selection are proposed:

- Real-life thematic content
- Useful knowledge
- Relevant problems
- True communication
- Personally engaging
- Self-motivation
- Lower- and higher-order thinking skills.

On the basis of the research study described earlier, and following the seven principles, a series of task-based course books entitled *New Notion English* was developed (Gong, 2014). These coursebooks were designed to be used as additional materials to state-school curricula, mostly, although not exclusively, in private schools. The book series consist of ten levels for students aged 7–12.

The tasks in *New Notion English* are too numerous to cover in any detail here, and the descriptions that follow are illustrative only. (More complete examples of teaching materials can be found in the website associated with this book.) One unit was based around hallway rules, a topic that related naturally to students' lives and which connected with areas beyond simply language. There was also a unit on growing taller. An adult's first reaction to this might be that this is an area controlled by genetics. But it was brought up by students as something important to them and so worth considering. It was possible to make this into a science topic, and explore relative contributions of genetics and such factors as lifestyle and diet. Other units, and associated tasks, were built around school bullying (of great importance to students), dealing with parents, conflict resolution, and becoming class leader. As is immediately clear here, the topics and ensuing tasks were driven by students' interests.

They were clearly part of the students' worlds, whether inner, knowledge, or future.

As indicated earlier, the content of the three goals are integrated when actual communication happens. For example: when students perform a hallway rules task, they have to practice opening the door, turning their heads to see if someone is behind them. If someone is following them, they are expected to hold the door open, and the other one should say "Thank you." This task involves not only language use, but also a way of thinking and virtues of being kind. So it integrates social and emotional well-being practice with language learning. Similarly, in doing a good listener task, students are expected to face the speaker, have eye contact, keep their hands and feet still, and nod their head.

As we have seen, the development of the thinking goal targets the development of thinking processes essential to a person in his or her lifelong learning and career, such as clarifying, comparing, reasoning, analyzing, and hypothesizing. Young learners will not be able to acquire such abstract thinking skills by merely being taught explicitly. Tasks, especially real-life tasks, in contrast, provide perfect opportunities to help them understand and develop thinking skills. For example, comparison tasks can be integrated into the materials. In a pet task, the decision-making process concerns whether it is better for a family to raise a dog or a cat. Students first compare the differences of living habits between a cat and a dog. They have to think about whether their family members have time to walk a dog twice a day. Then students have to think about their families. If they have busy parents and no grandparents, they may have to think about whether she or he has time to raise a dog. Finally, their local environment also needs to be considered regarding adequate space. For the outcome of the task, they make a decision as to whether they should adopt a dog or cat. This task involves not only thinking skills and decision-making skills, but also helps children learn responsibility and perspective-taking (Galinsky, 2011).

Clearly, the information from the earlier data-gathering research was vital for the selection of thematic content. Some of the topics we discussed might link naturally with many courses for school-age children (pets, becoming a good listener). Others (hallway rules) are perhaps examples from the present context relevant to general task-based teaching, such as Willis's (1982) suggestions for exploiting the classroom and school environment to find genuine communicative opportunities. Some topics, though, have rather surprising qualities (bullying, growing taller), and can be regarded as only discoverable through research of the sort described here. Others might be potentially general in nature but particularly appropriate for this Chinese context (becoming a class leader). This certainly demonstrates the contribution that such research can make to topic identification. As the accompanying website materials make clear, it was then possible to design tasks that build on these topics, and be more confident that the topics would stimulate interest.

11B.4   A Preliminary Evaluation of the Task-Based Course

The pedagogic innovation described above has been evaluated in two broad phases. In the first phase, ten schools were selected and data gathered between 2014 and 2016. Then, tasks were redesigned and these modified tasks were the basis for the second phase of the evaluation. In the main part of the second phase, approximately seventy primary schools, in more than fifteen provinces in China, were involved initially. Subsequently, more data have been collected since 2018, in ten schools, in five provinces.

The research methods for both phases include participant and nonparticipant observation, semi-structured interviews with students, parents, and teachers, collection of students' homework, and focus group interviews. The participants include local supervisors, school principals, schoolteachers, students, and parents. The data collected so far, particularly that from the second phase, have not been processed completely yet, and so the observations made here have an anecdotal quality. Even so, some interesting evidence was found to show that these tasks do have a positive influence on students' language achievement, character strengths, and thinking skills. Their language ability, in particular, is believed to be more rigorous and fluent than those of their peers in other schools.

Beyond language itself, some interesting insights have emerged to show that the tasks did have some influence on students' behaviors and their ways of thinking. A schoolteacher in Chengdu recounted that two students had a fight in the classroom, and other students came up and pulled them apart. One student even spoke in English and said "walk away from him," which came directly from a unit on conflict resolution in their textbook!

Evidence shows that throughout the school-based curriculum-implementation, learners show signs of positive thinking with a growth mindset. In the becoming class leader task learners are encouraged to analyze their own advantages and limitations. They compare the different personalities of potential leaders and indicate what kind of person they like best. "I was quite surprised that a shy girl like my daughter was able to bravely express herself and to talk about her advantages in order to run for class leader," was a remark shared by one of the parents from Chongqing.

In addition, while implementing the "Time to Speak Out" unit, which was originally designed to expose learners to the phenomenon and potential harm of bullying, the task was completely changed in response to learners' own orientation to the problem. When asked whether they think the suggestions for preventing school bullying are useful, they all said "No!" So, the teacher asked students to find their own solutions, and in doing this they talked extensively about the different ways of completing the task. A teacher working in a key primary school in Beijing observed that:

They questioned the definition provided in the book ... Therefore, I made up my mind to negotiate with them and change the task into discussing bullying in China and to provide possible solutions.

This also relates to the task-as-workplan and task-as-process distinction (Breen, 1989; Ellis, 2003). As Long (2005: 20) suggested "To be sure, learners sometimes not only wish to be consulted, but also are well informed."

11B.5 Conclusion

From this case study, we strongly believe that local educational goals and the needs of student growth must be one of the things to consider if TBLT is to be successfully implemented in curricula or course books for school-age learners who are learning English as a foreign language. As Ellis (2018: xii) argues "Researchers should focus more on the implementation of tasks in actual classrooms rather than on the design of tasks in carefully controlled experiments." Language skills and communicative competence are important for *surviving* in an English-speaking environment, but *thriving* within schools and beyond is perhaps more important for students in schools and classrooms. Students must be prepared for the future as global citizens. Language ability is not the only thing they need to acquire for successful communication with people in other nations. Behaviors, values, character strengths, virtues, and positive mindset all have positions in communication. Whether one has creative thinking or critical thinking skills also involves students' personalities (Csikszentmihalyi, 1996; Ruggiero, 2012). Researchers, teacher trainers and teachers in TBLT may have to learn other knowledge beside language-learning theories.

Further Reading

Butler, Y. G., Kang, K. I., Kim, H., and Liu, Y. (2018). "Tasks" appearing in primary school textbooks. *ELT Journal*, 72(3), 285–295.

Cook, V. (2007). The goals of ELT: Reproducing native-speakers or promoting multicompetence among second language users? In J. Cummins and C. Davison, eds. *International handbook of English language teaching*. New York: Springer, pp.237–48.

Garton, S. and Copland, F. (2018), eds. *Routledge handbook of teaching English to young learners*. Abingdon: Routledge.

McKay, S. (2006). *Assessing young language learners*. Cambridge: Cambridge University Press.

Nikolove, M. (2009), ed. *The Age Factors and Early Language Learning*. Berlin: Mouton de Gruyter.

Shehadeh, A. and Coombe, C. A. (2012). *Task-based language teaching in foreign language contexts*. Amsterdam: John Benjamins.

Van den Branden, K. (2006), ed. *Task-based language education*. Cambridge: Cambridge University Press

Willis, D. and Willis, J. (2007). *Doing task-based teaching*. Oxford: Oxford University Press.

Study Questions

1. The chapter discusses findings from mainland China. How different or similar do you think it would be if you did similar research and task development in your context?
2. It is argued that not only is there value in incorporating CLIL within task-based approaches in a school context, but also that the development of cognition and thinking skills should be an integral part of TBLT. Do you agree for school-age learners?
3. The authors propose three 'worlds': inner, knowledge, and future. Do you agree with this analysis? What alternatives could you suggest?
4. The chapter discusses three worlds, and then three goals, within a multi-goal curriculum. How satisfactory do you think the match is between the three worlds and the three goals?
5. The authors argue that successful communication involves personal character and thinking skills, in addition to classic four components of communicative competence. Do you agree with this idea?
6. Do you think it necessary and possible to assess young learners' language proficiency as well as their character strengths and thinking skills at the same time?

References

Breen, M. P. (1989). The evaluation cycle for language learning tasks. In R. K. Johnson, ed. *The second language curriculum*. Cambridge: Cambridge University Press, pp. 187–206.

Candlin, C. N. (2001). Afterword: Taking the curriculum to task. In M. Bygate, P. Skehan, and M. Swain, eds. *Researching pedagogical tasks: Second language learning, teaching and testing*. Harlow: Pearson Education Limited, pp. 229–43.

Csikszentmihalyi, M. (1996). *Creativity: flow and the psychology of discovery and invention*. New York: Harper Collins.

Dornyei, Z. (2019). Task motivation: What makes an L2 task engaging? In Z. Wen and M. Ahmadian, eds. *Researching L2 Task Performance and Pedagogy*. Amsterdam: John Benjamins, pp.53–66.

Dweck, C. (2006). *Mindset: The new psychology of success*. New York: Random House.

Ellis, R. (2003). *Task-based language learning and teaching*. Oxford: Oxford University Press.

Ellis, R. (2018). Towards a modular curriculum for using tasks. *Language Teaching Research*, 23(4): 454–75

Ellis, R., Skehan, P., Li, S., Shintani, N., and Lambert, C. (2020). *Task-based learning and Teaching*. Cambridge: Cambridge University Press.

Galinsky, E. (2011). *Mind in the making: The seven essential life skills every child needs*. New York: Willian Morrow.

Gong, Y. (2014). *New Notion English*. Beijing: Beijing Language Teaching and Research Press.

Graves, K. (1996). *Teachers as course developers*. Cambridge: Cambridge University Press.

Long, M. H. (2005), ed. *Second language needs analysis*. Cambridge: Cambridge University Press.

Long, M. (2015). *Second language acquisition and task-based language teaching*. Hoboken, NJ: John Wiley and Sons.

Markee, N. (1997). *Managing curricula innovation*. Cambridge: Cambridge University Press.

Nikuta, T. (2015). Hands-on tasks in CLIL science classrooms as sites for subject-specific language use and learning. *System*, 54, 14–27.

Ortega, L. (2015). Researching CLIL and TBLT interfaces. *System*, 54, 103–9.

Peterson, C. and Seligman, M. (2004). *Character strengths and virtues*. Oxford: Oxford University Press.

Ruggiero, V. R. (2012). *Beyond Feelings: A guide to critical thinking (Ninth Edition)*. New York: McGraw-Hill.

Van Gorp, K. and Van Den Branden, K. (2015). Teachers, pupils, and tasks: The genesis of dynamic learning opportunities. *System*, 54, 28–39.

Wagner, T. and Dintersmith, T. (2016) *Most likely to succeed: Preparing our kids for the innovation era*. New York: Scribner.

Wesche, M. B. and Skehan, P. (2002). Communicative, task-based, and content-based language instruction. In R. B. Kaplan, ed. *The Oxford handbook of applied linguistics*. Oxford: Oxford University Press, pp. 207–28.

Widdowson, H. G. (1979). *Explorations in applied linguistics*. Oxford: Oxford University Press.

Willis, J. (1982). *Teaching English through English*. London: Longman.

Part VI

The Teacher in Task-Based Language Teaching

12
Teacher Preparation and Support for Task-Based Language Teaching

Martin East

12.1 Introduction

Despite a relatively long history dating back to the 1980s, and strong theoretical and empirical support, it seems that task-based language teaching (TBLT) is still often viewed by teachers as something new and unknown, and to be treated with caution. TBLT invites the teacher to move away from the more familiar positioning of "sage on the stage" who leads and directs all classroom processes. Instead, in TBLT "task" becomes the central focus and learners' engagement in tasks becomes the fundamental goal of the communicative classroom. TBLT asks the teacher to embrace a quite different position of "guide on the side" who may provide learners with corrective feedback or direction when required, but who otherwise plays a principally non-interventionist role (at least while learners engage in the task).

Teachers are a key element and crucial variable in the success (or otherwise) of the TBLT endeavor. The implementation of TBLT by real teachers in real classrooms is frequently hindered by a history of pedagogical practices that have largely been teacher-led and expository, with teachers "still standing in front of a group of students with a piece of chalk in their hand" (Van den Branden, 2009: 659). Moreover, research among practitioners has revealed that teachers working in a variety of contexts and with different kinds of students demonstrate a range of understandings (and misunderstandings) about the construct of task for the purposes of TBLT and often resort to more traditional and teacher-fronted elements (see, e.g., Andon & Eckerth, 2009; Carless, 2003, 2007; Xiongyong & Samuel, 2011). Teachers, whether starting out or more established, therefore need to be supported to develop deeper understanding of, and greater certainty about, what TBLT is and how tasks can be implemented more successfully in real classrooms.

Drawing on aspects of my own practices as a language teacher educator, in this chapter I explore the teacher variable, and present some of the ways in which teachers' knowledge of and expertise in TBLT can be enhanced through teacher preparation and support initiatives, alongside some of the challenges that persist.

12.2 Fundamental Considerations

In this chapter, I take it as a given that teacher education initiatives, whether for beginner pre-service teachers or more experienced in-service teachers, are a necessary component of the successful implementation of TBLT in real classrooms, and that these initiatives will be led by those who believe in and understand the innovation at hand. Teacher preparation and support will take a variety of forms, depending on teachers' needs and experience. Indeed, in my own work as a teacher educator, I have been involved in teacher preparation for TBLT at several levels. These have included: a formal year-long initial teacher education (ITE) qualification as a pre-requisite for entry into the teaching profession at school level; short-term professional development opportunities that have focused practising teachers on key aspects of practice; and more in-depth post-ITE qualifications designed to upskill practising teachers working in a range of contexts. In what follows, I identify some of the fundamental considerations that have guided my work with teachers as I have sought to prepare them for implementing task-based ideas.

12.2.1 Establishing a Baseline: Teachers' Beliefs about Effective Pedagogy

A crucial starting point with regard to preparing teachers to implement TBLT is to make teachers more consciously aware of the beliefs about effective pedagogy that they currently hold, and the possible reasons for those beliefs. As Nunan (2004: 6) argued, although it might not be immediately apparent, the pedagogical choices teachers make in classrooms are "underpinned by beliefs about the nature of language, the nature of the learning process and the nature of the teaching act." Borg (2015: 8) likewise asserted that teachers do not operate as "mechanical implementers of external prescriptions." They are, rather, "active, thinking decision-makers." Fundamentally, what teachers *think* about teaching and learning, and what they *believe* to be pedagogical best practice, will have significant influence on what they choose to *do* in their classrooms.

The beliefs teachers hold may be strongly influenced by their own experiences as learners, and these early formed beliefs can become quite embedded and hard to shift. If early experiences in the language learning classroom have been largely influenced by behaviorist, teacher-dominated and grammar-focused practices (which is often the case), it should not surprise us if teachers come to view these practices as optimal or necessary for language acquisition. These experiences will continue to play a significant role in teachers' thinking even when they are being confronted with new ideas (Calderhead, 1996; Clark & Peterson, 1986; Pajares, 1993; Phipps & Borg, 2007; Van den Branden, 2009). However, there is also evidence to suggest that, through teacher education, beliefs can be changed (Borg, 2003; Cabaroglu & Roberts, 2000; Richards, Ho, & Giblin, 1996).

There are various ways in which an initial focus on teachers' beliefs can be facilitated in teacher preparation and support initiatives. One approach I have used with beginning teachers has been to present them, right at the start of a year-long program, with a series of belief statements, available as a photocopiable resource in Lightbown and Spada (2013: xvii–xviii), about how to promote effective second language acquisition. I asked the teachers to indicate individually their strength of agreement with the statements. Then they compared their responses with a partner. After that, we discussed the statements as a whole group, focusing particularly on those where a range of views on the expressed belief had emerged. Throughout this process, I made it clear that beliefs are neither right nor wrong; they simply are what they are. This provided a safe environment in which these beginning teachers could think about and aim to identify their own beliefs, enter into discussion about how these beliefs might differ across individuals, and consider possible reasons for that. This initial focus always led to rich and valuable discussions that helped participants (and me as the facilitator) to become more aware of the beliefs teachers hold right at the start of a teacher preparation program.

12.2.2 Critical Reflective Practice

Once teachers have been supported in making their own (current) beliefs about effective pedagogy more visible to them, the goal of teacher preparation and support for TBLT becomes one of critiquing existing beliefs in light of ideas that teachers may not have considered before. However, simply telling teachers that TBLT is a "good idea" or extolling the theoretical and/or empirically tested benefits of task use are not likely to shift teachers' beliefs very far.

Widdowson (1993: 271) early argued that "new ideas do need to be mediated effectively and appropriately, that is to say, evaluated for relevance by critical appraisal and application." For TBLT as innovation to be implemented most successfully, teachers need to engage *critically* with

TBLT in theory. That is, they need to be given space to question and interrogate its assumptions. They also need to be supported to *test out and evaluate* for themselves whether (and to what extent) something that seems like a good idea in theory or experimental research is also a good idea in practice. This theory and practice linked critical reflection has been described as "an essential element of professional 'becoming' in the journey of a teacher's development" (Brandenberg & Jones, 2017: 260), a process whereby teachers improve their teaching as they consider and analyze their practice (Williams & Grudnoff, 2011).

In East (2014a) I built on several classic definitions of reflective practice to make the case that three components of a reflective cycle will enable theory and practice to be linked effectively – reflection *for/in/on* action. Once I had established a baseline of current beliefs with the teachers with whom I was working, this three-component reflective cycle became the foundation for exploration of TBLT in theory and practice.

12.2.3 Reflection-for-Action

Killion and Todnem (1991) identified reflection-*for*-action as an important component of the reflective cycle. This, they argued, is a future-focused reflection, separate from the classroom. When it comes to teacher preparation for TBLT, reflection-for-action can take place before intending practitioners have even set foot in a classroom, or before practicing teachers begin a new teaching sequence. It creates the space for teachers to reflect on theory, and to consider what theory might mean for future pedagogical choices (Too, 2013). It also supports teachers (whether beginning or experienced) to think reflectively and analytically about their past and present beliefs in light of the theory (Bullock & Muschamp, 2004; Chien, 2013). Reflection-for-action is therefore a crucial starting point in the reflective process, and arguably lays the groundwork for future practices as teachers "step outside of their own definitions of the world and see new perspectives" (Davis, 2005: 18).

12.2.4 Task-Based Considerations (from a Theoretical Perspective)

When it comes to the *theory* about TBLT on which teachers might be encouraged to reflect for future action, decisions need to be made about what exactly teachers need to consider, and how exactly they are to consider it.

As I suggested earlier, exposing teachers to a whole range of theoretical arguments in favor of TBLT and empirical studies that demonstrate the efficacy of TBLT might be seen as useful, but (depending on the context and the amount of time available) it may well be overwhelming and counterproductive. It is important, therefore, to identify the key aspects of TBLT that appear to present the most problems for practitioners, and thus the dimensions that arguably require specific attention as teachers prepare for the TBLT classroom. In what follows, I outline several key task-based considerations that I have taken into account as I have worked with teachers who are preparing *for* action – the notion of "task"; the place of grammar; and task sequencing/lesson planning.

12.3 What Is a Task?

The construct of task is a crucial element for exploration (see Sasayama, this volume), and a foundational issue for teachers is to understand exactly what a task is for the purposes of TBLT. In this regard, tasks need to be distinguished from the kinds of communicative activity that teachers might draw on in the traditional communicative classroom. This is easier said than done. As Long (2016: 5) put it, both task and TBLT can mean "different things to different people" or, indeed, "anything the writer chooses." Long went on to explain that some commercial textbooks, for example, use the word "task" when in fact they are referring to "a traditional, linguistically focused exercise or activity." This has simply been "relabelled to keep up with language teaching (LT) fashion," presumably in order to make the textbook a more attractive proposition for teachers with a level of interest in TBLT.

In essence, the differentiation that teachers need to be made aware of runs something like this: in a communicative activity the focus is on using predetermined language and grammar to achieve a communicative goal (e.g., using a list of set phrases to carry out a role-play where a customer orders food and drink from a waiter in a café). The principal focus is on accurate use of appropriate (specified) language. In a task, the goal is to achieve a non-linguistic outcome using any language that is appropriate to that outcome (e.g., win the debate; win the game). The principal focus is on fluency or meaning. This is where things can get problematic for teachers. After all, it could be argued that ordering items in a café is outcome-oriented and could be achieved using any language the interlocutor chooses. Why, then, is it not a task? Or is it a task?

Over the years, a range of theoretical and working definitions of task has been developed (see, e.g., Samuda & Bygate, 2008, and this volume). Teacher preparation might focus on giving teachers one or several theoretical definitions of task. To promote critical reflection-*for*-action, teachers can be encouraged to use the definitions to evaluate (and justify) the strengths and limitations of example tasks. They can also be encouraged to create and critique their own tasks against the definitions. For example, teachers in a teacher preparation program, whether working individually or collaboratively, might be asked to come up with a task focused on a particular topic. In designing the task, teachers would be asked, at the beginning of the process, to keep in mind the theoretical definitions and, at the end, to justify their task as a task in light of those definitions. This approach helps to promote practical hands-on experience with task design that focuses on the teachers themselves and their developing understanding of a task. It also models a task-based approach.

After the teachers I was working with in the year-long teacher preparation program had explored their current beliefs about language pedagogy (and had also been introduced to theoretical standpoints that might have influenced those beliefs), the teachers were presented with three theoretical definitions of the task construct (Ellis, 2009: 223; Samuda and Bygate, 2008: 69; Willis & Willis, 2007: 13; see also East, 2018: 29). These were presented before the teachers were set to work in real classrooms.

Additionally, participants were introduced to Willis's (1996: 26–27) taxonomy of task types: (1) listing; (2) ordering and sorting; (3) comparing; (4) problem-solving; (5) sharing personal experiences; (6) creative tasks. These were first presented to the teachers with a level of explanation and examples.

In one activity I drew on to help the teachers to apply the Willis (1996) taxonomy, I asked them to work in small groups to come up with an example of a task that might fit one of the primary classifications (1–6). Each group worked for a short while on one classification, writing an example task on a large sheet of paper. Then the groups moved on to another classification, and each group added a new task to the list. By the end of the process, the groups returned to their original spot and reviewed the full list and range of examples. The completed lists were subsequently transcribed to become a participant-generated taxonomy of task types, which the teachers could draw on as they began their work in real classrooms.

In practice, the learner-centered and experiential application of theory that I facilitated as teachers thought about what a task was brought several challenges to the surface. Sometimes the distinction between task and communicative activity was not an easy one to make. This experience demonstrates that, as teachers prepare to implement TBLT, they need to be willing at times to live with ambiguity and come to realize that a given task proposal may be *relatively* rather than *absolutely* task-like, depending on its level of fit with defined criteria (see, e.g., Erlam, 2016). For teachers, the essential question does not have to be "is it a task?" but, rather, "how task-like is it?" Beyond that, teachers need to understand sufficient theory to be able to differentiate what is *clearly* a task from what is clearly a communicative language practice activity. As I argued in East (2017b: 416), "flexibility with the notion of task gives teachers considerable freedom to make context-specific choices about what they consider to be suitable tasks to foster student engagement, and how they will implement those tasks, and this is a potential strength." However, this strength becomes problematic "when there is misunderstanding about even the basic notion of task." A clear theoretical foundation needs to be laid for teachers' reflection-for-action, even if its application leads at times to a level of haziness.

12.4 What about the Grammar?

Alongside the issues that can come to the surface as teachers aim to determine what is and what is not a task, grammar instruction has been identified as a major source of anxiety for teachers. I have found this to be the case in my work with both preservice teachers (East, 2014a) and inservice teachers (East, 2014b; 2017a). This can be particularly troubling for teachers who are struggling to move from a teacher-led behaviorist model to a learner-centered experiential model. As Larsen-Freeman (2015: 263) argued, grammar instruction "has been relatively unaltered by research findings. It remains traditional for the most part, with grammar teaching centered on accuracy of form and rule learning, and with mechanical exercises seen as the way to bring about the learning of grammar." Teachers preparing for TBLT need to be given opportunities to consider carefully the role and place of grammar instruction in the task-oriented classroom.

As with tasks, teachers need to be confronted with theoretical perspectives on grammar, and their place in and for TBLT. An essential framework for teachers to consider is what we might label the forms-meaning-form trichotomy (e.g., Long, 2000). The important issues for teacher preparation are, first, to help teachers to identify their current beliefs about grammar instruction, and, second, to raise teachers' awareness of alternative perspectives. In particular, teacher preparation for TBLT requires theoretical engagement with a focus-on-form approach to grammar, and what this might mean for their own roles in the classroom when students perform a task. Issues of concern for teachers include: when to intervene and when not to intervene; or when to provide feedback and when to instruct.

12.5 Task Sequencing

As teachers prepare to move from theory to practice, a third fundamental consideration is determining and planning for when, where and how tasks fit into pedagogic sequences (see Gilabert and Malicka, this volume), and the implications for structuring a task-based lesson to maximum effect (Willis, 1996; Willis and Willis, 2007). Important here is not only a consideration of what might go into both individual lessons and series of lessons, but also how learners are to be supported to achieve task outcomes. Issues for teachers include: the kind of language input the students need to fulfill the task and how that is to be acquired (independent work? Collaborative work? Teacher input?); the mode of the task (output-based? Input-based? Integrated?); the ways in which the students will work on the task (individually? In pairs? In small groups? As a class?); the staging of the tasks (one large task? Several sub-tasks? Repeated tasks?); and addressing matters arising from task performance (focus on form).

It is arguably at the stage of task sequencing that teachers come up against the reality that opinion is divided about the execution of lessons in TBLT. Indeed, exploration of grammar is where teachers will have begun to grapple with conflicting theoretical perspectives, although arguably the limitations of a focus-on-forms approach will have been suitably critiqued. Contrasting viewpoints become more apparent as teachers consider planning a task-based lesson. That is, a "strong" view of TBLT is founded on task execution as "the necessary and sufficient condition of successful second language acquisition" (Nunan, 2004: 21) and "as adequate to drive forward language development" (Skehan, 1996: 39). In a "weaker" understanding of TBLT (which we might call task-*supported*), tasks, as Skehan put it, will be "preceded by focused instruction, and after use, may be followed by focused instruction which is contingent on task performance" (39). Skehan argued that the purpose of the pre-task phase, which, he suggested, may be achieved via explicit pre-teaching or more implicit (i.e., learner-centered) work, raises learners' awareness of language needed to perform the task. Willis (1996: 38) similarly suggested that, in this initial phase, the teacher "explores the topic with the class, highlights useful words and phrases, helps students understand task instructions and prepare."

Teachers being prepared for TBLT need to be encouraged to consider a range of ways in which learners can be set up to achieve task outcomes successfully, and not necessarily to assume that the default is some kind of direct instruction. They need also to recognize that, that, whatever else they might consider including, tasks are "the starting point, primary focus, and ultimate goal of a unit of instruction" and "the fundamental reference point" for teaching (Van den Branden et al., 2009: 9) – hence a central focus in teacher preparation on the construct of task. As Ellis (2009: 224) put it, "[a] task-based lesson can involve three phases (the pretask phase, the main task phase, and the post-task phase), although only one of these (the main task phase) is obligatory."

12.6 Reflection in and on Action

The essential purpose of reflection-for-action is to help practitioners to consider the theoretical implications of new ideas for practice. However, having laid a solid (and targeted) theoretical foundation, teacher preparation must provide opportunities for teachers to try all this out in real classrooms. Teachers' reflective work needs to continue as they go (or go back) into the classroom. When it comes to this on-going reflective work, I come back to the classic definitions I presented in East (2014a).

In the classroom itself, Schön (1983) differentiated between reflection-*in*-action and reflection-*on*-action. Reflection-in-action represents the reflection that might take place in the context of a particular lesson as teachers evaluate, on a moment-by-moment basis, what is happening in their classroom. In-action reflection might lead a teacher to make real-time adjustments to how that lesson is being implemented. Reflection-on-action represents the reflection that might take place *after* a lesson has been delivered – posing a "how did it go?" question that might lead teachers to decide to change their practices in some way in future lessons. Through reflection in and on action, teachers respond to what is going on in the classroom.

12.7 Task-Based Considerations (from a Practical Perspective)

In East (2014a, 2018) I explained how I supported the group of beginning teachers I was working with to engage in reflection in and on action from which these teachers could evaluate how tasks worked in practice. On their first practicum placement (where they would spend seven weeks in a school), participants were encouraged to use the task definitions they had been presented with, and (in later course iterations) the taxonomy of task types they had come up with themselves, to develop and implement a task for a real class with whom they were working. After the seven weeks were over, they came back to the university campus and shared with their peers how the task implementation had gone. In East (2018) I provided several early examples of these tasks and teachers' evaluations of their effectiveness.

As they shared their tasks with each other, the participants first had to justify to their peers how the task they used measured up against at least one theoretical definition (thus providing evidence of critical reflection-*for-*action). Then they were asked to present their evaluation of the effectiveness of the task, identifying what seemed to go well, and what seemed not to work so well. In these ways they provided evidence of critical reflection *in* and *on* action. Finally, they were required to speculate on what changes they might need to make to the task if it were to be used again – coming back to reflection *for* future action.

This presentation of tasks in practice thus provided the opportunity for these beginning teachers to engage in the reflective cycle. This enabled deeper consideration of the theory, illuminated by actual experience. The teachers were encouraged to ask several key reflective questions: if something worked, what made it work? If something did not work, why didn't it work? What could have been done differently? What does this mean for theory? It was made clear to the students that, even if the task had not worked very well in their perception, this was a learning opportunity for them. Lack of success on one occasion provided opportunities to consider trying things out in a different way and evaluating how that might go.

As these beginning teachers started to try out task-based ideas in real classrooms and engage critically with how that went, this began to raise a second layer of conflict between beliefs and practices. In the process of preparing teachers for TBLT, teachers may have thus far demonstrated openness to consider new and unfamiliar ideas and concepts and even to have begun to modify their beliefs about effective pedagogy. However, when it comes to applying these emerging beliefs in real classrooms, a range of contextual factors will play a part in shaping teachers' ongoing perspectives. These may include expectations imposed by their place of work, the beliefs and practices of other colleagues, things that happen in class, and dealing with individual differences in learners (Coe, Aloisi, Higgins, & Elliot Major, 2014). As Borg (2015: 321) put it, what teachers end up doing in classrooms is influenced by a range of "complex, practically-oriented, personalized, and context-sensitive networks of knowledge, thoughts and beliefs." Teachers reflecting in and on action will inevitably make pedagogical choices in real time, and in response to a range of contextual factors. Openness to new ideas in theory may become challenged by conflicting classroom realities, and these may hinder teachers' implementation of something new. A final consideration for teacher preparation and support for TBLT is how to help teachers to deal with the inevitable clashes that will emerge between theory and practice.

12.8 When Theory and Practice Clash

Despite a structured sequential program that scaffolds teachers as they begin to put tasks into practice, the implementation of TBLT can be a complicated business. Several authors underscore the reality I raised earlier in this chapter – that the notion of task can be hazy at times. Furthermore, the concept of TBLT has been interpreted and implemented in a wide variety of ways, making it difficult to pin down exactly what TBLT is or should be (Hall, 2018; Nunan, 2004; Richards, 2006). More broadly, Coe et al. (2014: 23), for example, made the claim that a learner-centered social/experiential approach such as the one on which TBLT is built "is not supported by research evidence, which broadly favours direct instruction." As Mitchell, Myles, and Marsden (2013: 11) put it, learning an additional language is a hugely complex process which is "coloured by debates on fundamental issues in human learning more generally" – to the extent that they concluded that, with regard to teaching, there can be "no 'one best method', however much research evidence supports it, which applies at all times and in all situations, with every type of learner" (406). As Long (2016:28) asserted, "[n]o approach to LT has proven 'correct' to date, and there should be no illusion as to TBLT's chances of breaking the tradition. Real issues remain."

As a consequence of arguments and counter-arguments about TBLT and its place in the wider discourse about effective language teaching and learning, there is a clash between tradition and innovation which at once creates both a crucial mediating role for teacher preparation and support and an immensely complex environment in which to try to enact pedagogical innovation with teachers, whether new or experienced. This raises the question of how the exploration of TBLT should be enacted most effectively in teacher preparation and support initiatives.

This chapter has thus far proposed a model for teacher preparation for TBLT that includes several key elements. These elements will give teachers opportunities to reflect critically on:

- their current beliefs about effective pedagogy, and where they might come from
- new ideas and theories before they try to enact them in classrooms – reflection-for-action
- how the innovation is going in real time – reflection-in-action
- how the innovation went in practice – reflection-on-action
- what teachers might change in the future, and what their experiences mean in the light of theory – reflection for (future) action.

But what happens when theory and practice clash? Ultimately, it is important for teachers to have opportunities to engage with contrasting theoretical arguments, to come to their own positions, and to take ownership for their own decisions. Brandenberg and Jones (2017: 264)) put it like this: "reflection is an *on-going* cycle of learning about one's teaching ... [that] does not necessarily resolve issues, but perhaps generates even more questions and problems" (my emphasis). When questions and problems are generated in the process of implementing something new, there is, of course, the risk that teachers may choose to abandon the innovation in favor of more tried and tested approaches. However, I believe we must not be afraid of that risk. I consider that it is worth taking if it means that, in the context of their own critical reflection, practitioners are more informed about contrasting perspectives.

For example, when the beginning teachers I worked with reached the end of their one-year program, I implemented an assignment that was designed to help teachers to confront some of the challenging issues that had emerged. I asked participants to select one issue for the successful implementation of TBLT that had occurred to them in the course of the year, to go away and research what others had to say about it by reading a few articles, and then to present their issue and their findings on it to their peers. I varied the way in which I operated this assignment, making this either a small group activity or an individual presentation. Fundamental, however, was that I wanted my students to be open to embrace controversies and to look at what these meant for on-going practice. This assignment thus rounded out what I had done at the beginning when I asked the teachers to critique their initial beliefs, both in theory and in practice. That is, I started the year by effectively saying "let's look at something new and different." I ended the year by allowing the students to critique the very innovation that I set out to introduce.

12.9 Conclusion

In this chapter, I have proposed that effective teacher preparation and support for TBLT should be founded on critical reflective practice that enables teachers, at whatever level, to consider and apply theory to practice and see how that works in real classrooms. Thus, the three dimensions of reflective practice (for/in/on action) can be theorized as working in a cyclical way: consider the theory; try it out; evaluate how that went; reconsider the theory, and so on. This three-component cycle is arguably a useful *modus operandi* for teacher exploration and evaluation of TBLT as innovation.

However, implementing TBLT as innovation in real classrooms is not an easy matter. First, and as Long (2016) reminded us, we must not underestimate the length of time and the amount of effort needed to build expertise and enable innovation to take stronger hold in classrooms. We need to recognize that shifting teachers' thinking and practices, both individually and collectively, will necessitate "an *unfolding* of experience and a *gradual development* of skill and sophistication in using the innovation" (Van den Branden, 2009: 665; my emphases).

Second, it may well be that clashes will emerge between theory and practice. There are two implications of these clashes.

On the one hand, the challenges that might emerge at the local level (genuine as these might be) should not be allowed to become reasons why an innovation cannot be pursued. Widdowson (1993) early acknowledged that taking local contexts into account should not be allowed to limit what could be done – teachers, in his view, needed to remain open to change and be challenged not to lean on the tried and tested as protections against new ideas. Considerably more recently, Hamilton and Pinnegar (2014: 139) asserted that "[w]e must position ourselves to seek out, understand, and enact emerging and evolving practices that take into account new content knowledge, new understandings of learning, and new ways of teaching." Teachers, whether starting out or more established, must be encouraged to consider and explore innovative ideas, and teacher educators must be open to facilitate that exploration.

On the other hand, Van den Branden (2009: 671) cautioned that "it is imperative that teachers' concerns and beliefs, as well as the characteristics and constraints of the local conditions in which they operate, are taken into account; otherwise, innovations are bound to cause only superficial change." Whilst teacher educators must help teachers to explore the "new content knowledge, new understandings of learning, and new ways of teaching" advocated by Hamilton and Pinnegar (2014), researchers must *also* position themselves, in Hamilton and Pinnegar's words, to "produce scholarship that contributes to the refinement and evolution of such knowledge" (139).

My own research into teacher preparation and support for TBLT, undertaken over several years, has been framed from the cyclical reflective perspective I have presented in this chapter. What I have concluded from this research is that a critically reflective focus on TBLT as innovation can successfully challenge and change existing beliefs, and can bring about successful changes to practice. Nevertheless, a focus on TBLT must occur in the context of on-going reflection to continually evaluate its success, and its theoretical claims, in light of evidence emerging from practice. In other words, those of us with a stake in teacher education informed by on-going research need to remain open to the conclusion regarding TBLT asserted by Long (2016: 28–29), that "[a]dvances in theory and research, coupled with further field trials, will assuredly refine current models, and quite probably identify needed changes." The role of the teacher in identifying these advances is crucial, and the role of teacher education is to maintain that crucial balance between supporting and critiquing innovation.

Further Reading

Andon, N. and Eckerth, J. (2009). Chacun à son goût? Task-based L2 pedagogy from the teacher's point of view. *International Journal of Applied Linguistics*, 19(3), 286–310.

Carless, D. (2009). Revisiting the TBLT versus P-P-P debate: Voices from Hong Kong. *Asian Journal of English Language Teaching*, 19, 49–66.

East, M. (2018). How do beginning teachers conceptualise and enact tasks in school foreign language classrooms? In V. Samuda, M. Bygate, and K. Van den Branden eds. *TBLT as a researched pedagogy*. Amsterdam: John Benjamins, pp. 23–50.

East, M. (2017). "If it is all about tasks, will they learn anything?" Teachers' perspectives on grammar instruction in the task-oriented classroom. In M. J. Ahmadian and M. P. García Mayo, eds. *Recent perspectives on task-based language learning and teaching*. Berlin: De Gruyter Mouton, pp. 217–31.

Ellis, R. (2009). Task-based language teaching: Sorting out the misunderstandings. *International Journal of Applied Linguistics*, 19(3), 221–46.

Erlam, R. (2016). 'I'm still not sure what a task is': Teachers designing language tasks. *Language Teaching Research*, 20(3), 279–99.

Study Questions

1. If TBLT is to be successfully enacted in classrooms, what do you see as the most pressing teacher preparation and support needs?
2. How do you think these needs might best be addressed?
3. What balance between theory and practice do you think should be maintained in teacher preparation and support programs?
4. How do you think teachers should be introduced to TBLT theories most effectively?

References

Andon, N. and Eckerth, J. (2009). Chacun à son goût? Task-based L2 pedagogy from the teacher's point of view. *International Journal of Applied Linguistics*, 19(3), 286–310.

Borg, S. (2003). Teacher cognition in language teaching: A review of research on what language teachers think, know, believe, and do. *Language Teaching*, 36, 81–109.

Borg, S. (2015). *Teacher cognition and language education: Research and practice*. London: Bloomsbury Academic.

Brandenberg, R. and Jones, M. (2017). Toward transformative reflective practice in teacher education. In R. Brandenberg, K. Glasswell, M. Jones, and J. Ryan, eds. *Reflective theory and practice in teacher education*. Singapore: Springer, pp. 259–73.

Bullock, K. and Muschamp, Y. (2004). Reflecting on pedagogy: Outcomes from a Beacon School Network. *Teacher Development*, 8(1), 29–44.

Cabaroglu, N. and Roberts, J. (2000). Development in student teachers' pre-existing beliefs during a 1-year PGCE programme. *System*, 28, 387–402.

Calderhead, J. (1996). Teachers: Beliefs and knowledge. In D. C. Berliner and R. C. Calfee, eds. *Handbook of educational psychology*. New York, NY: Macmillan, pp. 709–25.

Carless, D. (2003). Factors in the implementation of task-based teaching in primary schools. *System*, 31(485–500).

Carless, D. (2007). The suitability of task-based approaches for secondary schools: Perspectives from Hong Kong. *System*, 35(4), 595–608.

Chien, C.-W. (2013). Analysis of a language teacher's journal of classroom practice as reflective practice. *Reflective Practice: International and Multidisciplinary Perspectives*, 14(1), 131–43.

Clark, C. M. and Peterson, P. L. (1986). Teachers' thought processes. In M. C. Wittrock, ed. *Handbook of research on teaching*. 3rd ed. New York: Macmillan, pp. 255–96.

Coe, R., Aloisi, C., Higgins, S., and Elliot Major, L. (2014). *What makes great teaching? Review of the underpinning research*. London: The Sutton Trust.

Davis, S. (2005). Developing reflective practice in pre-service student teachers: What does art have to do with it? *Teacher Development*, 9(1), 9–19.

East, M. (2014a). Encouraging innovation in a modern foreign language initial teacher education programme: What do beginning teachers make of task-based language teaching? *The Language Learning Journal*, 42(3), 261–74.

East, M. (2014b). Mediating pedagogical innovation via reflective practice: A comparison of pre-service and in-service teachers' experiences. *Reflective Practice: International and Multidisciplinary Perspectives*, 15(5), 686–99.

East, M. (2017a). "If it is all about tasks, will they learn anything?" Teachers' perspectives on grammar instruction in the task-oriented classroom. In M. J. Ahmadian and M. P. García Mayo, eds. *Recent perspectives on task-based language learning and teaching*. Berlin, Germany: De Gruyter Mouton, pp. 217–31.

East, M. (2017b). Research into practice: The task-based approach to instructed second language acquisition. *Language Teaching*, 50(3), 412–24.

East, M. (2018). How do beginning teachers conceptualise and enact tasks in school foreign language classrooms? In V. Samuda, M. Bygate, and K. Van den Branden, eds. *TBLT as a researched pedagogy*. Amsterdam: John Benjamins, pp. 23–50.

Ellis, R. (2009). Task-based language teaching: Sorting out the misunderstandings. *International Journal of Applied Linguistics*, 19(3), 221–46.

Erlam, R. (2016). 'I'm still not sure what a task is': Teachers designing language tasks. *Language Teaching Research*, 20(3), 279–99.

Hall, G. (2011). *Exploring English language teaching: Language in action*. New York: Routledge.

Hamilton, M. L. and Pinnegar, S. (2014). Self-study of teacher education practices as a pedagogy for teacher educator professional development. In C. Craig and L. Orland-Barak, eds. *International teacher education: Promising pedagogies (part A). Advances in research on teaching*. Bradford: Emerald Publishing, pp. 137–52.

Killion, J. and Todnem, G. (1991). A process of personal theory building. *Educational Leadership*, 48(6), 14–16.

Larsen-Freeman, D. (2015). Research into practice: Grammar learning and teaching. *Language Teaching*, 48(2), 263–80.

Lightbown, P. and Spada, N. (2013). *How languages are learned*. 4th ed. Oxford: Oxford University Press.

Long, M. (2000). Focus on form in task-based language teaching. In R. D. Lambert and E. Shohamy, eds. *Language policy and pedagogy: Essays in honor of A. Ronald Walton*. Amsterdam: John Benjamins, pp. 179–92.

Long, M. (2016). In defense of tasks and TBLT: Nonissues and real issues. *Annual Review of Applied Linguistics*, 36, 5–33.

Mitchell, R., Myles, F. and Marsden, E. (2013). *Second language learning theories*. 3rd ed. New York and London: Routledge.

Nunan, D. (2004). *Task-based language teaching*. Cambridge: Cambridge University Press.

Pajares, F. (1993). Teachers' beliefs and educational research: Cleaning up a messy construct. *Review of Educational Research*, 62, 307–32.

Phipps, S. and Borg, S. (2007). Exploring the relationship between teachers' beliefs and their classroom practice. *The Teacher Trainer*, 21(3), 17–19.

Richards, J. C. (2006). *Communicative language teaching today*. Cambridge: Cambridge University Press.

Richards, J. C., Ho, B., and Giblin, K. (1996). Learning how to teach in the RSA Certificate. In D. Freeman and J. C. Richards, eds. *Teacher learning in language teaching*. Cambridge: Cambridge University Press.

Samuda, V. and Bygate, M. (2008). *Tasks in second language learning*. Basingstoke: Palgrave Macmillan.

Schön, D. A. (1983). *The reflective practitioner: How professionals think in action*. New York: Basic Books.

Skehan, P. (1996). A framework for the implementation of task-based instruction. *Applied Linguistics*, 17(1), 38–61.

Too, W. K. (2013). Facilitating the development of pre-service teachers as reflective learners: A Malaysian experience. *The Language Learning Journal*, 41(2), 161–74.

Van den Branden, K. (2009). Diffusion and implementation of innovations. In M. Long and C. Doughty, eds. *The handbook of language teaching*. Oxford: Wiley-Blackwell, pp. 659–72.

Widdowson, H. G. (1993). Innovation in teacher development. *Annual Review of Applied Linguistics*, 13, 260–75.

Williams, R. and Grudnoff, L. (2011). Making sense of reflection: A comparison of beginning and experienced teachers' perceptions of reflection for practice. *Reflective Practice: International and Multidisciplinary Perspectives*, 12(3), 281–91.

Willis, D. and Willis, J. (2007). *Doing task-based teaching*. Oxford: Oxford University Press.

Willis, J. (1996). *A framework for task-based learning*. Harlow: Longman Pearson Education.

Xiongyong, C. and Samuel, S. (2011). Perceptions and implementation of task-based language teaching among secondary school EFL teachers in China. *International Journal of Business and Social Science*, 2(24), 292–302.

12A

Connecting Teacher Training to Task-Based Language Teaching Implementation

A Case Study of Preservice Teachers in Honduran Bilingual Schools

Lara Bryfonski

12A.1 Introduction

With a focus on student-centered learning, interactive tasks and individualized instruction, task-based language teaching (TBLT) has at times been criticized for a lack of attention to the role of the language teacher in task-based classrooms (Van den Branden, 2016). Prior work examining TBLT implementations has mostly centered around the barriers, both cultural and pedagogical, teachers face when attempting to implement TBLT for the first time (e.g., Carless, 2004; McDonough & Chaikitmongkol, 2007), or has examined the role of the teacher in specific task performances (Samuda, 2001). Given TBLT's foundations in second language acquisition theories, teachers implementing TBLT require a substantial amount of background knowledge, creativity and expertise in order to successfully implement a task-based pedagogy. In order to accomplish this, they clearly require specialized training. However, we know that training teachers to design and implement authentic tasks is difficult and sometimes unsuccessful. For example, Erlam's (2016) aptly named study, "'I'm still not sure what a task is:' Teachers designing language tasks," found that after a year-long professional development course highlighting TBLT pedagogy, only half of the tasks teachers designed reflected the criteria they had learned about in their course.

Teachers' beliefs about pedagogical practices have also been shown to affect how they interpret TBLT (e.g., Chan, 2012; Ogilvie & Dunn, 2010). Despite teachers' difficulties in interpreting and applying TBLT principles, little empirical research has documented their experiences in task-based training programs and connected those experiences to subsequent TBLT implementation – the goal of the current study. In addition, prior work documenting program-level implementations has argued that TBLT is suitable for worldwide contexts (e.g., Müller-Hartmann & Schocker-von Ditfurth [2011] in Germany; McDonough & Chaikitmongkol [2007] in Thailand; Shintani [2018] in Japan; and Van den Branden [2006] in Belgium), yet it remains understudied in many regions, including Latin America, where the current study took place. To address these gaps, this chapter documents a task-based training program aimed at novice English teachers preparing to teach in a network of bilingual schools in Honduras. The case study aims to provide a detailed description of how the training unfolded, document teachers' reactions to the training, including their perceptions about the utility of the training, and examine any connections between these experiences and their subsequent implementations of tasks of their own design in a teaching practicum. The following questions are explored:

1. To what extent were teachers able to successfully implement TBLT in their classrooms following training?
2. How useful was the task-based training for the novice teachers?

12A.2 Context

This case study examined a group of English–Spanish bilingual schools located in Honduras. Historically, English–Spanish bilingualism has been perceived as a significant asset in Honduras, due, in part, to the region's proximity to the United States and its political and economic ties (Euraque, 1999). English language proficiency is recognized as an opportunity to access further education and employment, owing to the demand for English speakers in local call-centers, factories, and tourism industries (Soluri, 2005), positions that are often more lucrative and sustainable than typical local employment. With over 65 percent of Hondurans currently living below the poverty line (World Bank, 2017) and cities routinely topping the list of highest homicide rates in the world (US Department of State, 2016), because of gang- and drug-related violence, it is not surprising that over 18,000 unaccompanied Honduran minors migrated to the United States in 2014 alone (US Customs and Border Protection, 2016). While these figures have declined slightly in 2016 and 2017, due to increased border enforcement by the Mexican government (International Crisis Group, 2016), as well as reportedly, current policies and rhetoric of the Trump Administration (Raderstorf, Wilson, Zechmeister & Camilleri, 2017), AmericasBarometer (2016) reported that "intentions to move abroad have risen significantly in every country in Central American since 2014, especially in Honduras" (as cited in Raderstorf et al., 2017: 3).

The same survey also reported that 35 percent of Hondurans have considered migrating in the last twelve months because of insecurity. Bilingualism is often a means to escape the cyclical poverty present in Honduras that drives young Latin Americans to consider migration. Due to the desire to learn English and access higher-paying jobs in local industries, bilingual education is in high demand. However, the majority of bilingual schools are private and therefore only accessible to the financially secure, making opportunities for upward mobility rare.

The participating schools in the current project are battling these structural inequalities by providing English language teachers to local bilingual schools at very low or zero cost to the local community. Bilingual Education for Central America (BECA, becaschools.org name published with permission) is a US-based nonprofit that recruits, trains and supports proficient English-speaking volunteer teachers to staff a network of community-run bilingual schools in Honduras. These partnerships provide over 600 students from preschool through ninth grade access to quality bilingual education.

In BECA schools, English, math, and science are taught in English by English-speaking teachers, while social studies and Spanish classes are taught in Spanish by Honduran teachers. In this way, the schools' curricula have a CLIL approach (content and language integrated learning; see Ortega [2015] for an overview of TBLT/CLIL interfaces) as their foundation. However, recently, the schools have sought to adopt TBLT in an effort to further support language-learning outcomes and drive day-to-day lesson planning. In 2014 and 2015, a needs analysis and program evaluation were conducted with key stakeholders at the schools to identify target tasks for graduates. The needs analysis indicated most wanted to be able to successfully apply for jobs in English-speaking domains, such as call-centers, tourism or other local industries, translation, and English teaching. Administrators and instructors were interviewed as part of the needs analysis and local employers who hire English speakers were surveyed.

12A.3 Methods

12A.3.1 Participants

This case study examines one cohort of preservice and novice English-speaking teachers (n = 19) embarking on their first or second year teaching at one of the three partner schools. This group was predominantly female (84 percent, n = 16) and made up of recent university graduates with a mean age of 22 (see Table 12A.1). The teachers were a range of nationalities with variability in their prior teaching and learning experiences.

Table 12A.1 *Teacher backgrounds*

Demographic	Value	Number of teachers (n = 19)
Gender	Male	3
	Female	16
First language	English	7
	Spanish	11
	Garifuna[1]	1
Country of origin	United States	7
	Honduras	9
	Mexico	1
	Venezuela	1
	Dominican Republic	1
Previous teaching experience	Less than 6 months	1
	6 to 12 months	2
	1 to 2 years	8
	2 or more years	3
	None	5
Type of teaching credential	No prior formal teaching credential	10
	University degree in linguistics	2
	University degree in education	4
	TESOL certificate	2
	Teaching certification/license	2
Grade(s) teaching 2018-2019	Preschool	2
	1st–3rd Grades	9
	4th–6th Grades	6
	7th–9th Grades	5
	Administration	2

During the teaching practicum, participating teachers taught classes of students (n = 114) from one of the bilingual schools. Each classroom had an average of 16 students (range = 11–20) from kindergarten through sixth grade.

12A.3.2 Materials and Procedures

A variety of materials and procedures were used to encourage critical reflection throughout the training, which has been described as an important element of teacher professional development (Chan, 2012), as reflection enables teachers to consider and analyze their own beliefs and teaching practices. Reflection was a key component of the training – written and oral reflections were recorded to identify qualitative changes throughout the teachers' training experiences

12A.3.3 Training Lessons

The TBLT elements in the summer training course were part of an intensive four-week teaching institute for all first-year English-speaking

---

[1] Indigenous language spoken along the western cost of Central America.

teachers and administrators. The training was approximately 160 hours long and divided into two phases. In the first two weeks, teachers divided their time between working with a mentor on lesson planning for their grade-level and attending various training sessions. The second two weeks were a teaching practicum, where teachers designed and executed their own task-based lessons in classrooms. Teachers divided into grade-level teams and individually taught hour-long lessons to small groups of students while their group members and mentor teachers observed and provided feedback (see Figure 12A.1).

The training was itself task-based, in that the training sessions were all designed to be student-centered, modeling the execution of the session objectives. The training was therefore highly interactive, with teachers engaging and experiencing tasks designed for them first-hand. The novice teacher trainees were frequently treated as if they are the "students" by the trainer, in order to model a given objective. The teacher trainees were also

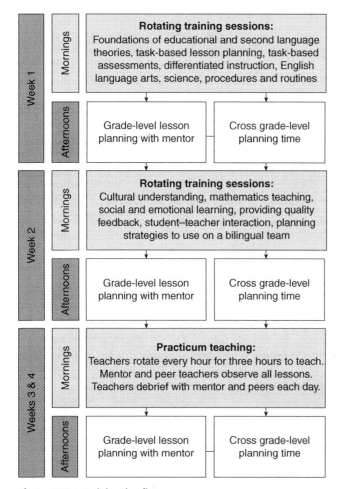

Figure 12A.1 Training timeline

Table 12A.2 *TBLT training*

Training topic	Training content
Theories of second language acquisition and bilingualism	• Discussion of first vs. second language acquisition • Mini-lessons on second language acquisition theories • Compare and contrast TBLT with alternatives (e.g., Krashen and Terrell's [1983] Natural Approach)
Task-based lesson planning	• Introduction to backwards design (Wiggins & McTighe, 2005) • Critique of different tasks and lesson plan designs • Creation of grade-level tasks and unit plans
Providing quality feedback	• Video analysis of oral and written feedback strategies • Role-play skits of corrective feedback
Planning for differentiated group work	• Discussion of ways to group students during tasks to promote peer interaction • Assessing student needs • Assessing task difficulty • Design grade-level-appropriate differentiation strategies
Task-based assessments	• Discussion of formative vs. summative assessments • Evaluation of example assessments • Creation of grade-level sample assessments

often asked to practice a given objective by modeling with a small group of other teachers. For example, in the foundations of second language education session, the teachers completed a "Gallery Walk" activity where they moved in small groups between posters that presented key points regarding contrasting language teaching approaches (TBLT vs. PPP [presentation, practice, and production] vs. Grammar Translation). The teachers left comments on each poster with sticky notes, connecting the pedagogic approach to their own beliefs or experiences, and rotating to read and react to comments left by others. After the activity, the teachers debriefed in new groups and were assigned interactive roles to encourage the flow of discussion. In this way, a variety of teaching techniques, management strategies and content were quickly and clearly disseminated to the teaching team. During these two weeks of course work and individual lesson planning time, teachers recorded self-reflections on their learning experience and shared them with the training team. See Table 12A.2 for an overview of the TBLT training.

Written Reflections

During the first two weeks of training (prior to the practicum), instructors submitted daily reflections on their experiences. At the end of each day, teachers wrote their positive reflections (takeaways) and their changes (suggestions for improvement) regarding the day's training sessions. Teachers were provided with five minutes at the end of each training day to reflect. Reflections were kept anonymous and digitally transcribed to track ongoing changes that occurred in teachers' perceptions of the training.

Video Recordings

Once during the two-week teaching practicum, teachers video-recorded an hour-long lesson of their choosing. For teacher-centered activities a digital camera was used to record the teachers' actions. For student-centered tasks, a Samsung 360-degree camera was set on a tripod in the center of the classroom and recorded both the teacher and students engaged in the tasks. Lesson outcomes captured on video were discussed with the teachers in subsequent interviews.

Interviews

The final week of the training, teachers took part in a semi-structured interview. They were asked a series of open-ended questions about their experiences during the course, areas they found most and least useful, specific outcomes they achieved and suggestion for improvement of the training.

12A.3.4 Analysis

Responses to written reflections and in oral interviews were transcribed and translated into English where necessary. Responses were then transferred to Nvivo (QSR International) and coded by both the researcher and two trained coders for emergent themes using a grounded approach (following suggestions in Mackey & Gass [2015]). Individual responses with themes were compared with independent participant variables, such as native-speaker/nonnative-speaker status, teaching experience, grade-level taught and teacher age. The video data was analyzed according to the degree to which teachers implemented TBLT based on the criteria for implementation outlined in Long's (2015) methodological principles.

12A.4 Findings and Discussion

12A.4.1 To What Extent Were Teachers Able to Successfully Implement Task-Based Language Teaching in Their Classroom following Training?

Sixteen teachers submitted video recordings of their class during the teaching practicum. Teachers taught hour-long lessons in English on a variety of topics including literacy skills, math topics (e.g., numbers, addition, word problems) or science (e.g., animals, sounds, the water cycle). Each lesson included one or more tasks that students engaged in, facilitated by the teacher. Overall, the videos represented a range of implementations of TBLT pedagogy, with some teachers' lessons well aligned with Long's methodological principles and others continuing to include grammar-based strategies and exercises to organize their lessons (see Bryfonski, 2021 for a quantitative discussion of these results). Two teachers' lessons and sample tasks are highlighted below to demonstrate this variability – Christina[2] is an example of a teacher whose lesson aligned with TBLT principles, and Raquel[2] is a teacher whose lesson continued to have a grammatical focus post-training.

Christina taught a third grade writing class on the topic of brainstorming. Her lesson plan had the objective of brainstorming ideas for an "All About Me" writing project. She began the lesson by modeling a web-diagram brainstorm whole-class on the white board using her own family as examples. Next she asked students to supply their own examples orally and by writing them on the board. She then asked students to work at their tables in groups to create their own web-diagrams, discussing their ideas with one another, while she circulated providing feedback and extra support to struggling students. Christina's lesson was aligned with TBLT principles in that it had a clear nonlinguistic outcome as its focus – second grade students need to practice writing, and this project is individualized to be about each child's family, fostering meaning-making. Learners needed to utilize their own linguistic resources, or those provided in the model (input), to create their web-diagrams, they were not provided word lists or required to include particular grammar forms. In her facilitative role as the teacher, Christina provided individualized corrective feedback and incidental focus on form as needed for struggling children. She reflected in her interview that she was concerned about student participation during the lesson and that she "was trying to get everybody, 100% involved" and indicated she was focused on promoting student output. During her interview, Christina reported that she connected with the style of the training and enjoyed reflecting each day. Her biggest takeaway from the training was the realization of how much she needed to elaborate classroom input to foster meaning-making. She said "I see how explicit directions need to be and the level of steps ... too many steps and kids get lost."

By contrast, Raquel struggled to implement tasks according to the training in her practicum class. Raquel taught a reading class to a group of fourth graders. Raquel indicated in her lesson plan that her lesson's objective was to teach the class how to retell a story. She began the lesson by discussing irregular and regular (-ed ending) verbs and asking students to identify regular and irregular verbs in a list of sentences on the board. She then asked students to work in groups to create their own past tense

---

[2] All names pseudonyms

sentences. She then explained steps to retell a story and asked the class to help her retell the story of *Cinderella* as she wrote it on the board. Raquel reflected in her post-video interview that she felt that a grammatical lesson on verbs was necessary before she could begin her lesson on retelling a story. She reflected: "How am I going to do my activity if I don't remind them about the verbs?" She also indicated in her post-training interview that she struggled with lesson planning and that she felt overwhelmed by the amount of information packed into the training. She said "It was too much information and I said, 'how is this going to help me if it is a lot of information?' I cannot get all this in my mind."

These results add further evidence to prior research demonstrating a mismatch between TBLT training and teacher implementation. In the study by Ogilvie and Dunn (2010), some teachers were also observed implementing lessons that lacked key principles of TBLT after attending training. The authors suggested that teachers did so because they did not perceive the epistemological value of TBLT. Additionally, teachers in that study reported the desire to adhere to their own cultural norms for teaching and learning. Raquel, in the example above, drew from her own beliefs rather than the TBLT training to decide that a grammatical lesson on verbs was necessary for student understanding. However, other teachers were documented effectively utilizing the techniques demonstrated in the TBLT training in their own lessons. These teachers most consistently demonstrated the ability to elaborate input (methodological principle 3 in Long [2015]) by using a variety of strategies to support input comprehension, such as including visuals, gestures, and music, and by activating prior knowledge or referencing prior learning.

Individual differences might also have played a role in these focal teachers' experiences in the training. Raquel acquired English as a foreign language as an adult in Honduras, whereas Christina was raised bilingually in Spanish and English in the United States. When asked about her experience in the training, Raquel said: "Some words are difficult and some of them speak so fast. So fast. Trainers and students. Slow down and use words that are not so difficult." In prior work, Warford and Reeves (2003) found that the effect of prior learning experiences, the "apprenticeship of observation," has a stronger effect on nonnative speakers teaching their second language, due to the fact that the nonnative speakers are living the language-learning experience as they teach, while native speakers are not. Additionally, Anderson (2016) found that native-speaker and nonnative-speaker teachers prioritize different components of course content during implementation. Raquel indicated that as a first-time teacher, she found the training overwhelming, which may have been further compounded by the fact that the training was conducted entirely in English, and could have factored into the observed outcomes in her lesson.

12A.4.2 How Useful Was the Training for the Teachers Immediately following Training and during Their First Year Teaching?

Through daily written reflections and end-of-training interviews, teachers described how useful various aspects of the training were for their own teaching. Two hundred reflections were gathered from the teachers during the first two weeks of training. Table 12A.3 below provides an overview of prominent themes that emerged from the teacher reflections.

These findings indicate that during the training, teachers connected with its student-centered, collaborative nature, but had concerns about the lack of resources and structure. These findings were echoed in semi-structured interviews teachers participated in during the final days of the teaching practicum. The task-based nature of the training was a prominent theme in the interviews. One teacher said:

> I liked how you modeled how to get our attention ... I think that stayed more in my brain than a list would. You modeling the mini lessons and what those looked like instead of just talking through them.

Table 12A.3 *Prominent daily reflection themes*

Positives/takeaways		Negatives/changes	
Theme	Illustrative quote	Theme	Illustrative quote
Mentorship	I like the one-on-one time with mentor, good space to ask questions.	Structure	I would also like a bit more lecturing on how to actively transfer this information to using it in the classroom.
Collaboration	Shar[ing] strategies with my fellow 1st grade teacher, I loved working in small groups and getting more individualized attention from the trainers.	Lesson planning	I think that the planning lesson should be a factor #1, how to do planning lessons and tasks, how to understand the curriculum better.
Modeling	I liked the way different methods and strategies were modeled. I like that we started with a bit of theory and immediately did activities that were modeled.	Resources	I would like a bit more concreteness. Right now, we are given information that is a bit general and are able to draw our own conclusions from it. Concrete ideas and tools, helpful handouts, etc. I would like to have something concrete in the trainings, not just theory, it makes it harder for me ...
Reflection	Making us reflect on our practice and personal life. I'm making more connections.	Strategies	More strategies/examples, the "watch me teach and take away ideas" method isn't going so well for me.

Other teachers described the utility of learning pedagogy and teaching techniques actively rather than passively. One teacher connected active learning from training to her experience in the practicum:

> I learn the best when I see someone do something and then I do it myself. Giving us a lot of examples of how we can do things. I took a lot of notes down on things I can do with my students, I think getting to try things out seeing and knowing that everything is step by step, but when you actually try to do it you're like "... I didn't think about that!" It's been great to see this and play around with it. [The practicum] is great because we get to explore and experience the real thing because when you have an idea it's just what's in your mind but you don't know how things will turn out.

Teachers also described how they appreciated that the training was differentiated for different grade levels and how teachers were given strategies to adapt techniques to work in their own classes. The utility of mentorship was also a prominent theme in the interviews. Teachers said they found individualized attention, time for reflection, observation by more experienced teachers and being provided feedback were all essential to their development as teachers. One teacher reflected: "The most useful thing was being re-taught how to teach and then immediately putting it into practice and getting feedback while it is fresh in my mind."

Teachers also were asked during their interviews which aspects of the training were the least useful or what areas they would change. The main theme to emerge from this portion of the training was the need to dedicate more training time to lesson planning. Teachers described their struggle in breaking down target tasks from the curriculum into individual unit and lesson plans. One teacher said:

> I wish we had done more on how to lesson plan how to plan out the [quarter], I would say something wish we had more of was a class or workshop on how to look through the curriculum and lesson plans and taking time to pick those apart and how to take a unit and spread it out to make a week or two weeks.

This finding echoes previous work (e.g., Erlam, 2016; Ogilvie & Dunn, 2010) which has found that teachers struggle to plan task-based lessons after professional development programs on TBLT. The teachers in this study suggested it would be beneficial to have more time for group planning and sharing ideas. Teachers said they also wanted more ideas on how to build in differentiation into their lesson plans, including planning for students with varied English proficiency levels and working with students with learning disabilities.

Another theme that emerged was the need for more concreteness in terms of examples and resources throughout the training. Teachers indicated that they wanted more specific strategies, examples and techniques, preferably in easy-to-use handouts or other resources. This reflects a documented difficulty in preparing teachers to enact TBLT (as overviewed in Long [2016]), which is that, unlike in traditional language programs where one textbook provides day-by-day activities and structure, TBLT requires more creativity and moment-to-moment decision-making on the part of the teacher. This may also be reflected in teachers' overall dissatisfaction with their preparation to write and enact task-based lesson plans.

12A.5 Implications and Conclusion

The results of the current study uncovered variation in the impact of the task-based teacher-training program on novice language teachers' TBLT implementations. Findings indicated that teachers did not experience the training uniformly and this may have led, in part, to the variability in their understanding and implementation of TBLT in the teaching practicum. Results suggest teacher trainers should pay attention to individual differences in prior experiences amongst teacher trainees and investigate the ways these differences could impact on how they experience TBLT training, especially for teachers like Raquel who teach and experience training in their second language.

The training that was implemented for teachers in the current study was itself task-based and included frequent modeling on the part of the trainers and the novice teachers, as well as participation in hands-on tasks and activities. Prior work has also encouraged this strategy, describing it as a way to promote a more holistic understanding of TBLT (Brandl, 2016; Han, 2018). Teachers studied here recognized the benefits of modeling, indicating they benefited from a task-based, reflective approach to TBLT training. Future programs could also offer training in a "TBLT style," modeling the techniques expected from teachers and promoting reflective practices.

Results also uncovered a variety of changes that teachers indicated would improve the quality of the task-based training they received. The most prominent theme to emerge from these data was the desire for more specific instruction on day-to-day lesson planning. Teachers in the current study indicated post-training that they continued to find it difficult to break down target tasks from the curriculum into individual lesson plans and wished they had more specific resources to use. The teachers' struggles with lesson planning and the lack of resources suggest that teacher trainers and school administration must find a way to marry the desire of teachers to be given pre-made lesson plans and lists of ready-to-use activities with the components of TBLT which focus on student language needs, reactivity, differentiation and individualization in language teaching. Programs should develop resources tailored to students in their specific context (according to the results of a needs analysis) and find ways to incorporate that information into materials that are accessible and usable by novice language teachers.

Further Reading

Han, J. (2018). Task-based learning in task-based teaching: Training teachers of Chinese as a foreign language. *The Annual Review of Applied Linguistics*, 38, 162–86.

McDonough, K. and Chaikitmongkol, W. (2007). Teachers' and learners' reactions to a Task- Based EFL course in Thailand. *TESOL Quarterly*, 41(1), 107–32.

Ogilvie, G. and Dunn, W. (2010). Taking teacher education to task: Exploring the role of teacher education in promoting the utilization of task-based language teaching. *Language Teaching Research*, 14(2), 161–81.

Révész, A. and Gurzynski-Weiss, L. (2016). Teachers' perspectives on second language task difficulty:Insights from think-alouds and eye tracking. *Annual Review of Applied Linguistics*, 36,182–204.

Stanton, S. and Fiszbein, A. (2019). Work in progress: English teaching and teachers in Latin America. The Inter-American Dialogue. Retrieved from: www.thedialogue.org/wp-content/uploads/2019/11/white-paper-2019-completo-final.pdf

Van den Branden, K. (2016). The role of teachers in task-based language education. *Annual Review of Applied Linguistics*, 36, 164–81.

Study Questions

1. What other individual differences of language teachers can you think of? How might these differences impact on how teachers experience TBLT training?
2. What do you think the next tasks in the sequence would be in Christina's class on writing? What suggestions would you make to Raquel to improve her lesson?
3. Why do you think the teachers in this case study felt limited by a lack of resources? How might this be remedied in other low-resource contexts like the one represented by this case study?

References

AmericasBarometer (2016). The Latin American Public Opinion Project (LAPOP). Retrieved from www.vanderbilt.edu/lapop/ab2016.php.

Anderson, J. (2016). Initial teacher training courses and non-native speaker teachers. *ELT Journal*, 70(3), 261–74.

Brandl, K. (2016). Task-based instruction and teacher training. In N. Van Deusen-Scholl and S. May, eds. *Second and foreign language education. Encyclopedia of language and education*. 3rd ed. Cham, Switzerland: Springer, pp. 1–14.

Bryfonski, L. (2021). From task-based training to task-based instruction: Novice language teachers' experiences and perspectives. *Language Teaching Research*.

Carless, D. (2004). Issues in teachers' reinterpretation of a task-based innovation. *TESOL Quarterly*, 38(4), 639–62.

Chan, S. P. (2012). Qualitative differences in novice teachers' enactment of task-based language teaching in Hong Kong primary classrooms. In A. Shehadeh, C. A. Coombe, eds. *Task-based language teaching in foreign language contexts: Research and implementation*. Amsterdam: John Benjamins, pp. 187–214.

Erlam, R. (2016). "I'm still not sure what a task is": Teachers designing language tasks. *Language Teaching Research*, 20(3), 279–99.

Euraque, D. (1999). *Reinterpreting the banana republic: Region & state in Honduras, 1870-1972*. Chapel Hill, NC: University of North Carolina Press.

International Crisis Group (2016). Easy Prey: Criminal Violence and Central American Migration. Brussels, International Crisis Group. Retrieved from www.crisisgroup.org/latin-america-caribbean/central-america/easy-prey-criminal-violence-and-central-american-migration.

Krashen, S. D. and Terrell, T. D. (1983). *The Natural Approach: Language acquisition in the classroom*. New York: Pergamon Press.

Long, M. H. (2015). *Second language acquisition and task-based language teaching*. John Wiley & Sons.

Long, M. H. (2016). In defense of tasks and TBLT: Nonissues and real issues. *Annual Review of Applied Linguistics*, 36, 5–33.

Mackey, A. and Gass, S. (2015). *Second language research: Methodology and design*. 2nd ed. New York: Routledge.

Müller-Hartmann, A. and Schocker-von Ditfurth, M. (2011). *Introduction to English language teaching: Optimize your exam preparation*. Stuttgart: Klett Lerntraining.

Müller-Hartmann, A. and Schocker, M. (2017). The challenge of thinking task-based teaching from the learners' perspectives – Developing teaching competences through an action research approach to teacher education. In M. J. Ahmadia and M. Pilar García Mayo, eds. *Recent perspectives on task-based language learning and teaching*. De Gruyter, pp. 233–58.

Ortega, L. (2015). Researching CLIL and TBLT interfaces. *System*, 54, 103–9.

Raderstorf, B., Wilson, C. J., Zechmeister, E. J., and Camilleri, M. J. (2017). Beneath the violence: How insecurity shapes daily life and emigration in Central America: A Report of the Latin American Public Opinion Project and the Inter-American Dialogue. Rule of Law Working Paper.

Samuda, V. (2001). Guiding relationships between form and meaning during task performance: The role of the teacher. In M. Bygate, P. Skehan, and M. Swain, eds. *Researching pedagogic tasks: Second language learning, teaching and testing*, London and New York: Routledge, pp. 119–40.
Shintani, N. (2018). Researching TBLT for young, beginner learners in Japan. In V. Samuda, K. Van den Branden and M. Bygate, eds. *TBLT as a researched pedagogy*. Amsterdam: John Benjamins, pp. 200-12.
Soluri, J. (2005). *Banana cultures: Agriculture, consumption, and environmental change in Honduras and the United States*. Austin: University of Texas Press.
US Customs and Border Protection. (2016, October). United States Border Patrol Southwest Family Unit Subject and Unaccompanied Alien Children Apprehensions Fiscal Year 2016. Retrieved from www.cbp.gov/newsroom/stats/southwest-border-unaccompanied-children/fy-2016
US Department of State. (2016). Country Information: Honduras. Retrieved from https://travel.state.gov/content/passports/en/country/honduras.html
Van den Branden, K. (2006). *Task-based language education: From theory to practice*. Cambridge: Cambridge University Press
Warford, M. K. and Reeves, J. (2003). Falling into it: Novice TESOL teacher thinking. *Teachers and Teaching*, 9(1), 47–65.
Wiggins, G. and McTighe, J. (2005). *Understanding by design*. Upper Saddle River, NJ: Prentice Hall.
World Bank. (2017). Honduras: World Development Indicators. Retrieved from http://data.worldbank.org/country/honduras

12B

Training for Tasks the Cooperative Way

An Online Tutored Task-Based Language Teaching Course for Teachers, Managers and Course Designers

Neil McMillan and Geoff Jordan

12B.1 Introduction

In this case study we discuss a small private online course (as defined by Fox (2013)), on task-based language teaching (TBLT), aimed at teachers, teacher educators, directors of studies and course designers. The small private online course is designed and run by members of the Spanish cooperative Serveis Lingüístics de Barcelona, SCCL (SLB), principally the authors of this case study. Michael Long (University of Maryland), Roger Gilabert (Universitat de Barcelona and member of SLB) and Glenn Fulcher (University of Leicester) are guest tutors on the course and informal consultants.

12B.2 Background

Set up in 2014, SLB is a *cooperativa de serveis*, or services cooperative, under Catalan law. The members (twenty at time of writing) are mainly freelance English teachers, translators, proofreaders and educational materials writers who contribute to and benefit from services such as legal and financial advice, continuous professional development workshops and teaching materials (see www.slb.coop). In addition, SLB has a commitment to serve the wider community in Barcelona, for example by campaigning for better pay and conditions for teachers in the private English language teaching (ELT) sector, and by collaborating with local organisations, such as the Federation Salut Mental Catalunya (Mental Health Catalonia 2020) and the Sense Gravetat network of community workshops (Zero Gravity 2020).

In 2015, SLB president Neil McMillan invited Geoff Jordan to deliver a workshop on TBLT to co-op members. This was based on Long's (2015) *Second Language Acquisition and Task-Based Language Teaching*, and by the time Jordan returned to give a second workshop in 2017, members had adopted elements of Long's approach in their classes, and SLB had begun offering tailored TBLT courses to new clients. Based on our perception of a strong interest in TBLT from teachers in our network, but a lack of training, we decided to design a training course based on Long's TBLT.

However, given the scope of Long's approach, which is designed to be implemented at an institutional level (Long, 2016: 28), we included curriculum managers and course designers as possible participants. Our knowledge of teachers' contexts in our local sector and beyond, as well as our own experiments implementing TBLT, led us to conclude that some participants would not be in a position to participate in a full TBLT implementation. This led us to develop a version of TBLT that compromises on some of Long's stipulations, for example, by doing needs analysis on an ongoing basis, or by having teachers design tasks and materials. We call this approach 'Long light'; it respects most (if not all) of Long's methodological principles, but is possibly more attractive to, and useful for, teachers working in restricted circumstances (i.e., with limited influence over course design and little institutional support).

Following the construction of our own online platform for delivering courses; a survey of currently available TBLT courses; the production of a sample unit; and consultation with SLB members, early in 2018, SLB decided to develop the course as a minimal viable product. McMillan and Jordan were charged with designing the course, with some support from Marc Jones, a Tokyo-based SLB member.

12B.3 Course Design

12B.3.1 The Model

Long and Crookes (1992) give an early indication of Long's view of TBLT, specifically, his criticisms of 'synthetic' syllabuses, as outlined in Wilkins (1976). Long and Crookes reject synthetic syllabuses, because they break the target language down into small items of grammar, lexis, pronunciation, etc., and present these items one by one in a linear sequence to learners, on the false assumption that learners can then re-assemble, or synthesise, them into a coherent knowledge of the language. Long (2015) demonstrates how such an approach contradicts robust findings of research on second language acquisition, and presents instead an alternative syllabus, where students are given practical hands-on experience with real-world tasks. Beginning with a needs analysis to identify 'target tasks' – the things learners will actually have to do in the second language (L2) – pedagogic tasks are designed to build learners' ability to perform the target tasks, often culminating in a full simulation of that task. Materials are selected on the principle of 'input elaboration' – improving the comprehensibility of relevant spoken or written texts by adding redundancy and regularity (see Long, 2020a). The syllabus consists of a sequence of pedagogic tasks implemented according to 'methodological principles' and locally-defined 'pedagogic procedures'. Key methodological principles include providing rich input, encouraging inductive 'chunk' learning, focus on form, respecting learner syllabi and developmental processes, and promoting cooperative, collaborative learning.

Long's TBLT stands in stark contrast to the approaches taken by Willis and Willis (2009); Nunan (2004); and R. Ellis (2009), and to the views of TBLT expressed by teacher trainers such as Harmer (2015) and Ur (2012), who all define tasks as 'communicative activities' and assume that tasks accompany or support explicit language teaching. While Skehan (2002) distinguishes between 'strong' and 'weak' versions of TBLT, Long (2016) talks about 'task-supported' language teaching as opposed to TBLT proper. Long sees 'weak' versions of TBLT as 'covert' linguistic syllabuses 'concealed' in communicative tasks, and criticises R. Ellis' 'dual structural and task hybrid':

> Tasks ... are the real-world communicative uses to which learners will put the L2 beyond the classroom – the things they will do in and through the L2 – and the task syllabus stands alone, not as one strand in a hybrid of some kind. (Long, 2016: 6)

We endorse Long's views, and agree that explicit teaching should be limited to 'focus on form' (Long, 2015: 316), where learners' attention is drawn to formal aspects of the language in harmony with the internal 'learner syllabus'. However, as indicated above, we recognised the demanding nature of Long's TBLT syllabus.

First, Long's TBLT rejects the established grammar-based syllabus, where explicit grammar and vocabulary teaching form a major part of the teacher's job. Could we realistically expect managers and teachers to accept such a radical demand? Would they not insist on grammar teaching and point out that students themselves demand it? Second, we advocated abandoning General English coursebooks like *Headway* and *English File*, which provide teachers with a convenient, coherent, multi-faceted tool for doing their job. And third, we replaced coursebooks with a syllabus and materials design process involving hundreds of hours of work. All this would need careful negotiation with course participants, and compromises would have to be made.

12B.3.2 The Course

The aims of the course were set out as seen in 12B.1.

The primary aim is to enable participants to be part of a full TBLT implementation, if not now, then at some point in the future.

Course aims

Overall, the course aims are to:

- ✓ introduce the theory behind task-based language teaching (TBLT)
- ✓ make the case for Long's TBLT as the optimum version, informed both by research and classroom experience
- ✓ develop lighter versions of this model for adoption in more restricted circumstances
- ✓ take you through the steps of designing a TBLT syllabus, from needs analysis to task designs and sequencing
- ✓ present a robust model for implementing and evaluating TBLT in the classroom

Figure 12B.1 Course aims

Meanwhile, the course provides tools and opportunities to experiment with lighter forms of TBLT in the classroom and with 'Long light' course design. Our course, like the course run by staff at the Universidad Nacional Autónoma de México (UNAM; see Solares-Altamirano 2010), seeks 'to make second language acquisition theory accessible and closer to teachers' everyday practice', and accepts, like them, that 'radical change is not considered an immediate course objective, but fostering teachers' awareness, questioning and reflection is' (Solares-Altamirano, 2010: 55). However, in contrast with UNAM, where no one definition or mode of TBLT is promoted, we adopt Long's approach. Furthermore, our course is also aimed at those responsible for course and materials design, and includes sessions on needs analysis and analysing target discourse (see Long, this volume; Sağdıç & Reagan, this volume; and Maie & Salen, this volume), with which teachers are not normally involved.

The course consists of twelve sessions, based on the twelve chapters of Long's (2015) book, which is the set text. (For a full description, see SLB, 2020a.)

1. Sample unit
2. How we learn an L2
3. Which TBLT?
4. Long's TBLT
5. The needs analysis: identifying target tasks
6. Analysing target discourse
7. Mulling it over with Mike Long
8. Syllabus design
9. Materials
10. Methodological and pedagogical principles
11. Focus on form
12. TBLT assessment and roundup

Following Van den Branden (2006: 242–43), we wanted to exploit the online platform to incorporate elements of TBLT into course design, for example, to make online activities task-like, and to promote collaborative learning by maximising synchronous and asynchronous interaction among participants and tutors. This led to the following structure for each session:

a) background reading/viewing
b) thirty-minute video presentation by the session tutor
c) short digital exercise checking comprehension of the topic or exploring a related topic
d) forum discussion task
e) sixty-minute video-conference tutorial
f) tutor-assessed 'Output task'.

A forum was open throughout the course. Stage (d) encouraged reflection and a critical assessment of the session's content by asking participants to reflect on a question; for example, 'share opinions on which version of TBLT is most appropriate or desirable for your context' (Session 3). Stage (e) aimed at clarifying the content, further encouraging reflection, and preparing participants for stage (f), which served formally as an assessment tool, but was intended to give participants an opportunity for further reflection, since tasks were often directed towards connecting theory and practice. For example, Session 9's Output task asks participants to produce a piece of material to support a pedagogic task. Overall, the assignment types vary from essays to commentaries on task discourse and video and audio reflections.

In terms of reflection, we wanted the course to facilitate both reflection *for* action and reflection *in/on* action (see East, this volume). This would help us meet one of Van den Branden's (2006: 237–38) key requirements for TBLT teacher education:

> For teachers it is crucial that they are given the chance to try out new ideas in the classroom and see how they work out. This again stresses the primacy of practice-oriented in-service training: it must lead to things that teachers can *do* in their classrooms (tasks they can perform), and if this is the case, teachers have a great need to reflect upon that practice afterwards.

However, unlike the in-service courses Van den Branden describes, where teachers are trained to actively implement a new TBLT syllabus, we anticipated that some participants would work in contexts where no such syllabus was in place, and would have limited or no opportunities to experiment. We therefore designed both forum and Output tasks with options for those unable, or perhaps unwilling, to reflect in/on action. The aforementioned Session 9 Output task, for example, provides participants with model material for a specific task, then asks them to adapt the material for a given variation in the task design. Alternatively, participants can choose their own target tasks related to their students' needs. Similarly, the Output task for Session 11 (focus on form) has participants record a task performed in their classroom, or review a video of a task provided by us, and then evaluate how focus on form was or could have been implemented.

Each session was estimated to require four hours of work by participants, and was scheduled to take place over a week. Session 1 was offered as a free sample unit, and the course proper ran over eleven weeks from 1 March to 7 June 7 2019, allowing for a two-week Easter break.

12B.4 Writing the Course

In dividing up the creation of content, Jordan took on the more theoretical sessions (e.g., the cognitive-interactionist model) and McMillan the more practical ones (e.g., focus on form and materials design). Additionally, McMillan acted as overall director and editor, which mainly involved editing the video presentations and assembling the component parts of each session onto the online platform. Roger Gilabert wrote a tutorial on the overall design and implementation of TBLT, based on the course for Catalan journalists described in Gilabert (2005). Michael Long contributed a recorded Q&A session, and two tutorials; one open, and one on syllabus design. Finally, Marc Jones wrote a guide to corpus creation and concordancing for Session 5, and helped produce content for Sessions 8 and 9.

12B.5 Marketing and Participants

Marketing was conducted primarily via social media. Followers of SLB's Twitter account had reached 1000 by March 2019, and among followers were significant numbers of our target participants. From November 2018, we programmed a series of tweets to promote the course and drive interested parties to the SLB website. We also used Google Ads, Facebook and LinkedIn to drive traffic to the site, email marketing to SLB newsletter subscribers, and blogposts by McMillan, Jordan and Jones.

A full course programme was published, and the first session of the course, 'Why TBLT?' (SLB, 2020b), was offered as a free sample. It features background reading, a video presentation by Jordan, and an interactive quiz, but there is no forum task or assignment.

An early-bird fee of 399 euros was offered until 1 January 2019, when the price rose to 475 euros. A minimum of eight paying customers was required to cover tuition, grading, course management, and the partial repayment of cooperative investors. We set the upper limit at sixteen, and three free spaces were allocated for SLB members.

The course began on 1 March 2019 with all nineteen places taken. Of the participants, five were based in the UK, four in Spain and two in Russia. The remainder were based in Ireland, Italy, Thailand, Serbia, New Zealand, Israel, France and Poland.

12B.6 First Implementation

Participants completed an orientation session and worked through Session 1 before the course started. The orientation session included a pre-course survey (see Appendix A), which served as a basic needs analysis. Fifteen participants responded.

Table 12B.1 shows that 80 per cent of respondents were teachers. Despite high levels of qualifications (see Table 12B.2), only four participants had studied TBLT academically, and only four had experimented with some form of TBLT. This led us to produce more video and audio examples of TBLT classes, providing chances to observe TBLT in action. While six participants taught English for Specific Purposes and five English for Academic Purposes, most taught coursebook-driven General English, justifying our decision to ensure that all our activities encouraging reflection on teaching practice came with an option to reflect on a given example (see Section 12B.3.2), as well as our provision of a 'Long light' option as an alternative approach.

12B.6.1 Engagement with Course Activities

Of the nineteen participants, two made no contributions to any forum, Output task or tutorial. The rest engaged well over the first sessions, with a high standard of contribution. The Session 2 forum task, adapted from Clandfield and Hadfield (2017: 25–26), enjoyed the highest participation (see Table 12B.3). By Session 5, five participants had dropped out, due to personal or work issues, and participation had started to decline. Early feedback confirmed that we had seriously underestimated the time required to complete activities, some requiring double the time. We responded by extending several sessions to two weeks, which did not

Table 12B.1 *Participants' working roles*

Language teacher	Teacher trainer	Director of studies	Course designer	Academic/ researcher	Pedagogic materials designer
12 (80%)	5 (33.3%)	4 (26.7%)	4 (26.7%)	2 (13.3%)	3 (20%)

Table 12B.2 *Participants' highest qualifications*

Master's degree	Diploma (DELTA or Trinity DipTESOL)	PG diploma in language teaching	Introductory certificate (CELTA, Cert TESOL)	None
7 (46.7%)	5 (33.3%)	1 (6.7%)	1 (6.7%)	1 (6.7%)

Table 12B.3 *Engagement in forum tasks*

Session	Task	Number of voices*	Number of posts
2: How we learn an L2	Introduce yourself and discuss questions about interests/concerns re TBLT with a partner.	15	66
3: Which TBLT?	Reflect on strong/weak versions of TBLT/task-supported language teaching. Which best suits your context?	9	46
4: Long's TBLT as a whole	Describe which aspects of Long's TBLT you would most/least like to be involved with. Why?	14	63
5: Identifying target tasks	Choose a target task relevant to your learners, research it and describe it in terms of type, steps etc.	6	16
6: Analysing discourse	Describe three discourse features of a familiar target task.	4	9
7: Mulling it over with Mike Long	Brainstorm questions for Long for the Q&A tutorial.	5	15
8: Syllabus design	Reflect on a syllabus type described by Long (2015: 207–23) and discuss your view of Long's evaluation.	4	12
9: Materials	Review the SLB prototype TBLT materials bank. Choose an evaluation question to respond to.	3	7
10: Methodological principles	Describe the pedagogical procedures you use to implement one of Long's methodological principles.	2	7
11: Focus on form	Discuss how you implement one of the pedagogical procedures for focusing on form described in the presentation.	3	8
12: Testing and evaluation	'Linguistic competence should not be taken into account when evaluating task performance'. Discuss.	4	6

*Not including tutors

suit everyone's schedule, but was considered necessary to give participants a fair chance of passing the course.

The inadequate time provision was probably even more acutely felt when we moved into more technical areas – needs analysis in Session 5, and analysing task discourse in Session 6 – both requiring specific expertise beyond the ken of most chalk-face teachers. Although we feel that teachers can be trained to take part in needs analysis, we acknowledge that this may have been too much for some.

12B.6.2 Completion Rates

To complete the course, participants were required to pass all Output tasks. In the end, six participants completed the full course, comprising 32 per cent of all participants and 35 per cent of participants active at the beginning. Among those still actively submitting Output tasks from Session 5 onwards, when the biggest drop-off occurred (see Table 12B.4), 86 per cent went on to complete the course. This compares favourably with figures for massive open online courses (MOOCs), which have a median completion rate of 12.6 per cent (Jordan, 2015: 341). Two of the six who completed were teachers only; two had additional roles of course designer and pedagogic materials writer; one was a director of studies; and another was an academic. The minimum teaching-related qualification held was the Cambridge or Trinity Diploma, while four held Master's degrees.

12B.6.3 Post-course Feedback

Seven participants gave post-course feedback via an anonymous evaluation (see Appendix B). Five were teachers and two were course managers. Feedback was largely positive: six of the seven agreed or strongly agreed that the course had helped them develop professionally, and most of the questions about course content got similar responses. Predictably, the time required to complete the work was deemed inadequate. Participants praised the course content (especially the quality of presentations and the sequencing of topics); the level of challenge of Output tasks and the feedback given to these; the usefulness of the practical elements of the course; and the knowledge and guidance of the tutors.

In general, five respondents (71.4 per cent) rated the course as excellent on a scale of 1–5 (1 = poor, 5 = excellent); one gave it 4/5, and the other 3/5. Individual sessions were also rated highly, with none receiving less than 3/5. The most highly rated session was Session 4, 'Long's TBLT as a whole', where Roger Gilabert gave a presentation on a real case of TBLT implementation. Five (71.4 per cent) rated this as excellent. Both this session and Session 7, where Michael Long responded to participants' questions, were highlighted in comments.

Table 12B.4 Completion of Output tasks

Session	Task	Submitted	Pass	Fail
2	Essay on beliefs and practice re explicit and implicit language teaching and learning.	15	15	0
3	Evaluation of a given or participant-provided pedagogic task sequence in relation to definitions of task and TBLT.	14	13	1
4	Proposal for a TBLT course for a given or participant-selected group of students.	14	13	1
5	Outline of needs analysis procedure based on Serafini et al. (2015).	7	7	0
6	Comment on discourse features of a given or participant-provided target task.	7	7	0
8	Analyse a target task or task-type and suggest a sequence of pedagogic tasks, justifying the order in terms of complexity or other relevant features.	6	6	0
9	Adapt or produce material to support a given or participant-selected series of pedagogic tasks.	6	6	0
10	Essay on participants' approach to Long's methodological principle 5 ('Encourage inductive "chunk" learning'), or proposal for a continuous professional development workshop covering one of Long's methodological principles.	6	6	0
11	Reflect on actual and possible approaches to focus on form in relation to a recording of students performing a task.	6	6	0
12	Outline a process for evaluating task performance for a task discussed earlier in the course.	6	6	0

When asked for advice for future course participants, most respondents mentioned setting aside adequate time for the course. One recommended reading Long (2015) before the course starts, while another counselled participants to simply enjoy the opportunity to engage with the course materials and learn from experts in the field.

It is likely that most of the respondents had completed the course, and more insights from those who did not would obviously have been valuable. One participant who dropped out told us informally that he found the academic demands of the course overwhelming, but added that he found the course engaging and continued as a passive participant.

We neglected to include specific questions about how and when participants might go on and implement TBLT in their practice. However, this can still be measured with a follow-up survey which we propose to carry out in June 2020, twelve months after the course ended.

12B.7 Second Implementation

For the second run, aware of the need to allow participants adequate time to get to grips with the materials and tasks, we increased the time for each session from 4 to 8 hours, and allotted two weeks for each session. This created a ninety-hour course, programmed to run between November 2019 and March 2020. A full description can be found at SLB (2020c)

Another major change was to offer three ways to complete the course. For teachers, the Output tasks on specialised activities like needs analysis (Session 5) are now optional, as are Output tasks relating to classroom practice, such as focus on form (Session 11), for participants in course design roles. More general or theory-based sessions remain mandatory for all participants. Finally, participants are free to try all Output tasks regardless of their work role. In this way they can achieve a certificate for overall completion, for completion of the teacher stream, or completion of the course design stream. This was done to lessen the overall workload for participants, and to cater more effectively to each of the main roles our course aimed to develop.

We also made some changes to course content. We refreshed reading lists and introduced more 'loop input' (Woodward, 2003) to the forum and tutorial tasks. This concept refers to the use of activities for teacher education which mirror the activities teachers are being trained to deliver to students, and has helped make our course more collaborative and task-based in itself (Van den Branden, 2006; Solares, 2010). For instance, the Session 5 forum activity 'Describe a target task for a chosen group of students' now leads on to a second stage where participants team up to develop needs analysis tools for that target task. Subsequent tutor feedback guides participants to reflect on the task they had just participated in, what its steps were, and how its structure might be used in tasks for language students.

Finally, as shown in Figure 12B.2, we created clearer rubrics for Output tasks, specifying the performance requirements for a pass grade (50–79 per cent) and a higher band (80 per cent and more). This mirrors TBLT evaluation practice.

Marketing began in September 2019, using the same channels as before. A commercial company was contracted to advertise the course using a variety of social media channels. The course is running at the time of writing, with seven participants.

12B.8 Discussion

We think the first iteration of our course was a qualified success. Time was the biggest issue; we advise those designing online courses to calculate the time required with care. Furthermore, what East (this volume) refers to as the clash between theory and practice was evident. Despite our efforts, some participants viewed Long's approach as unrealistic and felt unwilling to investigate it in depth. As Van den Branden (2016: 173) points out, 'teachers' classroom practice and beliefs are not dictated by the publications produced by second language acquisition researchers or language pedagogues' – even when those teachers sign up for a course based on such research! Nevertheless, our course took a serious, in-depth, critical look at ELT practice and provided a platform for both an ad-hoc, or 'Long light', implementation of classroom tasks, and for the design and implementation of full TBLT programmes. Its design was informed by current ideas of reflective practice (Farrell, 2018) and especially by our wish to make the course consistent with the principles of Long's TBLT.

We see a strong case for making our course compliant with the requirements for state training funds for Spanish workers, FUNDAE (2020). This would bring the course within reach of Spanish schools or institutions considering the implementation of TBLT. We should not expect teachers working in private or public institutions to pay for continuous professional development, and we were disappointed that only two of the seven who gave post-course feedback received funding from their institutions.

In the case of locally situated courses, the delivery mode could become blended and include elements of teacher observation to further focus on practice. At the same time, we feel there is still a place for a wholly distance, more open course like ours, and that the presence of people with diverse experiences is a help rather than a hindrance. Training can

A good answer (50–70%) will:	A very good answer (80–100%) will (also):
Briefly specify a group of learners, whether real or imagined, with some contextual information	
Refer explicitly to the table from Serafini (2015) and comment on the inclusion, exclusion and/or adaptation of needs analysis steps	Make reference to at least two further sources in support of arguments
Relate inclusions, exclusions and adaptations to means available and/or other factors	
Describe data-gathering methods to be used	Include samples of questions for students/domain experts
Be coherent and cohesive to a level that causes little or no strain on the reader	Be coherent, cohesive and well organised to a level that engages the reader

Figure 12B.2 Output task criteria, Session 5

still be practice-oriented: participants can try things out and report back; and video can be used for recording classroom experiments and reflecting on practice, for example. But we want the course to remain flexible enough to accommodate teachers unable or as yet unwilling to try out TBLT in their own environments.

Whatever the format, we feel that the course should more closely follow the principles of loop input: by organising itself more explicitly around tasks rather than topics, the course could reflect TBLT processes more faithfully, and better practise what it preaches. The aim should be to make the exploration of task-types and related issues of complexity, sequencing, etc., something that runs throughout the course. Furthermore, since the forum and Output tasks are already technology-mediated, more attention should be drawn to this aspect of TBLT implementation (see González-Lloret & Ortega, 2014). The session on needs analysis, for example, should direct participants towards including tools, digital literacies and access to technology in their needs analysis processes.

12B.9 Conclusion

We have presented a case study of an online course on TBLT which has already undergone some transformation, and we have suggested ways in which the course might be further transformed in the future. This is entirely in keeping with the development of TBLT courses themselves, which, being focused on the needs of their participants, must adapt in response to feedback and results. We hope to have contributed to the development of task-based teacher education, in particular in terms of the use of online delivery and the adoption of a framework derived from TBLT itself. And finally, we hope that the questions we have raised will be of use to future designers of courses of this nature. Just as Long (2015: 374) acknowledges that 'TBLT is a work in progress', we too are 'building the road as we travel' – towards a future in which practitioners are better placed to implement TBLT, and practitioner-run organisations such as SLB can play an important role.

Further Reading

Freeman, D. and Johnson, K. (1998) Reconceptualizing the knowledge-base of language teacher education. *TESOL Quarterly*, 32(3), 397–417.

Long, M.H. (2016). In defense of tasks and TBLT: Nonissues and real issues. *Annual Review of Applied Linguistics*, 36, 5–33.

Solares-Altamirano, M. E. (2010). Promoting teacher professional development through online task-based instruction. *International Journal of Virtual and Personal Learning Environments (IJVPLE)*, 1(4), 52–65.

Skehan, P. (2003). Task-based instruction. *Language Teaching*, 36(1), pp. 1–14.

Van den Branden, K. (2006). Training teachers: Task-based as well? In K. Van den Branden, ed. *Task-based language education. From theory to practice*. Cambridge: Cambridge University Press, pp. 217–48.

Van den Branden, K. (2016). The role of teachers in task-based language education. *Annual Review of Applied Linguistics*, 36, 164–81.

Study Questions

1. Is there a space for a distance-only, international small private online course on TBLT like this, or would such courses be more beneficial if situated and tailored?
2. What are the benefits and drawbacks of aiming to develop both teachers and course designers on the same course?
3. Does a course like this need to be less partisan (i.e., towards Long's TBLT) and more open to the use of task-supported language teaching, focused tasks, etc.?

References

Clandfield, L. and Hadfield, J. (2017). *Interaction Online: Creative activities for blended learning*. Cambridge: Cambridge University Press.

Ellis, R. (2009). Task-based language teaching: sorting out the misunderstandings. *International Journal of Applied Linguistics* 19(3), 221–46.

Farrell, T. (2018). Operationalizing Reflective Practice in Second Language Teacher Education. *Journal of Second Language Teacher Education*, 1(1) pp. 1–20.

Fox, A. (2013). From MOOCs to SPOCs. *Commun. ACM*, 56(12), 38–40.

FUNDAE (2020). Website of the Fundación Estatal para la Formación en el Empleo (State Foundation for Employment Training). www.fundae.es.

Gilabert, R. (2005). Evaluating the use of multiple sources and methods in needs analysis: A case study of journalists in the Autonomous Community of Catalonia (Spain). In M. Long, ed. *Second language needs analysis*. Cambridge: Cambridge University Press, pp. 182–99.

González-Lloret, M. and Ortega, L. (2014), eds. *Technology-mediated TBLT: Researching technology and tasks*. Amsterdam: John Benjamins.

Jordan, K. (2015). Massive open online course completion rates revisited: Assessment, length and attrition. *International Review of Research in Open and Distributed Learning*, 16(3), 341–58.

Harmer, J. (2015) *The practice of English language teaching*. London: Pearson.

Long, M. H. and Crookes, G. (1992). Three approaches to task-based syllabus design. *TESOL quarterly*, 26(1),27–56.

Long, M. H. (2015). *Second language acquisition and task-based language teaching*. Malden: John Wiley & Sons.

Long, M. H. (2016). In defense of tasks and TBLT: Nonissues and real issues. *Annual Review of Applied Linguistics*, 36, 5–33.

Long, M. H. (2020a). Optimal input for language learning: genuine, simplified, elaborated, or modified elaborated? *Language Teaching*, 53, 169–82.

Long, M. H. (2020b). The L in TBLT: Analyzing target discourse. *The Cambridge handbook for task-based language teaching*. Cambridge: Cambridge University Press.

Mental Health Catalonia (2020). Website. www.salutmental.org.

Nunan, D. (2004). *Task-based language teaching*. Cambridge: Cambridge University Press.

Serafini, E. J., Lake, J. B., and Long, M. H. (2015). Needs analysis for specialized learner populations: Essential methodological improvements. *English for Specific Purposes*, 40, 11–26.

Skehan, P. (2002). A non-marginal role for tasks. *English Language Teaching Journal* 56(3), 289–95.

SLB (2020a). The TBLT Course, March 2019. Retrieved from: https://learn.slb.coop/course/how-to-implement-task-based-language-teaching-tblt/.)

SLB (2020b). Session 1 of the TBLT course. Retrieved from: https://learn.slb.coop/lesson/1-why-tblt/.

SLB(2020c). TBLT Course, November 2019. Retrieved from: https://learn.slb.coop/course/tblt-from-theory-to-practice-nov2019/.

Solares-Altamirano, M. E. (2010). Promoting teacher professional development through online task-based instruction. *International Journal of Virtual and Personal Learning Environments* (IJVPLE), 1(4),52–65.

Ur, P. (2012). *A Course in English Language Teaching*. Cambridge: Cambridge University Press

Van den Branden, K. (2006). Training teachers: Task-based as well?. In K. Van den Branden, ed. *Task-based language education. From theory to practice*. Cambridge: Cambridge University Press, pp. 217–48.

Van den Branden, K. (2016). The role of teachers in task-based language education. *Annual Review of Applied Linguistics*, 36, 164–81.

Wilkins, D. A. (1976). *Notional syllabuses*. Oxford: Oxford University Press.

Willis, D. and Willis, J. (2009). Task-based language teaching. *The Language Teacher*. 33(3), 3–4.

Woodward, T. (2003) Loop Input. *English Language Teaching Journal*, 57(3), 301–4.

Zero Gravity (2020). Website of Sense Gravetat network of community workshops. https://redsingravedad.org/ca/.

Appendix A Pre-course survey

TBLT pre-course survey

We will use your responses to help adapt the course to your needs and to help us plan future courses. By answering the questions you give us the right to use the data for those purposes, as well as to refer to data anonymously in academic articles published about our course, and for no other purpose.

*Required

1. **Email address** *

2. **How did you find out about this course?** *
   Mark only one oval.
   - Twitter
   - Facebook
   - Search engine, e.g. Google
   - Recommendation from a friend/colleague
   - Other:

Your work

3. **How would you describe your current work? Please check all that apply.** *
   Check all that apply.
   - Language teacher
   - Teacher trainer
   - Director of studies
   - Course designer
   - Academic/researcher
   - Pedagogic materials designer
   - Other:

4. **What is the highest qualification related to language teaching that you currently hold?** *
   Mark only one oval.
   - PhD
   - Master's degree
   - BA degree
   - Diploma (DELTA or Trinity Dip TESOL)
   - Recognised Introductory certificate (CELTA or Trinity Cert)
   - Unrecognised introductory certificate ('TEFL')
   - None
   - Other:

Pre-course survey

5. **How many years have you been working in language education?** *
   Mark only one oval.

   - ○ 0-2
   - ○ 3-5
   - ○ 6-10
   - ○ 11-20
   - ○ 20+

Your learners
If you only write materials, please consider which kinds of learners you write for.

6. **If applicable, what category of learners do you usually work with? Please check all that apply.**
   Check all that apply.

   - ☐ Adults
   - ☐ Teenagers / secondary age students
   - ☐ Children / primary age students
   - ☐ Children / pre-primary age students

7. **Could you further categorise your learners?**
   Check all that apply.

   - ☐ English for academic purposes (EAP)
   - ☐ Exam English (e.g. Cambridge, TOEFL, IELTS etc.)
   - ☐ ESOL/ESL (English for life in an English-speaking country)
   - ☐ EFL / "General English"
   - ☐ English for schools (primary/secondary)
   - ☐ ESP (English for Specific Purposes)
   - ☐ Other: _____

8. **If you answered 'ESP' above, please state the specific purpose(s) below**

   _____
   _____
   _____
   _____

You and TBLT

(cont.)

9. **Please tell us something about your experience with TBLT, and/or why you are interested in developing in this area.** *

Tutorial times

10. **Finally, which days and times will be best for you to attend online tutorials? Please refer to times in CET (GMT+1) (https://time.is/CET) and give as many options as you can.**
    Check all that apply.

	Mondays	Tuesdays	Wednesdays	Thursdays	Fridays
9AM-10AM	☐	☐	☐	☐	☐
10AM-11AM	☐	☐	☐	☐	☐
11AM-12PM	☐	☐	☐	☐	☐
12PM-1PM	☐	☐	☐	☐	☐
1PM-2PM	☐	☐	☐	☐	☐
2PM-3PM	☐	☐	☐	☐	☐
3PM-4PM	☐	☐	☐	☐	☐
4PM-5PM	☐	☐	☐	☐	☐
5PM-6PM	☐	☐	☐	☐	☐
6PM-7PM	☐	☐	☐	☐	☐
7PM-8PM	☐	☐	☐	☐	☐
8PM-9PM	☐	☐	☐	☐	☐
9PM-10PM	☐	☐	☐	☐	☐

(cont.)

Appendix B Post-course evaluation

TBLT online course evaluation

An evaluation for SLB's inaugural TBLT training course, March-June 2019. This evaluation should take approximately 10 minutes of your time.

* Required

About you

1. **How would you describe yourself? Tick all that apply.** *
   Check all that apply.
   - [ ] Teacher
   - [ ] Teacher trainer
   - [ ] Director of studies
   - [ ] Course designer
   - [ ] Course manager
   - [ ] Materials writer
   - [ ] Other: _____

2. **Why did you choose our course?** *
   Mark only one oval.
   - ○ I already work with TBLT and wanted to learn more
   - ○ I have some curiosity about TBLT and wanted to develop in this area
   - ○ It was part of required CPD where I work
   - ○ Other: _____

3. **How did you fund the course?** *
   Mark only one oval.
   - ○ From my own funds
   - ○ Using my institution's CPD funds
   - ○ A mix of personal and institutional funds
   - ○ Other: _____

Course content
1= strongly disagree; 2=disagree; 3=neither agree nor disagree; 4= agree; 5= strongly agree

4. **The course content helped me develop professionally.** *
   Mark only one oval.

	1	2	3	4	5	
Strongly disagree	○	○	○	○	○	Strongly agree

Course evaluation

5. **The level of challenge was appropriate to the course objectives.** *
   Mark only one oval.

	1	2	3	4	5	
Strongly disagree	○	○	○	○	○	Strongly agree

6. **The amount of time required was as I expected.** *
   Mark only one oval.

	1	2	3	4	5	
Strongly disagree	○	○	○	○	○	Strongly agree

7. **How many hours, on average, did you spend on each session?** *

   _____

8. **The course presented content in a helpful sequence.** *
   Mark only one oval.

	1	2	3	4	5	
Strongly disagree	○	○	○	○	○	Strongly agree

9. **There was an appropriate balance of theory and practice.** *
   Mark only one oval.

	1	2	3	4	5	
Strongly disagree	○	○	○	○	○	Strongly agree

10. **The suggested reading helped my understanding of key concepts.** *
    Mark only one oval.

	1	2	3	4	5	
Strongly disagree	○	○	○	○	○	Strongly agree

11. **The presentations explained theory and practice clearly.** *
    Mark only one oval.

	1	2	3	4	5	
Strongly disagree	○	○	○	○	○	Strongly agree

12. **The forum and tutorial discussions complemented the main content.** *
    Mark only one oval.

	1	2	3	4	5	
Strongly disagree	○	○	○	○	○	Strongly agree

(cont.)

13. **The Output tasks were explained clearly.** *
    Mark only one oval.

	1	2	3	4	5	
Strongly disagree	○	○	○	○	○	Strongly agree

14. **The Output tasks gave me the opportunity to apply what I learned.** *
    Mark only one oval.

	1	2	3	4	5	
Strongly disagree	○	○	○	○	○	Strongly agree

15. **Please comment on the strengths of the course content.**

16. **Please give suggestions on how course content could be improved.**

Instruction
1= strongly disagree; 2=disagree; 3=neither agree nor disagree; 4= agree; 5= strongly agree

17. **The instructors presented concepts and strategies clearly.** *
    Mark only one oval.

	1	2	3	4	5	
Strongly disagree	○	○	○	○	○	Strongly agree

18. **The instructors presented material in an organised way.** *
    Mark only one oval.

	1	2	3	4	5	
Strongly disagree	○	○	○	○	○	Strongly agree

(cont.)

19. **The instructors provided appropriate guidance when required.** *

    Mark only one oval.

	1	2	3	4	5	
Strongly disagree	○	○	○	○	○	Strongly agree

20. **The instructors responded in a timely fashion to messages and discussion posts.** *

    Mark only one oval.

	1	2	3	4	5	
Strongly disagree	○	○	○	○	○	Strongly agree

21. **The instructors provided constructive feedback on Output tasks.** *

    Mark only one oval.

	1	2	3	4	5	
Strongly disagree	○	○	○	○	○	Strongly agree

22. **The instructors clearly articulated the standards of performance.** *

    Mark only one oval.

	1	2	3	4	5	
Strongly disagree	○	○	○	○	○	Strongly agree

23. **The instructors guided discussion well during tutorials.** *

    Mark only one oval.

	1	2	3	4	5	
Strongly disagree	○	○	○	○	○	Strongly agree

24. **Please comment on the strengths of instruction.**

    ....
    ....
    ....
    ....

25. **Please give suggestions on how instruction could be improved.**

    ....
    ....
    ....
    ....

The platform

(cont.)

1= strongly disagree; 2=disagree; 3=neither agree nor disagree; 4= agree; 5= strongly agree

26. The Learn.SLB platform was easy to use. *

Mark only one oval.

	1	2	3	4	5	
Strongly disagree	○	○	○	○	○	Strongly agree

27. It was easy to find the content I needed. *

Mark only one oval.

	1	2	3	4	5	
Strongly disagree	○	○	○	○	○	Strongly agree

28. Videos and links to reading content worked well. *

Mark only one oval.

	1	2	3	4	5	
Strongly disagree	○	○	○	○	○	Strongly agree

29. It was easy to complete online activities (e.g. categorisation tasks) *

Mark only one oval.

	1	2	3	4	5	
Strongly disagree	○	○	○	○	○	Strongly agree

30. It was easy to contribute to the forum. *

Mark only one oval.

	1	2	3	4	5	
Strongly disagree	○	○	○	○	○	Strongly agree

31. It was easy to send a message to a tutor or other participant. *

Mark only one oval.

	1	2	3	4	5	
Strongly disagree	○	○	○	○	○	Strongly agree

32. The tutorial platform Zoom was easy to use. *

Mark only one oval.

	1	2	3	4	5	
Strongly disagree	○	○	○	○	○	Strongly agree

(cont.)

33. **The tutorial platform Zoom was reliable in terms of connection.** *
    Mark only one oval.

	1	2	3	4	5	
Strongly disagree	○	○	○	○	○	Strongly agree

34. **Sound and video worked well during tutorials.** *
    Mark only one oval.

	1	2	3	4	5	
Strongly disagree	○	○	○	○	○	Strongly agree

35. **Please comment on the strengths of the platform.**

36. **Please give suggestions on how the platform could be improved.**

Summing up

37. **How would you rate the effectiveness of the course overall?** *
    Mark only one oval.

	1	2	3	4	5	
Poor	○	○	○	○	○	Excellent

(cont.)

38. **How would you rate each session from 1 (poor) to 5 (excellent)? Please rate each session that you participated in.**
    Check all that apply.

	1	2	3	4	5
Why TBLT?					
Long's cognitive-interactionist theory					
Which TBLT?					
Long's TBLT in detail					
The needs analysis					
Analysing target discourse					
Mulling it over with Mike Long					
Syllabus design					
Materials					
MPs and PPs					
Focus on form					
Testing and assessment					

39. **Choose a session you rated positively (if any) and tell us why you liked it.**

40. **Choose a session you rated negatively (if any) and tell us how we could improve it.**

41. **How would you rate your own participation in the course?** *
    Mark only one oval.

	1	2	3	4	5	
Poor	○	○	○	○	○	Excellent

42. **What advice would you give to someone taking this course?**

(cont.)

43. **If you are happy to be identified so that we can use your comments in publicity for future courses, please enter your email address below.**

(cont.)

Part VII

Task-Based Assessment and Program Evaluation

13

Task-Based Language Assessment

John M. Norris and Martin East

13.1 What Is, and What Isn't, Task-Based Language Assessment?

Norris (2016: 232) defines task-based language assessment (TBLA) as "the elicitation and evaluation of language use (across all modalities) for expressing and interpreting meaning, within a well-defined communicative context (and audience), for a clear purpose, toward a valued goal or outcome." Put more simply, in a task-based assessment, learners have to use their second language (L2) abilities to get things done. The 'things' that they do are communication tasks that involve a goal or purpose of some kind, and that occur within a specific setting, situation, or context. The kinds of tasks that appear in an assessment depend on what we want to know about the learner's L2 ability. For example, can she write an email, give a presentation, order a coffee, read and respond to a text message, follow instructions in an assembly manual, write an argumentative essay, or do a variety of other things? What distinguishes TBLA from other forms of language assessment is that we are genuinely interested in the extent to which learners can actually do the tasks in the assessment. Task-based performance, then, is evaluated according to what it means to do the task. For some tasks, that might be a simple yes/no distinction based on whether a given outcome was achieved (did the learner get the coffee?), while other tasks call for robust rubrics that set out the criteria by which the quality of performance is determined (was the presentation intelligible, fluently delivered, well organized, and so on?).

Task-based language assessment, then, is a particularly useful type of assessment when we want to know whether, and how well, learners can do things in the L2 – and there are many occasions when that is exactly what we want or need to know (see below; Norris, 2016). In order to make sound interpretations about what learners can do, TBLA places a premium on authenticity of both the nature of language use that is elicited and the situation within which the task is performed (Norris, Brown, Hudson, &

Yoshioka, 1998; Weideman, 2006). Thus, task-based assessments typically simulate or replicate key dimensions of the setting, participants, stakes, evaluative criteria, and other factors that characterize communication tasks as they occur outside of the assessment context. Because of these characteristics, TBLA has come to play an increasingly important role, not only as a key component of task-based approaches to language teaching, but also in the broad domain of language testing. The purpose of this chapter is to sketch out the origins, uses, and consequences of TBLA, and to highlight likely future developments.

So, what is *not* TBLA? Certainly, there are many uses for assessment in relation to language learning, and it is important to emphasize that different uses for assessment may call for quite distinct types of tests or other assessment tools (Bachman & Palmer, 2010; Norris, 2000). Sometimes we want to find out what learners know about the language, for example whether they understand certain grammatical rules or whether they have mastered frequent vocabulary terms. Or we may want to know about particular features of their language ability, such as whether they can distinguish certain phonemes in aural input or whether they can produce intonation patterns effectively in speech. For these kinds of interpretations about discrete knowledge or underlying abilities, other forms of assessment are likely to be more appropriate than TBLA; multiple-choice tests of decontextualized grammar and vocabulary knowledge, minimal pairs discrimination exercises, and sentence read-aloud activities are types of assessment that might better address the phenomena listed above. Additionally, it may be that certain purposes for assessment call for a heightened emphasis on efficiency, for example to make quick decisions about placing learners into appropriate levels of an instructional program. For these kinds of uses, efficient assessment types such as cloze, C-test, vocabulary size, or elicited imitation (to name a few) might better serve the purpose of quickly determining the general proficiency of learners or their fit to a particular level of instruction. Clearly, though, each of the assessment types mentioned here lacks one or more of the characteristics associated with TBLA. That is not to say that such assessments are inappropriate or useless; rather, it is to qualify that the design of an assessment should match the intended uses and interpretations that will ensue. Importantly, where there is a need to know what learners *can do* in the target language, then the assessment types listed above are unlikely to be a good fit, whereas task-based approaches provide a much more justifiable alternative.

13.2 Task-Based Language Performance Assessment: A Brief History

The origins of TBLA can be traced to developments both in educational assessment and in language teaching and testing. During the latter half of the twentieth century (see early interest in, for example, Ryan & Frederiksen [1951]), the theory and methods of educational assessment experienced considerable upheaval as traditions of practice – namely a heavy emphasis on the use of selected-response item types to test learners' knowledge of discrete facts – were challenged in terms of what they were and were not able to tell us about learners' abilities and the outcomes of education (Moss, 1992). These discrete-point, objective testing practices, prized for their efficiency in capturing large amounts of content in a quickly administered (and automatically scorable) format, had come to prominence in the era of large-scale minimal competency and accountability testing. Such tests were generally designed according to norm-referenced testing principles, with the goal of spreading learners into a normal distribution curve and thereby enabling decisions about relative strengths and weaknesses of learners, schools, school districts, and so on (Bond, 1996). However, along with expanding notions of assessment validity that incorporated an explicit focus on test uses, interpretations, and consequences (Messick, 1994; Shepard, 1993), these assessment traditions became the object of extensive critique. Key concerns had to do with: (a) their influence on teaching and learning, and the risk that assessments were narrowing the focus of education to only those phenomena that were amenable to discrete-point testing; and (b) the disconnect between desired outcomes of education, in the form of abilities to actually use knowledge and skills to do meaningful things, and the types of phenomena being tested.

In response, the alternative assessment movement proposed the use of a variety of other testing formats to counter perceived negative consequences and interpretive inadequacies of discrete-point testing (Herman, 1992). New assessment techniques included a host of more individualized or personalized formats (e.g., portfolios, journals, self-assessments), as well as a heightened emphasis on constructed-response and particularly performance-based assessments (Haertel, 1999; Moss, 1992). Performances (e.g., presentations, projects, extended essay writing, debates, and so on) provided the means of realizing the meaningful integration of domain-related knowledge, cognitive skills, and ability to do valued things (Khattri, Reeve, & Kane, 1998). According to Wiggins (1998), a prominent assessment reform advocate of the time, by having learners perform authentic tasks – the tasks that characterized particular domains of endeavor outside of the classroom – assessment would play a transformative, educative function of emphasizing the important connection between knowing and doing. The rise of performance assessment also dovetailed with a shift away from norm-referenced testing and toward criterion-referenced testing, especially for classroom and program assessment purposes (Popham, 1993). Rather than designing a test to rank learners, criterion-referenced testing designs emphasized the careful representation of a body of knowledge, skills, and abilities that learners were being taught, with the goal of determining the extent to which they had mastered the instructional content. This deep connection between teaching, learning, and assessment became a hallmark of the new era of educational assessment (Wiggins, 1998).

Parallel to these developments in educational assessment, evolving notions of effective language pedagogy and language testing practices also set the stage for TBLA. In language pedagogy, the rise of communicative language teaching marked a critical shift in our understandings of the goals of language learning, with a newfound commitment to developing learners' abilities to use the language rather than mere knowledge about the language. During this time, the emergence of influential national and international language proficiency scales and standards also pointed clearly to the development of communicative abilities as the core purpose of language learning (e.g., American Council on the Teaching of Foreign Languages, 1999; Centre for Canadian Language Benchmarks, 2000; Council of Europe, 2001). Importantly, all of these scales and frameworks portrayed language proficiency levels by way of *can-do* statements – what learners should be able to do with their language knowledge and skills – and in particular they emphasized the kinds of tasks learners at different proficiency levels would be able to accomplish. Task-based language teaching (TBLT), then, provided one systematic and evidence-based approach to planning and implementing language teaching with a focus on developing learners' abilities to do meaningful communication tasks in the target language (Long & Norris, 2000). By organizing curriculum, instruction – and assessment (see next section) – around communication tasks, the inextricable inter-relationship of language form, function, meaning, and context was foregrounded rather than left as an afterthought, and the experiential or "hands-on" orientation of task-based learning underscored the critical application of classroom learning to real-world use (see Norris, 2009; Long, 2015; Sasayama, this volume).

In language testing, similarly to educational assessment, the alternative assessment movement and expanding understandings of validity[1] opened the doors for discussions of diverse assessment formats in response to various intended uses, interpretations, and consequences (e.g., Lynch, 2001). Although performance assessments of particular kinds had been in evidence in language testing for some time (e.g., the Foreign Service Interview), a renewed interest in performance-based language testing evolved in hand with the re-orientation of language pedagogy and proficiency frameworks toward communicative language ability (Shohamy,

---

[1] In brief, validity of assessments was expanded to include a primary focus on how assessments were used and the kinds of interpretations that were to be made about examinees' knowledge and abilities, as well as the consequences that these uses and interpretations had on various assessment stakeholders. This more comprehensive view of validity led to increasing questions about the roles played by different item types (e.g., multiple-choice) and test formats, in particular as they were used within – and had an impact on – teaching and learning contexts (see review in Norris, 2008).

1995). The potential advantages of performance assessment were clear – they focused on what learners were (hopefully) learning to do in the language, and they aligned closely with the intended learning outcomes of communicative language teaching (Norris et al., 1998). Performance assessment also provided an additional benefit for language learning in the form of a rich data base of actual learner language production (e.g., recorded speech and writing), which opened a window for teachers and learners to use assessment formatively as a space for observing language use, raising awareness, and offering corrective feedback. Language performance assessment was not without its challenges, of course (McNamara, 1997). Namely, the complexity of assessment was heightened considerably, with a requirement to pay careful attention to the following components:

- Performance had to be elicited on the basis of a prompt, input, task, or other device, and the design of the elicitation approach turned out to have a substantial effect on the nature of language performance.
- The performance assessment had to be administered somehow, ideally in a systematic or standardized way to encourage fairness, but always demanding of time and resources as individuals or groups of learners engaged in the assessment.
- The resulting performance had to be scored, judged, or otherwise evaluated, typically necessitating a scale or rubric of some kind, often with an eye toward provision of formative feedback, and clearly open to the subjectivity of the rater or raters who were doing the scoring.

A focus on TBLA as one specific option in language performance assessment occurred in tandem with the rise of TBLT as a pedagogic approach (Brindley, 1994). It made consummate sense that a curriculum which targeted ability to accomplish certain kinds of needed communication tasks would feature a criterion-referenced task-based assessment as the key *summative* measure of learning outcomes (Long & Crookes, 1993). Where learners needed to develop the language abilities to benefit from industrial vocational training, for example, an assessment should put the learners through their paces on precisely those tasks typical of the vocational training environment (e.g., Van den Branden, DePauw, & Gysen, 2002). At the same time, the introduction of regular *formative* task-based assessments into a classroom context provided a meaningful space for learners and teachers to orient toward a common learning goal, establish clear performance targets, and focus feedback on high-priority dimensions of language performance (e.g., Byrnes, 2002).

While the beneficial use of TBLA in classroom and program contexts seemed apparent – where specific target tasks could be identified based on needs analyses and program learning outcomes – language testers expressed more concern when it came to implementing task-based approaches for large-scale standardized assessment purposes (e.g., Bachman, 2002). A key challenge here had to do with the extent to which performance on one task might be generalized to performance on other tasks (Linn & Burton, 1994), and whether tasks might be predictably categorized according to their inherent complexity or difficulty (Mislevy, Steinberg, & Almond, 2002; Norris, Brown, Hudson, & Bonk, 2002; Skehan, 1998). Another concern was whether performances on specific communication tasks could be rated reliably, and what types of rubrics, scales, and rater training might be required to ensure some degree of objectivity in the process (Bindley, 1994; Brown, Hudson, Norris & Bonk, 2002).

What became relatively clear, after an ensuing period of research, as well as debate, was that different types of TBLA were likely to be necessary in response to the specific intended uses, interpretations, and consequences of a given language assessment (Norris, 2002, 2016). Here, the notion of stronger versus weaker versions of language performance assessment (McNamara, 1996) played a useful role. Thus, a strong form of performance assessment would call for (a) a focus on specific target tasks that learners needed to be able to do, (b) simulating or replicating how those tasks were done in actual language use contexts, and (c) rating task performances according to highly task-specific criteria like those used in non-assessment settings. By contrast, weaker versions of performance assessment might emphasize tasks as devices or templates for eliciting language performances that could be rated according to broad qualities of language knowledge and ability (e.g., quality of delivery, grammatical accuracy), thereby enabling broader generalizations, alignment to generic language proficiency descriptors/scales, and standardized scoring (although diminishing the extent to which task-specific abilities might be assessed). As time has passed, it seems evident that many of the benefits of TBLA can accrue under this graduated approach to implementing weaker or stronger versions of communication tasks in language performance assessments, depending on the needs of test users (see Lockwood, 2015).

13.3 Putting Task-Based Language Assessment to Use

Emerging from these roots, TBLA has come to play an increasingly prominent role in response to a variety of assessment needs. The earliest and most persistent application of TBLA approaches has been in the context of language-learning classrooms and educational programs, where task-based assessments have been developed for both formative and summative purposes, as well as to align testing with a communicative focus of teaching and learning (Ellis, 2003; East, 2012; Norris, 2009; Norris et al., 1998; Skehan, 1998). Robinson and Ross (1996) offered an interesting early example of a task-based assessment used in the context of an intensive academic English training program at a US university. The target task for this assessment required students to utilize library research resources to first identify an academic journal article about a particular topic and then to locate the journal in the library and access the specific needed article. Interestingly, the assessment was administered at the full-class level, with the teacher serving as assessment monitor at a central location in the library, while the students worked individually through the procedures of the target task. Scoring was done by the teacher and based on whether students were able to complete each step successfully by bringing back evidence (e.g., the name and location of the journal, a copy of an article relevant to the topic). This assessment directly measured whether students were able to do one kind of task – and the specific steps in the task – that they would need to be able to do on their own in the context of university course work.

Typically, development of this kind of classroom-based TBLA has occurred hand-in-hand with language-educational reform efforts, either of the organic (program-internal) variety or inspired by shifts in educational policies. One comprehensive example of a policy-related TBLA initiative is the *Integrated Performance Assessment* approach which was introduced into US foreign language education contexts as a way of bringing assessment into closer alignment with the national Standards for Foreign Language Learning (see Adair-Hauck, Glisan, Koda, Swender & Sandrock, 2006). In this approach, learners work progressively through three phases of task-based performance: first individually, then interactively (with a partner), and finally in a more formalized presentational step. At each point, extensive task guidelines are provided to establish key dimensions of task purpose, audience, and situational authenticity; reflective and rating rubrics are provided, to encourage awareness-raising about linguistic and sociocultural dimensions of expected performance; guidance is given on how to assess one's own and others' performances, as a means for generating formative feedback; and clear criteria for scoring the final presentational task are provided as a means of scaffolding performance toward accomplishment. Figure 13.1 shows an example of the kind of initial prompt used to introduce students to the authentic tasks they will be doing in the assessment.

The explicit purpose of this approach to using tasks for assessment was to encourage "backwards design," that is, to ensure that instruction was oriented toward a concrete communicative goal; as well, it provided clear guidance on how task-based performances could be used formatively to promote learning (Adair-Hauck, Glisan & Troyan, 2014). Figure 13.2 shows a small portion of the rubric used by both teachers and learners to assess and provide feedback on learner performances during the "interpersonal" task described above in step two of the overall series of tasks. The full rubric elicits ratings on the same scale for the categories of language functions, text type, clarification strategies, comprehensibility, and

> You have been given the opportunity of a lifetime to apply for an athletic training camp in [foreign country], tuition free! This camp trains young people in all sports, from the extreme (snowboarding, bicycle motor cross, rollerblading) to team sports of all kinds (basketball to volleyball). You name it, they help you train for it! To be accepted into the camp, all applicants have to convince the admissions office that they have good exercise and nutrition habits. First, you will read about health and nutrition from the perspective of the [language]-speaking world. Then you will discuss your eating and exercise regimen with your partner to compare your nutrition and exercise, perhaps even to get some ideas. You will then write your application letter to the summer camp describing your nutrition and training regimen, convincing them that you are well prepared for the camp and need to be accepted.

Figure 13.1 Example prompt for an Integrated Performance Assessment (adapted from Adair-Hauck et al., 2006: 367)

Category	Exceeds expectations	Meets expectations Strong	Meets expectations Weak	Does not meet expectations
Communication Strategies Quality of engagement and interactivity; amount of negotiation of meaning; how one participates in the conversation and advances it.	Initiates and maintains conversation using a variety of strategies.	Maintains conversation by asking and answering questions.	Maintains simple conversation: asks and answers some basic questions (but still may be reactive).	Responds to basic direct questions. Asks a few formulaic questions (primarily reactive).

Figure 13.2 Portion of a rating rubric from an Integrated Performance Assessment (adapted from Adair-Hauck et al., 2006: 382).

language control, all features deemed important in performing the target interactive task.

In contrast to this broad effort at TBLA reform, Byrnes, Maxim, and Norris (2010) describe an integral role for TBLA in the bottom-up reform of a university German language program. Here, assessment tasks served numerous purposes: (a) as a means for clearly stating the learning outcomes valued by the program; (b) as a key summative assessment component that emphasized ability to use the target language in sophisticated ways; (c) as a mechanism for enabling teachers to establish multiyear and instructional-level-specific expectations for language development; and (d) as a systematic basis for eliciting learner performance and providing focused feedback. Of particular interest in this project were the robust

> **Task-based writing assessment template**
> [Curricular level, Theme, Topic]
>
> **Task: [Title]**
> [Description of the target task, purpose, audience, and typical elements]
> **Content:**
> [Description of the relevant content to be addressed in the piece of writing]
> **Language focus:**
> [Description of the developmentally expected levels of language ability emphasized in the target task]
>   Discourse level: [Overall expectations for organization and function of writing]
>   Sentence level: [Expected syntactic patterns and structures]
>   Lexicogrammatical level: [Expected vocabulary and grammar]
> **Writing process:**
> [Description of the iterative process of producing drafts and revisions of the writing task]
> **Assessment criteria:**
> [Description of how the writing task will be evaluated, including weighting of the components described above, as well as first draft and revisions]

Figure 13.3 Task-based assessment template from the Georgetown University German Department (Adapted from Byrnes, Maxim & Norris, 2010).

task-elicitation templates, used systematically across classes and program levels to situate learners and teachers to the linguistic, content/context, and performative emphases of tasks. Figure 13.3 shows an example of a task-elicitation template for target writing tasks.

The above examples highlight the close alignment between curriculum and learning, and both formative and summative assessment that is a key contribution of TBLA, especially where developing learners' abilities to do things in the target language is the goal. Other interesting examples highlight specific purposes of TBLA in relation to language classes and programs, including:

- outcomes assessment for university foreign-language programs in the European context (e.g., Fischer, Chouissa, Dugovičová, & Virkkunen-Fullenwider, 2011)
- highly focused formative assessment that raises awareness and provides meaningful linguistic and performative feedback to learners (e.g., in the Dutch second language context, Berben et al., 2008; Colpin & Gysen, 2006; in the Japanese English teaching context, Weaver, 2013)
- carefully designed tasks to enable and assess scaffolded interaction by young language learners (e.g., Butler & Zeng, 2014; Wolf, Lopez, Oh & Tsutagawa, 2017)
- the use of TBLA for diagnosing L2 literacy levels/needs and monitoring ongoing literacy development (e.g., in the South African higher education context, Weideman, 2006; in Finnish primary education, Alanen, Huhta & Tarnanen, 2010).

These and other examples point to a growing realization of the need to align testing practices with instructional practices and desired learning outcomes, despite the likely complexities involved (Van Gorp & Deygers, 2014).

Beyond task-based classes and programs, the most obvious application of a strong form of TBLA may be the use of specific, context-embedded tasks for assessing the L2 competency of candidates for various professions where communication is essential. From law enforcement to aviation to the medical professions, a high priority is given to determining what exactly candidates can do in on-the-job, real-life situations, and to certifying that they meet threshold expectations. For one example, the Canadian English Language Benchmark Assessment for Nurses (CELBAN) tests the extent to which international candidates for nursing certification can meet threshold levels of performance on daily tasks that are typically faced by members of this profession (Lewis & Kingdon, 2016). Candidates read doctors' notes, listen to descriptions of symptoms, take patient histories, and fill out medical charts (among many other tasks), and their performances are evaluated according to criteria that stipulate accomplishment of each task. Here, a TBLA approach uniquely enables the determination of examinees' abilities to do important, job-specific tasks in context, and for this reason TBLA has been advocated for use in a variety of other professional certification assessments (e.g., Alderson, 2009; Elder et al., 2012; Lockwood, 2015; Gysen & Van Avermaet, 2005).

Another important use of TBLA is in large-scale standardized testing of academic language proficiency for making university-admission decisions about international students. Here, the focus of assessment is not on determining examinees' abilities to accomplish specific job-related tasks; rather it is whether students have sufficient degrees of language proficiency to engage successfully with the types of tasks that typify university academic settings. For example, prominent English-language assessments like the Test of English as a Foreign Language™ Internet-Based Test (TOEFL iBT®) and the International English Language Testing System™ (IELTS) present examinees with prototypical task types that have been carefully selected to represent the common language use demands of university-level academic discourse. Examinees must read extended texts, listen to lectures, write essays, and speak on academic topics, thereby demonstrating their linguistic readiness to undertake these kinds of tasks in the real-world university setting. An innovative development for the TOEFL iBT® was the inclusion of multiple integrated task types, that is, tasks that require students to listen to and/or read authentic academic texts followed by writing or speaking about the content – these kinds of integrated task types have clear correlates in high-priority language use situations students commonly encounter in university classes (Chapelle, Jamieson & Enright, 2008). The assessment of performance on this variety of academic tasks across the four skills provides a robust basis for determining whether student applicants can effectively deal with the challenging uses of language they will encounter at university. For this reason, TBLA has been adopted for high-stakes admission assessments in a variety of other languages and contexts (see Eckes & Althaus, 2020; Norris, 2016).

Incorporating tasks into job-qualification or university-admission assessments makes a lot of sense, especially given the critical importance of being able to actually communicate successfully in specific ways in these life-shaping contexts. Beyond ensuring the likelihood that candidates have the language proficiency they will need in order to succeed, robust task-based assessments play another important function – they exert influence on how learners develop their language abilities in preparation for job or academic demands. This consequential aspect of deploying TBLA should not be overlooked as a key contribution toward improving language teaching and learning with the goal of effective communication in mind (Norris, 2018). Indeed, this close connection between task-based assessment and language teaching and learning inspired early attention to TBLA in the first place. We turn next to this integral relationship.

13.4 The Consequences of Task-Based Language Assessment

It should be clear by now that committing to TBLT has substantial implications, not only for language-teaching practices but also for language assessment. An ideal scenario is that, in contexts where TBLT is being encouraged or introduced, assessments of language learners' proficiency will reflect this pedagogical approach, creating a beneficial interface between the teaching and the assessment, or, put another way, a "constructive alignment of learning and outcomes" (Hattie, 2009: 259). Several of the examples introduced above demonstrate precisely this kind of close alignment.

At face value, constructive alignment between teaching and assessment through the use of tasks would lead to positive outcomes for learners. Nevertheless, using tasks for assessment purposes is not necessarily a straightforward process of introducing new types of tests and accruing the benefits (see, e.g., Carless, 2007). If TBLA is to be advocated or utilized as part and parcel of an overhaul of teaching programs, it is important to consider the range of outcomes or consequences for stakeholders of that overhaul.

13.4.1 Washback Effects in Language Testing
Fundamental to considering the consequences of introducing TBLA is the reality that tests and assessments have "washback." Washback refers to

the ways in which a particular assessment influences what goes on in classrooms as teachers prepare students for the assessment (see, e.g., Messick, 1996), and washback can be either positive or negative. A quick example of positive washback from TBLA can be traced to the introduction of new task types in the TOEFL iBT®, including, in particular, academic speaking tasks, as well as integrated read, listen, speak, and write tasks. Substantial longitudinal investigations by Wall and Horák (2006) demonstrated that these changes in the test led to a clear shift in instructional emphasis in test preparation classes in Europe, most specifically through a greater focus on teaching of language skills and strategies for productive task types and, in particular, speaking.

With regard to positive washback, if we look at what TBLA aims to achieve against the backdrop of a classic model of test usefulness proposed by Bachman and Palmer (1996), it is clear that meaningful language communication, or *authenticity*, is a key argument for (and intended positive washback effect of) including tasks as components of assessment. Bachman and Palmer argued that authenticity is a critical component of language tests because it enables scores on the test task to be generalized to the broader real-world domains that the test task aims to reflect. That is, authenticity describes the relationship of a test or assessment to what Bachman and Palmer referred to as "target language use" domains – the actual real-world contexts in which language users will need to use the language they have learned. As we argued above, there ideally needs to be a clear interface and reciprocal relationship between the tasks that students do in the language-learning classroom, the tasks we use for assessment purposes, and the tasks language users will carry out in the real world beyond the classroom. Put another way, tasks can aim to replicate *situational* authenticity.

Thus, one positive consequence of introducing TBLA is that, via its washback effect, it will raise awareness about, and enable a focus on, authentic (real-world) language use in classrooms. This is, however, not simply a matter of designing assessment tasks that aim to replicate target language use domains (such as ordering items in a café or checking into a hotel), although there are clear benefits to doing so when feasible. In many cases, though, real-world scenarios cannot be fully replicated in the test situation. That is, unless, for example, we actually take students to a café in the target language context, set them up with a task they need to fulfill in interaction with the waiting staff, and observe how they go, the testing of how someone deals with an interaction in this target language use domain will only ever be, at best, a simulation, as with a flight simulator. Of course, that is nearly always the case with any assessment, TBLA or otherwise, the assessment situation inherently affecting the nature of language use.

In addition to the importance of simulating or replicating real-life scenarios – which help establish critical linkages between language use and the realities of the contexts in which it happens – it can also be important to promote what Bachman and Palmer (1996) referred to as *interactional authenticity*, or what Nunan (2004) called an 'activational' rationale for a task. An interactionally authentic task is real-world, but in the sense that learners are required to draw on the kinds of skills that they might use in any real-life interactional situation outside of the task, such as co-operating, collaborating, expressing own points of view, or negotiating meaning (East, 2012). Here, too, tasks have a crucial role to play for assessment purposes.

The argument of authenticity is a valid (and positive) consequence of TBLA. However, the reality for many students is that they will face (and will therefore need to be prepared to face), tests and examinations that may not replicate or utilize communicative tasks. When summative assessments include activities that may be very different from the tasks that teachers might use in the task-based classroom, the alignment between teaching and assessment becomes more complex. Particularly when assessments are being used to make high-stakes decisions, students will inevitably want to do as well as they can on them. There is potential here for negative washback. Carless (2007) highlighted this kind of negative washback in the context of English education in Hong Kong, where TBLT-oriented reform efforts were not particularly successful at changing teaching and learning behaviors, due largely to the washback of high-stakes examinations that did not feature authentic language use tasks (i.e., leading learners to focus on learning for the exam rather than for communication). Another interesting example of negative washback was raised by Alderson (2010), who observed that the use of academic English proficiency assessments was inappropriate for testing in situations that required highly specific task-based abilities, like air traffic control communications. Alderson (2010: 63) pointed out that "[t]he consequences of inadequate language tests being made available to license pilots, air traffic controllers and other aviation personnel are almost too frightening to contemplate."

Essentially, then, assessments have washback, and, in the context of wishing to align TBLT with TBLA, this washback may be beneficial or detrimental. It is important to consider the potential consequences for stakeholders of introducing TBLA, both positive and negative.

13.4.2 Consequences for Stakeholders

For teachers, the most likely beneficial consequence of introducing TBLA is that it will encourage them to embrace a task-based approach, or at least to question the alignment of their own pedagogy with the things being emphasized in assessment. That is, if it is clear, and is made clear, that assessments aligned to a particular teaching program require language users to engage in some kinds of tasks, teachers will be more likely to facilitate opportunities for students to engage in tasks in the classroom because they will perceive this as vital preparation for forthcoming assessments. Thus, TBLA may become a positive motivator of task use in classrooms, among both the enthusiastic and the more reticent. By this argument, if we wish to promote TBLT as a beneficial pedagogical approach, we require language assessments that will influence teachers to embrace task use, and we should aim to introduce such assessments along with procedures for engaging teachers in their use (see an interesting example of this type of washback in Byrnes [2002]).

For learners, the most likely beneficial consequence of introducing TBLA is that assessments will promote greater opportunities for students to engage in tasks in the classroom, and thereby to enhance (and have opportunities to demonstrate) their communicative proficiency. Learners will also be able to perceive a clear relationship between what they do in the classroom and how they will be assessed, and potentially how they can use language effectively outside of the classroom. Coming back to the authenticity argument, Bachman and Palmer (1996) maintained that authenticity is an important consideration for the learners who will take the assessments because it contributes to the perceived relevance of the assessment to them. When assessments are seen as relevant by learners, this helps to encourage positive engagement with the assessment task, thereby helping those taking the assessment to perform at their best and demonstrate what they can do with language. By this argument, learners' interaction with the assessment task may conversely be affected negatively if they perceive that the assessment lacks authenticity or is not aligned with what goes on in their classrooms (or is not relevant to what they hope to do with language outside of the classroom), because they will fail to see its relevance to language use.

There are, however, situations where attempts to introduce TBLA may lead to negative consequences for stakeholders. As East (2012) reminded us, there are occasions when teachers are subject to the assessment requirements that are imposed on them by schools and high-stakes assessment regimes, and these requirements can sometimes conflict with TBLA. In these circumstances, the perceived relevance of TBLA may be compromised in the eyes of the learners, and teachers may find themselves having to adopt teaching practices that run counter to TBLT in order to meet more appropriately the demands and expectations of the tests which the students might subsequently take. We are left, then, with something of a two-edged sword for TBLA.

13.5 The Future of Task-Based Language Assessment

The idea of TBLA is deceptively simple – have learners perform communication tasks and evaluate how well they are able to do so. However, after several decades of experimenting with this approach to language assessment, we have developed a much more nuanced understanding of the complexities of TBLA, including its attendant challenges, as well as ways of reaping its benefits. Here, we point to a few key directions that will likely characterize the future of TBLA.

First, it seems evident that language classes and programs will continue to benefit from the practice of TBLA, especially where there is a genuine interest in developing learners' abilities to use the target language for communicative purposes. However, experience and evidence suggest that teachers and learners will both require support in understanding how to engage with task-based testing techniques, including the design of tasks and the expectations for engagement in them, the use of rating rubrics and criteria, and the provision of feedback. TBLA is about a lot more than simply having learners do tasks, if the goal is to inform teaching and learning. In this regard, the robust teacher and learner support (including materials, rubrics, procedures, coaching, etc.) described for Dutch second language education for young learners in Flanders is suggestive of the possibilities for encouraging effective implementation of TBLA at the classroom level (e.g., Berben et al., 2008; Van den Branden, 2006; Van Gorp & Deygers, 2014).

Second, TBLA has an important role to play in educational reform more broadly. As we explained above, over several decades educational thinking has moved us away from a static testing and examination culture toward a broader and more dynamic approach to educational assessment. That is, the once normative model of summative static tests and examinations has given way to a consideration of alternative forms of assessment in response to a variety of uses, and most recently in support of so-called learning-oriented assessment. This broader landscape, East (2016: 31) argued, "would include, in addition to standardized tests, a range of assessment instruments (such as classroom assessments, practical and oral assessments, coursework and portfolios) and a variety of approaches (norm-referenced, criterion-referenced, formative and performance-based)." Task-based language assessment is both a progenitor and a realization of this broader reforming process in assessment. Key here for the potential of TBLA and other assessment reforms to be realized is the need to help stakeholders of all kinds to understand the nuanced relationship between the kinds of consequences that are being sought from an assessment and the kinds of assessment designs that are implied. Not all assessments are created equally, and not all assessment uses will be realized by one monolithic "best" type of assessment. Even within TBLA, different versions (stronger, weaker; high-context, high-generalizability; can-do, help-to-do; etc.) of task-based tests will be called for to meet distinct uses. Certification of ability to do critical job-specific tasks should imply a very different design from a task-based assessment that is intended to promote learning (Norris, 2018), although both will benefit from the fundamental incorporation of authentic communication tasks.

Not to be missed, too, is the reality that introducing a task-based approach to assessment inevitably underscores the fundamental reality that language use is a social and context-embedded endeavor, just as it is a personal cognitive activity (McNamara & Roever, 2006). Communication is always about purposeful interaction, in one way or another, yet many forms of language assessment under-represent this dimension of language learning and use. With tasks, then, we are able to elicit and observe the extent to which learners understand and respond effectively to the communication environment, the interlocutor(s), the impact of their own communication efforts, and so on. There is no doubt that TBLA will be further exploited to take fuller advantage of the holistic and context-rich potential of tasks, emphasizing, for example, the important role played by pragmatic knowledge and abilities in navigating many kinds of interactive tasks (e.g., Timpe-Laughlin, 2018).

Third, the ongoing march of technology will continue to affect language assessment, and TBLA may work well in concert with key aspects of these developments. Technology already enables the simulation of a variety of communicative task types, through provision of rich context and visual/audio affordances and realia of various kinds, thereby bringing the "real-world" into the classroom or testing environment. Most recently, the substantial advances in automated interactive technologies may also hold the promise of machine-generated conversation as a basis for assessment, and certainly internet capabilities now allow for the connection of learners, interlocutors, and assessors of various kinds in various places around the world, all contributing to the increased feasibility of simulating, replicating, or simply doing real-world, context-embedded, authentic tasks in an assessment situation (Norris, Davis, & Timpe-Laughlin, 2017; Timpe-Laughlin, 2018). Technology may also be exploited to extend the types of assessment tasks to longer, sustained, coherent task-based experiences of the sort that have been advocated under the notion of scenario-based assessments (Purpura & Turner, 2014). The advantage here is to enable learner engagement over longer periods of time, within authentic and motivating environments, such that performance and learning can be observed longitudinally, scaffolded as needed, repeated, and evaluated for more than a mere one-time, all-or-nothing, test-taking effort (see examples in Wolf, Lopez, Oh, & Tsutagawa [2017]).

In the end, then, we will echo the assertion by Van den Branden, Bygate, and Norris (2009: 11) that tasks present "a uniquely powerful resource both for the teaching *and* testing of language" (our emphasis). In order to realize the potential benefits of task-based approaches to language assessment in interaction with language education, it will be important to continue learning from experiences and iterating exactly what we are trying to accomplish through tasks. Fundamentally, it will also help to keep in mind that we are still talking about an assessment, and there are core values and principles – never mind assumptions and impacts – that come along with any assessment. As Wajda (2011: 278) argued, "[t]he basic pragmatic and ethical premises of this orientation are accountability and fairness understood as objectivity and equal treatment of test-takers." Bachman and Dambӧck (2018) also spoke of accountability and fairness as two important requisites of valid assessment, noting that fairness is crucial if we want stakeholders to have trust in how assessments are being used. In this regard, if TBLT promotes meaningful and authentic language use, and if we view proficiency in using meaningful and authentic language as important goals for language-learning programs, it is only fair that students should be assessed on their ability to use language meaningfully and authentically.

Those of us who advocate TBLA as a viable and necessary adjunct to TBLT, never mind an essential type of assessment for meeting certain high-stakes uses, need to confront issues of fairness and accountability in ways that are convincing to those with a stake in language assessment, particularly in high-stakes contexts. This is not just among teachers and students as the primary stakeholders, but also among language testers and those who need to make decisions on the basis of assessment outcomes. Hamp-Lyons (2000: 32) asserted that "there is no one standpoint from which a test can be viewed as 'fair' or 'not fair.'" Seen from this perspective, there is plenty of scope for TBLA advocates to take up the challenge, and the potentially beneficial consequences of TBLA make its exploration a worthwhile endeavor.

Further Reading

East, M. (2015). Coming to terms with innovative high-stakes assessment practice: Teachers' viewpoints on assessment reform. *Language Testing*, 31(1), 101–20.

Norris, J. (2009). Task-based teaching and testing. In M. Long and C. Doughty, eds. *The handbook of language teaching*. Oxford: Wiley-Blackwell, pp. 578–94.

Norris, J. M. (2018). Task-based language assessment: Aligning designs with intended uses and consequences. *JLTA Journal*, 21, 3–20.

Van Gorp, K. and Deygers, B. (2014). Task-based language assessment. In A. Kunnan, ed. *The companion to language assessment*. Cambridge: Wiley-Blackwell, pp. 578–93.

Wiggins, G. (1998). *Educative assessment: Designing assessments to inform and improve student performance*. San Francisco: Jossey Bass.

Study Questions

1. How can "real-world" communication tasks be simulated or replicated within an assessment – what are the key aspects of the task that require representation?
2. What are the most important (and different) intended uses for TBLAs? What kinds of interpretations about language learners can/should be made on the basis of task-based assessments?
3. What do you see as the most important consequential advantages of using tasks for assessment purposes?
4. What do you see as the most urgent challenges associated with using tasks for assessment purposes, and how do you think they might be solved?
5. In what ways can teachers and learners best be supported to understand and make effective use of task-based assessments in language classrooms and programs?

References

ACTFL. (1999). *American Council on the Teaching of Foreign Languages Proficiency Guidelines*. Alexandria, VA: ACTFL.

Adair-Hauck, B., Glisan, E., Koda, K., Swender, E., and Sandrock, P. (2006). The Integrated Performance Assessment (IPA): Connecting assessment to instruction and learning. *Foreign Language Annals*, 39, 359–82.

Adair-Hauck, B., Glisan, E., and Troyan, F. (2014). *Implementing Integrated Performance Assessment*. Alexandria, VA: ACTFL.

Alanen, R., Huhta, A., and Tarnanen, M. (2010). Designing and assessing L2 writing tasks across CEFR proficiency levels. In I. Bartning, M. Martin, and I. Vedder eds. *Communicative proficiency and linguistic development: Intersections between language testing and SLA research*. EUROSLA Monograph, pp. 21–56.

Alderson, J. C. (2009). Air safety, language assessment policy, and policy implementation: The case of aviation English. *Annual Review of Applied Linguistics*, 29, 168–87.

Alderson, J. C. (2010). A survey of aviation English tests. *Language Testing*, 27, 51–72.

Bachman, L. F. (2002). Some reflections on task-based language performance assessment. *Language Testing*, 19(4), 453–76.

Bachman, L. F. and Damböck, B. (2018). *Language assessment for classroom teachers*. Oxford: Oxford University Press.

Bachman, L. F. and Palmer, A. (1996). *Language testing in practice: Designing and developing useful language tests*. Oxford: Oxford University Press.

Bachman, L. F. and Palmer, A. (2010). *Language assessment in practice: Developing language assessments and justifying their use in the real world*. Oxford: Oxford University Press.

Berben, M., Callebaut, I., Colpin, M., François, S., Geerts, M., Goethals, M., and Vanoosthuyze, S. (2008), eds. *TotemTaal: Inleiding en evaluatie 5*. Mechelen, Belgium: Wolters Plantyn.

Bond, L. A. (1996). Norm-and criterion-referenced testing. *Practical Assessment, Research & Evaluation*, 5(2), 120–25.

Brindley, G. (1994). *Task-centered assessment in language learning: The promise and the challenge*. ERIC Document # ED 386 045.

Brown, J. D., Hudson, T. D., Norris, J. M., and Bonk, W. (2002). *Investigating task-based second language performance assessment*. Honolulu, HI: University of Hawai'i Press.

Butler, Y. G. and Zeng, W. (2014). Young foreign language learners' interactions during task-based paired assessments. *Language Assessment Quarterly*, 11(1), 45–75.

Byrnes, H. (2002). The role of task and task-based assessment in a content-oriented collegiate foreign language curriculum. *Language Testing*, 19(4), 419–37.

Byrnes, H., Maxim, H., and Norris, J. M. (2010). *Realizing advanced FL writing development in collegiate education: Curricular design, pedagogy, assessment*. Cambridge: Wiley-Blackwell.

Carless, D. (2007). The suitability of task-based approaches for secondary schools: Perspectives from Hong Kong. *System*, 35(4), 595–608.

Centre for Canadian Language Benchmarks. (2000). *CLB 2000: Theoretical framework*. Ottawa: Centre for Canadian Language Benchmarks

Chapelle, C. A., Enright, M. K., and Jamieson, J. M. (2008), eds. *Building a validity argument for the Test of English as a Foreign Language*. New York: Routledge.

Colpin, M. and Gysen, S. (2006). Developing and introducing task-based language tests. In K. Van den Branden, ed., *Task-based language education: From theory to practice*. Cambridge: Cambridge University Press, pp. 151–74.

Council of Europe (2001). *Common European Framework of Reference for languages: Learning, teaching, assessment*. Cambridge: Cambridge University Press.

East, M. (2012). *Task-based language teaching from the teachers' perspective: Insights from New Zealand*. Amsterdam: John Benjamins.

East, M. (2016). *Assessing foreign language students' spoken proficiency: Stakeholder perspectives on assessment innovation*. Singapore: Springer.

Eckes, T. and Althaus, H. J. (2020). Language proficiency assessments in college admissions. In M. E. Oliveri and C. Wendler, eds. *Higher education admission and placement practices: An international perspective*. Cambridge: University of Cambridge, pp. 256–75

Elder, C., Pill, J., Woodward-Kron, R., McNamara, T., Manias, E., Webb, G., and McColl, G. (2012). Health professionals' views of communication: Implications for assessing performance on a health specific English language test. *TESOL Quarterly*, 46(2), 409–19.

Ellis, R. (2003). *Task-based language learning and teaching.* Oxford: Oxford University Press.

Fischer, J., Chouissa, C., Dugovičová, S., and Virkkunen-Fullenwider, A. (2011). *Guidelines for task-based university language testing.* Graz: European Centre for Modern Languages.

Gysen, S. and Van Avermaet, P. (2005). Issues in functional language performance assessment:The case of the Certificate Dutch as a Foreign Language. *Language Assessment Quarterly*, 2(1), 51–68.

Haertel, E. H. (1999). Performance assessment and education reform. *Phi Delta Kappan*, 80 (9), 662.

Hamp-Lyons, L. (2000). Fairnesses in language testing. In A. J. Kunnan, ed. *Fairness and validation in language assessment.* Cambridge: Cambridge University Press, pp. 30–34.

Hattie, J. (2009). The black box of tertiary assessment: An impending revolution. In L. H. Meyer, S. Davidson, H. Anderson, R. Fletcher, P. M. Johnston, and M. Rees, eds. *Tertiary assessment and higher education student outcomes: Policy, practice and research.* Wellington, NZ: Ako Aotearoa, pp. 259–75.

Herman, J. L. (1992). *A practical guide to alternative assessment.* Alexandria, VA: Association for Supervision and Curriculum Development.

Khattri, N., Reeve, A., and Kane, M. (1998). *Principles and practices of performance assessment.* Mahwah, NJ: Lawrence Erlbaum.

Lewis, C. and Kingdon, B. (2016). CELBANTM: A ten-year retrospective. *TESL Canada Journal*, 33, 69–82.

Linn, R. L. and Burton, E. (1994). Performance-based assessment: Implications of task specificity. *Educational Measurement: Issues and Practice*, 13(1), 5–8.

Lockwood, J. (2015). Language for specific purpose (LSP) performance assessment in Asian call centres: Strong and weak definitions. *Language Testing in Asia*, 5(3).

Long, M. (2015). *Second language acquisition and task-based language teaching.* Hoboken, NJ: John Wiley & Sons.

Long, M. H. and Crookes, G. (1993). Units of analysis in syllabus design: The case for task. In G. Crookes and S. Gass, eds. *Tasks in a pedagogical context: Integrating theory and practice.* Bristol: Multilingual Matters, pp. 9–54.

Long, M. H. and Norris, J. M. (2000). Task-based teaching and assessment. In M. Byram, ed. *Encyclopedia of language teaching.* London: Routledge, pp. 597–603.

Lynch, B. K. (2001). The ethical potential of alternative language assessment. In *Experimenting with uncertainty: essays in honour of Alan Davies.* Cambridge: Cambridge University Press, pp. 228–39.

McNamara, T. (1996). *Measuring second language performance*. New York: Longman.

McNamara, T. (1997). 'Interaction' in second language performance assessment: Whose performance? *Applied linguistics*, 18(4), 446–66.

McNamara, T. and Roever, C. (2006). *Language testing: The social dimension*. Malden, MA: Blackwell.

Messick, S. (1994). The interplay of evidence and consequences in the validation of performance assessments. *Educational Researcher* 23, 13–23.

Messick, S. (1996). Validity and washback in language testing. *Language Testing*, 13(3), 241–56.

Mislevy, R., Steinberg, L., and Almond, R. (2002). Design and analysis in task-based language assessment. *Language Testing*, 19(4), 477–96.

Moss, P. A. (1992). Shifting conceptions of validity in educational measurement: Implications for performance assessment. *Review of Educational Research*, 62(3), 229–58.

Norris, J. M. (2000). Purposeful language assessment. *English Teaching Forum*, 38(1), 18–23.

Norris, J. M. (2002). Interpretations, intended uses and designs in task-based language assessment. *Language Testing*, 19(4), 337–46.

Norris, J. M. (2008). *Validity evaluation in language assessment*. Frankfurt: Peter Lang.

Norris, J. M. (2009). Task-based teaching and testing. In M. Long and C. Doughty, eds., *Handbook of language teaching*. Cambridge: Blackwell, pp. 578–94.

Norris, J. M. (2016). Current uses for task-based language assessment. *Annual Review of Applied Linguistics*, 36, 230–44.

Norris, J. M. (2018). Task-based language assessment: Aligning designs with intended uses and consequences. *JLTA Journal*, 21, 3–20.

Norris, J. M., Brown, J. D., Hudson, T. D., and Bonk, W. (2002). Examinee abilities and task difficulty in task-based second language performance assessment. *Language Testing*, 19(4), 395–418.

Norris, J. M., Brown, J. D., Hudson, T. D., and Yoshioka, J. K. (1998). *Designing second language performance assessment*. Honolulu, HI: University of Hawai'i Press.

Norris, J. M., Davis, J., and Timpe-Laughlin, V. (2017). *Second language educational experiences for adult learners*. London: Routledge.

Nunan, D. (2004). *Task-based language teaching*. Cambridge: Cambridge University Press.

Popham, W. J. (1993). Educational testing in America: What's right, what's wrong? A criterion-referenced perspective. *Educational Measurement: Issues and Practice*, 12(1), 11–14.

Purpura, J. E. and Turner, C. E. (2014). *Learning-oriented assessment in language classrooms: Using assessment to gauge and promote language learning*. New York: Routledge.

Robinson, P. and Ross, S. (1996). The development of task-based assessment in English for academic purpose programs. *Applied Linguistics*, 17, 455–76.

Ryan, D. G. and Frederiksen, N. (1951). Performance tests of educational achievement. In E. F. Lindquist, ed. *Educational measurement*. Washington DC: American Council on Education, pp. 455–94.

Shepard, L. A. (1993). Evaluating test validity. *Review of research in education*, 19(1), 405–50.

Shohamy, E. (1995). Performance assessment in language testing. *Annual Review of Applied Linguistics* 15, 188–211.

Skehan, P. (1998). *A cognitive approach to language learning*. Oxford: Oxford University Press.

Timpe-Laughlin, V. (2018). Pragmatics in task-based language assessment: Opportunities and challenges. In N. Taguchi and Y. Kim, eds. *Task-based approaches to teaching and assessing pragmatics*. Amsterdam: John Benjamins, pp. 287–304.

Van den Branden, K. (2006), ed. *Task-based language education: From theory to practice*. Cambridge: Cambridge University Press.

Van den Branden, K., Bygate, M., and Norris, J. (2009). Task-based language teaching: Introducing the reader. In K. Van den Branden, M. Bygate, and J. Norris, eds. *Task-based language teaching: A reader*. Amsterdam, Netherlands: John Benjamins, pp. 1–13.

Van den Branden, K., Depauw, V., and Gysen, S. (2002). A computerized task-based test of second language Dutch for vocational training purposes. *Language Testing*, 19(2), 438–52.

Van Gorp, K. and Deygers, B. (2014). Task-based language assessment. In A. Kunnan, ed. *The Companion to Language Assessment*. Cambridge: Wiley-Blackwell, pp. 578–93.

Wajda, E. (2011). New perspectives in language assessment: The interpretivist revolution. In M. Pawlak, ed. *Extending the boundaries of research on second language learning and teaching*. Berlin: Springer, pp. 275–85.

Wall, D. and Horák, T. (2006). The impact of changes in the TOEFL examination on teaching and learning in Central and Eastern Europe: Phase 1, the baseline study. *ETS Research Report Series*, MS-34.

Weaver, C. (2013). Incorporating a formative assessment cycle into task-based language teaching. In A. Shehadeh and C. Coombe, eds. *Researching and implementing task-based language learning and teaching in EFL contexts*. Amsterdam: John Benjamin, pp. 287–312.

Weideman, A. (2006). Assessing academic literacy: A task-based approach. *Language Matters*, 37, 81–101.

Wiggins, G. (1998). *Educative assessment: Designing assessments to inform and improve student performance*. San Francisco, CA: Jossey Bass.

Wolf, M. K., Lopez, A., Oh, S., and Tsutagawa, F. S. (2017). Comparing the performance of young English language learners and native English speakers on speaking assessment tasks. *English language proficiency assessments for young learners*. New York: Routledge, pp. 171–190.

14

Evaluating Task-Based Language Programs

John M. Norris and John McE. Davis

14.1 Task-Based Language Teaching: A Programmatic Approach to Language Education

In this chapter, we address the variety of contributions that program evaluation can make to the theory and practice of task-based language education. As a starting point, we first consider the programmatic nature of task-based language teaching (TBLT) as a defining, if often overlooked, characteristic.

Since its inception in the 1980s, TBLT has been described, investigated, promoted, and critiqued from a number of perspectives. Each perspective portrays TBLT in a different light, typically emphasizing particular attributes or phenomena that are of specific theoretical or practical interest while underplaying other dimensions of TBLT (e.g., focusing on task design, as in Pica, Kanagy & Falodun [1993]; focusing on lesson structure, as in Willis & Willis [2007]; focusing on teacher practice, as in Butler [2011]). Seen as a holistic approach to language education, TBLT combines ideas and elements from these and other perspectives into a comprehensive means for designing and delivering intentional language-learning experiences (Norris, Davis & Timpe-Laughlin, 2017). Indeed, in its earliest conceptualizations (e.g., Long, 1985) and in its most robust (and likely most challenging) form, TBLT is an inherently programmatic undertaking (Norris, 2015). By programmatic we mean that the variety of elements that make up instructed language learning (teachers, learners, materials, lessons, syllabuses, assessments, and so on) are combined into a logical design that stipulates what kind of teaching takes place, how that is intended to influence learning, and what kinds of outcomes follow. By programmatic, we also mean that the entire educational package, with all of its constituent parts, should be the ultimate unit of analysis for any type of inquiry that seeks to make claims about the effectiveness of TBLT.

As we have suggested elsewhere (Norris, Davis & Timpe-Laughlin, 2017; Norris, 2015), program evaluation provides a fitting approach to inquiry that takes into account the complex yet holistic nature of task-based programs, establishes the high-priority questions that need to be answered for particular purposes, and points to appropriate methodologies for gathering the evidence to do so. Evaluation also sets out a systematic approach to informing decisions about task-based programs at distinct points in their lifecycle, from inception and design, to implementation, to effectiveness testing and long-term impact. According to Norris (2015: 41):

> This kind of approach to inquiry can at once address the actual educational scope of task-based programs, do so in ways that reflect the local realities of implementation and factors that influence it, and potentially – in illuminating the details of actual TBLT programs – reveal something more generally interpretable about how task-based education works, under what circumstances, and with what effects.

In the following, we sketch out several roles for task-based program evaluation that have been proposed in the TBLT domain. We then highlight the most common intended uses for evaluation, along with typical methods, and we point to a few useful examples of evaluation applied to TBLT programs. Finally, we consider the likely prospects for utilizing evaluation as a heuristic for understanding and improving task-based language education in the future.

14.2 Roles for Evaluation in Task-Based Language Education

Evaluation has been of considerable interest in task-based theory and practice since the earliest TBLT innovations, yet the conceptualization of evaluation, its purposes, and its methodology have taken a variety of forms. Of course, in some ways, any and all empirical research on task-based ideas and implementations can be considered evaluative, in the sense that the findings of research potentially contribute to improved understandings of TBLT as an approach to language teaching and learning. Yet research may be distinguished from evaluation in the essential purposes for each: research is about generating and testing theories per se, whereas evaluation is a pragmatic undertaking intended to inform decisions and actions (e.g., understanding and improving TBLT as an educational practice) (see discussion in Norris, 2016; Patton, 2008). The lines can become blurred, though, when the purpose of testing TBLT theory is, in fact, to recommend it over other "theories" or approaches to language education, so we return to theory testing as one specific use for TBLT evaluation below. Another type of pseudo-evaluation might be characterized best as "armchair" evaluation or "expert" critique. There can certainly be some value to well-informed individuals voicing their opinions about TBLT, potentially based on their experiences with or observations of task-based ideas in practice. At the same time, we would distinguish this activity from evaluation on the fundamental difference that evaluation is always an empirical endeavor; that is, evaluation is based on evidence gathered through a variety of data-collection methods (including collecting data on experts' opinions), whereas critique is most typically not evidence-based (e.g., Littlewood, 2004; Swan, 2005).

Evaluation – of the evidence-based, decision-oriented type – has been in evidence since some of the earliest publications on TBLT, and it figures into seminal accounts of TBLT as a scientific-educational domain. An early view focused on the idea that task-based or related innovations could be compared empirically with other types of language instruction in an effort to demonstrate the effectiveness of one versus the other (e.g., Beretta, 1990; Beretta & Davies, 1985; Prabhu, 1987). In the Bangalore Project, where elements of task-based instruction were packaged into a procedural syllabus, evaluation was operationalized in the form of a between-groups comparison, with one set of English classes receiving traditional language instruction and the other featuring task-based techniques. At the conclusion of multiple years of the intervention, a variety of posttests were employed to demonstrate that the classes with task-based activities performed as well as traditional classes on language knowledge assessments and that they outperformed traditional classes on performance assessments. This type of methods comparison evaluation is attractive in its potential to identify what works and guide educational decision making and reform, and it has remained a core interest of TBLT evaluation. However, it is also fraught with methodological challenges that threaten the interpretations about relative effectiveness of methods, and for that reason there have been few convincing TBLT evaluations of this sort (see discussion in Beretta, 1992; Long, 2015; Norris, 2015; Ellis, Skehan, Li, Shintani, & Lambert, 2019).

Both Ellis (2003) and Long (2015) devote substantial attention to evaluation in their influential books on TBLT. For Ellis (1997, 2003, 2015), evaluation can play multiple roles in relation to TBLT, ranging from macro- to micro-evaluation. On the macro end of the spectrum, in addition to methods comparison evaluations of the sort described above, evaluation is used to investigate task-based programs in order to determine their effectiveness and/or to identify needed improvements; evaluation of this sort is undertaken for accountability and quality-assurance purposes, and it focuses on the outcomes of programs. Micro-evaluations, by contrast, investigate the discrete elements of TBLT, from teacher and learner perspectives on their practices and participation, to materials design and utilization, and most specifically focusing on tasks and how they function in the classroom. Ellis is particularly interested in teachers evaluating tasks within their classroom practices, as a way of raising teacher awareness about different aspects of task design (e.g., learner responses to tasks, task processes that occur, learning outcomes) and identifying possibilities for improvement (Ellis, 2015).

For Long (2015), evaluation of TBLT ideally occurs at the program level and in specific educational contexts, where questions need to be answered about what is actually happening under the name of TBLT (i.e., the process that ensues during task-based instructional implementation) and what learning occurs as a result (i.e., the product or outcomes of instruction). Long emphasizes that particular care should be taken in evaluating the extent to which instruction is, in fact, TBLT, and he recommends the observation of a variety of classroom phenomena that distinguish task-based from other types of instruction as a way of verifying the TBLT intervention. Beyond holistic program evaluations of this sort, Long is also interested in the accumulation of evidence about discrete aspects of task-based practice, and in particular the findings from studies of what he terms the methodological principles that undergird task-based teaching and learning. These laboratory- or classroom-based studies provide a first, controlled step toward understanding the potential effectiveness of TBLT, after which actual program-level implementation should follow to determine effectiveness in actual practice. Long is also particularly interested in – though also cautious about – the potential contribution of carefully designed evaluations that compare TBLT with other approaches to language education.

Other prominent depictions of evaluation in TBLT have focused on its role as a key empirical and judgmental component of language teaching innovation (e.g., Ellis et al., 2019; Van den Branden, 2006; 2009). From this perspective, evaluation offers critical insights into the viability of task-based innovations as they are pursued in actual educational and cultural settings, with diverse stakeholders, for distinct and at times uncertain purposes. The role for evaluation is at once formative, in that it can help make innovation happen by identifying issues in need of consideration as TBLT is locally implemented, and summative, in that it can determine to what extent the innovation works and identify challenges or problems that determined its effectiveness. We return to this integrated view on evaluation- and task-based innovation as a likely trajectory for future endeavor below.

14.3 Putting Evaluation to Use in Task-Based Language Teaching

How does program evaluation contribute practically to task-based language education? Evaluation can be usefully defined as a process of "gathering of information about any of the variety of elements that constitute educational programs, for a variety of purposes that include primarily understanding, demonstrating, improving, and judging program value" (Norris, 2006: 579). Another important dimension of evaluation is that it should be a multimethodological endeavor employing the full range of information-collection techniques available to applied linguistics researchers and practitioners, ranging from the most technically psychometric (e.g., language testing statistics) to the most qualitatively situated (e.g., teacher observation), and all other data-collection methods in between (Norris, 2006). Evaluation conceived in these ways can play an important role in language education, providing educators and other stakeholders useful information about the effectiveness of language teaching and learning that is happening in their programs. Importantly, then, program evaluation is a tool of inquiry that can focus on language education in diverse ways, over long- or short-term time periods, to the satisfaction of different stakeholders, and shedding light on any and all of the processes happening in language education. Evaluation likewise provides a powerful approach to educational inquiry in TBLT programs. That is, evaluation can shed light on the full programmatic scope of task-based language education as conceived, implemented, and developed by teachers and other stakeholders in specific educational contexts. In the following, we sketch out four types of uses for evaluation that seem particularly salient for understanding and improving task-based education.

14.4 Evaluation for Developing Task-Based Programs

Evaluation can play a particularly important role even before any teaching or learning happens, that is, during the design and development of new TBLT educational programs, or with an eye toward the re-design of existing programs. Indeed, a fundamental feature of task-based language program design is to conduct a learner needs analysis that identifies the real-world tasks students will need to perform in targeted communication contexts. In TBLT, "target tasks" form the basis of materials, curriculum, teaching, and assessment design, and a systematic investigative effort is recommended to identify the target tasks needed by students (Long, 2005, 2015). Thus, a well-established genre of evaluation involves collecting information to identify relevant tasks using: (a) a variety of data-collection methods, such as informant interviews/questionnaires, analyses of relevant documents, and observations/recordings of target task performances; and (b) comparison of perspectives on learning needs across multiple sources of information, including learners themselves, but also other stakeholders, like teachers, domain experts, and local informants (Long, 2005; Van Avermaet & Gysen, 2006). Needs analysis, then, serves as a useful starting point for developing new TBLT programs, and it may also shed light on how well existing instruction is helping students reach important language-learning goals.

Iizuka (2019) offers an interesting example of task-based needs analysis in relation to a study abroad program for US learners of Japanese as a foreign language. Here, a primary use of the evaluation was to shed light on the extent to which the existing program was addressing the immediate language-learning needs of students during the study abroad experience, which included a homestay with a Japanese family as a critical component. Iizuka utilized interviews and questionnaires, across both student and host family sources, to identify the kinds of tasks that were particularly salient during the study abroad period. An interesting dimension to the methodology was the solicitation of input on both the importance of various tasks as well as the extent to which these tasks proved more or less problematic. Findings indicated that, although multiple tasks were deemed important (including some academic tasks), speaking tasks in general were perceived as most important, and small-talk, conversational, and social uses of language received the highest ratings. Small-talk with the host family was perceived to be the single most important task, though interestingly, these more social uses of Japanese were not deemed to be overly difficult, whereas reading and listening tasks, as well as more formalized speaking tasks, proved more challenging. Perhaps most interesting, it was in the homestay-oriented data where important discrepancies were identified between the host (particularly the host mother) and student perspectives, with cultural sensitivities (e.g., related to food, clothing, cleanliness) coming to the fore. Iizuka concludes the needs analysis by identifying a handful of target tasks that should be incorporated into the study abroad course in order to better tailor it to the actual needs and problems encountered by learners during this experience (for other examples of TBLT needs analysis see, González-Lloret & Nielson [2015]; Lambert [2010]; Long [2005]).

In a related developmental use of evaluation, in addition to identifying target tasks, TBLT program designers will typically need to know how well students can perform those tasks after receiving instruction, which calls for establishing learning benchmarks or student learning outcomes as key targets for language teaching and learning (Long & Norris, 2000; Norris, 2006, 2009). TBLT assessment calls for the use of target task performances as key indicators of language ability, these often conceived in terms of the specific language knowledge, skills, and dispositions (i.e., "can-do" statements) needed to perform real-world tasks (e.g., "Students will be able to present and support a position/opinion during a class presentation"). Below, we elaborate on how the assessment of student learning outcomes is itself an important evaluation genre. For now, we point out that student learning outcomes statements can be used as key building blocks for several program planning and pre-evaluation activities useful in developing TBLT education.

Getting to the heart of the programmatic undertaking that is (or should be) TBLT, a final developmental evaluation activity that plays a critical role involves conceptualizing an entire language program via a theory of change or logic model. A theory of change is a comprehensive description and illustration of how a desired change is expected to happen as a result of participation in an educational program. The theory of change will typically have several components, including the desired outcomes of a learning program, as well as the various program elements (resources, funding, materials, teaching activities, etc.) that combine to bring about the targeted learning/changes in participants. A commonly-used variety of theory of change is logic-modeling (Frechtling, 2007), which depicts a program framework by stating the long- and short-term program objectives, and then, working backward, lists the program inputs, outputs, and activities needed for the targeted outcomes to occur. Logic-modeling can be a first step in program design, used to set out the envisioned program aims and structure. In addition (and perhaps more commonly), logic-modeling can help reveal if an existing program is organized in a way conducive to achieving its goals.[1] Since TBLT programs are by their nature holistic and consist of several interconnected elements, delineating a TBLT program via logic-modeling can help to reveal whether all program elements are conceived in a rational way and contribute to learning effectively. However, despite the attractive possibilities of such an undertaking, to date, TBLT program designers and evaluators "have not sought to capture any kind of program theory or logic underlying innovations or interventions" (Long, 2015: 350). We return to this issue in discussing TBLT theory testing below.

14.5 Evaluation for Understanding and Improving the Implementation of Task-Based Programs

A particular variety of evaluation called "fidelity of implementation" can help TBLT educators know if TBLT-oriented program innovations are happening as planned. Fidelity of implementation evaluation involves investigating the extent to which a new program has been operationalized as designed, and whether implementation has deviated from intended planning in ways that undermine program effectiveness. Fidelity of implementation evaluation is most usefully conducted prior to any focus on effectiveness, to make sure that program outcomes are the result of the intended program design and not extraneous factors related to incomplete or lacking program implementation. Likewise, a newly designed TBLT program or course can be a novel educational innovation, the success of which depends on specific teaching and assessment practices. As

---

[1] In higher education, an equivalent process is "curriculum mapping," which involves developing a grid consisting of (a) learning outcomes (as the ultimate targets of a degree program), and (b) courses and assessments. A curriculum map provides an overview of a degree program to better understand whether it provides sufficient content and learning opportunities for students to reach targeted learning goals.

experience has shown, TBLT can call on teachers and students to engage in new and unfamiliar instructional practices (e.g., McDonough & Chaikitmongkol, 2007; Van den Branden, 2006). When introducing TBLT, then, into new teaching contexts, task-based instruction may be modified in unhelpful ways, or, not implemented at all. Fidelity of implementation evaluation helps educators to know if TBLT innovations are happening as intended.

Any of the several prescribed components of TBLT instructional programs are candidates for this type of evaluative inquiry, and TBLT educators engaging in evaluation stand to gain from the insights and feedback evaluation provides. Of the many evaluation benefits available to TBLT practitioners, perhaps a key theme among these is the ability of evaluation to shed light on the specifically (and perhaps uniquely) programmatic aspects of TBLT instruction, particularly since task-based programs are holistic in their intended design and consisting of several complex and interrelated program elements (Norris, 2015). Many potential foci for evaluation in TBLT programs are possible, but a handful of exemplary foci listed next highlight how some of the unique programmatic characteristics of TBLT education are usefully amenable to evaluative inquiry:

- *Learning sequences articulating with one another in ways that support effective task-based teaching and learning.* TBLT commonly includes the creation of specific learning sequences – either pedagogic tasks or articulated courses – that progress in complexity over time and build on previously learned abilities toward mastery of target task skills. Evaluation – using document review and different kinds of assessment of student performance (among other methods) – can shed light on whether learning is happening as intended over extended, sequential periods of instruction, particularly if evaluation is implemented repeatedly over longitudinal cycles of program inquiry.
- *Whether task-based materials are supporting language instruction effectively.* Typically TBLT calls for eschewing commercial textbooks and developing original materials in support of task-based instruction that develops language skills for performing authentic target tasks. The usefulness and effectiveness of instructor-designed TBLT materials within classes and over sequences of learning will be a perennial concern for practitioners and program stakeholders. Testimony from teachers and students (collected via interviews, questionnaires, and focus groups), observations of students use of materials in class, and careful document review of student work will reveal whether materials are supporting TBLT effectively.
- *The extent to which task-based assessment is functioning effectively.* TBLT typically calls for a specific approach to assessment in which students must demonstrate the specific language skills needed for performing target tasks (Long & Norris, 2000). Task-based assessment will commonly

involve the use of authentic assessment tasks and scoring criteria focused on successful task performance. Typically, such assessments will be designed by local educators and will be unique to local program aims. The efficacy and usefulness of task-based assessments (and related issues having to do with assessment quality) will be an important concern for TBLT practitioners, and one that evaluation can shed light on by periodically investigating the appropriateness and usefulness of assessment practices.

- *Teachers and students participating effectively in TBLT programs of instruction.* As noted prior, TBLT can be a novel undertaking for teachers and students alike. Teachers may react to TBLT methods in unexpected ways and may need training or awareness-raising to develop new skills or address resistance to TBLT techniques. Students also might fail to understand their responsibilities in a TBLT instructional approach and likewise may need training to understand how to engage with task-based instruction to make the most of TBLT's learning potential. Evaluation inquiring into teacher and student actions (e.g., through structured classroom observations) and attitudes (e.g., through introspective and retrospective interviews, focus groups, questionnaires) can identify and address these and other "human-factor" implementation issues known to arise in TBLT innovations.

- *TBLT programs effectively situated within – and in alignment with – the local instructional context.* A common (though perhaps unconvincingly supported) claim is that TBLT can be ill-suited to certain instructional contexts. The validity of these claims notwithstanding, TBLT will be most effective when it is cognizant of and situated appropriately within the local education context and culture (Norris, Davis & Timpe-Laughlin, 2017). Evaluative inquiry can help achieve this aim, investigating the feasibility and execution of TBLT practices against a backdrop of local cultural and educational norms, and especially when the evaluation approach is an inclusive and stakeholder-driven process inviting diverse voices and perspectives on how best to implement TBLT in specific locales for specific teachers and students.

Kim, Jung, and Tracy-Ventura (2017) report on one example of evaluating the implementation of an innovative task-based course in the context of a Korean university English program. The course itself was based on a needs analysis that indicated certain topical themes (work, travel, and school events) and associated target tasks, with a heavy emphasis on spoken interaction as both a learning goal and the primary pedagogic task type. Here, owing to the presumed novelty of the TBLT approach, the evaluation focused on a semester-long analysis of student perspectives on and participation in task-based learning. Evaluation data included repeated surveys of students after each unit of instruction, eliciting their perspectives on the usefulness of the task-based approach, their interest in this kind of learning, and the effectiveness of TBLT for particular learning foci. Additionally, one learner's complete semester-long portfolio of task engagement and performance was analyzed for various features, including motivation, enjoyment, difficulty, learning opportunities, and so on. Findings indicated that learners began the course with relatively lower perceptions of TBLT as an interesting and effective approach to language learning, but that they became noticeably more positive over the semester as they also became familiar with the format of the highly collaborative learning tasks. Additionally, learner perceptions indicated that distinct units of instruction (e.g., focusing on different target task types) were perceived to be variably effective, and that certain language-learning goals (e.g., development of grammatical accuracy) were not as convincingly incorporated into instruction as others. Among other implications, the evaluators conclude that the meta-cognitive development of learners is probably an important addition to future iterations of the course, as a way of reminding learners of the intended processes and outcomes of task-based learning (for another example of TBLT implementation evaluation, with similar patterns of findings, see McDonough & Chaikitmongkol [2007]).

14.5.1 Assessing Task-Based Student Learning Outcomes

Task-based language teaching programs are distinct in their primary focus on helping students develop language abilities for specific real-world tasks related to their personal and professional goals. A key feature of TBLT is assessing students' abilities to perform target tasks, which calls for unique assessment strategies for understanding whether students have learned the language skills and task-based competencies targeted in the program (Norris & East, this volume).

While task-based assessment is a fundamental component of TBLT instruction, its implementation also provides a ready-made framework of evaluation that educators can use for program accountability as well as improvement and development. If a program has (a) identified task-based learning outcomes as targeted aims for instruction, (b) designed articulated instruction to help students attain those outcomes, and (c) developed related student learning outcome assessments, then educators have put in place the essential building blocks of a prototypical evaluation methodology known outside language education as "objectives-based evaluation," an approach to evaluating teaching and learning dating back to the early twentieth century (Davis, 2016). Objectives-based evaluation involves judging the effectiveness of a program on the extent to which it has attained its learning or service-oriented objectives,[2] and, in instances

---

[2] Objectives are typically desired changes in program participants – that is, what participants do differently or better as result of the services provided by a program. Objectives can be a statement of a targeted change in circumstances, status, level of functioning, behavior, attitude, knowledge, or skills that a program aims to effect in program participants or clients.

where programs have failed to achieve their objectives, taking steps toward improving instruction, training, or other aspects of program delivery. Objectives-based evaluation is akin to a process in language education termed student learning outcomes assessment and involves a similar assessment-based approach to evaluating language education (Davis, 2015; Norris 2006). That is, student learning outcomes assessment typically involves (a) developing student learning outcomes for programmatic sequences of learning, (b) assessing student attainment of those outcomes, and (c), crucially, *using* assessment information on student performance to diagnose where instruction is functioning ineffectively and to make improvements.

Student learning outcomes assessment offers language educators a powerful tool for investigating whether teaching and learning in their TBLT programs are functioning effectively. There are relatively obvious targets for the outcomes of task-based learning, including: (a) the ability to perform a series of target-language tasks to specified criterion levels for accomplishment; (b) the qualities of language performance expected of learners and revealing of second language development (e.g., increases in their syntactic and lexical complexity, grammatical accuracy, fluency, pragmatic/cultural sensitivity, discourse familiarity, and so on); and (c) the extent to which learning transfers to "on-the-job" or other real-world application of language abilities (i.e., conveying a sense of the relevance as well as effectiveness of what was taught in the task-based program). Consistent cyclical review of student performance along these lines can shed light on programmatic functioning of TBLT in useful ways. Thus, assessment can be used toward many helpful ends, such as modifying or improving teaching and materials; aligning instruction with curriculum; engendering programmatic thinking in terms of sequential learning throughout a course or curriculum; clarifying expectations and providing clear learning and instructional targets for teachers and students; improving and streamlining assessments; demonstrating students' knowledge, abilities, and dispositions to various audiences; and, ultimately, improving student learning in targeted, systematic, locally valued ways.

González-Lloret and Nielson (2015) provide an interesting example of the use of student learning outcomes assessment to answer critical questions about an innovative task-based training program. The program context was a new Spanish course for US Border Patrol agents, designed on the basis of a needs analysis that identified critical target communication tasks, and implemented according to task-based learning principles. Key questions after the initial stage of implementation had to do with whether the course overall was effective in developing participants' language proficiency over the eight weeks of instruction, whether the students demonstrated better task-based language abilities than previous cohorts who had not experienced the new course, and to what extent participants found that they had developed the language abilities that were called for once they were in active job settings. Findings indicated that: (a) pre-post language development, measured using an independent speaking proficiency test, showed substantial gain; (b) learners in the innovative course demonstrated consistently superior task speaking abilities across multiple dimensions of performance (e.g., complexity, fluency) compared with previous cohorts; and (c) once on the job, learners felt well-prepared to handle the majority of Spanish speaking tasks encountered. Interestingly, participants also reported that additional task types, particularly related to social uses of the language, and more sustained conversational speaking practice would benefit future cohorts. Here, then, outcomes assessments of several varieties were utilized to demonstrate the effectiveness of the innovative course but also as a way of identifying areas in need of improvement (for another example of TBLT-related outcomes assessment, see Byrnes, Maxim & Norris [2010]).

14.5.2 Evaluation for Testing Task-Based Language Teaching Theory, Logic, and Claims

A final use for evaluation in relation to task-based education takes the form of what we might call theory testing. Here, questions like "does TBLT work?" or "is TBLT better than other approaches to language teaching" – or at greater depth "How does TBLT work?" or "Why is TBLT better than other approaches?" – focus more on the overall approach to language teaching and learning, rather than the specifics of a given program design or implementation. While evaluation offers several possibilities for answering such questions, doing so is by no means a straightforward endeavor (see Long, 2015; Norris, 2016; Beretta, 1992). A major challenge is that there are, at best, few examples of TBLT program designs (never mind other language educational approaches) that spell out a theory of change or present a logic model, yet without such a theoretical foundation it is essentially impossible to test whether it works. That is, unless there are clear predictions about how the distinct parts of a program (teachers, learners, materials, and assessments) work together to enable clearly specified learning outcomes to happen, then any observations of effectiveness or the lack thereof will remain uncertainly attributable. Could it have been that the learners were not engaged as intended? Did the teachers understand their instructional roles well enough? Was the assessment designed to support task-based learning or did it distract from that focus? A theory of change or logic model at least spells out what ought to happen among the many factors that affect learning, and it lays out a map for focusing evaluation on the various critical parts of the program.

A related and critical challenge, then, is that it is often uncertain what actually has been implemented under the name of TBLT. If we want to know whether TBLT works, or works better than other options, then we need to be certain that what we are testing is in fact TBLT. Here, it is essential to have a careful accounting of what actually happens in a TBLT program as it is implemented – what do the teachers and learners do, how well do materials function, what happens during assessment, how much time and effort is devoted to what kinds of learning activities, and so on. Document analyses and teacher/learner interviews or surveys, combined with intensive observations of the learning situation (e.g., Long, 2015), offer methods for keeping track of the ways in which TBLT (or another approach) was implemented, and they enable subsequent grounding of claims that learning outcomes were attributable to a particular theory as it was realized in practice. This kind of careful attention to the implementation of TBLT in practice also allows for unanticipated factors to be captured, that is, factors that might influence the ultimate outcomes but that have not been posited in the theory of change. One example here might be the undue influence that assessment can have on how teachers and learners engage with TBLT, especially where externally mandated assessments emphasize language abilities distinct from those in focus in the task-based instruction (e.g., Carless, 2007; East, 2012).

When it comes to making comparisons, to identifying the "best" method for language teaching, these kinds of challenges are exacerbated. Thus, to be able to draw a conclusion that one approach is more effective than another, the programs or theories under comparison must first be well understood (i.e., each has a theory of change) and there must be adequate documentation that the program is being implemented as intended (i.e., evidence for fidelity of implementation). Even then, a major additional challenge has to do with the comparability of conditions under which the programs are implemented. In other words, a variety of unanticipated factors may affect the outcomes of the learning programs such that the program theory, per se, is not the primary cause of any observed differences. A classic example is differences in the learners participating in the two conditions, where proficiency, motivation, or other learner individual differences may cause better or worse learning to happen. Another example would be differential preparation and experience of the teacher(s) to deliver a particular approach (see Beretta, 1992). Comparison evaluations, though of high interest as a means for guiding policy and practice, are fraught with complexities, hence there are very few trustworthy examples to date.

Despite the challenges, Shintani (2016) provides one useful example of a theory-driven comparison evaluation that can serve as a model for this type of inquiry. A key contribution of this work was the care taken to describe and account for the approaches under comparison as well as their implementation and outcomes. Shintani first carefully situates the study within a specific educational milieu and its attendant challenges – namely, the teaching of English as a foreign language to absolute beginners in a primary school setting in Japan. She then outlines the theoretical orientation and design of two teaching approaches, one based on the present, practice, produce (PPP) methodology and the other based on input-oriented TBLT (i.e., the primary pedagogic task type emphasized aural input from the teacher and student response through the manipulation of realia). These approaches, along with a true control condition, were implemented over a nine-week period, with pre-post-delayed assessments utilizing both discrete-point and task-based tests that sought to capture receptive as well as productive skills. Painstaking observation, recording, and discourse analysis of the actual instruction that occurred in the comparison conditions then established the fidelity of implementation of each approach. On the basis of these critical foundational steps, Shintani was able to support strong claims about the relative effectiveness of the PPP versus TBLT approaches, as demonstrated through outcomes assessments: (a) TBLT was as good as PPP for the development of receptive knowledge of nouns, and it was better than PPP for receptive knowledge and productive use of adjectives; and (b) TBLT was better than PPP for developing receptive knowledge of the plural -s and copula *be*. Again, owing to the careful design and observation of the instructional approaches as they were implemented, Shintani was also able to draw theoretical conclusions about particular contributions of TBLT (e.g., the role of negotiation of meaning and form, pushed output, and incidental learning of language), as well as practical implications for task-based pedagogy (e.g., the use of input-based tasks with beginning learners, the role and linguistic skills of the teacher).

14.6 Evaluation, Task-Based Language Teaching, and the Future of Language Education

In sum, there is a lot to recommend evaluation as an approach to understanding, improving, and validating TBLT. The unique contributions of evaluation are its capacity for observing and accounting for both theory and practice, its attention to the complexities of educational programs and the situations where they occur, and its explicit incorporation of stakeholders as arbiters of evaluation findings and uses. When pursued systematically and purposefully, evaluation provides a revealing window and broad perspective on the functioning of teaching and learning, shedding light on TBLT's theoretical concepts, its proposed instructional logic, and attendant claims of learning efficacy. A "wide-angle" perspective like this is useful, given a key feature of TBLT that recommends the sequencing of learning over series of pedagogic tasks, moving progressively toward mastery of target task abilities at terminal program junctures. Likewise, the necessarily concatenated and interconnected aspect of TBLT instruction – with various program components working together to develop target task student abilities – can be usefully illuminated and investigated using evaluation methods. For example, evaluation can help reveal if student needs are clearly known and reflected in TBLT instructional design. Similarly, evaluation of distinct task-based design elements, such as outcomes/objectives, materials, curricular/course sequences, assessment, teacher induction/training, and so on, can help investigate whether these elements are supporting language learning effectively. Along these lines, evaluation also can shed light on key aspects of TBLT delivery, such as teacher and learner understandings, plans, motivations, and engagement, helping to show how teachers and learners interact with, and react to, the TBLT instructional experience. Finally, evaluation (and student learning outcomes assessment in particular) can provide evidence of the efficacy of TBLT itself – as the preeminent research-based language pedagogy to date – using observable task-based student learning outcomes and demonstrated language development as evidence of TBLT's potential usefulness for instructed second language acquisition.

Evaluation, then, allows for a focus on the full scope of educational innovations and the conditions within which they occur, a focus that is essential if we hope to make sense of what works and what doesn't in language teaching (Byrnes, 2019). Importantly, evaluation also provides a means for enabling educational innovations to occur in the first place, as a type of empirical practice undergirding program design (e.g., in the form of needs analysis and logic-modeling for TBLT programs) and instructional delivery (e.g., in the form of fidelity of implementation investigations). This formative orientation of program evaluation may be of the most value for educators seeking a way of embarking systematically on a TBLT innovation.

Of course, the desire for theory testing of TBLT will continue, and there are two trajectories in this type of evaluative work that we might foresee. One will involve the comprehensive and painstaking observation of complex task-based programs as they are designed and implemented, and as they lead to specific outcomes (e.g., Shintani, 2016). Within these deep, rich, typically longitudinal descriptions of task-based theoretical ideas in practice, evaluators will be able to uncover locally situated truths that can nevertheless shed light on generalizable understandings about what really matters in trying to accomplish TBLT. A recent example of this kind of evaluation is Bryfonski's (2019, this volume) study, where a TBLT teacher training program was carefully investigated for its impact on teachers' beliefs and actions, both during training and subsequently in their teaching experiences; findings shed light on key teacher background factors that proved highly influential in determining their responses to the task-based training. An additional benefit of this kind of situated evaluation is that it has immediate utility for informing local practices where TBLT innovation is taking place, as indicated by interest and uptake from the local language education community in Bryfonski's study.

As TBLT program implementation and efficacy evaluations continue to accrue, another intriguing possibility for evaluation takes the form of meta-evaluation. While meta-analyses of particular domains of task-based research have been in evidence for some time (e.g., Keck, Iberri-Shea, Tracy-Ventura & Wa-Mbaleka, 2006), it is only recently that attempts have been made to synthesize findings across studies that investigated TBLT program-level effects. Bryfonski and McKay (2019) offer an interesting example of evaluating TBLT evaluations by combining effect sizes across all studies that operationalized a program-scale implementation and measured effects quantitatively. Though constrained by the typical insufficiencies in the reporting of program designs and their implementations, this meta-evaluation offers a first glimpse into the relatively strong and consistently positive effects, for both learning outcomes and student/teacher perceptions, that are associated with TBLT programs across a variety of educational contexts. Importantly, it also sheds light on the ways in which TBLT is being implemented, including likely gaps and other infelicities (e.g., lacking needs analysis), as well as the ways in which TBLT program evaluations are being reported (e.g., lacking thorough information on the nature of the implementation, the types of learners, and so on). Looking ahead, this type of regular meta-evaluation of TBLT program evaluations will play a heightened role, both in identifying broad needs for improvement in how TBLT theory is put into practice, and also as a convincing means for answering questions about what works in language education.

In the end, we would like to return to the idea that program evaluation is much more than a way of empirically testing TBLT theory as it is put into practice, although that is one important orientation for evaluative work. We suggest that program evaluation is, or should be, part and parcel of the TBLT innovation enterprise. In particular, where TBLT ideas are being used to introduce or otherwise encourage language educational reform, it is irresponsible not to include program evaluation from the outset. Thus, evaluation can and should be applied to the design of any TBLT program, to the identification of learner needs, to the specification of targeted learning outcomes, and to sketching out the logic according to which language learning should occur. Evaluation really must be employed to check on the fidelity with which task-based principles are being put into practice by teachers, through task materials and syllabus designs, through learner engagement and uptake, and in the types of assessment that are being used. And evaluation is essential to gauge the outcomes of task-based instruction, in terms of language development, stakeholder perceptions, and the ultimate impact of the educational experience on learners and those they encounter in their next steps in life. By thinking and acting evaluatively from the very beginning of TBLT design through to its culmination in language learning, we will be more likely to realize the potential contribution of TBLT to improving language education.

Further Reading

Beretta, A. (1992). What can be learned from the Bangalore Evaluation. In J. C. Alderson and A. Beretta, eds. *Evaluating second language education*. Cambridge: Cambridge University Press, pp. 250–71.

Norris, J. M. (2015). Thinking and acting programmatically in task-based language teaching: Essential roles for program evaluation. In M. Bygate, ed. *Domains and directions in the development of TBLT: A decade of plenaries from the international conference*. Amsterdam: John Benjamins, pp. 27–57.

Norris, J. M., Davis, J., and Timpe-Laughlin, V. (2017). *Second language educational experiences for adult learners*. London: Routledge.

Shintani, N. (2016). *Input-based tasks in foreign language instruction for young learners*. Amsterdam: John Benjamins.

Van den Branden, K. (2006). Training teachers: Task-based as well? In K. Van den Branden, ed. *Task-based language teaching in practice*. Cambridge: Cambridge University Press, pp. 217–73.

Study Questions

1. What are the elements of task-based language programs, and how do they interact with each other in shaping the language-learning experience?
2. What are the main differences between program evaluation and other types of research, and what does each have to contribute to TBLT?
3. In what ways can language teachers, learners, and other stakeholders participate in the evaluation of task-based language programs?
4. Which are the most important questions that should be answered by evaluation methods at different points in the development and implementation of TBLT?
5. What are the factors that make it difficult to "prove" the effectiveness of any approach to language teaching, including TBLT?

References

Beretta, A. (1990). Implementation of the Bangalore Project. *Applied Linguistics*, 11(4), 321–40.

Beretta, A. (1992). What can be learned from the Bangalore evaluation. In J. C. Alderson and A. Beretta, eds. *Evaluating second language education*. Cambridge: Cambridge University Press, pp. 250–71.

Beretta, A. and Davies, A. (1985). Evaluation of the Bangalore project. *ELT Journal*, 29, 121–27.

Butler, Y. G. (2011). The implementation of communicative and task-based language teaching in the Asia-Pacific region. *Annual Review of Applied Linguistics*, 31, 36–57.

Bryfonski, L. E. (2019). *Task-based teacher training: Implementation and evaluation in Central American bilingual schools.* Unpublished doctoral dissertation, Georgetown University: Washington DC.

Bryfonski, L. and McKay, T. H. (2017). TBLT implementation and evaluation: A meta-analysis. *Language Teaching Research*, 23, 603–32.

Byrnes, H. (2019). Affirming the context of instructed SLA: The potential of curricular thinking. *Language Teaching Research*, 23, 514–32.

Byrnes, H., Maxim, H., and Norris, J. (2010). Realizing advanced L2 writing development in a collegiate curriculum: Curricular design, pedagogy, assessment [Monograph]. *Modern Language Journal*, 94.

Carless, D. (2007). The suitability of task-based approaches for secondary schools: Perspectives from Hong Kong. *System*, 35(4), 595–608.

Davis, J. McE. (2015). The usefulness of accreditation-mandated outcomes assessment: Trends in university foreign language programs. In J. M. Norris and J. McE. Davis eds. *Student learning outcomes assessment in college foreign language programs.* Honolulu, HI: University of Hawai'i, National Foreign Language Resource Center, pp. 1–35.

Davis, J. McE. (2016). Toward a capacity framework for useful student learning outcomes assessment in college language programs. *Modern Language Journal*, 100(1), 377–99.

East, M. (2012). *Task-based language teaching from the teachers' perspective: Insights from New Zealand.* Vol. 3. Amsterdam: John Benjamins.

Ellis, R. (1997). The empirical evaluation of language teaching materials. *ELT Journal*, 51, 36–42.

Ellis, R. (2003). *Task-based language learning and teaching.* Oxford: Oxford University Press.

Ellis, R. (2015). Teachers evaluating tasks. In M. Bygate, ed. *Domains and directions in the development of TBLT: A decade of plenaries from the international conference.* Amsterdam: John Benjamins, pp. 247–70.

Ellis, R., Skehan, P., Li, S., Shintani, N., and Lambert, C. (2019). *Task-based language teaching: Theory and practice.* Cambridge: Cambridge University Press.

Frechtling, J. A. (2007). *Logic modeling methods in program evaluation.* San Francisco, CA: Jossey-Bass.

González-Lloret, M., Nielson, K. B. (2015). Evaluating TBLT: The case of a task-based Spanish program. *Language Teaching Research*, 19(5), 525–49.

Iizuka, T. (2019). Task-based needs analysis: Identifying communicative needs for study abroad students in Japan. *System*, 80, 134–42.

Keck, C.M., Iberri-Shea, G., Tracy-Ventura, N., and Wa-Mbaleka, S. (2006). Investigating the empirical link between interaction and acquisition: A quantitative meta-analysis. In J. Norris and L. Ortega. *Synthesizing research on language learning and teaching*. Amsterdam: John Benjamins, pp. 91–131.

Kim, Y., Jung, Y., and Tracy-Ventura, N. (2017). Implementation of a Localized Task-Based Course in an EFL Context: A Study of Students' Evolving Perceptions. *TESOL Quarterly*, 51(3), 632–60.

Lambert, C. (2010). A task-based needs analysis:Putting principles into practice. *Language Teaching Research*, 14(1), 99–112.

Littlewood, W. (2004). The task-based approach: Some questions and suggestions. *ELT Journal*, 58(4), 319–26.

Long, M. H. (1985). A role for instruction in second language acquisition: Task-based language teaching. In K. Hyltenstam and M. Pienemann, eds. *Modelling and assessing second language acquisition*. Bristol: Multilingual Matters, pp. 77–99.

Long, M. (2005). *Second language needs analysis*. Cambridge: Cambridge University Press.

Long, M. (2015). *Second language acquisition and task-based language teaching*. Oxford: Wiley-Blackwell.

Long, M. and Norris, J. M. (2000). Task-based teaching and assessment. In M. Byram, ed. *Encyclopedia of language teaching*. London: Routledge, pp. 597–603.

McDonough, K. and Chaikitmongkol, W. (2007). Teachers' and learners' reactions to a task-based EFL course in Thailand. *TESOL Quarterly*, 41, 107–32.

Norris, J. M. (2006). The why (and how) of assessing student foreign language programs. *Modern Language Journal*, 90, 590–97.

Norris, J. M. (2009). Task-based teaching and testing. In C. Doughty and M. Long, eds. *The handbook of language teaching*. Malden, MA: Wiley-Blackwell, pp. 578–94.

Norris, J. M. (2015). Thinking and acting programmatically in task-based language teaching: Essential roles for program evaluation. In M. Bygate, ed. *Domains and directions in the development of TBLT: A decade of plenaries from the international conference*. Amsterdam: John Benjamins, pp. 27–57.

Norris, J. M. (2016). Language program evaluation. *Modern Language Journal*, 100(s), 169–89.

Norris, J. M., Davis, J. McE., and Timpe-Laughlin, V. (2017). *Second language educational experiences for adult learners*. London: Routledge.

Patton, M. Q. (2008). *Utilization-focused evaluation*. 4th ed. Thousand Oaks, CA: Sage.

Pica, T., Kanagy, R., and Falodun, J. (1993). Choosing and using communicative tasks for second language instruction. In G. Crookes and S. M. Gass. eds. *Tasks in a pedagogical context*. Bristol: Multilingual Matters, pp. 9–34.

Prabhu, N. S. (1987). *Second Language Pedagogy*. Oxford: Oxford University Press.

Shintani, N. (2016). *Input-based tasks in foreign language instruction for young learners*. Amsterdam: John Benjamins.

Swan, M. (2005). Legislation by hypothesis: The case of task-based instruction. *Applied Linguistics*, 26(3), 376–401.

Van Avermaet, P. and Gysen, S. (2006). From needs to tasks: Language learning needs in a task-based approach. In K. Van den Branden, ed. *Task-based language education: From theory to practice*. Cambridge: Cambridge University Press, pp. 17–46.

Van den Branden, K. (2006), ed., *Task-based language education: From theory to practice*. Cambridge: Cambridge University Press.

Van den Branden, K. (2009). Diffusion and implementation of innovations. In M. Long and C. Doughty, eds. *The handbook of language teaching*. Oxford: Wiley-Blackwell, pp. 659–72.

Willis, D. and Willis, J. (2007). *Doing task-based teaching*. Oxford: Oxford University Press.

14A

Comparing the Effectiveness of Task-Based Language Teaching and Presentation-Practice-Production on Second Language Grammar Learning

A Pilot Study with Chinese Students of Italian as a Second Language

Ilaria Borro

14A.1 Rationale and Background

Second language grammar teaching is matter of an ongoing debate (Long, 2017). The practices advocated by the different positions involved can be seen as speaking to three issues, (1) the extent to which grammar is pivotal in the syllabus design, (2) the proportion of class time devoted to grammar, and (3) the degree of explicitness and implicitness of grammar instruction and corrective feedback.

The present contribution aims at evaluating and comparing task-based language teaching (TBLT) and the widespread pedagogical routine summarized by the acronym PPP (i.e., presentation, practice, production). In the aforementioned debate, PPP reflects a grammar-based syllabus, extensive and explicit grammar instruction position. Indeed, the focus on forms (FonFS) carried out in PPP deals with predefined grammar structures, which are the main focus of the lesson and are explicitly explained and practiced. On the other hand, TBLT involves no predefined grammar syllabus, as its focus on form (FonF) respects the learner's internal syllabus by being reactive. Moreover, FonF is incidental, thus keeping the main focus and most class time on meaning and content. These factors make grammar instruction in TBLT mostly implicit, which boosts the likelihood of it resulting in implicit knowledge of the language (Paradis, 1994; 2004).

Recent literature has acknowledged the priority of implicit over explicit knowledge as a goal for language teaching (Long, 2017; Whong et al., 2014), as well as the importance of employing tools capable of assessing both dimensions of knowledge (Godfroid & Kim, 2019). Nevertheless, studies evaluating the relative effectiveness of PPP and TBLT on grammar instruction have rarely employed specific, online measures to assess implicit knowledge of grammar. Mostly, researchers have measured learning by means of task-based assessments (e.g., Burwell et al., 2009; De Ridder et al., 2007; Gonzalez-Lloret & Nielson, 2014), explicit grammar tests (e.g., De la Fuente, 2006), or a combination of the two (e.g., Beretta & Davies 1985). Li and colleagues (2016) constitute an exception, since they measured both explicit and implicit knowledge by employing a grammaticality judgment test and an oral elicited imitation test, respectively. However, Suzuki (2017) pointed out that the oral elicited imitation test is more likely to measure automatized explicit knowledge than implicit knowledge, which was confirmed by Godfroid and Kim (2019). On the other hand, online tools, such as self-paced reading, eye tracking and priming, are acknowledged as possible measures of implicit competence (Godfroid & Kim, 2019; Suzuki, 2017), which makes it desirable for evaluation studies to employ them. The present contribution aims to address this gap, measuring participants' implicit knowledge by means of self-paced reading tests.

Moreover, the results of existing experiments on the relative effectiveness of TBLT and PPP on grammar learning point to the need for further research. In part of the literature, FonFS resulted in better performances than TBLT in offline grammar tests (e.g., De la Fuente, 2006; Li et al., 2016; Loewen et al., 2009), but not for grammatical structures that were not the explicit focus of the lesson (Beretta & Davies, 1985). However, task-based assessments often showed subjects treated with TBLT outperforming PPP groups on task performance (e.g., De Ridder et al., 2007; Beretta & Davies, 1985), while equaling them on accuracy (Burwell et al., 2009; Gonzales-Lloret & Nielson, 2014; Shintani & Ellis, 2010).

14A.2 Research Questions

Acknowledging the need for further research about FonF and grammar acquisition as well as the importance of including online measurements in evaluation studies, the following research questions were formulated.

Is there any difference in terms of effectiveness between TBLT (FonF) and PPP (FonFS) with regard to:

1 the creation of implicit knowledge of grammar?
2 the creation of explicit knowledge of grammar?
3 the performance of real-life tasks?

14A.3 Methodology

A between-group, pretest–posttest design was adopted. The sample of twenty young adult Chinese learners of Italian was randomized into two groups, which performed both online and offline pretests and then were exposed to either a TBLT or a PPP pedagogical treatment. The subjects then did both immediate and delayed posttests, with the same format as the pretests. The relative gains resulting from each treatment were then compared.

The main challenge was to design comparable modules, given that deeply different approaches to grammar teaching had to be applied (Long, 2015; Sasayama, this volume; Gilabert & Malicka, this volume). Specifically, in order to create the pretests and a proper PPP module, a target structure had to be chosen. However, a predetermined grammar target would have contradicted the TBLT principle of a reactive – and therefore largely unpredictable – focus on form. In order to be consistent with the principles of both approaches, a needs analysis was carried out first. Three target tasks were selected and authentic samples of language were collected accordingly. This linguistic material was then analyzed and the target structure for the experiment chosen on the basis of the analysis. Next, the experimental treatments (TBLT and PPP) were created. Details of each step in the procedure are described in the next sections.

14A.3.1 Context and Sample

Participants were Chinese learners of Italian as a second language enrolled in an exchange program (Marco Polo – Turandot) at the University of Pavia. The program involves ten months of twenty hours of language instruction per week in monolingual classes. After this language training, students enroll in bachelor's or master's degrees at Italian universities. At the time of the study, participants had spent six months in Italy and had reached a pre-intermediate proficiency level (A2 according to the CILS, the official certification test for Italian as a second language). Initially, a whole class of twenty students was included in the study, but only half of the students showed up at all of the sessions, so the final sample was composed of ten participants (six women, four men, with an average age of 21). Subjects were randomized in two experimental groups (five subjects per group in the final sample), which were exposed to the PPP and TBLT treatments.

14A.3.2 Needs Analysis

Two questionnaires about communicative needs and difficulties were administered to both the experimental subjects and their tutors. The tutors were Chinese students who have successfully completed the ten-month language training and then enrolled as BA or MA students at the University of Pavia. They are hired to help the Marco Polo – Turandot students deal with university, medical, and public institutions. Therefore, they are selected based on proficiency and integration in Italian society. Moreover, they have already experienced Italian university classes, which makes them especially aware of the linguistic needs their younger colleagues are going to face. Table 14A.1 shows the needs analysis outcome.

Target tasks highly relevant to the sample such as "chatting with Italian friends" and "understanding university lectures" had to be excluded for logistical and methodological reasons. First, acquiring recordings of genuine spontaneous chat among university students was not feasible. When it came to input from university lectures, the Chinese students had many different study areas. Therefore, choosing one of them for the experimental material would have affected the motivation of part of the sample, thus threatening the reliability of results. For these reasons, the three target tasks selected were (1) opening a bank account, (2) changing a mobile tariff plan, and (3) writing formal emails to professors.

14A.3.3 Target Feature

As the focus for the present pilot study was on grammar learning, a target feature needed to be selected. However, in line with TBLT principles, the choice was made not to pick one *a priori* but to extract it from the natural input produced by native speakers while performing the target tasks. Therefore, authentic linguistic material was collected: dialogues in a phone store and a bank were recorded, and email exchanges between university students and professors collected. The language samples were

Table 14A.1 *Needs analysis outcome*

Learners		Tutors	
Chatting with Italian friends	76%	Understanding university lectures	89%
Opening a bank account	61%	Writing formal emails to professors	67%
Changing mobile tariff plan in a shop	69%	Understanding textbooks	52%

analyzed in order to choose the target grammatical structure, which had to meet two main requirements: (1) it had to occur frequently in the input collected, in order for statistical and implicit learning to be possible; and (2) it must not already be part of the explicit knowledge. Third-person clitic pronouns, both direct and indirect, met these requirements and were therefore chosen as target structure for the experiment.

Italian clitic pronouns are known to be problematic even at intermediate levels of proficiency, for a number of reasons. First, they have low salience, because they are monosyllabic and both homographs and homophones of articles. Second, they have a complex morphology, as they need to agree in gender and number with the noun they refer to. Finally, on a syntactic level, second language speakers have difficulty even at advanced levels in choosing between direct and indirect pronouns according to the verb features. Taking into account the proficiency level of the students, only accuracy in gender and number agreement with the noun phrase was tested, while the direct/indirect issue was avoided.

14A.3.4 Treatments

Both the TBLT and the PPP group were exposed to 10 hours of instruction over two weeks, in three 3-hour lessons, plus a 1-hour follow-up.

The PPP treatment followed the presentation–practice–production sequence. The authentic linguistic material collected was transcribed and simplified, and unknown lexical and grammatical items were eliminated and replaced by known structures. Unavoidable vocabulary related to the communicative context was introduced with matching exercises before reading the text. Reading the simplified text was followed by comprehension questions, and then the FonFS activities. The teacher introduced and explicitly explained the grammar rule (presentation). Next, the subjects performed grammar exercises, such as drills and fill-in-the-blank exercises (practice). Finally, they were asked to write a text or to perform a dialogue where the use of the target structure was explicitly required (production). In the event of errors, metalinguistic feedback was provided. Taking into account the texts and the exercises, PPP group students were exposed to a total of fifty occurrences of the target structure.

For the TBLT group, the authentic input recorded was elaborated, not simplified. Low-frequency lexical items and complex grammatical structures were retained, and synonyms and paraphrases added in order to make them comprehensible. Moreover, the target structures were visually enhanced (bolded), in order to make them more salient (Gass et al., 2018; Long 2015; Sharwood Smith 1981, 1993). No lexical focus was conducted out of context before the students read and listened to the input. The lesson focus was always on meaning and content. The pedagogic tasks included information gaps, spotting differences between kinds of bank accounts or cellphone plans (authentic materials from the companies' websites), and matching dialogues with the correct flier among five or six describing special offers (real fliers from the shop and the bank). No explicit information about the grammar rule was provided, unless reactively and in context. The sequence of pedagogic tasks was concluded with a simulation of the target task. Corrective feedback was provided in the form of recasts. The TBLT group encountered thirty-nine occurrences of the target structure.

14A.3.5 Tests

The need to measure linguistic knowledge and skills beyond traditional pencil-and-paper, offline assessment is widely expressed in the literature (e.g., Godfroid & Kim, 2019; Rebuschat, 2013). With the aim of measuring both implicit and explicit knowledge, the experimental subjects were administered three different tests: a self-paced reading (SPR) test, an untimed grammaticality judgment test (UGJT) and an exit task. The exit task was only performed as a posttest. The SPR and UGJT were carried out before the treatment (pretest), right after it (immediate posttest) and then again two weeks later (delayed posttest).

Implicit knowledge was measured by means of an SPR test. Marsden and colleagues (2018: 1) define SPR as "an online computer-assisted research technique in which participants read sentences, broken into words or segments, at a pace they control by pressing a key." A computer software program (in this case, Paradigm) measures the time elapsed between each key-press, (i.e., the time the subject spends on each segment). This time is called reaction time; it is usually measured in milliseconds (ms), and it constitutes the main dependent variable provided by the SPR test. The rationale for analyzing reaction times lies in the premise that cognitive processes take time, and therefore observing how long it takes subjects to respond to stimuli allows inferences about the mechanisms involved in language processing (Jiang 2012). According to the anomaly-detection experimental paradigm, longer reaction times for violations than for correct structures may show implicit sensitivity to errors – i.e., the existence of implicit knowledge of the structure in exam (Keating & Jegerski 2015).

Different features of SPR enable researchers to be reasonably sure that the task taps implicit knowledge, with minimal, if any, involvement of explicit knowledge. First, the SPR task takes place online (i.e., while comprehension is ongoing) and subjects are required to read as fast as possible. This emphasis on the speed of performance and the transient nature of input display make it unlikely learners will use linguistic knowledge consciously in such a short time, which usually amounts to a few hundred milliseconds per segment (Suzuki 2017). Second, the receptive nature of the task does not require any production from the subject, and therefore removes a further reason to tap into explicit knowledge. Third, in a well-designed SPR task, participants read the sentences while focusing on their meaning, because comprehension questions follow each critical item. Therefore, they have no reason to pay conscious attention to language form. Additionally, subjects should not be aware of the linguistic structure the test addresses, which is achieved by adding distracter items.

In the present study, the SPR test consisted of thirty-six trials, including twelve sentences containing the target structure and twenty-four distracters. The test was validated with both native speakers and advanced Chinese learners of Italian as a second language. The validation process showed that simply ungrammatical sentences like example 1 failed to have a significant effect on learners' reaction times. However, semantically inconsistent sentences, such as example 2, did prolong the reaction times of subjects who processed them correctly. Consequently, half of the sentences containing the target structure in the SPR test were of this kind. The inconsistency of the sentences was always due to gender agreement.

(1) Le fragole costano poco, allora la compro.*
    Strawberries are cheap, so I buy it.*

(2) La nonna cucina ottimi biscotti: la mangio sempre.*
    Granny bakes good cookies: I always eat her.*

Sentences were composed of six to eight segments and employed familiar vocabulary and grammatical structures.

With the aim of providing the best conditions for implicit knowledge measurement, the SPR test was performed first, before the offline grammar test. Further, in order to keep subjects focused on meaning, they were required to answer a true/false comprehension question after every two sentences.

After the SPR test, participants performed the UGJT, which was aimed at measuring explicit knowledge of the target structure. It was a pencil-and-paper test consisting of thirty-six sentences, of which twelve contained the target items and twenty-four were distracters. For both the target and the distracter items, half of the sentences were grammatical, while the other half contained a violation. Subjects were required to state whether each sentence was grammatical or ungrammatical. They were not allowed to re-read the sentences or modify any part of the test that they had already completed. No time constraint was imposed.

Four versions of each test (SPR and UGJT) were created. Each target item varied, occurring in grammatical (consistent), ungrammatical (inconsistent), masculine and feminine versions, as shown in example 3. Item order was randomized in the four versions, which were equally distributed in the two experimental groups.

(3) Il treno di Diana è in ritardo, le telefono subito.
    Diana's train is late, I call her right now.

Il treno di Diana è in ritardo, gli telefono subito.*
Diana's train is late, I call it right now.*

La macchina di Carlo è rotta, gli telefono subito.
Carlo's car is broken, I call him right now.

La macchina di Carlo è rotta, le telefono subito.*
Carlo's car is broken, I call it right now.*

Finally, in order for the study to be consistent and comparable with the existing literature, a task-based assessment was included among the posttests. The subjects role-played the three target tasks with the teacher. The dialogue recordings and the formal email were then evaluated by five experienced raters using the functional-adequacy scale (Kuiken et al., 2010; Kuiken & Vedder 2014, 2016; Pallotti 2009).

14A.4 Results and Discussion

All data showed skewed distributions; therefore, nonparametric tests were run, namely, Mann-Whitney tests for independent samples and Wilcoxon signed-rank tests for repeated measures. However, no differences were statistically significant, which is consistent with the pilot nature of the study and its very limited sample size (only five subjects per group). The next sections therefore reports the descriptive statistics for each test, providing a synthesis of participants' behavioral responses. Future studies with a similar design and larger sample sizes are needed to provide more generalizable results.

14A.4.1 Self-paced Reading Test

When dealing with SPR test outcomes, it is informative to look at differences between reaction times to correct items and to violations. Longer reaction times to ungrammatical than to grammatical items are considered a sign of implicit knowledge of the correct form.

In the literature, reaction times related to different segments are taken into account as most informative, depending on the research design. The most relevant and common ones are:

1. the segment containing the target structure
2. the first and/or second following segment(s), where the so-called spill-over effect can be apparent, since the effects of a prolonged processing of the target segment affect reaction times to the following segments
3. the last segment of a sentence (wrap-up).

In relation to the present study design and test trials, the choice was made only to analyze reaction times relative to segments 2 and 3. Target segments (1) were excluded because at that point in the reading, the learners had no cues from which to detect the semantic inconsistency deriving from the grammatical violation (see examples 2 and 3). The spill-over segment (2) following the target item was analyzed, i.e., the first where the violation was apparent. The wrap-up segment (3) is usually avoided in SPR-test analyses because the cognitive act of recalling the whole sentence prolongs its reaction times (Jiang 2012). However, in the present study, violations created semantic inconsistencies affecting the whole sentence; therefore, it seemed reasonable that some effect would become apparent when the learners reached the end of the sentence and recalled its contents as a whole.

Table 14A.2 reports average reaction times for the two experimental groups to consistent and inconsistent sentences in the spill-over and wrap-up segments, during pretest and immediate and delayed posttests.

Outcomes relative to the spill-over segment showed an inconsistent pattern for both experimental groups: reaction times to violations were longer than reaction times to correct items in the pretest, with the difference decreasing or becoming negative after the treatment. Such results suggest that the spill-over segment might not be informative in this kind of test, which is likely due to the behavioral effect of violations not yet being apparent. Indeed, the violations to the target structure resulted in a semantic inconsistency affecting the whole sentence more than single phrases. For this reason, the wrap-up segment is especially informative in this context.

As expected, reaction times for wrap-up segments showed a clearer pattern. No sensitivity to inconsistency was apparent in the pretest, while in the immediate posttest, both groups showed longer reaction times to violation trials than to congruent sentences. This effect is lost in the delayed posttest for the PPP group, but not for subjects exposed to TBLT. Such an outcome is consistent with the widespread notion of meaning-focused activities being more effective than explicit grammar instruction for the creation and retention of implicit knowledge (e.g., Paradis, 2004).

An additional way to look at SPR data is to analyze the grammatical-sensitivity index (GSI; Granena, 2013), which is calculated for each participant by subtracting reaction times to grammatical items from reaction times to ungrammatical items (GSI = ungrammatical reaction time − grammatical reaction time). The rationale underpinning the GSI is that reaction times to violations should be longer than reaction times to correct forms in subjects who have internalized the target structure. Therefore, the stronger the knowledge, the larger the difference between reaction times to violations and correct items (i.e., the index value). Table 14A.3 reports average GSI values for the experimental groups, calculated at pretest and immediate and delayed posttests in both the informative segments.

The GSI values confirmed what emerged from the reaction times: spill-over segment data showed no learning effect. Conversely, according to the wrap-up segment GSI values, both treatments were effective at the

Table 14A.2 SPR test: mean reaction times (standard deviation) to consistent and inconsistent items in the three tests at the spill-over and wrap-up segments

		Pretest (ms)		Immediate posttest (ms)		Delayed posttest (ms)	
		Correct pronoun	Violation	Correct pronoun	Violation	Correct pronoun	Violation
TBLT group	Spill-over	1251 (950)	1414 (1230)	1422 (906)	1589 (1331)	1148 (949)	1268 (687)
	Wrap-up	1602 (1100)	1218 (834)	1390 (962)	1592 (1442)	1197 (837)	1303 (743)
PPP group	Spill-over	1409 (824)	1712 (1077)	1609 (1354)	1515 (1357)	1340 (919)	1572 (1659)
	Wrap-up	1937 (1057)	1689 (1357)	1541 (1313)	1626 (1184)	1646 (1088)	1350 (1214)

Table 14A.3 *GSI values*

	Pretest (ms)		Immediate posttest (ms)		Delayed posttest (ms)	
	Spill-over segment	Wrap-up	Spill-over segment	Wrap-up segment	Spill-over segment	Wrap-up segment
TBLT group	981	-2301	1606	1811	-9	42
PPP group	1822	-1490	1181	2192	58	-379

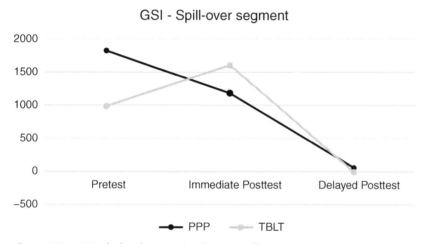

Figure 14A.1 GSI calculated on reaction times to spill-over segments

immediate posttest stage, while most knowledge appeared to have been lost after two weeks, especially in the PPP group (see Figures 14A.1 and 14A.2).

14A.4.2 Untimed Grammaticality Judgment Test

The UGJT is supposed to measure explicit knowledge, because it requires learners to provide metalinguistic information, and because it does not have any time constraint. Such features make it very likely that participants will tap into their explicit knowledge about the grammatical structures involved (Ellis et al., 2009). Table 14A.4 shows the test outcomes for the two groups.

Despite the randomization of the sample, the TBLT group showed lower scores in the pretest, which suggests uneven prior knowledge among the learners. Even so, the gain slope in the two groups is very similar, as clarified in Figure 14A.3, and knowledge seems to have been partially retained after two weeks. Although it is impossible to generalize from

Table 14A.4 *UGJT outcomes: mean scores (SD), k = 12*

	Pretest	Immediate posttest	Delayed posttest
TBLT group	5.4 (2.3)	6.5 (2.2)	6.1 (2.5)
PPP group	6.9 (1.4)	8.1 (1.8)	8.0 (2.1)

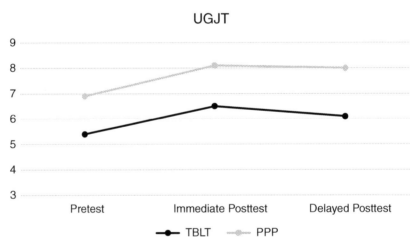

Figure 14A.2 GSI calculated on reaction times to wrap-up segments

Figure 14A.3 UGJT outcomes

these results, it is relevant to point out that reactive and incidental FonF seems to have improved both implicit and explicit grammatical knowledge as much as explicit FonFS.

Table 14A.5 *Functional-adequacy rates (median)*

	Oral tasks	Written task	Total
TBLT group	12	14	14
PPP group	6	13	10

14A.4.3 Exit Tasks

At the end of the treatment sessions, each participant performed a simulation of the target task with the teacher. The tariff-plan and bank-account tasks were performed orally, with the teacher acting as shop assistant and bank clerk. The information provided was based on real-life material collected by the researcher at shops and on the bank website. For the formal-email task, the students were required to write an email to a university professor, communicating prespecified content.

Both the recordings of oral tasks and the email texts were assessed by five experienced raters employing the functional-adequacy scale (Kuiken et al., 2010; Kuiken & Vedder, 2014, 2016; Pallotti, 2009). The functional-adequacy scale assesses four dimensions: content, task requirements, comprehensibility, and coherence-cohesion. Each was rated on a Likert scale of 1–6, so the maximum score for each participant was 24.

Interrater reliability was calculated both for consistency and agreement employing the Intraclass Correlation Coefficient, with a two-way random effects model (Shrout & Fleiss, 1979). Both interrater consistency and interrater agreement resulted acceptable (consistency = .86**; absolute agreement = .76**). Likert-scale scores are ordinal and not interval data, so instead of mean and standard deviation, the median was employed to describe the ratings outcomes (see Table 14A.5).

The TBLT group outperformed the PPP group in the target-tasks simulation, and especially on the oral tasks.

14A.5 Conclusions

The present pilot study was designed to compare the effectiveness of FonF and FonFS on the learning of a grammatical structure. At the same time, the relative effects of TBLT- and PPP-based instruction on learners' ability to perform real-life tasks were assessed.

The limited sample size of this pilot study resulted in statistically nonsignificant findings and makes it inappropriate to generalize results to a wider population. Rather, the intent was to pilot an experimental design tailored to TBLT principles, in order to provide future studies with indications about procedures and likely outcomes. Descriptive statistics were encouraging with regard to the effectiveness of a TBLT module for the improvement of both grammatical knowledge and the performance of real-life tasks.

To address the first research question, an SPR test was administered to assess implicit knowledge before and after the treatment. The most informative segment showed a similar learning pattern in the two groups, with the TBLT group displaying better retention of knowledge on the delayed posttest. The offline test administered to answer the second research question showed a similar pattern. Both groups improved their performance after the treatment, with the variation displaying a similar slope. In this case, the PPP group showed better retention of knowledge on the delayed posttest.

In sum, FonF and FonFS resulted in very similar improvements to both implicit and explicit knowledge. In other words, at the level of the immediate posttests, grammar instruction delivered reactively, in context and mainly implicitly, seemed as effective for this sample as traditional, explicit FonFS. Interestingly, the delayed posttest suggest the possibility that FonF leads to better retention of implicit knowledge and that explicit instruction is related to offline performance. In interpreting these results it is worth pointing out that they were achieved with adult Chinese students, known for their habits and expectations of strongly explicit and grammar-based teaching.

While TBLT and PPP show little differences at the level of grammar learning, this is not the case when it comes to performing a simulation of a real-life task. Indeed, according to the functional-adequacy ratings of target task performance, subjects exposed to the TBLT treatment outperformed the PPP group, especially in the oral tasks (i.e., those requiring online access to language).

These results, albeit requiring confirmation by larger-scale studies, may point to two main conclusions. First, FonF as part of task-based instruction can be as effective as traditional FonFS in improving grammatical knowledge, while better equipping learners for second language performance in real life. Second, it is crucial to measure both implicit and explicit knowledge of language (i.e., to employ both online and offline measurements), since different kinds of language abilities can be developed independently, affected by different pedagogical treatments.

Further Reading

Ellis, N. C. (2001). Memory for language. In P. Robinson, ed. *Cognition and second language instruction*. Cambridge: Cambridge University Press, pp. 33–68.

Ellis, N. C. (2005). At the interface: Dynamic interactions of explicit and implicit language knowledge. *Studies in Second Language Acquisition*, 27, 305–52.

Godfroid, A. and Kim, M. (2021). The contributions of statistical-implicit learning aptitude to implicit-second language knowledge. *Studies in Second Language Acquisition*, 1–29.

Kang, E. Y., Sok, S., and Han, Z-H. (2018). Thirty-five years of ISLA on form-focused instruction: A meta-analysis. *Language Teaching Research*, 23(4), 428–53.

Study Questions

1. To what extent is it useful for a language course to be designed according to a grammatical syllabus?
2. To what extent is it useful for instructors to deal with grammar teaching explicitly during their lessons?
3. Are there factors relative to the learners or the course aims that should be taken into account when answering the previous questions?
4. What are the pros and cons of employing online measurements of language knowledge?

References

Beretta, A. and Davies, A. (1985). Evaluation of the Bangalore Project. *English Language Teaching Journal*, 39, 121–27.

Burwell, G., Gonzalez-Lloret, M., and Nielsen, K. (2009). Evaluating a TBLT Spanish immersion program. Paper presented in the colloquium: Evaluating task-based language programs. Third biannual conference on TBLT. University of Lancaster, September 13–16.

De la Fuente, M. J. (2006). Classroom L2 vocabulary acquisition: investigating the role of pedagogical tasks and form-focused instruction. *Language Teaching Research*, 10, 263–95.

De Ridder, I., Vangehuchten, L., and Sesena Gomez, M. (2007). Enhancing automaticity through task-based language learning. *Applied Linguistics*, 28 (2), 263–95.

Ellis, R., Loewen, S., Elder, C., Erlam, R., Philp, J., and Reinders, H. (2009). *Implicit and explicit knowledge in second language learning, testing and teaching.* Bristol: Multilingual Matters.

Gass, S., Spinner, P., and Behney, J. (2018), eds. *Salience in second language acquisition.* London: Routledge.

Godfroid, A. and Kim, K.M. (2019). *Not aptitude but aptitudeS: examining the relationship between implicit- explicit learning aptitudes and implicit-explicit knowledge.* Paper presented at the 29th conference of the European Second Language Association. Lund University, August 28- 31.

Gonzalez-Lloret, M. and Nielson, K. (2014). Evaluating TBLT: The case of a task-based Spanish program. *Language Teaching Research* 19(5),525–49.

Granena, G. (2013). Individual differences in sequence learning ability and second language acquisition in early childhood and adulthood. *Language Learning* 63(4),665–703.

Jiang, N. (2012). *Conducting reaction time research in second language studies.* New York: Routledge.

Keating, G. D. and Jegerski, J. (2015). Experimental designs in sentence processing research. A methodological review and user's guide. *Studies in Second Language Acquisition*, 37, 1–32.

Kuiken, F., Vedder, I., and Gilabert, R. (2010). Communicative adequacy and linguistic complexity in L2 writing. In I. Bartning, M. Martin, I. Vedder, eds. *Communicative proficiency and linguistic development: Intersections between SLA and language testing research.* Eurosla Monographs Series, pp. 81–100.

Kuiken, F. and Vedder, I. (2014). Rating written performance: What do raters do and why? *Language Testing*, 31(3), 329–48.

Kuiken, F. and Vedder, I. (2016). Functional adequacy in L2 writing: towards a new rating scale. *Language Testing*, 34(3), 321–36.

Li, S., Ellis, R., and Zhu, Y. (2016). Task-based versus task-supported language instruction. An experimental study. *Annual Review of Applied Linguistics*, 36, 205–29.

Loewen, S., Erlam, R., and Ellis, R. (2009). *Implicit and explicit knowledge and second language learning: testing and teaching.* Bristol: Multilingual Matters.

Long, M. (2015). *Second language acquisition and task-based language teaching.* Oxford: Wiley-Blackwell.

Long, M. (2017). Instructed second language acquisition (ISLA): Geopolitics, methodological issues, and some major research questions. *Instructed Second Language Acquisition*, 1, 7–44.

Marsden, E., Thomson, S., and Plonsky, L. (2018). A methodological synthesis of self-paced reading in second language research. *Applied Psycholinguistics*, 39(5),861–904.

Pallotti, G. (2009). CAF: Defining, refining and differentiating constructs. *Applied Linguistics*, 30(4), 590–601.

Paradis, M. (1994). Neurolinguistic aspects of implicit and explicit memory: Implications for bilingualism and SLA. In N. Ellis, ed. *Implicit and explicit language learning.* London: Academic Press, pp. 393–419.

Paradis, M. (2004). *Neurolinguistic Theory of Bilingualism.* Amsterdam: John Benjamins.

Rebuschat, P. (2013). Measuring implicit and explicit knowledge in second language research. *Language Learning* 63(3),595–626.

Sharwood Smith, M. (1993). Input enhancement in instructed SLA: Theoretical bases. *Studies in Second Language Acquisition*, 15, 165–79.

Sharwood-Smith, M. (1981). Consciousness-raising and the second language learner. *Applied Linguistics* 2, 159–68.

Shintani, N. and Ellis, R. (2010). The incidental acquisition of English plural -s by Japanese children in comprehension-based and production-based lessons: A process-product study. *Studies in Second Language Acquisition*, 32 (4),607–37.

Shrout, P. and Fleiss, J. (1979). Intraclass correlations: Uses in assessing rater reliability. *Psychological Bulletin*, 86(2),420–28

Suzuki, Y. (2017). Validity of new measures of implicit knowledge: distinguishing implicit knowledge from automatized explicit knowledge. *Applied Psycholinguistics*, 38, 1229–61.

Whong, M., Gil, H.-G., and Marsden, E. (2014). Beyond paradigm: The 'what' and the 'how' of classroom research. *Second Language Research*, 30 (4),551–68.

14B

Examining High-School Learners' Experience of Task Motivation and Difficulty in a Two-Week Spanish Immersion Camp

Laura Gurzynski-Weiss, Lindsay Giacomino, and Dylan Jarrett

14B.1 Brief Review of Relevant Literature

14B.1.1 Task-Specific Motivation as a Dynamic Process

Dörnyei and Ottó (1998) developed a "process model of L2 [second language] motivation" for task-specific motivation in which they outline three stages of task completion. The first is the *pre-actional phase*, or the phase in which learners make a plan for how they intend to carry out the task. The second is the *actional phase*. This phase sees learners executing the task and carrying out the goals set during the pre-actional phase. The final phase, the *post-actional phase*, occurs after the task is completed and involves learner evaluation of task performance. According to Dörnyei and Ottó (1998), task-specific motivation will fluctuate during these three phases, situating the process model of L2 motivation within a dynamic framework of motivation.

14B.1.2 Correlation between Task-Specific Motivation and Student Engagement

As noted by Torres and Serafini (2016: 292–93), prior empirical work that adopts this model of task-specific motivation had measured learner

We would like to acknowledge Jonathan Caudell, Carlos Heber da Silva Viana, Megan DeCleene, Nofiya Denbaum, Genoveva Di Maggio Ferraro, Jingyi Guo, Juan Manuel Martínez Rodríguez and Enrique Rodríguez Sánchez, who collaborated in the needs analysis and original curriculum design, Carly Carver and Ángel Milla Muñoz, who expanded the design into individual tasks, and Julie Madewell, the SLIC Program Director, who collaborated in countless ways.

motivation during the pre-actional and actional phases of task completion, while no such attention had been paid to the post-actional phase. Studies such as Dörnyei and Kormos (2000), Kormos and Dörnyei (2004), and Yanguas (2011) looked at the correlation between task-specific motivation and learner engagement. Dörnyei and Kormos (2000) found that when English learners completed oral argumentative tasks in dyads, those with higher measures of task-specific motivation also produced a greater number of words and turns. Kormos and Dörnyei (2004), analyzing the same data from their 2000 study, also saw a positive correlation between high task-specific motivation and the production of counterarguments. Yanguas (2011), looking at heritage learners of Spanish completing a writing task, found a positive correlation between task-specific motivation and student engagement, operationalized as positive outlook throughout the task, fewer signs of distraction, and the creation of sub-tasks during the actional phase.

14B.1.3 Task-Specific Motivation and Needs Analysis

Torres and Serafini (2016) addressed two significant gaps in the literature. The first was the consideration of task-specific motivation measures during tasks which were designed following a detailed needs analysis. The researchers designed a Business Spanish course consisting of fourteen target tasks and five exit tasks designed and sequenced based on the perceived frequency and difficulty reported by business professionals and business majors. The second contribution related to Dörnyei and Ottó's (1998) process model of L2 motivation. Task-specific motivation was measured during the post-actional phase of each exit task over the course of the semester, the first time the post-actional phase was considered when measuring task-specific motivation.

The researchers hypothesized that task-specific motivation would be higher overall as a result of the needs analysis which considered the input of domain experts as compared to tasks that were designed only by researcher perceptions. Using a questionnaire that measured student interest, perceived relevance of the task, and satisfaction with performance, it was found that, as hypothesized, task motivation was high overall for all five exit tasks and showed less variability than previous studies without needs analyses.

14B.1.4 The Role of Task Complexity and the Distinction from Task Difficulty

In task-based course designs, pedagogic tasks are sequenced on the basis of their task complexity or difficulty, rather than on their linguistic or grammatical content (Long, 2015; Robinson, 2011; Skehan, 2009). Long (2015) states that while the task syllabus should be drawn from a needs analysis, pedagogic tasks should be the main unit of the syllabus, broken down into a series of smaller tasks sequenced from simpler to increasingly complex. This sequence of pedagogic tasks is scaffolded intentionally, so that the final task in each unit should be as similar as possible to the real-world task identified in the needs analysis.

Two of the most influential models, Robinson (2011) and Skehan (2009), differ in how they operationalize task complexity. Skehan (2009) delineates three factors that contribute to a task's difficulty: code complexity, or the lexical and syntactic difficulty of the input in the task design; cognitive complexity, the processing demands of the task; and communicative stress, which involves the task modality, the number of participants involved, and the time pressure. Robinson's (2011) model, on which we base our categorization, also conceptualizes the sequencing of tasks based on a triad of factors, but uniquely makes a distinction between the task complexity, the conditions under which the task is performed (e.g., with or without planning time), and task difficulty for particular learners (e.g., because of their higher or lower L2 proficiency). Robinson's notion of task complexity relates to the cognitive demands of the task on the learner, with the design of the task to be manipulated to lessen or decrease the learners' cognitive load. Task conditions involve the interaction features of the task, such as participant interaction.

Finally, for Robinson, task difficulty is concerned with the demands a task poses for particular learners, and is distinct from task complexity. Task difficulty is influenced by learners' affective factors (including anxiety and motivation to complete the task) and ability factors (such as aptitude or proficiency). Taking motivation as an example, learners with higher motivation to complete the task at hand may find the task easier to complete than learners with lower motivation, which in turn may result in differential task performance. In this study, we measure the difficulty of each pedagogical task to see how it relates to our researcher/designers' judgement of task complexity and the instructors' perception of task difficulty for their students.

While there are many ways to measure task difficulty, including self-assessment ratings (Robinson, 2001b), dual-task methodology (Révész, Sachs, & Hama, 2014; Révész, Michel, & Gilabert, 2016; Sasayama, 2016), time estimation (Baralt, 2010, 2013), and eye tracking (Révész, Sachs, & Hama, 2014), our selections were based on what would be the most ecologically valid for our domestic immersion program context and the least invasive during student task performance. To this end, we employed a questionnaire at the end of each task in each task cycle, as well as time estimation (i.e., asking students to estimate time on task and comparing their estimation to their actual time on task). These task difficulty methods, and our operationalization of task complexity according to the task design, are explained in Section 14B.3.

14B.2 Our Study

14B.2.1 Participants

The participants in the current study were eight high-school students of Spanish as an L2, three instructors, three activity coordinators, and two residential aids, all of whom were graduate students in the Department of Spanish and Portuguese at the hosting institution. Additionally, the program director participated in providing feedback. The authors of this paper were the director of curricular design, an activity coordinator, and a program instructor.

14B.2.2 Spanish Language Immersion Camp Program

The primary motivation for the creation of this program – the Spanish Language Immersion Camp (SLIC) – was to meet the needs of high-school students learning Spanish who were not able – financially and/or emotionally – to study abroad in a six-week immersion opportunity offered by Indiana University's High School Foreign Language Program. Additionally, Indiana University's program is only open to residents of the state of Indiana. We wished to offer a two-week, domestic program that allowed students an immersive Spanish experience and a chance to sample the Bloomington flagship campus of Indiana University. Research has shown that students who visit a campus are much more likely to attend, and we saw this program creation as both a service to the community and a potential recruiting tool for the Department of Spanish and Portuguese.

Following a needs analysis, the two-week program (ten days of instruction) were designed around five domains: *university life, social/recreation, #adulting, on the job,* and *travel*. As depicted in Figure 14B.1, some of the domains were the focus of more than one day.

Each morning students had three hours of instruction, which consisted of two to three task cycles (Willis, 1996). After each task cycle, students were given a questionnaire to complete, which is explained in detail in

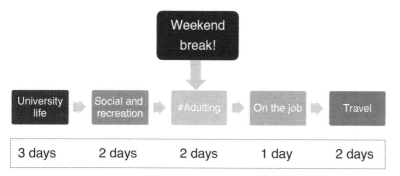

Figure 14B.1 SLIC program design

Section 14B.3. After the morning instructional time, students had lunch, followed by an exit task and extra-curricular activities. Lunchtime discussion topics and extra-curriculars were designed in support of each domain topic and to allow additional preparation for, and extension of, the exit tasks, respectively.

14B.2.3 Research Questions

The research questions for the current study were as follows:

1. How can we describe students' motivation during a two-week Spanish immersion camp for high schoolers?
2. How can we describe these students' experiences of task difficulty during the camp?

14B.3 Procedure and Instruments

To answer our first research question, all eight students completed a micro-evaluation following the completion of each of the three daily tasks for all ten days of instruction, amounting to a total of thirty tasks. Three items targeted task-specific motivation. These items were adapted from Torres and Serafini (2016) and also took into consideration the recommendations of Keller (1994), who posited four factors that affected task-specific motivation: interest, relevance, confidence, and satisfaction. As seen in Figure 14B.2, students were asked to indicate the degree to which they agreed with each of the three statements on a Likert scale of 1 to 5 (1 = not at all interested, 5 = very interested). One statement targeted student interest, one targeted student satisfaction, and one asked students explicitly to rate how motivated they were during task completion.

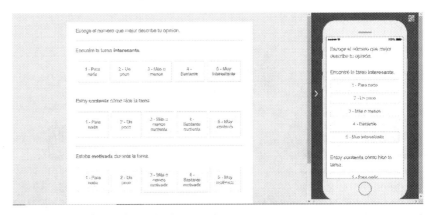

Figure 14B.2 Task-specific motivation questions

> Day 1: University Life – roommates
>
> Are you interested in attending university after graduating high school? Why or why not? What expectations do you have for a roommate? Are you excited to live with another person? Explain your response.
>
> Reflect on your first day at SLIC: think about all you have done both in and out of the classroom. What did you enjoy about the tasks from today? Was there something that you did not enjoy? What are your goals for your two weeks at SLIC? Explain your response.

Figure 14B.3 Example of a reflective journal prompt

Students also completed nightly reflective journals in which they responded to a prompt related to the theme of that day, as well as questions pertaining to their use of Spanish during their daily interactions and their experience with the tasks of the day. A sample prompt is shown in Figure 14B.3.

For the second research question, all eight students provided data on task difficulty and time estimation, asked immediately following the task-specific motivation, as explained above for research question 1. Three items in the survey measured task difficulty through a self-assessment of task difficulty and time estimation. The questionnaire items were developed following similar questionnaires in Robinson (2001b) and Sasayama (2016) and measured both perceived task difficulty and mental effort exerted. Students completed the following statements, presented in Spanish: (a) "I think this task was ... (difficulty assessment)," and (b) "This task required ... (effort assessment)." Students selected their responses via Likert scales ranging from 1 (very easy/no effort) to 5 (very difficult/extreme effort), with each number operationalized. A sample questionnaire is shown in Figure 14B.4.

After completing each task and rating the difficulty and their effort, students were asked to estimate the time they had spent on the task. Following similar protocols in Baralt (2010, 2013) and Sasayama (2016), students were asked, "How long did you take to complete the task?" and estimated their time in minutes. Given that students completed these assessments regularly after each task, it can be assumed that they knew in advance that they would be asked to assess their time on task after completing each task. Therefore, the students completed a prospective (rather than a retrospective) time estimation, which carries important implications for what shorter or longer time estimations – in comparison to actual time on task – means for how students view the complexity of the task. Prospective time estimation here, for example, hypothesizes that increased task demands lead to shorter estimated time on task. If the time estimation were retrospective (i.e., students were not expecting to estimate their time on task and had to recall it from memory), shorter time

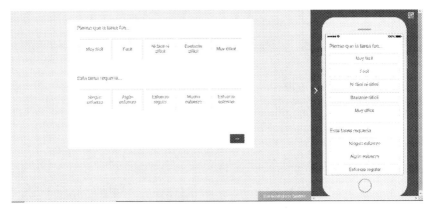

Figure 14B.4 Task difficulty questions

estimations would imply the opposite: that the task was perceived as easier by the student.

14B.4 Analysis

14B.4.1 Motivation

Mean Likert ratings were calculated for each of the tasks, in order to see (a) how task-specific motivation varied by day, and (b) how it varied by domain. Additionally, the nightly reflective journals were analyzed for student comments pertaining to the daily tasks, as well as interactions in Spanish, to provide insight into any spikes or dips in individual student measures of task-specific motivation.

14B.4.2 Complexity

Mean Likert ratings were calculated for each of the tasks, in order to see (a) global measures of task difficulty by day and domain, and (b) measures of difficulty by individual task. Afterwards, for each of the thirty tasks, students' time estimation was compared to the actual group time on task, as measured by the instructors.

In order to measure the researchers' (task designers') operationalization of task complexity in the curriculum, we used the bottom-up evaluation methods employed by Révész and Gurzynski-Weiss in their (2016) study of teachers' assessments of task difficulty. With each day divided into three tasks designed by the researchers to increase in complexity, we examined which factors emerged from the task design (see Figure 14B.5). These operationalizations of task complexity were compared to students' and teachers' perceptions of task difficulty to see if tasks were indeed scaffolded the way they were intended.

14B.5 Results and Discussion

14B.5.1 Motivation: Post-task Questionnaires

We first calculated mean Likert ratings for task-specific motivation by domain, seen in Table 14B.1.

The domain rated highest in terms of task-specific motivation was *recreation* ($\mu = 4.26$) and the lowest was *university life* ($\mu = 3.89$). *University life* also showed the most variability, with a standard deviation of .91. The *on the job* domain was also at the lower end in terms of motivation ($\mu = 3.95$), while *travel* was on the higher end ($\mu = 4.19$). Finally, *#adulting* was in the middle ($\mu = 4.06$). Importantly, none of the domains fell below a 3.5 rating, the lowest being 3.89. Based on the operationalization of our Likert scale, this means that no domain average fell below "*somewhat* interesting/satisfied/motivated" with three out of the five falling between "*pretty* interesting/satisfied/motivated" and "*very* interesting/satisfied/motivated." Much like Torres and Serafini (2016), we attribute this to the fact that tasks in each domain were designed following a detailed needs analysis.

Given that each domain spanned multiple days (with the exception of *on the job*) and between six and nine tasks, we also examined the average ratings by day, in order to see how motivation varied throughout the program. These results are presented in Table 14B.2.

Among the highest rated days were Day 4 ($\mu = 4.38$) within the *recreation* domain, Day 10 ($\mu = 4.22$) within the *travel* domain and Day 6 ($\mu = 4.19$) within

Table 14B.1 *Average ratings (standard deviation) for all students (n = 8) by domain*

	Domain				
	University life	Recreation	#Adulting	On the job	Travel
Mean (SD)	3.89 (.91)	4.26 (.72)	4.06 (.66)	3.95 (.57)	4.19 (.66)

Factors making a task less complex	Factors making a task more complex
• Model or template provided	• No model or template provided
• Planning time	• No planning time
• Closed task outcome (one solution)	• Open task outcome (multiple solutions)
• Decision alone/working alone	• Convergent decisions among student pairs/groups
• No reasoning demands	
• Few elements to consider	• Reasoning demands
• Familiar linguistic structure in the input	• Many elements to consider
	• Unfamiliar linguistic structure in the input

Figure 14B.5 Elements of task complexity

Table 14B.2 Average ratings (standard deviation) for all students (n = 8) by day

	Domain									
	University life		Recreation		#Adulting		On the job		Travel	
	Day 1	Day 2	Day 3	Day 4	Day 5	Day 6	Day 7	Day 8	Day 9	Day 10
Mean (SD)	3.88 (.85)	3.65 (1.09)	4.13 (.70)	4.38 (.68)	4.14 (.73)	4.19 (.76)	3.94 (.55)	3.95 (.57)	4.16 (.63)	4.22 (.70)

Table 14B.3 *Daily exit tasks for each domain of the immersion program*

	Domain				
	University life	Recreation	#Adulting	On the job	Travel
Tasks	• Find suitemates • Deliver an academic presentation • Meet with an academic advisor	• Write a restaurant review • Plan a group get together	• Grocery shopping • Healthy habits plan	• Carry out a job interview	• Pack a suitcase • Navigate a new city

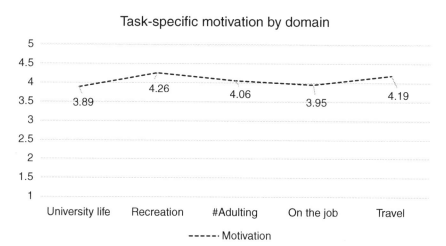

Figure 14B.6 Average ratings for all students (n = 8) by domain

the *#adulting* domain. The only days to fall below a 4.00 rating were Day 2 (μ = 3.65) and Day 1 (3.88) in the *university life* domain, Day 7 (μ = 3.94) in the *#adulting* domain and Day 8 (μ = 3.95), the only day in the *on the job* domain. The exit tasks for each of these domains can be found in Table 14B.3.

The results by both domain and day are represented graphically in Figures 14B.6 and 14B.7, in order better to see the changes in motivation over the course of the two weeks. Importantly, by analyzing the data by day, we are able to see that not every day of the *university life* domain was the least motivating during our program. Day 3 actually saw ratings above 4.00. It would appear that Day 2, specifically, was largely responsible for the lower motivation ratings seen for this domain. In the following section, we turn to our second data source to better understand why certain days were less motivating.

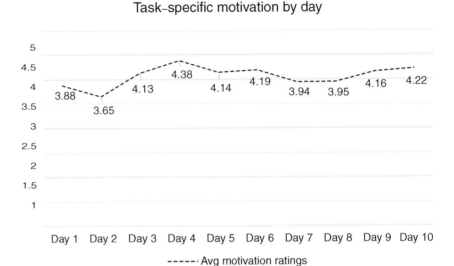

Figure 14B.7 Average ratings for all students (n = 8) by day

14B.5.2 Motivation: Reflective Journals

In order to better understand the patterns in the questionnaire data, we analyzed the nightly reflective journals with particular attention paid to days where motivation was highest or lowest.

Less Motivating Days

The following quotes were pulled from Days 1, 2, 7, and 8, the four days with average ratings below 4.00. Quotes are divided by theme.

Anxiety:

> "I didn't like presenting my work in front of the class."
> "I felt nervous each time I spoke."

Difficulty:

> "The tasks today were very difficult."
> "[The tasks] were difficult because I don't know a lot of medicine vocabulary."
> "I had problems during my interview when I couldn't think of particular words."
> "[The interview] was difficult when I couldn't remember the entire question and I didn't know how to respond."

Low satisfaction:

> "Today I think I did well, but I should try to do better."
> "I did poorly because I mentioned negative things that I can't do. I also said things that don't benefit anyone when they are working."

"I don't think I was successful, but I was close."

Low enjoyment:

"I don't like doing activity after activity after activity"
"I liked the tasks today, but they weren't my favorite."

More Motivating Days

The quotes for this section were pulled from Days 4 and 6, the two most motivating days of the two weeks. These quotes are also divided by theme.

Preparedness:

"I had a lot of confidence when ordering my food."
"The task before prepared me for my interactions when ordering food."

Low difficulty:

"Ordering was easier than I expected."

High satisfaction:

"I was successful ordering and interacting with the waiter."
"I'm very impressed with myself."

Enjoyment:

"I had a lot of fun in the restaurant; it was very interesting."
"It was fun speaking with the waiter only in Spanish."
"I felt more relaxed and I wasn't as stressed (speaking Spanish)."

Overall, the journals confirmed the importance of the four factors posited by Keller (1994): themes of interest, satisfaction, confidence, and relevance were present in several of the journal entries. In particular, it was seen in the journals that level of task interest and performance satisfaction patterned with levels of motivation, (i.e., lack of interest/low satisfaction led to lower motivation, high interest /high satisfaction led to higher motivation). Difficulty was another crucial factor affecting motivation. The difficulty of the job interviews on Day 8, for example, led to lower ratings of motivation.

Another important finding from the journal analysis were several comments that spoke to the motivating nature of task-based language teaching. Students regularly described tasks as "applicable," "important," and "different," with one student saying the tasks were "non-repetitive," and another saying that they were "more efficient than a textbook."

14B.5.3 Task Difficulty: Post-task Questionnaires

For task difficulty, we first considered the mean Likert ratings for perceived task difficulty and mental effort by domain, the results for which are presented in Table 14B.4.

Table 14B.4 *Average task difficulty/mental effort ratings for all students (n = 8) by domain*

	Domain				
	University life	Recreation	#Adulting	On the job	Travel
Difficulty mean (SD)	2.99 (1.03)	2.44 (.85)	2.79 (.99)	3.17 (.96)	2.71 (.65)
Mental effort mean (SD)	3.19 (.83)	2.77 (.75)	2.79 (.9)	3.08 (.93)	2.83 (.69)

The domain perceived as the most difficult overall was *on the job* ($\mu = 3.17$), and the domain perceived as easiest was *recreation* ($\mu = 2.44$). *University life*[1] also showed the most variability, with a standard deviation of 1.03, although the results for *#adulting* and *on the job* are similarly varied. *On the job* was also at the higher end of perceived difficulty ($\mu = 3.17$) while *travel* and *#adulting* were on the lower end ($\mu = 2.71$ and $\mu = 2.79$, respectively). These results pattern similarly with the patterns uncovered in the motivation by domain analysis from the previous section.

All of the average domain ratings fall between 2 and slightly above 3 points on the Likert scale. Based on the operationalization of our scale, this means that all domains were between "*easy*" and "*neither easy nor difficult.*" We take these scores to indicate that our tasks were designed at an appropriate level for students to engage with in each case, although adequate task sequencing can only be determined by the day level, presented in Table 14B.5.

The days rated as having the highest difficulty were Day 8 ($\mu = 3.17$) within the *on the job* domain, Day 7 ($\mu = 3.13$) within the *#adulting* domain, and Day 1 ($\mu = 3.13$) within the *university life* domain. The tasks for each of these domains can be found in Figures 14B.8–10.

The results by both domain and day are also represented graphically in Figures 14B.11 and 14B.12, in order better to see the changes in difficulty over the course of the two weeks. We see that while Day 1 of the program was initially somewhat difficult, overall perceived task difficulty generally decreased over the course of the week, increasing only on Days 7 and 8, when learners were asked to complete tasks that were not as applicable to their immediate lives.

14B.6 Conclusions and Future Directions

This study examined learners' task-specific motivation and experiences of task difficulty as a way of evaluating whether or not the task-based Spanish program functioned as designed. Overall, we found the program, designed

---

[1] While not the focus of this report, it is interesting to note that the greatest amount of perceived mental effort exerted occurred in the first domain, *university life* ($\mu = 3.19$). This may have been because it was the learners' first experience with tasks. This will be further explored in future analyses.

Table 14B.5 Average task difficulty/mental effort ratings for all students (n = 8) by day

	University life		Recreation		#Adulting		On the job	Travel	
	Day 1	Day 2	Day 3	Day 4	Day 5	Day 6	Day 7	Day 8	Day 9	Day 10
Difficulty Mean (SD)	3.13 (1.08)	3.04 (1.00)	2.79 (1.02)	2.33 (.76)	2.54 (.93)	2.46 (.88)	3.13 (.99)	3.17 (.96)	2.58 (.58)	2.83 (.70)
Mental Effort Mean (SD)	3.08 (.83)	3.50 (.88)	3.00 (.72)	2.79 (.66)	2.75 (.85)	2.58 (.88)	3.00 (.88)	3.08 (.93)	2.83 (.64)	2.83 (.76)

Target task: Students find and interview potential suitemates

Find a roommate (Simple)	Create a roommate contract (Complex)	Find suitemates (More complex)
Planning time: Write interview questions beforehand **Few elements** **Two participants** **Reasoning demands**	**Planning time:** Written mode **Many elements:** Added roommate complication **Two participants** **Reasoning demands**	**No planning time:** Instant response needed **Many elements:** compiling all information for interview **Four Participants** **Reasoning demands**

Figure 14B.8 Day 1 design (University life: "finding suitemates")

Target task: Students record video on healthy habits for college

Visit a doctor (Simple)	Create a healthy habits plan (Complex)	Make video (More complex)
Task outcome: Closed (One solution: diagnosis) **Two students** **Modality:** Oral	**Planning time:** Time to outline **Task outcome:** open **Many elements:** long list of requirements **Four students** **Modality:** Written	**No planning time** **Task outcome:** Open **Many elements** **Four students** **Modality:** Oral

Figure 14B.9 Day 7 design (#Adulting: "Healthy habits plan")

Target task: Students participate in job interview with activity coordinators

Choose a job (Simple)	Create a resume (Complex)	Carry out job interview (More complex)
Planning time: students write down questions about job **Modality:** Written **Task outcome:** Open **No prior knowledge** **Model provided**	**Some planning time:** Little amount of time for resume creation **Modality:** Written **Task outcome:** Open **No prior knowledge** **Model provided**	**No planning time:** Real-time interview **Interaction:** Equal (partner practice) to non-equal (coordinators) **Modality:** Oral **Task outcome:** Open **No prior knowledge** **Model provided**

Figure 14B.10 Day 8 design (On the job: "Carry out a job interview")

following a needs analysis, to be motivating in a domestic immersion context. It was also found that learners' experience with task difficulty was, with few exceptions, aligned with our intended designs of task

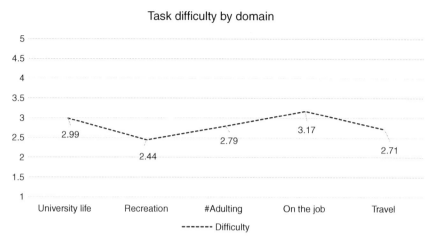

Figure 14B.11 Average difficulty ratings for all students (n = 8) by domain

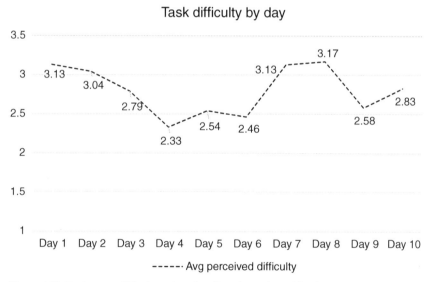

Figure 14B.12 Average difficulty ratings for all students (n = 8) by day

complexity. We used this information, as designed and collected within the program, to inform our decisions when making modest adjustments to the second iteration of the program. As all eight learners rated the inaugural iteration a 5/5 and said they would recommend it highly, the changes we make will be minimal.

In terms of changes based on the motivation data collected, we will be particularly prepared for the first-day challenge (i.e., explain the benefits of task-based language teaching to the students and provide greater than average positive feedback and encouragement). We are also considering just how far into the future students should project. For example, the *university* domain was motivating (more immediate future), whereas the *on the job* day was perhaps too far away (distal future) and/or needed to be spread over two days; we plan to reduce one of the *on the job* tasks and have students focus on an immediately applicable summer internship rather than a future career.

In terms of program changes we are considering based on task difficulty data, we will add a question requiring students to explain/justify their rating. We are also considering asking students to relate their perception of difficulty to their motivation (i.e., yes/the difficulty motivated me; yes/the difficulty demotivated me; no the difficulty didn't relate to my motivation). Most importantly, we will explicitly talk to students during orientation, explaining that how they engage with the program makes a difference, citing evidence from the pilot year as to how, regardless of incoming proficiency, etc., participants can have measurable gains if they honor their Spanish-only contract and persist through difficult moments.

In terms of future research directions, we will examine the information collected on individual differences in depth to see if patterns emerge and if they may further explain fluctuations in task-specific motivation. We will also compare how teachers perceived student difficulty and mental effort and what students report. Finally, we will unpack the ID data in general, particularly examining gains in proficiency alongside the data presented here.

Further Reading

Dörnyei, Z. and Ottó, I. (1998). Motivation in action: A process model of L2 motivation. *Working Papers in Applied Linguistics*, 4, 43–69.

Révész, A. and Gurzynski-Weiss, L. (2016). Teachers' perspectives on second language task difficulty: Insights from think-alouds and eye tracking. *Annual Review of Applied Linguistics*, 36, 182–204.

Robinson, P. (2011). Second language task complexity, the Cognition Hypothesis, language learning, and performance. In P. Robinson, ed., *Researching task complexity: Task demands, task-based language learning, and performance*. Amsterdam: John Benjamins, pp. 3–38.

Sasayama, S. (2016). Is a 'complex' task really complex? Validating the assumption of cognitive task complexity. *Modern Language Journal*, 100, 231–54.

Skehan, P. (2009). A Framework for the implantation of task-based instruction. In K. Van den Branden, M. Bygate, and J. Norris, eds., *Task-based language teaching*. Amsterdam: John Benjamins.

Torres, J. and Serafini, E. J. (2016). Micro-evaluating learners' task-specific motivation in a task-based business Spanish course. *Hispania*, 99(2), 289–304.

Study Questions

1. How do learners experience task difficulty in your language program? How does this differ from teacher perceptions and the program design?
2. How motivating are the lessons used in your language program? What data can you collect to evaluate and increase learners' task-specific motivation?
3. How do additional individual differences play a role in learners' task-specific motivation and perception of task difficulty?
4. Do learners' task-specific motivation and/or perception of task difficulty relate to proficiency gains?

References

Baralt, M. L. (2010). Task complexity, the Cognition Hypothesis, and interaction in CMC and FTF environments. Unpublished doctoral dissertation. Georgetown University, Washington DC.

Baralt, M. L. (2013). The impact of cognitive complexity on feedback efficacy during online versus face-to-face interactive tasks. *Studies in Second Language Acquisition*, 35, 689–725.

Candlin, C. N. (1987). Towards task-based language learning. In C. N. Candlin and D. Murphy, eds. *Language learning tasks*. Englewood Cliffs, NJ: Prentice Hall, pp. 5–22

Dörnyei, Z. and Kormos, J. (2000). The role of individual and social variables in performance. *Language Teaching Research*, 4(3), 275–300.

Dörnyei, Z. and Ottó, I. (1998). Motivation in action: A process model of L2 motivation. *Working Papers in Applied Linguistics*, 4, 43–69.

Keller, J. M. (2008). First principles of motivation to learn and e3-learning. *Distance Education*, 29(2), 175–85.

Kormos, J. and Dörnyei, Z. (2004). The Interaction of Linguistic and Motivational Variables in Second Language Task Performance. *Zeitschrift für Interkulturellen Fremdsprachenunterrichte*, 9(2), 1–21.

Long, M. H. (2015). *Second language acquisition and task-based teaching*. Oxford: Wiley-Blackwell.

Révész, A. and Gurzynski-Weiss, L. (2016). Teachers' perspectives on second language task difficulty: Insights from think-alouds and eye tracking. *Annual Review of Applied Linguistics*, 36, 182–204.

Révész, A., Michel, M., and Gilabert, R. (2016). Measuring cognitive task demands using dual-task methodology, subjective self-ratings, and expert judgements: A validation study. *Studies in Second Language Acquisition*, 38, 703–37.

Révész, A., Sachs, R., and Hama, M. (2014). The effects of task complexityand input frequency on the acquisition of the past counterfactual construction through recasts. *Language Learning*, 64, 615–50.

Robinson, P. (2001b). Task complexity, task difficulty, and task production: Exploring interactions in a componential framework. *Applied Linguistics*, 22, 27–57.

Robinson, P. (2011). Second language task complexity, the Cognition Hypothesis, language learning, and performance. In P. Robinson, ed. *Researching task complexity: Task demands, task-based language learning and performance*. Amsterdam: John Benjamins, pp. 3–38.

Sasayama, S. (2016). Is a 'complex' task really complex? Validating the assumption of cognitive task complexity. *Modern Language Journal*, 100, 231–54.

Skehan, P. (2009). A Framework for the implantation of task-based instruction. In K. Van den Branden, M. Bygate, and J. Norris, eds. *Task-based language teaching*. Amsterdam: John Benjamins, pp. 83–108.

Torres, J. and Serafini, E. J. (2016). Micro-evaluating learners' task-specific motivation in a task-based business Spanish course. *Hispania*, 99(2), 289–304.

Willis, J. (1996). *A framework for task-based learning*. Vol. 60. Harlow: Longman.

Yanguas, I. (2011). The dynamic nature of motivation during the task: Can it be captured? *Innovation in Language Learning and Technology*, 5(1), 35–61.

14C

Designing a Classroom-Based Task-Based Language Assessment Framework for Primary Schools

Blurring the Lines between Teaching, Learning, and Assessment

Koen Van Gorp

14C.1 Introduction

Task-based language assessment (TBLA) subscribes to a "can do" approach to language assessment by assessing, as directly as possible, whether language learners can perform specific language tasks in meaningful communicative settings. However, classroom-based TBLA can enable teachers to do more than acknowledge whether students have performed a specific task successfully. Task-based assessments have the potential to provide teachers with rich, useful information about students' progress in performing target tasks, and help them provide quality feedback to scaffold and advance students' learning. In order to reach its didactic potential, TBLA can rely on an assessment framework (exemplified in this case study) that generates rich and useful information to support in-class learning and inform teaching. By integrating a TBLA framework in a task-based language teaching (TBLT) curriculum, the use of tasks for assessment purposes and the use of assessment tasks for learning purposes becomes central to a task-based language pedagogy. Classroom-based TBLA has the potential to be a strong example of learning-oriented assessment, an approach that acknowledges the interrelationship between teaching, assessment, and learning (Turner & Purpura, 2015; Jones & Saville, 2016).

This case study focuses on the design of an assessment framework for a task-based language syllabus for both first language (L1) and second language (L2) speakers in Flemish primary education. It describes the choices a team of syllabus designers made with respect to task specifications, assessment criteria and teacher support and feedback guidelines. The case study further illustrates how an integral TBLT-TBLA approach can serve as a "bridge" between teaching and learning (Colby-Kelly & Turner, 2007).

14C.2 Setting the Scene: A Task-Based Language Syllabus for Primary Schools

14C.2.1 Valuable Lessons Learned from Implementing Task-Based Language Teaching in the 1990s

In 2005, the Centre for Language and Education at KU Leuven in Belgium was given the opportunity to create a new task-based syllabus for primary schools in Flanders and Brussels, called "TotemTaal." This opportunity provided it with a chance to put the valuable lessons it learned developing and implementing its first task-based syllabus "De Toren van Babbel" (a pun on the tower of Babel, "Babbel" being informal Dutch for "talking") into practice, and create a TBLT curriculum that would be a better fit with teacher expectations and teaching practices in Flanders.

The first TBLT syllabus was developed between 1992 and 1995, and implemented from 1995 onward (for a description, see Colpin & Van Gorp 2007). "De Toren van Babbel" provided a clear shift from a teacher-centered to a learner-centered syllabus (Van Avermaet, Colpin, Van Gorp, Bogaert & Van den Branden, 2006). Teachers and other stakeholders, like school advisors and principals, reported students being enthusiastic and motivated to perform the language tasks in the syllabus. However, over time, the adoption of the task-based methodology by the teachers was less successful (Van den Branden, 2006b; Colpin & Van Gorp, 2007). Most teachers adapted the motivating and challenging tasks to fit their more traditional teaching methods (see also Berben, Van den Branden & Van Gorp, 2007). In a 2005 study into perceptions and actions of seventy-three primary school teachers who used De Toren van Babbel, teachers indicated that they found the goals of the tasks insufficiently concrete and clear, and that the syllabus guidelines did not provide them with enough support to provide useful feedback on students' task performances and language development (François, 2005).

As a result of the study and accumulated experiences in the field, the syllabus design team for TotemTaal decided to address four challenges in creating a new, updated TBLT syllabus for Flemish primary education (Colpin & Van Gorp, 2007: 206):

1. Define clear and specific task goals
2. Provide a well-balanced collection of tasks which gradually increase in complexity

3. Integrate teacher and learner support in the teaching manual and provide differentiation guidelines
4. Assess tasks in such a way that both teachers and students can trace language development across tasks.

14C.2.2 Developing a New Task-Based Language Teaching Syllabus for Primary Schools

TotemTaal is a task-based, Dutch-language syllabus for Dutch-medium primary schools in Belgium (Berben et al., 2007a). The syllabus encompasses listening, speaking, reading, writing, spelling, and language-awareness tasks for both L1 and L2 speakers from Grade 2 to 6. In Flemish primary education, L1 Dutch speakers and L2 Dutch learners (i.e., students who mainly speak a language other than the language of instruction at home) share a classroom and are taught the same curriculum.

The syllabus was developed from 2005 to 2008 by a team of professional task-based syllabus designers at the Centre for Language and Education. It was commissioned by a commercial publisher and Priority Policy Brussels, a non-profit educational network of school advisors responsible for the support of Dutch-medium primary schools in the Brussels-Capital Region of Belgium (Devlieger & Goossens, 2007). This support was provided by school advisors, each of them working closely with six to seven primary schools. From the start, primary school teachers and school advisors from Priority Policy Brussels were involved in the development of TotemTaal as members of a feedback and pilot group.

The curriculum of TotemTaal focused on acquiring the language of schooling or the academic register as stated in the attainment targets or official standards dictated by the Flemish Department of Education. These Dutch-language standards consist of language-proficiency and language-awareness goals to be attained within the language arts program at the end of Grade 6 by L1 Dutch speakers and L2 Dutch learners. The number of L2 speakers in the Flemish educational system varies according to region (Flemish vs. Brussels-Capital Region) and areas (rural vs. urban). In the 2017–2018 school year, on average 18.5 percent of the students in primary education in Flanders were L2 learners; in the Brussels-Capital Region the average was 72.7 percent (Lokale Inburgerings- en Integratiemonitor, 2019). In Flanders, L2 Dutch learners are predominantly found in the cities. For example, in the 2017–2018 school year, the average percentage of L2 learners in Antwerp (the largest city in Flanders) was 44.8 percent, and in Ghent (the second largest city in Flanders), it was 33 percent (Lokale Inburgerings- en Integratiemonitor, 2019). In these cities most L2 learners are located in a small number of schools with large populations of Dutch learners: from 50 percent to more than 90 percent.

Despite the heterogeneity of the classes, the standards and the curriculum are the same for L1 and L2 speakers. Therefore, TotemTaal focused on language learning principles that apply for all learners having to learn the language of schooling. However, the syllabus created opportunities for differentiation and remediation for struggling L1 and L2 speakers based on the task-specification and assessment framework.

14C.3 Toward a Classroom-Based Task-Based Language Assessment Framework

In classroom-based language assessment, summative assessment or assessment *of* learning (e.g., for reporting purposes) is often distinguished from formative assessment or assessment *for* learning (e.g., for diagnostic purposes or to support students' ongoing learning processes; Rea-Dickins, 2006). Additionally, assessment is also about teaching; it is about teachers questioning the impact of their teaching on the basis of their students' assessment results (Hattie & Yates 2014). Recently, assessment specialists and educators have been promoting learning-oriented assessment as an approach to align instruction, assessment and learning and a way "in which teachers and learners can make use of assessments and capitalize on the generated information to guide and support the learning process" (Turner & Purpura, 2015: 255). A task-based approach is well placed to unite and integrate assessment *of* and *for* learning, as well as inform teachers about their teaching, and to become a model of learning-oriented assessment in the classroom.

In TBLT, students acquire language by performing authentic, meaning-oriented language tasks that have a clear and motivating goal (Van den Branden, 2006a). Tasks constitute the central unit of analysis for teaching and learning. They are essential pedagogic constructs that "drive" classroom activity (Samuda & Bygate, 2008), as well as targeted learning outcomes. As a critical component of TBLT, TBLA assesses whether, and how well, language learners can perform specific language tasks in meaningful communicative settings (Van Gorp & Deygers, 2014). Task-based assessments aim to simulate or reproduce key characteristics of communication tasks as they occur outside of the assessment context, such as participants and audience, purpose, communicative strategies, and language use (Norris & East, this volume). Through students' performances on tasks, teachers are able to gauge and, consequently, promote students' language development and growth holistically, as well as on a wide range of language dimensions, aspects, and features (Norris, 2016). This capability provides TBLA with a huge advantage over the more traditional testing of language as discrete items (predominantly grammatical and lexical) that is often used for achievement purposes, particularly when teachers want to use classroom-based assessment to monitor language growth and support students' language learning. However, assessing language learning and growth is by no means a simple task (Norris, 2016). This advantage can only be realized if TBLA enables teachers to interpret successful task performance in all its aspects, and provide useful quality feedback that can be used and acted upon by students to improve future task performances. Norris (2009: 587) states that TBLA has to provide "frameworks for tracking and interpreting important aspects of learner development over time." For Norris, this means that teachers should be made aware of task specifications, of expected task performance, and of task performance strategies, so they can help learners improve their performance. This links up with Harding, Alderson, and Brunfaut's (2015: 333) recent observation that "task-based language teaching pedagogy will need to identify a way to merge discrete diagnostic information with a holistic, task-outcome-focused approach."

Consequently, for teaching and assessment purposes, tasks should be conceptualized as a set of characteristics rather than holistic entities (Bachman, 2002). These characteristics will be inherent to the task itself but will also relate to learner characteristics. Task performance yields information about the interaction between learners and tasks in context, and it is precisely this information that teachers need to assess students' ability to perform target tasks, as well as their progress, and to formulate feedback that students can act upon in their next task performance. The potential strength of a theoretically sound, interpretive framework based on task specifications and expectations is that it allows for a symbiotic relationship or encourages the "deep connection" (Norris & East, this volume) between teaching, learning, and assessment, and, thereby, positions TBLA as a clear example of learning-oriented assessment. Considering that, "[u]ltimately, language learning does not depend on a few 'super moments,' but on thousands of interactional moments" (Van den Branden, 2010: 296), assessment can and should also not be limited to a handful of these "super moments," nor should it be the responsibility of the teacher as the sole stakeholder. Assessment tasks should function as much as possible as learning tasks (Carless, 2007) and, likewise, all learning tasks should be considered assessment tasks (Van Gorp & Deygers, 2014), that is, opportunities to evaluate students' language use and growth. Furthermore, classroom-based language assessment should also encompass alternative assessment components (e.g., observations, portfolios, and peer and self-assessment) in which all major stakeholders (teacher, learners, and peers) share the responsibility to assess task performances, and provide and respond to useful feedback. By involving all stakeholders and allowing every task to become a space for spontaneous or planned assessment and feedback, TBLA will help blur the lines between instruction, assessment, and learning.

14C.4 Meeting the Challenge: Designing a Task-Based Language Assessment Framework for TotemTaal

14C.4.1 Designing a Task-Specification Framework

To meet the four challenges described above and meet the needs of teachers teaching very heterogeneous student populations, the TotemTaal team designed a task-specification framework that would constitute the backbone of the TBLT syllabus and help teachers monitor and promote language learning.

The starting point of the task-based syllabus were the official attainment goals (Departement Onderwijs, 1998) and the curricula and timetables developed by the three major "educational networks" in Flanders (community education, subsidized, publicly run schools, and subsidized, privately run schools). These curricula are the instructional directives that schools must follow, while the attainment goals are the official standards that every pupil has to achieve at the end of Grade 6 (see Figure 14C.1).

Based on the attainment goals and the educational networks' curricula, target tasks were identified. For example, a target task capturing standard in Figure 14C.1 would be reading an informational text with the aim of selecting and ordering information according to a personal or a given criterion. Next, target tasks were addressed by a series of pedagogic tasks sequenced according to complexity. For example, students could be given illustrated cards describing different games and be asked to identify which game they would like to play in class and why. A more complex pedagogic task would be reading an informational text on different outdoor and indoor games, in order to identify a game that could be played both outdoors and indoors (depending on the weather), taking into account certain criteria for playing the game indoors and outdoors. Next, students could read a longer informational text on children's games in Ancient Egypt and decide which game would still be interesting for children today, based on their own criteria and criteria found in another informational text on successful present-day games for children. For students to learn to perform the target tasks linked to the standards, several encounters with relevant

---

Information level = structuring (i.e., being able to order the information in a text in a personal and clear way)

The students can order information in level- and age-appropriate (a) school and study texts and activity instructions; and (b) stories, novels, dialogues, poems, journals and encyclopedias.

Figure 14C.1 Extract from the Flemish attainment goals for reading proficiency (Departement Onderwijs, 1998)[1]

---

[1] Figures 14C.1 and 14C.3, as well as Tables 14C.1 and 14C.2, were originally published in Van Gorp (2018).

types of pedagogic tasks varying in degrees of complexity are necessary, in order to build up the linguistic abilities required for more difficult target-task performances. Therefore, tasks of the same task type, but differing in content and complexity, recur systematically and in a cyclical way throughout the syllabus, providing pupils with ample opportunity to gradually acquire the skills to perform these tasks.

To enable task sequencing, monitor task complexity, and track learning opportunities, a task-specification framework was created. This framework built on the Centre for Language and Education's research into task complexity and difficulty (Duran & Ramaut, 2006) and defined task characteristics by means of six parameters closely related to the attainment targets (reflecting the constructs intended in the standards). Each task challenges students to practice one or more of the four *language skills* while processing or producing a *text type* for a certain *audience*, about a specific topic, representing or revealing a *world*, with a certain *function* or *purpose*. In addition, dealing with the information in the text demands a certain *level of processing*. Furthermore, the text can be linguistically easy or difficult depending on vocabulary, syntax, structure, code, conventions, and so on. Table 14C.1 illustrates these parameters for the reading task "Family looking for a robot." In this reading task, the students have to match advertisements by manufacturers selling different types of robots with advertisements from families looking for particular robots. The students have to identify which robot is the best fit for a particular family's needs. Figure 14C.2 provides an example of matching advertisements.

The task-specification framework provided the syllabus designers with all the information they needed to incrementally build a task-based curriculum for primary education. It allowed the syllabus designers to keep a bird's eye view on the design of the syllabus from Grade 2 to 6 and ensure content relevance and representativeness for pedagogic and assessment tasks.

Table 14C.1 *Task-specification framework for the reading task "Family looking for a robot" (TotemTaal, Grade 4, Unit 1)*

Parameters	Settings
Skill	Reading
Level of processing	Evaluating
Text type	Advertisements
Audience	Peers
World	Recognizable fantasy world: Robots
Function	Selecting information
Attainment goals	The students can order information in level- and age-appropriate stories. (Dutch Language Standard 3.5)
	The students can evaluate information in advertisements. (Dutch Language Standard 3.7)

(Berben et al., 2007a: 42)

> **Family Kamperman's ad**
> We are a household of six. We are looking for a housekeeping robot. The robot should be able to do the dishes, prepare food and clean the house. We need a robot that helps us in all domestic tasks. The robot should also be able to entertain the kids. Does such a robot exist?
>
> **Manufacturer's ad for Robot Emu**
> Let me present Emu. Emu is the perfect house robot. He loves kids. He tells stories and plays games. He will oversee your children's tooth brushing and will put them to bed. Furthermore, he is an excellent cook. He will clean the house, and wash and iron your clothes. What are you waiting for? Buy Emu now.

Figure 14C.2 Matching advertisements (Berben et al., 2007a: 43–44; adapted)

14C.4.2 Developing an Assessment Framework

The assessment framework of TotemTaal consists of four components combining tasks and formats for summative and formative assessment purposes, and incidental (spontaneous) and intentional (planned) assessments. Table 14C.2 provides an overview of the four components.

This carefully planned multi-componential, interpretive framework provides varied and multiple opportunities to gather information about the students' developing language skills while performing tasks, to use that information to scaffold students' task performances, and to provide feedback that the student can use to improve future task performances. The four components have partly overlapping purposes and help establish trustworthy, accurate interpretations of students' performances over time by allowing for "corrections" and "reinterpretations" (see Figure 14C.5):

1. Observation of task performance in order to provide teacher support to students if necessary and to get an idea of what students can and cannot do with language
2. Observation and analysis of task performance and task outcome of individual students to gather systematic, detailed information of what students can and cannot do with language
3. Learner reflection and portfolio for self-assessment of task performance and language-proficiency level to add a different perspective and an extra layer of planned formative information to the previous component
4. Task-based tests for summative use.

The key element linking the four components is an analysis diagram for each of the language skills. The skill-specific analysis diagrams link all assessment tasks with the task-specification framework, on the one hand, and key processes related to listening, speaking, reading, and writing, on the other hand. It guides the teacher in the observation and analysis of all task performances and helps the teacher decide whether students can

Table 14C.2 Assessment framework in TotemTaal

Function	Component	Format	Who	Focus	Pedagogic tools	Documentation
Incidental formative assessment	1	Observation and support	Teacher	Students' task performance (process)	Guidelines for teacher support of four language skills	Not applicable (mental notes)
Planned formative assessment	2	Observation and analysis	Teacher	Students' task performance (process) and outcome (product)	Analysis diagram for the observation and analysis of four language skills	Systematized notes
	3	Reflection	Student and teachers	Own task performance (process) and outcome (product)	Teacher guidelines for reflective talks; Portfolio guidelines for students	Worksheets; Portfolio
Summative assessment	4	Tests	Student and teachers	Students' outcomes of task-based tests (product)	Task-based tests for listening, reading, writing, spelling and language awareness	Rating rubrics; Test score

(Berben et al., 2007b: 156)

> *Reading goal*: Is the student's reading goal-oriented?
> - Can the student perform the reading task with the text?
> - If so, has the student understood the reading task and read in such a way as to reach the reading goal?
>
> *Information processing*:
> Is the student able to find the information he or she is looking for?
>
> Describe   Can the student find explicitly mentioned information in the text?
> Structure   Can the student connect several pieces of explicitly mentioned information from the text?
> Structure   Can the student find implicit information in the text?
> Evaluate   Can the student compare information from the text with information from a second source, or evaluate the information based on his or her own personal frame of reference?
>
> If not, hold a conversation with the student where you try to find out what went wrong
> - Identifying reading goal   Can the student identify the reading goal?
> - Topic   Is the student familiar with the topic?
> - Strategies   Does the student go about the reading task in an adequate manner?
> - Other:
>
> *Overall*: How does the student perform with respect to
>
> Self-reliance   Does the student attempt to resolve the task on his or her own? Does the student make use of the tools (strategies) at his or her disposal?
> Attitudes   Willingness to read, reading pleasure, willingness to reflect on own reading behavior
> Reflective ability   Does the student gradually develop the ability to think about his or her own reading skills? Does he or she apply these insights in subsequent reading tasks?

Figure 14C.3 Analysis diagram for reading tasks (Berben et al., 2007b: 203–4)

perform the task independently or needs help from the teacher or another student. Figure 14C.3 presents the main elements of the analysis diagram for reading tasks.

The analysis diagram for reading tasks in Figure 14C.3 provides teachers with information about which aspects are essential to the performance of reading tasks in general, and allows them to systematically track this information for individual students over multiple tasks in an observation/analysis worksheet. The worksheet allows the teacher to identify whether the students themselves were able to read in a goal-oriented way or whether the teacher had to step in and scaffold the students' performance. The aspects that were identified as relevant, based on meta-analyses of effective reading programs, are reading goal, level of information processing, topic, reading strategies, self-reliance, attitudes, and reflection (National Reading Panel, 2000; Slavin, Lake, Chambers, Cheung & Davis, 2009; Slavin, 2013). Other aspects are technical reading skills (e.g., fluency and accuracy), conventions of the text type or genre, relations in the text (e.g., function words expressing grammatical relations), vocabulary, and visual aspects (e.g., illustrations, layout). These aspects, specifically the focus on functional goal, levels of processing, and strategies, are largely similar for all language skills in TotemTaal's assessment framework. For the other skills, the analysis diagrams were also based on meta-analyses or reviews of effective listening, speaking, and writing instruction. For example, for writing, the analysis diagram was based among others on the meta-analyses by Graham and Perin (2007a, b, c).

The analysis diagrams for the four language skills and all the other documentation needed to realize the four assessment components of the TBLA framework were made available to the teacher in the form of a binder. In this teacher manual, the guidelines for teacher support, observation and analysis, and student reflection specify how these aspects of the reading process can be realized in a specific pedagogic task and what realistic expectations are for students of a certain grade. Figure 14C.4 illustrates how the analysis diagram for reading was operationalized for the planned formative assessment task "Family looking for a robot" (Component 2 in Table 14C.2) and provides the teacher with task-specific guidelines or criteria to observe and analyze students' performances.

The alignment of all pedagogic tools in the syllabus with the task-specification framework and analysis diagrams should enable teachers to combine analysis and support, to integrate instruction and assessment, and link it to student learning. The task-specification framework and analysis diagrams provide teachers with an interpretive framework, or a "lens," to look at students' task performances (during all tasks, whether they are planned assessment tasks or not), draw valid inferences about a student's current proficiency level, and engage in contingent pedagogy to advance the student's language development. This approach helps teachers and students develop a shared language to speak about task performances. It helps teachers provide concrete feedback or information that "closes the gap" between where a student is and where the student needs to be (Sadler, 1989).

The scenario in Figure 14C.5 provides a telling example of how the assessment framework can work in a classroom. The scenario shows how a fourth grade teacher can use the TBLA framework in TotemTaal to its full potential. The teacher in the scenario combines information that he gathers over multiple performances to get a clear(er) picture of what a student can and cannot do with language while performing a certain task type (e.g., comparing and evaluating information from different sources, see Table 14C.1). This classroom assessment scenario is a retrospective account of a teacher using the assessment opportunities in the syllabus. The scenario is based on teachers' experiences while piloting the lesson materials. This

> See Analysis diagram for reading tasks [Figure 14C.3]:
>
> - *Reading goal*: Do the students succeed in selecting the right robot for every family? If needed, clarify that each robot can only be assigned to one specific family. Do the students understand what constitutes a good match? (The characteristics of the robot have to match the family's preferences.)
> - *Type of information*: The information needed to accomplish the task is mentioned explicitly in all ads. The students need to identify the relevant information in each ad, compare information across ads carefully, and decide on the best match.
> - *Reading strategies*: How do the students structure the task? Do they read all ads by the families first, and then start reading the robot ads? Do they start reading one "Looking to buy" ad first and look which robot fits that description best? Are the students able to identify the relevant information?
> - *Genre*: Do the students understand the difference in types of ads (looking to buy versus looking to sell)?
> - *Vocabulary*: Do the students understand the key words? Do they use context clues, or the occurrences of these words in other advertisements to assign meaning to an unfamiliar word?
> - *Self-reliance*: Do the students ask for help? Who do they turn to first (another student or teacher)?
> - *Attitudes*: Are the students motivated to match families with robots? Do the students get stuck if they are not able to identify a robot for a particular family?

Figure 14C.4 Reading task "Family looking for a robot" – guidelines for analysis (Berben et al., 2007a: 42–43)

and similar scenarios are provided in the teacher manual to illustrate the use and potential of the TBLA framework.

14C.5 Conclusion

Developing a new, task-based language syllabus for Dutch-medium primary schools in Flanders was the ideal moment to rethink classroom-based language assessment from a task-based perspective. The syllabus designers created a TBLA framework that integrated tests with alternative assessments, like observation, portfolios, self-reflection, and so on, allowing for diverse assessment formats that encourage a collaborative assessment practice. To link instruction, assessment, and learning, a multi-componential, interpretive framework was developed based on task specifications and analysis diagrams. This framework provided teachers with a "lens" through which to look at tasks and task performances. The task specifications and analysis diagrams helped teachers focus attention on important aspects of task performance (e.g., language goal, audience, level of information processing, strategies, and so on) and provided them with a systematic way of tracking and promoting these task-essential aspects in

> While the fourth grade class was working on the reading task "Family looking for a robot" in unit one of the syllabus, student A's task performance attracted the attention of the teacher. Student A started reading the different advertisements enthusiastically, trying to match the manufacturers' advertisements with the advertisements from families looking to buy a robot. However, when student A found out that not all of his solutions were correct, he indicated to the teacher that the task was too difficult. The teacher noticed that the student read the advertisements quickly without paying real attention to the content. The student seemed to understand the task instruction but stopped reading when he was able to match one random piece of information in the family's ad with the robot manufacturer's ad. The student did not check the information with other possible combinations and did not combine the multiple pieces of information needed in order to solve the reading task. The teacher decided to engage with the student and asked student B to explain how she tackled the reading task. Student B told A that she first read the whole ad and then looked for the right match. Additionally, the teacher provided student A with the reading strategy to underline the most important information (i.e., the qualities in a robot each family is looking for). By doing so, student A became aware that he had to look for different pieces of information in one text.
>
> In unit two, the student performed better on a comparable reading task in which he had to match photos of houses with descriptions of houses. He appeared to read in a more structured way. He first read the whole description of the house and then looked for the matching photo. Also the student put the teacher's tip into practice by underlining relevant information. In a short, reflective talk with the teacher, the student admitted that underlining information was a good strategy. However, he also pointed out that matching visual with textual information was easier than comparing information from two texts.
>
> Also in unit two, a reading test presented the teacher with an opportunity to see whether student A had learned from the previous reading tasks. In this test, the students had to read four letters from children looking for a house for their family. After each letter the students had to answer multiple-choice questions. Rating the reading performance from student A with the rubric told the teacher that student A answered the multiple-choice questions in which he had to combine different pieces of information wrongly. The analysis confirmed the teacher's observation in unit one.
>
> After these three reading tasks in the first two units of the syllabus, the teacher came to the following interpretation of the student's reading behavior, which he wrote down on the observation sheet for that student: "Student A tends to read too quickly, skipping important information. He is not able to identify what information needs to be combined to solve the task. Underlining information helps the student. Tasks that ask the student to combine information from two different modalities (e.g., textual and visual) can act as a stepping stone to more complex tasks. Keep an eye on A's reading and engage him in a reflective talk about task performance and reading strategies after another comparable reading task."

Figure 14C.5 A teacher's interpretation of student A's reading development (Berben et al., 2007b: 178–79)

students' performances. The TBLA framework not only allows for more comprehensive and accurate interpretations of the language development of the class group, as well as individual language learners, but also ensures a fair assessment practice in which the primary stakeholders, students and teachers, are given a voice, and can be held accountable. It encourages the development of a shared language to talk about the quality of students' task performances and allows for the formulation of useful feedback that help students close the gap between present, less successful and more effective, future task performances. The TBLA framework encouraged teachers to strive toward a better integration of instruction and assessment: using pedagogic tasks to inform assessment, and assessment tasks to inform teaching, and by doing so blurred the lines between teaching, learning, and assessment.

However, the purpose of the framework as intended by syllabus designers and other stakeholders, like school advisors, turned out to be a challenge for many teachers. Overall, teachers were not accustomed to such a comprehensive framework consisting of several components and offering a variety of formats and pedagogic tools. An explorative study into how the framework was received in Brussels (Van Gorp, 2018), revealed that school advisors were more convinced of the value and potential of the framework than teachers, who sometimes found it too much, too elaborate, and too complicated. Nevertheless, all schools were using the assessment framework in one way or another, and some teachers or school teams even developed their own, more context-specific analysis diagrams. Furthermore, in some schools the framework had an impact on important discussions within school teams: the scope of assessment (narrow or broad, classical test versus alternative forms), the link between instruction and assessment (how can assessment inform classroom practice/actions), and the schools' assessment policy (vision, mission, report cards, etc.) as part of the overall language-in-education policy. We know that implementing a school language policy is a long and winding road (Van den Branden, 2010; Van Gorp & Versteden, 2020). The merit of the TBLA framework is that it got at least some school teams discussing some important topics.

Despite implementation issues, we may conclude that a multicomponent framework based on language tasks provided teachers with a balanced assessment repertoire, allowing at least some of the teachers to integrate instruction, assessment, and learning more closely, encouraging them to adopt a learning-oriented assessment approach. The TBLA framework allows for multiple sources of assessment evidence and the collection of multiple performances over time (Norris, 2016) to provide evidence of growth and learning. Such a repertoire enables teachers to make a variety of inferences about students' capacities for language use, or about what they can or cannot yet do, and how to support students going forward – and it is then, and only then, that lines between teaching, learning, and assessment will start to fade.

Further Reading

Colpin, M. and Van Gorp, K. (2007). Task-based writing in primary education: The development and evaluation of writing skills through writing tasks, learner and teacher support. In K. Van den Branden, K. Van Gorp, and M. Verhelst, eds. *Tasks in action: Task-based language education from a classroom-based perspective*. Newcastle: Cambridge Scholars Publishing, pp. 194–234.

Norris, J. M. (2016). Current issues for task-based language assessment. *Annual Review of Applied Linguistics*, 36, 230–44.

Rea-Dickins, P. (2006). Currents and eddies in the discourse of assessment: a learning-focused interpretation. *International Journal of Applied Linguistics*, 16(2), 163–88.

Van Gorp, K. (2018). Task-based language assessment for L1 and L2 speakers in primary education. Designing a useful task-specification framework. In J. McE. Davis, J. Norris, M. Malone, T. McKay, and Y. A Son, eds. *Useful assessment and evaluation in language education*. Washington DC: Georgetown University, pp. 131–48.

Van Gorp, K. and Deygers, B. (2014). Task-based language assessment. In A. J. Kunnan, ed. *The companion to language assessment. Volume II. Approaches and development*. Malden, MA: Wiley-Blackwell, pp. 578–93.

Study Questions

1. How can TBLA inform teachers about the effectiveness of their teaching approach?
2. What kinds of interpretations about language learners can be made on the basis of TotemTaal's TBLA framework?
3. What kind of information would you as a teacher expect from a TBLA, and how would you use that information to support language learners?
4. What kind of guidelines and support would you expect from a task-based language syllabus in order to scaffold your students in their task performances?

References

Bachman, L. F. (2002). Some reflections on task-based language performance assessment. *Language Testing*, 19, 454–76.

Berben, M., Callebaut, I., Colpin, M., François, S., Geerts, M., Goethals, M., Vander Meeren, K., Vandommele, G., and Van Gorp, K. (2007a). *TotemTaal. Themahandleiding en kopieerbladen 4A*. Mechelen: Wolters Plantyn.

Berben, M., Callebaut, I., Colpin, M., François, S., Geerts, M., Goethals, M., Vander Meeren, K., Vandommele, G., and Van Gorp, K. (2007b). *TotemTaal. Inleiding en evaluatie 4*. Mechelen: Wolters Plantyn.

Berben, M., Van den Branden, K., and Van Gorp, K. (2007). We'll see what happens: Tasks on paper and tasks in a multilingual classroom. In K. Van den Branden, K. Van Gorp, and M. Verhelst, eds. *Tasks in action: Task-based language education from a classroom-based perspective*. Newcastle: Cambridge Scholars Publishing, pp. 32–67.

Carless, D. (2007).Learning-oriented assessment: Conceptual basis and practical implications." *Innovations in Education and Teaching International*, 44, 57–66.

Colby-Kelly, C. and Turner, C. E. (2007). AFL research in the L2 classroom and evidence of usefulness: Taking formative assessment to the next level. *Canadian Modern Language Review*, 64(1), 9–37.

Colpin, M. and Van Gorp, K. (2007). Task-based writing in primary education: The development and evaluation of writing skills through writing tasks, learner and teacher support. In K. Van den Branden, K. Van Gorp, and M. Verhelst, eds. *Tasks in action: Task-based language education from a classroom-based perspective*. Newcastle: Cambridge Scholars Publishing, pp. 194–234.

Departement Onderwijs (1998). *Ontwikkelingsdoelen en eindtermen. Informatiemap voor de onderwijspraktijk: gewoon basisonderwijs*. Brussels: Afdeling Informatie en Documentatie.

Devlieger, M. and Goossens, G. (2007). An assessment tool for the evaluation of teacher practice in powerful task-based language learning environments. In K. Van den Branden, K. Van Gorp, and M. Verhelst, eds. *Tasks in action: Task-based language education from a classroom-based perspective*. Newcastle: Cambridge Scholars Publishing, pp. 92–130.

Duran, G. and Ramaut, G. (2006). Tasks for absolute beginners and beyond: Developing and sequencing tasks at basic proficiency levels. In K. Van den Branden, ed. *Task-based language education: From theory to practice*. Cambridge: Cambridge University Press, pp. 47–105.

François, S. (2005). *Naar een nieuwe taakgerichte taalmethode voor het basisonderwijs: behoeftenonderzoek*. Unpublished research report. Leuven: Centre for Language and Education

Graham, S. and Perin, D. (2007a). A meta-analysis of writing instruction for adolescent students. *Journal of Educational Psychology*, 99, 445–76.

Graham, S. and Perin, D. (2007b). *Writing next: Effective strategies to improve writing of adolescent middle and high school*. Washington DC: Alliance for Excellence in Education.

Graham, S. and Perin, D. (2007c). What we know, what we still need to know: Teaching adolescents to write. *Scientific Studies in Reading*, 11, 313–36.

Harding, L., Alderson, J. C., and Brunfaut, T. (2015). Diagnostic assessment of reading and listening in a second or foreign Language: Elaborating on diagnostic principles. *Language Testing*, 32, 317–36.

Hattie, J. and Yates, G. C. R. (2014). *Visible learning and the science of how we learn*. New York: Routledge.

Jones, N. and Saville, N. (2016). *Learning oriented assessment. A systematic Approach*. Studies in Language Testing 45. Cambridge: Cambridge University Press.

Lokale inburgerings- en integratiemonitor (2019). Retrieved from: www.statistiekvlaanderen.be/nl/monitor-lokale-inburgering-en-integratie.

National Reading Panel (2000). *Reports of the National Reading Panel: Teaching children to read: An evidence-based assessment of the scientific research literature on reading and its implications for reading instruction: Reports of the subgroups*. Rockville, MD: NICHD Clearinghouse.

Norris, J. M. (2009). Task-based teaching and testing. In M. H. Long and C. J. Doughty, eds. *The handbook of language teaching*. Malden, MA: Wiley-Blackwell, pp. 578–94.

Norris, J. M. (2016). Current uses of task-based language assessment. *Annual Review of Applied Linguistics*, 36, 230–44.

Rea-Dickins, P. (2006). Currents and eddies in the discourse of assessment: a learning-focused interpretation. *International Journal of Applied Linguistics*, 16(2), 163–88.

Sadler, R. (1989). Formative assessment and the design of instructional systems. *Instructional Science* 18, 119–44.

Samuda, V. and Bygate, M. (2008). *Tasks in second language learning*. London: Palgrave Macmillan.

Slavin, R. E., Lake, C., Chambers, B., Cheung, A., and Davis, S. (2009). Effective reading programs for the elementary grades: A best-evidence synthesis. *Review of Educational Research*, 79, 1391–466.

Slavin, R. E. (2013). Effective programmes in reading and mathematics: Lessons from the best evidence encyclopaedia. *School Effectiveness and School Improvement: An International Journal of Research, Policy and Practice*, 24, 383–91.

Turner. C. E. and Purpura, J. E. (2015). Learning-oriented assessment in the classroom. In D. Tsagari and J. Banerjee, eds. *Handbook of second language assessment*. Boston, MA: DeGruyter Mouton, pp. 255–73.

Van Avermaet, P., Colpin, C., Van Gorp, K., Bogaert, N., and Van den Branden, K. (2006). The role of the teacher in task-based language teaching. In K. Van den Branden, ed. *Task-based language education: From theory to practice*. Cambridge: Cambridge University Press, pp. 175–96.

Van den Branden, K. (2006a). Introduction: Task-based language teaching in a nutshell. In K. Van den Branden, ed. *Task-based language education: From theory to practice*. Cambridge: Cambridge University Press, pp. 1–16.

Van den Branden, K. (2006b). Training teachers: Task-based as well? In K. Van den Branden, ed. *Task-based language education: From theory to practice*. Cambridge: Cambridge University Press, pp. 217–48.

Van den Branden, K. (2010). *Handboek Taalbeleid Basisonderwijs*. Leuven: ACCO.

Van Gorp, K. (2018). Task-based language assessment for L1 and L2 speakers in primary education. Designing a useful task-specification framework. In J. McE. Davis, J. Norris, M. Malone, T. McKay, and Y. A Son, eds. *Useful assessment and evaluation in language education*. Washington DC: Georgetown University, pp. 131–48.

Van Gorp, K. and Deygers, B. (2014). Task-based language assessment. In A. J. Kunnan, ed. *The companion to language assessment. Volume II Approaches and development*. Malden, MA: Wiley-Blackwell, pp. 578–93.

Van Gorp, K. and Versteden, P. (2020). Advising linguistically diverse schools on developing a school-wide language policy. In R. M. Beerkens, E. Le Pichon-Vorstman, J. D. ten Thije, and R. G. J. L. Supheert, eds. *Enhancing intercultural communication in organizations: Insights from project advisors*. Abingdon: Routledge, pp. 83–92.

Part VIII

Research Needs and Future Prospects

15

Methodological Approaches to Investigating Task-Based Language Teaching

Advances and Challenges

Andrea Révész

15.1 Introduction

In the area of instructed second language acquisition (SLA) research, the past three decades have seen a surge of interest in investigating tasks as a means of facilitating second language (L2) development. This increased interest has been motivated by a growing consensus among instructed SLA researchers that tasks have the capacity to create ideal circumstances for L2 learning by promoting the cognitive as well as social processes assumed to foster L2 development in instructed language learning contexts. Research attention to tasks has additionally been driven by the increasing acceptance of task-based language teaching (TBLT) as a valuable and feasible pedagogical approach to teaching second languages. As a result of the rising theoretical and practical importance of task-related research, a wide range of methods have been utilized by researchers, from laboratory experimental designs to classroom action research projects, to explore task-based learning. In this chapter, I will provide an overview of key methods that are used to examine the role of tasks in L2 development. I will also highlight innovative approaches and methodological challenges in investigating task-based performance and learning.

15.2 Types of Task-Based Language Teaching Research

15.2.1 Experimental and Quasi-experimental Research on Tasks and Task-Based Programs

Much of the existing research on task-based performance and development has been quasi-experimental or experimental in nature. The primary focus has been to explore how the manipulation of task factors may influence the incidence of interaction-driven L2 learning opportunities, linguistic performance, and L2 development. More recently, researchers have also begun to examine how task-related variables may affect the cognitive processes that underlie task-based performance and learning (e.g., Kim, Payant, & Pearson, 2015; Révész, Kourtali & Mazgutova, 2017; Torres, 2018). In this line of research, the independent variable is usually a task-related factor, whereas the typical dependent variables are linguistic outcome measures, interactional features, or process-oriented indices. Task-related factors that have received extensive attention are task types (e.g., narrative vs. decision-making, integrated vs. independent), interactive task conditions (e.g., whether participants need or do not need to reach a consensus; see Ellis [2003] and Mackey [2012] for a review of interactive conditions), and task complexity (i.e., the inherent cognitive demands of tasks).

A study by Michel, Révész, Lu, Kourtali and Borges (2020) is a recent example of a study investigating task type effects. The researchers operationalized task type as the distinction between independent and integrated writing tasks. The independent task involved writing an essay, whereas, in the integrated task, participants were asked to produce a written summary of a listening and a written passage while synthesizing the information from the two sources. Each participant completed two independent and two integrated tasks, the order of which was counterbalanced across participants. The dependent variables were the behaviors and associated cognitive processes of L2 writers, as captured by a variety of keystroke-logging and eye-tracking indices and qualitative comments gathered through stimulated recall protocols. The stimulated recall comments were elicited based on the last writing task participants had performed. As compared to the majority of previous studies on task type effects, a strength of this design was that the researchers included two rather than one version of each task type, which allowed for isolating the impact of task type from potential topic or prompt effects.

Lambert and Engler's (2007) research well illustrates how an experimental approach can be used to examine the impact of interactive conditions on L2 performance. The researchers utilized a 2×3 repeated-measures design, with goal orientation and information distribution as independent, within-subjects factors. The two levels of goal orientation were whether the task was open (i.e., the task did not have a predetermined outcome) or closed (i.e., the task had a predetermined outcome). Information distribution was operationalized as having three levels: shared, one-way (i.e., one person holds all the information), and two-way (i.e., the information is split between participants). The order of the six conditions was counterbalanced, with each participant being exposed to all six conditions. The dependent variables were measures of linguistic complexity, accuracy, and fluency. A noteworthy feature of the design was that the researchers were able to generalize about the effects of various interactive conditions, given that these were investigated across three task types (ordering pictures, deciding responsibility, and arranging times).

While task type and interactive conditions have attracted considerable attention from TBLT scholars, most task-based research in the experimental paradigm so far has focused on the effects of task complexity on L2 performance. This area of research has largely been inspired by two cognitive-interactionist models of task-based learning, Robinson's (2001) Cognition Hypothesis and Skehan's (1998, 2009) Limited Capacity Model. These models make partially different predictions about how manipulations along certain task complexity dimensions will affect linguistic performance and development. With a view to testing these models, experimental studies of cognitive task complexity typically entail the following steps. First, researchers select or design a pedagogic task. Then, they develop two or more versions of the task with the intention that the versions differ in terms of cognitive demands along a particular task feature. For example, researchers might design two task versions, one posing more and the other imposing fewer reasoning demands. Next, researchers usually determine whether the task conditions have resulted in superior outcomes. To date, studies have primarily captured outcomes employing linguistic performance indices of complexity, accuracy, and fluency (Housen & Kuiken, 2009; Michel, 2017). Increasingly, however, TBLT scholars are also concerned with investigating how cognitive complexity manipulations may affect L2 development in specific linguistic features (e.g., the use of conditionals [Baralt, 2013; Kim, 2012; Kourtali & Révész, 2020; Nuevo, 2006; Révész, 2009; Révész, Sachs, & Hama, 2014; Torres, 2018]), the frequency of language learning opportunities arising during interaction (e.g., negotiation of meaning and various types of feedback [Gilabert, Barón & Llanes, 2009; Kim, 2009; Révész, 2011]), and the cognitive processes in which learners engage during task performance (e.g., Kim et al., 2015; Révész et al., 2017; Torres, 2018).

Until recently, one methodological weakness of task complexity studies has been that researchers assumed rather than substantiated the validity of their task manipulations (Norris & Ortega, 2003; Révész, 2014). In other words, they failed to provide independent evidence that the task version they constructed to be more complex did indeed exert greater cognitive demands on the learners. To deal with this shortcoming, a growing number of studies incorporate independent measures of cognitive complexity to ensure that the task complexity conditions reflect the intended experimental manipulation (e.g., Baralt, 2013; Malicka & Levkina, 2012; Révész et al., 2014; Zalbidea, 2017). To date, researchers have relied on a number of techniques to assess task-generated cognitive demands, including subjective self-ratings, subjective time estimations, dual-task methodology, eye-tracking, and expert judgments. Some scholars have even investigated and compared the usefulness of various methods to measure task-induced cognitive demands (e.g., Lee, 2019; Révész, Michel, Gilabert, 2016; Sasayama, 2016) with the aim of guiding validation work in future task complexity research.

Another key development in task-related experimental research has been a more sophisticated measurement of linguistic complexity, accuracy, and fluency, constructs which are often included as the primary dependent variables in task-based studies. For example, in response to calls to capture the dynamic and multidimensional nature of syntactic complexity (Bulté & Housen, 2012; Housen & Kuiken, 2009; Norris & Ortega, 2009), recent TBLT studies often include measures of phrasal, clausal, and overall complexity rather than a single index of syntactic complexity. Similarly, TBLT researchers increasingly employ a variety of lexical diversity indices following recommendations in the literature (e.g., Jarvis, 2013).

While there have been many methodological advances in experimental task-related research, a gap that needs addressing includes a lack of studies that assess whether the findings obtained in experimental settings can be transferred to real classrooms. Although the experimental approach might lend itself best to laboratory studies, where researchers can control for a large array of potential confounding factors, it is also important to extend experimental research to real classroom settings. Otherwise, whether the findings obtained possess ecological validity remains unassessed. A few studies have examined the effects of task-related variables in actual classroom contexts. Kim (2012), for example, investigated how task complexity may affect L2 development and the incidence of interaction-driven language learning opportunities in Korean L2 English classrooms. Kim's research is noteworthy in that the tasks in which participants engaged came from the syllabus the students normally followed rather than being supplied and designed by the researcher for the purpose of the experiment.

Finally, it is worth highlighting, that the experimental research, albeit primarily focusing on task effects so far, can also be utilized to compare the TBLT approach as a whole with other types of instructional options. Such comparative method studies are highly challenging to conduct, thus often suffer from methodological shortcomings, such as lack of pretesting, failure to include a control and/or a comparison group, absence of control over possible teacher and learner effects, the use of biased instruments toward one instructional treatment, and a lack of evidence that the instruction was aligned with the intended methodological approach (Ellis, Skehan, Li, Shintani & Lambert, 2020; Ellis & Shintani, 2014; Long, 2015). Some recent comparative studies, however, have succeeded in avoiding many of these pitfalls. For example, De la Fuente (2006) investigated the relative effectiveness of the presentation-practice-production (PPP) approach and TBLT with or without explicit instruction. The study focused on the learning of L2 Spanish vocabulary items. Similar, Shintani (2013, 2015) compared the extent to which TBLT and PPP facilitated development in target vocabulary by Japanese child learners of L2 English. Shintani (2015) also examined the incidental learning of two grammatical features (plural -s and copula be). Besides having relatively robust designs, a strength of these three studies was the inclusion of process data (e.g., examination of interactional patterns), in addition to product-oriented pretest-posttest and pretest-delayed posttest measures (de la Fuente, 2006; Shintani, 2013, 2015).

15.2.2 Correlational/Associative Research on Learners and Tasks

Correlational, or associative, designs are another type of research that task-based scholars employ. Unlike experimental approaches, correlational designs do not involve manipulating variables with a view to establishing cause-effect relationships, but instead investigate associations among variables that remain unmanipulated. In task-based research, correlational designs have most frequently been used to explore how individual difference factors may relate to task-based outcomes. Typically, participants are measured in terms of an individual difference factor (e.g., anxiety, aptitude, creativity, motivation, or working memory) and indices of linguistic performance, L2 learning, or interactional features assumed to drive L2 learning. In the next step, statistical procedures are used to identify associations between the two sets of variables.

A study by Dörnyei and Kormos (2000) was among the first correlational studies in the field of TBLT. The researchers set out to determine the relationship between task engagement and a group of motivational variables, social factors (e.g., group cohesiveness), as well as willingness to communicate in the participants' first language. Task engagement was operationalized as the number of turns and amount of speech produced by the learners. Self-report questionnaires were administered to measure participants with regard to the individual difference variables. To answer the research questions, the researchers computed correlations between the individual difference indices and the measures of task engagement. Several TBLT studies have adopted similar designs when examining how these and other individual difference factors, including working memory (e.g., Mackey, Adams, Stafford, & Winke, 2010) and creativity (Albert & Kormos, 2004; McDonough, Crawford, & Mackey, 2015), may influence task performance.

Increasingly, researchers are also using complex statistical techniques (e.g., structural equation modeling) to explore the role of individual differences in the context of TBLT. For example, a recent study by Wang (2019) aimed to identify the underlying facets of task motivation and task anxiety and how these factors relate to L2 motivation and foreign language and trait anxiety respectively. The study additionally examined the extent to which these motivational and anxiety-related factors predicted linguistic performance, expressed in terms of linguistic complexity, accuracy, and fluency indices. The researcher used motivation and anxiety questionnaires to gain information about participants' motivational and anxiety profiles, and elicited linguistic performance data by means of a video narration task. Participants' responses to the questionnaires were first submitted to exploratory factor analyses. Next, structural equation modeling was conducted to examine the associations between task motivation and L2 motivation and between task anxiety, trait anxiety, and foreign-language anxiety. To address the links between the individual difference factors and the linguistic performance measures, a series of multiple regression analyses were carried out.

15.2.3 Aptitude-Treatment-Interaction Research

The past decade has also seen a growing number of TBLT studies adopting the aptitude-treatment-interaction (ATI) research paradigm. The aim of ATI studies is to determine how individual differences among learners may moderate the effectiveness of various types of L2 instructional treatments. In ATI research, scholars usually assess participants in terms of individual difference factors such as working memory, aptitude, creativity, motivation, willingness to communicate or anxiety. Then, the effectiveness of some type of instructional treatment (e.g., task manipulation) is investigated in relation to the individual difference variable(s), involving either correlational designs (e.g., Fu & Li, 2019; Granena & Yilmaz, 2019; Nielson & DeKeyser, 2019; Révész, 2011) or comparison groups defined according to the learner variables (e.g., Yilmaz, 2013). Thus, ATI studies can be considered a subcategory of experimental research, and may also bear features of correlational/associate research.

To illustrate, Révész (2011) investigated whether three individual difference factors – linguistic self-confidence, anxiety, and self-perceived communicative competence – affect the extent to which L2 learners allocate attention to form-meaning connections during task-based interaction in a classroom context. Participants from six intact classes carried out a simple and complex version of the same type of decision-making task. Focus on form-meaning connections were captured in terms of a specific measure of speech production (use of conjoined clauses); global measures of complexity, accuracy, and fluency; and incidence of language-related episodes. Self-report questionnaires were used to elicit information about the participants with regard to the three individual difference variables. To assess the potential moderating effects of the individual difference factors, a series of correlational analyses were conducted for the simple and complex conditions separately.

Yilmaz (2013) provides a good example of a study where a comparison group design was adopted for some of the statistical analyses. This experiment examined the extent to which working memory capacity and language analytic ability influence the impact of two types of feedback on L2 development. Participants were assigned to three groups (explicit correction, recasts, and control), and received feedback according to their respective conditions during task-based work. Oral production, comprehension, and recognition tests were employed to assess changes in learners' knowledge of the target constructions. The operation span task and a subtest of LLAMA were used to measure working memory capacity and language analytic ability, respectively. To gauge whether the individual difference factors moderated the effectiveness of feedback types, Yilmaz first ran a series of mixed-model analyses of covariance (ANCOVAs), with time as a within-subject variable, feedback group as a between-subjects factor, and working memory and language analytic ability as covariates. When the analyses yielded a significant ATI, the researcher converted the individual difference factor into a categorical variable, that is, divided the participants into two groups: learners with scores above the median were regarded as high, and learners with scores below the median were considered low with regard to the aptitude factor. Then, some follow-up analyses were carried out involving aptitude as a categorical variable.

15.2.4 Descriptive, Nonexperimental Research on Tasks

There has also been an increasing interest among TBLT researchers in conducting descriptive research that explores what happens during task-based interaction. Descriptive studies typically involve preparing audio-, video-, or screen-recordings of learners while they are engaged in pedagogic tasks. Then, researchers transcribe the recordings and analyze the data, adopting an approach aligned with the theoretical orientation of their research and the focus of their research questions.

The aim of some descriptive research has been to capture task-based work in actual, unmanipulated classroom contexts. In this line of research, scholars usually utilize analytical frameworks such as interaction, multimodal, or conversation analysis, often inspired by a sociocultural view of SLA. One focus of such studies has been to investigate how learners talk during task-based work, assuming an emic perspective. For example, Markee and Kunitz (2013) employed conversation analysis to study the interactional patterns of three Italian as a foreign-language learners. The students were recorded during task work in their regular Italian language classes. The data comprised about three hours of video recordings collected over three weeks. From this dataset, four speech events were chosen for further analysis, each involving the planning stage prior to task performance. The researchers analyzed the video transcripts in meticulous detail, focusing on conversational features such as repair and turn-taking; types of embodied action, like gestures, body posture, and eye-gaze behaviors; and use of tools external to the task, including the computer and the notes that learners had taken while engaged in task-based planning.

Other researchers have taken an etic viewpoint when analyzing natural task-based interaction in classroom settings, relying on predetermined coding schemes, either adopted or adapted from previous research. For instance, researchers often code task-based interaction for negotiation of meaning and feedback episodes, categories that are derived from cognitive-interactionist approaches to SLA. Following this approach, Gurzynski-Weiss and Révész (2012) examined the extent to which the provision and immediate use of instructor feedback was related to whether the feedback occurred during tasks or non-tasks, unfocused or focused tasks, or the pre-, during-, or post-task stages. Twenty-three lessons were video-recorded from Spanish foreign-language university courses. Next, the transcripts of the recordings were coded according to several interactional and task features based on a coding scheme that originated from theory and previous empirical findings.

In some descriptive classroom research, unlike in Markee and Kunitz (2013) and Gurzynski-Weiss and Révész (2012), where the interactions were naturally occurring, the task-based materials have been developed by the classroom teacher and the researcher(s) together. The aim of this type of collaborative approach is to explore tasks that are of theoretical or practical interest to the researcher, but at the same time ensure that they remain aligned with normal classroom activities, and that the design thereby maintains ecological validity. For example, Mackey's (2002) study included data from three 50-minute lessons where learners of English as a second language completed task-based activities co-designed by the researcher and teacher. Participants also took part in a stimulated recall interview after the three lessons were over. The data analysis involved coding transcripts of oral interaction and stimulated recall comments in terms of interactional processes. A more recent study by Oliver, Philp, and Duchesne (2017) also provides a good example of how task-based interaction can be explored in real classroom contexts through collaboration between teachers and researchers. As in Mackey (2002), the tasks used in the study were designed in cooperation with the classroom teachers. The dataset included transcriptions of interaction among children over five task-based sessions in their regular classroom context. The researchers adopted a bottom-up approach during the coding process by letting coding categories emerge from the data. Then, the resulting categories were labeled, informed by the existing literature on features of social interaction, task management, and cognitive involvement.

15.2.5 Case Studies of Teachers and Task-Based Programs

The case study is another approach to TBLT research. Case studies have been used to investigate how learners engage in task-based work, how teachers implement tasks, and how task-based programs work. The aim of this type of research has been to give a detailed picture of individual cases of learners, teachers, or programs by describing them holistically and in depth in their own task-based environments. Case studies typically combine various data-collection methods and analytical approaches to capture the characteristics of a case or multiple cases in task-based contexts.

Research by Baba and Nitta (2014) and Nitta and Baba (2018) well exemplify how the case study approach can be used to investigate learners in task-based contexts. From a larger dataset, the researchers observed the longitudinal effects of task repetition on two students' writing development. The students engaged in repeating a writing task thirty times, once every week over a period of one academic year. Each time the participants completed a ten-minute writing output followed by reflective comments. Baba and Nitta (2014) focused on changes in students' writing fluency. Nitta and Baba (2018), in addition, analyzed students' written outputs in terms of syntactic and lexical complexity, and considered their self-reflection from the perspective of self-regulation processes.

A seminal study by Samuda (2001) provides a good example of a case study considering the teacher's role in a task-based lesson. The researcher gathered audio and video recordings of an English for academic purposes teacher and her class, as well as samples of the students' writing throughout a semester, spending a morning every week observing the class and the teacher. Using transcripts of classroom discourse, the study gives an in-depth description of one task-based lesson from beginning to end, exploring how the teacher gradually draws learners' attention to new language in the context of task-based interaction.

A more recent study by Andon (2018) also illustrates how a case study approach can be used to investigate teachers from the perspective of TBLT. The goal of this research was to explore the extent to which TBLT principles were represented in the practices and beliefs of three teachers of English as a foreign language employed in UK private language school settings. Data collection involved the researcher observing lessons and conducting semi-structured ethnographic interviews with the teachers. The observations were carried out to gain information about the teachers' classroom practices and to gather a basis for comparing these with their perceived practices. The observational data were also used for eliciting participants' views on specific activities that had taken place in the lessons. The aim of the interview schedule was to elicit participants' views on tasks and TBLT, but the researcher also allowed the teachers to raise issues, which were followed up on when considered relevant to the focus of the study. Andon adopted a data-driven, inductive approach to data analysis, but the process was also informed by the researcher's understanding of the key characteristics and principles of task-based teaching.

The case study approach can also be employed to investigate task-based programs. Studies by McDonough and Chaikitmongkol (2007) and Carless (2004) provide good examples of this. Adopting a longitudinal design, McDonough and Chaikitmongkol (2007) aimed to investigate teachers' and learners' responses to a new task-based English as a foreign language program at a Thai university and to examine the ways in which any concerns raised by the teachers and students were handled in the program. During a 12-month period, the researchers collected data from multiple sources: learning notebooks, task and course evaluations, observations, field notes, and interviews. The data, oral and written, were subjected to qualitative, recursive analysis. In other words, the focus of the data collection was informed by the researchers' reflections on data that had been previously gathered. For example, the interview topics were guided by insights that had emerged from earlier class observations. Unlike McDonough and Chaikitmongkol, Carless (2004) primarily focused on teachers in his case study of a task-based program. This study employed a multiple case study approach to evaluate the behaviors and perspectives of three primary school teachers who were in the process of implementing a newly introduced task-based program in Hong Kong. Carless observed the teachers in three cycles, each cycle entailing five to six classroom observations. The teachers' views were tapped through an attitude scale and interviews. The triangulation of these sources led to an understanding of how the implementation of the program was influenced by the beliefs of the teachers and practical issues inherent in their institutional contexts.

15.2.6 Practitioner Research

Practitioner research is another type that can be used to study task-based teaching and learning. Practitioner research, as its name suggests, is typically carried out by teachers in their own instructional settings. Two types of practitioner research that have been employed to investigate TBLT are action research and micro-evaluation of tasks.

Action research involves teachers, collaboratively or individually, in rounds of identifying, reflecting on, and finding solutions to problems that occur in their own specific task-based contexts. Given the cyclic nature of action research, the focus frequently develops as the investigation proceeds, with the teacher-researcher engaging in continuous revision of their TBLT practice. A good example of a TBLT action research project is a study by Shart (2008). The context was a beginner-level German class at a Japanese university, where Shart was the course instructor. Over a period of one year, Shart prepared weekly reflections on how the class was progressing and produced a thorough description of all the sessions he taught. In addition, another researcher, not involved in teaching the class, conducted focus group and individual interviews with the students, obtained students' perceptions about the classes through email, and made classroom observations. The project was conducted in a number of stages. Shart first recognized the need for a language course that is aligned with the needs of his students. Drawing on his existing language teaching experience and understanding of the context, he decided that TBLT would be a suitable pedagogical approach. In the next step, he designed a project to investigate the TBLT course he was going to teach. In the stages to follow, the teacher-researcher continued to refine the course, taking into account his own reflections and perceptions, the observations of the outside researcher, and the insights gained from the students' emails and interview comments. This cyclic approach proved helpful in reaching an improved understanding of the benefits and challenges entailed in implementing task-based teaching in the teacher-researcher's own pedagogic context.

Micro-evaluations of tasks are concerned with exploring whether a task works as intended (Ellis, 2011, 2015; Ellis et al., 2020). According to Ellis (2011), a possible procedure for evaluating tasks involves the following steps. First, the researcher needs to provide a thorough description of the task, which can later be used as a basis for the evaluation. Next, the aims of the evaluation should be determined; for example, whether the task succeeds in achieving the teacher's goals and whether it leads to unanticipated processes and outcomes. Data collection can start before the task (e.g., establishing what learners already know or can do), can take place during task performance (e.g., documenting how learners perform the task), and may continue after task performance (e.g., obtaining students' comments and perceptions about the task). Then, the researcher analyzes the data, possibly through triangulation of various data sources. Based on the results of the analysis, the teacher-researcher can conclude whether the task was successful and what modification might need to be implemented to make it work better. Ellis (2015) describes a number of micro-evaluations of tasks, which were carried out by teachers as part of an MA-level TBLT course. The teachers followed the steps outlined in Ellis (2011), and took the form of what Ellis refers to as student-based and response-based evaluations. The teachers obtained student-based data largely through administering a short perception questionnaire to students. The response-based components involved the collection of either product- or process-based evidence. Investigation of the product was concerned with establishing whether the learners had achieved the intended task outcomes, whereas the process element examined the processes in which learners engaged during task performance (e.g., by looking at interactional patterns or task engagement).

Although there are many advantages to practitioner research, this type of design also has some limitations that need to be taken into account when interpreting the findings. One disadvantage is that the results often cannot be generalized to other contexts, given that the researchers typically develop action research plans to address their local problems or design tasks tailored to the particular characteristics of their students. Other issues specific to action research are that scholars cannot include control groups in their designs or control for extraneous factors inherent in classroom research. If such challenges cannot be overcome, the validity and reliability of the research will inevitably suffer, limiting the generalizability of findings. As Mackey and Gass (2015) note, for action research to be able offer insights for the broader community, it also needs to adhere to methodological standards accepted in the field. Nevertheless, in cases where this is not possible, the findings are still likely to prove interesting to fellow practitioners who work in similar contexts or need to deal with similar challenges (Mackey, 2017).

15.2.7 Systematic Research Syntheses

With the available research base growing, TBLT researchers increasingly use meta-analytic and synthetic techniques to summarize and review the results of empirical research on TBLT. Systematic research syntheses, such as meta-analyses and narrative reviews, intend to find, analyze, and scrutinize primary studies carried out on a specific research topic. The principal aim of systematic research syntheses is to give a comprehensive summary of existing findings, research foci, and/or methodological approaches in the area studied.

Meta-analyses, a particular type of systematic research synthesis, can be employed to synthesize the results of quantitative studies by means of statistical analyses. So far, a number of meta-analyses have been conducted on TBLT-related topics, such as task-based interaction (Cobb, 2010; Keck et al., 2006), task complexity (Jackson & Suethanapornkul, 2013; Sasayama, Malicka & Norris, 2015), and TBLT programs (Bryfonski & McKay, 2019). We will consider Jackson and Suethanapornkul (2013) in more detail to exemplify a TBLT research synthesis and meta-analysis. The authors set out to review previous empirical research on Robinson's (2001) Cognition Hypothesis, a framework proposed to model how task manipulations may affect L2 performance and development. The researchers focused on one prediction of the framework: when task complexity is increased along resource-directing dimensions, L2 production will be more complex and accurate but less fluent. First, the researchers conducted a comprehensive literature search, attempting to identify all studies that had investigated the Cognition Hypothesis before 2010. The authors found forty-seven studies with a focus relevant to the intended aims of the meta-analysis and synthesis. In the next step, they employed eight inclusion criteria to select studies for the synthesis, resulting in a pool of seventeen published studies. These were synthesized taking account of key design features, including the task variables studied, the outcome measures used, the task conditions investigated, and the modalities of tasks in the research. Then, nine studies, with comparable aims and designs, were chosen to be included in a meta-analysis. Finally, for this set of studies, the researchers calculated combined effect sizes to examine the effects of increasing task complexity on syntactic complexity, lexis, and accuracy.

Rather than conducting a meta-analysis of previous TBLT research findings, Plonsky and Kim (2016) carried out a systematic review of the foci of studies exploring task-based learner production and the methodological features employed in this line of research. The authors first identified eighty-five primary studies investigating language production during task-based work, published between 2006 and 2015. Next, the studies were coded for their research focus (e.g., interactional features, complexity, accuracy, and fluency measures), contextual factors (e.g., laboratory vs. class, institutional setting), and demographic variables (e.g., proficiency, age). In addition, Plonsky and Kim categorized the studies in terms of a number of methodological characteristics related to their design, the sampling and analytical procedures employed, and the level of transparency in reporting. Drawing on the results, the researchers put forward a number of suggestions for future TBLT research.

A qualitative research synthesis is a third type of systematic review that has been used to summarize and critique previous TBLT research. Chong and Reinders (2020) employed this approach to synthesize previous qualitative research on technology-mediated TBLT published between 2002 and 2017. Adopting a grounded theory approach, the authors synthesized the data obtained from sixteen primary studies that utilized either qualitative or mixed-methods designs. In the case of mixed-methods studies, the researchers only included the qualitative findings in the synthesis. While staying open to themes emerging from the data, the authors were interested in identifying themes with regard to the characteristics, opportunities provided by, and limitations of technology-mediated tasks. Relying on the qualitative software NVivo, the researchers created 332 initial codes, which generated four conceptual, ten descriptive, and thirty-one sub-categories. In addition to the topic prespecified by the researchers, the data also yielded insights into what factors influence the effectiveness of technology-mediated TBLT.

Conducting meta-analyses and other types of systematic reviews are clearly important for the field of TBLT, as they can offer recommendations for teachers based on the aggravated results of many studies on a TBLT-related issue. However, as Sato and Loewen (2019: 13) note, given that instructed SLA is a relatively new field, researchers often examine new factors and techniques; thus, narrative reviews are likely to be comparably useful for teachers, as these can provide them with information about new techniques that they could trial in their own practice.

15.3 Issues in Task-Based Language Teaching Research Methodology and Suggestions for Further Research

Having reviewed key methods that have been employed to study the role of tasks in L2 teaching, I will now discuss the current issues in TBLT research methods. Also considered is how some of the methodological challenges might be overcome in future research.

15.3.1 Addressing Tensions between Internal and Ecological Validity

As in other areas of instructed SLA research, a key challenge for TBLT researchers is to strike a balance between internal and ecological validity. While internal validity is concerned with the soundness of the design of empirical research, ecological validity has to do with the extent to which the research findings can be extended to real TBLT settings. Arguably, there is a need to conduct tightly controlled TBLT experiments, as these can help isolate variables that might affect task-based performance and development. However, the danger is that, due to the careful control for potential confounding factors, experimental studies become so artificial and removed from actual classrooms that the findings no longer seem to have implications for actual TBLT practice. To minimize this risk, researchers could start by observing the current practices and learner behaviors in the type of task-based settings for which they would like to draw implications. Then, the observations made could inform the development of the materials and procedures in subsequent experiments (Lightbown & Spada, 2019; Rogers & Révész, 2020). Ecological validity can also be enhanced through collaboration with teachers when developing tasks, task manipulations, and task-based lessons. As mentioned previously, a few TBLT studies have successfully adopted this approach (e.g., Kim, 2012; Mackey, 2002; Oliver, Philp & Duchesne, 2017). Finally, another way to deal with potential threat to ecological validity is to employ quasi-experimental rather than true experimental designs (Sato & Loewen, 2019). Given that quasi-experimental research often takes place in classrooms, it is likely to have greater potential for informing pedagogy. When conducting classroom studies, however, researchers need to make sure that they minimize the disruption of classroom activities, do their best to maintain objectivity, and comply with ethical issues pertinent to classroom research (Mackey, 2017).

15.3.2 Need for More Developmental and Longitudinal Research

Similar to other subfields of instructed SLA research, there is a lack of longitudinal studies on TBLT. Although the past two decades have seen a growth of studies investigating task-based development, most of the developmental research is still short-term, usually spanning not longer than two to four weeks. Also, these studies, the majority focusing on the effects of engaging in task-based interaction (see Cobb, 2010; Keck et al., 2006; Mackey & Goo, 2007 for meta-analyses), typically had a narrow focus, investigating the acquisition of specific linguistic features rather than improvement in global proficiency. One could argue that, to inform and guide TBLT pedagogy, it would be necessary to conduct studies that take academic terms and even years, gauging overall L2 development in actual TBLT settings. However, the issue with such long-term studies is that they "tend to (and perhaps must) prioritize ecological validity over predictive validity" (Ellis et al., 2020: 300). Over extended periods of time, it is challenging to control for the large array of extraneous factors that can potentially affect classroom learning. Another practical problem is that carrying out longitudinal studies is highly labor-intensive, requiring a lot of researcher time and strong institutional commitment. These are challenging to secure in most contexts, due to low availability of research funding and already high demands on teachers. In light of this, it would appear more realistic for researchers to strive to conduct longitudinal studies that last for shorter periods (e.g., six to ten weeks). Such studies will allow for observing development in specific areas of task-based performance, serving as useful stepping stones to establishing the longer-term effects of task-based learning and teaching.

15.3.3 Focus on Processes and Products

To date, TBLT research has primarily been concerned with the products of task-based use and learning, mainly employing outcome measures such as complexity, accuracy, and fluency or indices gauging the use or knowledge of specific linguistic features. For the purposes of theory construction and informing pedagogical practices, however, it is also important to examine the processes in which learners engage during task-based work (Révész, 2014). Process-oriented research is, for example, warranted to explore the cognitive processes in which learners engage when they perform tasks. As Révész (2019) reviewed, there are a number of techniques that TBLT researchers have at their disposal to examine task-generated cognitive processes, including subjective techniques (e.g., questionnaires, interviews, and think-aloud and stimulated recall protocols), as well as more objective tools (e.g., dual-task methodology, keystroke-logging, screen-recording, eye-tracking, and fMRI).

In addition to looking at task-based processes, it would also be beneficial for future studies to focus more on links between process- and product-based measures. While there has been an increased interest in process-product relationships in the larger field of instructed SLA (e.g., Godfroid, Boers, & Housen, 2013; Pellicer-Sánchez, 2016), relatively few studies have looked into them in the area of TBLT. Among the early examples are interactionist TBLT studies that have examined the extent to which the frequency of interactional features (e.g., Adams, 2007) and cognitive activities (e.g., Mackey, 2006) during task performance predict L2 development. More recently, a few researchers have also begun to investigate how task variables may affect relationships between task-generated cognitive processes and task-based performance and development (e.g., Kim et al., 2015; Révész et al., 2017).

15.3.4 Triangulation of Sources

While in some types of TBLT research, such as the case study paradigm, data triangulation is a core feature of research designs, this methodological practice has been less widespread in cognitively oriented TBLT research. However, in recent years, as in instructed SLA research in general (King & Mackey, 2016; Mackey & Gass, 2016), there has been an increasing trend toward collecting and triangulating multiple data sources. The rationale for utilizing designs with various data sources is that the combination of different data-collection techniques, due to inherent limitations associated with each, is likely to yield more valid and complete insights than use of a single method (Révész, 2019). As discussed earlier, task complexity researchers increasingly rely on and triangulate multiple measures when providing independent evidence for the validity of their task manipulations to enhance the credibility of their validity argument. Révész, Michel and Gilabert (2016; Michel, Révész & Gilabert, 2014) collected data through four methods – dual-task methodology, self-perception questionnaires, eye-tracking, and stimulated recall – to tap the effects of task complexity manipulations on task-generated cognitive processes. Researchers have also combined verbal protocol data, such as the stimulated recall procedure with keystroke-logging (Charoenchaikorn, 2019; Révész et al., 2017; Révész et al., 2019), eye-tracking (Révész et al., 2019), Google docs (Michel & Stiefenhöfer, 2019) and screen-recordings (Charoenchaikorn, 2019), to study task-based L2 writing processes. In each of these studies, triangulating various methods, as expected, allowed the researchers to achieve richer and more valid conclusions. In light of this, more widespread use of data triangulation would appear to benefit cognitively oriented TBLT research in the future.

15.3.5 Data Reporting and Transparency

In their methodological synthesis of research on task-based language production, Plonsky and Kim (2016) point to a number of problems in data reporting and make a series of recommendations that researchers should follow to improve reporting practices in quantitative TBLT research. For example, they found that not all studies reported and interpreted reliability statistics, and visual displays of data were often missing or were ineffective. Plonsky and Kim also called for more detailed reporting of descriptive statistics including confidence intervals and effect sizes. In addition to improving reporting practices, it is crucial that TBLT researchers, regardless of their methodological orientation, make it a practice to share their instruments and data in open-science platforms such as IRIS. This will help increase the transparency and replicability of TBLT research, while also facilitating the education of TBLT scholars.

Further Reading

DeCosta, P. I., Valmori, L., and Choi, I. (2017). Qualitative research methods. In S. Loewen and M. Sato, eds. *The Routledge handbook of second language acquisition*. New York: Routledge, pp. 522–40.

DeKeyser, R. (2019). Aptitude treatment interaction in second language learning [Special issue]. *Journal of Second Language Studies*, 2(2).

Dörnyei, Z. (2007). *Research methods in applied linguistics*. Oxford: Oxford University Press.

Loewen, S. and Philp, J. (2011) Instructed second language acquisition. A. Mackey, and S. Gass, ed. *Research methods in second language acquisition: A practical guide*. Malden, MA: Wiley-Blackwell, pp. 53–73.

Mackey, A. (2017). Classroom-based research. In S. Loewen and M. Sato, eds. *The Routledge handbook of second language acquisition*. New York: Routledge, pp. 541–61.

Mackey, A. and Gass, S. M. (2015). *Second language research: Methodology and design* 2nd ed. New York: Routledge.

McKinley, J. and Rose, H. (2020), eds. *The Routledge handbook of research methods in applied linguistics*. New York: Routledge.

Plonsky, L. and Kim, Y. (2016). Task-based learner production: A substantive and methodological review. *Annual Review of Applied Linguistics*, 36, 73–97.

Révész, A. (2014). Towards a fuller assessment of cognitive models of task-based learning: Investigating task-generated cognitive demands and processes. *Applied Linguistics*, 35, 87–92.

Révész, A., Michel, M., and Gilabert, R. (2016). Measuring cognitive task demands using dual task methodology, subjective self-ratings, and expert judgments: A Validation Study. *Studies in Second Language Acquisition*, 38, 703–37.

Study Questions

1. What do you see as the main benefits and disadvantages of conducting TBLT research in classroom and laboratory settings?

2. What data sources would you ideally triangulate to investigate a TBLT topic of interest to you?
3. In your view, what research designs should researchers use more extensively to help reach valid conclusions about the effectiveness of TBLT?

References

Adams, R. (2007). Do second language learners benefit from interacting with each other? In A. Mackey, ed. *Conversational interaction in second language acquisition*. Oxford: Oxford University Press, pp. 29–51.

Albert, Á. and Kormos, J. (2004). Creativity and narrative task performance: An exploratory study. *Language Learning*, 54, 277–310.

Andon, N. J. (2018). Optimal conditions for TBLT?: A case study of teachers' orientation to TBLT in the commercial EFL for adults sector in the UK. In V. Samuda, M. Bygate and K. Van den Branden, eds. *TBLT as a researched pedagogy*. Amsterdam: John Benjamins, pp. 132–64.

Baba, K. and Nitta, R. (2014). Phase transitions in development of writing fluency from a complex dynamic systems perspective. *Language Learning*, 64, 1–35.

Baralt, M. (2013). The impact of cognitive complexity on feedback efficacy during online versus face-to-face interactive tasks. *Studies in Second Language Acquisition*, 35, 689–725.

Bryfonski, L. and McKay, T. H. (2019) TBLT implementation and evaluation: A meta-analysis. *Language Teaching Research*, 23, 603–32

Bulté, B. and Housen, A. (2012). Defining and operationalising L2 complexity. In A. Housen, F. Kuiken, and I. Vedder, eds. *Dimensions of L2 performance and proficiency: Complexity, accuracy and fluency in SLA*. Amsterdam: John Benjamins, pp. 21–46.

Carless, D. (2004). Issues in teachers' reinterpretation of a task-based innovation in primary schools. *TESOL Quarterly*, 38, 639–62.

Charoenchaikorn, V. (2019). *L2 revision and post-task anticipation during text-based synchronous computer-mediated communication (SCMC) tasks*. Unpublished doctoral dissertation, Lancaster University, UK.

Chong S.W. and Reinders H. (2020). Technology-mediated task-based language teaching: A qualitative research synthesis. *Language Learning & Technology*, 24(3), 70–86.

Cobb, M. (2010). *Meta-analysis of the effectiveness of task-based interaction in form-focused instruction of adult learners in foreign and second language teaching*. Unpublished doctoral dissertation, University of San Francisco, CA.

De la Fuente, M. J. (2006). Classroom L2 vocabulary acquisition: Investigating the role of pedagogical tasks and form-focused instruction. *Language Teaching Research*, 10, 263–95.

Dörnyei, Z. and Kormos, J. (2000). The role of individual and social variables in oral task performance. *Language Teaching Research*, 4, 275–300.

Ellis, R. (2003). *Task-based language learning and teaching*. Oxford: Oxford University Press.

Ellis, R. (2011). Macro- and micro-evaluations of task-based teaching. In B. Tomlinson ed. *Materials development in language teaching*. Cambridge: Cambridge University Press, pp. 212–35.

Ellis, R. (2015). Teachers evaluating tasks. In M. Bygate, ed. *Domains and directions in the development of TBLT: A decade of plenaries from the international conference*. Amsterdam: John Benjamins, pp. 247–70.

Ellis, R. and Shintani, N. (2014). *Exploring language pedagogy through second language acquisition research*. London: Routledge.

Ellis, R., Skehan, P., Li, S., Shintani, N., and Lambert, C. (2020). *Theory and practice of task-based language teaching*. Cambridge: Cambridge University Press.

Fu, M. and Li, S. (2019). The associations between individual differences in working memory and the effectiveness of immediate and delayed corrective feedback. *Journal of Second Language Studies*, 2(2), 233–57.

Gilabert, R., Barón, J., and Llanes, A. (2009). Manipulating cognitive complexity across task types and its impact on learners' interaction during oral performance. *International Review of Applied Linguistics in Language Teaching*, 47, 367–95.

Godfroid, A., Boers, F., and Housen, A. (2013). An Eye for Words. Gauging the role of attention in L2 vocabulary acquisition by means of eye tracking. *Studies in Second Language Acquisition*, 35, 483–517.

Granena, G. and Yilmaz, Y. Corrective Feedback and the Role of Implicit Sequence-Learning Ability in L2 Online Performance. *Language Learning*, 69, 127–56.

Gurzynski-Weiss, L. and Révész, A. (2012). Tasks, teacher feedback, and learner modified output in naturally occurring classroom interaction. *Language Learning*, 62, 851–79.

Housen, A. and Kuiken, F. (2009) Complexity, accuracy and fluency in second language acquisition. *Applied Linguistics*, 30, 461–73.

Jackson, D. O. and Suethanapornkul, S. (2013). The Cognition Hypothesis: A synthesis and meta-analysis of research on second language task complexity. *Language Learning*, 63, 330–67.

Jarvis, S. (2013). Defining and measuring lexical diversity. In S. Jarvis and M. Daller, eds., *Vocabulary knowledge: Human ratings and automated measures*. Amsterdam: John Benjamins, pp. 13–45.

Keck, C., Iberri-Shea, G., Tracy, N., and Wa-Mbaleka, S. (2006). Investigating the empirical link between task-based interaction and acquisition: A meta-analysis. In J. M. Norris, and L. Ortega, eds. *Synthesizing research on language learning and teaching*. Amsterdam: Benjamins, pp. 91–131.

Kim, Y. (2009). The effects of task complexity on learner-learner interaction. *System*, 37, 254–68.

Kim, Y. (2012). Task complexity, learning opportunities, and Korean EFL learners' question development. *Studies in Second Language Acquisition*, 34, 627–58.

Kim, Y., Payant, C., and Pearson, P. (2015). The intersection of task-based interaction, task complexity, and working memory: L2 question development through recasts in a laboratory setting. *Studies in Second Language Acquisition*, 37, 549–81.

King, K. and Mackey, A. (2016). Research methodology in second language studies: Trends, concerns and new directions. *The Modern Language Journal*, 100(s), 209–27.

Kourtali, N. and Révész, A. (2020). The roles of recasts, task complexity, and aptitude in child second language development. *Language Learning*, 70, 179–218.

Lambert, C. P. and Engler, S. (2007). Information distribution and goal orientation in second Language task design. In M. P. Garcia-Mayo, ed. *Investigating tasks in formal language learning*. Bristol: Multilingual Matters, pp. 27–43.

Lee, J. (2019). Task complexity, cognitive load, and L1 speech. *Applied Linguistics*, 40, 506–39.

Lightbown, P. and Spada, N. (2019). *In it together: Teachers, researchers, and classroom SLA*. Plenary presented at the annual meeting of the American Association of Applied Linguistics. Atlanta, GA.

Long, M. H. (2015). *Second language acquisition and task-based language teaching*. Oxford: Wiley-Blackwell

Mackey, A. (2002). Beyond production: Learners' perceptions about interactional processes. *International Journal of Educational Research*, 37, 379–94.

Mackey, A. (2006). Feedback, noticing and instructed second language learning. *Applied Linguistics*, 27, 405–30.

Mackey, A. (2012). *Input, interaction, and corrective feedback in L2 learning*. Oxford: Oxford University Press.

Mackey, A. (2017). Classroom-based research. In S. Loewen and M. Sato, eds. *The Routledge handbook of second language acquisition*. New York: Routledge, pp. 541–61.

Mackey, A., Adams, R., Stafford, C., and Winke, P. (2010). Exploring the relationship between modified output and working memory capacity. *Language Learning*, 60, 501–33.

Mackey, A., and Gass, S. (2016). *Second language research: Methodology and design*. New York: Routledge.

Mackey, A. (2017). Classroom-based research. In S. Loewen and M. Sato, eds. *The Routledge handbook of instructed second language acquisition*. New York: Routledge, pp. 541–61.

Mackey, A. and Goo, J. (2007). Interaction research in SLA: A meta-analysis and research synthesis. In A. Mackey, ed. *Conversational interaction in SLA: A collection of empirical studies*. New York: Oxford University Press, pp. 408–52.

Malicka, A. and Levkina, M. (2012). Measuring task complexity:does L2 proficiency matter? In A. Shehadeh and C. Coombe, eds. *Task-based language teaching in foreign language contexts: Research and implementation.* Amsterdam: John Benjamins, pp. 43–66.

Markee, N. and Kunitz, S. (2013). Doing planning and task performance in second language acquisition: An ethnomethodological respecification. *Language Learning,* 63, 1–36.

McDonough, K. and Chaikitmongkol, W. (2007). Teachers' and learners' reactions to a task-based EFL course in Thailand. *TESOL Quarterly,* 41, 107–32.

McDonough, K., Crawford, W., and Mackey, A. (2015). Creativity and EFL learners' language use during a group decision-making task. *TESOL Quarterly,* 49, 188–98.

Michel, M. (2017). Complexity, accuracy, and fluency in L2 production. In S. Loewen and M. Masatoshi, eds. *The Routledge handbook of instructed second language acquisition.* New York: Routledge, pp. 66–84.

Michel, M., Révész, A., and Gilabert, R. (2014). *Eye movement prompts in stimulated recall: tapping cognitive processes based on audio vs. visual stimuli.* Paper presented at AILA, Brisbane, Australia.

Michel, M., Révész, A., Lu, X., Kourtali, N., Lee, M., and Borges, L. (2020). Investigating L2 writing processes across independent and integrated tasks: A mixed-methods study. *Second Language Research,* 36(3), 307–34.

Michel, M. and Stiefenhöfer, L. (2019). Priming Spanish subjunctives during synchronous computer-mediated communication: German peers' classroom-based and homework interactions. In M. Sato and S. Loewen, eds. *Evidence Based Second Language Pedagogy.* New York: Routledge, pp. 191–218.

Nielson, K. B. and DeKeyser, R. M. (2019). Working memory and planning time as predictors of fluency and accuracy. *Journal of Second Language Studies,* 2, 281–316.

Nitta, R. and Baba, K. (2018) Understanding benefits of repetition from a complex dynamic systems perspective: The case of a writing task. In M. Bygate, ed. *Language learning through task repetition.* Amsterdam: John Benjamins, pp. 279–309.

Norris, J. and Ortega, L. (2003). Defining and measuring SLA. In C. J. Doughty and M. H. Long, eds. *The handbook of second language acquisition.* Malden, MA: Blackwell, pp. 717–61.

Norris, J. M. and Ortega, L. (2009). Towards an organic approach to investigating CAF in instructed SLA: The case of complexity. *Applied Linguistics,* 30, 555–78.

Nuevo, A. (2006). *Task complexity and interaction: L2 learning opportunities and development.* Unpublished PhD dissertation, Georgetown University, Washington DC.

Oliver, R., Philp, J., and Duchesne, S. (2017). Children working it out together: A comparison of younger and older learners collaborating in task based interaction. *System,* 69, 1–14.

Pellicer-Sánchez, A. (2016). Incidental L2 vocabulary acquisition from and while reading: An eye-tracking study. *Studies in Second Language Acquisition*, 38, 97–130.

Plonsky, L. and Kim, Y. (2016). Task-based learner production: A substantive and methodological review. *Annual Review of Applied Linguistics*, 36, 73–97.

Révész, A. (2009). Task complexity, focus on form, and second language development. *Studies in Second Language Acquisition*, 31, 437–70.

Révész, A. (2011). Task complexity, focus on L2 constructions, and individual differences: A classroom-based study. *Modern Language Journal*, 95, 162–81.

Révész, A. (2014). Towards a fuller assessment of cognitive models of task-based learning: Investigating task-generated cognitive demands and processes. *Applied Linguistics*, 35, 87–92.

Révész, A. (2019). Investigating task-generated cognitive processes: Methodological advances and challenges. Plenary talk presented at the Biennial International Conference on Task-Based Language Teaching (TBLT), Ottawa, Canada.

Révész, A., Kourtali, N., and Mazgutova, D. (2017). Effects of task complexity on L2 writing behaviors and linguistic complexity. *Language Learning*, 67, 208–41.

Révész, A., Michel, M., and Gilabert, R. (2016). Measuring cognitive task demands using dual task methodology, subjective self-ratings, and expert judgments: A Validation Study. *Studies in Second Language Acquisition*, 38, 703–37.

Révész, A., Michel, M., and Lee, M. (2019). Exploring second language writers' pausing and revision behaviours: A mixed methods study. *Studies in Second Language Acquisition*, 41, 605–31.

Révész, A., Sachs, R., and Hama, M. (2014). The effects of task complexity and input frequency on the acquisition of the past counterfactual construction through recasts. *Language Learning*, 64, 615–50.

Robinson, P. (2001). Task complexity, cognitive resources, and syllabus design: A triadic framework for investigating task influences on SLA. In P. Robinson, ed. *Cognition and second language instruction*. New York: Cambridge University Press, pp. 287–318.

Rogers, J. and Révész, A. (2020). Experimental and quasi-experimental designs. In H. Rose and J. McKinley, eds. *The Routledge handbook of research methods in applied linguistics*. New York: Routledge, pp. 133–43.

Samuda, V. (2001). Guiding relationships between form and meaning during task performance: The role of the teacher. In M. Bygate, P. Skehan, and M. Swain, eds. *Researching pedagogic tasks: Second language learning, teaching and testing*. London: Longman, pp. 119–40.

Sasayama, S. (2016). Is a 'complex' task really complex? Validating the assumption of cognitive task complexity. *The Modern Language Journal*, 100, 231–54.

Sasayama, S., Malicka, A., and Norris, J. (2015). Primary challenges in cognitive task complexity research: Results of a comprehensive research synthesis. Unpublished paper presented at the 6th Biennial International Conference on Task-Based Language Teaching (TBLT), Leuven, Belgium.

Sato, M. and Loewen, S. (2019). Towards evidence-based second language pedagogy: Research proposals and pedagogical recommendations. In M. Sato and S. Loewen, eds. *Evidence-based second language pedagogy: A collection of instructed second language acquisition studies.* New York: Routledge, pp. 1–23.

Shart, M. (2008). What matters in TBLT: Task, teacher or team? An action research perspective from a beginning German language classroom. In J. Eckerth and S. Siekman, eds. *Task-based language learning and teaching.* Berlin: Peter Lang, pp. 47–66.

Shintani, N. (2013). The effect of focus on form and focus on forms instruction on the acquisition of productive knowledge of L2 vocabulary by young beginner learners. *TESOL Quarterly*, 47, 36–62.

Shintani, N. (2015). The incidental grammar acquisition in focus on form and focus on forms instruction for young, beginner learners. *TESOL Quarterly*, 49, 115–40.

Skehan, P. (1998). *A cognitive approach to language learning.* Oxford: Oxford University Press.

Skehan, P. (2009) Modelling second language performance: Integrating complexity, accuracy, fluency and lexis. *Applied Linguistics*, 30, 510–32.

Torres, J. (2018). The effects of task complexity on heritage and L2 Spanish development. *Canadian Modern Language Review*, 74, 128–52.

Wang, Q. (2019). Chinese EFL learners' motivation and anxiety in a task context and the effects of individual difference on task performance. Unpublished doctoral dissertation, University of Auckl and, Auckland, New Zealand.

Yilmaz, Y. (2013). Relative effects of explicit and implicit feedback: The role of working memory capacity and language analytic ability. *Applied Linguistics*, 34, 344–68.

Zalbidea, J. (2017). One task fits all? The roles of task complexity, modality, and working memory capacity in L2 performance. *The Modern Language Journal*, 101, 335–52.

16

Task-Based Language Teaching as an Innovation

A Task for Teachers

Kris Van den Branden

16.1 Introduction

When I was asked to contribute a chapter on task-based language teaching (TBLT) and innovation to this volume, I felt a bit hesitant. Can TBLT still be called an innovation? After all, its basic principles were described around forty years ago in seminal publications by Prabhu, Long, and others (for an overview, see Van den Branden, Bygate & Norris [2009]), even before the technological revolution and globalization changed billions of people's daily lives. From that perspective, TBLT can actually be considered "old school," rather than an innovation in tune with current societal and educational trends.

However, on second thoughts, that view could be refuted for several reasons. The first reason, which I will elaborate on in the next paragraph, is that what counts as an innovation in education is not determined by its initiators, but rather by its potential users. The second argument, which will be further developed in the second part of this chapter, is that ever since its inception, and particularly during the past fifteen years, TBLT has been modified and combined with other innovations, and in this way repeatedly been updated and connected with cutting-edge views, practices, methodologies, and research-based insights regarding language education. Over the past four decades, "*le nouveau TBLT est arrivé*" time and time again, and so, even though most of the fundamental principles described in the seminal publications still apply, TBLT in 2020 can be argued to differ from the approach that was originally described.

16.2 Innovation: A Task for Teachers

Rogers (2003: 12) has defined an innovation as "an idea, practice, or object that is *perceived as new* by an individual or other unit of adoption" (my emphasis). So, what exactly counts as an innovation for a language teacher is a matter of personal judgement. Rogers' reference to ideas, practices, and objects also makes clear that innovations may be related to a wide range of different aspects of language teaching, from the use of particular grouping formats to the implementation of a new curriculum, new tools, methods, tests, or course books.

Innovations have been distinguished from mere change. In this respect, Kennedy (1996) has suggested that while change can be unplanned, chaotic, and caused by circumstances that no one controls, an innovation implies some degree of deliberation and consciousness. Typically, innovations are designed and planned by someone with an intent to improve an existing practice. In many cases, innovations are planned by other parties than those who are expected to put them in practice. As a result, they will need to be diffused (i.e., information about the innovation needs to be transferred, understood, and accepted by users) and implemented (i.e., they need to become manifest in users' thinking and behavior in specific contexts). Much of the above is captured in Carless's (2013: 1) definition of an innovation as "an attempt to bring about educational improvement by doing something which is perceived by implementers as new or different."

In the case of TBLT, the innovation was originally designed and described by researchers, most of whom were applied linguists with a pedagogical interest and/or background, and was meant to be adopted by teachers in their second language (L2) classrooms. In other words, adopting TBLT can be conceived as a task for teachers. Drawing on my own generic definition of tasks as the real-life activities that people engage in with a view to reaching a particular goal (Van den Branden, 2006), educational innovations, and the adoption of TBLT in particular, will be approached in this chapter as the innovative activities related to (language) teaching or learning that teachers engage in to reach a particular goal. Their goal may be to improve the quality of their language teaching, much as the instigators of TBLT originally intended, but it may also be of another kind: for instance, a language teacher may just want to comply with her colleagues' adoption of a particular innovative method (that *the latter* think will improve the quality of *their* language education) to maintain their mutually rewarding social and professional relationships.

Innovations that are designed by researchers to be implemented by teachers are prone to being reinterpreted, reshaped, and aborted along the way. In the process of implementation, governmental boards, curriculum developers, syllabus designers, commercial publishers, teacher educators, in-service trainers, teacher councellors, test designers, school principals, and even parents all may take up the role of change agent, and change the shape, goal, or outlook of the innovation that the teacher will take into consideration. In fact, the implementation of TBLT constitutes an example *par excellence* of this:

> As so often happens in applied linguistics, however, it was not long before the original proposals [regarding TBLT] were diluted, changed beyond recognition in some cases, and repackaged in a form more acceptable to the powerful political and commercial interests that exert enormous influence over the way [language teaching] is conducted. (Long, 2015: 6)

In the quote above, "acceptable" is a crucial term. For most practitioners in the field, "top-down" innovations that are mandated from above or introduced by external change agents pose a *threat*, rather than an opportunity, if they deviate too much from the practitioners' current beliefs and practices. In this respect, the literature and research on the management of change in education, which has steadily grown over the past decades (cf. Fullan, 2007; Hargreaves & Fullan, 2012; Schleicher, 2018; Van den Branden, 2009; Waters, 2009) points out a number of factors that impact on teachers' adoption of innovations:

- Teachers' motivation to participate in an innovation is strongly influenced by their assessment of *how useful* the innovation will be. Teachers are likely to be more motivated to participate if they believe the innovation will be rewarding for both themselves and for their students.
- Teachers will be more motivated to participate in the innovation if they perceive the goals they associate with the innovation, and the adoption of the innovation, not only as rewarding, but also as *attainable*.
- Teachers will be more inclined to participate in the innovation if they have the feeling that their *self-competence* will not be damaged and there is little risk of losing face.
- Teachers will be more motivated if they are allowed some degree of *autonomy* in determining the timing, modalities, and conditions under which they will approach the innovation.
- Innovations are more likely to reach the classroom if *proper support structures* are set up for the teachers involved. Whether it comes in the shape of in-service training, online modules, or coaching on the floor, teachers benefit the most from the kind of support that helps them to forge strong connections between theory and practice. One-shot training sessions that mainly offer theoretical background information have only limited effects compared to support that incorporates the demonstration of particular methods or approaches, and also offers the participating teachers extensive chances to try them out in their own classrooms and receive feedback on what they are doing.

- Adopting and implementing an innovation usually takes *time*. Teachers should be granted the time and space to try out new classroom practices, make mistakes, and learn from them.
- The implementation of innovation can be greatly enhanced by *collegial observation, interaction with fellow staff members, and team teaching*. Based on findings from the TALIS research, Schleicher (2018) concludes that these are the kinds of activities that teachers believe contribute the most to their professional development. Peers and colleagues can give teachers the contextualized cognitive, emotional, and motivational support it often takes to persist in implementing an innovation and keep on believing in it.

The above-mentioned factors interact in complex ways and reinforce each other. For example, in the recent ICILS study (Fraillon et al., 2019), teachers around the world were found to be more inclined to integrate computer and information literacy in their regular courses if (a) they had positive attitudes to ICT; (b) felt confident about their own ICT-skills; and (c) their schools fostered a climate of collaborative learning among staff members. In the next paragraph, I will focus on how the above-mentioned factors play out with regard to the implementation of TBLT.

16.3 Reinterpreting Task-Based Language Teaching

Over the past decades, TBLT has gained considerable momentum as a researched approach to L2 education, even to the extent that a growing number of governments recommend it as the most favored approach to L2 education. A number of studies are available which show how teachers, in different educational contexts across the world, approach the adoption and implementation of TBLT (e.g., Adams & Newton, 2009; Carless, 2004; East, 2012; McDonough & Chaikitmongkol, 2007; Shehadeh & Coombe, 2012; Van den Branden, 2006). Together, those studies make clear that, for most teachers, the implementation of TBLT is a complex and highly challenging project, and that in the process of adopting TBLT, they face a number of obstacles.

First, many teachers have reported the lack of task-based resources, and the lack of time to plan and design tasks, as a major obstacle (Erlam, 2016; Hu, 2013; Zheng and Borg, 2014). Many teachers who are interested in TBLT have to work with a structural syllabus, in which discrete linguistic items are taught explicitly before students are asked to perform communicative tasks, and the items come in a predetermined order. Secondly, and often in combination with the first concern, teachers report that they experience a serious clash between the task-based rationale and the high-stakes tests or national exams for which they have to prepare their students and in which the explicit knowledge of discrete linguistic items needs to be demonstrated (Adams & Newton, 2009; Hu, 2013; East, 2014; Nguyen, Jaspaert & Van den Branden, 2018; Zheng & Borg, 2014). Many teachers in the above-mentioned studies also acknowledge that they personally endorse the view that L2 learners should first acquire discrete linguistic elements before they are ready to perform meaningful tasks. In other words, not only do they use structural syllabi because there are no task-based alternatives, but also because they believe this is the way an L2 should be taught. In a number of studies, particularly those carried out in Asian contexts, this perception is tied up with strong feelings about the status of the teacher as expert, whose main task it is to transmit knowledge, provide direct instruction, and correct students' errors (Adams & Newton, 2009; Carless, 2004).

Besides the lack of adequate resources, class size is often seen as a major practical concern with the implementation of TBLT. In addition, teachers' fears that students will use their mother tongue while performing tasks in pairs or groups has a negative impact on many teachers' motivation to work with tasks. In some cases, teachers are hesitant because of certain misconceptions they have. For instance, in Flanders, the implementation of TBLT, which was largely conceived and planned from above by the government and university-based expert centers, was slowed down and obstructed by teachers who conceived of TBLT as an exclusively meaning-focused approach (cf. Van den Branden, 2006). As much as this idea runs counter to the symbiosis of meaningful communication and focus on form advocated in the TBLT-related theoretical discourse, it may create strong resistance with language teachers and, in some cases, lead to their decision to abolish it altogether. The same applies to some teachers' conviction that TBLT is unsuitable for beginner learners, because the latter are believed to lack the proficiency to produce meaningful utterances in the target language (Erlam, 2016). However, this view ignores the fact that many tasks are input-based, rather than output-based, and that some productive tasks at beginner level require little in terms of syntax and accuracy, or may be successfully performed by using unanalyzed chunks. If teachers primarily associate TBLT with output-based tasks and meaningful classroom interaction, they may also be reluctant to fully endorse it is because they have doubts about their own target language proficiency (Carless, 2004). Commercial publishers are very sensitive to teachers' entrenched beliefs. Even though they are keen on being associated with the latest trends in research and governmental educational policies ("Yes, our syllabus is task-based"), at the same time, they refrain from producing coursebooks that teachers are expected to perceive as too distant from their current classroom practice and their key beliefs about effective language education (Jordan & Grey, 2019; Tomlinson, 2013). As a result, Tomlinson (2013: 204) notes that, despite many changes in the L2 pedagogic theory, "coursebooks for teaching English as an L2 have remained little changed. They have more or less stuck with a commercially successful script of PPP [present, practice, produce] activities focusing on discrete teaching points." Language teachers and commercial publishers mutually influence and reinforce each other in their respective beliefs and their actions. As a result, educational practice constitutes a domain where innovations that are considered by practitioners as too revolutionary, cumbersome, challenging, or complex tend to be neutralized, or where creative compromises are struck. These compromises often consist of infusing existing classroom practice with some digestible proportion of the "new." A prime example of the latter is "task-supported language teaching" (cf. Ellis, 2003), which, although based on TBLT and communicative language teaching, is strongly compatible with structural approaches like PPP. In TSLT, the first two stages of PPP (i.e., present and practice) tend to be preserved, while the third stage (produce) is extended by incorporating the performance of meaningful tasks. While TSLT has been called a "weak" form of TBLT, Samuda (2015) has argued that it would do more justice to practitioners to see it as one of the many creative ways in which tasks can be put to use in a great diversity of complex and demanding educational settings.

16.4 Enriching Task-Based Language Teaching

To fully grasp the above-mentioned argument developed by Samuda, and to fully understand some teachers and commercial publishers' reluctance to endorse a strong version of TBLT, it should be realized that in 2020, implementing TBLT entails much more than using tasks as the basic unit of analysis for defining goals and organizing daily classroom practice. As demanding as that in itself may sound, in the TBLT-related theoretical and pedagogical literature that has developed over the past two decades, the implementation of TBLT seems to take the shape of a substantial package deal: working with tasks in the L2 classroom is linked with, and even presupposes the simultaneous, integrated implementation of a bunch of other innovations, including:

- the incorporation of modern technology in the L2 classroom
- the incorporation of cooperative learning in task-based classroom interaction
- the breaking down of barriers between language courses and other subjects in the curriculum and between language learning at school and outside school
- the enhancement of students' self-regulation skills while performing tasks
- the implementation of alternative and formative approaches to assessment.

Below, I will comment on those innovations and discuss how they are related to TBLT.

16.4.1 The Integration of Modern Technology in Language Education

The list of potential benefits of integrating digital technology in the language classroom, as described by those advocating this innovation, is impressive (cf. Beetham & Sharpe, 2013; Dudeney & Hockly, 2007). No wonder this innovation has also been directly linked to TBLT, and this has been done for several reasons (cf. Gonzalez-Lloret and Ortega, 2014):

- As a result of the technological revolution, a growing number of the target language tasks that L2 learners need to be able to perform in real life are mediated by modern technology. So, integrating modern technology in the (task-based) language classroom helps to update the curriculum.
- Integrating modern technology in the language classroom may enhance students' language learning motivation. For instance, through the integration of task-based language learning opportunities in digital applications and tools that students find appealing (such as games, computer-mediated communication, and virtual environments), they may be willing to invest more energy in the performance of tasks.
- While performing tasks, modern technology can aid teachers to expose their students to rich, elaborate, high-quality, authentic input, including input produced by native speakers. Moreover, modern technology offers a great range of options (including visual support, multimodal input, captions, subtitling, and online dictionaries) to make the task-based input comprehensible.
- Content can be provided to students through the use of modern technology, allowing the teacher to focus on monitoring individual learners' progress and interactionally supporting task performance.
- Modern technology presents students with a wide range of exciting opportunities to produce target language output for functional purposes, for instance through mobile phone applications, social media, correspondence classes, Skype, email, wikis, and so on. It also allows students to engage in authentic interaction with native speakers, pen pals, and other students outside their own classroom. Online applications and courses also extend opportunities for students to receive feedback and discuss their course work with other students.

From the above, it can be inferred that the implementation of TBLT quite naturally, and according to some inevitably, entails the integration of modern technology in language education. This, however, is not to say that all language teachers act upon this piece of advice, and that they do so in a way that maximally benefits their students' (language) development. Empirical research into the effects of integrating modern technology in the (language) classroom on students' development has produced mixed results. In some cases, the results have been downright disappointing:

"The results … show no appreciable improvement in student achievement in reading, mathematics and science in countries that had invested heavily in ICT for education. And perhaps the most disappointing finding of the report is that technology is of little help in bridging the skills divide between advantaged and disadvantaged students." (OECD, 2015)

The crux of the matter appears to lie in the extent to which the integration of modern technology is consistent with principles of effective instruction. For second language acquisition, and technology-mediated TBLT in particular, Ziegler (2016) and Gonzalez-Lloret (2017), amongst others, have pointed out that the integration of modern technology should, first and foremost, be informed by second language acquisition research and research into the effectiveness of language education. In other words, if modern technology does not cater for a productive symbiosis of meaningful tasks and focus on form; for rich, comprehensible input; for extensive output opportunities and formative feedback; and for rich opportunities for interaction and negotiation, the chances that modern technology will have a positive impact on L2 development are likely to suffer. If, however, the integration of modern technology *does* comply with principles of effective language teaching, then TBLT and modern technology can indeed be powerful allies, in view of all the above-mentioned advantages.

Evidently, all this also applies to the growing range of technology-driven resources (some of which are hinging on artificial intelligence) that foster independent and personalized L2 learning. Here too, it remains to be seen to what extent these AI-driven environments are truly capable of reaching beyond the level of discrete-unit teaching, and offer students a personalized menu of meaningful *tasks* (rather than exercises on discrete items), feedback on various dimensions of the students' output (rather than only accuracy), and truly communicative opportunities to develop L2 interaction skills.

16.4.2 Cooperative Learning

Group and pair work have been advocated in the literature on L2 pedagogy for a long time, particularly when it comes to offering students rich opportunities to develop their productive skills. Amongst others, they have been claimed to multiply speaking opportunities (because more than one student can speak at the same time), offer a safer climate to students and so encourage risk-taking, and give students chances to learn from each other. No wonder they feature highly in the pedagogical literature on TBLT. A substantial body of empirical research has been carried out into the kinds of tasks that foster the richest interaction and negotiation among students, and the conditions under which peer interaction benefits L2 learning the most (Ellis & Shintani, 2014; Hattie, 2009; Long, 2015;

Mitchell, 2014). It shows that particularly those types of group and pair work that are subsumed under "cooperative learning" have a positive impact on students' language development. Cooperative learning is characterized by five key features:

- positive interdependence, which refers to the fact that group members rely on each other to accomplish the task (as, for instance, in information gap tasks)
- group and individual accountability, which refers to the fact that each member can be held accountable for the group's success
- direct interaction, which involves all group members in discussing, negotiating, and actively participating
- group processing, which means that all members should contribute to handling the task management
- interpersonal skills, which refers to the fact that group members should develop the competences to listen to each other with respect and deal with conflicts.

Despite the great empirical support for its positive effects, cooperative learning is still seen by many teachers around the world as a challenging innovation. It tends to be associated with high noise levels, the use of the mother tongue (instead of the target language), off-task student behavior, and a threat to the position and role of the teacher. In the final part of this chapter, we will discuss how this kind of teacher resistance can be dealt with.

16.4.3 Language Learning across the Curriculum, and Beyond

Today, the default setting of language education is still to have it taught as a separate subject by a teacher who is specifically trained to teach languages. But, because so many language teachers tend to stick to structure-oriented approaches (as mentioned above), alternatives have been sought outside the traditional language classroom. In some of those innovative practices, the boundaries between the language classroom and other subjects in the curriculum are crossed, while in others those between the language classroom and the world outside the school are.

For instance, in content-and-language integrated learning (CLIL), a subject like geography, history, or sciences is taught through the medium of a foreign/second language by a teacher who is, first and foremost, an expert in teaching that subject. Through CLIL, students are believed to develop both subject-related and target language competences (Coyle, Hood, & Marsh, 2010; also see Mayo's chapter in this book). Particularly in higher education, CLIL has taken high flight with the growing number of courses that are taught in a language that is not the students' mother tongue. CLIL has been presented, amongst others by the European Commission (2014), as more than a way to find more hours for languages in an already crowded curriculum; it has been claimed to provide learners with more extensive, and better, opportunities to perform relevant tasks (i.e., to use the target language for meaningful communication and put language knowledge to immediate, functional practice). This, in fact, can be seen as a fundamental critique on the practice of teaching language as a subject. The available research (cf. Dalton-Puffer, 2008; Perez-Cañado, 2012) shows that, on the whole, CLIL indeed has a positive impact on target language development, although many of the studies may suffer from a selection bias (e.g., the most motivated students participate in CLIL-programs) and the research designs often do not allow to tease out the unique contribution of the CLIL program.

An even more extensive scope on language learning across the curriculum is taken in "language-aware schools" and school-based policies related to "language across the curriculum" (Corson, 1999). These are based on the premise that all teachers, regardless of the subject they teach, can ask their L2 students (so, the students who did not acquire the medium of instruction as their mother tongue) to perform writing, reading, listening, and speaking tasks in the L2, and can support their students in acquiring L2 competences. For instance, when a teacher of economics asks L2 students to write a letter of complaint to a firm, or a history teacher asks L2 students to write a critical essay, they too can provide their students with feedback on their drafts, model writing strategies, negotiate the meaning of the students' output, or discuss the meaning of infrequent vocabulary (with or without the aid of the students' mother tongue). In language-aware schools, language teachers often take the lead to conceptualize and design a school-based language policy plan, or support their colleagues with regard to offering students stimuli for language development.

In the same vein, Van den Branden (2019) describes examples of collaborative projects in which language teachers and teachers of other subjects connect some of their lesson activities to the same thematic content, which spontaneously leads to the integration of task-based language learning and subject learning. For instance, in a project involving a temporary cooperation between the teacher of physical education and English as a foreign language, thirteen-year old students are first asked to read an excerpt from a Harry Potter volume to learn the rules of Quidditch, which constitutes a motivating, goal-oriented, reading comprehension task. Next, the students negotiate and write down (again in English) the rules of a variant that can be played by human beings who cannot fly on brooms (an example of an L2 writing task). Next, the students try out their rules during physical education after which they refine and rewrite the rules (in English) on the basis of their experiment. While doing all this, they develop their physical skills and gain insight in the rules of fair play.

In a similar vein, L2 education has been integrated with vocational training courses, both for adolescent L2 learners in the vocational and technical strands of secondary education and adult L2 learners in higher education and vocational training courses. Many of these courses are prime examples of needs-based language teaching: students learn to perform the language tasks that are directly relevant to their needs, particularly with regard to (future) work and employment. In some cases, vocational training and language education are completely integrated in that stimuli for language development are given as they spontaneously present themselves during the vocational training. In other cases, what happens on the vocational training floor is taken as the basis for short, language-focused interventions "on the side." Language education can also be integrated in projects aiming to enhance the learners' social and cultural integration in society. In those cases, language teachers or coaches do not operate in language classrooms, but they accompany and support the L2 learner(s) while they are engaging in real-life interaction in their neighborhood, in community networks and services, in the school of their children, or in leisure-time activities. This comes close to what Eskildsen and Theodórsdóttir (2017) have called "language learning in the wild."

16.4.4 Integrating Language Learning with the Development of Twenty-First Century Skills

Since the beginning of the century, a wide range of publications have been issued by international organizations, researchers, and policy makers advocating the integration of twenty-first-century skills into modern-day curricula (for an overview see Van den Branden [2019]). Mainly inspired by societal changes driven by the technological revolution, climate change, and globalization, most lists include competences related to creative thinking, problem-solving, using modern technology, lifelong learning, interpersonal and intercultural communication, citizenship, adapting to change, and sustainable development. Almost all lists also include language competences, more particularly communicative competences in both the mother tongue and at least one foreign language, as well as the competence to deal with information overload in a critical, efficient, and goal-directed way.

In response, an increasing number of governments around the world are now engaged with curricular innovation: they are preparing updated curricula in which the development of twenty-first-century competences assumes a central position. This, however, poses a great challenge for policy makers, researchers, and practitioners alike, because the traditional way to deal with new competences is to stack them unto the existing curriculum. However, as Van den Branden (2019: 27) has argued, "including twenty-first-century competences in the curriculum is a matter of integration, rather than accumulation." All the above-mentioned competences need to be linked to specific content to be properly taught. The above-mentioned twenty-first-century competences *permeate* the traditional subjects, rather than coming on top of them in the shape of additional subjects. Mother tongue and L2 courses, and particularly task-based language courses, lend themselves admirably well to fostering twenty-first-century skills in an integrated manner, because (a) most of the above-mentioned twenty-first-century skills are strongly mediated through the use of language, and (b) TBLT departs from a holistic approach in which language is used for the kind of purposes that, often quite automatically, imply the application of other twenty-first-century competences. For instance, students who debate a current societal problem on the basis of a task-based reading assignment (allowing them to prepare their arguments) and are subsequently asked to present their innovative solution for the problem at hand to the other students, do a lot of task-based work, but at the same time get rich opportunities to develop their creative thinking skills, digital literacy competences, and interpersonal skills.

However, amongst language teachers, the integration of TBLT with a curriculum oriented around twenty-first-century skills may cause great unease because they tend to associate it with curriculum overload, a loss of autonomy, the fear of not having the right competences to teach those twenty-first-century competences, the lack of inspiring materials, and fundamental concerns with the way they should be assessed.

16.4.5 Alternative Views on Assessment

In 1989, Mendelsohn stated that "the goal of testing today ... is to see what someone *can do* with the language" (96; emphasis in original). This credo clearly resonates with the basic principles of performance-based and task-based language assessment, and has guided the development of many language tests issued by commercial publishers and professional test developers in the twenty-first century. This focus has further been enhanced by a number of influential frameworks and policy papers in which standards for language competence are described in the shape of meaningful tasks (e.g., the Common European Framework of Reference, the Canadian Language Benchmarks). In contrast to tests that focus on the explicit knowledge of discrete linguistic units, tests focusing on meaningful language use tend to be more time-consuming and labor-intensive in terms of design, administration, evaluation, and grading, which may be one of the reasons why so many teachers and commercial publishers still stick to more traditional, form-focused tests. This may slow down the implementation of TBLT, particularly in a context where high-stake tests and centralized exams have a strong impact on what needs to be taught.

Equally innovative (at least, in the heads of many practitioners) has been the alternative take on the purpose, timing, and impact of assessment. Whereas the traditional view on assessment is summative, in the sense that learners are tested at the end of an instructional unit to evaluate how much, and what, they have learned, the main purpose of more "formative" views on assessment is to foster (language) development. This typically occurs through the provision of feedback that is informed by the evaluative practice. In meta-analyses and review studies on the impact of education on development, feedback systematically ranks very high as one of the main variables that teachers can manipulate to foster learning (Hattie, 2009; Mitchell, 2014). Feedback has been shown to have particularly strong positive effects on (language) learning if the following conditions are met (Hattie & Timperley, 2007; Long, 2015; Mackey & Goo, 2007):

- The feedback is provided in a timely manner (i.e., preferably when the student can make use of it, so during the task performance);
- The feedback is clear and easy to interpret by the learner;
- The feedback relates to the quality of task performance rather than to the personality of the language user;
- The feedback contains information that can help the student to improve task performance.

All of this clearly resonates with the basic principles of TBLT. The implementation of TBLT even *implies* the implementation of performance-based types of assessment and the provision of task-oriented feedback, because task is "the unit of analysis in all stages of TBLT – from needs analysis to *student assessment*." (Long, 2015: 305; my emphasis). Every teacher with the ambition to implement TBLT, then, may face the challenge to fundamentally (re)consider their approach to assessment.

16.4.6 Metacognitive Awareness and Self-regulation

Much in line with alternative views on assessment, empirical support for the positive impact of enhancing the learner's metacognitive self-regulation on learning and development has accumulated (Hattie, 2009; Fadell, Bialik & Trilling, 2015). In general, "metacognition" refers to the process of thinking about thinking, while "metacognitive self-regulation" usually refers to the extent to which learners plan, monitor, and evaluate their own learning processes. In language education, the students' self-regulating skills can be enhanced by explicitly teaching them strategies to perform L2 reading, writing, speaking, and listening tasks, and teaching them how to select and adopt the proper strategy when facing problems during language use (Plonsky, 2011). For listening and reading tasks, strategies such as mobilizing prior knowledge, setting clear listening and reading goals, inferring the meaning of difficult words from the context, and negotiating with other listeners/readers have been shown to promote L2 performance (Vandergrift & Goh, 2009). For writing and speaking, students may, amongst others, benefit from planning, gaining insight in the criteria for successful task performance, and revising their first drafts on the basis of feedback (e.g., Graham & Sandmel, 2011; Plonsky, 2011).

As Clarke (2014) illustrates, students who have a clear view of the criteria for the successful performance of a writing task, can monitor their own work, provide peers and themselves with feedback on their drafts, revise their own work accordingly, and derive metalinguistic knowledge that will guide them when performing similar tasks in the future. One of the drawbacks of this approach (at least, in the heads of those who see this as innovative) is that it may turn the performance of L2 tasks into an extremely time-consuming effort.

16.4.7 Fundamental Changes

A version of TBLT that embraces and incorporates many, if not all of, the above-mentioned innovations potentially challenges certain well-established teacher views on (a) the role of students and teachers, (b) language, and (c) language learning, and do so in a fundamental way. The emphasis on the learner's agency and self-regulation, combined with the optimistic view on the benefits of peer interaction, may leave the teacher wondering what remains their proper role and where their true expertise and role in the language classroom lies (Van den Branden, 2016). Likewise, the emphasis on meaningful communication, including task performance outside the language classroom, runs counter to many teachers' basic intuitions that students first need to gain explicit knowledge about elements of the language before they are able to engage in proper communication. At the same time, a focus on authentic tasks and learners' needs may give rise to heated debate as to which variety of the language should be taught in the classroom: a standard variety of the target language as spoken by native speakers in a country far away, or a local variety that the students are more likely to encounter and need to use once they leave their classrooms and enter the real world. Particularly for a global language like English, the native speaker model is currently challenged by the growing number of "Englishes" around the world that deviate to an increasing extent from British or American standard varieties, but that constitute the base variety for real-life interpersonal and intercultural communication. In addition, the ubiquity of translation tools through online resources, and recent views on the value of translanguaging (Garcia, 2009) may challenge traditional views on the permanent use of the target language, let alone a particular standard, in the L2 classroom.

16.5 Implementing Task-Based Language Teaching in the Twenty-First Century: Making It Happen

In light of the above, for many language teachers today, the implementation of TBLT tends to take the shape of a revolution that turns the familiar world of the language classroom upside down. This, however, is not how successful innovations in education are usually realized. To the contrary, the available research (cf. Fullan, 2007; Hargreaves & Fullan, 2012; Schleicher, 2018; Van den Branden, 2009) strongly suggests that successful innovations in education usually take the shape of relatively slow, gradual evolutions. Furthermore, they only stand a reasonable chance of sustainable impact if local actors at the school level take charge of planning, monitoring, and evaluating their own innovation process. In other words, top-down initiated innovations may inspire, nudge or push practitioners, but they need to be redesigned at the grassroots level. This is not only so because granting autonomy to local change agents has been shown to enhance their motivation and drive to innovate, but also because for innovations to make a difference in the local classroom, they should be contextualized: they should be fine-tuned with the history, local culture, background, needs, ambitions, and competences of the agents who are meant to take action. Context is key: it largely defines what will be seen as innovative in the first place, largely dictates under what infrastructural, material, political, cultural, and social conditions the innovation will need to be implemented, and it may even determine which goals will be set and how they will be evaluated. Context will often also provide a discourse in which the innovation is framed. Context, in other words, will largely determine the goals, modalities, feasibility, and usefulness of the innovation task, and who will be involved, called upon, required, or motivated to perform it. Thirdly, educational innovations stand a higher chance of success if teachers are supported in developing their professional competence. In this regard, Kennedy (2013) advocates an ecological model of innovation and change in education: the innovation is approached as a system-wide endeavor, which means that change agents at different levels of the educational system all take their responsibility to make a contribution to the success of the innovation, and strong linkages between the different levels are maintained.

This is exactly what can be inferred from the documented cases in which the implementation of TBLT has turned out to be relatively successful. For instance, in an early account of the implementation of TBLT on a nationwide scale in Flanders, Van den Branden (2006) reviewed a number of studies documenting the stepwise, messy, and gradual way in which Flemish teachers got acquainted with the basic principles of TBLT, overcame some of their early resistance, and tried it out in their classrooms. His conclusion was clear:

> Regionwide, ambitious educational innovations can only succeed if sustained efforts are made: task-based language teaching takes a number of years to become fully incorporated in school practice. Furthermore, the incorporation will have better chances of success if many different partners, who can potentially act as supportive agents for school teams (e.g. school counsellors, syllabus developers, in-service trainers, school

inspectors, and educational policy makers) operate along agreed principles, and have the means and the competence to intensively coach and train the school teams that are involved." (Van den Branden, 2006: 248)

If teachers are properly supported, they can move from one zone of proximal development to the next, and gradually realize profound change. This process starts with building a proper understanding of the basic claims and principles of TBLT, and clearing up any misconceptions of TBLT teachers might have. The latter is also illustrated in East's account of New Zealand teachers' adoption of TBLT as a means of realizing the aims of the new curriculum that was introduced by the government (East, 2012). East's case studies powerfully attest to the basic insight that to engage with TBLT, teachers first need to gain firm knowledge about it and relate it to their own practice. They need to assign personal meaning to their understanding of TBLT and discover what benefits they and their students can derive from adopting it. This is entirely consistent with the basic view that adopting TBLT is goal-oriented activity: it is a task that a teacher or a school team sets themselves. So, to engage with that task, teachers need to identify relevant goals that are clear and rewarding for themselves and their students. East's case studies indicate that to do so, many teachers will need the support of meaningful others (like advisors, teacher educators, or colleagues) to cope with the cognitive conflict that innovation necessarily brings along. In some cases, those meaningful others need to gently push teachers to a point where they are ready to face the conflict and "be confronted, at a personal level, with what they were *currently* doing, what they could *potentially* be doing, and the *differences* that this might make, otherwise many teachers might conclude for themselves, with regard to TBLT, that 'that's what we do'" (East, 2012:195; original emphasis).

A number of studies also indicate that teachers are more willing to face that conflict, explore the potential rewards of change, and try out tasks in their classroom if their students give indications that they, too, see the benefits of (more) task-based work in the classroom (Adams & Newton, 2009; Van den Branden, 2006). It could be particularly worthwhile for teachers, then, to ask their students more frequently what surplus value they associate with tasks. In addition, to really put TBLT to practice, teachers are in dire need of practice-oriented support in the shape of inspiring task-based tools and syllabi. Virtually all the available studies in the implementation of TBLT show that skillfully designed materials and tests can make a crucial difference in terms of showing teachers what tasks can look like and how they can guide classroom practice and student evaluation (Adams & Newton, 2009; East, 2012; Shehadeh & Coombe, 2012; Van den Branden, 2006; Zheng & Borg, 2014). While experimenting with tasks, teacher can strongly benefit from coaching on the floor, particularly the kind that helps teachers to reflect on their own performance of task-based work in their classrooms. This kind of practice-based support can also come from colleagues, particularly the ones who are involved in the same innovation. In general, the implementation of TBLT stands a much greater chance of success if it is taken on by a school team, rather than by a scattered bunch of isolated, individual teachers (Van den Branden, 2006). If a team of practitioners together defines joint goals, plans actions, executes them, reflects on them, evaluates the effects on their own practice and their students' development, and determines the next steps in the innovation process accordingly, they can gradually develop into a full-blown learning community (DuFour, 2004; Hargreaves and Fullan, 2012). Cooperative learning works as well for teachers as for students. So, ultimately, one of the most profound innovations that many language teachers across the world may need to adopt is to work more closely together. In this respect, Hargreaves and Fullan (2012) have stated that the most abused research finding of the past twenty years is that the individual teacher makes the greatest difference: Teams make the greatest difference, not individual teachers.

16.6 Conclusion

The implementation of TBLT is not a goal in its own right, it is a means to an end. Ideally, it is the result of teachers' joint design, action, and evaluation meant to better serve the students' language learning needs. When trying to get acquainted with, and adopt, TBLT, teachers should not be left to their own devices. Given that the empirical research base underpinning the efficacy of TBLT for fostering students' language development has steadily grown (cf. Bryfonski & McKay, 2019; Keck et al., 2006), now more than ever, the implementation of TBLT needs to be approached as a system-wide endeavor. In essence, the implementation of TBLT does not differ from other educational innovations in being gradual, messy, and incoherent; in taking the shape of a relatively slow evolution, which requires a lot of time, a lot of persistence, and a substantial degree of teacher support and collaboration to make things happen, and to make a true difference for the students involved. If all that is taken into account, a lot of change can occur for the better. Because, as Fullan (2007: 117) has stated, "recognizing the limitations of planning is not the same thing as concluding that effective change is unattainable."

Further Reading

Carless, D. (2013). Innovation in language teaching. In C. A. Chapelle, ed. *The Encyclopedia of Applied Linguistics*. Oxford: John Wiley and Sons.
East, M. (2012). *Task-based language teaching from the teachers' perspective*. Amsterdam:John Benjamins Publishing.

Hyland, K. and Wong, L. (2013). *Innovation and change in English language education*. New York: Routledge.

Van den Branden, K. (2006). Training teachers: task-based as well? In K. Van den Branden, ed. *Task-based language education: from theory to practice*. Cambridge: Cambridge University Press, pp. 217–48.

Van den Branden, K. (2016). The role of the teacher in task-based language teaching. *Annual Review of Applied Linguistics*, 36, 164–81.

Study Questions

1. Do you think innovation in language education should be initiated by practitioners or by governments?
2. Which measures do you think might further the implementation of TBLT the most?
3. What do you think is the contribution that researchers and commercial publishers can make to the implementation of TBLT?
4. Do you believe that TBLT is the most crucial innovation that needs to be realized in the language education of the twenty-first century? Or, are there other, more crucial innovations?

References

Adams, R. and Newton, J. (2009). TBLT in Asia: Opportunities and constraints. *Asian Journal of English Language Teaching*, 19, 1–17.

Beetham, H. and Sharpe, R. (2013). *Rethinking pedagogy for a digital age*. New York: Routledge.

Bryfonski, L. and McKay, T. (2019). TBLT implementation and evaluation: A meta-analysis. *Language Teaching Research*, 23, 603–32.

Carless, D. (2004). Issues in teachers' reinterpretation of a task-based innovation in primary schools. *TESOL Quarterly*, 38(4), 639–62.

Carless, D. (2013). Innovation in language teaching. In C. A. Chapelle, ed. *The encyclopedia of applied linguistics*. Oxford: John Wiley and Sons.

Clarke, S. (2014). *Outstanding formative assessment: Culture and practice*. London: Hodder Education.

Corson, D. (1999). *Language policy across the curriculum*. Bristol: Multilingual Matters.

Coyle, D., Hood, P., and Marsh, D. (2010). *Content and language integrated learning*. Cambridge: Cambridge University Press.

Dalton-Puffer, C. (2008). Outcomes and processes in content and language integrated learning (CLIL): Current research from Europe. In W. Delanoy and L. Volkmann, eds. *Future perspectives for English language teaching*. Heidelberg: Carl Winter, pp. 139–57.

Dudeney, G. and Hockly, N. (2007). *How to teach English with technology*. Harlow: Pearson Education Limited.

DuFour, R. (2004) What is a professional learning community? *Educational Leadership*, 61(8), 6–11.

East, M. (2012). *Task-based language teaching from the teachers' perspective*. Amsterdam: John Benjamins.

Edwards, C. and Willis, J. (2005). *Teachers exploring tasks in English language teaching*. Basingstoke: Palgrave MacMillan.

Ellis, R. (2003). *Task-based language learning and teaching*. Oxford: Oxford University Press.

Ellis, R. and Shintani, N. (2014). *Exploring language pedagogy through second language acquisition research*. New York: Routledge

Erlam, R. (2016). 'I'm still not sure what a task is': Teachers designing language tasks. *Language Teaching Research*, 20, 279–99.

Eskildsen, S. and Theodórsdóttir, G. (2017). Constructing L2 learning spaces: Ways to achieve learning inside and outside the classroom. *Applied Linguistics*, 38, 143–64.

European Commission (2014). Improving the effectiveness of language learning: CLIL and CALL. Retrieved from: https://www.ecml.at/Portals/1/resources/Articles%20and%20publications%20on%20the%20ECML/CLIL%20and%20CALL%20report_July.2014.pdf?ver=2017-07-11-151504-977.

Fadel, C., Bialik, M., and Trilling, B. (2015). *Four-dimensional education: The competencies learners need to succeed*. Boston, MA: Centre for Curriculum Redesign.

Fraillon, J., Schulz, J., Friedman, W., and Duckworth, T. (2019), eds. *Preparing for life in a digital world*. Amsterdam: IEA.

Fullan, M. (2007). *The new meaning of educational change*. 4th ed. Abingdon: Routledge.

Garcia, O. (2009). *Bilingual education in the 21st century: A global perspective*. Sussex: Wiley.

González-Lloret, M. (2017). Technology for task-based language teaching. In C. A. Chapelle and S. Sauro, eds. *The handbook of technology and second language teaching and learning*. First edition. Hoboken, NJ: John Wiley & Sons, pp. 234–47.

González-Lloret, M. and Ortega, L. (2014). *Technology-mediated TBLT: Researching technology and tasks*. Amsterdam: John Benjamins

Graham, S. and Sandmel, K. (2011). The process writing approach: a meta-analysis. *Journal of Educational Research*, 104, 396–407.

Hargreaves, A. and Fullan, M. (2012). *Professional capital. Transforming teaching in every school*. New York: Routledge.

Hattie, J. (2009). *Visible learning: A synthesis of over 800 meta-analyses relating to achievement*. New York: Routledge.

Hattie, J. and Timperley, H. (2007). The power of feedback. *Review of Educational Research*, 77, 81–112

Hu, R. (2013). Task-based language teaching: Responses from Chinese teachers of English. *TESL-EJ*, 16, 1–21.

Hyland, K. and Wong, L. (2013). *Innovation and change in English language education*. New York: Routledge.

Jordan, G. and Gray, H. (2019). We need to talk about coursebooks, *ELT Journal*, 73, 438–46.

Kekh, C. et al. (2006). Investigating the empirical link between interaction and acquisition: A quantitative meta-analysis. In L. Ortega and J. Norris, eds. *Synthesizing research on language learning and teaching*. Amsterdam: John Benjamins, pp. 91–131.

Kennedy, C. (1996). *MA TEFL/TESL Open Learning Programme: ELT Management*. University of Birmingham: Centre for Language Studies.

Kennedy, C. (2013). Models of innovation and change. In C. Kennedy, K. Hyland, and L. Wong, eds. *Models of change and innovation. Innovation and change in English language education*. Abingdon: Routledge, pp. 13–27.

Long, M. (2015). *Second language acquisition and task-based language teaching*. Malden, MA: Wiley-Blackwell.

Mackey, A. and Goo, J. (2007). Interaction research in SLA: A meta-analysis and research synthesis. In A. Mackey, ed. *Conversational Interaction in Second Language Acquisition*. Oxford: Oxford University Press, pp. 407–52.

McDonough, K. and Chaikitmongkol, W. (2007). Teachers' and learners' reactions to a task-based EFL course in Thailand. *TESOL Quarterly*, 41, 107–32.

Mendelsohn, D. (1989). Testing should reflect teaching. *TESL Canada Journal*, 7(1), 95–108.

Mitchell, D. (2014). *What really works in special and inclusive education: Using evidence-based teaching strategies*. New York: Routledge.

Murray, D. (2008), ed. *Planning change, changing plans: Innovations in second language teaching*. Ann Arbor, MI: University of Michigan Press.

Nguyen, T., Jaspaert, K., and Van den Branden, K. (2018). EFL Teachers' perceptions of task-based language teaching in Vietnam. *European Journal of Applied Linguistics and TEFL*, 7, pp. 73–90.

OECD. (2015). *Students, computers and learning. Making the connection*. Paris: OECD Publishing.

Pérez-Cañado, M. (2012). CLIL research in Europe: past, present and future. *International Journal of Bilingual Education and Bilingualism*, 15(3), 315–41.

Plonsky, L. (2011). The effectiveness of second language strategy instruction: A meta-analysis. *Language Learning*, 61, 993–1038.

Rogers, E. (2003). *Diffusion of innovations*. 5th ed. New York: Free Press.

Samuda, V. (2015). Tasks, design and the architecture of pedagogical spaces. In M. Bygate ed. *Domains and directions in the development of TBLT*. Amsterdam: John Benjamins, pp. 271–301.

Schleicher, A. (2018). *World Class. How to build a 21st-century school system*. Paris: OECD Publishing.

Shehadeh, A. and Coombe, C. (2012), eds. *Task-based language teaching in foreign language contexts. Research and implementation*. Amsterdam: John Benjamins.

Tomlinson, B. (2013). Innovation in materials development. In K. Hyland and L. Wong, eds. *Innovation and change in English language education*. New York: Routledge, pp. 203–17.

Hyland, K. and Wong, L. (2013). *Innovation and change in English language education*. New York: Routledge.

Van den Branden, K. (2006). Training teachers: task-based as well? In K. Van den Branden, ed. *Task-based language education: From theory to practice*. Cambridge: Cambridge University Press, pp. 217–48.

Van den Branden, K. (2009). Diffusion and implementation of innovations. In M. Long and C. Doughty, eds. *The handbook of language teaching*. Oxford: Blackwell Publishers, pp. 659–72.

Van den Branden, K. (2016). The role of the teacher in task-based language teaching. *Annual Review of Applied Linguistics*, 36, 164–81.

Van den Branden, K. (2019). *Rethinking schools and renewing energy for learning. Research, principles and practice*. New York: Routledge.

Van den Branden, K., Bygate, M., and Norris, J. (2009). *Task-based language teaching: a reader*. Amsterdam: John Benjamins.

Vandergrift, L. and Goh, C. (2009). Teaching and testing listening comprehension. In M. Long and C. Doughty, eds. *The Handbook of Language Teaching*. Sussex: Wiley Blackwell, pp. 395–411.

Waters, A. (2009). Managing innovation in English language education. *Language Teaching*, 42, 421–58.

Zheng, X. and Borg, S. (2014). Task-based learning and teaching in China: Secondary school teachers' beliefs and practices. *Language Teaching Research*, 18, 205–21.

Ziegler, N. (2016). Taking technology to task: Technology-mediated TBLT, performance, and production. *Annual Review of Applied Linguistics*, 36, 136–63.

17

The Adoption of Task-Based Language Teaching in Diverse Contexts

Challenges and Opportunities

Jonathan Newton

17.1 Introduction

This chapter argues the case for context being both of theoretical and practical importance for task-based language teaching (TBLT) and outline the implications of a focus on context for research and prospects for the field. The virtual invisibility of context in the early decades of TBLT research[1] produced context-free, ostensibly universally applicable claims as to the value of TBLT. When drawn on to frame policy and practice in diverse contexts, these claims have often fallen foul of context, a point well illustrated in the failure of task-based curriculum reforms in Hong Kong primary and high-school English as a foreign language (EFL) programs in the 1990s (Adamson & Davison, 2003; Carless, 2009). In taking context seriously, researchers have the opportunity to contribute to the adoption of TBLT in contexts in which it has hitherto struggled to gain a foothold or has been unknown. Context-sensitive TBLT research can also help the field to evolve through drawing on the innovations and adaptations teachers make as they implement tasks in real-world classrooms. In essence I am arguing for an ecologically sensitive, situated approach to TBLT, as captured in the proposal that TBLT be viewed as a "researched pedagogy" (Samuda, et al., 2018).

I begin the chapter by making the case for context in TBLT research. I then discuss three different ways in which context is implicated in TBLT

---

[1] There are clearly exceptions, just a sample of which include Cortazzi and Jin (1996), Littlewood (2007), and Van den Branden (2006).

research, illustrating each with a discussion of selected studies. Drawing on this body of research, I conclude by identifying what I see as important research needs and prospects for TBLT in diverse contexts.

17.2 The Case for Context

Much of the early research and scholarship in TBLT in the 1980s and 1990s was oriented toward theoretical questions drawn from second language acquisition,[2] questions which concern, for example, the roles of input, interaction, negotiation for meaning and output (and associated mental corollaries of attention and noticing) in learning a second/foreign language. This research sought to understand the relationship between tasks (and task types), learning behaviors (e.g., task-based interaction and negotiation for meaning), and learning outcomes (evidence of acquisition). The primary goal was to provide empirical evidence for the role of language-learning tasks in language acquisition and to establish TBLT empirically as a viable methodological innovation. This research tradition has often treated context as an extraneous variable to be rendered invisible in the search for answers to theoretically interesting questions, which by their very nature exclude cultural and contextual considerations.

Predictably, the dominant role of second language acquisition in early TBLT research ensured that much of this research was conducted in settings proximate to the epicenters of second language acquisition research in North American universities (and their equivalents in other western countries), namely pre-sessional English as a second language (ESL) programs in which students are typically post-beginner, post-childhood, educated, from a range of first language (L1) backgrounds, and learning English for the specific purpose of entering into a mainstream tertiary program.[3] Classes in such programs are often small, held in well-equipped classrooms, embedded in an English-speaking setting, taught intensively for relatively short periods of time (i.e., weeks or months), and taught by teachers who have a graduate qualification in TESOL, are native speakers of English (or are at least highly proficient speakers of English), and are usually not proficient speakers of the learners' L1s.

On most if not all of these variables, pre-sessional programs are atypical of the diverse contexts in which second/foreign languages are learned worldwide and particularly of the dominant language-learning sector worldwide, that of *foreign* language programs situated in compulsory sector education

---

[2] Even in second language acquisition experimental studies, classroom tasks were usually used, and Long (1985, 2009, 2015) has long advocated for TBLT on the basis of its value in both syllabus design and teaching methodology.

[3] There have also been a few TBLT programs in very different settings, such as those represented in the case studies in this volume, including vocational training for Australian aborigines, for Syrian and other refugees, and in native-American language revival settings.

Table 17.1 *Dimensions of context*

Dimension	Pre-sessional ESL program in North America	Elementary school EFL in China
Class size	Small	Large
Resources	Variable, but often relatively resource rich	Resource poor
Exposure to English beyond the classroom	Extensive	Little, nonexistent in many rural contexts
English learning time	Intensive short courses	2–3 hours per week across five years
Teacher proficiency	High (often native speakers)	Variable and often quite low (A2–B1)
Teacher qualifications	Minimum MA in TESOL	Bachelor's degree in English studies (often with little pedagogic content)
Learners	Young adults	Children
Learning purpose	Entry into tertiary study	No obvious purpose beyond following the mandated curriculum
Classroom teaching and learning	Learner-centered classrooms: Group work and collaborative learning	Teacher-centered classrooms: transmission mode and didactic teaching style

(primary and secondary/high schools).[4] As presented in Table 17.1 below, a closer comparison of the contextual features typical of pre-sessional programs in the United States and elementary school EFL classes in China is instructive.

The striking differences between these two contexts highlights how important contextual factors are for understanding TBLT, a point not always acknowledged in formative TBLT research and scholarship. As Shehadeh (2012: 3) puts it, " knowledge about TBLT in [second language] contexts gets naturalized inadvertently as being about TBLT in general, with the implication that it is universally valid and easily generalizable across other contexts." The comparison in Table 17.1 brings us to the main point of this chapter, that if we are to advocate for and apply research-based pedagogic proposals concerning TBLT to diverse real-world classrooms, context and the contextual adaptions of TBLT need to be treated as theoretically interesting and worthy of research. It follows that implementation issues, rather than being background noise, constitute a central focus of TBLT as a researched pedagogy. It seems to me that the purpose of such research is twofold; one, to establish empirically the claim made by Long (2015) and others that the essential malleability of TBLT makes it suitable for teaching languages in diverse contexts; and two, to identify how and in what ways particular contextual factors impinge on the implementation and success of TBLT, so as to account for these factors in evolving models of task-based

---

[4] There are, for example, around 121 million elementary school learners in China, all of whom attend EFL classes.

teaching. As Butler (2011: 51) points out, "effective practice, whatever that denotes conceptually, is grounded in context and has never been static." Similarly, Bygate, Norris and Van den Branden (2009: 297) argue that the field needs classroom and program-based evidence and researched development of "ranges of materials for the instruction of language both through written and spoken media, at different levels of proficiency, and for different ages, for different needs, and for different cultural contexts, showing how the options can impact on language development."

The rehabilitation of context in TBLT research involves a dialectic flow of information between theory and practice; just as classroom practice needs to be informed and enriched by theoretically derived and research-based pedagogic proposals, so too, research and theory can be refined and reconstituted through evidence of the process and outcomes of TBLT as implemented in diverse real-world classrooms. This point dovetails with Ortega's (2011) call for a situated view of knowledge in second language acquisition and Long's (2009, 2015) position that TBLT is, by definition, local and situated since classroom tasks are derived from an analysis of the tasks any particular group of learners need to perform in the target language. As Long argues, "detailed classroom studies of the ways teachers and students perform classroom lessons" are "obvious areas in need of serious research effort" (Long, 2015: 371). Such effort is much in evidence in the rapidly expanding body of research on the adoption of TBLT in diverse contexts (e.g., Butler, 2015, 2017; Jackson & Burch, 2017; Lambert & Oliver, 2020; Shehadeh & Coombe, 2012; Thomas & Reinders, 2015).

17.3 Perspectives on Context in Task-Based Language Teaching Research

I see two main ways in which TBLT research has engaged with diverse contexts. I refer to these as "TBLT research *in* diverse contexts" and "TBLT research *about* diverse contexts." Studies of the first kind, while situated in a growing range of educational contexts, treat context as a backdrop for carrying out conventional confirmatory experimental or quasi-experimental research. Studies of this kind are not a primary concern of this chapter and so will only be dealt with in brief.

My focus is on research of the second type, that is "TBLT research *about* diverse contexts." The focus is less on theory building than on understanding the local contingent factors that influence uptake and adaption of TBLT. Studies in this category can be either top-down or bottom-up. Top-down studies focuses on uptake and responses by teachers and learners to TBLT as mandated in language education policy and/or curriculum statements. Bottom-up studies focus on specific instances of task-based adoption and innovation at the classroom or program level. These distinctions are presented in Figure 17.1 and discussed in the following sections.

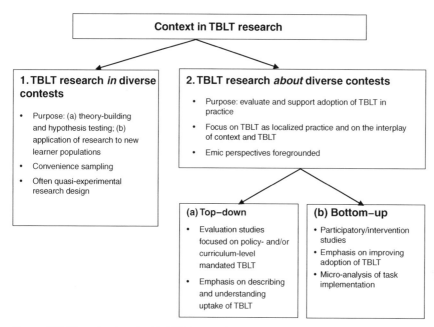

Figure 17.1 The role of context in TBLT research

Inevitably, there will be TBLT studies that don't fit easily into these categories or that straddle more than one category.

17.4 Task-Based Language Teaching Research *in* Diverse Contexts

TBLT research *in* diverse contexts treats context as a backdrop rather than a central concern. By and large, studies of this kind are carried out to test hypotheses derived from theoretical models of second language acquisition. Task performance data is typically collected outside of classroom lessons and ongoing programs of study, and results are interpreted in relation to theoretical constructs such as task complexity, planning time effects on the complexity, accuracy, and fluency of learner language production, and task type effects of negotiation for meaning (e.g., Sasayama, 2016). Context – beyond its role as a proxy for diverse learner populations – is itself usually a secondary factor of interest and is often little more than a convenient source of learners willing or available to participate in the research. The first five studies reported in Shehadeh and Coombe's (2012) edited collection of TBLT studies in EFL contexts are grouped together by the editors to reflect just this distinction, that is, studies sited in foreign language contexts, such as high-school EFL learners in Japan (Sasayama & Izumi, 2012) and university EFL students in Turkey (Genc, 2012), but with data drawn from decontextualized task performance outside of a program of study.

Research such as this contributes to the field by testing the generalizability of established findings to different contexts and learner populations, such as EFL learners (e.g., Shehadeh & Coombe, 2012), learners at different ages – and particularly young learners (e.g., García Mayo, 2017; García Mayo & Ibarrola 2015; MacKay & Silver, 2005; Pinter, 2005; Shintani, 2016) – learners of second languages (L2s) other than English (e.g., Bao & Du [2015] for Mandarin Chinese; de la Fuente [2002] for Spanish), and beginners/preschool learners (Shintani, 2016; Zhou, 2016). This expansion of experimental research into diverse contexts has been important for establishing the viability of TBLT beyond its roots in ESL contexts. But it provides limited evidence as to how TBLT is implemented in classrooms and programs of study in diverse contexts. For this we need to turn to TBLT research *about* diverse contexts.

17.5 Task-Based Language Teaching Research *about* Diverse Contexts

TBLT research *about* diverse contexts is the main focus of this chapter. This research seeks to provide empirically based insights into TBLT as a researched pedagogy situated in local language-learning ecologies – what Jackson and Burch (2017) refer to as "localized TBLT." Classroom realities and contextual adaptations of TBLT are central concerns, as are questions of how TBLT is (re)constituted in language policy, in needs analysis for task-based courses, in the minds of teachers and learners, and in classroom practice. As noted above, TBLT research *about* diverse contexts can be either top-down (i.e., focused on uptake of policy) or bottom-up (i.e., focused in innovation at the classroom or program level).

17.5.1 Top-down Task-Based Language Teaching Research about Diverse Contexts

Top-down studies seek to measure the success, uptake, and/or impact of TBLT reforms, usually within contexts in which TBLT has been advocated or mandated in language education policy. Typically, this research generates proposals for improving the implementation of TBLT but does not subject the proposals to empirical investigation. A prime example is research carried out on task-based reforms to primary and high-school ESL in Hong Kong in the 1990s (Carless, 2004, 2007; Adamson and Davison, 2003). The researchers found that these reforms faced contestation and resistance on the part of teachers who cited problems with learner reliance on the L1 to complete tasks, discipline issues, non-task-based examinations, and perceived conflicts with cultural norms (see also Butler, 2011, 2017; Littlewood, 2007). In other words, top-down task-based initiatives were hamstrung by contextual factors which had not been sufficiently accounted for in the rollout of the curriculum innovation. Similar problems have been reported with regard to attempts to mandate task-based teaching in China (Cortazzi & Jin, 1996; Deng & Carless, 2009; Luo & Xing, 2015; Zheng & Borg, 2014), Vietnam (Le & Barnard, 2009), Hong Kong (Chan, 2014), and Japan (Nishino & Watanabe, 2008; Sato, 2010).

A commonly cited factor that constrains or facilitates uptake of TBLT in these studies is teacher attitudes and understanding of TBLT. For example, in their survey of 228 middle-school teachers in Korea, Jeon and Hahn (2006) found that while teachers had a "reasonable" knowledge of what TBLT was, over half were negatively disposed toward it, seeing it as requiring too much preparation time and making classroom management difficult. (See McAllister, Narcy-Combes and Starkey-Perret [2012] for similar concerns by teachers in a Business English program at a university in France). They were also concerned that it exposed their own lack of communicative proficiency in English, was difficult to assess, and would be difficult for learners because of their own unfamiliarity with the approach. In Vietnam, Nguyen (2014) came to similar conclusions in a study which investigated the teaching practices and preferences of high-school teachers who were required to use mandated textbooks that were "task-based," at least according to the teacher's books and curriculum guidelines. Classroom observation and interview data revealed a clear preference for forms-focused instruction and a reluctance to adopt meaning-focused, task-based teaching. The teachers were convinced that their students need to be taught grammatical features before they can communicate effectively.

Offering more positive prospects, Chan (2012) adopted a multiple case-study approach to analyze the practices of ten Hong Kong primary school EFL teachers as they implemented the mandated task-based curriculum. Findings show considerable diversity among the teachers, but also revealed six pedagogic strategies that appeared crucial to the successful implementation of TBLT, namely: (1) strategic use of visual support to manage task demands; (2) contextualizing input to make connections between old and new knowledge; (3) simultaneous attention to task demands for progression in complexity; (4) provision of scaffolding through task sequencing and adjustment of task variables; (5) creating conditions for noticing form and salient features; and (6) creating conditions for restructuring to occur (207). With the recent expansion of EFL into the early primary school years in countries across Asia such as Japan and China, we can anticipate continued expansion of the already sizable body of recent research on TBLT for young learners.

Evaluative studies on task-based curriculum reforms are not limited to EFL. East (2012), for example, conducted an in-depth investigation into how practicing foreign language teachers and curriculum advisors in New Zealand interpreted TBLT after a curriculum renewal process in which TBLT was promoted (although not unambiguously). He found congruence between the new curriculum and the opportunities offered by TBLT, but also the usual challenges: lack of knowledge of TBLT among practitioners, and concerns about how learning occurs through tasks and about how task-based teaching could meet the demands of high stakes assessments. In response to these issues, East argues that top-down TBLT policy is likely to be counter-productive and that a more feasible solution is for curriculum leaders to take responsibility for providing teachers with relatable information about TBLT (including its theoretical bases and empirical evidence) and practical guidance for putting TBLT into practice in time-constrained circumstances.

The studies discussed above provide valuable insights into context-specific opportunities and constraints for TBLT in diverse contexts. These insights in turn provide a starting point for follow-up research into the nature and uptake of localized adaptions to TBLT designed to address the factors in question and provide evidence of classroom learning outcomes. The next section discusses research of this nature.

17.5.2 Bottom-up Task-Based Language Teaching Research about Diverse Contexts

Bottom-up studies focus on innovation at the classroom or program level and so by definition are context-focused. Often the researcher(s) is also a teacher in the context or plays a participatory role in designing and/or implementing a task-based innovation alongside teachers within an ongoing program of study. Outside of ESL contexts, most such studies have been conducted in EFL contexts, although there are some notable exceptions, which I discuss below. While the top-down studies discussed above typically focus on compulsory schooling contexts (primary and secondary schools), intervention studies are more often sited in tertiary-level programs, at least in the EFL sector. This is not surprising, since teachers in tertiary contexts are likely to have more autonomy and to teach to curricula and syllabi that are less tightly constrained by nation or state-wide education policy mandates. Reflecting the diverse contexts in which TBLT is being practiced, this section showcases selected studies covering tertiary EFL, primary school and preschool EFL, an ESL English for occupational purposes course, and two heritage language contexts.

Two studies, ten years apart, provide models of context-sensitive TBLT in tertiary EFL contexts. In the first, a notable forerunner of bottom-up studies, McDonough and Chaikitmongkol (2007) were part of a team which developed, pilot tested and implemented a year-long task-based EFL course at a Thai university. Of particular interest is the way the researchers addressed the issue of identifying authentic tasks for learners in general EFL classes. To do this, the team identified topics that students were interested in, while also mindful of expectations from the Thai government that English would be used to raise awareness of Thai culture and society. They then developed tasks that met these criteria as well as mimicked real-world activities that the learners might engage in in English outside the classroom. These included, for example, attending a youth seminar about social and environmental issues, and applying for an international cultural exchange program. They found that despite initial concerns, at the end of the semester, teachers and learners viewed the TBLT syllabus positively, noting how it increased learner independence, introduced useful learning strategies and was perceived as more relevant than previous courses to the real-world academic needs of the learners.

Ten years later, in a similarly longitudinal study, Kim, et al. (2017) tracked the evolving perspectives of learners at a South Korean university as they participated in a semester-long task-based general English skills course. Longitudinal data were collected from survey responses and portfolios and were analyzed qualitatively (thematic analysis of portfolio entries) and quantitatively (repeated-measures analyses of variance [ANOVAs] on survey data). Findings showed the students' perceptions of TBLT changed over the course of the trimester, with an overall gradual increase in interest toward TBLT. Of note is the way the researchers identified what count as authentic tasks for learners in general skills classes. They interviewed instructors and students as part of a needs analysis and identified upcoming local and university-based events of note during the semester. On this basis, they identified three main themes (work, travel, and school events) and then developed tasks for each theme. The researchers argued that building tasks around students' real-life experiences in this way is a viable option for needs analysis in EFL contexts.

These two studies provide valuable models for localized TBLT. They highlight three important lessons for research into the implementation of TBLT in programs of study: (1) the need for longer time scales to observe how learners adjust to TBLT over time; (2) the value of tracking student experiences and perspectives; and (3) the viability of designing tasks that are "authentic" for learners in general English skills EFL classes, for example by focusing on topics such as local cultural events that the students are familiar with and could conceivably be asked to explain to people from other countries.

Less common are context-focused studies involving preschool learners, with Shintani (2016) being a notable exception. Shintani developed a series of teacher-led input-based tasks for small classes of Japanese preschool children who had had very little, if any, exposure to English prior to their participation in the research. By including a comparison group who received PPP-based instruction (presentation, practice, production) and a control group, Shintani was able to provide empirical evidence for the relative efficacy of the three different modes of instruction. Her findings show superior learning outcomes for the TBLT group for both grammar and vocabulary. Because detailed task performance data were collected, Shintani was able to relate these outcomes to the different patterns of participation in the lessons under the different experimental conditions. In comparison to the PPP lessons, interaction in the TBLT lessons was acquisition rich, in that it resembled natural conversations in which the teacher and learners frequently engaging in collaborative dialogue and in which learners frequently negotiated for meaning and engaged in self-initiated repair. This study offers two valuable insights to counter common misconceptions of TBLT, especially as perceived in EFL contexts. First, it highlights the value of TBLT implemented through *input-based tasks* in which the emphasis is on comprehending message-focused input rather than on communicating in the L2. This approach is a valuable counter to the default assumption that TBLT necessarily involves learners performing communication tasks in groups. As Ellis (2009) argues, individual and whole-class work need be no less important than pair and group work for TBLT. For contexts involving large classes and/or beginner-level learners, this is a valuable option that deserves to be better understood by teachers. A second related point is that the teacher played a central role in Shintani's tasks as "a crucial interactional partner" (Van den Branden, 2009: 284). Again, this point counters a common misconception that in TBLT the teacher is relegated to the sidelines (Ellis, 2009; Van der Branden, 2016).

In one of few intervention studies in primary school contexts, Zhu (2020) reports on an action research project in the context of primary school education in China where the mandatory textbook series features tasks only nominally and does not provide adequate guidance on how to teach with tasks. In the study, a primary school teacher and the teacher educator (the author) worked together to design, implement and evaluate two task-based lessons (involving four tasks) that were repeated in two different classes, thus allowing two action research cycles of planning, action, and reflection for both lessons. A valuable aspect of this study was the way it modeled a systematic multidimensional approach to evaluating the effectiveness of task-based teaching that included:

- learning-based evaluation (receptive and productive vocabulary tests)
- student-based evaluation (questionnaire)
- response-based evaluation (how well the task outcomes were achieved)
- community-based evaluation (feedback from colleagues who observed the lessons).

Drawing on these data, Zhu was able to show how the four tasks were more successfully implemented when revised and taught to a second class, thus highlighting the value of systematic formative evaluation of task-based lessons and of opportunities for guided experiential teacher professional learning. A valuable insight for building teacher expertise in TBLT is that the community-based evaluation sessions in which other teachers were involved moved beyond evaluating the lessons and instead functioned, as Zhu reports, "more like a professional development seminar, with the tasks being evaluated in ways that inspired other [teachers] to consider the tasks in relation to their own classrooms" (2020: 18).

As with Zhu's study, Calvert and Sheen (2015) adopted an action research methodology to investigate the design and implementation of a TBLT lesson in an English for occupational purposes course for refugees in the United States. With support from the researcher (second author), the teacher for the course (first author) worked through a cycle of developing, implementing, critically reflecting on, modifying, and reusing a language-learning task. To evaluate the success of the task, the teacher collected two types of data: student-based data from a questionnaire, which gauged students' perceptions of the task, and response-based data in the form of an analysis of how well the task outcomes were achieved. She then critically reflected on the findings of the evaluation with reference to Skehan and Foster's (2001) distinction between code complexity factors, cognitive complexity factors and communicative stress factors. After a first, unsuccessful experience of teaching with the task, the authors carried out a systematic empirically based evaluation, which revealed the following problems: underestimating the linguistic demands of the task for low proficiency learners; failing to factor in the implicit unfamiliar cultural schemata built into the task (which involved using checklists); lack of learner familiarity with doing classroom tasks; and the need for much more teacher scaffolding to get the task underway. After modifications to address these issues, a second experience of teaching with the task proved successful and led to positive changes in how the teacher viewed task-based teaching. The authors concluded by emphasizing the benefits of action research as a means of helping teachers refine their task-based teaching.

One of the issues that is particularly salient for TBLT in EFL contexts is the widespread use of textbooks, which are typically organized around a synthetic syllabus. This raises the question of how teachers, with appropriate training, might be guided to develop the skills of adapting textbooks to reflect a stronger orientation to TBLT, for example by placing a stronger emphasis on "learning by doing" (methodological principle 2 in Long, [2009, 2015]). Dao and Newton (2021) investigated this question with respect to the use of an ostensibly task-based textbook, *New Cutting Edge Intermediate* (Cunningham & Moore, 2007), in EFL classes at a university in the North of Vietnam. In the first phase of the study, three EFL teachers were observed implementing the textbook in three 90-minute lessons each in classes for low proficiency non-English major students. Observations were followed by stimulated recall interviews and in-depth interviews with the teachers and focus-group discussions with students from each class. The analysis revealed the extent to which each teacher strengthened, maintained, or undermined (i.e., "detasked") the activities and tasks in the textbook. While the textbook contained a high proportion of communicative activities (many of which meet the criteria proposed by Ellis [2018] for being considered as tasks), all three teachers consistently either overlooked these tasks or de-tasked them by, for example, turning an interactive problem-solving task into teacher-fronted didactic teaching. All three teachers also added activities to the lessons that were not in the textbook, and in all cases these activities were grammar-focused and noncommunicative. Interview data revealed that the teachers had no awareness of the task-based nature of the textbook or of principles of TBLT. The students expressed a strong dispreference for this kind of teacher-centric language study. For these teachers at least, the presence of tasks and communicative activities in a textbook did little to shift their teaching practices from a traditional teacher-centered focus-on-forms approach. The second phase of the study involved a participatory action research project in which the teachers were helped to develop expertise in task-based teaching and to apply this expertise to their teaching from the textbook. Analysis of data from this second phase is still underway at time of writing, but there are indications of a dramatic increase in meaning-focused interactive task work in the class and a successful shift from pre-teaching grammar to reactive focus on form.

In a welcome change from studies focused on English as a second or foreign language, Riestenberg and Sherris (2018, this volume) evaluate the adoption of TBLT in two language revitalization projects, both involving Indigenous language-teaching contexts: the Macuiltianguis Zapotec classroom in Oaxaca, Mexico, and a workshop for teachers of Salish Qlipse in the state of Montana. The analysis involved identifying intersections in the two programs between Long's (2009, 2015) ten methodological principles for TBLT and Darvin and Norton's (2015) model of investment, which draws on concepts of identity, capital, and ideology to explain language-learning motivation. These two studies illustrate the diverse ideologies and patterns of investment in the communities within which such language revitalization programs are sited. In the case of the Zapotec project, for example, stakeholders included language activists, older community members, and a younger generation whose interactions at home and work are likely to be English-dominant and who may have only a passing interest in language revitalization. The findings of the two studies revealed how TBLT was able to bridge diverse ideology settings and to promote learner investment in the language, as evidenced, for example, in an increase in spoken interaction in the Zapotec classroom and in "unanimously positive feedback" from teachers of Salish Qlipse on their experience of a TBLT workshop (455).

However, the study also identified challenges unique to adopting TBLT in such programs. First, the needs analysis process is not straightforward because learners may have few tasks that they "need to do in the language," especially if the language is no longer intergenerationally transmitted, older speakers are bilingual, and there are few opportunities to use the language beyond the classroom (Riestenberg & Sherris, 2018: 440). As the authors note, "For task-based Indigenous language instruction to be successful, new social practices for Indigenous language use must be defined. Community members must invest in changing current linguistic habits and creating new spaces of language use through which authentic communicative tasks can emerge" (439). In the Zapotec context, this challenge was addressed through interviewing various members of the Zapotec community to identify patterns of language use. From these data, three target tasks were identified – salutations, small talk, and making purchases.

A second challenge is the enormous investment of effort required on the part of speakers in the community and teachers in order to, among other things, identify authentic communicative tasks and develop these into target language resources. Related to this issue is the scarcity of funding for ongoing support of such programs. As these points show, the exploration of TBLT in the two Indigenous language settings in this study is a rich source of insights into the unique cultural implementation issues faced when TBLT is introduced in diverse contexts. A final point worth making about this study is the way that it models the use of Long's ten methodological principles (Long 2015) as an analytic tool for evaluating alignment of implementation decisions with TBLT.

17.6 Summary

We see a contrast between the findings from top-down and bottom-up studies. Research on uptake from top-down mandated TBLT-based curriculum reforms (in Asia especially) has painted a somewhat negative picture of teacher resistance and implementation failure (c.f., Chan, 2012). On the other hand, bottom-up studies into smaller-scale context-sensitive implementation of TBLT show consistently positive outcomes in terms of teacher and learner evaluations and classroom learning processes. In many cases, these studies report on positive outcomes in contexts where top-down studies have previously shown poor uptake and understanding of TBLT (e.g., the contrasting perspectives on teaching with tasks in EFL in China seen in Luo & Xing [2015] and Zhu [2020]). A key characteristic of these bottom-up studies is that they treat teachers as active participants in task-based innovations rather than passive recipients of imposed policy. Perhaps then, the adoption of TBLT in diverse contexts is less about "context" and more about how teachers are afforded agency and ownership.

17.7 Research Needs and Future Directions

Research to date offers valuable insights into the adoption of TBLT in these diverse contexts and the factors that account for success or failure in initiatives to adopt TBLT in these contexts. In reviewing this research (and with a particular focus on what I have referred to as bottom-up studies), four points warrant comment:

1. These studies adopt a range of research methods, although most are qualitative in orientation. Methodologies include action research (Calvert & Sheen, 2015; Zhu, 2020); quasi-experimental design (Shintani, 2016); multiple case studies (Chan, 2012); mixed methods (Kim, et al., 2017); and descriptive curriculum analysis (Riestenberg & Sherris, 2018).
2. Multiple sources of data are typical of most of the research on TBLT in diverse contexts. These include surveys and interviews (teachers and learners), classroom observations, analysis of task performance and task and learning outcomes, lesson plan analysis, and teacher reflective diaries.
3. In keeping with a qualitative orientation, these studies often adopt a longitudinal design in which data are collected over a semester or full year of study (e.g., Kim, et al., 2017). This is an important trend in understanding how TBLT practices evolve over time and as a consequence of the experience and growing expertise by teachers and learners. Given that TBLT constitutes an often radical departure from traditional approaches, time is needed for teachers to move through the process of adapting their practices. As Carless (2004: 659) points out, "[t]eachers mould innovations to their own abilities, beliefs, and experiences; the immediate school context; and the wider sociocultural environment." Research that helps us understand this process can make a valuable contribution to the field.
4. Micro-analysis of task-based lessons is a feature of recent research (e.g., Calvert & Sheen, 2015; Zhu, 2020). This approach draws on the three dimensions of micro-evaluation of tasks proposed by Ellis (2018: 236): student-based, response-based, and learning-based. Student-based evaluations involve self-report by students on their perception of the value of a task and how motivated they were by it. Response-based evaluations focus on the process of task performance, identifying, for example, process features of task-based interaction, and, crucially, the success the learners had in achieving the task outcome. Learning-based evaluations are concerned with evidence that learners have acquired some new language or gained greater control over their existing language resources, and they are carried out through either pre- and posttests, or analysis of recordings and transcripts of task performances. Except for Shintani (2016), few of the studies discussed above

sought evidence of learning outcomes associated with TBLT. The lack of learning-based evaluations of TBLT in these studies is a gap to be addressed in future research.

In terms of future directions, a promising approach is adopted by Riestenberg and Sherris (2018, this volume) who use Long's ten methodological principles as an analytic tool to guide and evaluate implementation of TBLT in an atypical context. These principles allow teachers and researchers to move beyond a focus on the features of individual tasks and toward a more systemic approach to TBLT, wherever it is adopted. This approach addresses what I see as a problem in the field to date, namely an overemphasis on tasks as free-standing activities rather than treating TBLT as a methodological approach that informs all of curriculum design, including planning, whole lesson implementation, and assessment of learning outcomes. A focus on single tasks can too easily lead to slippage, such that TBLT becomes little more than a series of communicative games, a point that Wingate (2018) makes in her assessment of modern foreign language teaching in English secondary schools.

A second direction I see as productive for understanding TBLT in diverse contexts is moving to dual-phase research that begins with an exploratory study designed to understand the context and follows this up with a confirmatory research or intervention study in which issues identified in the first phase become the focus of empirical data collection in the second. We adopted this approach in Newton and Nguyen (2019), a study into the use of tasks in high-school EFL classes in Vietnam. The first phase involved a descriptive analysis of the naturalized task practices of the EFL teachers at a high school. We found that teachers had replaced the teacher-led, form-focused instruction traditionally used to begin a lesson with the localized practice of engaging learners in meaning-focused task rehearsal in pairs or groups, then following this with public performance of the rehearsed speaking tasks by pairs or groups in front of the class. The lessons usually concluded with feedback on language by the teachers. Based on their experience, the teachers understood how public performance motivated learning and solved the oft-cited difficulties of over-reliance on the L1 (Carless, 2004) and the demotivating effect of an absence of oral proficiency assessment in high stakes exams (Butler, 2011).

In the second phase of the research, we reintroduced these same practices into the teachers' classrooms in a quasi-experimental study so as to investigate more thoroughly the effect of different task types and different learner groupings, the learning processes taking place during rehearsal and performance and the learning outcomes that resulted from them. Because the research sought to understand the actual practices of teachers and students in a specific setting a Vietnamese high school, it also has something to say about this setting; it shows how the teachers had successfully adapted task-based teaching to fit within contextual constraints. The follow-up phase confirmed the teachers' intuitions concerning the value of public performance for language acquisition. Comparing these findings to Butler's (2011) claim that adaption of TBLT in Asian contexts typically resulted in a watered-down task-supported version of TBLT, the evidence from this school was indeed of adaptation. But it was adaptation that *strengthened* rather than diluted the task-based nature of instruction.

An issue highlighted by Newton and Nguyen (2019) concerns the role of multilingual teachers and management of L1 use in TBLT in foreign language contexts. This two-pronged issue has received limited attention in TBLT research as carried out in ESL contexts, where the assumption seems to be that all learning will take place in the target language and where the teacher is unlikely to share the first language(s) of learners (c.f. Moore, 2017). Plonsky and Kim's (2016) meta-analysis of eighty-five TBLT studies involving learner production found that only six explicitly accounted for L1 use in the data. We can conclude from this analysis that the majority of TBLT studies involving learner production either design L1 use out of the data (e.g., by requiring tasks to be performed in the L2 only), do not report it, or exclude it from analysis when it does occur. As Seals, et al. (2020) point out, the invisibility of the L1 in TBLT research has been perpetuated by the siloing of TBLT within the contexts of English for specific purposes and school- or institution-based second (and more recently, foreign) language learning. The failure to articulate a role for multilingualism is unsustainable if TBLT is to be more widely adopted in bilingual and multilingual settings.

17.8 Conclusions

In 2009, Van den Branden, et al. (2009: 11) made the following oft-cited and strong claim for the value of TBLT in diverse contexts:

> There are theoretical grounds, and empirical evidence, for believing that tasks might be able to offer all the affordances needed for successful instructed language development, whoever the learners might be, and *whatever the context* (emphasis added).

The body of research discussed in this chapter has, by and large, been conducted subsequent to this claim being made, a period during which we have seen two important trends: (1) a promising expansion of the contexts in which TBLT is being adopted and researched; and (2) growing interest in the mediating impact of context on how TBLT is constituted in practice. Consistently, across the studies reviewed in this chapter, we see positive signs of TBLT being successfully adopted and adapted in contexts in which, hitherto, TBLT has made few inroads. Notably, in most of the studies, successful adoption of TBLT is shown to depend on opportunities for teachers to be provided with appropriate guidance and to actively participate in determining how TBLT will be implemented. Teacher agency is clearly a vital component in uptake of TBLT (East, this volume; Van den Branden, 2016) and even more so when TBLT is being adopted in contexts where it diverges markedly from traditional practices and cultural values (e.g., Oliver, this volume; Riestenberg & Sherris, 2018, this volume).

To conclude, several limitations concerning the ground covered in this chapter need to be acknowledged. First, my own experience and expertise is in working mostly with EFL teachers in Asian contexts, and this has invariably resulted in some bias toward these contexts. Likewise, I have only drawn on research published in English. There is also a deeper underlying bias inherent in published research. Context-oriented TBLT research studies that experience failure or resistance by teachers and/or education authorities are much less likely to be completed, let alone published, and this creates a natural confirmation bias in favor of studies that report positively on the adoption of TBLT in diverse settings. Despite these limitations, this chapter has, I hope, argued the case convincingly for the value of TBLT research that engages with diverse contexts and treats the mediating effect of context factors on the uptake of TBLT as worthwhile topics for TBLT research.

Further Reading

Ahmadian, M. and Mayo, M. d. P. G. (2017). *Recent perspectives on task-based language learning and teaching*. Vol. 27. Berlin: Walter de Gruyter.

Long, M. H. (2015). *Second language acquisition and task-based language teaching*. Hoboken, NJ: John Wiley and Sons.

Newton, J. and Bui, T. (2020). Low-proficiency learners and task-based language teaching. In C. P. Lambert and R. Oliver eds. *Using tasks in second language teaching: Practice in diverse contexts*. Bristol: Multilingual Matters, pp. 28–40.

Samuda, V., Van der Branden, K., and Bygate, M., eds. (2018). *TBLT as a researched pedagogy*. Amsterdam: John Benjamins.

Seals, C. A., Newton, J., Ash, M., and Nguyen, T. B. T. (2020). Translanguaging and TBLT: Cross-overs and challenges. In Z. Tian, L. Aghai, P. Sayer, and J. Schissel, eds. *Envisioning TESOL through a translanguaging Lens – Global perspectives*. New York: Springer, pp. 275–92.

Study Questions

1. Read two or more of the case studies in the current volume and compare the contextual factors that were taken into account in adopting TBLT in each case, as well as the measures taken to address these factors.

2. Choose two or three of the dimensions of context in Table 17.1 and identify how each of these dimensions might be taken into account in TBLT.
3. What are the future prospects for TBLT in an L2 teaching and learning context that you are familiar with? What are the barriers to change and how might these be addressed?

References

Adamson, B. and Davison, C. (2003). Innovation in English language teaching in Hong Kong: one step forward, two steps sideways? *Prospect*, 18(1), 27–41.

Bao, R. and Du, X. Y. (2015). Implementation of task-based language teaching in Chinese as a foreign language: benefits and challenges. *Language Culture and Curriculum*, 28(3), 291–310.

Butler, Y. G. (2011). The implementation of communicative and task-based language teaching in the Asia-Pacific Region. *Annual Review of Applied Linguistics*, 31, 36–57.

Butler, Y. G. (2015). English language education among young learners in East Asia: A review of current research (2004–2014). *Language teaching*, 48 (3), 303–42.

Butler, Y. G. (2017). Communicative and task-based language teaching in the Asia-Pacific region. *Second and Foreign Language Education*, 327–38.

Calvert, M. and Sheen, Y. (2015). Task-based language learning and teaching: An action-research study. *Language Teaching Research*, 19(2), 226–44.

Carless, D. R. (2004). Issues in teachers' reinterpretation of a task-based innovation in primary schools. *TESOL Quarterly*, 38(4), 639–62.

Carless, D. R. (2007). Student use of the mother tongue in the task-based classroom. *ELT Journal*, 62(4), 331–38.

Carless, D. R. (2009). Revisiting the TBLT versus PPP debate: Voices from Hong Kong. *Asian Journal of English Language Teaching*, 19, 49–66.

Chan, W. L. (2014). Hong Kong secondary school English teachers' beliefs and their influence on the implementation of task-based language teaching. In D. Coniam, ed. *English Language Education and Assessment: Recent Developments in Hong Kong and the Chinese Mainland*. Singapore: Springer pp. 17–34.

Cortazzi, M. and Jin, L. (1996). Cultures of learning: Language classrooms in China. In H. Coleman, ed. *Society and the language classroom*. Cambridge: Cambridge University Press, pp. 169–206.

Cunningham, S. and Moor, P. (2007). *New Cutting Edge Intermediate*. 2nd ed. London: Longman.

Dao, H. and Newton, J. (2021). TBLT perspectives on teaching from an EFL textbook at a Vietnam university. *Canadian Journal of Applied Linguistics*.

Darvin, R. and Norton, B. (2015). Identity and a model of investment in applied linguistics. *Annual Review of Applied Linguistics*, 35, 36–56.

de la Fuente, M. J. (2002). Negotiation and oral acquisition of L2 vocabulary: The roles of input and output in the receptive and productive acquisition of words. *Studies in second language acquisition*, 24(1), 81–112.

Deng, C. and Carless, D. R. (2009). The communicativeness of activities in a task-based innovation in Guangdong, China. *Asian Journal of English Language Teaching*, 19, 113–34.

East, M. (2012). *Task-based language teaching from the teachers' perspective: Insights from New Zealand*. Amsterdam: John Benjamins.

Ellis, R. (2009). Task-based language teaching: sorting out the misunderstandings. *International Journal of Applied Linguistics*, 19(3), 221–46.

Ellis, R. (2018). *Reflections on task-based language teaching*. Bristol: Multilingual Matters.

García Mayo, M. d. P. (2017). *Learning foreign languages in primary school: Research insights*. Bristol: Multilingual Matters.

García Mayo, M. d. P. and Ibarrola, A. L. (2015). Do children negotiate for meaning in task-based interaction? Evidence from CLIL and EFL settings. *System*, 54, 40–54.

Genc, Z. S. (2012). Effects of strategic planning on the accuracy of oral and written tasks in the performance of Turkish EFL learners. In A. Shehadeh and C. A. Coombe, eds. *Task-based language teaching in foreign language contexts*. Amsterdam: John Benjamins, pp. 67–88.

Jackson, D. O. and Burch, A. R. (2017). Complementary Theoretical perspectives on task-based classroom realities. *TESOL Quarterly*, 51(3), 493–506.

Jeon, I.-J. and Hahn, J.-W. (2006). Exploring EFL teachers' perceptions of task-based language teaching: A case study of Korean secondary school classroom practice. *Asian EFL Journal*, 8(1), 123–43.

Kim, Y., Jung, Y., and Tracy-Ventura, N. (2017). Implementation of a localized task-based course in an EFL context: A study of students' evolving perceptions. *TESOL Quarterly*, 51(3), 632–60.

Lambert, C. P, and Oliver, R. (2020). *Using tasks in second language teaching: Practice in diverse contexts*. Bristol: Multilingual Matters.

Le, V. C. and Barnard, R. (2009). Curricular innovation behind closed classroom doors: A Vietnamese case study. *Prospect*, 24(2), 20–33.

Littlewood, W. (2007). Communicative and task-based language teaching in East Asian classrooms. *Language teaching*, 40(3), 243–49.

Long, M. H. (1985). A role for instruction in second language acquisition: Task-based language teaching. In K. Hylstenstam and M. Pienemann, eds. *Modelling and assessing second language acquisition*. Bristol: Multilingual Matters, pp. 77–99

Long, M. H. (2009). Methodological principles for language teaching. In M. H. Long and C. Doughty, eds. *The handbook of language teaching*. Oxford: Wiley-Blackwell, pp. 373–94.

Long, M. H. (2015). *Second language acquisition and task-based language teaching*. Hoboken, NJ: John Wiley & Sons.

Luo, S. and Xing, J. (2015). Teachers' perceived difficulty in implementing TBLT in China. In M. Thomas and H. Reinders, eds, *Contemporary task-based language teaching in Asia*. London: Bloomsbury, pp. 139–55.

Mackey, A. and Silver, R. E. (2005). Interactional tasks and English L2 learning by immigrant children in Singapore. *System*, 33(2), 239–60.

McAllister, J., Narcy-Combes, M.-F., and Starkey-Perret, R. (2012). Language teachers' perceptions of a task-based learning programme in a French University. In A. Shehadeh and C. A. Coombe, eds. *Task-based language teaching in foreign language contexts: Research and implementation*. Amsterdam: John Benjamins, pp. 313–42.

McDonough, K. and Chaikitmongkol, W. (2007). Teachers' and learners' reactions to a task-based EFL course in Thailand. *TESOL Quarterly*, 41(1), 107–32.

Moore, P. J. (2017). Unwritten rules: Code choice in task-based learner discourse in an EMI context in Japan. In *English medium instruction in higher education in Asia-Pacific*. Singapore: Springer, pp. 299–320.

Newton, J. and Nguyen, B. T. T. (2019). Task repetition and the public performance of speaking tasks in EFL classes at a Vietnamese high school. *Language Teaching for Young Learners*, 1(1), 34–56.

Nguyen, G. V. (2014). Forms or meaning? Teachers' beliefs and practices regarding task-based language teaching: A Vietnamese case study. *The Journal of Asia TEFL*, 11(1), 1–36.

Nishino, T. and Watanabe, M. (2008). Communication-oriented policies versus classroom realities in Japan. *TESOL Quarterly*, 42(1), 133–38.

Ortega, L. (2011). SLA after the social turn: Where cognitivism and its alternatives stand. In D. Atkinson, ed. *Alternative approaches to second language acquisition*. Abingdon: Routledge, pp. 179–92.

Pinter, A. (2005). Task repetition with 10-year old children. In C. Edwards and J. Willis, eds. *Teachers exploring tasks in English language teaching*. London: Palgrave Macmillan, pp. 113–26.

Plonsky, L. and Kim, Y. (2016). Task-based learner production: A substantive and methodological review. *Annual Review of Applied Linguistics*, 36, 73–97.

Riestenberg, K. and Sherris, A. (2018). task-based teaching of Indigenous languages: Investment and methodological principles in Macuiltianguis Zapotec and Salish Qlispe revitalization. *Canadian Modern Language Review*, 74(3), 434–59.

Samuda, V., Van der Branden, K., and Bygate, M. (2018), eds. *TBLT as a researched pedagogy*. Amsterdam: John Benjamins.

Sasayama, S. (2016). Is a 'complex' task really complex? Validating the assumption of cognitive task complexity. *The Modern Language Journal*, 100(1), 231–54.

Sasayama, S. and Izumi, S. (2012). Effects of task complexity and pre-task planning on Japanese EFL learners' oral production. In A. Shehadeh and C. A. Coombe, eds. *Task-based language teaching in foreign language contexts. Research and implementation*. Amsterdam: John Benjamins, pp. 23–42.

Sato, R. (2010). Reconsidering the effectiveness and suitability of PPP and TBLT in the Japanese EFL classroom. *JALT journal*, 32(2), 189–200.

Seals, C. A., Newton, J., Ash, M., and Nguyen, T. B. T. (2020). Translanguaging and TBLT: Cross-overs and challenges. In Z. Tian, L. Aghai, P. Sayer, and J. Schissel, eds. *Envisioning TESOL through a translanguaging Lens – Global perspectives*. Singapore: Springer.

Shehadeh, A. (2012). Introduction. In A. Shehadeh and C. A. Coombe, eds. *Task-based language teaching in foreign language contexts: Research and implementation*. Amsterdam: John Benjamins, pp. 1–20.

Shehadeh, A. and Coombe, C. A. (2012). *Task-based language teaching in foreign language contexts: Research and implementation*. Amsterdam: John Benjamins.

Shintani, N. (2016). *Input-based tasks in foreign language instruction for young learners* Amsterdam: John Benjamins.

Skehan, P. and Foster, P. (2001). Cognition and tasks. In P. Robinson, ed. *Cognition and second language instruction*. Cambridge: Cambridge University Press, pp. 183–205.

Thomas, M. and Reinders, H. (2015). *Contemporary task-based language teaching in Asia*. London: Bloomsbury Publishing.

Van den Branden, K. (2006), ed, *Task-based education*. Cambridge: Cambridge University Press.

Van den Branden, K. (2009). Mediating between predetermined order and chaos: the role of the teacher in task-based language education. *International Journal of Applied Linguistics*, 19(3), 264–85.

Van den Branden, K. (2016). The role of teachers in task-based language education. *Annual Review of Applied Linguistics*, 36, 164–81.

Van der Branden, K., Bygate, M., and Norris, J. M. (2009). *Task-based language teaching: A reader*. Amsterdam: John Benjamins.

Wingate, U. (2018). Lots of games and little challenge–a snapshot of modern foreign language teaching in English secondary schools. *The Language Learning Journal*, 46(4), 442–55.

Zheng, X. and Borg, S. (2014). Task-based learning and teaching in China: Secondary school teachers' beliefs and practices. *Language Teaching Research*, 18(2), 205–21.

Zhou, Y. (2016). Applying task-based language teaching in introductory level Mandarin language classes at the college of the Bahamas. *International Journal of Bahamian Studies*, 22, 34–42.

Zhu, Y. (2020). Implementing tasks in young learners' language classrooms: A collaborative teacher education initiative through task evaluation. *Language Teaching Research*.

Conclusion

Mohammad J. Ahmadian and Michael H. Long

In the Introduction, we asked, "If TBLT is so good, why isn't it more widely used?" In this closing chapter, we address a number of areas where further exploration might increase its acceptance and adoption.

Developing Teachers' Understanding of Genuine Task-Based Language Teaching

Teacher cognition (i.e., what teachers know, believe, and think about a pedagogical phenomenon) has been shown to be of paramount importance in what and how teachers teach in the classroom (Borg, 2003). When it comes to TBLT, teachers play a significant role in the extent to which it comes to life (East, this volume; Van den Branden, 2016). However, much previous research has almost exclusively zeroed in on teachers' perceptions and attitudes towards task-supported language teaching, rather than their *understanding* of what *genuine* TBLT is and of the theory, research, and methodological principles that underpin it. If teachers are not familiar with the underpinnings of TBLT, investigating their perceptions and attitudes toward it makes little sense. Therefore, what is needed is a principled and practice-oriented attempt at training teachers and familiarizing them with what TBLT is, why it is considered the closest we have ever had to a researched approach to language pedagogy, and, finally, how it should be implemented in the classroom. Excellent examples of such systematic training have been presented by Bryfonski and East in this volume. East has drawn on his research over the past ten years to showcase a wide range of practices that could be used to enhance teachers' understanding of TBLT and to facilitate the early involvement of language teachers. Bryfonski's study illustrates the importance of following up with classroom observations to see the extent to which training leads to changes in classroom practices.

Task-Based Language Teaching and Teaching Online

We are writing this closing section as much of the world is in lockdown because of the COVID-19 crisis. Despite the catastrophic health and socioeconomic ramifications that COVID-19 has had for the world, it has raised our awareness as to how volatile our face-to-face teaching could be. As of July 2020, school systems and virtually all language centers and higher education institutions in many parts of the world have switched to online instruction. Van den Branden (this volume) rightly points out that integrating modern technology in TBLT is quite natural and inevitable. However, we now need to consider how TBLT programs could be designed and delivered fully online. The chapter by Gonzalez Lloret and Ziefler and the accompanying case studies in Part IV illustrate some of these possibilities. This will involve investigating what a fully online TBLT program looks like, what additional challenges it will introduce in the implementation of TBLT, what additional training language teachers need, and what forms of assessment and program evaluation could be utilized to assess learners' progress, as well as the quality of the program. The same is true of the components and effectiveness of online teacher education for TBLT (see Jordan & McMillan, this volume).

Task-Based Language Teaching, Curriculum, and Change

One of the most significant reasons behind cynicism around implementation of TBLT is the fact that, in many parts of the world, the curriculum and, in turn, teaching methodology, are imposed from above/through coursebooks, with teachers or local administrators having little control over what or how they teach. Changing the status quo in such settings could prove very difficult. Waters (2009: 434) reviews a number of models of educational change. Change could take place in several ways:

1. In what he calls a "center-periphery" model, the power of the innovation center pushes adoption of the new approach.
2. In a Research, Development and Diffusion model, educational change follows the same pattern as in (1), except that the center of innovation draws on scientific evidence and empirical findings to promote the adoption of the new curriculum or methodology.
3. In a problem-solving model, "the innovation process centers on the 'problem-owner' rather than being controlled by outside agencies/individuals."
4. In Markee's (1997) contingency view of innovation, the situation will mandate the best model to be used.

Van den Branden (this volume) argues that, given the scientific evidence which underpins the methodological principles of TBLT, its implementation needs to be approached as a system-wide attempt which is, by virtue of its nature, slow and gradual. The amount of time required is usually a function of the degree of "reculturing" (Fullan, [2008], as cited in Wedell [2011]) that is involved in the change. Yet, regardless of the model used and irrespective of the amount of time required, implementing the change could ultimately be construed as "a task for teachers" and other frontline professionals (Van den Branden, this volume). Therefore, a prerequisite of successful implementation of TBLT is that teachers perceive the change as useful, that their sense of self-competence is not impaired by the change, and that proper support structures have been anticipated and are in place to scaffold teachers in the process of change (Van den Branden, this volume). Future TBLT research could look at how these prerequisites could be fulfilled in different contexts, what challenges could hinder the process, and how they could be tackled.

Task-Based Language Teaching and English as a Lingua Franca

Obviously, TBLT is not limited to teaching English. However, given the intense interest in learning English as an additional language by people who may never meet a native speaker of English, a group of researchers and teacher educators have started to question the viability and utility of drawing on English native speaker norms for language-teaching materials development. At the heart of this trend is the notion of intelligibility and the ways in which it could be enhanced by following lingua franca core features rather than native speaker models (Kiczkowiak, 2020). Traditionally, TBLT program developers have tended to create their course materials according to native speaker norms. This is partly because most clients still prefer the native speaker model, but mainly because it is not yet clear "what ELF [English as a lingua franca] is, who the ELF speaker is, and what ELF is understood to be for" (Park & Wess, 2011:361). This notwithstanding, in order for TBLT to thrive in all contexts, including those where ELF norms are preferred, more research and scholarship is indeed needed on how text selection, input elaboration (see Long, this volume) and feedback provision might work with reference to ELF core features (no matter how nebulous those features may be). Of course, ELF raises similar questions for all approaches to language teaching, not just TBLT.

Task-Based Language Teaching in Traditional and Exam-Oriented Contexts

Traditional and exam-oriented contexts are perhaps most impervious to the adoption and enactment of TBLT. This makes intuitive sense and has been documented in several studies, mainly conducted in South East Asia and Asia-Pacific regions (Carless, 2007, Butler, 2011). Therefore, an important research task is to explore how TBLT, or at least a fraction of the methodological principles of TBLT (rather than the so-called "weak version of TBLT"), could be implemented in these contexts. McDonough (2015) puts forth the idea of *localized TBLT*, which refers to task-based instruction developed within specific instructional programs. Drawing on McDonough's proposal, Kim, et al. (2017) have conducted a study aimed at implementing, and then canvassing learners' perceptions of, a localized TBLT in South Korea. The study shows that students perceptions of a task-based course, which had begun with a fairly thorough needs analysis, changed positively throughout the semester. Localized task-based courses like that appear to be attractive initiatives, as long as they do not lead to TBLT being diluted or misrepresented.

Although many criticisms leveled at TBLT lack substance, some have merit and serve to raise our awareness of important unresolved issues, as well as of lacunae in understanding of the approach in some quarters. Task-based language teaching is a work in progress. We are building the road as we travel. Our hope is that *The Cambridge Handbook of Task-Based Language Teaching* will help us along the way.

References

Borg, S. (2003). Teacher cognition in language teaching: A review of research on what language teachers think, know, believe, and do. *Language Teaching*, 36(2), 81–109.

Butler, Y. G. (2011). The implementation of communicative and task-based language teaching in the Asia-Pacific region. *Annual Review of Applied Linguistics*, 31, 36–57.

Carless, D. (2007). The suitability of task-based approaches for secondary schools: Perspectives from Hong Kong. *System*, 35(4), 595–608.

Kiczkowiak, M. (2020). Seven principles for writing materials for English as a lingua franca. *ELT Journal*, 74(1), 1–9.

Kim, Y., Jung, Y., and Tracy-Ventura, N. (2017). Implementation of a Localized Task-Based Course in an EFL Context: A Study of Students' Evolving Perceptions. *TESOL Quarterly*, 51(3), 632–60.

Long, M. H. (2016). In defense of tasks and TBLT: Nonissues and real issues. *Annual Review of Applied Linguistics*, 36, 5–33.

Markee, N. (1997).Managing curricular innovation. Vol. 198. Cambridge: Cambridge University Press.

McDonough, K. (2015). Perceived benefits and challenges with the use of collaborative tasks in EFL contexts. In M. Bygate, ed. *Domains and directions in the development of TBLT*. Amsterdam: John Benjamins, pp. 225–45.

Park, J. S. Y. and Wee, L. (2011). A practice-based critique of English as a Lingua Franca. *World Englishes*, 30(3), 360–74.

Van den Branden, K. (2016). The role of teachers in task-based language education. *Annual Review of Applied Linguistics*, 36, 164–81.

Waters, A. (2009). Managing innovation in English language education, state of the art review. *Language Teaching*, 42(4), 421–58.

Wedell, M. (2011). More than just 'technology': English language teaching initiatives as complex educational changes. In H. Coleman, ed. *Dreams and realities: Developing countries and the English language*. London: British Council, pp. 275–296.

Index

Aboriginal students, 87, 96, 99–100, 103, 108
accessibility principle, 35, 41, 44
affective, 15, 89, 133, 214–215, 331–332, 568
aptitude, xx, 48, 51, 170, 211, 216, 218, 222–223, 308, 310, 318–319, 322, 324, 374, 444, 563, 568, 609–611, 624
authentic tasks, 84, 108, 328, 463, 509, 513, 522, 641, 656–657
automaticity, 215

China, ix, xi, xvii, xviii, xxi, 23, 70–71, 82, 135–142, 144, 146–147, 149–150, 228, 248, 399, 410, 432, 434–436, 441–444, 462, 648, 651, 655, 658, 661, 666–669
content and language integrated learning, x, xxvi, 229, 397–398, 401–408, 410–420, 424–425, 429–431, 439, 443–444, 465, 476, 636, 645–647, 667
Cognition Hypothesis, x, 13–15, 20–21, 24–25, 205, 213–214, 216–218, 221–225, 248, 266, 269, 288, 333–335, 343, 390, 582–584, 607, 616, 623
computer-mediated, xviii, xxi, 63, 199–200, 235, 314, 320–321, 326, 330, 334–335, 338–344, 622, 634
conceptualisation, 10, 14
course books, 432, 436, 439, 442, 629
criterion-referenced performance, xi, 66

declarative knowledge, 29
discourse sample, 180

elaborated input, 170, 363, 370
English for academic purposes, 76, 94, 200–201, 291, 613
experiential learning, 329, 434
explicit learning, 4, 19, 308–309, 322, 324, 563

fluency, 4–7, 12–14, 18–19, 21–23, 26–27, 62, 84, 124–125, 133, 210, 212, 214, 217, 219, 221, 247, 249, 268–269, 271, 333, 402, 404, 407, 409, 414–415, 433, 451, 539–540, 595, 607–608, 610, 613, 622–623, 625, 627, 653

focus on form, 21–22, 27, 30, 38–39, 41–42, 46, 48, 198, 221, 251, 271, 287, 296–297, 306, 320–322, 324–325, 328, 331, 342, 365–366, 369, 381, 384, 409, 453–454, 470, 480, 482–483, 488, 551, 626–627, 632, 635
formulator, 14, 17
functional adequacy, 561–562

gaming, 225, 241, 326, 329, 331–332, 337, 340, 343

implicit learning, xxi, 4, 8, 19, 308, 310, 324, 387, 553, 563
Indigenous, x, xix, xx, 87–88, 92, 96, 100, 108, 359–360, 365, 369–372, 477, 660–661, 668
individual differences, 11, 49–50, 222–223, 322, 324, 471, 564
information gap, 267, 274
innovation, 28, 45, 51–52, 70, 82, 86, 89, 91, 149–150, 258, 335, 432, 441, 444, 448–449, 457–459, 461, 525, 532, 535, 543–544, 622, 628–631, 634, 636, 638, 642–645, 648, 650, 652, 654–656, 666–667, 672, 674–675
intentional reasoning, 211–212, 217, 223, 234
Interaction Hypothesis, 7, 62, 266, 307, 309, 313
Italian, x, xi, xix, xxvi, 170, 250–258, 417, 549, 551–553, 555, 611

jigsaw, 63, 333, 403

L2 pragmatics, xviii, xix, 189, 200–201
language analysis, 175
language exchange, 252–253, 257
learner needs, xxviii, 44, 55, 68, 74–77, 79, 82–83, 88–92, 96, 129, 134, 137, 171, 185, 293, 306, 533, 544
Levelt, 14, 17, 22, 24, 42, 49
lexical diversity, 332, 608, 623

methodological principles, 75, 92, 97, 331, 360, 362, 369–370, 372, 469, 479–480, 532, 660–661, 671–672, 674
modified elaborated, 165, 167, 171–172, 186, 493

needs analysis, ix, x, xxviii, xxix, 3, 53, 57, 59, 67–68, 73–74, 76, 80, 92–98, 108, 110, 118, 120, 122, 124–125, 127, 131–135, 137–138, 140, 142, 146–147, 150–151, 169–171, 173, 184–186, 189, 200–201, 208, 221, 226–230, 232, 236, 238, 240, 245, 247–249, 251, 264, 286, 291, 340, 348, 355–356, 374–376, 378–379, 382, 384, 389–390, 444, 465, 475, 479, 481, 484, 491–493, 533–534, 537, 539, 543–544, 546–547, 551–552, 567, 569, 573, 580, 583, 640, 654, 657, 660, 674
Noticing Hypothesis, 307

pedagogic tasks, x, xxvi, xxix, 22, 45, 50, 56, 58–68, 84, 107, 118, 120, 125, 127–130, 142, 151, 154, 168, 189, 205, 214, 216, 223, 225, 229–231, 240, 255, 264, 288–288, 293, 295, 300–301, 313, 320, 328, 479, 487, 536, 542, 553, 567, 590, 598, 611, 626
performance assessment, 66, 288, 508–509, 511–512, 524–527, 599
post-task, 7, 10–11, 15, 18–19, 23–24, 26, 39, 240, 295–296, 298, 300, 454, 612, 622
pre-task, 6, 9–10, 20, 296, 345
primary schools, xi, 70, 149, 401–402, 441, 460, 585–587, 596, 622, 666
program design, x, 61, 67–68, 250, 533, 535, 540, 543, 569, 583
program evaluation, xi, xvii, xix, 69, 72, 287, 465, 529–530, 532, 543–547, 672

reflective practice, 449–450, 458, 460–461, 489
refugees, ix, x, xxix, 73, 85–86, 109, 111, 117, 153, 228, 290–292, 297, 299–302, 659
reliability, xxviii, 77, 79, 82, 113, 156, 191, 419, 552, 561, 565, 616, 620
researched pedagogy, xxvi, 46, 49, 61, 69, 97, 149, 283–285, 287–289, 459, 461, 622, 649, 651, 654, 665, 669
resource directing, 16
restructure, 16, 19–20, 216

Salish, xx, 87–88, 92, 97, 360, 362–366, 369–373, 660, 668
school age, 432
simplified input, 166
spatial reasoning, 210–213, 225

SSARC Model, x, 13, 15–16, 20, 205–206, 248
structural syllabus, xxxi, xxxii, 206, 208, 220, 306, 631
sub-tasks, 125, 157, 159, 162, 167–169, 188, 190, 193, 196–198, 200, 227, 229, 233, 237, 244, 256, 293, 454

target discourse, x, 78, 91, 96, 117–118, 120, 151, 153–156, 158, 168, 171–173, 176, 183, 185–186, 188–189, 191, 200, 239, 375, 481, 493
task characteristics, 5, 8, 11, 17, 20–21, 209–210, 214, 225, 591
task complexity, xvii, xx, 15, 17–18, 21, 23–25, 117, 154, 209–214, 216, 218–221, 223, 225, 231, 241–244, 259, 293, 300, 333–335, 343, 389–390, 567–568, 572–573, 581–582, 584, 591, 606–608, 616, 620, 623–627, 653, 669
task design, x, xix, xx, 14, 18, 72, 96, 133, 171, 189, 205, 217–218, 222–223, 225–230, 232, 234, 236–241, 243–245, 247–249, 251, 259–260, 262–267, 269, 271–277, 280, 282–284, 288, 293, 301, 332, 334–335, 337, 432, 439, 452, 482, 529, 532, 568, 572, 624, 659, 666
task repetition, 10, 22, 47–50, 286, 336, 375, 401, 404, 408–409, 412, 414, 613, 625
task sequencing principle, 16
task-as-workplan, 273, 275–277, 298, 442
task-supported language teaching, 46, 75, 77, 399, 633, 671
teacher support, 139, 147, 586, 592–593, 595, 599–600, 644
teacher training, xi, xvii, xx, xxi, 55, 137, 141, 144, 146, 297, 335, 463, 476, 543, 546
telecollaboration, 250, 257, 259–260
Trade-off Hypothesis, 407

washback, xxviii, 517–520, 527
Web, 326, 342, 344

young learners, xviii, xxix, 50, 288, 301, 343, 403–404, 408–410, 412–414, 442–443, 521, 528, 545, 548, 654–655, 666, 669–670

Zapotec, 87–88, 92, 97, 360–363, 365–366, 369–372, 660–661, 668

Printed in the United States
by Baker & Taylor Publisher Services